3rd Workshop on NLP for Conversational AI (NLP4ConvAI 2021)

Online
10 November 2021

ISBN: 978-1-7138-9177-2

Printed from e-media with permission by:

Curran Associates, Inc.
57 Morehouse Lane
Red Hook, NY 12571

Some format issues inherent in the e-media version may also appear in this print version.

Printed with permission by Curran Associates, Inc. (2024)

For permission requests, please contact the Association for Computational Linguistics at the address below.

Association for Computational Linguistics
209 N. Eighth Street
Stroudsburg, Pennsylvania 18360

Phone: 1-570-476-8006
Fax: 1-570-476-0860

acl@aclweb.org

Additional copies of this publication are available from:

Curran Associates, Inc.
57 Morehouse Lane
Red Hook, NY 12571 USA
Phone: 845-758-0400
Fax: 845-758-2633
Email: curran@proceedings.com
Web: www.proceedings.com

EMNLP 2021

NLP for Conversational AI

Proceedings of the 3rd Workshop

November 10, 2021

Introduction

Welcome to the 3rd Workshop on NLP for Conversational AI, at EMNLP 2021.

Ever since the invention of the intelligent machine, hundreds and thousands of mathematicians, linguists, and computer scientists have dedicated their career to empowering human-machine communication in natural language. Although the idea is finally around the corner with a proliferation of virtual personal assistants such as Siri, Alexa, Google Assistant, and Cortana, the development of these conversational agents remains difficult and there still remain plenty of unanswered questions and challenges.

Conversational AI is hard because it is an interdisciplinary subject. Initiatives were started in different research communities, from Dialogue State Tracking Challenges to NIPS Conversational Intelligence Challenge live competition and the Amazon Alexa prize. However, various fields within the NLP community, such as semantic parsing, coreference resolution, sentiment analysis, question answering, and machine reading comprehension etc. have been seldom evaluated or applied in the context of conversational AI.

The goal of this workshop is to bring together NLP researchers and practitioners in different fields, alongside experts in speech and machine learning, to discuss the current state-of-the-art and new approaches, to share insights and challenges, to bridge the gap between academic research and real-world product deployment, and to shed the light on future directions. "NLP for Conversational AI" will be a one-day workshop including keynotes, spotlight talks, posters, and panel sessions. In keynote talks, senior technical leaders from industry and academia will share insights on the latest developments of the field. An open call for papers will be announced to encourage researchers and students to share their prospects and latest discoveries. The panel discussion will focus on the challenges, future directions of conversational AI research, bridging the gap in research and industrial practice, as well as audience-suggested topics.

With the increasing trend of conversational AI, NLP4ConvAI 2021 is competitive. We received 92 submissions, and after a rigorous review process, we only accepted 32. There are a total of 26 accepted regular workshop papers, 1 extended abstract, and 5 cross-submissions. The workshop overall acceptance rate is about just under 35%. We hope you will enjoy NLP4ConvAI 2021 at EMNLP and contribute to the future success of our community!

NLP4ConvAI 2021 Organizers
Alexandros Papangelis, Amazon Alexa AI
Pawel Budzianowski, PolyAI
Bing Liu, Facebook
Elnaz Nouri, Microsoft Research
Abhinav Rastogi, Google Research
Yun-Nung (Vivian) Chen, National Taiwan University

Organizing Committee:

Alexandros Papangelis, Amazon Alexa AI
Pawel Budzianowski, PolyAI
Bing Liu, Facebook
Elnaz Nouri, Microsoft Research
Abhinav Rastogi, Google Research
Yun-Nung (Vivian) Chen, National Taiwan University

Program Committee:

Abhinav Arora, Facebook
Yuan Cao, Google
Iñigo Casanueva, PolyAI
Daniel Cer, Google
Ta-Chung Chi, Carnegie Mellon University
Aleksandr Chuklin, Google
Samuel Coope, PolyAI
Paul Crook, Facebook
Aditya Gupta, Google
Sonal Gupta, Facebook
Raghav Gupta, Google
Dilek Hakkani-Tur, Amazon
Chao-Wei Huang, National Taiwan University
Ni Lao, Apple
Stefan Larson, SkySync
Wenqiang Lei, National University of Singapore
Ben Levin, PolyAI
Xiujun Li, University of Washington
Zhaojiang Lin, HKUST
Yang Liu, Amazon
Xiaohu Liu, Amazon
Andrea Madotto, HKUST
Shikib Mehri, Carnegie Mellon University
Gaurav Menghani, Google
Pranab Mohanty, Facebook
Seungwhan Moon, Facebook
Wei Peng, Huawei
Julien Perez, Naver Labs
Elahe Rahimtoroghi, Google
Anirudha Rayasam, Google
Marek Rei, Imperial College London
Lina M. Rojas Barahona, Orange Labs
Adithya Sagar, Facebook
Chinnadhurai Sankar, Facebook
Lei Shu, Amazon
Shang-Yu Su, National Taiwan University
Kai Sun, Cornell University
Ryuichi Takanobu, Alibaba
Gokhan Tur, Amazon

Stefan Ultes, Daimler AG
David Vandyke, Apple
Ivan Vulić, University of Cambridge
Peng Wang, AlphaSense
Zhiguang Wang, Facebook
Chien-Sheng Wu, Salesforce
Hu Xu, Facebook
Zi Yang, Google
Yi-Ting Yeh, Carnegie Mellon University
Emine Yilmaz, University College London
Lili Yu, Facebook
Hamed Zamani, University of Massachusetts Amherst
Xiaoxue Zang, Google
Hongyuan Zhan, Facebook
Bin Zhang, Google
Su Zhu, AISpeech

Invited Speakers:

Pascale Fung, Hong Kong University of Science & Technology
Koichiro Yoshino, Institute of Physical and Chemical Research (RIKEN)
Mona Diab, George Washington University
Idan Szpektor, Google
Tsung-Hsien Wen, PolyAI

Table of Contents

Taking Things Personally: Third Person to First Person Rephrasing
Marcel Granero Moya and Panagiotis Agis Oikonomou Filandras 1

Few-Shot Intent Classification by Gauging Entailment Relationship Between Utterance and Semantic Label
Jin Qu, Kazuma Hashimoto, Wenhao Liu, Caiming Xiong and Yingbo Zhou 8

Personalized Extractive Summarization Using an Ising Machine Towards Real-time Generation of Efficient and Coherent Dialogue Scenarios
Hiroaki Takatsu, Takahiro Kashikawa, Koichi Kimura, Ryota Ando and Yoichi Matsuyama 16

Multilingual Paraphrase Generation For Bootstrapping New Features in Task-Oriented Dialog Systems
Subhadarshi Panda, Caglar Tirkaz, Tobias Falke and Patrick Lehnen 30

Overcoming Conflicting Data when Updating a Neural Semantic Parser
David Gaddy, Alex Kouzemtchenko, Pavankumar Reddy Muddireddy, Prateek Kolhar and Rushin Shah 40

Not So Fast, Classifier – Accuracy and Entropy Reduction in Incremental Intent Classification
Lianna Hrycyk, Alessandra Zarcone and Luzian Hahn 52

On the Robustness of Intent Classification and Slot Labeling in Goal-oriented Dialog Systems to Real-world Noise
Sailik Sengupta, Jason Krone and Saab Mansour 68

Amendable Generation for Dialogue State Tracking
Xin Tian, Liankai Huang, Yingzhan Lin, Siqi Bao, Huang He, Yunyi Yang, Hua Wu, Fan Wang and Shuqi Sun 80

What Went Wrong? Explaining Overall Dialogue Quality through Utterance-Level Impacts
James D. Finch, Sarah E. Finch and Jinho D. Choi 93

XPersona: Evaluating Multilingual Personalized Chatbot
Zhaojiang Lin, Zihan Liu, Genta Indra Winata, Samuel Cahyawijaya, Andrea Madotto, Yejin Bang, Etsuko Ishii and Pascale Fung 102

Collaborative Data Relabeling for Robust and Diverse Voice Apps Recommendation in Intelligent Personal Assistants
Qian Hu, Thahir Mohamed, Zheng Gao, Xibin Gao, Radhika Arava, Xiyao Ma and Mohamed AbdelHady 113

Semi-supervised Intent Discovery with Contrastive Learning
Xiang Shen, Yinge Sun, Yao Zhang and Mani Najmabadi 120

CS-BERT: a pretrained model for customer service dialogues
Peiyao Wang, Joyce Fang and Julia Reinspach 130

PLATO-KAG: Unsupervised Knowledge-Grounded Conversation via Joint Modeling
Xinxian Huang, Huang He, Siqi Bao, Fan Wang, Hua Wu and Haifeng Wang 143

Improving Dialogue State Tracking by Joint Slot Modeling
Ting-Rui Chiang and Yi-Ting Yeh 155

Learning to Learn End-to-End Goal-Oriented Dialog From Related Dialog Tasks
Janarthanan Rajendran, Jonathan K. Kummerfeld and Satinder Baveja 163

Personalized Search-based Query Rewrite System for Conversational AI
Eunah Cho, Ziyan Jiang, Jie Hao, Zheng Chen, Saurabh Gupta, Xing Fan and Chenlei Guo . . . 179

Dialogue Response Generation via Contrastive Latent Representation Learning
Shuyang Dai, Guoyin Wang, Sunghyun Park and Sungjin Lee 189

AuGPT: Auxiliary Tasks and Data Augmentation for End-To-End Dialogue with Pre-Trained Language Models
Jonáš Kulhánek, Vojtěch Hudeček, Tomáš Nekvinda and Ondřej Dušek 198

Investigating Pretrained Language Models for Graph-to-Text Generation
Leonardo F. R. Ribeiro, Martin Schmitt, Hinrich Schütze and Iryna Gurevych 211

Style Control for Schema-Guided Natural Language Generation
Alicia Tsai, Shereen Oraby, Vittorio Perera, Jiun-Yu Kao, Yuheng Du, Anjali Narayan-Chen, Tagyoung Chung and Dilek Hakkani-Tur 228

Using Pause Information for More Accurate Entity Recognition
Sahas Dendukuri, Pooja Chitkara, Joel Ruben Antony Moniz, Xiao Yang, Manos Tsagkias and Stephen Pulman 243

Think Before You Speak: Learning to Generate Implicit Knowledge for Response Generation by Self-Talk
Pei Zhou, Behnam Hedayatnia, Karthik Gopalakrishnan, Seokhwan Kim, Jay Pujara, Xiang Ren, Yang Liu and Dilek Hakkani-Tur 251

Teach Me What to Say and I Will Learn What to Pick: Unsupervised Knowledge Selection Through Response Generation with Pretrained Generative Models
Ehsan Lotfi, Maxime De Bruyn, Jeska Buhmann and Walter Daelemans 254

Influence of user personality on dialogue task performance: A case study using a rule-based dialogue system
Ao Guo, Atsumoto Ohashi, Ryu Hirai, Yuya Chiba, Yuiko Tsunomori and Ryuichiro Higashinaka 263

Towards Code-Mixed Hinglish Dialogue Generation
Vibhav Agarwal, Pooja Rao and Dinesh Babu Jayagopi 271

Towards Zero and Few-shot Knowledge-seeking Turn Detection in Task-orientated Dialogue Systems
Di Jin, Shuyang Gao, Seokhwan Kim, Yang Liu and Dilek Hakkani-Tur 281

Conference Program

Taking Things Personally: Third Person to First Person Rephrasing
Marcel Granero Moya and Panagiotis Agis Oikonomou Filandras

Few-Shot Intent Classification by Gauging Entailment Relationship Between Utterance and Semantic Label
Jin Qu, Kazuma Hashimoto, Wenhao Liu, Caiming Xiong and Yingbo Zhou

Personalized Extractive Summarization Using an Ising Machine Towards Real-time Generation of Efficient and Coherent Dialogue Scenarios
Hiroaki Takatsu, Takahiro Kashikawa, Koichi Kimura, Ryota Ando and Yoichi Matsuyama

Multilingual Paraphrase Generation For Bootstrapping New Features in Task-Oriented Dialog Systems
Subhadarshi Panda, Caglar Tirkaz, Tobias Falke and Patrick Lehnen

Overcoming Conflicting Data when Updating a Neural Semantic Parser
David Gaddy, Alex Kouzemtchenko, Pavankumar Reddy Muddireddy, Prateek Kolhar and Rushin Shah

Not So Fast, Classifier – Accuracy and Entropy Reduction in Incremental Intent Classification
Lianna Hrycyk, Alessandra Zarcone and Luzian Hahn

On the Robustness of Intent Classification and Slot Labeling in Goal-oriented Dialog Systems to Real-world Noise
Sailik Sengupta, Jason Krone and Saab Mansour

Amendable Generation for Dialogue State Tracking
Xin Tian, Liankai Huang, Yingzhan Lin, Siqi Bao, Huang He, Yunyi Yang, Hua Wu, Fan Wang and Shuqi Sun

What Went Wrong? Explaining Overall Dialogue Quality through Utterance-Level Impacts
James D. Finch, Sarah E. Finch and Jinho D. Choi

XPersona: Evaluating Multilingual Personalized Chatbot
Zhaojiang Lin, Zihan Liu, Genta Indra Winata, Samuel Cahyawijaya, Andrea Madotto, Yejin Bang, Etsuko Ishii and Pascale Fung

Collaborative Data Relabeling for Robust and Diverse Voice Apps Recommendation in Intelligent Personal Assistants
Qian Hu, Thahir Mohamed, Zheng Gao, Xibin Gao, Radhika Arava, Xiyao Ma and Mohamed AbdelHady

Semi-supervised Intent Discovery with Contrastive Learning
Xiang Shen, Yinge Sun, Yao Zhang and Mani Najmabadi

No Day Set (continued)

CS-BERT: a pretrained model for customer service dialogues
Peiyao Wang, Joyce Fang and Julia Reinspach

PLATO-KAG: Unsupervised Knowledge-Grounded Conversation via Joint Modeling
Xinxian Huang, Huang He, Siqi Bao, Fan Wang, Hua Wu and Haifeng Wang

Improving Dialogue State Tracking by Joint Slot Modeling
Ting-Rui Chiang and Yi-Ting Yeh

Learning to Learn End-to-End Goal-Oriented Dialog From Related Dialog Tasks
Janarthanan Rajendran, Jonathan K. Kummerfeld and Satinder Baveja

Personalized Search-based Query Rewrite System for Conversational AI
Eunah Cho, Ziyan Jiang, Jie Hao, Zheng Chen, Saurabh Gupta, Xing Fan and Chenlei Guo

Dialogue Response Generation via Contrastive Latent Representation Learning
Shuyang Dai, Guoyin Wang, Sunghyun Park and Sungjin Lee

AuGPT: Auxiliary Tasks and Data Augmentation for End-To-End Dialogue with Pre-Trained Language Models
Jonáš Kulhánek, Vojtěch Hudeček, Tomáš Nekvinda and Ondřej Dušek

Investigating Pretrained Language Models for Graph-to-Text Generation
Leonardo F. R. Ribeiro, Martin Schmitt, Hinrich Schütze and Iryna Gurevych

Style Control for Schema-Guided Natural Language Generation
Alicia Tsai, Shereen Oraby, Vittorio Perera, Jiun-Yu Kao, Yuheng Du, Anjali Narayan-Chen, Tagyoung Chung and Dilek Hakkani-Tur

Using Pause Information for More Accurate Entity Recognition
Sahas Dendukuri, Pooja Chitkara, Joel Ruben Antony Moniz, Xiao Yang, Manos Tsagkias and Stephen Pulman

Think Before You Speak: Learning to Generate Implicit Knowledge for Response Generation by Self-Talk
Pei Zhou, Behnam Hedayatnia, Karthik Gopalakrishnan, Seokhwan Kim, Jay Pujara, Xiang Ren, Yang Liu and Dilek Hakkani-Tur

Teach Me What to Say and I Will Learn What to Pick: Unsupervised Knowledge Selection Through Response Generation with Pretrained Generative Models
Ehsan Lotfi, Maxime De Bruyn, Jeska Buhmann and Walter Daelemans

No Day Set (continued)

Influence of user personality on dialogue task performance: A case study using a rule-based dialogue system
Ao Guo, Atsumoto Ohashi, Ryu Hirai, Yuya Chiba, Yuiko Tsunomori and Ryuichiro Higashinaka

Towards Code-Mixed Hinglish Dialogue Generation
Vibhav Agarwal, Pooja Rao and Dinesh Babu Jayagopi

Towards Zero and Few-shot Knowledge-seeking Turn Detection in Task-orientated Dialogue Systems
Di Jin, Shuyang Gao, Seokhwan Kim, Yang Liu and Dilek Hakkani-Tur

Taking Things Personally: Third Person to First Person Rephrasing

Marcel Granero-Moya
Amazon Alexa AI
Cambridge, UK
marcel.graneromoya@gmail.com

Agis Oikonomou Filandras
Amazon Alexa AI
Cambridge, UK
filandp@amazon.co.uk

Abstract

The recent advancement of digital assistant technologies has opened new possibilities in the experiences they can provide. One of them is the ability to converse with a persona, e.g., celebrities, famous fictional characters, etc. This experience requires that the replies are answered from the point of view of the persona, i.e., the first person. Since the facts about characters are typically found expressed in the third person, there is a need to rephrase them to the first person in order for the assistant not to break character and the experience to remain immersive. However, the automatic solution to such a problem is largely unexplored by the community. In this work, we present a new task for NLP: third person to first person rephrasing. We define the task and analyze its major challenges. We create and publish a novel dataset with 3493 human-annotated pairs of celebrity facts in the third person with their rephrased sentence in the first person. Moreover, we propose a transformer-based pipeline that correctly rephrases 92.8% of sentences compared to 76.2% rephrased by a rule-based baseline system.

1 Introduction

The emergence of digital assistant technologies has opened new possibilities like creating conversational personas that impersonate celebrities or fictional characters and chat with users. When asked about themselves, these personas can respond with answers created manually by experts or taken straight from knowledge bases, which are usually stored in the third person. In order to not break character, we aim to rephrase automatically these third person replies to first person while preserving the original information.

The task can be thought of as a special case of controlled text rephrasing (Logeswaran et al., 2018; Xu et al., 2020) and text style transfer (Fu et al., 2018; Shen et al., 2017). Similarly to the above, third to first person rephrasing aims to transform a sentence while preserving the content. In our case instead of trying to change the style of the sentence, e.g. formality (Wang et al., 2019), sentiment (Li et al., 2018; Zhang et al., 2018), or politeness (Madaan et al., 2020), we want to change the point of view of the sentence narrator.

We define the task of Third to First Person Rephrasing. The task's goal is to rephrase a sentence about someone in the third person point of view to the first person point of view as if that person was talking about themself. The task has a number of challenges. Firstly, we can have text in quotes that should remain unchanged. Secondly, reported statements should be converted to personal statements, e.g., "He said that he loves ..." → "**I** love ...". Thirdly, there could be multiple subjects in the sentences, e.g., "Samuel and Ron went to ..." → "Ron and **I** went to ...". Finally, the point of view should be modified only on the mentions to the target persona. Thus, references and co-references have to be identified and rephrased, while keeping unchanged other third person mentions that refer to another subject. This is a known problem called coreference resolution, that aims to find the same entities present in text with a number of proposed solutions in literature (Clark and Manning, 2015, 2016; Lee et al., 2017; Joshi et al., 2019; Xu and Choi, 2020).

For instance, the sentence about Samuel L. Jackson *"His characters often feature the color purple: Jackson chose to have Doyle Gipson wear a purple hat in Changing Lanes; Mace Windu, upon request by Jackson to George Lucas, wielded a purple lightsaber in Star Wars; and Lazarus, his character in Black Snake Moan, plays a purple Gibson guitar."* should be rephrased to *"**My** characters often feature the color purple: **I** chose to have Doyle Gipson wear a purple hat in Changing Lanes; Mace Windu, upon **my** request to George Lucas, **I** wielded a purple lightsaber in Star Wars;*

Proceedings of the Third Workshop on Natural Language Processing for Conversational AI, pages 1–7
November 10, 2021. ©2021 Association for Computational Linguistics

*and Lazarus, **my** character in Black Snake Moan, plays a purple Gibson guitar.*". The rephraser needs to be able to disambiguate between the different subjects in complicated sentences and rephrase appropriately.

The contributions of this work are threefold:

- Definition and analysis of the task. We define the goal of rephrasing third person text to first person in order to impersonate a persona, and we identify the main challenges.
- Creation and distribution of a novel supervised dataset specific for the task. The source sentences are scrapped from a website containing facts from celebrities, and the target sentences are annotated with Amazon Mechanical Turk.
- Proposal of a rephrasing model and exploration of several pre-processing techniques. The proposed pipeline establishes a benchmark for future work.

2 Methodology

In this section, we will explain how we created our dataset for the task and present two solutions to the problem, a rule-based one and a deep learning based one.

2.1 Dataset

We built a supervised dataset with third person sentences rephrased to the first person. The source sentences were collected from TheFactSite[1], a website with celebrities facts like "*J.K. Rowling is 54 years old.*" and "*She was born on July 31st, 1965 in Yate, Gloucestershire.*". The data was collected filtering out groups and bands.

After collecting the facts, they were paired with their first person equivalents. The pairs were created manually, using Amazon Mechanical Turk. We defined microtasks (See Appendix A) containing an original fact, extracted from TheFactSite, to be rephrased to the first person point of view. The target celebrity and a link to the source webpage were provided to help MTurkers with the annotations. MTurkers were asked to change the target celebrity to a first person point of view, to preserve all the initial content in the rephrased sentence, and keep the word order. The last two instructions aimed to reach higher inter-annotator agreement. Each task was annotated by three MTurkers from the UK or the US, with more than 98% HIT Approval Rate, and more than 5000 HITs approved.

The results from MTurk were post-processed in three different steps to collect the final annotations. First, direct annotation; whenever at least two MTurkers agreed on the transformation, the answer was assumed to be correct. 3352 facts were directly annotated, from which 2307 had full agreement between annotators and 1045 where only two annotators coincided on the rephrasing. At this point, 359 sentences had no agreement between MTurkers. Answers that were not directly annotated in the previous step were simplified by lowercasing, removing final punctuation, and substituting contractions by expanded forms. Thanks to this process, 73 facts were annotated.The remaining 68 facts were annotated by hand. The result is a supervised dataset that consists of 3493 celebrity facts in the third person and the first person point of view.

The dataset contains facts from 117 different celebrities of which 85 are male and 32 are female. There are 2563 pairs for male celebrities and 930 for females. On average, each celebrity has 29.9 facts and each fact has 16.3 words. Table 1 shows an illustrative example of a data pair. It contains the celebrity and the celebrity's gender, as well as the source and the target fact.

celebrity	Shawn Mendes **gender** male
source	in some of *his* videos that *he has* uploaded to youtube, *shawn* just *sings* in them and *lets* other musicians collaborate with *him* by playing instruments.
target	in some of *my* videos that *i have* uploaded to youtube, *i* just *sing* in them and *let* other musicians collaborate with *me* by playing instruments.

Table 1: Example of a fact containing the celebrity name, its gender, the source sentence and the target. In italics, words that differ between source and target.

The most frequently substituted pairs from the original celebrity fact to the transformed first-person fact as expected are personal pronouns. More specifically, the top 5 substituted pairs are the following: his $\rightarrow$ my, he $\rightarrow$ I, her $\rightarrow$ my, she $\rightarrow$ I, him $\rightarrow$ me. As the dataset is unbalanced in gender, over two thirds of the substituted personal pronouns are masculine, and one third are feminine.

[1] www.thefactsite.com/celebrities/

2.2 Rephrasing Pipeline

To solve the problem, we investigated two possible alternatives. First a rule-based system and second we used a data-driven deep learning approach.

2.2.1 Rule-Based System

We implemented a rule-based system with dictionaries to rephrase text from third person to first person. First, it spots and tags the subject's name, then, replaces pronouns based on the subject's gender, and finally, applies substitution dictionaries with over 100 rules (e.g., "He has"→"I have", "with <subject>"→"with me") based on the most common substitutions in the dataset.

2.2.2 Deep Learning System

We used GPT-2, a large transformer-based language model with 1.5 billion parameters, trained on a dataset of 8 million web pages, (Radford et al., 2019). Specifically, we finetuned the 'gpt2' model from the Hugging Face open source library, (Wolf et al., 2019), on the collected dataset.

Before feeding our inputs to the model, we used a reference recognizer. It adds a tag before and after any of the target celebrity possible names (name, surname, acronym, nickname). This ensures that the model knows, what is the subject whose point of view it is trying to change. Also, we provide the subject's gender by prepending a gender token *<female>* or *<male>* to help the model disambiguate gendered pronouns. Thirdly, we tried another pre-processing step that dealt with the pronoun resolution. NeuralCoref (Clark and Manning, 2015), a neural network that resolves coreference clusters, was used to identify personal pronouns that refer to the target celebrity. Table 2 illustrates the two pre-processing steps, and shows examples of the input to the model.

Finally, the dataset was augmented to provide more training samples to the model, and to decorrelate celebrity names to specific facts. Thus, leveraging the substituted words between the source and target facts, celebrity names were changed in the source while keeping the rest of the fact. Personal pronouns had to change when the original and the new celebrity differed on gender. An example of data augmentation is depicted in Table 3. Male facts were expanded to 4 new male celebrities and 5 new female celebrities, whereas female celebrity facts were only expanded to 4 new female celebrities due to the ambiguity of the word *her*, which can be a personal pronoun replaced by *him* or a possessive replaced by *his*.

Celebrity	Billie Eilish
Gender	female
Source	Billie Eilish never smiles in photographs because she says it makes her feel " weak and powerless . "
Reference	<cel> Billie Eilish </cel> never smiles in photographs because she says it makes her feel " weak and powerless . "
Coreferences	<cel> Billie Eilish </cel> never smiles in photographs because <ref> she </ref> says it makes <ref> her </ref> feel " weak and powerless . "
Target	I never smile in photographs because it makes me feel " weak and powerless . "

Table 2: Example of reference recognizer and coreference resolution pre-processing steps. Tags *<cel>* and *<ref>* stand for celebrity and coreference respectively.

Original	<male> <cel> Post Malone </cel> 's first single was released during his illness. <cel> Post </cel> says it was thanks to his father.
Augmented A	<male> <cel> Nicholas Hoult </cel> 's first single was released during his illness. <cel> Nicholas </cel> says it was thanks to his father.
Augmented B	<female> <cel> Ariana Grande </cel> 's first single was released during her illness. <cel> Ariana </cel> says it was thanks to her father.

Table 3: Example of data augmentation by changing a male's fact to different male and female celebrities.

3 Experiments & Results

The dataset (see Section 2.1) was split 80% for training, 10% for evaluation and 10% for test. As the number of edits we wanted the model to do in a sentence were few, we evaluated results with a sentence accuracy metric where a rephrased sentence is correct if it perfectly matches the target sentence, and wrong otherwise. Table 5 shows the correct rephrasing for a fact and a possible wrong rephrasing.

Initially, we tried the rule-based system, as discussed in Section 2.2, model #0. We found it got 76.2% accuracy in the test set by handling most straightforward cases, i.e., when the subject was attached to the verb and when all pronouns and possessives referred to the celebrity. Also, it had problems with homographs, e.g., "her" can either be a pronoun or a possessive, so it can be replaced by "me" or "my" respectively.

We investigated using the GPT-2 model to solve

the task. Initially we trained the model without any preprocessing and by finetuning on the non-augmented dataset, model #1. We saw an increase in accuracy by 5.2%. The model could disambiguate between homographs without requiring any explicit input. It still had trouble though when there were multiple possible subjects.

We hypothesized that by providing the model with gender and the name of the subject we wanted it to rephrase, we would see an improvement. Thus, we first prepended a gender token (<female> or <male>) to the source text, model #2, and then, added the reference recognizer pre-processing step as described in section 2.2, model #3. Compared to GPT-2 without any preprocessing step, the accuracy was raised by 6.1% and 8.6% respectively. Our following hypothesis was that by using a coreferencing model, we would be able to help the model with cases where the pronouns were ambiguous, and it wasn't editing properly the text. By adding the coreference preprocessing step to the GPT-2 along with the reference recognizer and specified gender, model #4 decreased the accuracy compared to model #3. We surmised, this tiny accuracy drop was due to the limited amount of data. We did data augmentation, as discussed in section 2.2, to provide the model with more training examples of those ambiguous cases. By facing multiple similar examples with different subject names and pronouns, the model would have to take into account the subject name and the coreferences provided by the preprocessing steps. Data augmentation worked, models #5 and #6, resulting in an accuracy increase compared to model #3. It is very interesting to note that the deep learning model can achieve 91.4% high accuracy without using any dependency parsing and without the coreferencing model. The best model (#6) reached 92.8% of accuracy by leveraging all the preprocessing techniques. Gender-wise, model (#6) achieves 93.2% accuracy for masculine subjects and 92.0% for feminine ones. Table 4 shows a comparison of all our hypotheses and their results (see appendix C for further finetuned models).

We analyzed our best model's errors (#7) and categorized them. 24% of mistakes happened due to the removal or addition of an unrelated context words (e.g., predicted *"My dog"* instead of *"Brady, my dog"*). Regarding reference disambiguation, other subjects were rephrased 20% of times (*"I am Drake's only child."* instead of *"He is my only child."*), and 23% of times the reference recognition failed because the subject was not identified by the reference recognizer or not rephrased by the model (*"PewDiePie is ... "* instead of *"I am ... "*), or the subject was referred in plural along with other subjects (*"helped me"* instead of *"helped us"*), or the subject was not referred by its name (e.g., *"the player"* or *"the actor"*). Finally, there were two kinds of mistakes that could be counted as correct. In 20% of the cases, the subject reported its own statement and the report was omitted (*"I like chocolate"* instead of *"I said I like chocolate"*); and 6.8% for synonyms generated by the model (*"nearly"* instead of *"almost"*).

Model	Gender	Ref	Coref	Aug	Accuracy
#0					76.2%
#1					81.4%
#2	X				87.5%
#4	X	X	X		90.0%
#3	X	X			90.9%
#5	X	X		X	91.4%
#6	X	X	X	X	**92.8%**

Table 4: Accuracy results for the baseline (#0) and the different GPT2 models finetuned (#1-#6). An *X* is marked if the gender token is provided (Gen), reference recognizer used (Ref), coreferences annotated (Coref), and augmented dataset used for training (Aug).

Source	Post credits his father for introducing him to diverse music genres.
Correct prediction	I credit my father for introducing me to diverse music genres.
Wrong prediction	I credits my father for introducing me to diverse music genres.

Table 5: Example of correct prediction and a possible wrong prediction for a given source fact.

4 Conclusions

This work presented a novel NLP task: third person to first person rephrasing. We explored the challenges of the task, when impersonating a celebrity talking about themselves. We presented a supervised corpus of celebrity facts in the first and third person. We also proposed fine-tuning GPT-2 using the dataset and explored a number of techniques that helped the model achieve 92.8% of accuracy in the test split of our dataset, a 16.6% improvement compared to the rule-based baseline. Finally, we leave for future work the exploration of further refinements to our pipeline, extending our solution to other languages and augmenting the dataset.

References

Kevin Clark and Christopher D Manning. 2015. Entity-centric coreference resolution with model stacking. In *Proceedings of the 53rd Annual Meeting of the Association for Computational Linguistics and the 7th International Joint Conference on Natural Language Processing (Volume 1: Long Papers)*, pages 1405–1415.

Kevin Clark and Christopher D Manning. 2016. Deep reinforcement learning for mention-ranking coreference models. *arXiv preprint arXiv:1609.08667*.

Zhenxin Fu, Xiaoye Tan, Nanyun Peng, Dongyan Zhao, and Rui Yan. 2018. Style transfer in text: Exploration and evaluation. In *Proceedings of the AAAI Conference on Artificial Intelligence*, volume 32.

Mandar Joshi, Omer Levy, Daniel S Weld, and Luke Zettlemoyer. 2019. Bert for coreference resolution: Baselines and analysis. *arXiv preprint arXiv:1908.09091*.

Kenton Lee, Luheng He, Mike Lewis, and Luke Zettlemoyer. 2017. End-to-end neural coreference resolution. *arXiv preprint arXiv:1707.07045*.

Juncen Li, Robin Jia, He He, and Percy Liang. 2018. Delete, retrieve, generate: A simple approach to sentiment and style transfer. *arXiv preprint arXiv:1804.06437*.

Lajanugen Logeswaran, Honglak Lee, and Samy Bengio. 2018. Content preserving text generation with attribute controls. *arXiv preprint arXiv:1811.01135*.

Aman Madaan, Amrith Setlur, Tanmay Parekh, Barnabas Poczos, Graham Neubig, Yiming Yang, Ruslan Salakhutdinov, Alan W Black, and Shrimai Prabhumoye. 2020. Politeness transfer: A tag and generate approach. *arXiv preprint arXiv:2004.14257*.

Alec Radford, Jeffrey Wu, Rewon Child, David Luan, Dario Amodei, and Ilya Sutskever. 2019. Language models are unsupervised multitask learners. *OpenAI blog*, 1(8):9.

Tianxiao Shen, Tao Lei, Regina Barzilay, and Tommi Jaakkola. 2017. Style transfer from non-parallel text by cross-alignment. *arXiv preprint arXiv:1705.09655*.

Yunli Wang, Yu Wu, Lili Mou, Zhoujun Li, and Wenhan Chao. 2019. Harnessing pre-trained neural networks with rules for formality style transfer. In *Proceedings of the 2019 Conference on Empirical Methods in Natural Language Processing and the 9th International Joint Conference on Natural Language Processing (EMNLP-IJCNLP)*, pages 3564–3569.

Thomas Wolf, Lysandre Debut, Victor Sanh, Julien Chaumond, Clement Delangue, Anthony Moi, Pierric Cistac, Tim Rault, Rémi Louf, Morgan Funtowicz, et al. 2019. Huggingface's transformers: State-of-the-art natural language processing. *arXiv preprint arXiv:1910.03771*.

Lei Xu, Ivan Ramirez, and Kalyan Veeramachaneni. 2020. Rewriting meaningful sentences via conditional bert sampling and an application on fooling text classifiers. *arXiv preprint arXiv:2010.11869*.

Liyan Xu and Jinho D Choi. 2020. Revealing the myth of higher-order inference in coreference resolution. *arXiv preprint arXiv:2009.12013*.

Yi Zhang, Jingjing Xu, Pengcheng Yang, and Xu Sun. 2018. Learning sentiment memories for sentiment modification without parallel data. *arXiv preprint arXiv:1808.07311*.

A Data Collection Instructions with MTurk

The dataset was collected via MTurk, a crowdworking platform owned by Amazon. In order to help the annotator change the target celebrity from third person to first person, the celebrity name and a link to the celebrity facts webpage were provided. Moreover, two constraints were specified; first, to keep all the content present in the rephrased sentence and ensure no information was deleted. Although the annotations would lack diversity of written form, we specified to keep the same word order in an attempt to reach more inter-annotator agreement which would help to choose the ground truth rephrased sentence.

On the platform, there was a button to open a window with the instructions and illustrative examples showing correct and incorrect annotations. We specified that all HITs (Human Intelligence Tasks) would be reviewed to ensure proper annotations from MTurkers.

MTurk HIT

Instructions

Rephrase a celebrity's fact (3rd person) into a personal sentence (1st person).

Remember:

- The celebrity must be changed to a **1st person point of view**
- **All the content** must be present in the rephrased sentence.
- Keep the **same word order**

ALL HITS WILL BE REVIEWED

Example:

Facts from: j k rowling facts

Celebrity's fact: **J.K. Rowling** named **her** daughter, Jessica, after Jessica Mitford who was an English author and one of **J.K.s** heros.

Rephrased sentence: **I** named **my** daughter, Jessica, after Jessica Mitford who was an English author and one of **my** heros.

Your task

Rephrase the following fact (3rd person) into a personal sentence (1st person).

Fact from: niall horan facts

Celebrity's fact: His guitar was the best Christmas present he ever received.

Rephrased sentence:

<Text box for the answer>

<Submit button>

Figure 1: MTurk microtask

B Dataset's Most Frequently Substituted Pairs

In this section, we provide further details about the substituted pairs from the original dataset. Table 6 illustrates the 20 most substituted pairs from the original dataset. Note that masculine pronouns are twice as frequent as feminine pronouns, evidencing again the gender bias. Figure 2 shows the log-log distribution for the substituted pairs.

#	original	transformed	counts
1	his	my	1039
2	he	i	966
3	her	my	464
4	she	i	414
5	he is	i am	138
6	him	me	136
7	he has	i have	123
8	they	we	65
9	she is	i am	54
10	her	me	52
11	she has	i have	51
12	justin	i	35
13	their	our	33
14	has	have	30
15	himself	myself	25
16	he does	i do	21
17	he loves	i love	19
18	he 's	i 've	18
19	shawn	i	17
20	has	i have	16

Table 6: Most substituted pairs in the original (non-augmented) dataset.

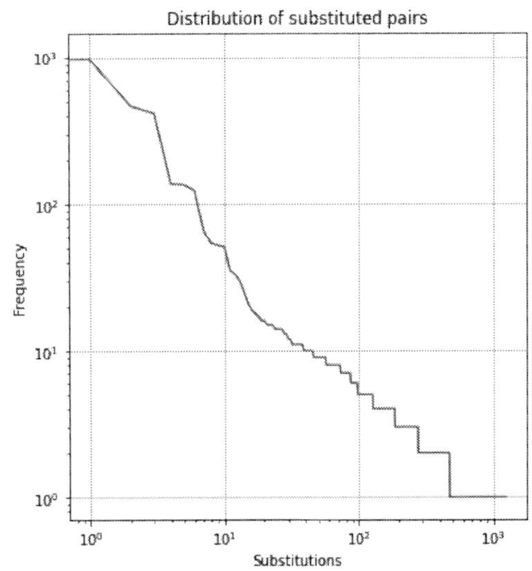

Figure 2: Log-log distribution of substituted pairs for the original dataset

C Further Model Results

We provide a table with the results for all the models. First, the baseline model (#0), and second, the finetuned GPT2 models which differ on the preprocessing steps applied. The models with a number are explained in section 3. The rest of models provide a wider understanding on how the preprocessing steps help the GPT2 model to rephrase from third to first person. Notice that the coreference resolution has to be used along with the reference recognizer.

Model	Gender token	Reference recognizer	Coreference resolution	Data augmentation	Accuracy
#0					76.2%
#1					81.4%
-				X	82.8%
-		X	X		85.3%
-		X			85.9%
-		X		X	86.1%
-	X			X	86.4%
-		X	X	X	87.0%
#2	X				87.5%
#4	X	X	X		90.0%
#3	X	X			90.9%
#5	X	X		X	91.4%
#6	X	X	X	X	**92.8%**

Table 7: Accuracy results for the rule-based baseline (#0) and the different finetuned GPT2 models. The GPT2 models differ on the preprocessing steps that were applied to the data before finetuning the GPT2 model. An *X* means that the column's preprocessing step was used for that model's finetuning.

Few-Shot Intent Classification by Gauging Entailment Relationship Between Utterance and Semantic Label

Jin Qu, Kazuma Hashimoto*, Wenhao Liu, Caiming Xiong, Yingbo Zhou
Salesforce Research, Palo Alto, CA, USA
{jqu,k.hashimoto,wenhao.liu,cxiong,yingbo.zhou}@salesforce.com

Abstract

Zhang et al. (2020) proposed to formulate few-shot intent classification as natural language inference (NLI) between query utterances and examples in the training set. The method is known as discriminative nearest neighbor classification or DNNC. Inspired by this work, we propose to simplify the NLI-style classification pipeline to be the entailment prediction on the utterance-semantic-label-pair (USLP). The semantic information in the labels can thus been infused into the classification process. Compared with DNNC, our proposed method is more efficient in both training and serving since it is based upon the entailment between query utterance and labels instead of all the training examples. The DNNC method requires more than one example per intent while the USLP approach does not have such constraint. In the 1-shot experiments on the CLINC150 (Larson et al., 2019) dataset, the USLP method outperforms traditional classification approach by >20 points (in-domain accuracy). We also find that longer and semantically meaningful labels tend to benefit model performance, however, the benefit shrinks as more training data is available.

1 Introduction

Many methods have been considered for few-shot intent classification. A simple but often effective approach is to simply generate more data through data augmentation. Wei and Zou, 2019 and Kumar et al., 2019 explored data augmentation at token- and feature-level to boost model performance. Meta-learning has also been studied extensively for few-shot learning. For instance, Induction Network (Geng et al., 2019) tried to learn general class representations via episode-based meta training and predict utterance labels based on the relation score between the query utterance and classes. Furthermore, large-scale pre-trained language models are often employed to mitigate the lack of annotated data for the target task. Schick and Schütze, 2021 leveraged pre-trained RoBERTa (Liu et al., 2019) and XLM-R (Conneau et al., 2020) to learn to generate task descriptions on small labeled datasets. They then use the trained models to produce descriptions and soft labels on large, task-specific unlabeled datasets and use them to train classifier. Although this approach has been proven to be effective, it requires extra unlabeled data and additional human supervision on description generation task. DNNC (Zhang et al., 2020) reformulates few-shot text classification as NLI-style pairwise comparison between training example and query utterance. However, DNNC requires at least two examples per intent for training and has to make $M \times$N (M: number of intents; N: number of training examples per intent) pairwise comparisons for each classification. Along the line of NLI-based classification, Yin et al. (2019) explored to leverage short semantic labels. However, this work is limited to zero-short setting and doesn't provide extensive analysis on how semantic information in labels affects model performance.

However, the DNNC work ignores one valuable and readily available supervision in the training data, the semantics in the labels. Our work is largely motivated by the hypothesis that semantic labels may carry valuable information about the intents and could benefit few-shot learning. There are prior works exploring how to leverage semantic labels in NLP tasks. For examples, Hou et al. (2020b) has proposed to improve the Prototypical Network (Snell et al., 2017) by directly embedding semantic labels; Hou et al. (2020a) has tried to use semantic information in labels for few-shot slot tagging. To our knowledge, however, there is no known work that has explored to leverage semantic labels for NLI-style intent classification. Neither has any work been done to study how model per-

*Work was done when the author was a full time research scientist at Salesforce Research, now works at Google

Proceedings of the Third Workshop on Natural Language Processing for Conversational AI, pages 8–15
November 10, 2021. ©2021 Association for Computational Linguistics

formance changes with regard to the interplay of data augmentation, different labeling, and number of training examples.

Based upon DNNC, our proposed method, utterance-semantic-label-pair (USLP), also leverages NLI-style classification. Instead of computing the entailment relationship between query sentence and the example sentences in the support set, we use the model to gauge the entailment relationship between query text and semantic labels. The semantic information in the labels can be perfectly infused into the classification process in this way. The pairwise entailment prediction is also reduced to M times per classification compared with the DNNC's $M \times$N. Figure 1 provides a few examples to illustrate the difference between USLP and DNNC.

In the following 1-shot experiments on the CLINC150 (Larson et al., 2019) dataset, we show that the USLP method outperforms the standard classification approach over 20 points with respect to in-domain accuracy. It is noteworthy that the predecessor of USLP, DNNC requires more than one example per intent for training. Although DNNC could do self-entailment training in 1-shot setting, our preliminary results show that the in-domain accuracy of multiple runs is extremely low (best result is below 20 from multiple runs). We also show that data augmentation, longer and more descriptive labeling, and NLI pre-training could boost model performance in few shot setting. However, as more training data is available, the efficacy of these performance boosters tends to shrink or even becomes negative. Our contributions can be summarized in two fold: 1, we proposed a new intent classification pipeline, USLP, and showed its effectiveness especially in 1-shot setting; 2, we studied how data augmentations, different labeling methods, and NLI pre-training might impact model performance in different few shot scenarios.

2 Method

2.1 Natural Language Inference

Natural Language Inference, or NLI, is a fundamental NLP task that aims to identify the relationship between a premise and a hypothesis. The relationship can be binary, (entailment and non-entailment) or ternary (entailment, contradiction, and neutral). Pre-trained transformer models such as BERT (Devlin et al., 2019) and RoBERTa (Liu et al., 2019) have achieved promising results on NLI tasks. Here the NLI task is treated as a textual sequence classification problem, where the premise and hypothesis sentences are concatenated as $[CLS], premise, [SEP], hypothesis, [SEP]$ (depending on the tokenizer, the concatenated text might be slightly different) and fed into the model. The last hidden state of the $[CLS]$ token is commonly used for classification.

2.2 Utterance-Semantic-Label-Pair

The utterance-semantic-label-pair (USLP) approach builds on top of NLI framework as aforementioned. In USLP, utterances in training data are treated as premise while semantic labels are considered as hypothesis. We use binary entailment relationship for USLP, namely entailment and non-entailment. During training, an utterance-label pair is treated as a positive or entailment example if the label is the assigned intent for the utterance. Similarly, if the label is not the right intent label for the utterance, the pair is considered as a negative or non-entailment example. Although the USLP method does not necessarily require intent labels to have semantic meaning, detailed and semantically meaningful labels can benefit in-domain classification, which will be demonstrated in the following experiments. The DNNC (Zhang et al., 2020) method is also based upon NLI-style classification, the major difference is, it predicts the entailment relationship between the query utterance and examples in the training set. We provide Figure 1 to compare the two methods with more details.

For inference, we first generate all the possible query utterance and label pair and compute the entailment probability scores. The pair with the highest score has the predicted label for the utterance. To accommodate out-of-scope (OOS) prediction, we can either treat it same as an additional intent class like the other intent labels, or set up a threshold T, if the maximum entailment probability score is over T, we assign the corresponding label as the prediction, otherwise we assign OOS as the prediction for the query utterance.

3 Experiments

3.1 Datasets

3.1.1 General NLI corpus for pre-training

To unleash the full potential of transformer model on NLI task, we follow the data processing and training pipeline provided by Zhang et al. (2020) to combine three NLI corpus (SNLI (Bowman

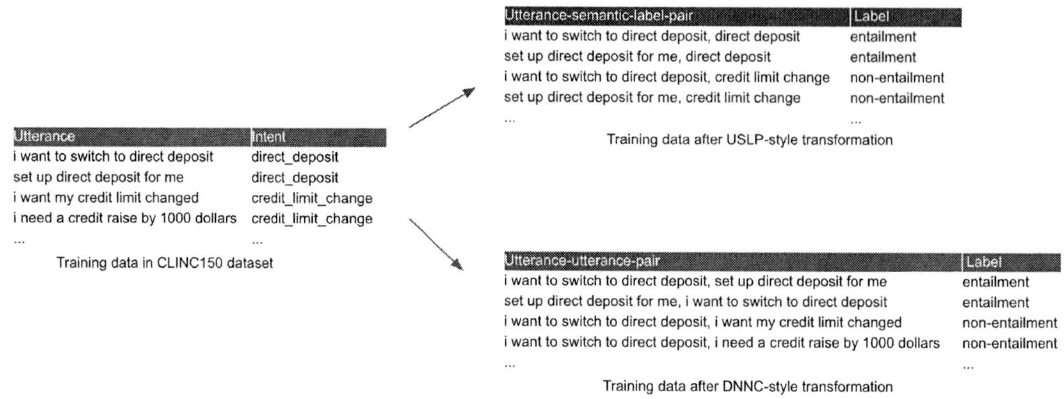

Figure 1: An illustration of training data in USLP and DNNC

et al., 2015), MNLI (Williams et al., 2018), and WNLI (Levesque, 2011)) from the GLUE benchmark (Wang et al., 2018) and use them for NLI pre-training.

3.1.2 CLINC150

CLINC150, introduced by Larson et al. (2019), is a multi-domain dataset for intent classification task. It has three dataset variants for in-domain and out-of-scope (OOS). We use the **small** dataset, which contains 150 intents, 50 examples/intent and 100 OOS examples for training. The original labeling has hyphen between each token in the label, we replace hyphen with empty space to format the label as short phrase. To simulate 1-, 5-, and 10-shot experiment, we randomly draw examples from the **small** dataset. We run each experiment five times with different seeds to capture the variations in random samplings. We remove dev set to simulate real few-shot scenario and use the original testing set for final results.

3.1.3 Schema-Guided Dialogue Dataset

SGD (Rastogi et al., 2019), or "Schema-Guided Dialogue Dataset", is a dataset about task-oriented dialogue. Its intent labels have detailed description, which is ideal for evaluating if detailed semantic labeling can help improve model performance. Since the original SGD dataset is not designed for few-shot intent classification, we went through a few data processing steps to customize the dataset for our use case. More details about the data processing steps can be found in Appendix B. We ended up with a subset of SGD dataset with 25 intents and 110 OOS utterances.

3.2 Data augmentation

We use the nlpaug library (Ma, 2019) for token-level data augmentation. In-domain utterances are augmented 4 times using random insertion, cBERT-based substitution, random swapping, and synonym replacement API. More details about the configurations can be found in Appendix A.

3.3 Training

We use the transformer library (4.5.1) (Wolf et al., 2020) by Huggingface for modeling. In NLI pre-training, we use the pre-trained roberta-base[1] model and follow the pre-training pipeline provided by Zhang et al. (2020). For downstream few-shot training, we use AdamW optimizer and linear scheduler, learning rate as 5e-5, epochs as 100, and train batch size as 128. We learnt this hyper-parameter set to be effective from our previous experiments with our in-house dataset. To simulate a real few shot setting, where dev set is often unavailable for hyper-parameter tuning and to demonstrate that the proposed method can be easily generalized into different datasets, we disregard all the dev sets in the following experiments and simply use the same hyper-parameter set without any further hyper-parameter tuning.

Balanced sampling Since the NLI reformulation of text classification results in much more negative examples than positive ones, we sample equal number of positive and negative examples for every batch to keep the model been exposed the balanced training examples. Furthermore, to prevent overfitting, each epoch iterates through all the positive examples while the negative examples are randomly

[1]https://huggingface.co/roberta-base

sampled to form batchs with positive examples. This data sampling strategy leads to better performance based upon previous empirical results on other in-house datasets. The previous DNNC (Zhang et al., 2020) work doesn't enforce balanced sampling, the positive and negative examples are mixed together and sampled randomly. We apply this sampling strategy to all the following experiments.

4 Results

4.1 Benchmark Results on CLINC150

USLP outperforms other methods by a large margin in 1-shot setting. Results from Table 1 show that USLP-T-A outperforms traditional classification approach by 20, 10, and 15 points in terms of in-domain accuracy, OOS recall, and OOS precision. The DNNC approch requires more than 1 example per class to start with, so it is out of the comparison. Compared with the 100-shot BERT-large results reported in Larson et al. (2019), the USLP-T-A achieves about 75% of the in-domain performance and has significantly higher OOS-recall score. Noticeably, within different USLP methods, the USLP-T has much better performance for in-domain accuracy (~20 points) and OOS-precision (>30 points) than USLP-O, but the USLP-O outperforms USLP-T by around 30 points for OOS-recall. One potential reason is the extremely unbalanced data; there are only one example per in-domain class, and in total we have 150 in-domain examples, but 100 examples for OOS. The USLP-O treats OOS as an extra class, but the OOS class has overwhelmingly more examples than other classes do, which could make the model favor OOS prediction. USLP-T approach, however, uses threshold to control in-domain and OOS prediction. Our experiments use 0.01 as the threshold, which tend to favor in-domain predictions and alleviates the extreme unbalance issue. Data augmentation can help improve in-domain classification and OOS-precision, but its impacts on OOS-recall and OOS-precision are opposite for USLP-T-A and USLP-O-A.

As we add more in-domain data into the experiments, in 5-shot and 10-shot experiments, we see the traditional classifier and DNNC in general perform better than USLP in terms of in-domain classification, but USLP has better and more balanced OOS-recall and OOS-precision scores. For example, in 10-shot experiments, CLS-T has the best in-domain accuracy, but it is unable to make OOS detection; DNNC has slightly better in-domain and OOS-precision result than USLP, but its OOS-recall is below that of USLP-T by around 30 points. Data augmentation seems to be more effective with USLP; it tends to hurt CLS and DNNC performance. Applying data augmentation on DNNC 10-shot training takes too much time (10+ hours on a single V-100 GPU), so we omit DNNC-A 10-shot experiment. Although the data augmentation continues to boost USLP in-domain performance for 5-shot and 10-shot experiments, it hurts OOS-recall. We believe that this is because the data augmentation will cause the model to be trained for more iterations due to fixed number of epochs and we sample 1/4 of batch size from OOS examples for every batch during training. As a result, the model is likely to overfit to the 100 OOS training examples.

4.2 The Role of Labeling Technique, Data Augmentation, and NLI pre-training

We use the SGD dataset to further study how relevant factors like labeling technique, data augmentation, and NLI pre-training on general corpus might impact USLP-T performance in different few-shot settings. Results are shown in Table 2.

Descriptive labeling can help improve USLP in-domain accuracy and OOS-precision. The SGD dataset provides intent labels as well as detailed descriptions for each label. To figure out the role of different labeling techniques in USLP-based intent classification, we set up three experiments with different labeling, 1) short labels, which are simply the original intent label. They are composed of either single words or short phrases and have limited semantic meaning; 2) long labels, which is the label description. Each description is usually a longer sentence than short labels and therefore can carry more semantic information; 3) symbolic labels. We convert labels into symbols like "0" and "1", which carry no semantic information. The results in Table 2 show that, long labels can effectively improve model performance. Especially at extreme low-resource scenario (1-shot), the long labels boost both in-domain accuracy and OOS-precision by 8+ points. Interestingly, long labels hurt model performance on OOS-recall. We hypothesize that long labels can boost model confidence on positive predictions resulting in producing higher prediction score favoring in-domain prediction.

	1-shot			5-shot			10-shot		
Method	In-Acc[3]	OOS-R[4]	OOS-P[5]	In-Acc	OOS-R	OOS-P	In-Acc	OOS-R	OOS-P
CLS-T[1]	51.56(1.31)	0.00(0.00)	NA	87.72(0.64)	0	NA	**92.52(0.41)**	0	NA
CLS-T-A[1]	51.44(1.61)	0.00(0.00)	NA	86.70(0.94)	0	NA	91.07(0.18)	0	NA
CLS-O[2]	43.41(3.17)	59.38(1.32)	48.20(4.82)	86.79(0.84)	42.98(2.36)	90.69(1.49)	91.95(0.50)	42.92(1.99)	95.05(1.01)
CLS-O-A[2]	45.31(2.28)	55.4(1.23)	51.03(5.00)	86.27(1.01)	43.18(1.81)	**92.84(1.75)**	91.18(0.40)	36.24(1.21)	**96.87(1.40)**
DNNC	NA	NA	NA	**88.49(1.00)**	61.46(6.10)	87.06(3.95)	91.21(0.61)	42.6(3.87)	92.69(1.39)
DNNC-A	NA	NA	NA	85.40(1.36)	20.30(10.33)	88.46(4.68)	NA	NA	NA
USLP-T	69.7(1.01)	62.62(3.07)	**66.92(3.64)**	83.96(1.45)	65.90(3.58)	84.32(3.26)	88.68(0.83)	**70.96(2.78)**	86.27(1.31)
USLP-T-A	**71.83(1.13)**	70.14(3.44)	65.18(5.08)	85.86(0.58)	65.47(2.81)	80.95(5.55)	90.29(0.44)	55.42(3.50)	89.23(2.30)
USLP-O	49.82(2.26)	**92.56(1.35)**	35.09(1.47)	79.28(1.11)	**67.06(2.34)**	72.61(2.45)	86.68(0.90)	56.70(3.81)	86.48(2.50)
USLP-O-A	66.84(1.05)	74.3(2.73)	55.67(3.40)	85.27(0.60)	54.18(3.83)	85.69(1.31)	90.22(0.59)	42.34(3.76)	94.51(1.40)
BL-100shot$_a$	96.9	40.3	NA						
BL-100shot$_b$	96.2	52.3	NA						

Table 1: CLINC150 few-shot benchmark results. [1] "CLS": traditional classifier using [CLS] token embedding for classification; "T": threshold, for all the experiments we use 0.01 as the threshold; "A": data augmentation; [2] "O": treating OOS as an additional class; BL-100shot$_a$ and BL-100shot$_b$ are based on bert-large model, reported by Larson et al. (2019). All other methods are based on roberta-base model. [3] "In-Acc", [4] "OOS-R", and [5] "OOS-P" stands for in-domain accuracy, OOS-recall, and OOS-precision respectively, numbers in the brackets represent standard deviation from multiple runs. DNNC requires >1 examples/intent for training and its 10-shot experiment with data augmentation takes >10 hours on a single V-100 GPU, so the corresponding experiments are skipped and results are shown as NA.

	1-shot			5-shot			10-shot		
Method	In-Acc	OOS-R	OOS-P	In-Acc	OOS-R	OOS-P	In-Acc	OOS-R	OOS-P
Short[1]	67.76(2.48)	**84.58(3.70)**	58.04(2.54)	85.54(1.18)	**74.53(6.63)**	89.84(2.33)	86.66(0.97)	**75.20(2.94)**	89.69(2.28)
Short-Aug[1]	69.68(3.51)	69.78(4.65)	60.35(4.34)	85.54(1.87)	67.96(5.17)	84.93(3.06)	85.46(1.00)	60.84(5.24)	84.85(2.27)
Long[2]	**76.24(2.47)**	77.2(3.96)	70.16(5.20)	**88.37(0.54)**	70.71(1.68)	**93.68(2.53)**	**88.59(0.61)**	74.80(4.11)	88.40(2.91)
Long-Aug[2]	74.22(1.14)	76.09(3.42)	**70.30(3.07)**	85.78(1.68)	74.00(5.03)	83.34(2.43)	87.14(0.83)	63.82(6.94)	86.44(2.05)
Symb[3]	4.58(1.02)	0	NA	7.94(1.71)	0	NA	58.90(8.18)	0	NA
Non-NLI[4]	64.64(3.74)	79.51(6.85)	62.96(1.21)	82.88(0.98)	62.00(3.55)	92.52(1.32)	88.26(0.51)	67.16(3.88)	**92.76(1.91)**

Table 2: USLP-T few-shot results on SGD dataset. [1] "short": original intent labels, which are either short phrases or single words; "Aug": data augmentation; [2] "long": detailed intent descriptions are used to replace short label to form utterance-label-pair; [3] "Symb": symbolic labels encoded as symbols like "0", "1", etc. They are converted from semantic labels; [4] "Non-NLI": the model is not fine-tuned on general NLI corpus.

Data augmentation is not always helpful. Quite different from the CLINC150 results, data augmentation fails to improve performance. In fact, data augmentation play a negative role in most experiments here. We tend to think that the effect of data augmentation is task-dependent, it might work well on some datasets but fail on other datasets. When developing few-shot applications with USLP, developers should be careful about applying data augmentation if no dev set is available.

NLI pre-training can boost performance in low-shot setting, but might have adverse effect when more training data is available. Our original hypothesis is that by exposing transformer model to NLI pre-training, the model can be more adapted into NLI related tasks and achieves better performance compared with the model without NLI pre-training. In 1-shot and 5-shot setting, we do observe that NLI pre-trained model can improve in-domain accuracy and OOS recall. But in 10-shot experiments, the NLI pre-trained model has weaker performance in terms of in-domain accuracy and OOS-precision.

5 Conclusion

We have created a new few-shot intent classification method, USLP, based upon NLI-style prediction. The USLP approach significantly outperforms traditional classification method by a large margin on 1-shot CLINC150 dataset and achieves about 75% of the 100-shot traditional classifier on in-domain classification with better OOS performance. This outstanding result indicates that the USLP approach can be an effective solution for developers who want to quickly build an intent classifier with extremely limited amount of training data. We have also found that detailed description can further boost USLP performance, but detailed labeling also requires labelers to have deeper understanding of each intent class and thus prolongs labeling process.

Acknowledgements

We would like to thank all the reviewers for their helpful comments. We would also like to thank Shashank Harinath, Shilpa Bhagavath, and Mridul Gupta for their insightful discussions on data augmentation methods.

References

Samuel R. Bowman, Gabor Angeli, Christopher Potts, and Christopher D. Manning. 2015. A large annotated corpus for learning natural language inference. In *Proceedings of the 2015 Conference on Empirical Methods in Natural Language Processing*, pages 632–642, Lisbon, Portugal. Association for Computational Linguistics.

Alexis Conneau, Kartikay Khandelwal, Naman Goyal, Vishrav Chaudhary, Guillaume Wenzek, Francisco Guzmán, Edouard Grave, Myle Ott, Luke Zettlemoyer, and Veselin Stoyanov. 2020. Unsupervised cross-lingual representation learning at scale. In *Proceedings of the 58th Annual Meeting of the Association for Computational Linguistics*, pages 8440–8451, Online. Association for Computational Linguistics.

Jacob Devlin, Ming Wei Chang, Kenton Lee, and Kristina Toutanova. 2019. BERT: Pre-training of deep bidirectional transformers for language understanding. *NAACL HLT 2019 - 2019 Conference of the North American Chapter of the Association for Computational Linguistics: Human Language Technologies - Proceedings of the Conference*, 1(Mlm):4171–4186.

Ruiying Geng, Binhua Li, Yongbin Li, Xiaodan Zhu, Ping Jian, and Jian Sun. 2019. Induction networks for few-shot text classification. In *Proceedings of the 2019 Conference on Empirical Methods in Natural Language Processing and the 9th International Joint Conference on Natural Language Processing (EMNLP-IJCNLP)*, pages 3904–3913, Hong Kong, China. Association for Computational Linguistics.

Yutai Hou, Wanxiang Che, Yongkui Lai, Zhihan Zhou, Yijia Liu, Han Liu, and Ting Liu. 2020a. Few-shot slot tagging with collapsed dependency transfer and label-enhanced task-adaptive projection network. In *Proceedings of the 58th Annual Meeting of the Association for Computational Linguistics*, pages 1381–1393, Online. Association for Computational Linguistics.

Yutai Hou, Yongkui Lai, Yushan Wu, Wanxiang Che, and Ting Liu. 2020b. Few-shot Learning for Multi-label Intent Detection.

Varun Kumar, Hadrien Glaude, Cyprien de Lichy, and Wlliam Campbell. 2019. A Closer Look At Feature Space Data Augmentation For Few-Shot Intent Classification. pages 1–10.

Stefan Larson, Anish Mahendran, Joseph J. Peper, Christopher Clarke, Andrew Lee, Parker Hill, Jonathan K. Kummerfeld, Kevin Leach, Michael A. Laurenzano, Lingjia Tang, and Jason Mars. 2019. An evaluation dataset for intent classification and out-of-scope prediction. In *Proceedings of the 2019 Conference on Empirical Methods in Natural Language Processing and the 9th International Joint Conference on Natural Language Processing (EMNLP-IJCNLP)*.

Hector J Levesque. 2011. Levesque - The Winograd Schema Challenge. (1989).

Yinhan Liu, Myle Ott, Naman Goyal, Jingfei Du, Mandar Joshi, Danqi Chen, Omer Levy, Mike Lewis, Luke Zettlemoyer, and Veselin Stoyanov. 2019. RoBERTa: A Robustly Optimized BERT Pretraining Approach. (1).

Edward Ma. 2019. Nlp augmentation. https://github.com/makcedward/nlpaug.

Abhinav Rastogi, Xiaoxue Zang, Srinivas Sunkara, Raghav Gupta, and Pranav Khaitan. 2019. Towards Scalable Multi-domain Conversational Agents: The Schema-Guided Dialogue Dataset.

Timo Schick and Hinrich Schütze. 2021. Exploiting cloze-questions for few-shot text classification and natural language inference. In *Proceedings of the 16th Conference of the European Chapter of the Association for Computational Linguistics: Main Volume*, pages 255–269, Online. Association for Computational Linguistics.

Jake Snell, Kevin Swersky, and Richard Zemel. 2017. Prototypical networks for few-shot learning. *Advances in Neural Information Processing Systems*, 2017-Decem:4078–4088.

Alex Wang, Amanpreet Singh, Julian Michael, Felix Hill, Omer Levy, and Samuel Bowman. 2018. GLUE: A multi-task benchmark and analysis platform for natural language understanding. In *Proceedings of the 2018 EMNLP Workshop BlackboxNLP: Analyzing and Interpreting Neural Networks for NLP*, pages 353–355, Brussels, Belgium. Association for Computational Linguistics.

Jason Wei and Kai Zou. 2019. EDA: Easy data augmentation techniques for boosting performance on text classification tasks. In *Proceedings of the 2019 Conference on Empirical Methods in Natural Language Processing and the 9th International Joint Conference on Natural Language Processing (EMNLP-IJCNLP)*, pages 6382–6388, Hong Kong, China. Association for Computational Linguistics.

Adina Williams, Nikita Nangia, and Samuel Bowman. 2018. A broad-coverage challenge corpus for sentence understanding through inference. In *Proceedings of the 2018 Conference of the North American Chapter of the Association for Computational Linguistics: Human Language Technologies, Volume*

1 (Long Papers), pages 1112–1122, New Orleans, Louisiana. Association for Computational Linguistics.

Thomas Wolf, Lysandre Debut, Victor Sanh, Julien Chaumond, Clement Delangue, Anthony Moi, Pierric Cistac, Tim Rault, Rémi Louf, Morgan Funtowicz, Joe Davison, Sam Shleifer, Patrick von Platen, Clara Ma, Yacine Jernite, Julien Plu, Canwen Xu, Teven Le Scao, Sylvain Gugger, Mariama Drame, Quentin Lhoest, and Alexander M. Rush. 2020. Transformers: State-of-the-art natural language processing. In *Proceedings of the 2020 Conference on Empirical Methods in Natural Language Processing: System Demonstrations*, pages 38–45, Online. Association for Computational Linguistics.

Wenpeng Yin, Jamaal Hay, and Dan Roth. 2019. Benchmarking zero-shot text classification: Datasets, evaluation and entailment approach. In *Proceedings of the 2019 Conference on Empirical Methods in Natural Language Processing and the 9th International Joint Conference on Natural Language Processing (EMNLP-IJCNLP)*, pages 3914–3923, Hong Kong, China. Association for Computational Linguistics.

Jianguo Zhang, Kazuma Hashimoto, Wenhao Liu, Chien-Sheng Wu, Yao Wan, Philip Yu, Richard Socher, and Caiming Xiong. 2020. Discriminative nearest neighbor few-shot intent detection by transferring natural language inference. In *Proceedings of the 2020 Conference on Empirical Methods in Natural Language Processing (EMNLP)*, pages 5064–5082, Online. Association for Computational Linguistics.

A Data Augmentation Methods

API name	action	model
WordEmbsAug	insert	GoogleNews-vectors-negative300
ContextualWord-EmbsAug	substitute	bert-base-uncased
RandomWordAug	swap	NA
SynonymAug	NA	ppdb-2.0-s-all

Table 3: Detailed configurations for nlpaug APIs.

B SGD Data Processing

We first extract utterances, intents, and detailed intent descriptions from the training set. The original labels formatted as tokens been concatenated together with the first letter capitalized, we introduce an empty space between each token. In the original dataset, the label set of the testing set does not fully overlap with the training set, so we keep the utterances with overlapped intents (25 intents) for in-domain and use the utterances with non-overlapped intents for OOS training (11 intents). Since our goal of using the SGD dataset is to explore how different labeling techniques might impact final results, we want to use the same training set to exclude the confounding factor of random training data sampling, so we sample 1-, 5-, 10-shot in-domain and 110 OOS (10 utterances/non-overlapped intent) utterances from the processed training set for all the SGD experiments. The original testing set has 11,105 utterances, which is expensive to run through for evaluation. So we sample 50 utterances per overlapped intents for in-domain testing set and 50 utterances per non-overlapped intents (9 non-overlapped intents) for OOS testing set, resulting in a testing set with 1,250 in-domain and 450 OOS utterances.

Personalized Extractive Summarization Using an Ising Machine Towards Real-time Generation of Efficient and Coherent Dialogue Scenarios

Hiroaki Takatsu[1] **Takahiro Kashikawa**[2] **Koichi Kimura**[2] **Ryota Ando**[3] **Yoichi Matsuyama**[1]
[1]Waseda University, Tokyo, Japan
[2]FUJITSU LIMITED, Kanagawa, Japan
[3]Naigai Pressclipping Bureau,Ltd., Tokyo, Japan
takatsu@pcl.cs.waseda.ac.jp {kashikawa, k.kimura}@jp.fujitsu.com
ando@naigaipc.co.jp matsuyama@pcl.cs.waseda.ac.jp

Abstract

We propose a personalized dialogue scenario generation system which transmits efficient and coherent information with a real-time extractive summarization method optimized by an Ising machine. The summarization problem is formulated as a quadratic unconstraint binary optimization (QUBO) problem, which extracts sentences that maximize the sum of the degree of user's interest in the sentences of documents with the discourse structure of each document and the total utterance time as constraints. To evaluate the proposed method, we constructed a news article corpus with annotations of the discourse structure, users' profiles, and interests in sentences and topics. The experimental results confirmed that a Digital Annealer, which is a simulated annealing-based Ising machine, can solve our QUBO model in a practical time without violating the constraints using this dataset.

1 Introduction

As mobile personal assistants and smart speakers become ubiquitous, the demand for dialogue-based media technologies has increased since they allow users to consume a fair amount of information via a dialogue form in daily life situations. Dialogue-based media is more restrictive than textual media. For example, when listening to an ordinary smart speaker, users can not skip unnecessary information or skim only for necessary information. Thus, it is crucial for future dialogue-based media to extract and efficiently transmit information that the users are particularly interested in without excess or deficiencies. In addition, the dialogue scenarios generated based on the extracted information should be coherent to aid in the proper understanding. Generating such efficient and coherent scenarios personalized for each user generally takes more time as the information source size and the number of target users increase. Moreover, the nature of conversational experiences requires personalization in real time. In this paper, we propose a personalized extractive summarization method formulated as a combinatorial optimization problem to generate efficient and coherent dialogue scenarios and demonstrate that an Ising machine can solve the problem at high speeds.

As a realistic application of the proposed personalized summarization method for a spoken dialogue system, we consider a news delivery task (Takatsu et al., 2018). This news dialogue system proceeds the dialogue according to a primary plan to explain the summary of the news article and subsidiary plans to transmit supplementary information though question answering. As long as the user is listening passively, the system transmits the content of the primary plan. The personalized primary plan generation problem can be formulated as follows:

> From N documents with different topics, sentences that may be of interest to the user are extracted based on the discourse structure of each document. Then the contents are transmitted by voice within T seconds.

Specifically, this problem can be formulated as an integer linear programming (ILP) problem, which extracts sentences that maximize the sum of the degree of user's interest in the sentences of documents with the discourse structure of each document and the total utterance time T as constraints. Because this ILP problem is NP-hard, it takes an enormous amount of time to find an optimal solution using the branch-and-cut method (Mitchell, 2002; Padberg and Rinaldi, 1991) as the problem scale becomes large.

In recent years, non-von Neumann computers called Ising machines have been attracting attention as they can solve combinatorial optimization problems and obtain quasi-optimal solutions instantly (Sao et al., 2019). Ising machines can solve combi-

Proceedings of the Third Workshop on Natural Language Processing for Conversational AI, pages 16–29
November 10, 2021. ©2021 Association for Computational Linguistics

natorial optimization problems represented by an Ising model or a quadratic unconstrained binary optimization (QUBO) model (Lucas, 2014; Glover et al., 2019). In this paper, we propose a QUBO model that generates an efficient and coherent personalized summary for each user. Additionally, we verify that our QUBO model can be solved by a Digital Annealer (Aramon et al., 2019; Matsubara et al., 2020), which is a simulated annealing-based Ising machine, in a practical time without violating the constraints using the constructed dataset.

The contributions of this paper are three-fold:

- The ILP and QUBO models for the personalized summary generation are formulated in terms of efficient and coherent information transmission.
- To evaluate the effectiveness of the proposed method, we construct a Japanese news article corpus with annotations of the discourse structure, users' profiles, and interests in sentences and topics.
- Experiments demonstrate that a Digital Annealer, which is a simulated annealing-based Ising machine, can solve our QUBO model in a practical time without violating the constraints.

The rest of this paper is organized as follows. Section 2 discusses the related work. Section 3 overviews the annotations of the discourse structure and interest data collection. Section 4 details the proposed method. Section 5 describes the Digital Annealer. Section 6 evaluates the performance of the proposed method. Section 7 provides the conclusions and prospects.

2 Related work

2.1 Discourse structure corpus

Typical datasets for discourse structure analysis are RST Discourse Treebank (Carlson et al., 2001), Discourse Graphbank (Wolf and Gibson, 2005), and Penn Discourse Treebank (Prasad et al., 2008). RST Discourse Treebank is a dataset constructed based on rhetorical structure theory (Mann and Thompson, 1988). Some studies have annotated discourse relations to Japanese documents. Kaneko and Bekki (2014) annotated the temporal and causal relations for segments obtained by decomposing the sentences of the balanced corpus of contemporary written Japanese (Maekawa et al., 2014) based on segmented discourse representation theory (Asher and Lascarides, 2003). Kawahara et al. (2014) proposed a method to annotate discourse relations for the first three sentences of web documents in various domains using crowdsourcing. They showed that discourse relations can be annotated in many documents over a short amount of time. Kishimoto et al. (2018) confirmed that making improvements such as adding language tests to the annotation criteria of Kawahara et al. (2014) can improve the annotation quality.

When applying discourse structure analysis results to tasks such as document summarization (Hirao et al., 2013; Yoshida et al., 2014; Kikuchi et al., 2014; Hirao et al., 2015) or dialogue (Feng et al., 2019), a dependency structure, which directly expresses the parent-child relationship between discourse units, is preferable to a phrase structure such as a rhetorical structure tree. Although methods have been proposed to convert a rhetorical structure tree into a discourse dependency tree (Li et al., 2014; Hirao et al., 2013), the generated trees depends on the conversion algorithm (Hayashi et al., 2016). Yang and Li (2018) proposed a method to manually annotate the dependency structure and discourse relations between elementary discourse units for abstracts of scientific papers, and then constructed SciDTB.

In this study, we construct a dataset suitable to build summarization or dialogue systems that transmit personalized information while considering the coherence based on the discourse structure. Experts annotated the inter-sentence dependencies, discourse relations, and chunks, which are highly cohesive sets of sentences, for Japanese news articles. Users' profiles and interests in the sentences and topics of news articles were collected via crowdsourcing.

2.2 Personalized summarization

As people's interests and preferences diversify, the demand for personalized summarization technology has increased (Sappelli et al., 2018). Summaries are classified as generic or user-focused, based on whether they are specific to a particular user (Mani and Bloedorn, 1998). Unlike generic summaries generated by extracting important information from the text, user-focused summaries are generated based not only on important information but also on the user's interests and preferences. Most user-focused summarization methods rank sentences using a score calculated considering user's characteristics and subsequently generate a summary by extracting higher-ranked sentences

(Díaz and Gervás, 2007; Yan et al., 2011; Hu et al., 2012). However, such conventional user-focused methods tend to generate incoherent summaries. Generic summarization methods, which consider the discourse structure of documents, have been proposed to maintain coherence (Kikuchi et al., 2014; Hirao et al., 2015; Xu et al., 2020).

To achieve both personalization and coherence simultaneously, we propose ILP and QUBO models to extract sentences based on the degree of user's interest and generate a personalized summary for each user while maintaining coherence based on the discourse structure.

3 Datasets

We constructed a news article corpus with annotations of the discourse structure, users' profiles, and interests in sentences and topics. Experts annotated the inter-sentence dependencies, discourse relations, and chunks for the Japanese news articles. Users' profiles and interests in the sentences and topics of news articles were collected via crowdsourcing.

3.1 Discourse structure dataset

Two web news clipping experts annotated the dependencies, discourse relations, and chunks for 1,200 Japanese news articles. Each article contained between 15–25 sentences. The articles were divided into six genres: sports, technology, economy, international, society, and local. In each genre, we manually selected 200 articles to minimize topic overlap. The annotation work was performed in the order of dependencies, discourse relations, and chunks. The discourse unit was a sentence, which represents a character string separated by an ideographic full stop.

3.1.1 Dependency annotation

The conditions in which sentence j can be specified as the parent of sentence i are as follows:

- In the original text, sentence j appears before sentence i.
- The flow of the story is natural when reading from the root node in order according to the tree structure and reading sentence i after sentence j.
- The information from the root node to sentence j is the minimum information necessary to understand sentence i.
- If it is possible to start reading from sentence i, the parent of sentence i is the root node.

3.1.2 Discourse relation annotation

A discourse relation classifies the type of semantic relationship between the child sentence and the parent sentence. We defined the following as discourse relations: *Start*, *Result*, *Cause*, *Background*, *Correspondence*, *Contrast*, *Topic Change*, *Example*, *Conclusion*, and *Supplement*.

An annotation judgment was made while confirming whether both the definition of the discourse relation and the dialogue criterion were met. The dialogue criterion is a judgment based on whether the response is natural according to the discourse relation. For example, the annotators checked whether it was appropriate to present a child sentence as an answer to a question asking the cause, such as "Why?" after the parent sentence.

3.1.3 Chunk annotation

A chunk is a highly cohesive set of sentences. If a parent sentence should be presented with a child sentence, it is regarded as a chunk.

A *hard chunk* occurs when the child sentence provides information essential to understand the content of the parent sentence. Examples include when the parent sentence contains a comment and the child sentence contains the speaker's information or when a procedure is explained over multiple sentences.

A *soft chunk* occurs when the child sentence is useful to prevent a biased understanding of the content of the parent sentence, although it does not necessarily contain essential information to understand the parent sentence itself. An example is explaining the situation in two countries related to a subject, where the parent sentence contains one explanation and the child sentence contains another.

3.2 Interest dataset

Participants were recruited via crowdsourcing. They were asked to answer a profile questionnaire and an interest questionnaire. We used 1,200 news articles, which were the same as those used in the discourse structure dataset. We collected the questionnaire results of 2,507 participants. Each participant received six articles, one from each genre. The six articles were distributed so that the total number of sentences was as even as possible across participants. Each article was reviewed by at least 11 participants.

3.2.1 Profile questionnaire

The profile questionnaire collected the following information: gender, age, residential prefecture, occupation type, industry type, hobbies, frequency of checking news (daily, 4–6 days a week, 1–3 days a week, or 0 days a week), typical time of day news is checked (morning, afternoon, early evening, or night), methods to access the news (video, audio, or text), tools used to check the news (TV, newspaper, smartphone, etc.), newspapers, websites, and applications used to check the news (Nihon Keizai Shimbun, LINE NEWS, SNS, etc.), whether a fee was paid to check the news, news genre actively checked (economy, sports, etc.), and the degree of interest in each news genre (not interested at all, not interested, not interested if anything, interested if anything, interested, or very interested).

3.2.2 Interest questionnaire

Participants read the text of the news article and indicated their degree of interest in the content of each sentence. Finally, they indicated their degree of interest in the topic of the article. The degree of interest was indicated on six levels: 1, not interested at all; 2, not interested; 3, not interested if anything; 4, interested if anything; 5, interested; or 6, very interested.

4 Methods

We propose an integer linear programming (ILP) model and a quadratic unconstraint binary optimization (QUBO) model for the personalized summary generation in terms of efficient and coherent information transmission.

4.1 Integer linear programming model

We considered a summarization problem, which extracts sentences that user u may be interested in from the selected N documents and then transmits them by voice within T seconds. The summary must be of interest to the user, coherent, and not redundant. Therefore, we formulated the summarization problem as an integer linear programming problem in which the objective function is defined by the balance between a high degree of interest in the sentences and a low degree of similarity between the sentences with the discourse structure as constraints. This is expressed as

$$\max. \sum_{k \in D_N^u} \sum_{i<j \in S_k} b_{ki}^u b_{kj}^u (1 - r_{kij}) \, y_{kij} \tag{1}$$

Table 1: Variable definitions in the interesting sentence extraction method

x_{ki}	Whether sentence s_{ki} is selected
y_{kij}	Whether both s_{ki} and s_{kj} are selected
b_{ki}^u	Degree of user u's interest in s_{ki}
r_{kij}	Similarity between s_{ki} and s_{kj}
t_{ki}	Utterance time of s_{ki} (seconds)
T	Maximum summary length (seconds)
L	Maximum bias in the number of extracting sentences between documents
$f_k(i)$	Function that returns the parent ID of s_{ki}
D_N^u	IDs of the selected N documents for user u
S_k	Sentence IDs contained in document d_k
C_{km}	Sentence IDs contained in chunk m of d_k

s.t.

$$\forall k, i, j: \ x_{ki} \in \{0,1\}, \ y_{kij} \in \{0,1\}$$

$$\sum_{k \in D_N^u} \sum_{i \in S_k} t_{ki} x_{ki} \leq T \tag{2}$$

$$\forall k < l: \ \left| \sum_{i \in S_k} x_{ki} - \sum_{i \in S_l} x_{li} \right| \leq L \tag{3}$$

$$\forall k, i: \ j = f_k(i), \quad x_{ki} \leq x_{kj} \tag{4}$$

$$\forall k, m, i \in C_{km}: \ \sum_{j \in C_{km}} x_{kj} = |C_{km}| \times x_{ki} \tag{5}$$

$$\forall k, i, j: \ y_{kij} - x_{ki} \leq 0 \tag{6}$$

$$\forall k, i, j: \ y_{kij} - x_{kj} \leq 0 \tag{7}$$

$$\forall k, i, j: \ x_{ki} + x_{kj} - y_{kij} \leq 1 \tag{8}$$

Table 1 explains each variable. Here, the i-th sentence of the k-th document is expressed as s_{ki}. r_{kij} represents the cosine similarity between the bag-of-words constituting s_{ki} and s_{kj}.

Equation 2 is a constraint restricting the utterance time of the summary to T seconds or less. Equation 3 is a constraint restricting the bias of the number of extracting sentences between documents to L sentences or less. Equation 4 is a constraint in which the parent s_{kj} of s_{ki} in the discourse dependency tree must be extracted when s_{ki} is extracted. Equation 5 is a constraint requiring other sentences in the chunk to be extracted when extracting s_{ki} in a chunk. Equations 6–8 are constraints that set $y_{kij} = 1$ when s_{ki} and s_{kj} are selected.

The maximum bias in the number of extracting sentences between documents L is calculated by the following formulas, which are based on the maximum summary length T, the number of documents N, and the average utterance time of the sentences $\bar{t}$.

$$L = \left\lfloor \frac{\bar{n}}{\sqrt{N}} + 0.5 \right\rfloor \quad (9)$$

$$\bar{n} = \frac{T}{\bar{t} \times N} \quad (10)$$

$\bar{n}$ represents the expected number of sentences to be extracted from one document. L is the value obtained by dividing $\bar{n}$ by the square root of the number of documents and rounding the result.

4.2 Quadratic unconstrained binary optimization model

To solve the combinatorial optimization problem with an Ising machine, the problem must be formulated with the Ising model or the quadratic unconstraint binary optimization (QUBO) model (Lucas, 2014; Glover et al., 2019). The energy functions of the Ising model and the QUBO model are described by the quadratic form of spin variables $\{-1, +1\}$ and binary variables $\{0, 1\}$, respectively. Ising machines search for the lowest energy state of the Ising model or the QUBO model. Here, we formulated the QUBO model based on the above ILP model. The energy function (or Hamiltonian) $\mathcal{H}$ of the QUBO model is defined as

$$\mathcal{H} = \mathcal{H}_0 + \lambda_1 \mathcal{H}_1 + \lambda_2 \mathcal{H}_2 + \lambda_3 \mathcal{H}_3 + \lambda_4 \mathcal{H}_4 \quad (11)$$

$$\mathcal{H}_0 = -\sum_{k \in D_N^u} \sum_{i<j \in S_k} b_{ki}^u b_{kj}^u \left(1 - r_{kij}\right) x_{ki} x_{kj} \quad (12)$$

$$\mathcal{H}_1 = \left(T - \sum_{k \in D_N^u} \sum_{i \in S_k} t_{ki} x_{ki} - \sum_{n=0}^{\lfloor \log_2 (T-1) \rfloor} 2^n y_n \right)^2 \quad (13)$$

$$\mathcal{H}_2 = \sum_{k<l \in D_N^u} \left(L - \left(\sum_{i \in S_k} x_{ki} - \sum_{i \in S_l} x_{li}\right) - \sum_{n=0}^{\lfloor \log_2 (L-1) \rfloor} 2^n z_n \right)^2 \quad (14)$$

$$\mathcal{H}_3 = \left(x_{ki} - x_{ki} x_{kj=f_k(i)}\right)^2 \quad (15)$$

$$\mathcal{H}_4 = \sum_{k \in D_N^u} \sum_{m \in C_k} \sum_{i \in C_{km}} \left(\sum_{j \in C_{km}} x_{kj} - |C_{km}| \times x_{ki}\right)^2 \quad (16)$$

where y_n and z_n are slack variables introduced to convert inequality constraints into equality constraints, λ_1, λ_2, λ_3, and λ_4 are the weight coefficients for each constraint.

QUBO models are solved by a simulated annealing-based method (Aramon et al., 2019) or parallel tempering (known as replica-exchange Monte Carlo) (Matsubara et al., 2020). In these methods, multiple solution candidates can be obtained by annealing in parallel with different initial values. However, these methods do not guarantee that constraint violations will not occur. Therefore, the solution candidate with the lowest constraint violation score and the highest score of the objective function is adopted. The constraint violation score E_{total} is calculated as

$$E_{total} = E_{dep} + E_{chunk} + E_{bias} + E_{time} \quad (17)$$

$$E_{bias} = \max\left(\hat{L} - L, 0\right) \quad (18)$$

$$E_{time} = \max\left(\hat{T} - T, 0\right) \quad (19)$$

where E_{dep} is the number of dependency errors, E_{chunk} is the number of chunk errors, $\hat{L}$ is the maximum bias in the number of extracted sentences between documents, $\hat{T}$ is the total utterance time of the extracted sentences.

5 Digital Annealer

Quantum computing technologies are categorized into two types: quantum gate computers (Arute et al., 2019; Gyongyosi, 2020) and Ising machines. Quantum gate computers are for universal computing, whereas Ising machines specialize in searching for solutions of combinatorial optimization problems. Ising machines can be subdivided into two categories: quantum annealing machines (Johnson et al., 2011; Bunyk et al., 2014; Maezawa et al., 2019) and simulated annealing machines (Yamaoka et al., 2016; Okuyama et al., 2017; Aramon et al., 2019; Matsubara et al., 2020). Quantum annealing machines search solutions using quantum bits, which are made of quantum devices such as a superconducting circuit. By contrast, simulated annealing machines use a digital circuit. Digital Annealer (Aramon et al., 2019; Matsubara et al., 2020) is a type of simulated annealing machines with a new digital circuit architecture, which is designed to solve combinatorial optimization problems efficiently.

This study uses a Digital Annealing Unit (DAU) of the second generation Digital Annealer. The

DAU has an annealing mode (Aramon et al., 2019) or parallel tempering mode (Matsubara et al., 2020) to solve QUBO models. It can handle up to 4,096 binary variables with 64-bit precision or as many as 8,192 binary variables with 16-bit precision. Hereinafter, the DAU in the annealing mode is referred to as DAU-AM, and the DAU in the parallel tempering mode is referred to as DAU-PTM.

6 Experiments

Using the constructed dataset, we evaluated the performance of the personalized summarization method for dialogue scenario planning. The ILP model was solved by the branch-and-cut method[1] (Mitchell, 2002; Padberg and Rinaldi, 1991) on the CPU. Hereinafter, this method is referred to as CPU-CBC. We used CPU-CBC as a benchmark and compared the performance of CPU-CBC, DAU-AM and DAU-PTM.

6.1 Experimental setup

We used 2,117 participants data which the answer time of the six articles was between 5 and 30 minutes. The performance was evaluated for two cases. The first transmitted $N = 6$ articles in $T' = 450$ seconds and the second transmitted the top $N = 3$ articles with high interest in the topic in $T' = 270$ seconds. Sentences in the news articles was synthesized by AITalk 4.1[2] to calculate the duration of speech. The maximum summary length T was calculated as $T = T' - (N-1) \times (q_d - q_s)$, where T' denotes the total utterance time of the primary plan, q_s denotes the pause between sentences, and q_d denotes the pause between documents. Here, $q_s = 1$ second and $q_d = 3$ seconds. The value obtained by adding q_s to the playback time of the synthesized audio file was set as t_{ki}.

The PULP_CBC_CMD solver of the PuLP[3], which is a Python library for linear programming optimization, was used to solve the ILP model. Python and PuLP versions were 3.7.6 and 2.4, respectively. The parameter for the number of threads of PULP_CBC_CMD was set to 30. The execution time of the solving function was measured on the Google Compute Engine[4] with the following settings: OS, Ubuntu 18.04; CPU, Xeon (2.20 GHz, 32 cores); Memory, 64 GB.

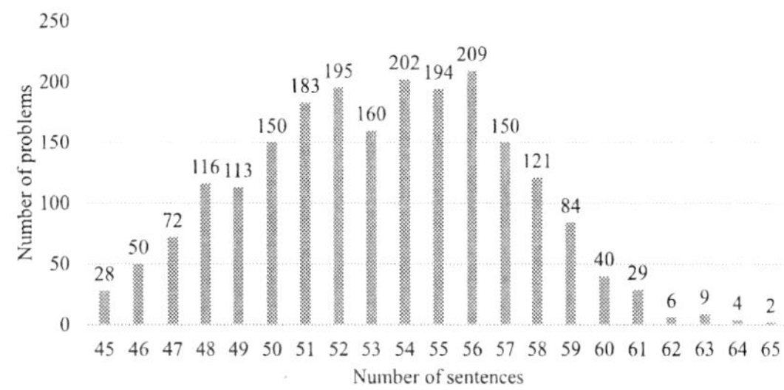

Figure 1: Number of problems for a given number of sentences when $N = 3$

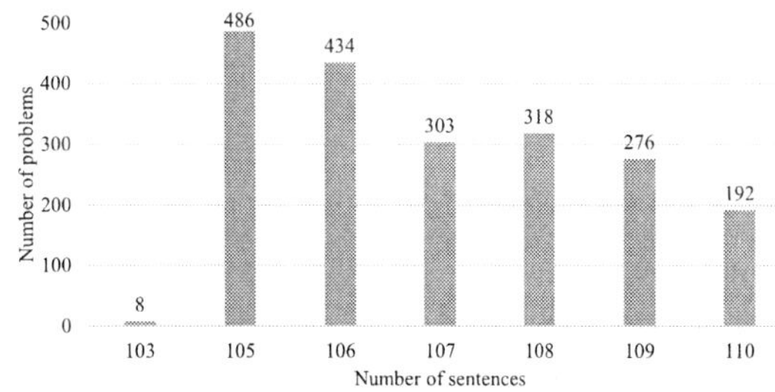

Figure 2: Number of problems for a given number of sentences when $N = 6$

Figure 1 shows the number of problems for a given number of sentences when $N = 3$. These are the top three articles with the highest degree of interest in the topic among the six articles distributed to each participant. Figure 2 shows the number of problems for a given number of sentences when $N = 6$. Since the six articles were distributed so that the total number of sentences was as even as possible across participants, the variation in the number of sentences was small.

The DAU must set the number of bits parameter from 1,024, 2,048, 4,096, or 8,192, depending on the problem size. In the experimental setting of $N = 3, T' = 270$, the 2,090 QUBO problems were less than 2,048 bits and the 27 QUBO problems were less than 4,096. On the other hand, in the experimental setting of $N = 6, T' = 450$, the 2,017 QUBO problems were less than 4,096 bits and the 100 QUBO problems were less than 8,192. In the latter experiment, these 100 participants data were excluded because the calculation precision of the DAU decreased when the problem size exceeds 4,096 bits.

The number of replicas in DAU-PTM and the number of runs of annealing in DAU-AM were 128. Since the performance of the DAU mainly depended on λ and the number of searches in one annealing (#iteration), these parameters were adjusted to prevent constraint violations.

[1] https://projects.coin-or.org/Cbc

[2] https://www.ai-j.jp/product/voiceplus/manual/

[3] https://coin-or.github.io/pulp/

[4] https://cloud.google.com/compute/?hl=en

Table 2: Information transmission efficiency of the summaries ($N = 3, T' = 270$)

	Parameters of the Digital Annealer					Efficiency of information transmission				Processing
	λ_1	λ_2	λ_3	λ_4	#iteration	Coverage	Exclusion rate	EoIT_1	EoIT_2	time (sec)
CPU-CBC (30 threads)	-	-	-	-	-	0.687	0.726	0.672	0.696	18.9
DAU-AM	10^2	10^6	10^{10}	10	10^3	0.638	0.612	0.584	0.593	0.0570
DAU-PTM	10^2	10^5	10^9	10	10^3	0.656	0.637	0.608	0.618	0.245
					10^4	0.669	0.661	0.627	0.639	1.76

Table 3: Information transmission efficiency of the summaries ($N = 6, T' = 450$)

	Parameters of the Digital Annealer					Efficiency of information transmission				Processing
	λ_1	λ_2	λ_3	λ_4	#iteration	Coverage	Exclusion rate	EoIT_1	EoIT_2	time (sec)
CPU-CBC (30 threads)	-	-	-	-	-	0.638	0.667	0.639	0.651	102
DAU-AM	10^2	10^6	10^{10}	10	10^3	0.538	0.585	0.552	0.568	0.199
DAU-PTM	10^2	10^5	10^9	10	10^3	0.553	0.577	0.556	0.565	0.749
					10^4	0.570	0.591	0.572	0.580	6.44

6.2 Evaluation metrics

We used EoIT_β (efficiency of information transmission) (Takatsu et al., 2021) as the evaluation metric. When C is the coverage of sentences annotated as "very interested," "interested," or "interested if anything," and E is the exclusion rate of the sentences annotated as "not interested at all," "not interested," or "not interested if anything," EoIT_β is defined based on the weighted F-measure (Chinchor, 1992) as

$$\mathrm{EoIT}_\beta = \frac{(1+\beta^2) \times C \times E}{\beta^2 \times C + E} \quad (20)$$

When $\beta = 2$, the exclusion rate is twice as important as the coverage. Compared to textual media, which allows readers to read at their own pace, dialogue-based media does not allow users to skip unnecessary information or skim necessary information while listening. Consequently, we assumed that the exclusion rate is more important than the coverage in information transmission by spoken dialogue and set $\beta = 2$.

6.3 Experimental results

Tables 2 and 3 show the results of $N = 3, T' = 270$ and $N = 6, T' = 450$, respectively. The values of the evaluation metrics and processing times represent the average. DAU-AM had a shorter processing time than DAU-PTM for the same number of iterations. However, in terms of the EoIT, DAU-PTM was higher than DAU-AM. The EoIT of DAU-PTM improved as the number of iterations increased, but the processing time also increased. On the other hand, increasing the number of iterations did not improve the EoIT of DAU-AM.

Figures 3 and 4 show the distributions of processing time for each number of sentences in the experimental settings of $N = 3, T' = 270$ and $N = 6, T' = 450$, respectively. The number of iterations for DAU-AM and DAU-PTM was 1,000. The processing time of CPU-CBC became longer as the number of sentences increased. Even if the number of sentences was the same, the processing time varied widely. On the other hand, the processing time of DAU-AM and DAU-PTM changed according to the size of the QUBO problems and the number of iterations, regardless of the number of sentences. At $N = 6$, the size of all QUBO problems was less than 4,096, and the processing time of DAU was almost constant regardless of the number of sentences. At $N = 3$, the size of the QUBO problems was less than 2,048 when the number of sentences was 59 or less, and less than 4,096 when the number of sentences was 63 or more. On the other hand, when the number of sentences was between 60 and 62, problems with less than 2,048 and problems with less than 4,096 were mixed due to the number of chunks.

Although the DAU is inferior to CPU-CBC in the EoIT, its processing time is considerably shorter than CPU-CBC. In addition, the processing time of the DAU can be estimated in advance based on the size of the QUBO problems and the number of iterations.

6.4 Discussion

The DAU does not guarantee that constraint violations will not occur. Although the DAU did not induce constraint violations in the parameter settings shown in the Tables 2 and 3, constraint

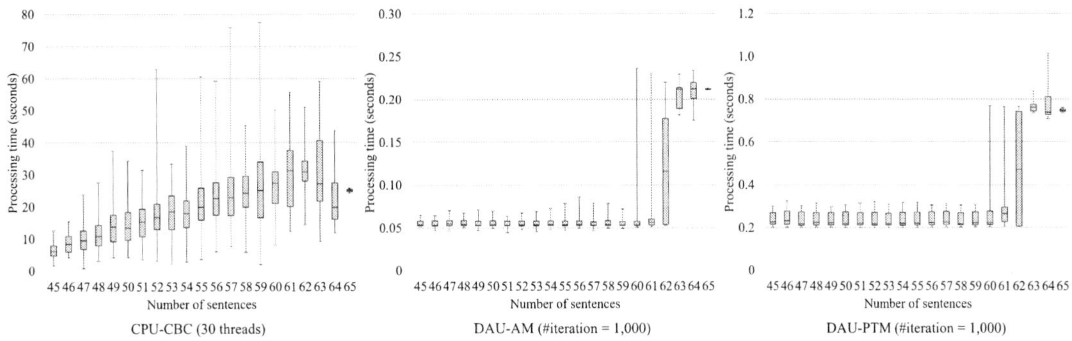

Figure 3: Processing time for each number of sentences ($N = 3, T' = 270$)

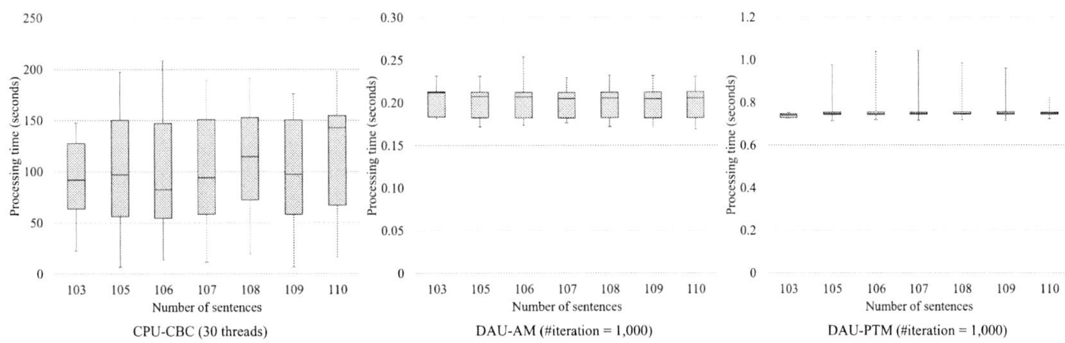

Figure 4: Processing time for each number of sentences ($N = 6, T' = 450$)

violations occurred when the number of iterations was too small or the value of λ was inappropriate.

In the case that delivers six articles consisting of 15 to 25 sentences, one DAU can generate personalized summaries on the scale of 100,000 users within 6 hours since about 0.2 seconds per person was necessary to generate a summary. In other words, an application with 100,000 users can prepare personalized summaries of the previous night's news by the next morning.

The second generation Digital Annealer can only handle problems up to 8,192 bits. However, a third generation Digital Annealer, which can solve problems on the scale of 100,000 bits, is currently under development (Nakayama et al., 2021). Spoken dialogue systems capable of extracting and presenting personalized information for each user from a huge amount of data in real time will be developed in the near future.

7 Conclusion

This paper proposed a quadratic unconstraint binary optimization (QUBO) model for the real-time personalized summary generation in terms of efficient and coherent information transmission. The model extracts sentences that maximize the sum of the degree of user's interest in the sentences of documents with the discourse structure of each document and total utterance time as constraints. To evaluate the effectiveness of the proposed method, we constructed a Japanese news article corpus with annotations of the discourse structure, users' profiles, and interests in sentences and topics. Experiments demonstrated that our QUBO model could be solved by a Digital Annealer, which is a simulated annealing-based Ising machine, in a practical time without violating the constraints using the dataset. In the future, we will verify the effect of personalized scenarios on the spoken dialogue system.

Acknowledgments

This work was supported by Japan Science and Technology Agency (JST) Program for Creating STart-ups from Advanced Research and Technology (START), Grant Number JPMJST1912 "Commercialization of Socially-Intelligent Conversational AI Media Service."

References

Maliheh Aramon, Gili Rosenberg, Elisabetta Valiante, Toshiyuki Miyazawa, Hirotaka Tamura, and Helmut G. Katzgraber. 2019. Physics-inspired optimization for quadratic unconstrained problems using a Digital Annealer. *Frontiers in Physics*, 7(48):1–14.

Frank Arute, Kunal Arya, Ryan Babbush, Dave Bacon, Joseph C. Bardin, Rami Barends, Rupak Biswas, Sergio Boixo, Fernando G. S. L. Brandao, David A. Buell, Brian Burkett, Yu Chen, Zijun Chen, Ben Chiaro, Roberto Collins, William Courtney, Andrew Dunsworth, Edward Farhi, Brooks Foxen, Austin Fowler, Craig Gidney, Marissa Giustina, Rob Graff, Keith Guerin, Steve Habegger, Matthew P. Harrigan, Michael J. Hartmann, Alan Ho, Markus Hoffmann, Trent Huang, Travis S. Humble, Sergei V. Isakov, Evan Jeffrey, Zhang Jiang, Dvir Kafri, Kostyantyn Kechedzhi, Julian Kelly, Paul V. Klimov, Sergey Knysh, Alexander Korotkov, Fedor Kostritsa, David Landhuis, Mike Lindmark, Erik Lucero, Dmitry Lyakh, Salvatore Mandrà, Jarrod R. McClean, Matthew McEwen, Anthony Megrant, Xiao Mi, Kristel Michielsen, Masoud Mohseni, Josh Mutus, Ofer Naaman, Matthew Neeley, Charles Neill, Murphy Yuezhen Niu, Eric Ostby, Andre Petukhov, John C. Platt, Chris Quintana, Eleanor G. Rieffel, Pedram Roushan, Nicholas C. Rubin, Daniel Sank, Kevin J. Satzinger, Vadim Smelyanskiy, Kevin J. Sung, Matthew D. Trevithick, Amit Vainsencher, Benjamin Villalonga, Theodore White, Z. Jamie Yao, Ping Yeh, Adam Zalcman, Hartmut Neven, and John M. Martinis. 2019. Quantum supremacy using a programmable superconducting processor. *Nature*, 574(7779):505—-510.

Nicholas Asher and Alex Lascarides. 2003. *Logics of conversation: Studies in natural language processing*. Cambridge University Press.

Paul I. Bunyk, Emile M. Hoskinson, Mark W. Johnson, Elena Tolkacheva, Fabio Altomare, Andrew J. Berkley, Richard Harris, Jeremy P. Hilton, Trevor Lanting, Anthony J. Przybysz, and Jed Whittaker. 2014. Architectural considerations in the design of a superconducting quantum annealing processor. *IEEE Transactions on Applied Superconductivity*, 24(4):1–10.

Lynn Carlson, Daniel Marcu, and Mary Ellen Okurovsky. 2001. Building a discourse-tagged corpus in the framework of rhetorical structure theory. In *Proceedings of the 2nd SIGdial Workshop on Discourse and Dialogue*, pages 1–10.

Nancy Chinchor. 1992. MUC-4 evaluation metrics. In *Proceedings of the 4th conference on Message understanding*, pages 22–29.

Alberto Díaz and Pablo Gervás. 2007. User-model based personalized summarization. *Information Processing and Management*, 43(6):1715–1734.

Song Feng, Kshitij Fadnis, Q. Vera Liao, and Luis A. Lastras. 2019. DOC2DIAL: A framework for dialogue composition grounded in business documents. In *Proceedings of the 33rd Conference on Neural Information Processing Systems*, pages 1–4.

Fred Glover, Gary Kochenberger, and Yu Du. 2019. Quantum bridge analytics I: A tutorial on formulating and using QUBO models. *4OR: A Quarterly Journal of Operations Research*, 17(4):335—-371.

Laszlo Gyongyosi. 2020. Unsupervised quantum gate control for gate-model quantum computers. *Scientific Reports*, 10(1):1–16.

Katsuhiko Hayashi, Tsutomu Hirao, and Masaaki Nagata. 2016. Empirical comparison of dependency conversions for RST discourse trees. In *Proceedings of the 17th Annual Meeting of the Special Interest Group on Discourse and Dialogue*, pages 128–136.

Tsutomu Hirao, Masaaki Nishino, Yasuhisa Yoshida, Jun Suzuki, Norihito Yasuda, and Masaaki Nagata. 2015. Summarizing a document by trimming the discourse tree. *IEEE/ACM Transactions on Audio, Speech and Language Processing*, 23(11):2081–2092.

Tsutomu Hirao, Yasuhisa Yoshida, Masaaki Nishino, Norihito Yasuda, and Masaaki Nagata. 2013. Single-document summarization as a tree knapsack problem. In *Proceedings of the 2013 Conference on Empirical Methods in Natural Language Processing*, pages 1515–1520.

Po Hu, Donghong Ji, Chong Teng, and Yujing Guo. 2012. Context-enhanced personalized social summarization. In *Proceedings of the 24th International Conference on Computational Linguistics*, pages 1223–1238.

M. W. Johnson, M. H. S. Amin, S. Gildert, T. Lanting, F. Hamze, N. Dickson, R. Harris, A. J. Berkley, J. Johansson, P. Bunyk, E. M. Chapple, C. Enderud, J. P. Hilton, K. Karimi, E. Ladizinsky, N. Ladizinsky, T. Oh, I. Perminov, C. Rich, M. C. Thom, E. Tolkacheva, C. J. S. Truncik, S. Uchaikin, J. Wang, B. Wilson, and G. Rose. 2011. Quantum annealing with manufactured spins. *Nature*, 473(7346):194–198.

Kimi Kaneko and Daisuke Bekki. 2014. Building a Japanese corpus of temporal-causal-discourse structures based on SDRT for extracting causal relations. In *Proceedings of the EACL 2014 Workshop on Computational Approaches to Causality in Language*, pages 33–39.

Daisuke Kawahara, Yuichiro Machida, Tomohide Shibata, Sadao Kurohashi, Hayato Kobayashi, and Manabu Sassano. 2014. Rapid development of a corpus with discourse annotations using two-stage crowdsourcing. In *Proceedings of the 25th International Conference on Computational Linguistics*, pages 269–278.

Yuta Kikuchi, Tsutomu Hirao, Hiroya Takamura, Manabu Okumura, and Masaaki Nagata. 2014. Single document summarization based on nested tree structure. In *Proceedings of the 52nd Annual Meeting of the Association for Computational Linguistics*, pages 315–320.

Yudai Kishimoto, Shinnosuke Sawada, Yugo Murawaki, Daisuke Kawahara, and Sadao Kurohashi. 2018. Improving crowdsourcing-based annotation of Japanese discourse relations. In *Proceedings of the 11th International Conference on Language Resources and Evaluation*, pages 4044–4048.

Sujian Li, Liang Wang, Ziqiang Cao, and Wenjie Li. 2014. Text-level discourse dependency parsing. In *Proceedings of the 52nd Annual Meeting of the Association for Computational Linguistics*, pages 25–35.

Andrew Lucas. 2014. Ising formulations of many NP problems. *Frontiers in Physics*, 2(5):1–15.

Kikuo Maekawa, Makoto Yamazaki, Toshinobu Ogiso, Takehiko Maruyama, Hideki Ogura, Wakako Kashino, Hanae Koiso, Masaya Yamaguchi, Makiro Tanaka, and Yasuharu Den. 2014. Balanced corpus of contemporary written Japanese. *Language Resources and Evaluation*, 48(2):345–371.

Masaaki Maezawa, Go Fujii, Mutsuo Hidaka, Kentaro Imafuku, Katsuya Kikuchi, Hanpei Koike, Kazumasa Makise, Shuichi Nagasawa, Hiroshi Nakagawa, Masahiro Ukibe, and Shiro Kawabata. 2019. Toward practical-scale quantum annealing machine for prime factoring. *Journal of the Physical Society of Japan*, 88(6).

Inderjeet Mani and Eric Bloedorn. 1998. Machine learning of generic and user-focused summarization. In *Proceedings of the 15th National / 10th Conference on Artificial Intelligence / Innovative Applications of Artificial Intelligence*, pages 820–826.

William C. Mann and Sandra A. Thompson. 1988. Rethorical structure theory: Toward a functional theory of text organization. *Text*, 8(3):243–281.

Satoshi Matsubara, Motomu Takatsu, Toshiyuki Miyazawa, Takayuki Shibasaki, Yasuhiro Watanabe, Kazuya Takemoto, and Hirotaka Tamura. 2020. Digital Annealer for high-speed solving of combinatorial optimization problems and its applications. In *Proceedings of the 25th Asia and South Pacific Design Automation Conference*, pages 667—-672.

John E. Mitchell. 2002. Branch-and-cut algorithms for combinatorial optimization problems. *Handbook of Applied Optimization*, pages 65–77.

Hiroshi Nakayama, Junpei Koyama, Noboru Yoneoka, and Toshiyuki Miyazawa. 2021. Description: Third generation Digital Annealer technology. `https://www.fujitsu.com/jp/group/labs/en/documents/about/resources/tech/techintro/3rd-g-da_en.pdf`.

Takuya Okuyama, Masato Hayashi, and Masanao Yamaoka. 2017. An Ising computer based on simulated quantum annealing by path integral Monte Carlo method. In *Proceedings of the 2017 IEEE International Conference on Rebooting Computing*, pages 1–6.

Manfred Padberg and Giovanni Rinaldi. 1991. A branch-and-cut algorithm for the resolution of large-scale symmetric traveling salesman problems. *SIAM Review*, 33(1):60–100.

Rashmi Prasad, Nikhil Dinesh, Alan Lee, Eleni Miltsakaki, Livio Robaldo, Aravind Joshi, and Bonnie Webber. 2008. The penn discourse treebank 2.0. In *Proceedings of the 6th International Conference on Language Resources and Evaluation*, pages 2961–2968.

Masataka Sao, Hiroyuki Watanabe, Yuuichi Musha, and Akihiro Utsunomiya. 2019. Application of Digital Annealer for faster combinatorial optimization. *FUJITSU SCIENTIFIC & TECHNICAL JOURNAL*, 55(2):45–51.

Maya Sappelli, Dung Manh Chu, Bahadir Cambel, David Graus, and Philippe Bressers. 2018. SMART journalism: Personalizing, summarizing, and recommending financial economic news. *The Algorithmic Personalization and News (APEN18) Workshop at ICWSM*, 18(5):1–3.

Hiroaki Takatsu, Ishin Fukuoka, Shinya Fujie, Yoshihiko Hayashi, and Tetsunori Kobayashi. 2018. A spoken dialogue system for enabling information behavior of various intention levels. *Journal of the Japanese Society for Artificial Intelligence*, 33(1):1–24.

Hiroaki Takatsu, Mayu Okuda, Yoichi Matsuyama, Hiroshi Honda, Shinya Fujie, and Tetsunori Kobayashi. 2021. Personalized extractive summarization for a news dialogue system. In *Proceedings of the 8th IEEE Spoken Language Technology Workshop*, pages 1044–1051.

Florian Wolf and Edward Gibson. 2005. Representing discourse coherence: A corpus-based study. *Computational Linguistics*, 31(2):249–287.

Jiacheng Xu, Zhe Gan, Yu Cheng, and Jingjing Liu. 2020. Discourse-aware neural extractive text summarization. In *Proceedings of the 58th Annual Meeting of the Association for Computational Linguistics*, pages 5021–5031.

Masanao Yamaoka, Chihiro Yoshimura, Masato Hayashi, Takuya Okuyama, Hidetaka Aoki, and Hiroyuki Mizuno. 2016. A 20k-spin Ising chip to solve combinatorial optimization problems with CMOS annealing. *IEEE Journal of Solid-State Circuits*, 51(1):303–309.

Rui Yan, Jian-Yun Nie, and Xiaoming Li. 2011. Summarize what you are interested in: An optimization framework for interactive personalized summarization. In *Proceedings of the 2011 Conference on Empirical Methods in Natural Language Processing*, pages 1342–1351.

An Yang and Sujian Li. 2018. SciDTB: Discourse dependency treebank for scientific abstracts. In *Proceedings of the 56th Annual Meeting of the Association for Computational Linguistics*, pages 444–449.

Yasuhisa Yoshida, Jun Suzuki, Tsutomu Hirao, and Masaaki Nagata. 2014. Dependency-based discourse parser for single-document summarization. In *Proceedings of the 2014 Conference on Empirical Methods in Natural Language Processing*, pages 1834–1839.

Appendix

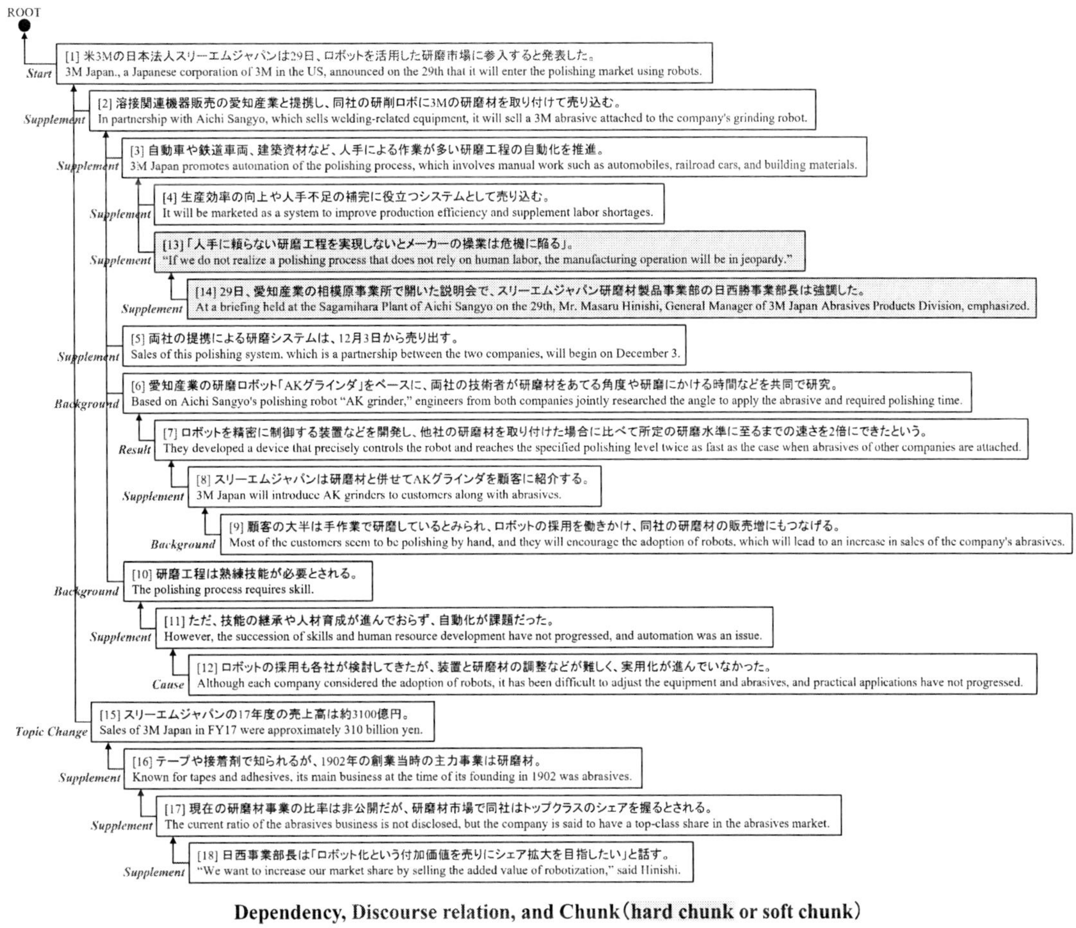

Figure 5: Annotation example of the discourse structure. [∗] indicates the sentence position in the original text. Dependency annotation, discourse relation annotation, and chunk annotation criteria are described in 3.1.1, 3.1.2, and 3.1.3, respectively.

Definition of the discourse relations

Start means that the parent of the sentence is the root node. *Result* means that the child sentence is the result of the parent sentence. *Cause* means that the child sentence is the cause of the parent sentence and includes event origin, the basis of the author's claim, and the reason. *Background* means that the parent sentence states facts or events, and the child sentence provides the background or premise. *Correspondence* means that the child sentence answers the question in the parent sentence. It also includes countermeasures or examinations of problems or issues. *Contrast* means that the parent sentence and the child sentence have a contrasting relationship. *Topic Change* means that the topic of the parent sentence changes in the child sentence, which includes a subtopic level change. *Example* means that the child sentence provides an instance to support the statement in the parent sentence. *Conclusion* means that the child sentence is a summary or conclusion of the story up to the parent sentence. *Supplement* means that the child sentence provides details or supplementary information about what is stated in the parent sentence. In a broad sense, although the above discourse relations are also included in supplement, herein, *Supplement* covers the inter-sentence relations that are not included in the aforementioned discourse relations.

Quality of the discourse annotations

A one-month training period was established, and discussions were held until the annotation criteria of the two annotators matched. To validate the inter-rater reliability, the two annotators annotated the same 34 articles after the training period. The Cohen's kappa of dependencies, discourse relations, and chunks were 0.960, 0.943, and 0.895, respectively. To calculate kappa of the discourse relations, the comparison was limited to the inter-sentence dependencies in which the parent sentence matched. To calculate kappa of the chunks, we set the label of the sentence selected as the hard chunk, soft chunk, and other to "1, 2, and 0," respectively. Then we compared the labels between sentences. Given the high inter-rater reliability, we concluded that the two annotators could cover different assignments separately.

Table 4: Example answers of the interest questionnaire. Interest level in the topic is assigned to the title [0]. (1, not interested at all; 2, not interested; 3, not interested if anything; 4, interested if anything; 5, interested; 6, very interested)

	U_1	U_2	···	U_{12}	U_{13}
[0] 研磨工程ロボ化、3Mが愛知産業と提携 Polishing process robotization, 3M partners with Aichi Sangyo	5	4		3	3
[1] 米3Mの日本法人スリーエムジャパンは29日、ロボットを活用した研磨市場に参入すると発表した。 3M Japan., a Japanese corporation of 3M in the US, announced on the 29th that it will enter the polishing market using robots.	5	4		3	4
[2] 溶接関連機器販売の愛知産業と提携し、同社の研削ロボに3Mの研磨材を取り付けて売り込む。 In partnership with Aichi Sangyo, which sells welding-related equipment, it will sell a 3M abrasive attached to the company's grinding robot.	3	3		3	1
[3] 自動車や鉄道車両、建築資材など、人手による作業が多い研磨工程の自動化を推進。 3M Japan promotes automation of the polishing process, which involves manual work such as automobiles, railroad cars, and building materials.	6	4		3	4
[4] 生産効率の向上や人手不足の補完に役立つシステムとして売り込む。 It will be marketed as a system to improve production efficiency and supplement labor shortages.	6	4		5	4
[5] 両社の提携による研磨システムは、12月3日から売り出す。 Sales of this polishing system, which is a partnership between the two companies, will begin on December 3.	3	4		3	1
[6] 愛知産業の研磨ロボット「AKグラインダ」をベースに、両社の技術者が研磨材をあてる角度や研磨にかける時間などを共同で研究。 Based on Aichi Sangyo's polishing robot "AK grinder", engineers from both companies jointly researched the angle to apply the abrasive and required polishing time.	6	3		3	1
[7] ロボットを精密に制御する装置などを開発し、他社の研磨材を取り付けた場合に比べて所定の研磨水準に至るまでの速さを2倍にできたという。 They developed a device that precisely controls the robot and reaches the specified polishing level twice as fast as the case when abrasives of other companies are attached.	5	3		3	1
[8] スリーエムジャパンは研磨材と併せてAKグラインダを顧客に紹介する。 3M Japan will introduce AK grinders to customers along with abrasives.	3	4		2	1
[9] 顧客の大半は手作業で研磨しているとみられ、ロボットの採用を働きかけ、同社の研磨材の販売増にもつなげる。 Most of the customers seem to be polishing by hand, and they will encourage the adoption of robots, which will lead to an increase in sales of the company's abrasives.	4	4		4	1
[10] 研磨工程は熟練技能が必要とされる。 The polishing process requires skill.	5	4		4	1
[11] ただ、技能の継承や人材育成が進んでおらず、自動化が課題だった。 However, the succession of skills and human resource development have not progressed, and automation was an issue.	5	4		3	1
[12] ロボットの採用も各社が検討してきたが、装置と研磨材の調整などが難しく、実用化が進んでいなかった。 Although each company considered the adoption of robots, it has been difficult to adjust the equipment and abrasives, and practical applications have not progressed.	5	3		3	1
[13]「人手に頼らない研磨工程を実現しないとメーカーの操業は危機に陥る」。 "If we do not realize a polishing process that does not rely on human labor, the manufacturing operation will be in jeopardy."	5	3		4	1
[14] 29日、愛知産業の相模原事業所で開いた説明会で、スリーエムジャパン研磨材製品事業部の日西勝事業部長は強調した。 At a briefing held at the Sagamihara Plant of Aichi Sangyo on the 29th, Mr. Masaru Hinishi, General Manager of 3M Japan Abrasives Products Division, emphasized.	3	3		3	1
[15] スリーエムジャパンの17年度の売上高は約3100億円。 Sales of 3M Japan in FY17 were approximately 310 billion yen.	3	3		3	1
[16] テープや接着剤で知られるが、1902年の創業当時の主力事業は研磨材。 Known for tapes and adhesives. its main business at the time of its founding in 1902 was abrasives.	4	4		3	1
[17] 現在の研磨材事業の比率は非公開だが、研磨材市場で同社はトップクラスのシェアを握るとされる。 The current ratio of the abrasives business is not disclosed, but the company is said to have a top-class share in the abrasives market.	4	4		3	1
[18] 日西事業部長は「ロボット化という付加価値を売りにシェア拡大を目指したい」と話す。 "We want to increase our market share by selling the added value of robotization," said Hinishi.	4	3		3	1

Table 5: Examples of user profiles

		U_1	U_{13}
Gender		Male	Female
Age		Forties	Twenties
Address		Kanagawa Prefecture	Mie Prefecture
Occupation type		Administrative worker	Professional / technical worker
Industry type		Manufacturing industry	Medical or welfare
Frequency of checking news		Daily	Daily
Typical time of day news is checked		Morning, night	Morning, evening
Methods to access the news		Video, text	Video
Tools used to check the news		TV, newspaper, smartphone / tablet	TV, smartphone / tablet
Newspapers, websites, and applications used to check the news		Yomiuri Shimbun, NHK, LINE NEWS, SmartNews, Yahoo! News	NHK, LINE NEWS
Whether a fee was paid to check the news		Free	Free
News genre actively checked		Politics, economy, international, society, sports, entertainment	Incident / accident, science / medical, sports, entertainment
Degree of interest in each news genre	Politics	Very interested	Not interested if anything
	Economy	Very interested	Not interested if anything
	International	Very interested	Not interested if anything
	Society	Interested if anything	Not interested if anything
	Local	Interested if anything	Not interested if anything
	Incident / accident	Interested if anything	Interested
	Science / medical	Not interested if anything	Interested
	Sports	Very interested	Interested
	Entertainment	Interested if anything	Interested
Hobbies		Watching sports, watching movies, watching dramas, listening to music, board games, video games / computer games / smartphone games, gambling, driving / touring	Sports / exercise, watching sports, watching movies, watching dramas, watching anime, eating out / visiting cafes, fashion, shopping, taking photos or videos, SNS, traveling

Statistics of the dataset

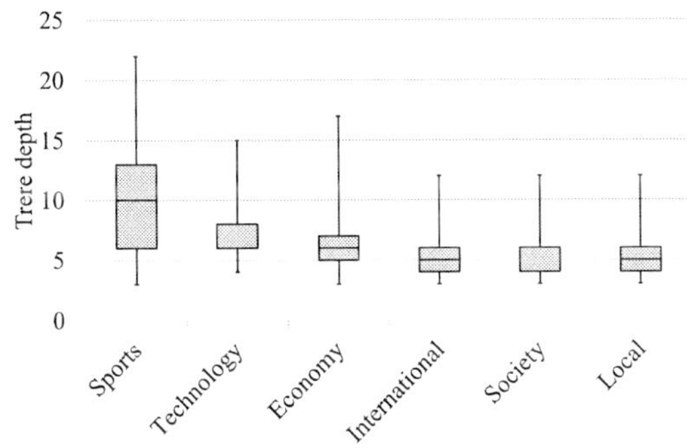

Figure 6: Tree depth distribution, which is the maximum number of sentences from the root node to the leaf nodes for each article. Average tree depth per article is 6.5 sentences.

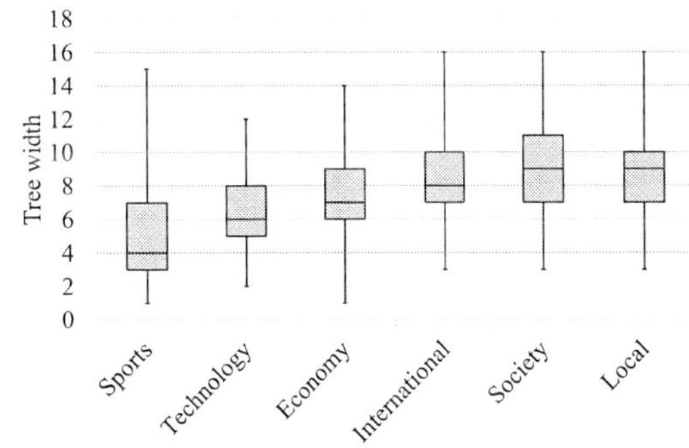

Figure 7: Tree width distribution, which is the number of leaf nodes for each article. Average tree width per article is 7.5 sentences.

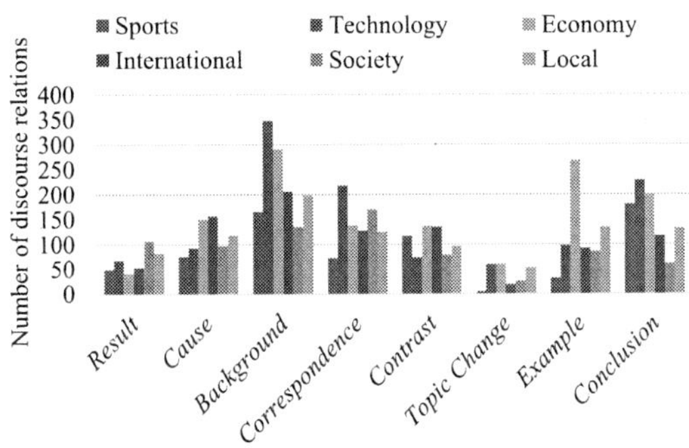

Figure 8: Frequencies of discourse relations in the dataset: *Start* = 1,221; *Result* = 400; *Cause* = 691; *Background* = 1,343; *Correspondence* = 851; *Contrast* = 638; *Topic Change* = 220; *Example* = 709; *Conclusion* = 920; and *Supplement* = 14,609.

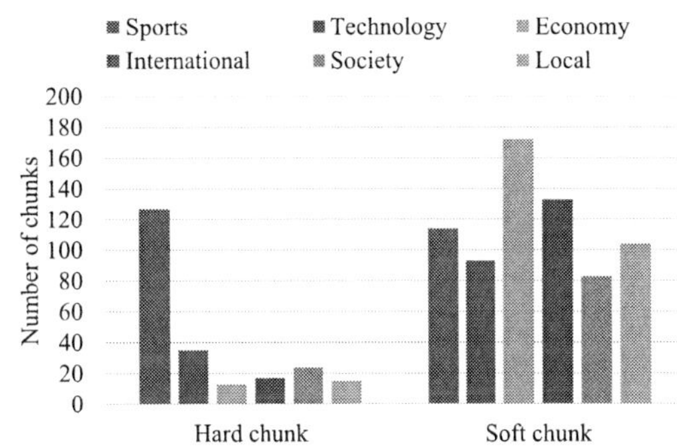

Figure 9: Frequencies of chunks in the dataset. There are 231 hard chunks and 699 soft chunks. Average number of sentences per chunk is 2.15.

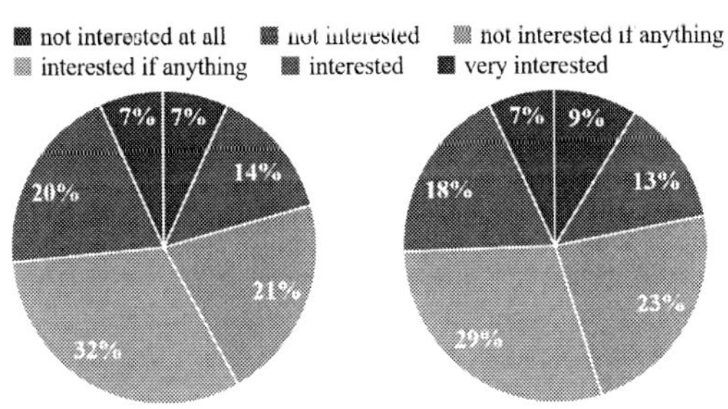

(a) Percentage of interest level in the topic

(b) Percentage of interest level in the sentence

Figure 10: Percentage of each interest level calculated from the questionnaire results, which includes 15,042 articles and 268,509 sentences.

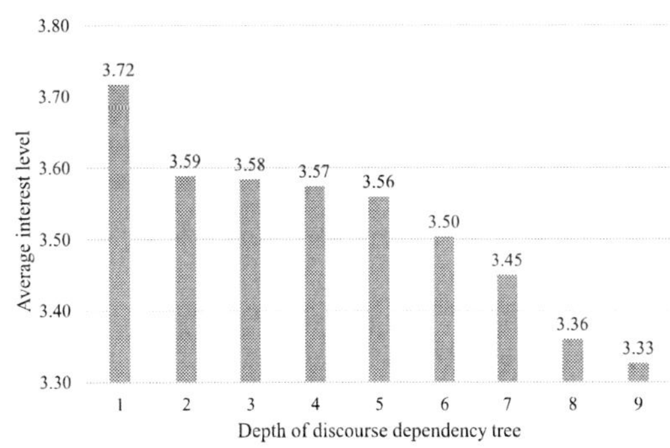

Figure 11: Average interest level of the sentences for each depth of the discourse dependency tree.

Multilingual Paraphrase Generation For Bootstrapping New Features in Task-Oriented Dialog Systems

Subhadarshi Panda[1,*], **Caglar Tirkaz**[2], **Tobias Falke**[2] and **Patrick Lehnen**[2]
[1]Graduate Center, City University of New York, USA
[2]Amazon Alexa AI, Germany
spanda@gc.cuny.edu, {caglart,falket,plehnen}@amazon.com

Abstract

The lack of labeled training data for new features is a common problem in rapidly changing real-world dialog systems. As a solution, we propose a multilingual paraphrase generation model that can be used to generate novel utterances for a target feature and target language. The generated utterances can be used to augment existing training data to improve intent classification and slot labeling models. We evaluate the quality of generated utterances using intrinsic evaluation metrics and by conducting downstream evaluation experiments with English as the source language and nine different target languages. Our method shows promise across languages, even in a zero-shot setting where no seed data is available.

1 Introduction

Spoken language understanding is a core problem in task oriented dialog systems with the goal of understanding and formalizing the intent expressed by an utterance (Tur and De Mori, 2011). It is often modeled as intent classification (IC), an utterance-level multi-class classification problem, and slot labeling (SL), a sequence labeling problem over the utterance's tokens. In recent years, approaches that train joint models for both tasks and that leverage powerful pre-trained neural models greatly improved the state-of-the-art performance on available benchmarks for IC and SL (Louvan and Magnini, 2020; Weld et al., 2021).

A common challenge in real-world systems is the problem of *feature bootstrapping*: If a new feature should be supported, the label space needs to be extended with new intent or slot labels, and the model needs to be retrained to learn to classify corresponding utterances. However, labeled examples for the new feature are typically limited to a small set of seed examples, as the collection of more annotations would make feature expansion costly and slow. As a possible solution, previous work explored the automatic generation of paraphrases to augment the seed data (Malandrakis et al., 2019; Cho et al., 2019; Jolly et al., 2020).

In this work, we study feature bootstrapping in the case of a *multilingual dialog system*. Many large-scale real-world dialog systems, e.g. Apple's Siri, Amazon's Alexa and Google's Assistant, support interactions in multiple languages. In such systems, the coverage of languages and the range of features is continuously expanded. That can lead to differences in the supported intent and slot labels across languages, in particular if a new language is added later or if new features are not rolled out to all languages simultaneously. As a consequence, labeled data for a feature can be available in one language, but limited or completely absent in another. With multilingual paraphrase generation, we can benefit from this setup and improve data augmentation for data-scarce languages via cross-lingual transfer from data-rich languages. As a result, the data augmentation can not only be applied with seed data, i.e. in a *few-shot* setting, but even under *zero-shot* conditions with no seeds at all for the target language.

To address this setup, we follow the recent work of Jolly et al. (2020), which proposes to use an encoder-decoder model that maps from structured meaning representations to corresponding utterances. Because such an input is language-agnostic, it is particularly well-suited for the multilingual setup. We make the following extensions: First, we port their model to a transformer-based architecture and allow multilingual training by adding the desired target language as a new input to the conditional generation. Second, we let the model generate slot labels along with tokens to alleviate the need for additional slot projection techniques. And third, we introduce improved paraphrase decoding methods that leverage a model-based selec-

*The first author worked on this paper during an internship at Amazon Alexa AI.

Proceedings of the Third Workshop on Natural Language Processing for Conversational AI, pages 30–39
November 10, 2021.

tion strategy. With that, we are able to generate labeled data for a new feature even in the zero-shot setting where no seeds are available at all.

We evaluate our approach by simulating a cross-lingual feature bootstrapping setting, either few-shot or zero-shot, on MultiATIS, a common IC/SL benchmark spanning nine languages. The experiments compare against several alternative methods, including previous work for mono-lingual paraphrase generation and machine translation. We find that our method produces paraphrases of high novelty and diversity and using it for IC/SL training shows promising downstream classification performance.

2 Related work

Various studies have explored paraphrase generation for dialog systems. Bowman et al. (2016) showed that generating sentences from a continuous latent space is possible using a variational autoencoder model and provided guidelines on how to train such a generation model. However, our model uses an encoder-decoder approach which can handle the intent and language as categorical inputs in addition to the sequence input. Malandrakis et al. (2019) explored a variety of controlled paraphrase generation approaches for data augmentation and proposed to use conditional variational autoencoders which they showed obtained the best results. Our method is different as it uses a conditional seq2seq model that can generate text from any sequence of slots and does not require an utterance as an input. Xia et al. (2020) propose a transformer-based conditional variational autoencoder for few shot utterance generation where the latent space represents the intent as two independent parts (domain and action). Our approach is different since it models the language and intent of the generation that can be controlled explicitly. Also, our model is the first to enable zero-shot utterance generation. Cho et al. (2019) generate paraphrases for seed examples with a transformer seq2seq model and self-label them with a baseline intent and slot model. We follow a similar approach but our model generates utterances from a sequence of slots rather than an utterance, which enables an explicitly controlled generation. Also the number of seed utterances we use is merely 20 for the few shot setup unlike around 1M seed para-carrier phrase pairs in Cho et al. (2019).

Several other studies follow a text-to-text approach and assume training data in the form of paraphrase pairs for training paraphrase generation models in a single language (Gupta et al., 2018; Li et al., 2018, 2019). Our approach is focused towards generating utterances in the dialog domain that can generate utterances from a sequence of slots conditioned on both intent and language.

Jolly et al. (2020) showed that an interpretation-to-text model can be used with shuffling-based sampling techniques to generate diverse and novel paraphrases from small amounts of seed data, that improve accuracy when augmenting to the existing training data. Our approach is different as our model can generate the slot annotations along with the the utterance, which are necessary for the slot labeling task. Our model can be seen as an extension of the model by Jolly et al. (2020) to a transformer based model, with the added functionality of controlling the language in which the utterance generation is needed, which in turn enables zero shot generation.

Using large pre-trained models has also been shown to be effective for paraphrase generation. Chen et al. (2020) for instance show the effectiveness of using GPT-2 (Radford et al., 2019) for generating text from tabular data (a set of attribute-value pairs). Our model, however, does not rely on pre-trained weights from another model such as GPT-2, is scalable, and can be applied to training data from any domain, for instance, dialog domain.

Beyond paraphrase generation, several other techniques have been proposed for feature bootstrapping. Machine translation can be used from data-rich to data-scarce languages (Gaspers et al., 2018; Xu et al., 2020). Cross-lingual transfer learning can also leverage use existing data in other languages (Do and Gaspers, 2019). If a feature is already being actively used, feedback signals from users, such as paraphrases or interruptions, can be used to obtain additional training data (Muralidharan et al., 2019; Falke et al., 2020).

3 Proposed method

We want to augment existing labeled utterances by generating additional novel utterances in a desired target language. In our case, existing data consists of feature-unrelated data (intents and slots already supported) spanning all languages and feature-related data, which is available in a source language but is small (few-shot) or not available (zero shot) in other languages. For generation, we first extract

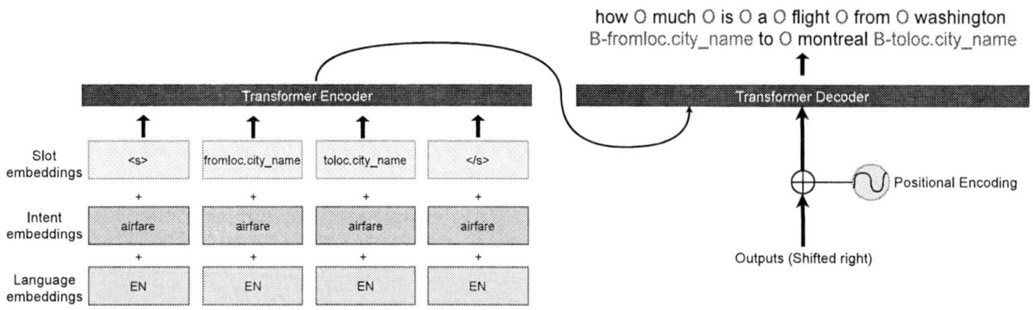

Figure 1: **Overall architecture of the multilingual paraphrase generation model.** The slot, intent and language embeddings are added at the slot level to obtain representations to input to the encoder. The <s> and </s> tags are necessary as they enable handling cases where we want to generate paraphrases having no associated slots. The decoder generates the slot labels along with the paraphrase tokens.

the intent and slot types from the available data. We then generate a new utterance by conditioning a multilingual language model on the intent, slot types and the target language. We refer to utterances that have the same intent and slot types as *paraphrases* of each other since they convey the same meaning in the context of the SLU system.

3.1 Paraphrase Generation Model

In order to generate paraphrases, we train a multilingual paraphrase generation model that generates a paraphrase given a language, an intent and a set of slot types. The model architecture is outlined in Figure 1. The model uses self-attention based encoder and decoder similar to the transformer (Vaswani et al., 2017). The encoder of the model receives as input the language embedding and the intent embedding, which are added to the slot embedding. Unlike the transformer model (Vaswani et al., 2017), we do not use the positional embedding in the encoder. This is because the order of the slot types in the input sequence does not matter and is thus made indistinguishable for the encoder.

In order to generate paraphrases which can be used for data augmentation, we would need the slot annotations and the intents of the generations. Note that we already know the intent of the generated paraphrase since it is the same intent as specified while generating it. The slot annotations, however, are not readily obtained from the input slot types. We can make the slot annotations part of the output sequence by generating the slot label in BIO format in every alternate time step, which would be the slot label for the token generated in the previous time step. This enables the model to generate the slot annotations along with the paraphrase. An illustrative example is shown in Figure 1.

3.2 Decoding Techniques

Generating the output sequence token-by-token can be done by using greedy decoding where given learned model parameters θ, the most likely token is picked at each decoding step as $x_t =$ argmax $p_\theta(x_t|x_{<t})$. Such a generation process is deterministic. For our task of generating paraphrases, we are interested in generating diverse and novel utterances. Non-deterministic sampling methods such as top-k sampling has been used in related work (Fan et al., 2018; Welleck et al., 2020; Jolly et al., 2020) to achieve this. In top-k random sampling, we first scale the logits z_w by using a temperature parameter τ before applying softmax.

$$p(x_t = w|x_{<t}) = \frac{\exp(z_w/\tau)}{\sum_{w' \in V} \exp(z_{w'}/\tau)}, \quad (1)$$

where V is the decoder's vocabulary. Setting $\tau > 1$ encourages the resulting probability distribution to be less spiky, thereby encouraging diverse choices during sampling. The top-k sampling restricts the size of the most likely candidate pool to $k \leq |V|$.

3.3 Balanced Augmentation

The generated paraphrases can be used to augment the existing training data. Since the training data we use is highly imbalanced, data augmentation might lead to disturbance in the original intent distribution. To ensure that the data augmentation process does not disturb the original intent distribution, we compute the number of samples to augment using the following constraint: the ratio of target intent to other intents for the target language should be the same as the ratio of target intent to other intents in the source language. Sometimes, using the above constraint results in a negligible number of samples for augmentation, in which cases we use a minimal number of samples (see experiments).

3.4 Paraphrase Selection

In addition to deciding how many paraphrases to augment, it is also crucial to decide which paraphrases to use. Preliminary experimental results showed that samping uniformly from all generated paraphrases does not lead to improvement over the baseline. Upon manual examination we found that not all the paraphrases belong to the desired target intent. To cope with that problem, we use the baseline downstream intent classification and slot labeling model, which is trained only on the existing data, to compute the likelihood of the generated paraphrases to belong to the target intent. We rank all the generated paraphrases based on these probabilities and select from the top of the pool for augmentation of the seed data.

4 Experimental setup

We evaluate our approach by simulating few-shot and zero-shot feature bootstrapping scenarios.

4.1 Data

We use the MultiATIS++ data (Xu et al., 2020), a parallel IC/SL corpus that was created by translating the original English dataset. It covers a total of 9 languages: English, Hindi, Turkish, German, French, Portuguese, Spanish, Japanese and Chinese. The languages encompass a diverse set of language families: Indo-European, Sino-Tibetan, Japonic and Altaic.

Choosing target intents To reduce the number of experiments, we only choose three different intents for simulating the feature bootstrapping scenario. The MultiATIS++ dataset is highly imbalanced in terms of intent frequencies. For instance, 74% of the English training data has the intent *atis_flight* and as many as 9 intents have less than 20 training samples. The trend is similar for the non-English languages. For choosing target intents for simulating the zero shot and few shot training data, we therefore consider the following three target intents: (a) *atis_airfare*, which is highly frequent, (b) *atis_airline*, which has medium frequency, and (c) *atis_city* which is scarce.

Preprocessing We remove the samples in the MultiATIS++ data for which the number of tokens and the number of slot values do not match.[1] We also only consider the first intent for the samples that have multiple intent annotations. We show the data sizes after preprocessing in Table 1.

Training setup To simulate the feature bootstrapping scenario, we consider only 20 samples (**few shot setup**) or no samples at all (**zero shot setup**) from the MultiATIS++ data for a specific target intent in a target language.[2]

Language setup We use English as the source language and consider 8 target languages (Hindi, Turkish, German, French, Portuguese, Spanish, Japanese, Chinese) simultaneously. This encourages the model parameters to be shared across all the 9 languages including the source language English. The purpose of this setup is to enable us to study the knowledge transfer across multiple target languages in addition to that from the source language. We train a single model for paraphrase generation on all the languages as well as a single multi-lingual downstream IC/SL model.

4.2 Models and Training Details

Paraphrase generation training Since the training data is imbalanced, we balanced the training data by oversampling the intents to match the frequency of the most frequent intent.[3] For both the encoder and the decoder, the multi-head attention layers' hidden dimension was set to 128 and the position-wise feed forward layers' hidden dimension was set to 256. The number of encoder and decoder layers was set to 3 each. The number of heads was set to 8. Dropout of 0.1 was used in both the encoder and the decoder. The model parameters were initialized with Xavier initialization (Glorot and Bengio, 2010). The model was trained using Adam optimizer (Kingma and Ba, 2014) with a learning rate of 5e-4 and a gradient clipping of 1. The training was stopped when the development loss did not improve for 5 epochs.

Generating paraphrases For generating paraphrases in the target intent in the target language,

[1] This leads to removal of 0.6% of the total samples.

[2] For cases that have less than 20 samples to pick from, we consider all the samples which are available.

[3] Experiments with the original imbalanced training data resulted in generating paraphrases which belongs to one of the frequent intents, even if the desired intent was one with a low frequency in the training data.

Language	Train	Dev	Test	Unique intents (Train)	Unique slots (Train)
DE	4,487	490	892	17	79
EN	4,488	490	893	17	79
ES	4,484	489	813	17	79
FR	4,413	489	791	17	79
HI	1,495	160	893	16	70
JA	4,487	490	886	17	78
PT	4,478	489	892	17	79
TR	626	60	715	15	62
ZH	4,487	490	893	17	79

Table 1: MultiATIS++ data statistics.

we used the slots appearing in the existing training data in the target intent. We used greedy decoding and top-k sampling with $k = 3, 5, 10$ and $\tau = 1.0, 2.0$. For a given input, we generated using the top-k random sampling three times with different random seeds. We finally combined all generations and ranked the candidates using the baseline downstream system's prediction probability. The number of paraphrases that are selected is determined as in 3.3, with 20 as the minimum.

Methods for comparison We compare our method against four alternatives:
(a) Baseline: No data augmentation at all. The downstream model is trained using just the available seed examples for the target intent.
(b) Oversampling: We oversample the samples per intent uniformly at random to match the size of the augmented training data using the proposed method. This is only applicable to the few shot setup since for the zero shot setup, there are no existing samples in the target intent in the target language to sample from.
(c) CVAE seq2seq model: We generate paraphrases using the CVAE seq2seq model by Malandrakis et al. (2019). The original CVAE seq2seq model as proposed by Malandrakis et al. (2019) defines the set {domain, intent, slots} as the *signature* of an utterance and denotes the carrier phrases for a given signature to be paraphrases. These carrier phrases are then used to create input-output pairs for the CVAE seq2seq model training. Since the original formulation does not take into account the language of generation, we adapt the method for our case by defining the signature as the set {language, intent, slots}. We set the model's hidden dimension to 128, used the 100-dimensional GloVe embeddings (Pennington et al., 2014) pretrained on Wikipedia, and trained the model without freezing embeddings using early stopping with a patience of 5 epochs by monitoring the development loss. Finally we generated 100 carrier phrases for each carrier phrase input in the target intent in the target language. Paraphrases were obtained by injecting the slot values to the generated carrier phrases. The pool of all paraphrases was sorted using the baseline downstream system's prediction probabilities. The CVAE seq2seq model was only applicable to the few shot setup since in the zero shot setup there are no existing carrier phrases in the target language in the target intent that can be used to sample from.
(d) Machine translation: We augmented the translations generated from English using the MT+fast-align approach from the MultiATIS++ paper (Xu et al., 2020). For the few shot setup, we added all the translated utterances except the ones that correspond to those utterances we already picked as the few shot samples. For the zero shot setup, we added all the translated utterances.

Downstream training Unlike the paraphrase generation model training, we do not balance the simulated training data by oversampling based on intent. This choice was made to make sure that the original intent distribution was preserved for the downstream model training. We used the BERT base multilingual cased model (Devlin et al., 2019)[4] and added an intent head and a slot head on top for joint intent classification and slot labeling. Each head uses a hidden size of 256 and ReLU activation. The model was trained using Adam optimizer with a learning rate of 0.1. The training was stopped when the development semantic error rate (Su et al., 2018) did not improve for 3 epochs.

4.3 Intrinsic evaluation metrics

We evaluate the quality of the generated paraphrases using the following metrics. Let S be the set of input slot types and G be the set of generated slot types.

[4] `https://github.com/google-research/bert/blob/master/multilingual.md`

Few shot results:

Generation method	All retrieval score	Exact match	Partial match	F1 slot score	Jaccard index	Novelty	Diversity
greedy	0.58	0.43	0.94	0.76	0.68	0.96	0
τ = 1.0, topk = 3	0.54	0.4	0.9	0.71	0.64	0.98	0.92
τ = 1.0, topk = 5	0.52	0.37	0.87	0.69	0.61	0.98	0.94
τ = 1.0, topk = 10	0.52	0.38	0.87	0.69	0.61	0.98	0.96
τ = 2.0, topk = 3	0.49	0.3	0.86	0.64	0.55	0.99	0.98
τ = 2.0, topk = 5	0.44	0.23	0.86	0.59	0.49	0.99	1
τ = 2.0, topk = 10	0.44	0.23	0.84	0.57	0.48	1	1

Zero shot results:

Generation method	All retrieval score	Exact match	Partial match	F1 slot score	Jaccard index	Novelty	Diversity
greedy	0.41	0.22	0.78	0.56	0.48	1	0
τ = 1.0, topk = 3	0.4	0.26	0.78	0.58	0.5	1	0.95
τ = 1.0, topk = 5	0.4	0.22	0.78	0.56	0.48	1	0.96
τ = 1.0, topk = 10	0.39	0.19	0.77	0.53	0.44	1	0.98
τ = 2.0, topk = 3	0.38	0.16	0.76	0.5	0.41	1	0.99
τ = 2.0, topk = 5	0.35	0.1	0.73	0.45	0.35	1	1
τ = 2.0, topk = 10	0.34	0.12	0.72	0.43	0.34	1	1

Table 2: Intrinsic evaluation scores for different generation methods in few shot and zero shot scenarios.

Language	Few shot						Zero shot		
	Lang. detection score		Novelty		Diversity		Lang. detection score	Novelty	Diversity
	CVAE	Ours	CVAE	Ours	CVAE	Ours	Ours		
DE	0.69	0.95	0.43	0.97	0.33	0.81	0.97	1	0.85
ES	0.71	0.91	0.48	0.98	0.44	0.82	0.93	1	0.83
FR	0.78	0.94	0.47	0.98	0.36	0.82	0.95	1	0.85
HI	0.69	0.97	0.5	0.97	0.28	0.81	0.97	1	0.81
JA	0.83	0.96	0.52	1	0.39	0.85	1	1	0.85
PT	0.5	0.75	0.55	0.97	0.38	0.81	0.86	1	0.85
TR	0.01	0.34	0.25	0.99	0.22	0.85	0.53	1	0.84
ZH	0.57	0.68	0.61	1	0.52	0.85	0.62	1	0.85

Table 3: Intrinsic evaluation scores for different target languages in few shot and zero shot scenarios.

All retrieval score The all retrieval score r measures if all the input slots were retrieved in the generation.

$$r = \begin{cases} 1 & \text{if } |S \cap G| = |S| \\ 0 & \text{otherwise} \end{cases} \quad (2)$$

Exact match The exact match score r measures if all the input slots and output slots exactly match (Malandrakis et al., 2019).

$$r = \begin{cases} 1 & \text{if } S = G \\ 0 & \text{otherwise} \end{cases} \quad (3)$$

Partial match The partial match score r measures if at least one output slot matches an input slot.

$$r = \begin{cases} 1 & \text{if } |S \cap G| > 0 \\ 0 & \text{otherwise} \end{cases} \quad (4)$$

F1 slot score The F1 slot score F_1 measures the set similarity between S and G using precision and recall which are defined for sets as follows.

$$\text{precision} = \frac{|S \cap G|}{|G|}, \text{recall} = \frac{|S \cap G|}{|S|} \quad (5)$$

Jaccard index Jaccard index measures the set similarity between S and G as their intersection size divided by the union size.

Novelty Let P be the set of paraphrases generated from a base utterance u.

$$\text{novelty} = \frac{1}{|P|} \sum_{u' \in P} \Big(1 - \text{BLEU4}(u, u')\Big) \quad (6)$$

Diversity The diversity is computed using the generated paraphrases P.

$$\text{diversity} = \frac{\sum_{u' \in P, u'' \in P, u' \neq u''} \Big(1 - \text{BLEU4}(u', u'')\Big)}{|P| \times (|P| - 1)} \quad (7)$$

Language detection score We are interested in quantifying if a generated paraphrase is in the target language. We use `langdetect`[5] to compute $p(\text{lang} = \text{target lang})$. Higher scores denote better language generation.

[5] `https://github.com/Mimino666/langdetect`

	Method	Intent classification								
		DE	ES	FR	HI	JA	PT	TR	ZH	AVG.
Few shot	Baseline	95.3	79.2	**86.0**	72.9	69.6	80.4	66.3	56.7	75.8
	Oversampling	93.6	80.6	84.4	78.2	**76.9**	83.7	63.1	62.3	77.8
	CVAE	94.1	84.7	83.7	71.7	63.8	**85.6**	**69.1**	55.8	76.1
	MT	91.3	**86.7**	81.6	**83.4**	70.9	82.8	64.0	56.0	77.1
	Paraphrasing	**97.1**	79.5	84.4	75.9	74.1	80.8	65.5	**66.8**	**78.0**
Zero shot	Baseline	48.7	44.8	51.6	15.0	3.1	33.8	8.0	1.0	25.8
	MT	**75.6**	**87.8**	**77.9**	**86.4**	**8.3**	**82.8**	**57.6**	**23.8**	**62.5**
	Paraphrasing	56.9	50.5	51.6	34.3	7.4	26.9	12.3	4.0	30.5

Table 4: Downstream intent classification accuracies (%). Each score shown is the average score of 10 runs.

	Method	Slot labeling								
		DE	ES	FR	HI	JA	PT	TR	ZH	AVG.
Few shot	Baseline	**98.0**	**85.0**	91.3	74.6	89.6	**92.2**	79.6	90.6	**87.6**
	Oversampling	96.2	84.6	**91.7**	**76.9**	89.9	90.0	81.3	90.3	**87.6**
	CVAE	97.3	83.5	90.0	75.8	**90.8**	91.6	**82.1**	89.6	**87.6**
	MT	95.0	78.8	90.9	73.0	90.8	82.9	77.9	88.8	84.8
	Paraphrasing	97.2	80.8	89.7	76.2	90.2	91.3	78.6	**91.6**	86.9
Zero shot	Baseline	**93.9**	**84.5**	89.3	72.5	89.1	88.7	77.3	87.8	85.4
	MT	92.0	79.9	88.5	**73.3**	**92.1**	82.1	76.2	**88.7**	84.1
	Paraphrasing	93.1	84.1	**90.5**	70.3	89.5	**91.5**	**77.6**	87.2	**85.5**

Table 5: Downstream slot labeling F1 scores (%). Each score shown is the average score of 10 runs.

5 Experimental results

5.1 Intrinsic Evaluation

For both the few shot and zero shot setups, the paraphrases used for intrinsic evaluation are generated in the target intent and the target language only. For the top-k sampling based generation, we generate for each input three times with different random seeds and compute novelty and diversity scores.

Table 2 shows intrinsic evaluation results for different generation methods. For the few shot setup, the all retrieval, exact match, partial match, F1 slot and Jaccard index scores decrease upon increasing top-k and temperature. The highest scores for the above metrics are obtained for the greedy generation, which indicates that the generated slot types are most similar to the input slot types in that case. However, it is the opposite for the novelty and diversity metrics where the scores are higher with larger top-k and temperatures. For the zero shot setup, the overall trend is similar to the few shot setup. The slot similarity based metrics are lower in general, which indicates that even as little as 20 samples in the few shot setup improve the generation of desired slots. The novelty scores for the zero shot setup are 1 as we would expect.

In Table 3, we show that the intrinsic evaluation results using the proposed approach are consistently better than the CVAE seq2seq paraphrase generation model (Malandrakis et al., 2019). The language detection score varies across languages, which may be due to the vocabulary overlap between languages, e.g., *San Francisco* appears in both English and German utterances. Interestingly we also observe code switching, i.e. mixed-language generations, while using our approach.

5.2 Downstream Evaluation

We evaluate the downstream intent classification using accuracy and the slot labeling using F1 score. Since we are interested in measuring the variation in scores for the target intents, we only report the scores for the test samples in the target intents in Tables 4 and 5. We run each downstream training experiment 10 times and report the mean scores for each language and also the average across languages in the AVG column in Tables 4 and 5. We are also interested in tracking the scores for the test samples having intents other than the target intents since we need to ensure that the scores on the other intents does not go down. We found that the effect on the scores (both intent classification and slot labeling) for the other intents is negligible using paraphrasing and other methods.[6]

In Tables 4 and 5, our paraphrasing results outperform the baseline scores on average. In the few shot setup, our paraphrasing approach outperforms the CVAE seq2seq approach in 6 (DE, ES, FR, HI, JA, ZH) out of 8 languages in intent classification and overall obtains an improvement of 1.9% intent classification accuracy across all target languages.

[6]The maximum drop in score was less than 1% absolute.

Input	airline and flight number from columbus to minneapolis
DE	Zeige mir alle Fluglinien, die von Toronto nach Boston fliegen
ES	Qué aerolineas vuelan desde Atlanta hasta Filadelfia
FR	Quelles compagnies volent de Toronto à San Francisco
HI	जो एयरलाइन डेन्वर से अटलांटा तक उड़ान भरती है
JA	デンバー から ピッツバーグ まで飛んでいる航空会社を教えて
PT	Mostre todas companhias aéreas voam de Denver
TR	hangi havayolu boston pittsburgh ' a ucar
ZH	从 丹佛 到 旧金山 航班的航空公司

Table 6: Examples of paraphrases generated using the multilingual paraphrase generation model for *airline* and slots *fromloc* and *toloc*. The paraphrases shown are cherry picked from a set of generations.

Both oversampling and MT approaches are competitive. Oversampling performs the best for JA whereas MT performs the best for ES and HI. Our paraphrasing approach results in the best intent classification scores overall (78%). In terms of slot F1 scores, we see mixed results with no clear best method (baseline, oversampling and CVAE all result in 87.6% F1 score). Notably, the MT approach results in the lowest overall slot F1 score of just 84.8% on average.

In the zero shot setup, the MT approach outperforms our paraphrasing approach by a large margin in intent classification (62.5%). However we note that the paraphrasing approach requires no dependencies on other models or other data, unlike the MT approach which requires a parallel corpus to train the MT model. In terms of slot F1 scores, our paraphrasing approach and the baseline approach both result in almost similar overall scores (85.5% and 85.4%), both higher than the MT approach. The lower slot F1 scores using the MT approach in few and zero shot setups indicate that the fast align method to align slots in source and translation might result in noisy training data affecting the SL model.

5.3 Examples

Paraphrases generated in different languages for a given input are shown in Table 6. The intent is *airline* and the slots are *fromloc.city_name* for *columbus* and *toloc.city_name* for *minneapolis*. For this intent and the slots, the generated paraphrase in German (translated to English) is *Show me all the airlines that fly from Toronto to Boston*. The desired intent, that is *airline* is realized in the generated paraphrase. Additionally, *Toronto* and *Boston* are the slot values respectively for the slot types *fromloc.city_name* and *toloc.city_name*. For Spanish, the generated paraphrase (translated to English) is *Which Airlines Fly from Atlanta to Philadelphia*. The *airline* intent is realized in the generated paraphrase and also *Atlanta* and *Philadelphia* are the slot values produced associated with the desired slot types. As illustrated by the examples, the model is free to pick a specific slot value during generation, leading to variations across languages, but all are consistent with the slot type.

6 Conclusion

In this paper, we proposed a multilingual paraphrase generation model that can be used for feature bootstrapping with or without seed data in the target language. In addition to generating a paraphrase, the model also generates the associated slot labels, enabling the generation to be used directly for data augmentation to existing training data. Our method is language agnostic and scalable, with no dependencies on pre-trained models or additional data. We validate our method using experiments on the MultiATIS++ dataset containing utterances spanning 9 languages. Intrinsic evaluation shows that paraphrases generated using our approach have higher novelty and diversity in comparison to CVAE seq2seq based paraphrase generation. Additionally, downstream evaluation shows that using the generated paraphrases for data augmentation results in improvements over baseline and related techniques in a wide range of languages and setups. To the best of our knowledge, this is the first successful exploration of generating paraphrases for SLU in a cross-lingual setup.

In the future, we would like to explore strategies to exploit monolingual data in the target languages to further refine the paraphrase generation. We would also like to leverage pre-trained multilingual text-to-text models such as mT5 (Xue et al., 2020) for multilingual paraphrase generation in the dialog system domain.

Acknowledgements

We would like to thank our anonymous reviewers for their thoughtful comments and suggestions that improved the final version of this paper.

References

Samuel R. Bowman, Luke Vilnis, Oriol Vinyals, Andrew Dai, Rafal Jozefowicz, and Samy Bengio. 2016. Generating sentences from a continuous space. In *Proceedings of The 20th SIGNLL Conference on Computational Natural Language Learning*, pages 10–21, Berlin, Germany. Association for Computational Linguistics.

Zhiyu Chen, Harini Eavani, Wenhu Chen, Yinyin Liu, and William Yang Wang. 2020. Few-shot NLG with pre-trained language model. In *Proceedings of the 58th Annual Meeting of the Association for Computational Linguistics*, pages 183–190, Online. Association for Computational Linguistics.

Eunah Cho, He Xie, and William M. Campbell. 2019. Paraphrase generation for semi-supervised learning in NLU. In *Proceedings of the Workshop on Methods for Optimizing and Evaluating Neural Language Generation*, pages 45–54, Minneapolis, Minnesota. Association for Computational Linguistics.

Jacob Devlin, Ming-Wei Chang, Kenton Lee, and Kristina Toutanova. 2019. BERT: Pre-training of deep bidirectional transformers for language understanding. In *Proceedings of the 2019 Conference of the North American Chapter of the Association for Computational Linguistics: Human Language Technologies, Volume 1 (Long and Short Papers)*, pages 4171–4186, Minneapolis, Minnesota. Association for Computational Linguistics.

Quynh Do and Judith Gaspers. 2019. Cross-lingual transfer learning with data selection for large-scale spoken language understanding. In *Proceedings of the 2019 Conference on Empirical Methods in Natural Language Processing and the 9th International Joint Conference on Natural Language Processing (EMNLP-IJCNLP)*, pages 1455–1460, Hong Kong, China. Association for Computational Linguistics.

Tobias Falke, Markus Boese, Daniil Sorokin, Caglar Tirkaz, and Patrick Lehnen. 2020. Leveraging user paraphrasing behavior in dialog systems to automatically collect annotations for long-tail utterances. In *Proceedings of the 28th International Conference on Computational Linguistics: Industry Track*, pages 21–32, Online. International Committee on Computational Linguistics.

Angela Fan, Mike Lewis, and Yann Dauphin. 2018. Hierarchical neural story generation. In *Proceedings of the 56th Annual Meeting of the Association for Computational Linguistics (Volume 1: Long Papers)*, pages 889–898, Melbourne, Australia. Association for Computational Linguistics.

Judith Gaspers, Penny Karanasou, and Rajen Chatterjee. 2018. Selecting machine-translated data for quick bootstrapping of a natural language understanding system. In *Proceedings of the 2018 Conference of the North American Chapter of the Association for Computational Linguistics: Human Language Technologies, Volume 3 (Industry Papers)*, pages 137–144, New Orleans - Louisiana. Association for Computational Linguistics.

Xavier Glorot and Yoshua Bengio. 2010. Understanding the difficulty of training deep feedforward neural networks. In *Proceedings of the Thirteenth International Conference on Artificial Intelligence and Statistics*, volume 9 of *Proceedings of Machine Learning Research*, pages 249–256, Chia Laguna Resort, Sardinia, Italy. PMLR.

Ankush Gupta, Arvind Agarwal, Prawaan Singh, and Piyush Rai. 2018. A deep generative framework for paraphrase generation. In *Proceedings of the AAAI Conference on Artificial Intelligence*, volume 32.

Shailza Jolly, Tobias Falke, Caglar Tirkaz, and Daniil Sorokin. 2020. Data-efficient paraphrase generation to bootstrap intent classification and slot labeling for new features in task-oriented dialog systems. In *Proceedings of the 28th International Conference on Computational Linguistics: Industry Track*, pages 10–20, Online. International Committee on Computational Linguistics.

Diederik P. Kingma and Jimmy Ba. 2014. Adam: A method for stochastic optimization. Cite arxiv:1412.6980Comment: Published as a conference paper at the 3rd International Conference for Learning Representations, San Diego, 2015.

Zichao Li, Xin Jiang, Lifeng Shang, and Hang Li. 2018. Paraphrase generation with deep reinforcement learning. In *Proceedings of the 2018 Conference on Empirical Methods in Natural Language Processing*, pages 3865–3878, Brussels, Belgium. Association for Computational Linguistics.

Zichao Li, Xin Jiang, Lifeng Shang, and Qun Liu. 2019. Decomposable neural paraphrase generation. In *Proceedings of the 57th Annual Meeting of the Association for Computational Linguistics*, pages 3403–3414, Florence, Italy. Association for Computational Linguistics.

Samuel Louvan and Bernardo Magnini. 2020. Recent neural methods on slot filling and intent classification for task-oriented dialogue systems: A survey. In *Proceedings of the 28th International Conference on Computational Linguistics*, pages 480–496, Barcelona, Spain (Online). International Committee on Computational Linguistics.

Nikolaos Malandrakis, Minmin Shen, Anuj Goyal, Shuyang Gao, Abhishek Sethi, and Angeliki Metallinou. 2019. Controlled text generation for data augmentation in intelligent artificial agents. In *Proceedings of the 3rd Workshop on Neural Generation and Translation*, pages 90–98, Hong Kong. Association for Computational Linguistics.

Deepak Muralidharan, Justine Kao, Xiao Yang, Lin Li, Lavanya Viswanathan, Mubarak Seyed Ibrahim, Kevin Luikens, Stephen Pulman, Ashish Garg, Atish

Kothari, and Jason Williams. 2019. Leveraging User Engagement Signals For Entity Labeling in a Virtual Assistant. *arXiv*, 1909.09143.

Jeffrey Pennington, Richard Socher, and Christopher Manning. 2014. GloVe: Global vectors for word representation. In *Proceedings of the 2014 Conference on Empirical Methods in Natural Language Processing (EMNLP)*, pages 1532–1543, Doha, Qatar. Association for Computational Linguistics.

Alec Radford, Jeff Wu, Rewon Child, David Luan, Dario Amodei, and Ilya Sutskever. 2019. Language models are unsupervised multitask learners.

Chengwei Su, Rahul Gupta, Shankar Ananthakrishnan, and Spyros Matsoukas. 2018. A re-ranker scheme for integrating large scale nlu models. In *2018 IEEE Spoken Language Technology Workshop (SLT)*, pages 670–676.

Gokhan Tur and Renato De Mori. 2011. *Spoken Language Understanding: Systems for Extracting Semantic Information from Speech*. John Wiley and Sons.

Ashish Vaswani, Noam Shazeer, Niki Parmar, Jakob Uszkoreit, Llion Jones, Aidan N Gomez, Ł ukasz Kaiser, and Illia Polosukhin. 2017. Attention is all you need. In *Advances in Neural Information Processing Systems*, volume 30. Curran Associates, Inc.

H. Weld, X. Huang, S. Long, J. Poon, and S. C. Han. 2021. A survey of joint intent detection and slot-filling models in natural language understanding. *arXiv*, 2101.08091.

Sean Welleck, Ilia Kulikov, Stephen Roller, Emily Dinan, Kyunghyun Cho, and Jason Weston. 2020. Neural text generation with unlikelihood training. In *International Conference on Learning Representations*.

Congying Xia, Caiming Xiong, Philip Yu, and Richard Socher. 2020. Composed variational natural language generation for few-shot intents. In *Findings of the Association for Computational Linguistics: EMNLP 2020*, pages 3379–3388, Online. Association for Computational Linguistics.

Weijia Xu, Batool Haider, and Saab Mansour. 2020. End-to-end slot alignment and recognition for cross-lingual NLU. In *Proceedings of the 2020 Conference on Empirical Methods in Natural Language Processing (EMNLP)*, pages 5052–5063, Online. Association for Computational Linguistics.

Linting Xue, Noah Constant, Adam Roberts, Mihir Kale, Rami Al-Rfou, Aditya Siddhant, Aditya Barua, and Colin Raffel. 2020. mT5: A massively multilingual pre-trained text-to-text transformer.

Overcoming Conflicting Data when Updating a Neural Semantic Parser

David Gaddy
University of California, Berkeley*
dgaddy@berkeley.edu

Alex Kouzemtchenko, Pavankumar Reddy Muddireddy, Prateek Kolhar,
and **Rushin Shah**
Google Assistant
{kuza,mpavan,pkolhar,rushinshah}@google.com

Abstract

In this paper, we explore how to use a small amount of new data to update a task-oriented semantic parsing model when the desired output for some examples has changed. When making updates in this way, one potential problem that arises is the presence of conflicting data, or out-of-date labels in the original training set. To evaluate the impact of this under-studied problem, we propose an experimental setup for simulating changes to a neural semantic parser. We show that the presence of conflicting data greatly hinders learning of an update, then explore several methods to mitigate its effect. Our multi-task and data selection methods lead to large improvements in model accuracy compared to a naive data-mixing strategy, and our best method closes 86% of the accuracy gap between this baseline and an oracle upper bound.

1 Introduction

Most work in semantic parsing (and NLP in general) considers a scenario where the desired outputs of a model are static and can be specified with a large, fixed dataset. However, when deploying a semantic parsing model in a real world virtual assistant, it is often necessary to update a model to support new features or to enable improvements in downstream processing. For example, creators of a media assistant may want to add new commands specialized towards new media types like podcasts, or those of a navigation assistant might like to add a new feature to allow users to specify roads to avoid. Such changes require that the structures output by the model are updated, either by introducing a new intent (a representation of a desired action) or re-configuring arguments of existing intents. In this work, we investigate the best way to make updates to the intents and arguments of a task-oriented neural semantic parsing model.

To make an update, new data annotations must be collected to specify the new form that is desired for model outputs. Because changes can be quite frequent, we would like to be able to collect a small amount of data for each update (on the order of 50 examples) and merge the new information with a much larger existing dataset. Naively, we might hope to simply combine new data in with the old and train on the combination. However, this approach has the problem that some of the older data with out-of-date labels may conflict with the new labeling. These conflicts occur whenever inputs that would be affected by a change appear in the original dataset. For example, when introducing a new intent for podcasts, the original dataset may have included podcast examples labeled with a more generic media intent or a label indicating that the feature is unsupported. When introducing a new argument, say 'roads to avoid', there may be instances in the original dataset that should have this argument labeled but do not because they were annotated before the argument was introduced. This conflicting data can confuse the model and cause it to predict labels as they were before an update rather than after. Unfortunately, this problem of conflicting data during model updates is understudied in the academic literature.

To enable exploration of this problem on publicly available datasets, we propose a method to easily create simulated updates with conflicts (Section 3.3) and release our update data. The idea behind our method is to form updates in the reverse direction, relabeling instances of a particular intent or argument to simulate out-of-date labels. Using our proposed setup, we demonstrate how conflicting data greatly hinders learning of updates (Section 5).

In addition, we explore several methods for mitigating the negative effects of conflicting data by modifying how we combine the old and the new data (Section 6). One approach is to keep the old

* Work performed during an internship at Google.

Proceedings of the Third Workshop on Natural Language Processing for Conversational AI, pages 40–51
November 10, 2021.

and new datasets separate, but to share information indirectly with either fine-tuning or multi-task learning. Another approach is to explicitly filter data that is likely to conflict using a learned classifier. Each of these methods substantially improves performance compared to naively mixing in new data, establishing strong baselines for future work on this task.

In summary, the contributions of this work are 1) establishing an experimental setup to test updates with conflicting data, 2) demonstrating that conflicting data leads to large losses in model performance if left unmitigated, and 3) exploring several possible approaches to mitigate this problem.

2 Related Work

There has been a substantial amount of prior work on making updates to neural models (Xiao et al., 2014; Rusu et al., 2016; Li and Hoiem, 2016; Kirkpatrick et al., 2017; Castro et al., 2018), demonstrating a recognition in the community that the ability to update models is important. However, most of these works consider a setting where none of the original data conflicts with the new labels. Thus these works, and the general continual learning and class-incremental learning literature, assume that the space of inputs affected by a change does not appear at all in the original data. In many scenarios, this assumption does not hold because the original dataset will aim to cover the full distribution of inputs a model might encounter. Because of the non-conflicting assumption, this body of prior work focuses on other questions such as what can be done when the original data is no longer available.

One paper that does consider updates with label conflicts is Chen and Moschitti (2019). Although they do not intentionally set out to study conflicting-data updates, in their NER task locations where new labels apply are tagged with special "outside" labels prior to the update, which cause conflicts with the new labels. While their work avoids the conflicting data problem by considering a setting where the original data is no longer available, our experiments show that it can be advantageous to instead keep the original data around and use more direct methods to avoid problems of conflicting data.

Our work also has parallels to the concept drift literature (Tsymbal, 2004; Lu et al., 2018). However, concept drift work focuses on unintentional changes to a natural data distribution over time, while our work is concerned with intentional restructuring of the output representation space, leading to very a different setup and choice of methods. In particular, that work operates over a stream of examples where changes often occur gradually, does not generally include structured prediction tasks, and does not allow the practitioner to introduce additional structure on the types of annotation given (as we do in Section 3.2).

Finally, our work relates to work on training with noisy labels (Sukhbaatar et al., 2014; Veit et al., 2017; Jiang et al., 2018), since the incorrect labels from conflicting data could be viewed as a type of noise. However, it is important to evaluate the problem of conflict-causing updates separately from other noisy label problems because the distribution of incorrect labels due to an update will be very different from most other sources of label noise. While not all noisy-label methods can directly apply to our task (as many are designed for classification as opposed to structured prediction) and may not take full advantage of the additional structure of our problem, we believe this line of work can still serve as a source of inspiration for future exploration on our task.

3 Task Setup

3.1 Preliminaries - Task-oriented Semantic Parsing

The experiments in this paper focus on a semantic parsing task where the goal is to generate a tree structure conditioned on an input sentence. We use the task formulation and data from Gupta et al. (2018) as the basis of our setup. Output trees are made up of intents and arguments (aka slots), where intents come from a fixed inventory of labels, and arguments consist of an argument-type label along with a value. Argument values may either be free-form text selected from the input sentence, or a nested intent to form a hierarchical structure. In this work, we represent these trees with a linearized form using nested brackets, which allows for the use of standard sequence-to-sequence models (see Section 4 for details of our base model and Figure 1 below for some example inputs and outputs).

3.2 Data Updates

In this paper, we focus on the task of making a single update to the intent and argument structure output by a model, where the update is specified by collecting a small amount of additional data.[1] Accordingly, our task setup expects two sets of data: a large amount of data from before a change, which we will call the **V1** (version one) set, and a small amount of data from after a change, which we call the **V2** set. The V1 set represents the current state of the system with any data collected in the past, while the new V2 set is collected specifically for the purpose of introducing a particular update. For the purposes of testing methods in this paper, we will form these two sets synthetically, as described in Section 3.3 below.

Because the V2 set is gathered explicitly for the purpose of introducing a particular update, we would like the input distribution of this data to be targeted rather than uniformly covering the full input space. Ideally, a substantial portion of this data should be examples whose labels will actually change after the update. We will call this portion of data the ***changed*** set. However, it is also useful to specify some examples that are not affected by a change, so that we can accurately determine the scope of a change. We will call inputs whose label would be the same under the new and old label scheme ***unchanged*** examples. We will include a set of *unchanged* examples in the V2 data to show that these labels have been confirmed under the V2 labeling scheme.

Many types of changes that we care about only apply to examples labeled in a particular way in the original V1 data. For example, a new argument can often only be used for specific intents, or a new intent may only apply to examples previously labeled as unsupported. By taking advantage of this information, we may be able to avoid some unwanted side effects of our model updates. To help us handle this information, we define a third category of examples: ***trivially-unchanged***. The *trivially-unchanged* partition contains all examples which we can determine to be unaffected based solely on the original V1 labels and some simple hand-defined rule like a list of affected intents. By identifying these examples, we can directly include them in the updated training set without causing label conflicts. In the remainder of this paper, we reserve the term *unchanged* to refer specifically to unchanged examples that do not fall into the *trivially-unchanged* category. Thus, the *unchanged* partition represents the remaining hard examples that are difficult to distinguish from the *changed* set in the V1 data. See Figure 1 for examples of how our three data partitions apply to particular updates.

In some instances, it is also useful to talk about the data in the original V1 set in terms of the three partitions (*changed*, *unchanged*, and *trivially-unchanged*). In this case, these labels refer to whether an example *would* change if we had gathered new labels for them. In actuality, the *changed* subset will have out-of-date labels in V1, and we call these examples *conflicting data*. Our experiments show that conflicting data causes substantial problems when learning an update (see Section 5 and 7), but unfortunately, the examples that make up the conflicting set cannot be easily identified in the V1 data.

3.3 Creating Synthetic Changes

To enable exploration of the conflicting data problem, we demonstrate a method for easily simulating updates with conflicts on an existing publicly available dataset. We form our synthetic updates in the reverse direction – the data from the original dataset represents the final V2 form, and we modify some examples to represent a V1 (pre-update) form. We aim to make changes that can be done automatically in the reverse direction, while still being interesting to learn in the forward direction.

To form our updates, we select a particular intent or argument from the dataset to simulate the introduction of. We sample a set of examples labeled with the selected intent or argument to form the primary part of the V2 training set. For other examples with this intent or argument, we will keep them as part of the V1 training set, but re-label them to some form they may have taken before the new intent or argument was introduced. These re-labeled examples act as conflicting data.

For example, suppose we would like to simulate the creation of the intent `GET_INFO_TRAFFIC`, as shown at the top of Figure 1. After selecting a subset of `GET_INFO_TRAFFIC` examples for the V2 training set, we form a conflicting set in the V1 data by re-labeling `GET_INFO_TRAFFIC` examples to use the related intent `GET_INFO_ROAD_CONDITION`. For this particular change, we kept the arguments the same when updating, but for others we remove

[1] While handling a stream of updates may pose additional challenges, we leave an investigation of that scenario to future work. What qualifies as a single update is somewhat open to interpretation, but our methods are not overly sensitive to how it is defined.

New intent from related

Changed

Query: *Where is there construction on the highway?*

V1 Label:	V2 Label:
`(IN:GET_INFO_ROAD_CONDITION (SL:LOCATION "the highway" ) )`	`(IN:GET_INFO_TRAFFIC (SL:LOCATION "the highway" ) )`

Unchanged

Query: *Are roads icy?*

V1 Label:	V2 Label:
`(IN:GET_INFO_ROAD_CONDITION (SL:ROAD_CONDITION "icy" ) )`	`(IN:GET_INFO_ROAD_CONDITION (SL:ROAD_CONDITION "icy" ) )`

Trivially-unchanged

Examples not labeled with `IN:GET_INFO_ROAD_CONDITION` in V1 are trivially-unchanged.

New intent from unsupported

Changed

Query: *If I leave right now, can I get to New York City before one o'clock PM?*

V1 Label:	V2 Label:
`(IN:UNSUPPORTED_NAVIGATION )`	`(IN:GET_ESTIMATED_ARRIVAL (SL:DATE_TIME_DEPARTURE "right now" ) (SL:DESTINATION "New York City" ) )`

Unchanged

Query: *What major city has the worst traffic?*

V1 Label:	V2 Label:
`(IN:UNSUPPORTED_NAVIGATION )`	`(IN:UNSUPPORTED_NAVIGATION )`

Trivially-unchanged

Examples not labeled with `IN:UNSUPPORTED_NAVIGATION` in V1 are trivially-unchanged.

New argument

Changed

Query: *Which route to work has less traffic?*

V1 Label:	V2 Label:
`(IN:GET_DIRECTIONS (SL:DESTINATION "work" ) )`	`(IN:GET_DIRECTIONS (SL:DESTINATION "work" ) (SL:OBSTRUCTION "traffic" ) )`

Unchanged

Query: *What is the best route to get to Atlanta to see my brother Mark?*

V1 Label:	V2 Label:
`(IN:GET_DIRECTIONS (SL:DESTINATION "Atlanta" ) )`	`(IN:GET_DIRECTIONS (SL:DESTINATION "Atlanta" ) )`

Trivially-unchanged

Examples not labeled with one of the seven intents that allow the `SL:OBSTRUCTION` slot are trivially-unchanged.

Figure 1: Examples from different types of updates that we simulate. To simulate updates, we use the original dataset as the V2 form, and modify some examples to a V1 form in a way that is not easily reversed. We describe our data in terms of three partitions: *changed*, *unchanged*, and *trivially-unchanged* – as described in Section 3.2. Note that while *trivially-unchanged* examples can be easily identified from their V1 labels, *changed* and *unchanged* examples cannot be easily distinguished in V1.

arguments or relabel them in the V1 set.

Because the examples with our "new" intent or argument are different between the V1 and V2 data, those examples make up the *changed* subset. Recall that we would also like to include some *unchanged* examples in the V2 training set. To select examples for this partition, we find other examples labeled with the intent that we re-labeled our conflicting set to have. For our `GET_INFO_TRAFFIC` intent example, this means finding some examples with the label `GET_INFO_ROAD_CONDITION`, since these examples look similar to the re-labeled conflicting examples but should have the same labels in V1 and V2. Since all of the examples where this update applies are labeled as `GET_INFO_ROAD_CONDITION` in the V1 training set, any example with a different V1 label can be considered *trivially-unchanged.*

In total, we form five different synthetic updates to use in our experiments.[2] Figure 1 also shows examples for two other types of updates: introducing a new intent for previously unsupported inputs and introducing a new argument. The updates are formed from the TOP dataset, which contains over 40,000 English queries about navigation or events labeled with tree-based semantic parses (Gupta et al., 2018).

4 Base Model

The semantic parsing model we use for our experiments is a sequence-to-sequence model based on the transformer architecture (Vaswani et al., 2017). We use a sequence-to-sequence model because of their flexibility and widespread use in semantic parsing (Jia and Liang, 2016; Dong and Lapata, 2016; Rongali et al., 2020) and NLP in general. Our model encodes a language input using a pretrained 12-layer BERT model (Devlin et al., 2019), then decodes a parse tree flattened by depth-first traversal. At each step, the decoder can generate either 1) a labeled bracket representing an intent or argument label 2) a closing bracket or 3) an index of an input token to be copied. The hyperparameters of our model architecture and training can be found in Appendix A.

[2]Data for our synthesized updates can be downloaded from `https://github.com/google/overcoming-conflicting-data/`, and Appendix B summarizes the partition sizes for each of these changes.

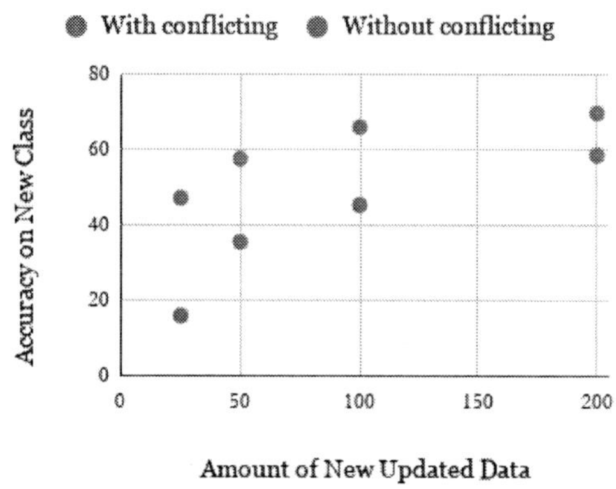

Figure 2: Accuracy as a function of data size with conflicting data compared to accuracy when an oracle removes the conflicts, averaged across five different updates.

5 Effect of Conflicting Data

Before we describe and test our methods for mitigating conflicts, this section will briefly explore how conflicting data affects learning. We evaluate model updates both with and without conflicting data, and compare accuracies as we vary the amount of new V2 data being introduced. The non-conflicting setting represents an oracle where all conflicting data is removed, which we can easily simulate in our synthetic data-creation process but is generally not achievable on real-world data without additional manual annotation.

More precisely, when evaluating updates with conflicting data, we include 50 examples with out-of-date labels in the *changed* category. We mix these examples with a full set of *unchanged* and *trivially-unchanged* examples to represent a V1 training set from before an update. We then introduce different amounts of *changed* examples with updated labels to act as the V2 training set, with sizes ranging from from half the conflicting set size (25) to four times as much (200). For each data size, we measure accuracy using an exact match metric, meaning the entire tree output by the model must match the reference to be considered correct. For the non-conflicting setting, we do not include the 50 examples with out-of-date labels, but otherwise use the same setup.

The results for this experiment are shown in Figure 2, after averaging over five different changes (a detailed breakdown of results can be found in Appendix C). To the left of the graph, we see that when the amount of conflicting data is greater than the size of the new data being added, we get less than half of the accuracy we would get without conflicting data. While the gap narrows somewhat with more data, even when we introduce four times as much new data as there are conflicting examples, the presence of conflicting data still leads to a loss of over 10% accuracy. These results show just how detrimental conflicting data can be to the learning of a model update.

6 Mitigation Methods

In this work, we consider three methods to alleviate the problems caused by conflicting data: fine-tuning, multi-task learning with separate decoder heads, and data filtering with a learned classifier.

6.1 Fine-tuning

Our first and simplest method for handling conflicting data is fine-tuning. For this approach, we first train a model on only the V1 training data, then after training completes, we take the final parameters and use those as initialization for training with the V2 data. This approach can alleviate the conflicting data problem because the second stage of training does not include any conflicting data and the model will have less confusion about how to label *changed* examples. By first training on the V1 data, we are also able to benefit indirectly from the larger amount of data contained in it.

During the second stage of training, we train on the *changed* and *unchanged* data in the V2 training set, as well as the *trivially-unchanged* examples from the V1 training set. *Trivially-unchanged* data from the V1 data can be included in V2 training because it can be easily identified and is known to not conflict.

6.2 Multi-task

For our next method, we use an approach from multi-task learning where multiple decoder heads are used for different sets of data (Caruana, 1997; Fan et al., 2017). Our two "tasks" correspond to the V1 data and the V2 data, and we use a separate set of parameters for the final pre-softmax layer of the decoder for each of the versions (as illustrated in Figure 3). The V1 head is only trained with V1 data and the V2 head is only trained with V2 data, but the encoder layers and decoder transformer are shared between both. This way, the V2 head is never trained on conflicting examples from V1, but the overall V2 model can still benefit from some information in V1 data indirectly through the shared encoder and decoder transformer layers. After training, the V1 head can be discarded, and the V2 head is used to make decisions. We train on both versions simultaneously, with each batch containing some of both types of data. As with our other methods, the V2 head is also trained on *trivially-unchanged* data from the V1 data.

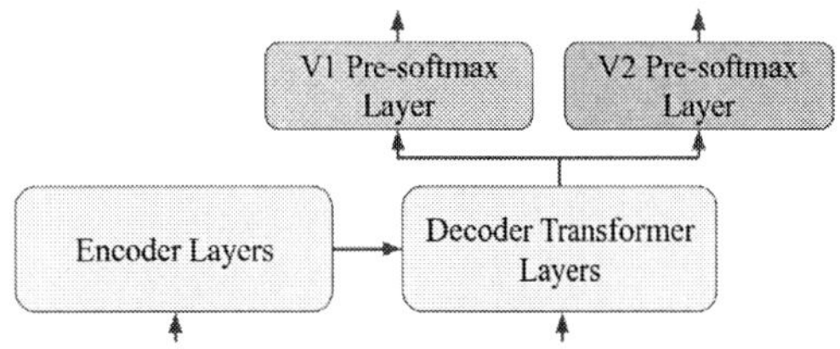

Figure 3: In our multi-task method, we feed the new V2 data to a separate decoder head to separate it from the possibly-conflicting data in the original V1 training set. The encoder layers and decoder transformer layers are shared between V1 and V2.

The goal behind this approach is similar to that of fine-tuning: to avoid training the V2 model directly on the possibly-conflicting V1 data while still sharing some amount of information through model parameters. However, unlike fine-tuning, which is liable to forget information from V1 as training progresses, the simultaneous training for the multi-task method keeps the V1 information active for better sharing.

6.3 Classifier-based Data Selection

The final method we explore in this work is classifier-based data selection. The idea behind the data selection strategy is to explicitly select examples from the original V1 data that we don't think will conflict. Using the small amount of V2 data, we train a classifier to predict whether an example will be *changed* or *unchanged*, and then apply this classifier to the V1 data, as illustrated in Figure 4. We can then include the selected examples in our updated training set, allowing us to take advantage of more information from the original training set while filtering out many of the problematic conflicting examples.

We first train a classifier on the V2 data to learn a binary decision between *changed* and *unchanged* examples. This training requires that we can distinguish between which examples are *changed* and *unchanged*, which can either be specified as part of the annotation process, or can be estimated by

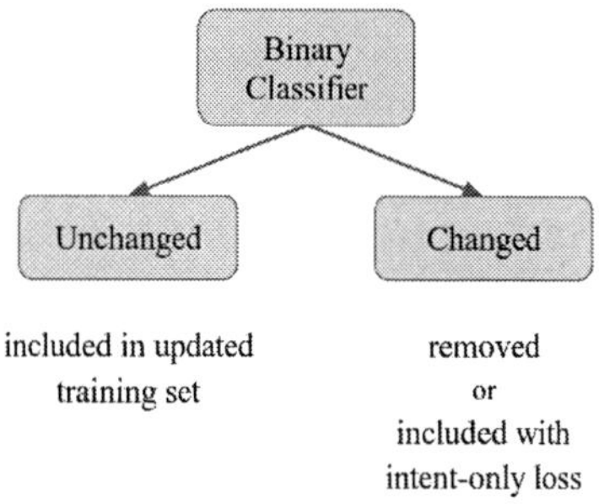

Figure 4: Our selection classification method uses a binary classifier to filter the original V1 data based on whether it is likely to be out-of-date.

	Overall Accuracy
Baselines	
Train on V1 data	49.2
Train on V2 data	51.8
Direct mixing	49.9
Methods	
Fine-tune	59.9
Multi-task	69.7
Selection (drop changed)	65.6
Selection (intent only)	**71.5**
Oracle	
Relabel all examples	74.7

Table 1: Exact match accuracies of our methods for mitigating the effects of conflicting data, averaged across five different updates. Our methods greatly outperform the baselines and close a substantial portion of the gap to the oracle upper bound.

running an existing V1 model to predict old labels for the provided V2 examples (in this work we use the annotation method, as part of our synthetic data-creation process). Our classifier uses the same BERT encoder as our sequence-to-sequence parsing model and is initialized with parameters from a parsing model for the V1 data. Representations of this encoder are averaged across time before feeding into a small feedforward network with a hidden dimension of 512. After training on the V2 set, the binary classifier is run on the V1 training set (excluding the *trivially-unchanged* examples, which can be automatically included as-is for V2 training). This creates a categorization of predicted-changed and predicted-unchanged, which we hope will closely approximate the true *changed* and *unchanged* sets. For many of the changes we tested, the classifiers performed quite well, with accuracies above 90% on held-out data. For examples in predicted-unchanged, we will include them in the set of training examples used to train our updated model. For examples in predicted-changed, we do not want to directly include them, and consider two possible solutions: 1) remove them completely or 2) include the examples with an intent-only loss, as described below.

6.3.1 Intent-only Loss

The idea of the intent-only loss variant of the data selection method is to try to take advantage of more information about the predicted-changed examples without requiring us to know the full form of the tree after a change. While we know that these examples are likely to have changed, in general we do not know if or how the full argument structure will change for all examples. However, it is usually possible to know what the intent should be for the *changed* examples. If the update is introducing a new intent, we can use this new intent for the predicted-changed examples. If the update only affects arguments, we can keep the original intents for the examples. Which of these cases applies can be specified manually (as we do in our experiments), or could likely be determined automatically by running a V1 model on the V2 data and comparing the intents. Once we have determined the new top-level intent for the predicted-changed examples, we will include them as special training examples that only receive a loss on their intent. Since the intent is the first token to be predicted by the sequence-to-sequence decoder, we can simply mask out the loss for the rest of the tokens in the sequence. With this masking, argument structure prediction will be unaffected by these examples, and the model must defer to other examples, such as those in the V2 training set, to learn argument labeling.

One case that this approach does not currently handle are updates that introduce multiple new intents simultaneously, and we leave an exploration of that case to future work. To use an intent-only loss on those updates, more fine-grained classifications are needed to determine what the correct intent for the *changed* examples are.

7 Evaluation

In this section, we describe the evaluation of our methods for mitigating the conflicting data problem.

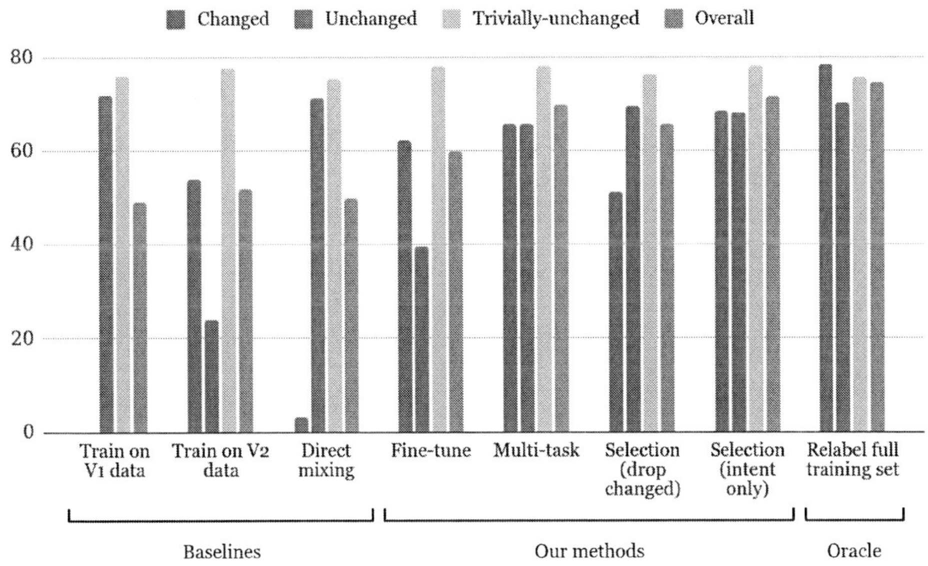

Figure 5: A break down of results across the three data partitions.

For each update, we form a test set by randomly selecting 100 examples from each of the three data partitions (*changed*, *unchanged*, and *trivially-unchanged*), and a V2 training set by selecting 50 *changed* and 50 *unchanged* examples. All remaining examples are placed into the V1 training set and *changed* examples are relabeled appropriately. Note that unlike in Section 5 where we used a fixed-size conflicting set of 50 examples in V1, in this setup we use all remaining examples available after sampling a subset for V2, which results in larger conflicting sets ranging from hundreds to thousands of examples. The large sizes of the conflicting sets further amplifies the effect of the conflicting data. We report results in terms of exact match accuracy between the predicted and target parse structure. Results are aggregated across 5 different updates, giving us a total of 1500 test examples for each method (5 updates × 3 partitions × 100 examples). We also average across 5 different runs for each method to reduce variance.

We compare against three baselines: training only on the original V1 data, training only on the new V2 data, and directly mixing the two data versions together into a single dataset.[3] We also compare to an upper bound where the entire V1 training set is re-annotated with updated labels. For many updates, this upper bound requires thousands of new annotations, as compared to the one hundred labels used by our methods.

7.1 Results

The results of our evaluation are shown in Table 1. All of our methods substantially outperform the baselines. Our best method, the selection classifier with an intent-only loss on changed examples (§ 6.3), obtains an accuracy of 71.5%, covering 86% of the gap between the best baseline and the oracle upper bound.

To see a more clear picture of what is happening, we also break down results by data partitions, as shown in Figure 5 (an even more detailed breakdown across different updates is provided in Appendix D). In this chart, we can see that the base line that mixes the V1 and V2 data without accounting for conflicts performs extremely poorly on the *changed* examples, echoing our results in Section 5. On the other hand, training only on the small set of V2 data throws away all the information from the original V1 training set, limiting its performance (particularly on *unchanged* examples). Our methods provide an effective way to combine information in both datasets without overwhelming *changed* data with out-of-date labels.

8 Conclusion

This work has shown that in order to make effective updates to the outputs of a neural semantic

[3] We also tried a variant of the direct mixing baseline where the V2 data is upsampled to try to account for differences in size, but this obtained almost identical results, indicating that upsampling is not an effective method for overcoming conflicting data (not shown in main results; see Appendix D).

parsing model by adding new data, it is important to consider the effect of conflicting examples in the original data. Conflicting data is likely a problem in many different scenarios where outputs to a model must be updated, and we believe that further study into methods for mitigating the effects of conflicting data is an important direction to allow practitioners to handle the constantly-changing needs of real-world machine learning applications.

References

Rich Caruana. 1997. Multitask learning. *Machine learning*, 28(1):41–75.

Francisco M Castro, Manuel J Marín-Jiménez, Nicolás Guil, Cordelia Schmid, and Karteek Alahari. 2018. End-to-end incremental learning. In *Proceedings of the European conference on computer vision (ECCV)*, pages 233–248.

Lingzhen Chen and Alessandro Moschitti. 2019. Transfer learning for sequence labeling using source model and target data. In *Proceedings of the AAAI Conference on Artificial Intelligence*, volume 33, pages 6260–6267.

Jacob Devlin, Ming-Wei Chang, Kenton Lee, and Kristina Toutanova. 2019. BERT: Pre-training of deep bidirectional transformers for language understanding. In *Proceedings of the 2019 Conference of the North American Chapter of the Association for Computational Linguistics: Human Language Technologies, Volume 1 (Long and Short Papers)*, pages 4171–4186, Minneapolis, Minnesota. Association for Computational Linguistics.

Li Dong and Mirella Lapata. 2016. Language to logical form with neural attention. In *Proceedings of the 54th Annual Meeting of the Association for Computational Linguistics (Volume 1: Long Papers)*, pages 33–43, Berlin, Germany. Association for Computational Linguistics.

Xing Fan, Emilio Monti, Lambert Mathias, and Markus Dreyer. 2017. Transfer learning for neural semantic parsing. In *Proceedings of the 2nd Workshop on Representation Learning for NLP*, pages 48–56, Vancouver, Canada. Association for Computational Linguistics.

Sonal Gupta, Rushin Shah, Mrinal Mohit, Anuj Kumar, and Mike Lewis. 2018. Semantic parsing for task oriented dialog using hierarchical representations. In *Proceedings of the 2018 Conference on Empirical Methods in Natural Language Processing*, pages 2787–2792, Brussels, Belgium. Association for Computational Linguistics.

Robin Jia and Percy Liang. 2016. Data recombination for neural semantic parsing. In *Proceedings of the 54th Annual Meeting of the Association for Computational Linguistics (Volume 1: Long Papers)*, pages 12–22, Berlin, Germany. Association for Computational Linguistics.

Lu Jiang, Zhengyuan Zhou, T. Leung, L. Li, and Li Fei-Fei. 2018. Mentornet: Learning data-driven curriculum for very deep neural networks on corrupted labels. In *ICML*.

James Kirkpatrick, Razvan Pascanu, Neil Rabinowitz, Joel Veness, Guillaume Desjardins, Andrei A Rusu, Kieran Milan, John Quan, Tiago Ramalho, Agnieszka Grabska-Barwinska, et al. 2017. Overcoming catastrophic forgetting in neural networks. *Proceedings of the national academy of sciences*, 114(13):3521–3526.

Zhizhong Li and Derek Hoiem. 2016. Learning without forgetting. In *European Conference on Computer Vision*, pages 614–629. Springer.

Jie Lu, Anjin Liu, Fan Dong, Feng Gu, Joao Gama, and Guangquan Zhang. 2018. Learning under concept drift: A review. *IEEE Transactions on Knowledge and Data Engineering*, 31(12):2346–2363.

Subendhu Rongali, Luca Soldaini, Emilio Monti, and Wael Hamza. 2020. Don't parse, generate! a sequence to sequence architecture for task-oriented semantic parsing. In *Proceedings of The Web Conference 2020*, WWW '20, page 2962–2968, New York, NY, USA. Association for Computing Machinery.

Andrei A Rusu, Neil C Rabinowitz, Guillaume Desjardins, Hubert Soyer, James Kirkpatrick, Koray Kavukcuoglu, Razvan Pascanu, and Raia Hadsell. 2016. Progressive neural networks. *arXiv preprint arXiv:1606.04671*.

Sainbayar Sukhbaatar, Joan Bruna, Manohar Paluri, Lubomir Bourdev, and Rob Fergus. 2014. Training convolutional networks with noisy labels. *arXiv preprint arXiv:1406.2080*.

Alexey Tsymbal. 2004. The problem of concept drift: definitions and related work. *Computer Science Department, Trinity College Dublin*, 106(2):58.

Ashish Vaswani, Noam Shazeer, Niki Parmar, Jakob Uszkoreit, Llion Jones, Aidan N Gomez, Łukasz Kaiser, and Illia Polosukhin. 2017. Attention is all you need. In *Advances in neural information processing systems*, pages 5998–6008.

Andreas Veit, Neil Alldrin, Gal Chechik, Ivan Krasin, A. Gupta, and Serge J. Belongie. 2017. Learning from noisy large-scale datasets with minimal supervision. *2017 IEEE Conference on Computer Vision and Pattern Recognition (CVPR)*, pages 6575–6583.

Tianjun Xiao, Jiaxing Zhang, Kuiyuan Yang, Yuxin Peng, and Zheng Zhang. 2014. Error-driven incremental learning in deep convolutional neural network for large-scale image classification. In *Proceedings of the 22nd ACM international conference on Multimedia*, pages 177–186.

A Model Hyperparameters

Hyperparameter	Value
Decoder layers	1
Decoder dimension	256
Decoder feedforward dimension	256
Batch size	512
Training steps	50000
Learning rate	3e-4
Learning rate warmup	10000

These hyperparameters were kept constant across all experiments and were selected based on defaults from an existing implementation. Model parameter counts are dominated by the BERT encoder, with approximately 100 million parameters. Training was performed on TPUs and took several hours per run.

B List of changes with data sizes

The table below briefly describes the five updates we test on with the sizes of each data partition *changed*, *unchanged*, and *trivially-unchanged*. For our primary experiments, 100 examples from each partition are placed in the test set, 50 examples from *changed* and *unchanged* are placed in the V2 training set, and the remainder are used for the V1 training set.

Update type	Changed	Unchanged	Trivially-unchanged
New intent from unsupported	1719	1756	32266
New intent from related + argument name change	3625	3776	28340
New argument	635	21114	13992
New intent from related	10044	422	25275
New intent from multiple intents in V1	285	3942	31514

C Effect of Conflicting Data Results Detail

The table below details the results for the experiment described in Section 5 and summarized in Figure 2. We vary the size of updated data in the V2 *changed* partition while holding constant a set of 50 conflicting examples in the original V1 data.

Change	New data size	Accuracy (%)	
		Conflicting	No Conflicting
New from unsupported	25	21	42
	50	27	51
	100	54	60
	200	61	71
New from related + arg change	25	17	59
	50	44	73
	100	52	74
	200	66	75
New argument	25	11	54
	50	44	54
	100	45	68
	200	67	67
New from related	25	16	41
	50	29	56
	100	42	56
	200	54	71
New from multiple sources	25	15	40
	50	34	54
	100	34	72
	200	45	65
Average	25	16	47.2
	50	35.6	57.6
	100	45.4	66
	200	58.6	69.8

D Main Results Detail

The following table breaks down our main results across the different updates tested. These results are described in Section 7 and summarized in Figure 5.

Update	Partition	Accuracy (%)								
		V1 only	V2 only	Dir mix	Upsampl	Fine-tu	Multi-t	Sel (rm)	Sel (io)	Oracle
A	Change	0.0	53.6	0.8	0.0	58.2	66.8	51.4	68.2	80.2
	Unchange	75.4	20.8	70.0	74.8	35.0	61.6	72.8	69.8	72.2
	Triv-unch	78.8	77.2	77.8	77.6	78.8	82.0	78.0	79.4	78.0
B	Change	0.0	59.6	0.0	0.6	66.2	70.6	60.2	64.6	81.8
	Unchange	68.4	15.2	69.3	66.6	35.2	62.2	66.6	65.2	67.0
	Triv-unch	79.6	83.0	79.3	80.0	82.8	81.2	80.0	81.8	77.2
C	Change	0.0	31.2	1.8	2.8	45.4	39.0	43.8	59.2	73.4
	Unchange	79.0	25.4	81.0	80.6	42.4	79.2	77.2	80.8	81.4
	Triv-unch	73.4	75.0	72.3	73.6	74.2	74.8	72.4	74.6	73.6
D	Change	0.0	55.0	0.0	0.0	69.0	85.6	55.2	83.4	86.8
	Unchange	64.6	41.4	66.2	64.8	52.2	61.6	60.8	56.8	59.0
	Triv-unch	70.0	74.4	70.4	73.0	73.2	71.8	71.8	73.0	72.0
E	Change	0.0	69.6	13.0	13.4	71.8	65.4	46.2	66.0	69.8
	Unchang	71.0	17.4	69.8	72.2	33.4	63.0	69.0	68.2	70.6
	Triv-unch	78.2	78.6	77.3	77.6	80.8	80.2	79.2	81.2	77.2
Avg	Change	0.0	53.8	3.1	3.4	62.1	65.5	51.4	68.3	78.4
	Unchange	71.7	24.0	71.2	71.8	39.6	65.5	69.3	68.2	70.0
	Triv-unch	76.0	77.6	75.4	76.4	78.0	78.0	76.3	78.0	75.6

Update key: A: New intent from unsupported, B: New intent from related with argument relabeling, C: New argument, D: New intent from related with same arguments, E: New intent from multiple intents in V1

Not So Fast, Classifier – Accuracy and Entropy Reduction in Incremental Intent Classification

Lianna Hrycyk
LumenVox GmbH
Lianna.Hrycyk@LumenVox.com

Alessandra Zarcone
HumAIn, Fraunhofer IIS
zce@iis.fraunhofer.de

Luzian Hahn
Semantic Audio Processing, Fraunhofer IIS
hal@iis.fraunhofer.de

Abstract

Incremental intent classification requires the assignment of intent labels to partial utterances. However, partial utterances do not necessarily contain enough information to be mapped to the intent class of their complete utterance (correctly and with a certain degree of confidence). Using the final interpretation as the ground truth to measure a classifier's accuracy during intent classification of partial utterances is thus problematic. We release inCLINC, a dataset of partial and full utterances with human annotations of plausible intent labels for different portions of each utterance, as an upper (human) baseline for incremental intent classification. We analyse the incremental annotations and propose entropy reduction as a measure of human annotators' convergence on an interpretation (i.e. intent label). We argue that, when the annotators do not converge to one or a few possible interpretations and yet the classifier already identifies the final intent class early on, it is a sign of overfitting that can be ascribed to artefacts in the dataset.

1 Introduction

In non-incremental spoken dialogue systems (SDS), modules process complete utterances sequentially: the Automatic Speech Recognition (ASR) module must detect an end of turn before the transcribed speech can be processed by the Natural Language Understanding (NLU) module, in which utterances are often assigned an intent label. The sequential execution of such systems not only increases response latency, but also affects the perceived naturalness of the interaction. Natural conversations typically proceed incrementally: people rely on multiple cues to build partial interpretations of incomplete input, check if the communication is successful, and adapt their production accordingly (Clark, 1996), sometimes completing the interlocutor's turn, barging in, or responding before the turn is over (Jaffe and Feldstein, 1970; Brady, 1968).

Incremental dialogue systems, on the other hand, make use of incremental processors to enable more efficient, flexible, and effective interactions with users (Schlangen and Skantze, 2011). For example, the ASR module of an incremental, task-oriented SDS continuously processes incoming speech signals and posts hypothesized transcriptions. Then, the downstream NLU module analyses the increasingly longer portions of the final utterance, before the user finishes their turn. These early hypotheses produced by an incremental NLU (iNLU) module can in turn be consumed by downstream modules as soon as they are posted. Thanks to incremental processing, an SDS can approximate various characteristics of human dialogue, such as timing backchannel responses or optimizing turn-taking between speakers (Baumann and Schlangen, 2011; Skantze and Hjalmarsson, 2013; Lala et al., 2017; Khouzaimi et al., 2018, *inter alia*). Incremental processing can also improve the computational efficiency of an SDS, for example by accessing time-consuming external services (e.g. database queries) before the end of a user's turn.

What's more, incremental processing enables new types of interactions between a dialogue system and its users. For example, Kennington and Schlangen (2016) developed a personal assistant that could communicate its incremental understanding of the user's ongoing speech and its prediction states by graphically displaying a branching tree. At the start of the interaction, a tree with one branch per supported intent is displayed. Once the user's intent is recognized by the system, the tree is adjusted and its associated slots are displayed as subbranches to its node. This visual feedback increases the transparency of both the system's capabilities and current understanding; it also guides the user to provide values for all required slot for the task.

iNLU is not just relevant to spoken dialogue systems: recent work has enabled incremental processing in the NLU pipeline of RASA, a widely-

Proceedings of the Third Workshop on Natural Language Processing for Conversational AI, pages 52–67
November 10, 2021.

used, open-source framework for building chat and voice-based virtual assistants (Rafla and Kennington, 2019; Bocklisch et al., 2017). When equipping a text-based dialogue system with incremental capabilities, iNLU processing is not limited by the rate at which the ASR posts intermediate results: user text can be processed as it is typed.

Intent classification, a common task assigned to the NLU module of a task-oriented SDS, poses the problem of identifying the point of the utterance where the intent has been classified with a given degree of certainty. An early identification of the correct intent, however, is not necessarily a sign of an effective classifier: when an iNLU module identifies the correct intent label before a human can (for example, after processing a not yet informative partial utterance such as "I'd like to"), then its "success" may likely be caused by the presence of artefacts in the training set.

In order to provide an upper baseline for incremental intent classification, we present inCLINC[1], a dataset of crowd-sourced incremental intent annotations, where utterances are broken into increasingly longer partial utterances by identifying peaks and troughs in surprisal (Shannon, 1948; Hale, 2001) as boundaries. We then compare the performance of human annotators to that of a Transformer-based classifier (Vaswani et al., 2017). We propose entropy reduction (between the different intent interpretation hypotheses) as a measure of uncertainty reduction during human incremental intent identification. We show that, for a substantial amount of the partial utterances, the final intent label is not yet identifiable to humans, and that a reduction in uncertainty (as annotators converge on an interpretation) is typically associated with an increase in accuracy for the annotators. We argue that, when the human annotators do not converge to one or a few possible interpretations and yet the classifier already identifies the final intent class early on, it is a sign of overfitting that can be ascribed to artefacts in the dataset.

1.1 Previous Work

The NLU module of a task-oriented SDS is commonly tasked with intent classification, where an utterance's most likely intent label is predicted. Intent can be operationalised as the main goal that one wants to achieve with a particular speech act

	Word	Predicted Intent	Correct?
w_1	I	SearchCWork	No
w_2	want	SearchCWork	No
w_3	to	SearchCWork	No
w_4	hear	PlayMusic	Yes
w_5	any	PlayMusic	Yes
w_6	tune	PlayMusic	Yes
w_7	from	PlayMusic	Yes
w_8	the	PlayMusic	Yes
w_9	Twenties	PlayMusic	Yes

Table 1: Intent of SNIPS utterance incrementally predicted by a DistilBERT classifier. *SearchCreativeWork* is abbreviated as *SearchCWork*. "Correct?" indicates whether the predicted label would be considered as accurate in a typical incremental intent classification evaluation framework, where the complete utterance's label is assigned to each of its partial utterances.

(Cohen, 2019; Allen and Perrault, 1980). Such information is found on a pragmatic level: it reflects the overall meaning communicated by a person in a particular context. Accordingly, incremental intent classification is typically framed as a *predictive* task: based on the information present in a partial utterance, a classifier must predict what information will be present in the complete utterance.

Measuring Incremental Performance Accuracy and word savings are the most commonly reported metrics in studies on incremental intent classification in the literature. An incremental prediction is typically evaluated as *accurate* when the predicted label for a partial utterance matches the ground truth label of its complete utterance. *Word savings* are then used to show the point in an ongoing utterance at which a classifier first makes an accurate prediction. If a complete utterance has 12 words and a classifier successfully predicts its label after 10 words (w_{10}), then two words are saved. Additionally, Schlangen and Skantze (2011) and Baumann et al. (2011) present metrics specifically for incremental processors. As incremental intent classification involves the prediction of a single label (i.e. one "information unit"), *edit overhead* (EO $\in [0, 1]$) is most relevant[2]. It describes the ratio of unnecessary changes in label predictions to the total number of changes.

In the literature, different types of models have been applied to the task of intent classifi-

[1]`https://fordatis.fraunhofer.de/handle/fordatis/213`

[2]Other metrics are less relevant when only one IU is predicted. For example, correctness is equivalent to accuracy on the set of complete and partial utterances in this case.

cation for incremental NLU (e.g. DeVault et al., 2009; Manuvinakurike et al., 2018; Constantin et al., 2019; Coman et al., 2019; Madureira and Schlangen, 2020, *inter alia*). A typical approach is to segment complete utterances into increasingly longer partial utterances. Each partial utterance is then assigned the ground truth label of the complete utterance. This method, however, is overly simplistic, because a partial utterance does not necessarily contain enough information to be mapped to the given intent class of its complete utterance. Table 1 presents an utterance from the popular SNIPS dataset (Coucke et al., 2018). The classifier predicts *PlayMusic* for partial utterance $w_4 =$ "I want to hear". However, this partial context is arguably not restrictive enough to be predictive of the class *PlayMusic*, especially for a SDS which may play back different kinds of information beyond music. It is not until the mention of "tune" in w_6 that the utterance arguably has enough semantic information to reasonably belong to the class *PlayMusic*. Until then, utterances beginning with "I want to hear" could easily be assigned to other intent classes. However, the phrase "I want to hear" is exclusively found in utterances belonging to the *PlayMusic* class in SNIPS. Rather than an important semantic distinction between intents, this characteristic reflects an artefact of the dataset, arising from an arbitrary choice of intent labels.

Existing approaches in the literature would view w_4 as correctly classified, as it matches the complete utterance's ground truth label. This approach inflates the assessment of classifier's accuracy and other performance metrics; the external validity of its performance on utterances outside of the dataset should be questioned. The example in Table 1 emphasises how *a*) adopting the complete utterance's label is inappropriate for many partial utterances and *b*) the performance of models in studies that do so risk being inflated by over-fitting.

1.2 Incremental Processing in Humans

Communication between human speakers and listeners is incremental on many levels. A speaker delivers information incrementally by speaking words one after the other. Exchanges of information between speakers and listeners unroll rapidly: human listeners interpret these incoming linguistic signals incrementally (Tanenhaus et al., 1995), rapidly forming both partial hypotheses based on what they hear, as they hear it (Marslen-Wilson, 1973), as well as expectations about the next signal.

The view of human language processing as being expectation-based has gained considerable support over the last 30 years in psycho-linguistic research. Research has shown that comprehenders form expectations at different levels of granularity (Zarcone et al., 2016): about the next upcoming word (Ehrlich and Rayner, 1981; McDonald and Shillcock, 2003), about its semantic category (Federmeier and Kutas, 1999), about the next event to follow in an ongoing sequence (Chwilla and Kolk, 2005), about verb selectional restrictions (Altmann and Kamide, 1999), and more. Crucially, hypotheses about the correct syntactic parse of the ongoing sentence are not only revised each time a new word is encountered; new predictions are also proactively made about the upcoming syntactic structure once this new information is integrated (Hale, 2001; Levy and Jaeger, 2007). Highly-predictable input is easier to process, as it matches the comprehender's expectations, but is also less informative. Conversely, input conveying more information given the context requires higher cognitive effort to process (Hale, 2001; Jaeger and Tily, 2011). More effort is required to process input when it results in a revision of these hypotheses than that which conforms with prior expectations (e.g. Sturt et al., 1999). The relationship between information content and processing difficulty has been described on a computational level (Marr, 1982) using Surprisal and Entropy Reduction.

Surprisal Surprisal defines the predictability of a linguistic unit (e.g. a word) in terms of its conditional probability given the context in which it appears (Shannon, 1948; Hale, 2001). Specifically, the Surprisal S of word w_t in a sentence given preceding words $(w_1, ..., w_{t-1})$ is equal to:

$$S(w_t) = -\log P(w_t|(w_1, ..., w_{t-1}, Ctxt)) \quad (1)$$

where $Ctxt$ represents extra-sentential information (e.g. visual cues, Knoeferle et al., 2008). Surprisal has been shown to be an effective complexity metric for the prediction of human sentence comprehension difficulty (Boston et al., 2008; Demberg and Keller, 2008; Frank, 2013; Levy and Jaeger, 2007; Levy, 2008). As a word's predictability is inversely proportional to its information content, we adopt Surprisal as a measure of information content at the word level - information which can contribute to the intent interpretation of an utterance.

Entropy Reduction Entropy is defined as the average amount of uncertainty at a given state associated with a random variable's possible outcomes (Shannon, 1948). If I is the set of all possible interpretations of a sentence, then the entropy of all possible interpretations can be expressed as:

$$H(I) = -\sum_{i \in I} P(I) \log_2 P(I) \quad (2)$$

Entropy is high when an ongoing sentence has many probable interpretations and is maximal when all possible interpretations have the same probability (the sentence is ambiguous). As words come in, they are "either helpful or unhelpful in narrowing down the interpretation" (Yun et al., 2015). Each new word w_t carries a certain amount of information, which can be used to *a*) revise existing hypotheses about the correct interpretation of an ongoing sentence and *b*) predict the interpretation of the remainder of the sentence (Hale, 2001; Levy and Jaeger, 2007).

Entropy reduction is then a measure of how much a given word w_t decreases the amount of uncertainty about the ongoing sentence being processed (Hale, 2003, 2006). It can be expressed as the difference in the entropy at state $t-1$ and the entropy at state t, i.e. before and after w_t:

$$\Delta H(w_t) = H(t-1) - H(t) \quad (3)$$

A greater reduction in uncertainty at a given step results in higher processing difficulty (Hale, 2006; Yun et al., 2015). Entropy reduction been shown to predict processing difficulty independently from Surprisal (Frank, 2013; Linzen and Jaeger, 2016). More specifically, two types of uncertainty can be identified, namely *a*) uncertainty about the next prediction step and *b*) uncertainty about the full sentence. Linzen and Jaeger (2016) investigated how both types impacted readers' parsing performance and showed that increased reading times were correlated with the *reduction* of uncertainty about the overall structure of an ongoing sentence but not with an *increase* in uncertainty about the next prediction step.

We adopt entropy reduction as a measure of how much a given word decreases the amount of uncertainty about the possible intent interpretation of the complete utterance. While Surprisal defines a word's information content from its conditional probability (estimated from co-occurrences), Entropy Reduction measures the changes in the human hypotheses at the (higher) intent level, at different stages in the utterance, and is estimated from the (partial) intent interpretations.

1.3 Uncertainty in Neural Networks

Uncertainty is not only relevant to human language processing; the estimation of uncertainty in deep neural networks is also an important field of research. For completeness, we will briefly introduce uncertainty and its estimation in this context. We refer the interested reader to a recent survey by Gawlikowski et al. (2021) for more information.

At its core, machine learning is interested in using data to extract models to then make predictions about unseen data (Hüllermeier and Waegeman, 2019). Such predictions are accompanied by predictive uncertainty, which can be distinguished as *aleatoric* and *epistemic* uncertainty (Kiureghian and Ditlevsen, 2009; Hüllermeier and Waegeman, 2019). For example, consider a neural network intent classifier that approximates an intent class $c \in C$ as a region in its sentence embedding space. Aleatoric uncertainty arises when such regions belonging to different intents in C overlap, whereas epistemic uncertainty is high for utterances that occur in regions in the input space sparsely populated by training instances. Points with high epistemic uncertainty could constitute an outlier or an out-of-scope utterance.

Perhaps the simplest way to estimate the predictive uncertainty of a deep neural network is to interpret its softmax output as a probability distribution. However, the softmax output distributions of deep neural networks are often poorly calibrated (Guo et al., 2017). Monte Carlo Dropout (MCD) is an alternative method for use in networks trained with dropout (Gal and Ghahramani, 2016). It interprets dropout as a Bayesian optimization approach that samples from the approximate posterior distribution of the model's parameters given the training data. Essentially, applying different dropout masks to drop different neurons from a single network can be viewed as creating an ensemble of different networks, which are treated as Monte Carlo samples from the space of all possible models for the task. By enabling dropout during inference, a prediction is generated by each network in this ensemble. The distribution of these predictions can be analysed to determine the predictive mean and the associated predictive uncertainty (e.g. the variance of this distribution) of an unseen sample at test time. Finally, deep ensembles constitute another sampling-based approach, where an ensemble of neural networks with the same architecture are trained after being initialised with different values (Lakshminarayanan et al., 2016). As with MCD, the softmax outputs across all models is aggregated to quantify the uncertainty of the prediction.

2 Proposed Approach

We propose the theory of Entropy Reduction as a lens through which to view the problem of incremental intent classification. The theory suggests that more cognitive effort is needed to process an encountered word that greatly reduces the probable interpretations of the complete sentence, as compared to a word which does not. Like human listeners, iNLU modules form (multiple) early predictions (in this case, intent predictions) for partial utterances during incremental processing, which can be revised or revoked as more words arrive.

Of course, the computational cost of a typical iNLU module does not vary as a function of an input's Surprisal or the Entropy Reduction that it triggers. However, identifying which parts of an utterance trigger a considerable reduction in the set of plausible intent interpretations may be helpful when evaluating the performance of such a module. When the set of interpretations is too open (i.e. a partial utterance could conceivably belong to almost any intent), identifying one correct answer (and potentially acting upon it) does not make sense. As this set narrows, comparing the human hypotheses with the classifier's hypotheses may help understand the classifier's decisions.

Intent labels for complete utterances do not show how intent interpretations by humans change as an utterance progresses. To the best of our knowledge, however, there is no (publicly-available) dataset with incremental annotations of utterances with intent labels. Our first contribution is a dataset of partial and full utterances with human annotations of plausible intent labels at different portions of each utterance, which can provide an upper baseline for incremental intent classification. As a second contribution, we use the collected annotations for an analysis of the performance of a Transformer-based classifier on an equivalent task of incremental intent classification (Vaswani et al., 2017). We hypothesise that humans will outperform the classifier, achieving a higher overall accuracy and higher word savings due to correct early predictions. Responses from the humans are then used to examine over-fitting versus under-performance of the classifier.

Lastly, to showcase the application of our dataset, we present an analysis of the relationship between entropy reduction and increases in accuracy during incremental intent classification. Based on previous research, such as that by Linzen and Jaeger (2016), we hypothesise that a reduction in entropy between two subsequent partial utterances are more frequently associated with increases in accuracy than between partial utterances with no changes/increases in entropy.

3 Methods

inCLINC Dataset Clinc150 is a challenging intent classification dataset with utterances from 150 classes spanning across 10 different domains, plus out-of-scope (OOS) queries (Larson et al., 2020). Adapting it to an incremental setting, we created *inCLINC*, with utterances spanning a smaller number of intents (37 intents plus OOS) so that human annotators could become familiar with the task more quickly. OOS utterances were also included proportionally. Some intent names were modified to increase transparency, while avoiding the addition of key words that appear in the utterances themselves and could bias participants (see Appendix A). inCLINC was created from Clinc150's published test set[3]. Complete utterances were first split based on the presence of white space characters. An incrementalised set of partial utterances was then created for each full utterance w_n of length *n*: w_n was segmented into a set of *n* partial utterances, such that a partial utterance w_t contained *t* words. The complete utterance w_n was also included as a control. As this method produced a large set of stimuli ($>$ 9000), we sought to identify a smaller set of partial utterances that were likely to introduce relevant (based on Surprisal) and thus potentially intent-relevant information, so that they could be shown to participants as stimuli.

3.1 Annotation Study

Stimulus selection We first computed the Surprisal of each token w_t in inCLINC by estimating their conditional probability using a pre-trained DistilGPT-2 model. We restricted the set of complete utterances by removing outliers (extremely

[3]The complete utterances from the original training and validation subsets (100 and 20 per intent, respectively) were reserved for training our intent classifier.

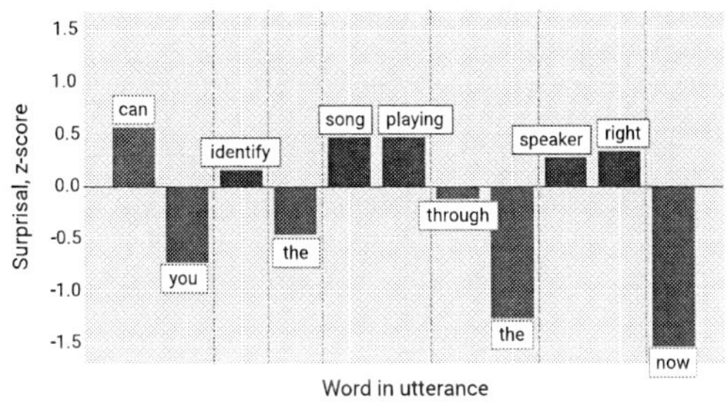

Figure 1: Segmenting an utterance into stimuli (six partial utterances plus one complete utterance) based on peaks in Surprisal.

high-surprisal words > 2.5 SD from the standardized mean), utterances with less than 4 words, utterances starting with a keyword (belonging to a list of lemmatized intents names) and utterances that did not contain at least one peak in Surprisal (see below). We randomly selected four utterances per intent from this set.

We identified peaks in Surprisal to help select a subset of partial utterances (see example in Figure 1). Peaks were detected as (consecutive) words with a positive Surprisal z-score. The onset of a peak was marked as the transition point between a negative to positive z-score, whereas its offset was marked during the switch from positive to negative. The first word in an utterance always had high Surprisal: as such, it was only included in a peak if the second word also has a positive z-score. We selected partial utterance stimuli by breaking the utterances before and after each peak's onset.

In the end, a total of 630 partial and complete utterances were presented to participants, representing 152 distinct complete utterances across 37 intent classes, plus a OOS class.

Data Collection Stimuli were randomly divided across 17 batches of 37-38 stimuli each. Stimuli from the incrementalised set of the same complete utterance were put in separate batches. Each batch contained eight to nine complete utterances as controls. For each batch, a questionnaire was created using SoSciSurvey (Leiner, 2014), presenting one stimulus per page, along with a table listing the possible intents (see screenshot in Appendix B, Figure 3). The order of presentation of the stimuli and of the intent categories was randomized across participants and between stimuli.

Participants were instructed to predict the most likely intent of the complete query, based on the incomplete text provided. An attention check was included to confirm participants read the instructions. To familiarize them with the task, two example items were also presented. The intent of the first example was clear and was used as a control question for data cleaning. The second ("are you able to") was used to illustrate how multiple possible intents could match its complete query.

Participants Participants were recruited through Amazon Mechanical Turk[4] and redirected to the annotation questionnaires. They were paid for their participation and were informed that they were free to stop the task and delete their data at any point. They were asked to confirm their English fluency: those who did not were excluded from participation. Participants could complete multiple batches. We collected nine annotations per batch.

Data Cleaning We removed stimuli belonging to ambiguous complete utterances. A complete utterance was deemed ambiguous if the classifier's prediction did not match the ground truth label and/or $< 50\%$ of participants selected the same intent for a given complete utterance. We also excluded all answers from participants who either failed the attention checks and/or selected an incorrect intent for ≥ 3 unambiguous control stimuli.

3.2 Intent Classifier

A DistilBERT[5] Transformer model with a linear layer classification head was fine-tuned to classify the intent class of the pooled output (CLS token) (Sanh et al., 2019). DistilBERT was selected to mimic a feasible set-up for an online, incremental processing setting. All weights were trained for 2 epochs (for more details, see Appendix C).

3.3 Annotated Dataset

After data cleaning, the inCLINC dataset included 121 distinct utterances in their complete form (121) and in partial form (417), for a total of 538 annotated utterances. After data cleaning, each utterance (partial or complete) had six to nine annotations. Each utterance was then assigned a predicted human label as the response with the highest number of votes. In case of a tie, we assigned the label of the complete query or, if this was not among the list of intent labels with the most votes, then the predicted intent label was randomly selected from

[4] `https://www.mturk.com/`

[5] Checkpoint from *Hugging Face* library `https://huggingface.co/transformers/`

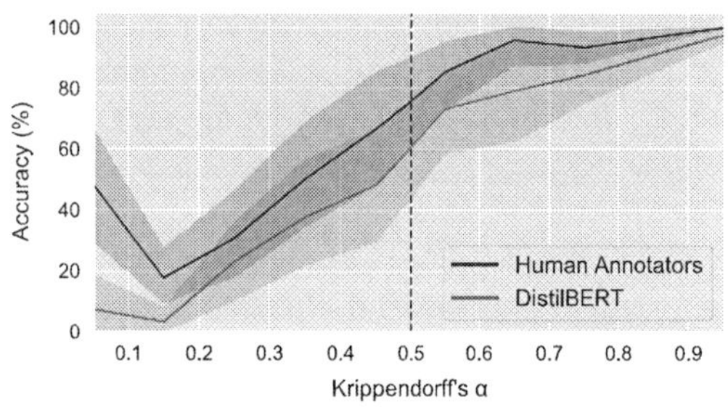

Figure 2: Mean accuracy at different levels of agreement. Stimuli were divided into 10 equal-sized bins based on $\alpha \in [0, 1]$ (shadow shows standard deviation).

	Accuracy	EO	WC Savings
Annotators	66.43%	0.39	2.43
DistilBERT	56.35%	0.45	1.94

Table 2: Performance on partial utterance stimuli.

the top-voted list. inCLINC with its annotations (majority-vote labels, as well as single labels) has been made publicly available[6]. 365 unique words appear in the inCLINC dataset. For descriptive statistics of the stimuli, see Table 5 in Appendix A.

4 Results

Annotation reliability To verify response reliability, we measured participant agreement on the set of complete utterances using Krippendorff's α (Krippendorff, 2011). On these control stimuli, participant responses reached $\alpha = 0.80$, reflecting substantial to perfect agreement (Artstein and Poesio, 2008). Figure 2 shows a positive trend between α and accuracy for both participants' and DistilBERT's predictions, supporting task validity: the more participants agree on the label for a partial utterance, the more often they identify the complete utterance's intent label.

Accuracy For the complete utterances in Clinc150's test set[7], DistilBERT achieved an accuracy of 94.56%. However, for inCLINC, Table 2 shows that the annotators outperformed DistilBERT by over 10% for partial utterances. What's more, the annotators "only" reached an accuracy of 66%: for many partial utterances, the complete utterance's intent is not discernible.

[6]https://fordatis.fraunhofer.de/handle/fordatis/213

[7]Utterances from the original test subset that belong to a class included in inCLINC.

	↑ Accuracy	↓ Accuracy
ER < 0	85	143
ER ≥ 0	10	179

Table 3: Frequency table showing entropy reduction (ER) of stimuli and associated increases/decreases in accuracy, as compared to the previous partial utterance.

Word Chunk (WC) Savings Complete utterances were chunked based on Surprisal peaks and troughs, and thus sequential partial utterances differed by a variable number of words. As such, rather than the absolute number of words saved, we examine *word chunk savings* (WC savings), i.e. how many stimuli earlier than the complete utterance was the final intent first predicted. As shown in Table 2, human annotators achieved a higher mean WC savings than DistilBERT. Despite their superior performance, human annotators met an upper bound: they had zero WC savings for about 6% of utterances (13% for DistilBERT), whereas only 1 WC was saved for about 28% of utterances (28% for DistilBERT).

Edit Overhead (EO) Table 2 reports a lower Edit Overhead (EO) for annotators than DistilBERT. Participants not only predicted the final label earlier, but were also more consistent with their predictions throughout an utterance.

Entropy Reduction (ER) Entropy reduction (ER) was considered as an independent variable with categories ER < 0 and ER ≥ 0. We tested whether a difference in outcomes across these ER categories exists, where the possible outcomes were *a*) an increase in accuracy between processing the sequential partial utterances (i.e. predicted label was incorrect for the previous partial utterance before but was correct for the following partial utterance) *b*) a decrease/no change in accuracy. McNemar's test was performed using the binomial probability distribution (McNemar, 1947). The frequencies in Table 3 differed significantly across ER categories ($p < 0.001$, one-sided). More specifically, partial utterances characterised by Entropy Reduction (ER < 0) were more frequently accompanied by an increase in participant accuracy than by an increase in entropy/no change (ER ≥ 0).

5 Discussion

Humans as an Upper Baseline Bender and Koller (2020) debate how much *meaning* a trained neural language model *understands* and argue that, when a system outperforms inter-annotator agreement, the task likely contains artefacts that do not represent meaning. As such, over-fitting in the context of incremental intent prediction can be assessed by examining the cases where DistilBERT predicts the complete label for an earlier partial utterance than the annotators. Conversely, areas where a model could be improved can be studied by looking at utterances where the annotators predicted the complete utterance's intent earlier. We looked at partial utterances whose complete label was predicted by either the annotators or the classifier, but not both. These disagreements, found in 16% of partial utterances, were used to examine over-fitting and under-performance.

Evidence for Overfitting For eight partial utterances, DistilBERT predicted the complete utterance's label, but the majority of participants did not. These partial utterances included: "tell my", "i have to", and "on the" (complete list in Table 7, Appendix D). None of these utterances can be clearly assigned to a specific intent: this prediction is a "lucky guess" based on artefacts distinguishing classes. Popular NLU intent benchmarks with notably fewer classes, such as ATIS and SNIPS (Hemphill et al., 1990; Coucke et al., 2018), may contain more such artefacts, which would speak against the generalisability of the results obtained on them. Furthermore, existing studies that label partial utterances with the complete utterance's label do not distinguish between such "lucky guesses" and points where the intent is identifiable: reported performance could be inflated by overfitting.

Evidence for Under-Performance 61 utterances were correctly predicted by the participants but not by DistilBERT. Of these, 24 had at least moderate agreement ($\alpha \geq 0.50$) between participants (values reported in Appendix D). These utterances do not represent the point where intent is identifiable by a vast majority of participants. Rather, they represent subtle differences in formulation of utterances that humans, but not the classifier, might associate with a certain intent class, which results in a considerable amount of (but not all) participants predicting the final intent.

A few interesting observations can be made. First, "i need milk" was correctly assigned to *Update/add to shopping list* by participants, while DistilBERT predicted *Place an order*. People are probably more likely to buy perishable items such as milk at a store in-person: a failure to "understand" this real-world knowledge might have caused the classifier to miss this prediction. Next, the familiarity of participants with the well-known expression "how's the weather" is visible in the agreement of $\alpha = 1.0$ for the partial utterance "how's the" and class *Get Weather*. The completion "how's the" to "how's the weather" suggests that "how's the" is a high-cloze phrase (Taylor, 1953) and "weather" is a highly-predictable continuation. Note that the missing word "weather" is also found in the label for its intent, and that "how's the weather" matches an utterance one would expect to hear in the context of a task-oriented SDS with inCLINC's supported intents. This example can be considered the human-equivalent of the artefact in Table 1. However, humans make such a prediction by generalising over their own statistical experience accumulated over a lifetime of language exposure, while a model only has access to the patterns it has learned to represent based on those found in the (domain-specific, limited) data on which it was trained.

Entropy Reduction During incremental intent classification, not all steps contribute equally to the final interpretation. We identified Surprisal peaks and troughs as relevant points to break the utterances into informative incremental chunks, as informed by the token's conditional probability. We then proposed ER (computed from the human interpretations) as a metric to demonstrate the incremental narrowing of the set of plausible final intents at these breaking points.Utterances accompanied by a reduction in entropy are more frequently associated with an increase in accuracy compared to those with no changes/increases in entropy. ER serves as a tangible metric of how much certain (chunks of) words, driven by information content, restrict the set of plausible final intents and is thus accompanied by increased prediction accuracy.

Limitations Changes in ER across partial utterances could be affected by *a*) different representations of the intent classes across participants and/or *b*) their differing language abilities. This limitations arises as our (relatively small number of) participants were recruited online and their English fluency was self-reported[8]. With six to nine annotations per item, each response has significantly influence the set of annotations for a given item. Collecting more annotations would be beneficial to

[8]Fluency was indirectly verified by excluding participants who gave incorrect responses for multiple control utterances.

reduce fluctuations in the distribution of responses triggered by individual participants and to allow for a more in-depth study of the role of Entropy Reduction in incremental intent classification (controlling for e.g. the Surprisal and the predictability of the next word, the position in which reductions of entropy are expected, etc.). Additionally, when the complete utterance's label was among those with the most votes, then this label was selected as the prediction: this is a biased selection of a favourable answer. 3.5% of stimuli were resolved using this heuristic and annotators' accuracy in Table 2 is arguably inflated by this amount. Finally, only one classifier was used in the presented work. Comparing different models' performance to our human upper baseline would be interesting.

6 Conclusion

Assigning an utterance's ground-truth label to its partial utterances is a common oversimplification of incremental intent classification. Existing studies report global performance metrics across partial utterances and fail to distinguish between those not containing enough information to be representative of the final intent and those who do. It is then unclear to what degree a classifier's performance is attributable to overfitting to the evaluated dataset versus to a generalisable representation of intent classes. We proposed an alternate lens to view this task: evaluating a model of incremental intent classification should not just be a matter of *getting the intent right*. Rather, it should be about predicting a set of plausible labels for an ongoing utterance and communicating with what certainty the final intent has been classified at this point.

As an alternative to simply adopting the complete utterance's label, we presented a new dataset with annotated incrementalised utterances. We proposed a novel method for determining plausible intent annotations at relevant points – from an information-theoretic point of view – in an ongoing utterance. With humans as an upper baseline, the performance of incremental intent classifiers may be evaluated against our labeled annotations. The remainder of our work then focused on the evaluation of a Transformer-based intent classifier in an incremental setting. To analyse our dataset, we proposed ER as a metric to detect the incremental narrowing of intent interpretations by human annotators. Our analysis showed that ER more frequently accompanied increased prediction accuracy for the annotators compared to decreases/no changes in accuracy. ER has the potential to identify the earliest point of understanding, before which accuracy and word savings are not informative measures to evaluate the performance of an incremental classifier, as before this point the upper performance bound is unknown.

While our work did not focus on the training of incremental intent classifiers, inCLINC opens up several new possibilities. For example, its annotations could be used to assess and improve the confidence calibration (in the strong sense, see Vaicenavicius et al., 2019) of multi-class classifiers to ensure that their softmax output more reliably estimates the uncertainty about the (final) intent at a given point in an ongoing utterance. Providing strongly-calibrated confidence scores alongside predictions would help increase model interpretability, facilitate its integration into other probabilistic models (Guo et al., 2017), and help coordinated processing across modules in an incremental SDS (Schlangen and Skantze, 2011). Alternatively, the annotations could be used as labels in a multi-intent classification setting for partial utterances[9]. This approach would circumvent the problem of assigning a complete utterance's label to a partial utterance with not yet enough semantic information relevant to the target class: all plausible labels could be trained for partial utterances. Finally, ER in a SDS could be monitored across ongoing utterances to learn points at which the entropy of possible interpretations is low enough for the given task. A dataset with annotations such as inCLINC could provide useful labels for this paradigm. All in all, models which are able to overcome the challenges of incremental intent classification could have the potential to learn more robust and generalisable class representations, which will could conceivably improve their performance in a real-life applications.

Acknowledgements

This research was carried out while the first author was affiliated with the Fraunhofer IIS, as a member of the Semantic Audio Processing department. It was funded by the German Federal Ministry for Economic Affairs and Energy (BMWi) through the SPEAKER project (FKZ 01MK19011).

[9]E.g. "I need to cancel my" could represent many inCLINC intents, such as *Cancel a reservation*, *Update/add to reminders*, and *Update/add to to-list*.

References

James F. Allen and C. Raymond Perrault. 1980. Analyzing intention in utterances. *Artificial Intelligence*, 15(3):143–178.

Gerry T.M. Altmann and Yuki Kamide. 1999. Incremental interpretation at verbs: Restricting the domain of subsequent reference. *Cognition*, 73(3):247–264.

Ron Artstein and Massimo Poesio. 2008. Inter-Coder Agreement for Computational Linguistics. *Computational Linguistics*, 34(4):555–596.

Timo Baumann, Okko Buß, and David Schlangen. 2011. Evaluation and optimisation of incremental processors. *Dialogue and Discourse*, 2(1):113–141.

Timo Baumann and David Schlangen. 2011. Predicting the micro-timing of user input for an incremental spoken dialogue system that completes a user's ongoing turn. In *Proceedings of the 12th Annual Meeting of the Special Interest Group on Discourse and Dialogue (SIGDIAL)*, pages 120–129.

Emily M Bender and Alexander Koller. 2020. Climbing towards NLU: On Meaning, Form, and Understanding in the Age of Data. In *Proceedings of the 58th Annual Meeting of the Association for Computational Linguistics*, 2, pages 5185–5198.

Tom Bocklisch, Joey Faulkner, Nick Pawlowski, and Alan Nichol. 2017. Rasa: Open Source Language Understanding and Dialogue Management. *arXiv preprint arXiv:1712.05181*.

Marisa Ferrara Boston, John Hale, and Reinhold Kliegl. 2008. Parsing costs as predictors of reading difficulty: An evaluation using the Potsdam Sentence Corpus. *Journal of Eye Movement Research*, 2(1):1–12.

Paul T Brady. 1968. A statistical analysis of on-off patterns in 16 conversations. *Bell System Technical Journal*, 47(1):73–91.

Dorothee J. Chwilla and Herman H.J. Kolk. 2005. Accessing world knowledge: Evidence from N400 and reaction time priming. *Cognitive Brain Research*, 25(3):589–606.

Herbert H Clark. 1996. *Using Language*. Cambridge University Press.

Philip R. Cohen. 2019. Foundations of collaborative task-oriented dialogue: What's in a slot? In *Proceedings of the - 20th Annual Meeting of the Special Interest Group Discourse Dialogue - Proceedings of the Conference (SIGDIAL)*, September, pages 198–209.

Andrei C. Coman, Koichiro Yoshino, Yukitoshi Murase, Satoshi Nakamura, and Giuseppe Riccardi. 2019. An incremental turn-taking model for task-oriented dialog systems. In *Proceedings of the 20th Annual Conference of the International Speech Communication Association (INTERSPEECH)*, pages 4155–4159.

Stefan Constantin, Jan Niehues, and Alex Waibel. 2019. Incremental processing of noisy user utterances in the spoken language understanding task. In *Proceedings of the 5th Workshop on Noisy User-generated Text (W-NUT 2019)*, pages 265–274.

Alice Coucke, Alaa Saade, Adrien Ball, Théodore Bluche, Alexandre Caulier, David Leroy, Clément Doumouro, Thibault Gisselbrecht, Francesco Caltagirone, Thibaut Lavril, Maël Primet, and Joseph Dureau. 2018. Snips Voice Platform: an embedded Spoken Language Understanding system for private-by-design voice interfaces.

Vera Demberg and Frank Keller. 2008. Data from eye-tracking corpora as evidence for theories of syntactic processing complexity. *Cognition*, 109(2):193–210.

David DeVault, Kenji Sagae, and David Traum. 2009. Can I Finish? Learning when to respond to incremental interpretation results in interactive dialogue. In *Proceedings of the 10th Annual Meeting of the Special Interest Group on Discourse and Dialogue (SIGDIAL)*, pages 11–20.

Susan Ehrlich and Keith Rayner. 1981. Contextual Effects on Word Perception and Eye Movements during Reading. *Journal of Verbal Learning and Verbal Behavior*, 20(6):641–655.

Kara D. Federmeier and Marta Kutas. 1999. A Rose by Any Other Name: Long-Term Memory Structure and Sentence Processing. *Journal of Memory and Language*, 41(4):469–495.

Stefan L. Frank. 2013. Uncertainty Reduction as a Measure of Cognitive Load in Sentence Comprehension. *Topics in Cognitive Science*, 5(3):475–494.

Yarin Gal and Zoubin Ghahramani. 2016. Dropout as a Bayesian approximation: Representing model uncertainty in deep learning. *33rd International Conference on Machine Learning, ICML 2016*, 3:1651–1660.

Jakob Gawlikowski, Cedrique Rovile Njieutcheu Tassi, Mohsin Ali, Jongseok Lee, Matthias Humt, Jianxiang Feng, Anna Kruspe, Rudolph Triebel, Peter Jung, Ribana Roscher, et al. 2021. A survey of uncertainty in deep neural networks. *arXiv preprint arXiv:2107.03342*.

Chuan Guo, Geoff Pleiss, Yu Sun, and Kilian Q. Weinberger. 2017. On calibration of modern neural networks. In *Proceedings of the 34th International Conference on Machine Learning (ICML)*, pages 2130–2143.

John Hale. 2001. A probabilistic Earley parser as a psycholinguistic model. In *Proceedings of the Second meeting of the North American Chapter of the Association for Computational Linguistics (NAACL)*, pages 1–8.

John Hale. 2003. The information conveyed by words in sentences. *Journal of Psycholinguistic Research*, 32(2):101–123.

John Hale. 2006. Uncertainty about the rest of the sentence. *Cognitive Science*, 30(4):643–672.

Charles T. Hemphill, John J. Godfrey, and George R. Doddington. 1990. The ATIS spoken language systems pilot corpus. In *Speech and Natural Language: Proceedings of a Workshop Held at Hidden Valley, Pennsylvania, June 24-27, 1990*, pages 96–101.

Eyke Hüllermeier and Willem Waegeman. 2019. Aleatoric and Epistemic Uncertainty in Machine Learning: An Introduction to Concepts and Methods. *arXiv preprint arXiv:1910.09457*.

T Florian Jaeger and Harry Tily. 2011. On language 'utility': Processing complexity and communicative efficiency. *Wiley Interdisciplinary Reviews: Cognitive Science*, 2(3):323–335.

J. Jaffe and S. Feldstein. 1970. *Rhythms of dialogue*. Academic Press, New York, NY.

Casey Kennington and David Schlangen. 2016. Supporting spoken assistant systems with a graphical user interface that signals incremental understanding and prediction state. In *Proceedings of the 17th Annual Meeting of the Special Interest Group on Discourse and Dialogue*, pages 242–251.

Hatim Khouzaimi, Romain Laroche, and Fabrice Lefèvre. 2018. A methodology for turn-taking capabilities enhancement in Spoken Dialogue Systems using Reinforcement Learning. *Computer Speech and Language*, 47:93–111.

Armen Der Kiureghian and Ove Ditlevsen. 2009. Aleatory or epistemic? Does it matter? *Structural Safety*, 31(2):105–112.

Pia Knoeferle, Boukje Habets, Matthew W. Crocker, and Thomas F. Münte. 2008. Visual scenes trigger immediate syntactic reanalysis: Evidence from ERPs during situated spoken comprehension. *Cerebral Cortex*, 18(4):789–795.

Klaus Krippendorff. 2011. Computing Krippendorff's Alpha-Reliability. Departmental Papers (ASC).

Balaji Lakshminarayanan, Alexander Pritzel, and Charles Blundell. 2016. Simple and scalable predictive uncertainty estimation using deep ensembles. *arXiv preprint arXiv:1612.01474*.

Divesh Lala, Pierrick Milhorat, Koji Inoue, Masanari Ishida, Katsuya Takanashi, and Tatsuya Kawahara. 2017. Attentive listening system with backchanneling, response generation and flexible turn-taking. In *Proceedings of the 18th Annual Meeting of the Special Interest Group on Discourse and Dialogue (SIGDIAL)*, pages 127–136.

Stefan Larson, Anish Mahendran, Joseph J. Peper, Christopher Clarke, Andrew Lee, Parker Hill, Jonathan K. Kummerfeld, Kevin Leach, Michael A. Laurenzano, Lingjia Tang, and Jason Mars. 2020. An evaluation dataset for intent classification and out-of-scope prediction. In *Proceedings of the 2019 Conference on Empirical Methods in Natural Language Processing and 9th International Joint Conference on Natural Language Processing (EMNLP-IJCNLP 2019)*, pages 1311–1316.

Dominik J Leiner. 2014. SoSci survey (version 2.4. 00-i).

Roger Levy. 2008. Expectation-based syntactic comprehension. *Cognition*, 106(3):1126–1177.

Roger Levy and T Florian Jaeger. 2007. Speakers optimize information density through syntactic reduction. In *Advances in neural information processing systems (NIPS)*, volume 19, page 849–856. MIT Press.

Tal Linzen and T. Florian Jaeger. 2016. Uncertainty and Expectation in Sentence Processing: Evidence From Subcategorization Distributions. *Cognitive Science*, 40(6):1382–1411.

Ilya Loshchilov and Frank Hutter. 2019. Decoupled weight decay regularization. In *Proceedings of the 7th International Conference on Learning Representations (ICLR)*.

Brielen Madureira and David Schlangen. 2020. Incremental processing in the age of non-incremental encoders: An empirical assessment of bidirectional models for incremental NLU. In *Proceedings of the 2020 Conference on Empirical Methods in Natural Language Processing (EMNLP)*, pages 357–374, Online. Association for Computational Linguistics.

Ramesh Manuvinakurike, Trung Bui, Walter Chang, and Kallirroi Georgila. 2018. Conversational image editing: Incremental intent identification in a new dialogue task. In *Proceedings of the 19th Annual SIGdial Meeting on Discourse and Dialogue*, pages 284–295, Melbourne, Australia. Association for Computational Linguistics.

David Marr. 1982. *Vision: A Computational Investigation Into the Human Representation and Processing of Visual Information*. W. H. Freeman, San Francisco, CA, USA.

William Marslen-Wilson. 1973. Linguistic structure and speech shadowing at very short latencies. *Nature*, 244(5417):522–523.

Scott A. McDonald and Richard C. Shillcock. 2003. Eye movements reveal the on-line computation of lexical probabilities during reading. *Psychological Science*, 14(6):648–652.

Quinn McNemar. 1947. Note on the sampling error of the difference between correlated proportions or percentages. *Psychometrika*, 12(2):153–157.

Andrew Rafla and Casey Kennington. 2019. Incrementalizing RASA's Open-Source Natural Language Understanding Pipeline. *arXiv preprint arXiv:1907.05403*.

Victor Sanh, Lysandre Debut, Julien Chaumond, and Thomas Wolf. 2019. DistilBERT, a distilled version of BERT: smaller, faster, cheaper and lighter. In *Proceedings of EMC2: 5th Edition Co-located with NeurIPS 2019*.

David Schlangen and Gabriel Skantze. 2011. A General, Abstract Model of Incremental Dialogue Processing. *Dialogue & Discourse*, 2(1):83–111.

C. E. Shannon. 1948. A Mathematical Theory of Communication. *Bell System Technical Journal*, 27(3):379–423.

Gabriel Skantze and Anna Hjalmarsson. 2013. Towards incremental speech generation in conversational systems. *Computer Speech and Language*, 27(1):243–262.

Patrick Sturt, Martin J. Pickering, and Matthew W. Crocker. 1999. Structural Change and Reanalysis Difficulty in Language Comprehension. *Journal of Memory and Language*, 40(1):136–150.

Michael K. Tanenhaus, Michael J. Spivey-Knowlton, Kathleen M. Eberhard, and Julie C. Sedivy. 1995. Integration of visual and linguistic information in spoken language comprehension. *Science*, 268(5217):1632–1634.

Wilson L. Taylor. 1953. "Cloze Procedure": A New Tool for Measuring Readability. *Journalism Quarterly*, 30(4):415–433.

Juozas Vaicenavicius, David Widmann, Carl Andersson, Fredrik Lindsten, Jacob Roll, and Thomas B. Schön. 2019. Evaluating model calibration in classification. In *Proceedings of the 22nd International Conference on Artificial Intelligence and Statistics (AISTATS)*, pages 3459—-3467.

Ashish Vaswani, Noam Shazeer, Niki Parmar, Jakob Uszkoreit, Llion Jones, Aidan N. Gomez, Łukasz Kaiser, and Illia Polosukhin. 2017. Attention is all you need. In *Advances in Neural Information Processing Systems*, pages 5999–6009.

Jiwon Yun, Zhong Chen, Tim Hunter, John Whitman, and John Hale. 2015. Uncertainty in processing relative clauses across East Asian languages. *Journal of East Asian Linguistics*, 24(2):113–148.

Alessandra Zarcone, Marten Van Schijndel, Jorrig Vogels, and Vera Demberg. 2016. Salience and attention in surprisal-based accounts of language processing. *Frontiers in Psychology*, 7:844.

A Description of inCLINC

The original training/validation/test subsets published in Larson et al. (2020) were used to create inCLINC. Expanded intent names were created for some of the labels in inCLINC to clarify their meaning. The addition of key words that appear in the utterances themselves was avoided. As well, intent labels were grouped into six categories (plus OOS) for presentation to participants. Table 4 shows the mapping of the original labels to their expanded labels and their assigned category. Descriptive statistics for stimuli in inCLINC are presented in Table 5.

B Presentation of Task

Figure 3 shows how a partial utterance was displayed to participants during Experiment 2. The intent categories were randomly shuffled between the presentation of each stimulus.[10] The order in which intents within a given category were displayed was not shuffled. This design choice was made to reduce the cognitive load of participants: as participants were not familiar with the dataset, shuffling the order of items within the category could be frustrating and discourage participants from making thoughtful predictions about the intent for short utterances, especially when intent is not clear (e.g. for the utterance "I want").[11] This choice has the added advantage that similar intents are always grouped, encouraging participants to make fine-grained decisions between similar intents.[12]

C Training DistilBERT

The intent classifier used HuggingFace's implemented *DistilBertForSequenceClassification* architecture. The final linear layer of the model consisted of 38 output neurons: one for each 37 in-scope classes, plus an additional neuron for the out-of-scope class. The weights in the classifier's task-specific classification head were randomly initialized; the weights in the encoder layers were loaded from the pre-trained model. The weights in the dropout layer had a probability $p = 0.2$ of

[10]The intent categories are the headers of the blue boxes: *Shopping, Events & Tasks, Music, Out-of-Scope, Restaurant, Cooking, Tools & Utilities*.

[11]Participants were made familiar with the displayed intents in three practice rounds before the presentation of experimental stimuli.

[12]For example, *Update/add to calendar* is always presented under *Ask about calendar*.

inCLINC Category	Clinc150 Domain	inCLINC Label	Clinc150 Label
Cooking	Kitchen and Dining	Ask about calories	calories
Cooking	Kitchen and Dining	Ask about cook time	cook time
Cooking	Kitchen and Dining	How long food lasts	food last
Cooking	Kitchen and Dining	Ingredients for recipes	ingredient list
Cooking	Kitchen and Dining	Ingredient substitution	ingredient substitution
Cooking	Kitchen and Dining	Ask for meal suggestion	meal suggestion
Cooking	Kitchen and Dining	Nutrition information	nutrition info
Cooking	Kitchen and Dining	Get recipe	recipe
Events & Tasks	Home	Ask about calendar	calendar
Events & Tasks	Home	Update/add to calendar	calendar update
Events & Tasks	Home	Ask about reminders	reminder
Events & Tasks	Home	Update/add to reminders	reminder update
Events & Tasks	Home	Ask about to-do list	todo list
Events & Tasks	Home	Update/add to to-do list	todo list update
Events & Tasks	Home	Update/add to playlist	update playlist
Music	Tools and Utilities	Calculator	calculator
Music	Home	Next song	next song
Music	Home	Play music	play music
Music	Home	Identify song	what song
Restaurant	Kitchen and Dining	Accept a reservation	accept reservations
Restaurant	Kitchen and Dining	Cancel a reservation	cancel reservation
Restaurant	Kitchen and Dining	Confirm a reservation	confirm reservation
Restaurant	Kitchen and Dining	How busy is restaurant	how busy
Restaurant	Kitchen and Dining	Make a reservation	restaurant reservation
Restaurant	Kitchen and Dining	Ask for restaurant review	restaurant reviews
Restaurant	Kitchen and Dining	Ask for restaurant suggestion	restaurant suggestion
Shopping	Home	Place an order	order
Shopping	Home	Ask about order status	order status
Shopping	Home	Ask about shopping list	shopping list
Shopping	Home	Update/add to shopping list	shopping list update
Utilities	Tools and Utilities	Ask about date	date
Utilities	Tools and Utilities	Find phone	find phone
Utilities	Tools and Utilities	Make call	make call
Utilities	Tools and Utilities	Share location	share location
Utilities	Home	Smart home function	smart home
Utilities	Tools and Utilities	Text	text
Utilities	Tools and Utilities	Weather	weather
Out-Of-Scope	Out-Of-Scope	Out-Of-Scope	OOS

Table 4: Mapping of original labels from Clinc150 to categories and labels in inCLINC.

Figure 3: Stimulus Presentation in Experiment 2. The complete utterance is "i need buy a birthday gift for sue taken off my calendar", belonging to the intent class *Update/add to calendar*.

	Stimuli	Mean	SD	Min	Max
Length (# words)	Full Utterances	8.83	3.02	5.00	20.00
	Partial Utterances	5.35	3.11	1.00	19.00
# of Partials Utterances	Full Utterances	3.45	1.74	1.00	12.00
	Partial Utterances	–	–	–	–
# of Annotations	Full Utterances	7.47	0.82	6.00	9.00
	Partial Utterances	7.41	0.83	6.00	9.00
Δ Entropy	Full Utterances	-0.23	0.46	-1.49	0.45
	Partial Utterances	-0.31	0.59	-1.95	1.15
Krippendorff's α	Full Utterances	0.89	0.16	0.46	1.00
	Partial Utterances	0.57	0.35	0.00	1.00
z-Surprisal	Full Utterances	0.12	1.02	-1.66	2.49
	Partial Utterances	0.06	1.01	-1.65	2.49

Table 5: Descriptive statistics for inClinc stimuli. Length refers to the number of whitespace-separated words in a stimulus. z-Surprisal refers to the Surprisal value for the last word in the stimulus, standardized based on all Surprisal values computed from utterances in the original Clinc150 dataset.

being dropped. All weights were fine-tuned using the complete utterances in the training subset.

Model fit during training was evaluated with respect to the NLL loss for the validation subset. The classifier was trained for 5 epochs, using an initial learning rate of 2e$-$5 that was linearly decreased by a factor of 0.2. An AdamW optimizer was used, which performs gradient bias correction and weight decay to improve regularization (Loshchilov and Hutter, 2019). Optimization was performed with respect to the NLL on the validation subset.

Validation NLL was the lowest after epoch 2; this is the model that was retained for testing. After training, the classifier had a 94.56% accuracy on the complete utterances on the test set.[13]

D Disagreement between Participants and DistilBERT

The partial utterances whose complete label was either successfully predicted by either the coders or the classifier, but not both, were inspected. These disagreements were found in 69 presented stimuli out of 538 (12.82%). For 61 of these stimuli, the coders successfully predicted the correct complete label while the classifier did not; the agreement of 24 of these utterances surpassed the threshold of moderate agreement $\alpha = 0.50$. These 24 utterances are presented in Table 6. For the remaining eight of 69 disagreements, the classifier was the one with the successful prediction. These stimuli are presented in Table 7. Note that none of the stimuli reported in Table 6 involved ties.

[13]Here, the test set refers to all complete utterances from the original Clinc150 test split, before sampling the select stimuli to be presented to participants.

#	Partial Utterance	Predicted, DistilBERT	Label, Complete Utterance	α
1	i need milk	Place an order	Update/add to shopping list	0.51
2	put the dishes on my	Smart home function	Update/add to to-do list	0.51
3	please give me the name of a few good options	Ask for meal suggestion	Ask for restaurant suggestion	0.51
4	i'll be confirming	Share location	Confirm a reservation	0.52
5	please put chips	Ingredient Substitution	Update/add to shopping list	0.52
6	what is the solution	OOS	Calculator	0.58
7	what events do i have going on on	Ask about to-do list	Ask about calendar	0.65
8	can you help me hunt for my missing	Ask about reminders	Find phone	0.65
9	please give me the name of a few good options	Identify song	Ask for restaurant suggestion	0.65
10	do they serve good tacos	Ask for meal suggestion	Ask for restaurant review	0.65
11	what events	OOS	Ask about calendar	0.70
12	after how much time is it still safe	Ask about date	How long food lasts	0.70
13	get reservations	Accept a reservation	Make a reservation	0.70
14	i need a table	Cancel a reservation	Make a reservation	0.74
15	please identify	Share location	Identify song	0.74
16	will this recipe still be good if i use	Get recipe	Ingredient Substitution	0.74
17	please identify the	Share location	Identify song	0.74
18	can you identify	Share location	Identify song	0.74
19	i don't need mowing the lawn on my	Cancel a reservation	Update/add to to-do list	0.74
20	get reservations at	Accept a reservation	Make a reservation	1.00
21	get reservations at olive garden	Accept a reservation	Make a reservation	1.00
22	can i store bread	Ingredient Substitution	How long food lasts	1.00
23	how's the	OOS	Weather	1.00
24	can you identify this	Share location	Identify song	1.00

Table 6: Stimuli where only the majority of human annotators successfully predicted the final intent, but DistilBERT made an incorrect prediction. α refers to Krippendorff's α for the responses of the annotators for the presented stimuli. Only stimuli with $\alpha \geq 0.50$ are presented. OOS represents the "out-of-scope" class label.

#	Partial Utterance	Predicted Label, Humans	Label, Complete Utterance	α
1	tell my	Text	Share location	0.29
2	i have to	OOS	Cancel a reservation	0.31
3	set the	OOS	Smart home function	0.38
4	what things are on my	OOS	Ask about to-do list	0.38
5	tell me what tomorrow's	Weather	Ask about date	0.46
6	on the	OOS	Smart home function	0.51
7	i have a reservation for strip house for jennifer that i'd	Cancel a reservation	Confirm a reservation	0.70
8	put the dishes on my list	Update/add to shopping list	Update/add to to-do list	0.70

Table 7: Partial utterances where DistilBERT successfully predicted the complete utterance's label (column 4), but not the majority of human annotators. α refers to the agreement of human annotators for each stimuli. OOS represents the "out-of-scope" class label.

On the Robustness of Intent Classification and Slot Labeling in Goal-oriented Dialog Systems to Real-world Noise

Sailik Sengupta*, **Jason Krone***, **Saab Mansour**
amazon aws AI
{kronej,sailiks,saabm}@amazon.com

Abstract

Intent Classification (IC) and Slot Labeling (SL) models, which form the basis of dialogue systems, often encounter noisy data in real-word environments. In this work, we investigate how robust IC/SL models are to noisy data. We collect and publicly release a test-suite for seven common noise types found in production human-to-bot conversations (abbreviations, casing, misspellings, morphological variants, paraphrases, punctuation and synonyms). On this test-suite, we show that common noise types substantially degrade the IC accuracy and SL F1 performance of state-of-the-art BERT-based IC/SL models. By leveraging *cross-noise robustness transfer* – training on one noise type to improve robustness on another noise type – we design aggregate data-augmentation approaches that increase the model performance across all seven noise types by +10.8% for IC accuracy and +15 points for SL F1 on average. To the best of our knowledge, this is the first work to present a single IC/SL model that is robust to a wide range of noise phenomena.

1 Introduction

Intent classification (IC) and slot labeling (SL) tasks (shown in Table 1) form the backbone of goal-oriented dialog systems. In recent times, deep-learning models have achieved impressive performance, reporting accuracies above 95% (Chen et al., 2019) on public IC/SL benchmarks such as ATIS (Hemphill et al., 1990) and SNIPS (Coucke et al., 2018). These datasets, commonly used in the academia, are clean while real-world data is often noisy. Extensive prior work on robustness has focused on identifying noise-types that affect NLP systems and suggesting methods to improve robustness to individual noise types. However, two key questions remain – (1) what noise types are seen in real-world goal-oriented dialog systems, and (2) how can we construct a single model robust to all real-world noise variants?

Input Utterance	**Play a song by Bob Dylan**
Slot Labels (SL)	**O O O O** artist artist
Intent Class (IC)	**PlayMusic**

Table 1: Example input and outputs for IC & SL tasks.

In this work, we identify and evaluate the impact of seven noise types frequently observed in a production – casing variation, misspellings, synonyms, paraphrases, punctuation, abbreviations, and morphological variants – on IC and SL performance. In this regard, we collect a suite of realistic ATIS and SNIPS test data for these phenomena. We find that noise reduces the IC/SL performance of state-of-the-art BERT based IC/SL models by an average of −13.5% for IC accuracy and −18.9 points for SL F1. We show that strategic augmentation and regularization approaches can offset these losses, improving performance on noisy benchmarks by +10.8% for IC and +15 points for SL F1 on average by leveraging cross-noise robustness transfer while minimally effecting accuracy on the original test-data. We emphasize that these improvements are for a single IC/SL model that is robust to all noise types. This is a substantial improvement in generalization over existing methods, which train separate models for each noise type.

To summarize our contributions:

(1) We publicly release a bench-marking suit of IC/SL test data for seven noise types seen in real-world goal oriented dialog systems. [1]

(2) We show that training data augmentation with one noise type (eg. synonyms) can improve robustness to unseen noise types (eg. paraphrases) substantially (eg. ATIS IC: +12.6); we call this *cross-noise robustness transfer*.

* Equal Contribution.

[1]**Dataset**: github.com/amazon-research/real-world-noisy-benchmarks-for-natural-language-understanding

Proceedings of the Third Workshop on Natural Language Processing for Conversational AI, pages 68–79
November 10, 2021. ©2021 Association for Computational Linguistics

Phenomena	Train Generation	Test Generation	Examples
Abbreviations	Rule Based	Human	book a flight from San Jose 2 NYC
Casing	Rule Based	Rule Based	BOOK A FLIGHT FROM SAN JOSE TO NYC
Misspellings	(Hasan et al., 2015)	Public DB	book a flite from San Jose to NYC
Morph.	Internal DB + LM	Human	start booking a flight from San Jose to NYC
Paraphrasing	Back Translation	Human	can you book me a flight from San Jose to NYC
Punctuation	(Tilk and Alumäe, 2016)	Human	book a flight from San Jose to NYC.
Synonyms	WordNet + LM	Human	reserve a flight from San Jose to NYC

Table 2: Summary of methods to generate noisy data for training and testing purposes. As an example, we provide a noised version of the sentence (in ATIS) 'book a flight from San Jose to NYC' for each category.

(3) We present a single IC/SL model that improves robustness to all seven noise types that we study by an average of +10.5% for IC accuracy and +15 points for SL F1.

2 Related Work

Prior works demonstrate the brittleness of neural systems in NLP to different noise types. Adversarial NLP focuses on construction of examples that impair a model's performance (Jia and Liang, 2017; Ribeiro et al., 2018; Ebrahimi et al., 2017; Cheng et al., 2019). A parallel thread of research investigates the behavior of models towards real-word noise types. Machine Translation (MT) systems perform poorly in the presence of synthetic and natural character-level changes (eg. character swaps, typographical errors, misspellings) (Belinkov and Bisk, 2018; Karpukhin et al., 2019); similar conclusions hold for casing noise (Niu et al., 2020). Other works investigate robustness of NLP models to paraphrases (Einolghozati et al., 2019), misspellings (Pruthi et al., 2019), and morphological variants (Tan et al., 2020a). The most common approach to improving model robustness is data augmentation, either at pre-training or training time. For example, in (Tan et al., 2020a), augmentation with adversarial examples and a single epoch of pre-training can improve robustness of the model for Question Answering (QA) and MT tasks; a comprehensive summary of DA techniques can be found in (Feng et al., 2021). Recent works present frameworks for comprehensive model-agnostic testing of NLP systems to grammatical and noise variants (Ribeiro et al., 2020; Goel et al., 2021). All of these prior works focus on either (1) improving robustness to individual noise types or (2) simply evaluating model performance on synthetically-generated noise variants. In contrast, we construct a single model that is robust to all seven noise types seen in real-world systems.

Dataset	Phenom.	#Utt	#IC	#SL	#SV	BLEU
ATIS	Original	893	20	69	288	1.00
	Abbrev.	99	13	44	135	0.66
	Case.	893	20	69	288	0.00
	Misspl.	893	20	69	350	0.80
	Morph.	115	15	45	154	0.59
	Para.	217	18	56	185	0.42
	Punc.	243	14	49	212	0.68
	Syn.	225	18	57	191	0.64
Snips	Original	700	7	39	1571	1.00
	Abbrev.	98	6	35	334	0.63
	Case.	700	7	39	1474	0.00
	Misspl.	700	7	39	1623	0.83
	Morph.	101	6	36	335	0.65
	Para.	197	6	36	585	0.54
	Syn.	201	6	36	592	0.73

Table 3: Statistics on utterance (Utt), intent (IC), slot label (SL), and slot value (SV) counts as well as the average BLEU score between the original and noised utterances for ATIS and SNIPS.

Beyond training-data augmentation, pre-training robust word-embeddings is a popular defense against adversarial examples (Zhu et al., 2020), misspellings (Piktus et al., 2019), and character ordering (Malykh et al., 2018). In (Kudo, 2018), authors investigate the impact of different subword tokenization techniques on model robustness. Effective regularization has also been shown to improve the robustness of IC/SL models to paraphrases (Einolghozati et al., 2019). Yet many of the techniques to improve robustness are not comparable due to evaluation on different test sets. Hence, we provide high-quality noisy test data to serve as a common test bed.

3 Noise Categories

We consider seven types of noise that are prevalent in the traffic of a task oriented dialogue service – namely, misspellings, casing, synonyms, paraphrases, punctuation, morphological variants, and abbreviations (see Table 2). With the exception of misspellings and casing, we employ trained data associates to collect test sets that are representative of naturally occurring noise. For the misspelling and casing phenomena, we automatically generate our test sets because (1) high-quality generation is possible for English and (2) purposeful introduction of misspellings is not a natural task. Generating noisy data using human experts is expensive. Therefore, it is not suitable for the purpose of training augmentation. Thus, all of our training augmentation experiments rely upon automatically generated phenomena. In this section, we provide details about the manual data collection process and describe the automatic generation procedure leveraged for training data augmentation. In Table 3, we showcase statistics for ATIS and SNIPS noisy test sets.

3.1 Manual Test Data Collection

We employ trained data associates to introduce synonyms, paraphrases, morphological variants, and abbreviations in ATIS and SNIPS. We also use data associates to punctuate ATIS. ATIS requires special treatment for punctuation as it is unpunctuated, while SNIPS is punctuated and does not require manual collection for the punctuation noise type. Due to cost constraints, we noise a subset of approximately 200 utterances for each dataset. We instruct the data associates to introduce the given phenomena into the carrier phrase portion of each utterance (i.e. the spans that do not correspond to slot values). In instances where the associates are unable to come up with a viable modification to an utterance, the utterance is excluded from the evaluation set. For this reason, our test sets for some phenomena, namely abbreviations and morphological variants, contain fewer than 200 utterances. We perform quality assurance on the collected data, using internal data specialist that ensure at least 95% of the examples in a sample containing 25% of each noisy test set are realistic and representative of the given noise type.

3.2 Synthetic Data Generation

Casing Casing variation is common in text modality human-to-bot conversations. Consider for example, the responses "john" vs. "John" vs. "JOHN" to a bot prompt "Can I have your first name?". Given that the training data is mostly small-cased (for ATIS) and true-cased (for SNIPS), we evaluate the impact of capitalizing all characters in the test set; we simply capitalize all test utterances. For training augmentation, we inject all-caps noise into 50% of training tokens.

Misspellings Misspelling test sets contain 15% misspelled words, sourced from a collection of public, human misspelling-correction pairs[2]. Using human misspelling pairs produces a more natural test set, but it does not generalize well to new languages or domains. Thus, for augmentation, we utilize a probabilistic approach to generate synthetic misspellings put forward in (Hasan et al., 2015). This method introduces errors based on induction probabilities mined from natural data and bases character level edits on the QWERTY keyboard layout.

Synonyms We augment the training data with synonyms using a two step approach. First, we obtain a list of candidate synonyms via word net. Second, we introduce the synonym candidate that results in the lowest perplexity, as measured by DistilGPT2 (Sanh et al., 2020), into the utterance. This perplexity filter ensures greater fluency.

Paraphrases For training data augmentation, we considered using paraphrased generated using back-translation, from English to Chinese and back (Mallinson et al., 2017; Einolghozati et al., 2019). For preserving slot-labels, we annotate the slot values in the back-translated text if they match the slot values in the original text, ignoring casing differences. In contrast to other noise types that are injected at the token-level, this is injected at the utterance level.

Punctuation For ATIS, we augment the training data by using a bi-directional recurrent neural network with attention proposed in (Tilk and Alumäe, 2016). We note that the punctuation added to ATIS test sets are clearly noise or *irrelevant punctuation* (Ek et al., 2020) as the absence of these in the original test-sets does not impact intent or slot value classification. While some punctuation can be considered for complex scenarios in NLU (eg. use of comma to separate consecutive slot values), the idea of *relevant punctuation* is currently not well explored in the context of NLU systems. We do not experiment with the punctuation phenomena on the Snips dataset, since snips already contains punctuation in both the training and test splits.

Morphological Variants We generate morphological variants for training data augmentation in a similar manner to synonyms. Namely, we first

[2]www.dcs.bbk.ac.uk/ ROGER/corpora.html

produce a list of candidate morphological variants, using an internal curated database of 120,000 morphological variant pairs sourced by human experts and then select the candidate with the lowest perplexity. While this is similar to the MORPHEUS approach described in (Tan et al., 2020b), it has two major differences. First, the list of morphed candidates in our case are chosen based on an internal curated database as opposed to the LemmInflect package[3]. Second, our approach is a model-agnostic approach that can work regardless of how the model is trained, whereas (Tan et al., 2020b) uses a model-in-the-loop approach to generate morphed inputs that are adversarial in nature (i.e. flip the model's prediction).

Abbreviations To synthetically construct abbreviations for augmenting the training data, we consider first a knowledge base of common abbreviations (Beal, 2021) and follow certain rule-based approaches to drop vowels from tokens (eg. 'people' → 'ppl') or include common abbreviation mappings between numerals and words which share phonetics (e.g., "2" and "to").

4 Approach

In this section, we highlight the various approaches we consider to construct a single model robust to various noise types seen in live traffic.

4.1 Model Setup

We evaluate the robustness of a BERT based joint intent classification and slot labeling model, which is currently SOTA on the Snips and ATIS benchmarks (Chen et al., 2019). Similar to (Chen et al., 2019), we add an additional feed forward layers on top of the [CLS] and sub-token hidden representations to predict the IC and SL tags, respectively.[4] We use the cased BERT checkpoint pre-trained on the Books and Wikipedia corpora.

4.2 Data Augmentation

Training Data Augmentation (DA) For each noise type, we consider augmenting the training data with noised versions of utterances in the original training set along-with the same intent and similar slot labels. For this purpose, we leverage the synthetic approaches described in subsection 3.2.

Aggregate Data Augmentation (A-DA) We explore two augmentation strategies that consider all noise types: *Uniform (Uni) Aggregation* and *Best Proportion (BP) Aggregation*. *Uni* augments the training set with 10% for each noise type (i.e. 10% abbreviation, 10% casing, 10% synonyms, etc.). *BP* tunes the training augmentation proportions based on the best performance observed on a validation set (15% abbreviation, 50% casing, 10% synonyms, etc.).

4.3 Regularization

BERT-based Sub-word Regularization (B-SR) There exists multiple options when splitting word tokens into sub-words. In (Kudo, 2018), authors propose stochastic sub-word tokenization and show that this can improve the robustness of a Machine Translation system. Given we use a pre-trained BERT model with a fixed vocabulary, we consider an adaptation of this method– we first consider an index-based split of each word followed by BERT-based tokenization of each split. Then, we sample each such token with $\frac{1}{4}$-th the probability of the original word tokenization. We call this method BERT-based Sub-word Tokenization (B-ST). For example, consider the word 'fly', the subwords and the sampling probabilities are as follows.

Manual Splits	BERT sub-word(s)	Sampling Pr
None	'fly'	0.666
'f','ly'	'f', 'ly'	0.167 (0.666/4)
'fl','y'	'f', 'l', 'y'	0.167 (0.666/4)

Adversarial Logit Pairing (ALP) In (Einolghozati et al., 2019), authors proposed the use of data augmentation (data generated via back-translation) along with regularization terms that penalize (via L_2 distance) the model for outputting different intent and slot labeling logits for a training sample and its noise-augmented version. We adapt this approach for our setting, where the A-DA training set is augmented with multiple noise types. For each mini-batch with K_I pairs of samples derived from an input utterance x and K_S pairs of slot values, the loss function looks as follows,

$$\mathcal{L}=\frac{1}{K_I}\sum_{i=0}^{K_I}||I(x)-I(\tilde{x})||+\frac{1}{K_S}\sum_{i=0}^{K_S}||S(x)-S(\tilde{x})||$$

where I and S represents the intent and slot labeling logits respectively.

5 Experiments

We first evaluate the trade-off between use of data augmentation during pre-training vs. fine-tuning

[3] github.com/bjascob/LemmInflect

[4] Implemented using the gluon tutorial: nlp.gluon.ai/model_zoo/intent_cls_slot_labeling/index.html

Model	ATIS				Snips			
	IC Acc.		SL F1		IC Acc.		SL F1	
	Orig.	Noisy	Orig.	Noisy	Orig.	Noisy	Orig.	Noisy
BERT	98.8	97.3	95.6	86.5	99.0	98.7	96.3	91.2
+MLM Aug.$^{5\%}$	**98.7**	97.4	**95.6**	86.8	98.8	98.4	**96.6**	91.9
+Train Aug.$^{20\%}$	**98.7**	**97.8**	95.5	**94.6**	**99.1**	**98.8**	96.4	**95.3**
+MLM & Train Aug.	98.6	97.6	95.5	94.5	99.0	**98.8**	96.0	95.1

Table 4: Robustness of BERT with and without augmentation (Aug.) of misspellings at pre-training time (MLM) and IC/SL training time (Train.) to misspelling phenomena in the ATIS and Snips datasets measured by intent classification accuracy (IC Acc.) and slot labeling F1 (SL F1) scores.

time. We focus the majority of our analysis on fine-tuning time augmentation as we show it outperforms pre-training augmentation.

5.1 Pre-training *vs.* Fine-tuning DA for Synthetic Misspellings

We pre-train BERT on the Wikipedia and Books corpus augmented with synthetic misspellings at a rate of 5% for an additional 9,500 steps using the standard MLM objective. Our results, shown in Table 4, empirically demonstrate that noisy pre-training does not perform better than training augmentation (esp. on the noisy data). While noisy pre-training generates marginal improvements on SL F1 (avg. +0.3), training time augmentation produces substantially larger gains (+6.1 on SL F1 and +0.5% on IC acc). Due to this finding, we only consider data augmentation at the fine-tuning stage in the experiments that follow.

5.2 Results

Table 5 highlights the performance of the various methods (represented by the different rows) for IC accuracy and SL F1 on the original test set (averaged over the control sets for each noise type), treatment sets for the individual noise types, and an average gain over the control and treatment sets of each approach over the BERT IC-SL baseline. Figures in **bold** indicate the best performance for each column.

The diagonal cells under the data augmentation (DA) section, highlighted in yellow, represent the effect of augmentation with a particular noise type and testing on it. While this idea of *Noise-Aligned Data Augmentation (NADA)* has been extensively explored in prior work, we observe that only 5 of the yellow cells (namely, punc. IC, casing SL for ATIS and casing IC, abbrev. SL, misspell SL for Snips) result in the best performing models (out of 26 metrics on noised-test sets). This indicates that augmentation with other noise types (cross-noise) has beneficial (side-)effects on the robustness to a particular noise type; we term this phenomena as *Cross-noise Robustness Transfer*.

We discuss the results of our experiments in three sections. First, we summarize the performance gains of the different models across all the test sets. Then we analyze the performance on original test sets. Lastly, we analyze performance on the noisy test data.

5.2.1 Overall Performance

Data-augmentation approaches (DA) We find that A-DA with BP aggregation outperforms all the approaches on ATIS (IC:+8.4%, SL:+14.4) and SNIPS (IC:+13.1%, SL:+15.6). NADA approaches, while often successful for a particular noise type, do not perform well against all noise types and hence, aggregate DA methods are deemed necessary. Further, we observe that injecting a particular noise in training data provides robustness against other noise types. Thus, we attribute the success of the A-DA BP approach to this cross-noise robustness transfer. We find that uniform sampling of noise types for aggregate data-augmentation (A-DA Uni) is always worse than best-proportion aggregation (A-DA BP), whether used by itself or in conjunction with the regularization approaches. Thus, we only showcase the results of using A-DA BP with regularization approaches in Table 5.

BERT-based Sub-word Regularization (B-SR) B-SR, by itself, provides marginal gains for ATIS (IC:+2.7%, SL:+2.3) and degrades the performance of the baseline on SNIPS (IC:−0.8%, SL:−3.3). For ATIS, the gains stem from minor improvements seen on paraphrase and synonym test-data; for SNIPS, we see a consistent degradation in performance for both the original data and all noise types. In contrary, when coupled with A-

Dataset	Model	IC Accuracy orig.^{E}	abv.	case	spl.	mor.	para.	punc.	syn.	gain^E	SL F1 orig.^{E}	abv.	case	spl.	mor.	para.	punc.	syn.	gain^E
ATIS	**BERT IC/SL**	97.9	85.5	72.2	97.4	**97.4**	77.8	98.9	76.8	0.0	94.5	78.0	22.7	86.5	94.7	89.8	87.8	91.0	0.0
	+B-SR	95.7	84.8	74.7	97.6	96.2	87.2	98.5	87.8	+2.6	92.8	83.6	38.5	92.7	93.1	87.7	84.1	88.4	+2.3
	+DA																		
	abbrev. (15%)	97.8	88.2	72.7	97.3	97.1	78.1	**99.2**	78.1	+0.7	94.1	90.8	36.2	90.0	94.7	89.9	85.7	**91.6**	+4.0
	casing (50%)	97.2	84.5	98.2	97.0	95.4	83.6	**99.2**	82.3	+4.8	93.4	81.1	**94.9**	88.4	92.9	88.5	85.8	89.8	+9.9
	misspl. (20%)	97.4	86.2	75.4	97.6	96.5	84.1	**99.2**	81.7	+2.0	94.5	87.8	50.1	94.6	94.9	89.4	87.1	90.7	+6.3
	morph. (10%)	97.6	85.5	72.2	97.2	96.2	77.5	**99.2**	75.7	-0.4	94.6	77.9	18.6	86.9	94.8	89.5	89.1	91.0	-0.4
	para. (15%)	97.3	85.2	70.8	97.1	96.5	**91.4**	98.1	**91.8**	+3.5	93.2	75.6	27.3	85.9	93.9	88.8	93.1	90.1	+0.4
	punc. (15%)	97.8	86.9	67.9	96.8	96.8	87.5	**99.2**	85.6	+2.0	93.1	77.2	14.3	85.4	93.8	88.2	93.5	89.8	-1.4
	syn. (10%)	**97.9**	88.2	72.4	97.0	96.5	91.0	98.9	90.5	+4.1	**94.8**	78.3	24.2	87.7	94.8	**90.4**	89.5	91.1	+0.8
	+A-DA																		
	Uniform (Uni)	97.3	87.5	89.5	97.5	95.9	89.8	**99.2**	90.2	+6.1	94.5	90.6	85.3	93.3	**95.0**	89.6	93.9	90.8	+12.6
	Best Proportion (BP)	97.5	89.2	**98.3**	**98.0**	97.1	**91.4**	**99.2**	91.7	**+8.3**	94.5	**92.0**	**94.9**	**95.0**	**95.0**	89.4	**94.4**	90.5	**+14.4**
	+A-DA + ALP	97.0	86.5	89.2	97.2	95.1	91.0	98.9	90.2	+5.9	94.2	88.0	84.2	92.8	94.7	89.2	93.3	91.5	+11.9
	+A-DA + B-SR	97.3	**91.6**	97.9	97.5	96.5	89.3	**99.2**	88.4	+7.7	93.8	90.9	94.5	94.6	93.8	89.4	94.0	89.7	+13.7
	+A-DA + ALP + B-SR	96.8	89.2	97.7	97.3	95.9	89.9	98.9	89.3	+7.3	93.5	90.4	94.3	94.4	93.5	89.3	94.0	88.8	+13.3
		orig.^{E}	abv.	case	spl.	mor.	para.	punc.	syn.	gain^E	orig.^{E}	abv.	case	spl.	mor.	para.	punc.	syn.	gain^E
SNIPS	**BERT IC/SL**	98.3	97.6	23.3	98.7	98.0	98.5	–	98.5	0.0	**97.0**	88.1	5.0	91.2	96.5	94.9	–	**96.3**	0.0
	+B-SR	98.2	98.3	20.2	98.4	98.0	96.8		98.3	-0.8	93.9	84.6	3.0	92.2	91.6	91.1		92.5	-3.3
	+DA																		
	abbrev. (15%)	98.3	98.3	24.7	98.1	98.3	98.1	–	98.3	+0.2	96.8	**96.0**	3.0	92.7	**97.4**	**95.2**	–	96.1	+1.4
	casing (50%)	98.6	98.0	**98.7**	98.2	98.3	98.3	–	98.0	+12.5	96.1	89.6	90.2	91.5	97.2	93.8	–	94.3	+14.0
	misspl. (20%)	98.7	97.3	24.6	98.9	98.3	98.8	–	98.7	+0.4	96.6	91.3	+5.1	**94.9**	97.0	95.0	–	95.9	+1.1
	morph. (10%)	98.3	98.3	19.4	98.4	98.0	98.3	–	98.7	+2.7	96.8	85.6	1.4	91.3	96.8	95.1	–	96.0	-2.7
	para. (15%)	98.6	97.6	29.1	98.3	98.0	98.5	–	98.2	+0.9	94.3	84.6	9.2	88.1	96.0	92.5	–	93.5	-1.8
	syn. (10%)	98.3	98.0	21.1	98.5	98.3	98.1	–	98.8	-0.3	96.7	87.5	5.5	91.2	97.2	94.2	–	95.5	-0.2
	+A-DA																		
	Uniform (Uni)	98.6	97.6	91.2	**99.0**	98.3	98.8	–	98.3	+11.5	96.4	94.3	67.1	93.9	96.7	94.7	–	95.3	+11.6
	Best Proportion (BP)	98.8	98.6	98.6	98.9	**98.7**	**99.2**	–	98.8	+13.1	95.8	95.7	**90.4**	94.6	96.6	94.8	–	95.0	**+15.6**
	+A-DA + ALP	98.9	98.6	98.6	98.7	**98.7**	99.0	–	99.2	+13.1	95.8	94.8	86.5	94.6	96.6	94.8	–	94.9	+14.8
	+A-DA + B-SR	**99.2**	**99.0**	98.5	98.9	98.0	**99.2**	–	**99.3**	**+13.2**	95.2	94.3	89.5	94.0	94.7	93.7	–	94.5	+14.5
	+A-DA + ALP + B-SR	98.8	98.6	98.5	99.0	98.3	99.0	–	**99.3**	+13.1	95.0	93.5	87.9	94.1	94.5	92.9	–	94.1	+13.8

Table 5: Intent Classification (IC) and Slot Labeling (SL) metrics for the different approaches on ATIS and SNIPS averaged over 3 seed runs. The column with the Orig.^{E} header reports average accuracy over the different phenomena control sets, the red-highlighted columns showcase results on the noised-sets and the Gain^E shows the average gain over the BERT IC/SL baseline across all datasets. The percentage of augmented data for the (DA) methods is shown in brackets. Yellow cells highlight performance of Noise-Aligned Data Augmentation (NADA) approaches. As SNIPS lacks a punctuation noised-set, the results are omitted for this condition.

DA BP approach, it produces the best performing model on SNIPS IC (+13.2%) marginally edging out A-DA's gain (+13.1%) and a fraction behind the best performing models in other categories.

Adversarial Logit Pairing (ALP) While ALP coupled with A-DA BP boosts performance when compared to the (BERT IC-SL) baseline model on ATIS (IC:+5.9%, SL:+11.9) and SNIPS (IC:+13.1%, SL:+14.8) data, it does not yield the best-performing model robust to all noise types.

An amalgamation of the approaches, although better than the baseline on ATIS (IC:+7.3%, SL:+13.3) and SNIPS (IC:+13.1%, SL:+13.8) data, lacks behind the best-performing models. This indicates that the approaches A-DA, ALP, and B-SR don't provide complimentary benefits and thus, cannot simply be combined to construct a more robust model.

5.2.2 Performance on the Original Test Sets

Owing to the lack of linguistic diversity in the original test-sets, we do not observe models trained on grammatically-correct noise data (eg. paraphrase, morphological variance, synonyms) clearly outperform the joint-BERT baseline. Yet, synonym-based DA results in the best performing model on both IC and SL performance for ATIS. A key reason for this is that ATIS has domain-specific vocabulary– eg. training data maps utterances with the word 'flight' to atis_flight and 'plane' to atis_aircraft even though the two words can be used interchangeably in test utterances. Synonym-based DA helps the model to generalize better by allowing the model to avoid this spurious co-relations between words and intents and consider the larger context of the sentence/utterance. For SNIPS, which has a more diverse vocabulary, well distributed over the test and training set compared to ATIS, the original BERT IC-SL performs the best on SL F1, whereas the model A-DA (BP) + B-SR performs the best on IC accuracy. The diverse tokenization of words, caused by both A-DA and B-SR, ensures that words in movie/book/song names, which may often be indistinguishable, does not impact the model's IC capabilities and the model pays more attention to the carrier phrases.

5.2.3 Performance on Noised Test Sets

For each noise type, we design a control set that contains only the clean version of the noised utterances in the treatment set. While we only list average performance on the original/control test sets in Table 5, our discussion below often analyzes the model performance on the treatment set and compares it to the corresponding control test set (an opposed to only drawing inference based on the average metrics).

Abbreviations Abbreviation degrades IC (-12.34% for ATIS, -0.7% for SNIPS) and SL performance (-16.47 for ATIS, -8.87 for SNIPS). Note that the degradation on ATIS is of higher magnitude than on SNIPS. Upon investigation, we observe that ATIS abbreviations are often specific to the travel domain (e.g., "tix" vs. "tickets"), whereas abbreviations for SNIPS are more general (e.g., "@" vs. "at"). We hypothesize that BERT is more likely to have been trained on the abbreviations present seen in the SNIPS noised set than for ATIS, and therefore more robust on SNIPS.

Augmentation with only abbreviation data boosts performance on SL-F1 but provides small gains on IC accuracy. We find that the coverage of test abbreviations (injected manually) in the augmented training data (injected synthetically) is far lower for ATIS than for SNIPS (40% vs. 74%) and this results in a higher disparity between IC performance on clean (97.86%) *vs.* noised (88.22%) test-set for ATIS even after augmentation. Further, we observe that augmentation with synonyms also provides a boost in IC accuracy for abbreviation injected test-data for both ATIS and SNIPS. This cross-noise robustness transfer further boosts the accuracy when the model is trained with BP A-DA (that contains 15% abbreviation and 10% synonym data). When further coupled with B-SR, the best performing model achieves an IC accuracy of 91.58% for ATIS (+5.06%) and 99.25% (+0.93%) for SNIPS. For SL, BP performs the best for ATIS while training data augmentation with abbreviation performs the best for SNIPS.

Casing IC and SL performances drop substantially on the noised test set because the Bert tokenizer fails to identify fully capitalized words in the vocabulary and instead breaks them down to often match character-level sub-word tokens (eg. 'would' $\rightarrow$ {'W', 'O', 'U', 'LD'}). Without the use of augmentation, where half-of-the training data is injected with capitalized form of words, the classifier is not able to associate these sub-token representations to the correct intent classes or the slot-labels. Unfortunately, casing noise is orthogonal to all the other noise types (as injection other noise types does not improve model performance on casing test-set) and thus, does not benefit from cross noise-robustness transfer. While the best performing model for ATIS (IC: 98.28%, SL: 94.88) and SNIPS SL (90.37) is the BP A-DA, it is only marginally better (< 0.2) than the training data augmentation approach, which is a better for SNIPS IC. Note that as the BP A-DA approach considers augmented data will all the noise types, it significantly increases the training time per epoch (see appendix for run-times of the various approaches). Hence, if one desires a model to only be robust to casing noise, we suggest using training data augmentation with capitalized words.

Misspelling Test-time misspellings do not impact IC accuracy more than 0.2% points; a misspelled word in the utterances changes the sub-token breakdown of that word ('what' *vs.* {'wa','t'}) that, in turn, does not change the intent of the sentence. While majority of the noise in the test set is in the carrier phrase tokens (as opposed to the tokens representing slot values), we notice a large drop in SL F1 (ATIS: -8.6, SNIPS: -5.1). For ATIS, we noted that slot values for slot labels such at period of day (eg. 'night' *vs.* 'nite') are more prone to mis-classification when injected with misspelled noise in comparison to slot values such as day names ('sunday' *vs.* 'suntday'). Augmentation of training data with 20% misspellings increases SL F1 (ATIS: +8, SNIPS: +3) making it within 1.2 points of performance on the control set. As the sub-tokens of misspelled words are now better recognized as slot values. This result demonstrates training on synthetic misspellings (Hasan et al., 2015) can improve generalization to natural misspelling noise seen at test time. Further, we observe that other noise types such as abbreviation, which also increases the model's familiarity to sub-word tokens, also boosts the model's accuracy to test-time misspelling; this cross-noise robustness transfer makes BP A-DA the best performing model for ATIS. Given tokenization is a key issue for the performance drop, we observe B-SR provides a boost in model performance, but comparatively less than A-DA approaches. Also, coupling A-DA + B-SR doesn't necessarily boost the accuracy further.

Morphological Variants In contrast to the lack of robustness seen on various NLP tasks in the presence of morphological noise (Tan et al., 2020b), IC and SL models evaluated on ATIS and SNIPS data are pretty robust to morphological variation at test-time, deviating from test-time performance on clean data by at most -1.1 points. We notice that synonyms and paraphrase noise injected at training time helps in improving the models robustness to morphological variance at test time. Upon using A-DA BP, we observe that this cross-noise robustness transfer boosts the model's performance beyond the baseline model's performance on the clean data.

Synonyms Synonyms decrease the model's performance on ATIS (IC: -19.8%, SL:-2.8), while the impact on SNIPS IC/SL is negligible. We note that the model picks up word to intent correlations ('fare' $\rightarrow$ 'atis_airfare', 'flight(s)' $\rightarrow$ 'atis_flight', 'plane(s)' $\rightarrow$ 'atis_aircraft') and when these words are replaced with a synonym in the test data, the model misclassfies the intent. For example, changing the word 'flight(s)' to the word 'plane(s)' where they can be used as synonyms, the model's intent prediction flips from 'atis_flight' to 'atis_aircraft'. We conjecture that this difference in effect size is the result of over-fitting on less diverse ATIS carrier phrases. This lack of diversity is evidenced by the fact that ATIS contains roughly half as many unique carrier phrase tokens as Snips (430 *vs.* 842), despite having longer utterances on average (11.3 *vs.* 9.1 words). While introducing synonyms into the ATIS training data boosts IC (+13.7%) and SL (+0.7) performance, the best performing models are the ones augmented with paraphrase data (for ATIS IC) and abbreviation data (for ATIS SL). In this setting, the benefit of cross-noise robustness transfer is more pronounced where other noise types can boost the accuracy more than the particular noise type observed at test time. This is also due to the fact that data augmentation with synonyms generated via word-net + language models does not align as well with human-injected synonym noise seen at test time.

Paraphrase Paraphrases lead to a significant drop in ATIS performance (IC: -18.6%, SL:3.0) and a marginal drop for SNIPS (IC:-0.2, SL:-1.9). Similar to the cases of synonyms, we posit that ATIS is impacted due to (1) the lack of diverse carrier phrases in the training set and (2) a greater degree of dis-similarity between the original and the paraphrased test-sets (evident from the 0.12 lower BLEU score compared to SNIPS). While, training augmentation with back-translated paraphrases yields comparable scores to the baseline system, ALP (Einolghozati et al., 2019) coupled with Uni A-DA yields the best IC accuracy for both ATIS and SNIPS. For SL, cross-noise robustness transfer with synonyms (for ATIS) and abbreviation (for SNIPS) aids the model in achieving the best performance.

Punctuation As mentioned earlier, SNIPS training data already has (is naturally augmented with) punctuation tokens for a sub-set of utterances, we do not consider punctuation as a noise and hence, do not create a test set for SNIPS. BERT makes models robust to punctuation-based noise on IC accuracy, but we observe a 8.6 point difference on SL F1. This happens due to either the (1) over-prediction of punctuation tokens after a slot value as a slot-value (eg. in an uttearnce '... to Pittsburgh .' both 'Pittsburgh' and '.' are identified as city names) or (2) missing out slot values when a punctuation is present around it (eg. in an utterance '... from Columbus, Ohio to ... ', the model fails to recognize Columbus and Ohio as slot values). While augmenting with punctuation data boosts model performance, we also noticed a similar boost in SL F1 when augmenting training data with back-translated paraphrase data because machine translation often automatically introduced punctuation tokens. Hence, when coupled together in the A-DA approaches, we observe the best model performance with BP A-DA on ATIS' SL F1.

6 Conclusion

In this paper, we show that SOTA BERT based IC/SL models are not robust to many real world noise types found in production. We further demonstrate that cross-noise robustness transfer – training on one noise type to improve model robustness on another noise type – yields gains for a number of noise type pairs. Through Aggregate Data Augmentation (A-DA), we leverage cross-noise robustness transfer to improve the model's average performance by +10.8% on IC and +15 points on SL F1. Despite the gains we obtain, our benchmark provides substantial headroom to improve model performance on the abbreviation, synonym, and paraphrase noise types. We hope that our benchmark will support future research in this direction and enable the design of robust IC/SL models for goal-oriented dialogue systems.

Acknowledgements We would like to thank the anonymous reviewers at multiple venues and the Amazon Lex team for their insightful feedbacks and constructive suggestions.

References

Vangie Beal. 2021. The complete list of 1500+ common text abbreviations & acronyms.

Yonatan Belinkov and Yonatan Bisk. 2018. Synthetic and natural noise both break neural machine translation. *ICLR*.

Qian Chen, Zhu Zhuo, and Wen Wang. 2019. Bert for joint intent classification and slot filling.

Yong Cheng, Lu Jiang, and Wolfgang Macherey. 2019. Robust neural machine translation with doubly adversarial inputs. In *Proceedings of the 57th Annual Meeting of the Association for Computational Linguistics*, pages 4324–4333, Florence, Italy. Association for Computational Linguistics.

Alice Coucke, Alaa Saade, Adrien Ball, Théodore Bluche, Alexandre Caulier, David Leroy, Clément Doumouro, Thibault Gisselbrecht, Francesco Caltagirone, Thibaut Lavril, Maël Primet, and Joseph Dureau. 2018. Snips voice platform: an embedded spoken language understanding system for private-by-design voice interfaces. *CoRR*, abs/1805.10190.

Javid Ebrahimi, Anyi Rao, Daniel Lowd, and Dejing Dou. 2017. Hotflip: White-box adversarial examples for text classification. *arXiv preprint arXiv:1712.06751*.

Arash Einolghozati, Sonal Gupta, Mrinal Mohit, and Rushin Shah. 2019. Improving robustness of task oriented dialog systems. *arXiv preprint arXiv:1911.05153*.

Adam Ek, Jean-Philippe Bernardy, and Stergios Chatzikyriakidis. 2020. How does punctuation affect neural models in natural language inference. In *Proceedings of the Probability and Meaning Conference (PaM 2020)*, pages 109–116.

Steven Y. Feng, Varun Gangal, Jason Wei, Sarath Chandar, Soroush Vosoughi, Teruko Mitamura, and Eduard Hovy. 2021. A survey of data augmentation approaches for nlp. Association for Computational Linguistics.

Karan Goel, Nazneen Rajani, Jesse Vig, Samson Tan, Jason Wu, Stephan Zheng, Caiming Xiong, Mohit Bansal, and Christopher Ré. 2021. Robustness gym: Unifying the nlp evaluation landscape. *arXiv preprint arXiv:2101.04840*.

Saša Hasan, Carmen Heger, and Saab Mansour. 2015. Spelling correction of user search queries through statistical machine translation. In *Proceedings of the 2015 Conference on Empirical Methods in Natural Language Processing*, pages 451–460, Lisbon, Portugal. Association for Computational Linguistics.

Charles T Hemphill, John J Godfrey, and George R Doddington. 1990. The atis spoken language systems pilot corpus. In *Speech and Natural Language: Proceedings of a Workshop Held at Hidden Valley, Pennsylvania, June 24-27, 1990*.

Robin Jia and Percy Liang. 2017. Adversarial examples for evaluating reading comprehension systems. *arXiv preprint arXiv:1707.07328*.

Vladimir Karpukhin, Omer Levy, Jacob Eisenstein, and Marjan Ghazvininejad. 2019. Training on synthetic noise improves robustness to natural noise in machine translation. In *Proceedings of the 5th Workshop on Noisy User-generated Text (W-NUT 2019)*, pages 42–47, Hong Kong, China. Association for Computational Linguistics.

Taku Kudo. 2018. Subword regularization: Improving neural network translation models with multiple subword candidates. *arXiv preprint arXiv:1804.10959*.

Jonathan Mallinson, Rico Sennrich, and Mirella Lapata. 2017. Paraphrasing revisited with neural machine translation. In *Proceedings of the 15th Conference of the European Chapter of the Association for Computational Linguistics: Volume 1, Long Papers*, pages 881–893, Valencia, Spain. Association for Computational Linguistics.

Valentin Malykh, Varvara Logacheva, and Taras Khakhulin. 2018. Robust word vectors: Context-informed embeddings for noisy texts. In *Proceedings of the 2018 EMNLP Workshop W-NUT: The 4th Workshop on Noisy User-generated Text*, pages 54–63, Brussels, Belgium. Association for Computational Linguistics.

Xing Niu, Prashant Mathur, Georgiana Dinu, and Yaser Al-Onaizan. 2020. Evaluating robustness to input perturbations for neural machine translation. In *Proceedings of the 58th Annual Meeting of the Association for Computational Linguistics*, pages 8538–8544, Online. Association for Computational Linguistics.

Aleksandra Piktus, Necati Bora Edizel, Piotr Bojanowski, Edouard Grave, Rui Ferreira, and Fabrizio Silvestri. 2019. Misspelling oblivious word embeddings. In *Proceedings of the 2019 Conference of the North American Chapter of the Association for Computational Linguistics: Human Language Technologies, Volume 1 (Long and Short Papers)*, pages 3226–3234, Minneapolis, Minnesota. Association for Computational Linguistics.

Danish Pruthi, Bhuwan Dhingra, and Zachary C. Lipton. 2019. Combating adversarial misspellings with robust word recognition. In *Proceedings of the 57th Annual Meeting of the Association for Computational Linguistics*, pages 5582–5591, Florence, Italy. Association for Computational Linguistics.

Marco Tulio Ribeiro, Sameer Singh, and Carlos Guestrin. 2018. Semantically equivalent adversarial rules for debugging NLP models. In *Proceedings of the 56th Annual Meeting of the Association for Computational Linguistics (Volume 1: Long Papers)*, pages 856–865, Melbourne, Australia. Association for Computational Linguistics.

Marco Tulio Ribeiro, Tongshuang Wu, Carlos Guestrin, and Sameer Singh. 2020. Beyond accuracy: Behavioral testing of NLP models with CheckList. In *Proceedings of the 58th Annual Meeting of the Association for Computational Linguistics*, pages 4902–4912, Online. Association for Computational Linguistics.

Victor Sanh, Lysandre Debut, Julien Chaumond, and Thomas Wolf. 2020. Distilbert, a distilled version of bert: smaller, faster, cheaper and lighter.

Samson Tan, Shafiq Joty, Min-Yen Kan, and Richard Socher. 2020a. It's morphin' time! Combating linguistic discrimination with inflectional perturbations. In *Proceedings of the 58th Annual Meeting of the Association for Computational Linguistics*, pages 2920–2935, Online. Association for Computational Linguistics.

Samson Tan, Shafiq Joty, Min-Yen Kan, and Richard Socher. 2020b. It's morphin'time! combating linguistic discrimination with inflectional perturbations. *arXiv preprint arXiv:2005.04364*.

Ottokar Tilk and Tanel Alumäe. 2016. Bidirectional recurrent neural network with attention mechanism for punctuation restoration. In *Interspeech 2016*.

Chen Zhu, Yu Cheng, Zhe Gan, Siqi Sun, Thomas Goldstein, and Jingjing Liu. 2020. Freelb: Enhanced adversarial training for language understanding. *ICLR*.

A Appendix

A.1 Hyper Parameter Settings

We fine-tune BERT for up to 40 epochs with a batch size of 32. To prevent over fitting, we use early stopping on the validation loss. We optimize BERT parameters using gluonnlp's bertadam optimizer with a learning rate of 5e-5 and no weight decay. These are the default hyper-parameters provided in the gluon tutorial for intent classification and slot labeling. [5]

A.2 Hyper Parameter Tuning

We use the default BERT joint IC/SL hyper-parameters mentioned above in all experiments, for both the baseline or training augmentation approaches. Using these fixed hyper-parameters, we tune the noise rate used for IC/SL training data augmentation. We tune the training data augmentation noise rate in the ranges listed below for each noise type. We select the noise rate that provides the best trade-off between performance on the control and treatment sets. The noise rates used in our final results are shown in the results table as a superscript.

Noise Rate Search Range by Noise Type:

- Casing: {15%, 25%, 50%, 100%}
- Misspellings: {10%, 15%, 20%, 25%, 30% }
- Abbreviations: {10%, 15%, 20%, 25%}
- Morphological Variants: {10%, 20%, 25%, 30% 50%}
- Synonyms: {10%, 20%, 25%, 30%, 50%}
- Paraphrases: {5%, 10%, 15%, 20%}

A.3 Compute Environment

We run all experiments on p3.2xlarge GPU instances using the AWS Deep Learning AMI (Ubuntu 16.04).

A.4 Packages Used in Experimentation

We utilize the following packages to train and evaluate our models as well as generate synthetic noise for training augmentation:

5 https://nlp.gluon.ai/model_zoo/intent_cls_slot_labeling/index.html

Dataset	Model Type	≈Time Taken
ATIS	BERT IC-SL	13m
	+ B-SR	17m
	+ Uni A-DA	22m
	+ Uni A-DA + B-SR	27m
	+ Uni A-DA + ALP	37m
	+ Uni A-DA + ALP + B-SR	58m
	+ BP A-DA	57m
	+ BP A-DA + B-SR	65m
	+ BP A-DA + ALP	125m
	+ BP A-DA + ALP + B-SR	207m
SNIPS	BERT IC-SL	23m
	+ B-SR	29m
	+ Uni A-DA	37m
	+ Uni A-DA + B-SR	42m
	+ Uni A-DA + ALP	59m
	+ Uni A-DA + ALP + B-SR	70m
	+ BP A-DA	102m
	+ BP A-DA + B-SR	110m
	+ BP A-DA + ALP	186m
	+ BP A-DA + ALP + B-SR	227m

Table 6: Table showing the time taken to run 30 epochs of a model training + inference on test data. As the test data size varies based on the noise type (since different treatment sets have different number of utterances), all numbers are shown for the abbreviation control set.

```
nltk==3.3
gluonnlp==0.8.1
mxnet==1.3.0
numpy==1.14.3
scikit-learn==0.23.1
scipy==1.1.0
torch==1.7.1
transformers==4.2.2
seqeval==0.0.12
```

Listing 1: requirements.txt

A.5 Evaluation Metrics

We compute slot labeling F1 score using the seqeval library (https://github.com/chakki-works/seqeval). We utilize the evaluation function provided in the gluonnlp intent classification and slot labeling tutorial to compute intent classification accuracy (https://nlp.gluon.ai/model_zoo/intent_cls_slot_labeling/index.html).

A.6 Model Training and Inference Times

Training for 40 epochs plus inference on the test set takes approximately 13 minutes on the ATIS data-set and 23 minutes for the SNIPS data-set for both the baseline and training augmentation approaches. The time taken significantly increased for the other

Noise Type	Probability	Example	Char. Edit
Original	1.0 - p	list *flights* from las vegas to phoenix	N/A
Insertion	$p * 0.33$	list *fljights* from las vegas to phoenix	$+$j
Deletion	$p * 0.18$	list *flghts* from las vegas to phoenix	$-$i
Substitution	$p * 0.43$	list *flithts* from las vegas to phoenix	g $\rightarrow$ t
Transposition	$p * 0.06$	list *filghts* from las vegas to phoenix	l $\leftrightarrow$ i

Table 7: Instances of insertion, deletion, substitution, and transposition noise types for the example utterance (Original), "list flights from las vegas to phoenix". We sample each noise type with the given probability to construct noisy pre-training and IC/SL training datasets, where p is the noise rate. We inject noise into the token *"flights"* in each example and provide the character level edit (Char. Edit) that transforms the original token to the noised token.

model types and are listed in Table 6.

A.7 Synthetic Misspelling Generation

We build on prior work by (Hasan et al., 2015) to generate synthetic misspellings that are representative of natural misspellings. Hasan et al. present a taxonomy of misspelling types and induction probabilities mined from natural noise. This taxonomy consists of four noise types, substitution, insertion, deletion, and transposition.

Character choice in substitution and insertion operations is based on the QWERTY keyboard layout. Given a character c (e.g., "d"), we substitute or insert a character the appears next to c on the QWERTY keyboard (e.g. "f", "s", "e", "c"). We provide examples of each noise type and list the probability with which we introduce these types of noise in Table 7.

Amendable Generation for Dialogue State Tracking

Xin Tian, Liankai Huang, Yingzhan Lin, Siqi Bao, Huang He, Yunyi Yang, Hua Wu, Fan Wang, Shuqi Sun
Baidu Inc., China
{tianxin06,huangliankai,linyingzhan01,baosiqi,hehuang, yangyunyi01,wu_hua,wang.fan,sunshuqi01}@baidu.com

Abstract

In task-oriented dialogue systems, recent dialogue state tracking methods tend to perform one-pass generation of the dialogue state based on the previous dialogue state. The mistakes of these models made at the current turn are prone to be carried over to the next turn, causing error propagation. In this paper, we propose a novel **A**mendable **G**eneration for **D**ialogue **S**tate **T**racking (**AG-DST**), which contains a two-pass generation process: (1) generating a primitive dialogue state based on the dialogue of the current turn and the previous dialogue state, and (2) amending the primitive dialogue state from the first pass. With the additional amending generation pass, our model is tasked to learn more robust dialogue state tracking by amending the errors that still exist in the primitive dialogue state, which plays the role of reviser in the double-checking process and alleviates unnecessary error propagation. Experimental results show that AG-DST significantly outperforms previous works in two active DST datasets (MultiWOZ 2.2 and WOZ 2.0), achieving new state-of-the-art performances.

1 Introduction

Dialogue state tracking (DST) is a crucial task in task-oriented dialogue systems, as it affects database query results as well as the subsequent policy prediction (Chen et al., 2017). It extracts users' goals at each turn of the conversation and represents them in the form of a set of (*slot*, *value*) pairs, i.e., dialogue state.

Traditional methods of DST mainly rely on a predefined ontology which includes all possible slots and corresponding values. These models predict the value for each slot as a classification problem (Mrkšić et al., 2017; Zhong et al., 2018; Ramadan et al., 2018). However, in practical applications, some slot values appearing in the conversations cannot be predefined, and it is infeasible to acquire a fully predefined ontology or transfer to other domains with fixed predefined ontology. To address such challenges, open-vocabulary DST has been proposed, where the value of each slot is directly generated or extracted from the dialogue history (Chao and Lane, 2019; Hosseini-Asl et al., 2020; Ham et al., 2020; Heck et al., 2020). Although this approach offers scalability and is capable of handling unseen slot values, many of the previous models are not efficient enough as they need to predict the dialogue state from scratch based on the dialogue history.

On the merits of utilizing the previous dialogue state as a compact representation of the previous dialogue history, some recent methods choose to take the previous dialogue state into consideration when generating the slot values. One direction is to decompose DST into two explicit sub-tasks: State Operation Prediction and Value Generation (Kim et al., 2020; Zeng and Nie, 2020). At each turn, whether or how to modify the value in the previous dialogue state is determined by the discrete operations from the state operation prediction, so the accuracy of state operation prediction holds back the overall DST performance (Kim et al., 2020). Another direction of recent works recasts dialogue state tracking into a single causal language model by using the dialogue of the current turn and the previous dialogue state as input sequence (Lin et al., 2020; Yang et al., 2021), where the current dialogue state is generated by jointly modeling the state operation prediction and value generation in a implicit fashion. While it is more effective and reasonable to use the previous dialogue state under the Markov assumption, the mistakes of these models made during the prediction of the current turn are prone to be carried over to the next turn, causing error propagation. These carried-over mistakes are unlikely to be fixed in the next turn. Essentially, these models perform a one-pass generation process and lack a double-checking process to amend the mistakes of

Proceedings of the Third Workshop on Natural Language Processing for Conversational AI, pages 80–92
November 10, 2021. ©2021 Association for Computational Linguistics

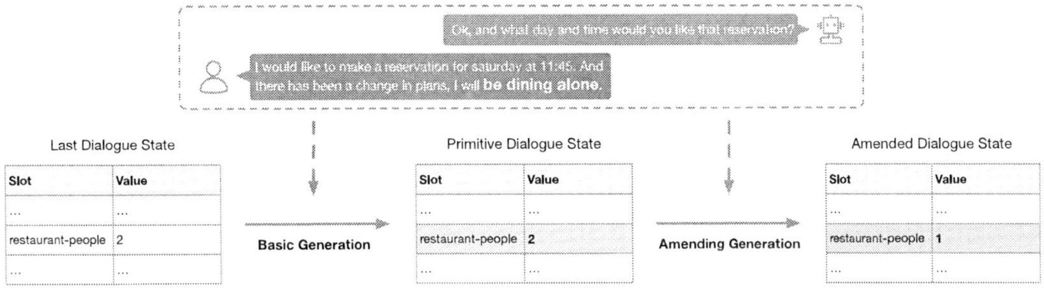

Figure 1: An example of AG-DST with two-pass generation process. In this example, the user wants to change *restaurant-people* from 2 to 1 by "*... a change in plans, I will be dining alone*". In the two-pass generation process, the amending generation obtains corresponding information to correct mistake in the basic generation.

the current turn. Missing such amending process would result in some potential mistakes being left unfixed.

To nip the mistakes in the bud and alleviate the error propagation problem, we propose **A**mendable **G**eneration for **D**ialogue **S**tate **T**racking (**AG-DST**), a pretrained language model that generates the dialogue state based on the dialogue of the current turn and previous dialogue state. In contrast to previous one-pass generation process (Kim et al., 2020; Zeng and Nie, 2020; Lin et al., 2020; Yang et al., 2021), AG-DST employs a two-pass generation process consisting of a basic generation and an amending generation, where the first pass uses the dialogue of the current turn and the previous dialogue state to generate a primitive dialogue state, and second pass utilizes the dialogue of the current turn to amend the primitive dialogue state. With the additional amending generation pass, our model is tasked to learn more robust dialogue state tracking by amending the errors that still exist in the primitive dialogue state. These errors are more challenging to fix and relatively scarce during training. Therefore, we further design a negative sampling mechanism to exploit more challenging errors and facilitate the effective learning of the amending generation pass. With such two-pass generation process, AG-DST is less likely to generate false dialogue state for the next turn, and thus reduces error propagation. Figure 1 illustrates a complete dialogue state generation process of AG-DST.

Experimental results show that AG-DST consistently outperforms all prior works on MultiWOZ 2.2 and WOZ 2.0. Especially on MultiWOZ 2.2, AG-DST achieves 57.26% joint goal accuracy, 2.86% higher than the previous state-of-the-art performance. Besides, we provide ablation study and the attention visualization to demonstrate the effectiveness of the amending generation, and analyze the types of mistakes that can be corrected by the amending generation. Our models and code will be released for further research.[1]

2 Methodology

In this section, we introduce AG-DST in the following aspects: the basic generation, the amending generation and the training objective.

2.1 Basic Generation

A dialogue with T turns can be represented as $D = \{D_1, D_2, \dots, D_T\}$, where D_t is the dialogue at turn t consisting of system response R_t and user utterance U_t. We denote the dialogue states at every turn as $\mathcal{B} = \{\mathcal{B}_1, \mathcal{B}_2, \dots, \mathcal{B}_T\}$. For multi-domain DST, the dialogue state at turn t is denoted as $\mathcal{B}_t = \{(S^i, V_t^i) | 1 \leq i \leq I\}$, in which S^i is the slot and V_t^i is its corresponding value (I is the number of all slots in different domains). Particularly, S^i is represented as a special token concatenated by domain and slot (i.e. <domain-slot>) following most previous works. We use special tokens <nm> and <dc> to indicate *not mentioned* and *don't care* in slot value respectively.

We leverage the dialogue of the current turn and the previous dialogue state to generate the current dialogue state. The dialogue of the current turn D_t is used in the input tokens under the Markov assumption. To a certain extent the previous dialogue state B_{t-1} could be viewed as a compact representation of the previous dialogue history (Kim et al., 2020). Specifically, we denote the dialogue at turn t as:

$$D_t = [R_t; U_t] \quad (1)$$

[1] https://github.com/PaddlePaddle/Knover/tree/develop/projects/AG-DST

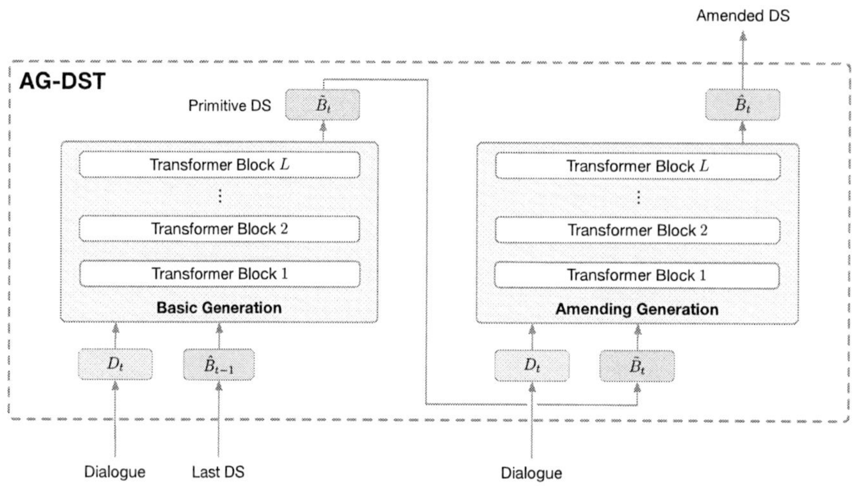

Figure 2: The overview of the proposed AG-DST. In the basic generation, AG-DST takes the dialogue of the current turn D_t and the previous dialogue state $\hat{B}_{t-1}$ as input and generates the primitive dialogue state $\tilde{B}_t$. In the amending generation, AG-DST takes the dialogue of the current turn D_t and the primitive dialogue state $\tilde{B}_t$ as input and outputs the amended dialogue state $\hat{B}_t$.

where R_t and U_t are system response and user utterance accordingly. Special tokens <con/> and </con> are added around D_t for marking the boundary of the dialogue context, and special tokens <sys> and <usr> are added before R_t and U_t respectively to indicate the role. The dialogue state at turn t is denoted as

$$B_t = [B_t^1; B_t^2; \ldots; B_t^I] \tag{2}$$

where $B_t^i = [S^i; V_t^i]$ is the concatenation of i-th slot and its value. Similar to the dialogue context, two special tokens <ds/> and </ds> are added around the whole dialogue state.

The overview of AG-DST is illustrated in Figure 2. AG-DST is a generation model based on transformer (Vaswani et al., 2017; Dong et al., 2019). In the basic generation of AG-DST, the input sequence is composed of the current turn dialogue and the previous dialogue state, and the primitive dialogue state is predicted by:

$$\tilde{B}_t = Transformer(D_t, B_{t-1}) \tag{3}$$

where <gen/> and </gen> are added around the whole input sequence to indicate the first pass generation process.

As shown in Figure 3, the input embedding of each token is the sum of token embedding, position embedding, role embedding and segment embedding. Among them, position embedding is added to discriminate input token positions; role embedding is employed to distinguish the characters of the speaker in the dialogue; segment embedding is used for different types of sequence.

2.2 Amending Generation

To amend the potential errors in the primitive dialogue state, we propose a novel amending generation that takes the dialogue of the current turn and the primitive dialogue state predicted by the basic generation as input, and generates the amended dialogue state:

$$\hat{B}_t = Transformer(D_t, \tilde{B}_t) \tag{4}$$

where the new input sequence of amending generation is consisted of the current turn dialogue and the primitive dialogue state, $\hat{B}_t$ is the amended dialogue state. The amending generation shares the same parameters with the basic generation model. To differentiate this two-pass generation process, the special tokens <amend/> and </amend> are added around the new input sequence in Equation 4 as opposed to the <gen/> and </gen> in Equation 3.

Negative Sampling To facilitate effective learning of the amending generation process, we propose a negative sampling strategy that actively mines the examples on which the model is prone to make mistakes (i.e., generating the wrong slot values, or failing to update some slots). Specifically, we performs negative sampling on the dialogue state with changed slot values between turns

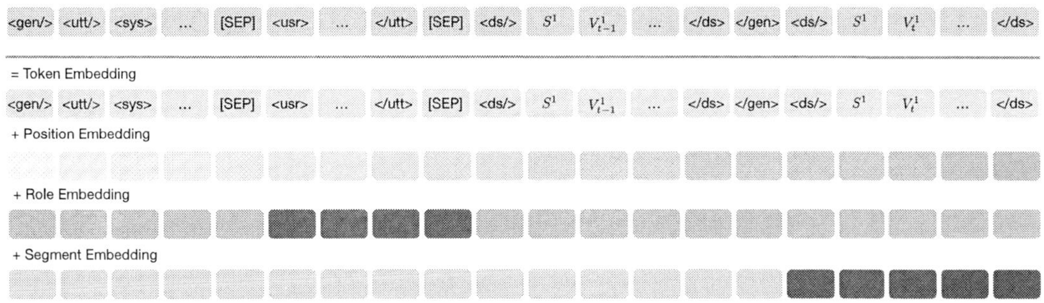

Figure 3: An example of input representation. The input embedding of each token is the sum of token embedding, position embedding, role embedding and segment embedding.

$\Delta\mathcal{B}_t = \mathcal{B}_t - \mathcal{B}_t \cap \mathcal{B}_{t-1}$, where these slot values are randomly replaced by `<nm>`, `<dc>` or some wrong values. During training, the dialogue state after negative sampling is used as the primitive dialogue state $\tilde{B}_t$ in the amending generation to encourage the model to lay more emphasis on error correction.

2.3 Training Objective

The training objective of the basic generation is the negative log-likelihood loss given the dialogue of the current turn and the previous dialogue state:

$$\mathcal{L}_{basic} = -\log P(B_t|D_t, B_{t-1}) \tag{5}$$

Similar to the basic generation, the loss of the amending generation is also the negative log-likelihood loss:

$$\mathcal{L}_{amending} = -\log P(B_t|D_t, \tilde{B}_t) \tag{6}$$

The total objective of AG-DST is to minimize the sum of the above two losses:

$$\mathcal{L} = \mathcal{L}_{basic} + \mathcal{L}_{amending} \tag{7}$$

3 Experiments

3.1 Datasets

We conduct our experiments on both multi-domain dataset MultiWOZ 2.2 (Zang et al., 2020) and single-domain dataset WOZ 2.0 (Wen et al., 2017). MultiWOZ (Budzianowski et al., 2018) is a large-scale multi-domain dialogue dataset with human-human conversations including over 10,000 dialogues. It is a widely used benchmark for dialogue state tracking. MultiWOZ 2.2 (Zang et al., 2020) is a new version of MultiWOZ 2.1 (Eric et al., 2019), in which a number of dialogue state annotation errors across 17.3% of the utterances have been fixed.

Statistics	MultiWOZ 2.2	WOZ 2.0
# domains	5	1
# slots	30	3
# dialogues	10424	1200
# train dialogues	8426	600
# valid dialogues	998	200
# test dialogues	1000	400
Avg. turns per dialogue	13.71	8.35
Avg. tokens per turn	16.86	13.18

Table 1: Statistics of the datasets in the experiments.

Following Wu et al. (2019), due to the absence of *hospital* and *police* domains in the validation and test datasets, there are only 5 domains (*attraction*, *hotel*, *restaurant*, *taxi* and *train*) and 30 corresponding domain-slot pairs in our experiments. WOZ 2.0 (Wen et al., 2017) is a well-known single-domain DST dataset, where 3 slots (*area*, *food* and *price range*) are involved in the *restaurant* domain. Table 1 summarizes the statistics of the above two datasets.

3.2 Implementation Details

Our AG-DST approach can be easily deployed with many pre-trained generation models (such as GPT-2 (Radford et al., 2019), T5 (Raffel et al., 2020), PLATO-2 (Bao et al., 2021)). In this paper, we employ the GPT-2 and PLATO-2 to initialize our model parameters. GPT-2 is a large causal language model, and PLATO-2 is a large-scale open-domain dialogue model trained on the Reddit comments. Specifically, GPT-2 has 117M parameters containing 12 transformer blocks, 12 attention heads and 768 hidden units, and PLATO-2 has 310M parameters containing 24 transformer blocks, 16 attention heads and 1024 hidden units.[2] Adam optimizer (Kingma and Ba, 2015) is employed for optimization in all experiments. For the hyper-parameters we used in the best model, the PLATO-2 is fine-tuned with a dynamic batch size of 8192 tokens, a learning rate of $1e-5$, warmup steps of 1000 and a learning rate decay rate of 0.01. For GPT-2, we set the batch size of 6, a learning rate of $5e-5$ with no warmup and learning rate decay. All the models are trained on 4 Nvidia Telsa V100 32G GPU cards for 40 epochs and early stop according to the performance on the validation set. All the reported results of AG-DST are averages over five runs.

3.3 Baselines

We compare our approach with the following methods:

Neural Belief Tracker (Mrkšić et al., 2017) learns the distributed representation of system responses and user utterances from pre-trained word vectors, and decides which slot-value pairs are required by the user.

Belief Tracking (Ramadan et al., 2018) proposes a model that utilizes semantic similarity between ontology terms and utterances and shares the information across domains.

GLAD (Zhong et al., 2018) uses global modules to share parameters across slots and local modules to learn the features which take into account the specific slot.

StateNet (Ren et al., 2018) proposes a model that composes a representation of the dialogue history and measures the distances between the representation and the value vectors.

TRADE (Wu et al., 2019) uses a state operation with an utterance encoder and a dialogue state generator to handle the cross domain phenomenon.

DS-DST (Zhang et al., 2020) proposes a dual strategy: picklist-based and span-based. The span-based strategy includes a slot-gate classifier and span-based slot-value prediction.

BERT-DST (Chao and Lane, 2019) adopts BERT to encode dialogue context and extracts slot values by the state operation prediction and the span prediction.

SOM-DST (Kim et al., 2020) proposes an efficient decoder by updating dialogue state as a memory to reduce the burden of the decoder.

COMER (Ren et al., 2019) adopts two sequential decoders to generate dialogue state. The first decoder is used to generate state sketch (i.e. domains and slots), and the second one is used to generate slot values by conditioning on the dialogue history and state sketch.

SGD-baseline (Rastogi et al., 2020) adapts BERT to obtain the schema embeddings (including intents, slots and possible values of categorical slots) and utterance embeddings and uses different strategies for non-categorical and categorical slots.

SimpleTOD (Hosseini-Asl et al., 2020) changes sub-tasks of task-oriented dialogue into a single causal language model which generates dialogue state, system action and system response successively.

Seq2Seq-DU (Feng et al., 2021) applies schema descriptions to deal with unseen domains with a sequence-to-sequence framework.

3.4 Experimental Results

We use joint goal accuracy (Joint Acc) as our main evaluation metric for dialogue state tracking. Joint goal accuracy measures the percentage of *correct* in all dialogue turns, where a turn is considered as *correct* if and only if all the slot values are correctly predicted. We also show the slot accuracy for each domain which measures the accuracy of all the slot values in that specific domain.

Table 2 shows the performance of the AG-DST in comparison to the baselines. We can observe that the AG-DST consistently outperforms all baselines on both MultiWOZ 2.2 and WOZ 2.0 datasets, achieving a new state-of-the-art performance. On MultiWOZ 2.2, AG-DST achieve 57.26% joint goal accuracy, by 2.86% significant improvement on the top of the Seq2Seq-DU (Feng et al., 2021), the latest sequence-to-sequence generation model. In addition, the domain-specific results of our approach are also provided in Table 3. On the single-domain dataset, WOZ 2.0, we obtain joint goal accuracy of 91.37%, which indicates that our model is also effective in a relatively simple scenario. We

[2] Unless otherwise specified in subsequent experiments, the pre-trained backbone we used is PLATO-2 as it carries out better results.

Model	MultiWOZ 2.2	WOZ 2.0
Neural Belief Tracker	-	84.20
Belief Tracking	-	85.50
GLAD	-	88.10
StateNet	-	88.90
TRADE	45.40†	-
DS-DST	51.70†	-
BERT-DST	-	87.70
SOM-DST	53.81‡	-
COMER	-	88.60
SGD-baseline	42.00†	-
SimpleTOD	54.02‡	-
Seq2Seq-DU	54.40	91.20
AG-DST	**57.26**	**91.37**

Table 2: Joint goal accuracy of AG-DST and baselines on MultiWOZ 2.2 and WOZ 2.0 datasets. AG-DST consistently outperforms all baselines. †: the results borrowed from Zang et al. (2020). ‡: our reproduction results by official code.

Domain	Joint Acc	Slot Acc
multi-domain	57.26	97.48
attraction	89.91	96.26
hotel	82.31	97.16
restaurant	89.00	97.97
taxi	96.09	98.31
train	89.15	97.51

Table 3: Joint goal accuracy and slot accuracy of AG-DST on MultiWOZ 2.2 by domains.

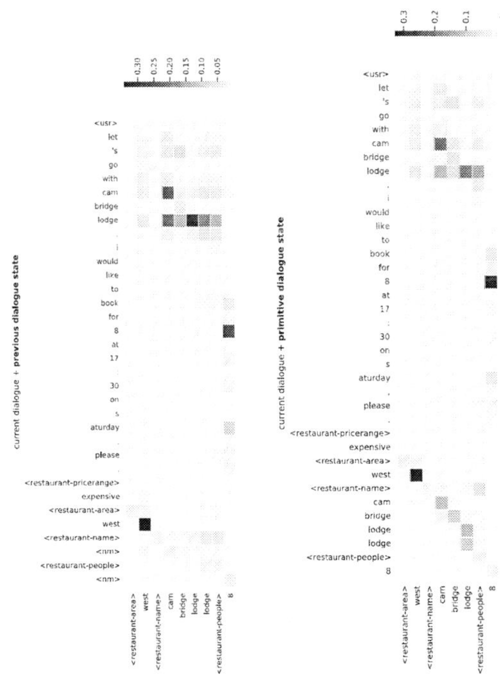

(a) Basic Generation (b) Amending Generation

Figure 4: The attention visualization of (a) basic generation and (b) amending generation on an example from MultiWOZ 2.2. Note that in both figures, the abscissa and ordinate are a fraction of whole input and output sequence respectively because of limited space.

will analyse the strengths of AG-DST in the subsequent section.

4 Analysis

4.1 Amending Generation

As shown in Table 4, we conduct ablation study to investigate the effectiveness of the proposed amending generation. The results show that the amending generation has a significant improvement on the basic generation, where the model gets extra joint goal accuracy of 0.87%. When we perform negative sampling to facilitate effective learning of the amending generation process, it will lead to an increase by 1.06%. Furthermore, we implement heuristic negative sampling which exchanges some correlated slot values (such as *leave at* and *arrive by*, *departure* and *destination*, *area* in different domains) on MultiWOZ 2.2. While using this further heuristic negative sampling, the model achieves the best joint goal accuracy of 57.35%. Essentially, the amending generation process amends the challenging mistakes that still exists after the basic generation and provides a more accurate prediction of the dialogue state of the current turn, which effectively alleviate the error propagation problem. To the best of our knowledge, AG-DST is the first DST method that involves a two-pass generation process to amend the primitive dialogue state.

Visualization Figure 4 shows the attention visualization of the basic generation and the amending

Model	Joint Acc
basic generation	56.20
+ amending generation	57.07 (+0.87)
+ amending generation w/ NS	57.26 (+1.06)
+ amending generation w/ NS^{+}	57.35 (+1.15)

Table 4: The ablation study of the amending generation on MultiWOZ 2.2 with joint goal accuracy. NS means the negative sampling mentioned in Section 2.2, as well as NS^{+} performs a heuristic negative sampling.

generation on an example of MultiWOZ 2.2. In the basic generation, the value of slot *restaurant-area* is copied from previous dialogue state and the value of slot *restaurant-people* is predicted from user utterance accurately. However, for the *restaurant-name*, although the model pays attention to the corresponding tokens in the dialogue of the current turn, it generates a wrong slot value. In the amending generation, the *restaurant-name* and its value attend to both the corresponding tokens in the user utterance and slot value in the primitive dialogue state with high weight, which indicates that the amending generation can utilize both the dialogue of the current turn and the primitive dialogue state for reference to correct the mistakes in the primitive dialogue state.

Error Analysis In our analysis, we found three frequent errors in a one-pass generation model of DST. (1) The slot value is not updated, as the model fails to obtain the key information in the dialogue, an example can be seen in Figure 1. (2) Some common mistakes occur in generation model. For example, *cambridge lodge* is predicted to *cambridge lodge lodge*, and *camboats* is predicted to *cambots*. (3) There is confusion between correlated slots, such as *leave at* and *arrive by*, *departure* and *destination*. As reported in Figure 5, we make the statistics of error types by random sampling on MultiWOZ 2.2, which indicates that 51% of the error comes from the first type, 4% comes from the second type, 3% comes from the third type, 36% is due to the inconsistent annotation, and 6% is due to others. Furthermore, we show that the proposed amendable generation can greatly correct these errors and improve the overall performance of DST with concrete examples of the amending generation are shown in Table 9 of Appendix B.

4.2 Effect of Previous Dialogue State

As shown in Table 5, we compare three types of input sequence formations: only dialogue history, dialogue history and previous dialogue state, current turn dialogue and previous dialogue state. We find that using the previous dialogue state (i.e. dialogue state memory) performs better than using only dialogue history, which confirms that the previous dialogue state can be served as a compact representation of the dialogue history and utilizing the previous dialogue state is more effective than performing DST from scratch. The results also show that using the current turn dialogue instead of the whole dialogue history barely hurts the performance, yet it greatly improves the efficiency, which justifies our use of the current turn dialogue and previous dialogue state as the input sequence.

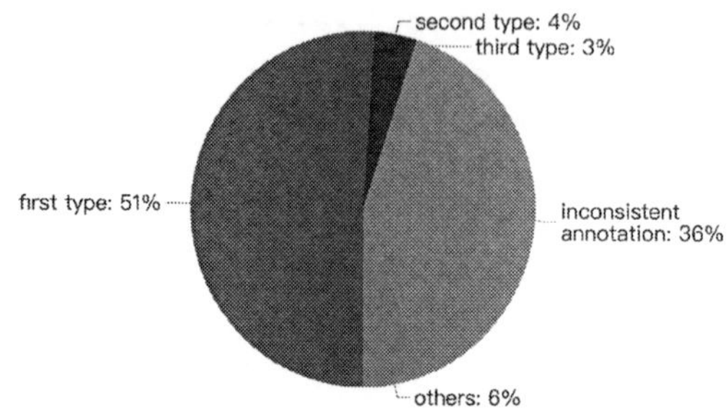

Figure 5: Error type statistics of the basic generation. first type: slot value not updated; second type: common mistakes of generation; third type: confusion between correlated slots.

Structure	Joint Acc
$(B_t \mid D)$ †	54.02
$(B_t \mid D, B_{t-1})$	**56.27**
$(B_t \mid D_t, B_{t-1})$	56.20

Table 5: Joint goal accuracy of different structures of generation model on MultiWOZ 2.2. The structures with dialogue state memory perform better than the rest which uses only dialogue context. †: we reuse the result of SimpleTOD in Table 2.

4.3 Effect of Pre-training

In prior works, GPT-2 is often the pre-trained backbone in generation model (Hosseini-Asl et al., 2020; Ham et al., 2020; Yang et al., 2021). We also analyze the ability of GPT-2 on MultiWOZ 2.2 (see Table 6), where only token embedding and position embedding are added as input embedding. Results show that our approach initialized with GPT-2 surpasses the SimpleTOD (a generation model initialized by GPT-2) and Seq2Seq-DU (the prior state-of-the-art), and obtains similar results

Model	Joint Acc
SimpleTOD	54.02
Seq2Seq-DU	54.40
GPT-2 w/ basic generation	55.24
GPT-2 w/ amending generation	55.85
GPT-2 w/ amending generation + NS	56.09
PLATO-2 w/ basic generation	56.20
PLATO-2 w/ amending generation	57.07
PLATO-2 w/ amending generation + NS	**57.26**

Table 6: The ablation study of the pre-trained model on MultiWOZ 2.2 with joint goal accuracy.

Model	Joint Acc
basic generation	**56.20**
- name special token	55.34 (-0.86)
- utterance special token	55.70 (-0.50)
- DS special token	54.50 (-1.70)
- above three	54.41 (-1.79)

Table 7: The ablation study of the absence of different special tokens on MultiWOZ 2.2 with joint goal accuracy.

with the PLATO-2 initialization. This indicates our approach's ability to universally improve the performances of other pretrained models.

4.4 Effect of Special Tokens

Special tokens are important for identifying different input components (Hosseini-Asl et al., 2020). In our experiments, similar to prior works, we use the utterance special token and dialogue state special token to differentiate each part. Besides, to boost the extraction of entity names on MultiWOZ 2.2, we add special tokens `<name/>` and `</name>` around the candidate entity names. Table 7 shows the joint goal accuracy reduction caused by the absence of various special tokens, which further confirms the neccesity of using special tokens.

5 Related Work

Traditional methods regard DST as a classification task, in which an encoder is employed for obtaining a representation of utterances and a classifier is utilized for predicting a slot value from a pre-defined ontology (Mrkšić et al., 2017; Zhong et al., 2018; Ramadan et al., 2018). However, it is difficult to obtain a full ontology in a real scenario. Some open-vocabulary DST models extract or generate the dialogue state from the dialogue history at each turn (Chao and Lane, 2019; Hosseini-Asl et al., 2020; Ham et al., 2020; Heck et al., 2020). These methods predict the dialogue state from scratch at each turn, which undoubtedly puts a great burden on the model.

To address this problem, some recent methods consider to utilize the previous dialogue state and recent dialogue history as input information. Specifically, the DST is separated into two components, where a component named State Operation Prediction is used to encode utterance and previous dialogue state, as well as predict the operation of state at each turn, and the other component named Value Generation predicts the value for each slot (Kim et al., 2020; Zeng and Nie, 2020). Kim et al. (2020) encodes the dialogue history of the last two turns and the previous dialogue state by BERT and predicts four kinds of state operations: *carryover*, *delete*, *dontcare* and *update*. For *update* operation, a GRU-based value generation is used to decode the slot value. Zeng and Nie (2020) reuses a fraction of the hidden states of the encoder in the decoder to build a flat model for effective parameter updating. Besides, some methods treat dialogue state tracking as a causal language model by using the dialogue of the current turn and previous dialogue state as input sequence (Lin et al., 2020; Yang et al., 2021). Lin et al. (2020) utilizes an encoder-decoder framework to generate dialogue state and system response sequentially, where minimal slot value pairs are generated for efficiently tracking. Yang et al. (2021) models task-oriented dialogs on a dialog session level, which generates dialogue state, dialogue action and system response sequentially based on the whole previous dialogue context, including the generated dialogue states and dialogue actions. Moreover, some schema-guided DST methods leverage schema descriptions to deal with unseen schemas with new domains and slots (Zhu et al., 2020; Feng et al., 2021; Noroozi et al., 2020).

6 Conclusion

In this paper, we propose a novel amendable generative approach for dialogue state tracking, which learns implicit state operation prediction and value generation jointly in a single model to reduce the error propagation. Meanwhile, our model offers an opportunity to amend the primitive dialogue state in the amending generation. Experimental results show that our model outperforms previous works on both MultiWOZ 2.2 and WOZ 2.0 datasets, achieving state-of-the-art performance. The ablation study and attention visualization demonstrate that the proposed amending generation is significantly effective. Moreover, we analyze the types of mistakes that can be resolved by the amending generation and provide some examples to illustrate them in the Appendix. In the future, we will try to integrate schema descriptions into our architecture and explore a generative approach to support end-to-end task-oriented dialogue system.

References

Siqi Bao, Huang He, Fan Wang, Hua Wu, Haifeng Wang, Wenquan Wu, Zhen Guo, Zhibin Liu, and Xinchao Xu. 2021. PLATO-2: Towards building an open-domain chatbot via curriculum learning. In *Findings of the Association for Computational Linguistics: ACL-IJCNLP 2021*, pages 2513–2525, Online. Association for Computational Linguistics.

Paweł Budzianowski, Tsung-Hsien Wen, Bo-Hsiang Tseng, Iñigo Casanueva, Stefan Ultes, Osman Ramadan, and Milica Gašić. 2018. MultiWOZ - a large-scale multi-domain Wizard-of-Oz dataset for task-oriented dialogue modelling. In *Proceedings of the 2018 Conference on Empirical Methods in Natural Language Processing*, pages 5016–5026, Brussels, Belgium. Association for Computational Linguistics.

Guan-Lin Chao and Ian Lane. 2019. BERT-DST: Scalable End-to-End Dialogue State Tracking with Bidirectional Encoder Representations from Transformer. In *Proc. Interspeech 2019*, pages 1468–1472.

Hongshen Chen, Xiaorui Liu, Dawei Yin, and Jiliang Tang. 2017. A survey on dialogue systems: Recent advances and new frontiers. *Acm Sigkdd Explorations Newsletter*, 19(2):25–35.

Li Dong, Nan Yang, Wenhui Wang, Furu Wei, Xiaodong Liu, Yu Wang, Jianfeng Gao, Ming Zhou, and Hsiao-Wuen Hon. 2019. Unified language model pre-training for natural language understanding and generation. In *Advances in Neural Information Processing Systems 32: Annual Conference on Neural Information Processing Systems 2019, NeurIPS 2019, December 8-14, 2019, Vancouver, BC, Canada*, pages 13042–13054.

Mihail Eric, Rahul Goel, Shachi Paul, Abhishek Sethi, Sanchit Agarwal, Shuyag Gao, and Dilek Hakkani-Tur. 2019. Multiwoz 2.1: Multi-domain dialogue state corrections and state tracking baselines. *arXiv preprint arXiv:1907.01669*.

Yue Feng, Yang Wang, and Hang Li. 2021. A sequence-to-sequence approach to dialogue state tracking. In *Proceedings of the 59th Annual Meeting of the Association for Computational Linguistics and the 11th International Joint Conference on Natural Language Processing (Volume 1: Long Papers)*, pages 1714–1725, Online. Association for Computational Linguistics.

Donghoon Ham, Jeong-Gwan Lee, Youngsoo Jang, and Kee-Eung Kim. 2020. End-to-end neural pipeline for goal-oriented dialogue systems using GPT-2. In *Proceedings of the 58th Annual Meeting of the Association for Computational Linguistics*, pages 583–592, Online. Association for Computational Linguistics.

Michael Heck, Carel van Niekerk, Nurul Lubis, Christian Geishauser, Hsien-Chin Lin, Marco Moresi, and Milica Gasic. 2020. TripPy: A triple copy strategy for value independent neural dialog state tracking. In *Proceedings of the 21th Annual Meeting of the Special Interest Group on Discourse and Dialogue*, pages 35–44, 1st virtual meeting. Association for Computational Linguistics.

Ehsan Hosseini-Asl, Bryan McCann, Chien-Sheng Wu, Semih Yavuz, and Richard Socher. 2020. A simple language model for task-oriented dialogue. In *Advances in Neural Information Processing Systems 33: Annual Conference on Neural Information Processing Systems 2020, NeurIPS 2020, December 6-12, 2020, virtual*.

Sungdong Kim, Sohee Yang, Gyuwan Kim, and Sang-Woo Lee. 2020. Efficient dialogue state tracking by selectively overwriting memory. In *Proceedings of the 58th Annual Meeting of the Association for Computational Linguistics*, pages 567–582, Online. Association for Computational Linguistics.

Diederik P. Kingma and Jimmy Ba. 2015. Adam: A method for stochastic optimization. In *3rd International Conference on Learning Representations, ICLR 2015, San Diego, CA, USA, May 7-9, 2015, Conference Track Proceedings*.

Zhaojiang Lin, Andrea Madotto, Genta Indra Winata, and Pascale Fung. 2020. MinTL: Minimalist transfer learning for task-oriented dialogue systems. In *Proceedings of the 2020 Conference on Empirical Methods in Natural Language Processing (EMNLP)*, pages 3391–3405, Online. Association for Computational Linguistics.

Nikola Mrkšić, Diarmuid Ó Séaghdha, Tsung-Hsien Wen, Blaise Thomson, and Steve Young. 2017. Neural belief tracker: Data-driven dialogue state tracking. In *Proceedings of the 55th Annual Meeting of the Association for Computational Linguistics (Volume 1: Long Papers)*, pages 1777–1788, Vancouver, Canada. Association for Computational Linguistics.

Vahid Noroozi, Yang Zhang, Evelina Bakhturina, and Tomasz Kornuta. 2020. A fast and robust bert-based dialogue state tracker for schema-guided dialogue dataset. *arXiv preprint arXiv:2008.12335*.

Alec Radford, Jeffrey Wu, Rewon Child, David Luan, Dario Amodei, and Ilya Sutskever. 2019. Language models are unsupervised multitask learners. *OpenAI blog*, 1(8):9.

Colin Raffel, Noam Shazeer, Adam Roberts, Katherine Lee, Sharan Narang, Michael Matena, Yanqi Zhou, Wei Li, and Peter J. Liu. 2020. Exploring the limits of transfer learning with a unified text-to-text transformer. *Journal of Machine Learning Research*, 21(140):1–67.

Osman Ramadan, Paweł Budzianowski, and Milica Gašić. 2018. Large-scale multi-domain belief tracking with knowledge sharing. In *Proceedings of the 56th Annual Meeting of the Association for Computational Linguistics (Volume 2: Short Papers)*, pages 432–437, Melbourne, Australia. Association for Computational Linguistics.

Abhinav Rastogi, Xiaoxue Zang, Srinivas Sunkara, Raghav Gupta, and Pranav Khaitan. 2020. Towards scalable multi-domain conversational agents: The schema-guided dialogue dataset. *Proceedings of the AAAI Conference on Artificial Intelligence*, 34(05):8689–8696.

Liliang Ren, Jianmo Ni, and Julian McAuley. 2019. Scalable and accurate dialogue state tracking via hierarchical sequence generation. In *Proceedings of the 2019 Conference on Empirical Methods in Natural Language Processing and the 9th International Joint Conference on Natural Language Processing (EMNLP-IJCNLP)*, pages 1876–1885, Hong Kong, China. Association for Computational Linguistics.

Liliang Ren, Kaige Xie, Lu Chen, and Kai Yu. 2018. Towards universal dialogue state tracking. In *Proceedings of the 2018 Conference on Empirical Methods in Natural Language Processing*, pages 2780–2786, Brussels, Belgium. Association for Computational Linguistics.

Ashish Vaswani, Noam Shazeer, Niki Parmar, Jakob Uszkoreit, Llion Jones, Aidan N. Gomez, Lukasz Kaiser, and Illia Polosukhin. 2017. Attention is all you need. In *Advances in Neural Information Processing Systems 30: Annual Conference on Neural Information Processing Systems 2017, December 4-9, 2017, Long Beach, CA, USA*, pages 5998–6008.

Tsung-Hsien Wen, David Vandyke, Nikola Mrkšić, Milica Gašić, Lina M. Rojas-Barahona, Pei-Hao Su, Stefan Ultes, and Steve Young. 2017. A network-based end-to-end trainable task-oriented dialogue system. In *Proceedings of the 15th Conference of the European Chapter of the Association for Computational Linguistics: Volume 1, Long Papers*, pages 438–449, Valencia, Spain. Association for Computational Linguistics.

Chien-Sheng Wu, Andrea Madotto, Ehsan Hosseini-Asl, Caiming Xiong, Richard Socher, and Pascale Fung. 2019. Transferable multi-domain state generator for task-oriented dialogue systems. In *Proceedings of the 57th Annual Meeting of the Association for Computational Linguistics*, pages 808–819, Florence, Italy. Association for Computational Linguistics.

Yunyi Yang, Yunhao Li, and Xiaojun Quan. 2021. Ubar: Towards fully end-to-end task-oriented dialog system with gpt-2. In *Proceedings of the AAAI Conference on Artificial Intelligence*, volume 35, pages 14230–14238.

Xiaoxue Zang, Abhinav Rastogi, Srinivas Sunkara, Raghav Gupta, Jianguo Zhang, and Jindong Chen. 2020. MultiWOZ 2.2 : A dialogue dataset with additional annotation corrections and state tracking baselines. In *Proceedings of the 2nd Workshop on Natural Language Processing for Conversational AI*, pages 109–117, Online. Association for Computational Linguistics.

Yan Zeng and Jian-Yun Nie. 2020. Multi-domain dialogue state tracking–a purely transformer-based generative approach. *arXiv preprint arXiv:2010.14061*.

Jianguo Zhang, Kazuma Hashimoto, Chien-Sheng Wu, Yao Wang, Philip Yu, Richard Socher, and Caiming Xiong. 2020. Find or classify? dual strategy for slot-value predictions on multi-domain dialog state tracking. In *Proceedings of the Ninth Joint Conference on Lexical and Computational Semantics*, pages 154–167, Barcelona, Spain (Online). Association for Computational Linguistics.

Victor Zhong, Caiming Xiong, and Richard Socher. 2018. Global-locally self-attentive encoder for dialogue state tracking. In *Proceedings of the 56th Annual Meeting of the Association for Computational Linguistics (Volume 1: Long Papers)*, pages 1458–1467, Melbourne, Australia. Association for Computational Linguistics.

Su Zhu, Jieyu Li, Lu Chen, and Kai Yu. 2020. Efficient context and schema fusion networks for multi-domain dialogue state tracking. In *Findings of the Association for Computational Linguistics: EMNLP 2020*, pages 766–781, Online. Association for Computational Linguistics.

A Error Propagation Analysis

Our model learns simultaneously the implicit state operation prediction and value generation by a single generation model with dialogue state memory. Indeed, such joint learning can boost the performance of the *update* gate. Because the traditional method needs to predict the state operation firstly, and then use another component to predict the corresponding value, which leads to error propagation. The *update* gate accuracy and the value generation F1 under the *update* gate are given in Table 8.[3] Compared with the SOM-DST, our AG-DST attains better results of both gate accuracy and value F1. This implies that the coupling structure we used is beneficial to learning *update* gate and corresponding value prediction.

B Case Study

Table 9 indicates the the amendable ability of the AG-DST. On the test set of MultiWOZ 2.2, the total number of improved examples for the three error types is 313. AG-DST was able to amend the slot value during the amending generation, when the basic generation decoded nothing or a wrong value.

[3]Note that for our model, the state operation can be concluded from the difference between last and current dialogue states.

Model	Acc	F1
SOM-DST	70.50	78.58
AG-DST	**72.77**	**79.84**

Table 8: The comparison of *update* gate accuracy and corresponding value generation F1 between SOM-DST (Kim et al., 2020) and our basic generation on MultiWOZ 2.2.

C Attention Visualization of State Operation Prediction

Figure 6 shows the attention visualization of different state operations on test set of MultiWOZ 2.2. From the *update* gate and *dontcare* gate attention visualizations in Figure 6a and 6b, we can easily find that the slot values attend to the corresponding tokens in the utterance with a highest weight. Figure 6c indicates that an implicit copy mechanism is used for the *carryover* gate. Figure 7 shows the attention visualization of *delete* gate and *coreference* phenomenon. For *delete* gate in Figure 7a, it is easily seen that the model can grasp the information in the user utterance to generate appropriate <nm> slot value. As shown in Figure 7b, when the user only said "from the restaurant to the hotel", the model can extract the corresponding restaurant and hotel names from DS memory. This indicates that our model is able to handle the *coreference* operation. Most examples of this *coreference* phenomenon appear in *taxi* domain.

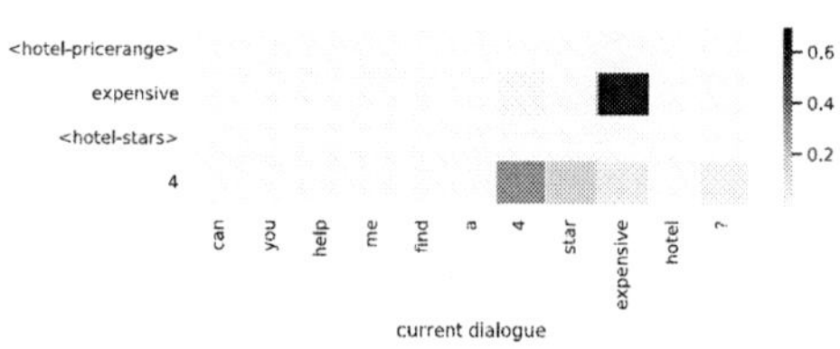

(a) *update* gate

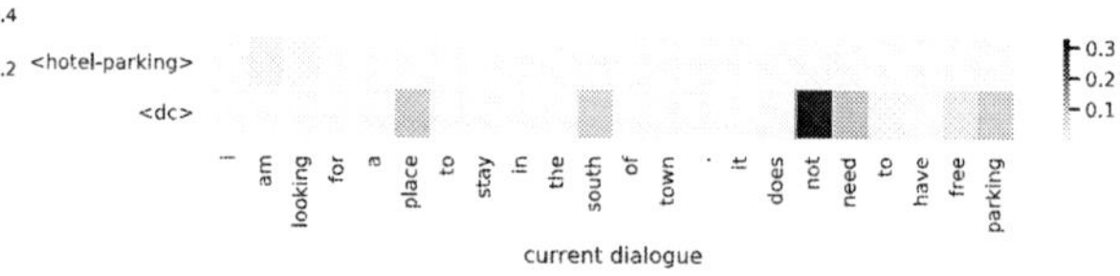

(b) *dontcare* gate

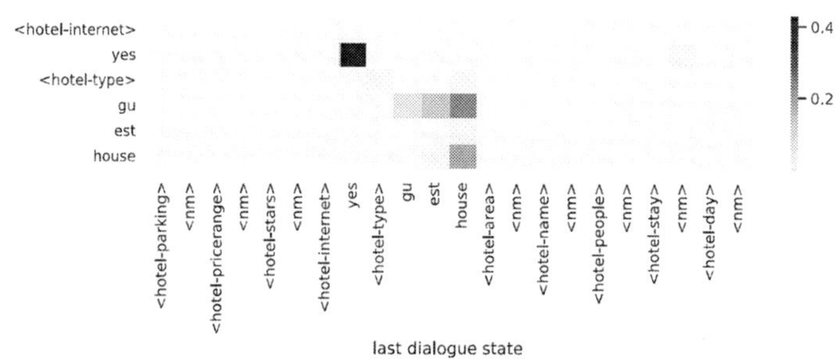

(c) *carryover* gate

Figure 6: The attention visualization of state operation on MultiWOZ 2.2.

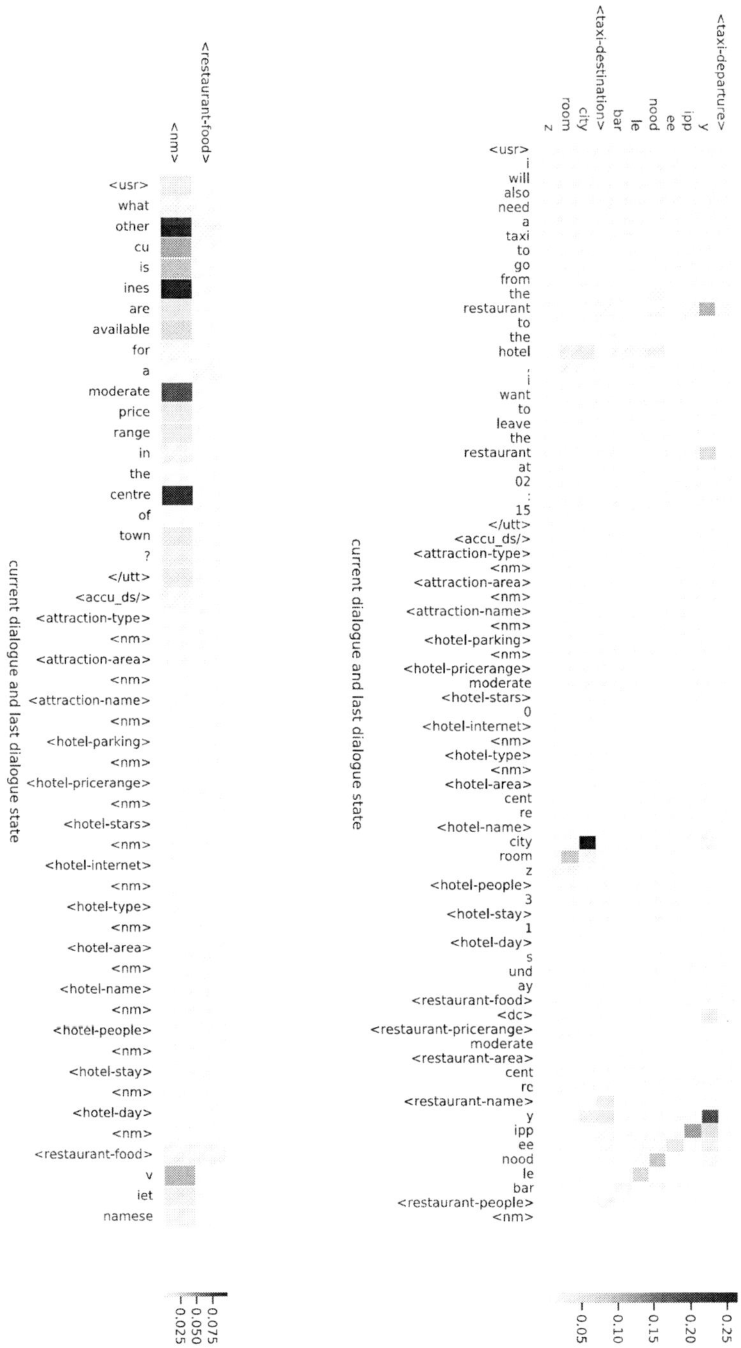

(a) *delete* gate (b) *coreference* phenomenon

Figure 7: The attention visualization of *delete* gate and *coreference* phenomenon on MultiWOZ 2.2.

Current Turn Dialogue	Previous Dialogue State $\hat{B}_{t-1}$	Primitive Dialogue State $\tilde{B}_t$	Amended Dialogue State $\hat{B}_t$
R_t: no , i am sorry . i am searching for a 4 star hotel in the centre for 2 nights on saturday . is that correct ? U_t: i need the hotel for *3 nights* starting on saturday please .	hotel-stay-2	hotel-stay-2	hotel-stay-3
R_t: ok , and what day and time would you like that reservation ? U_t: i would like to make a reservation for saturday at 11:45 . and there has been *a change in plans , i will be dining alone* .	restaurant-people-2	restaurant-people-2	restaurant-people-1
R_t: hello . U_t: i am looking for info on expensive *south indian* restaurant -s in cambridge .	restaurant-food-<nm>	restaurant-food-indian	restaurant-food-south indian
R_t: ok , so you would like a taxi from the restaurant to the park ? could you please let me know your desired departure and arrival times ? U_t: i am sorry , i would like a taxi from *wandlebury country park* to taj tandoori . i would like the taxi to pick me up at 10:15 .	taxi-departure-byard art	taxi-departure-byard art	taxi-departure-wandlebury country park
R_t: yes , <name/> *wandlebury country park* </name> is in the south . in order to help you book a taxi between the park and your hotel , i need to know what hotel you are at . U_t: i want a taxi from the restaurant that i am at	taxi-destination-kohinoor	taxi-destination-kohinoor	taxi-destination-wandlebury country park
R_t: i am sorry , i am experiencing a system error . could you please restate your request ? U_t: i want a place to go in the south , *a swimmingpool . or another type of entertainment* , if there is no pool ?	attraction-type-swimmingpool	attraction-type-entertainment	attraction-type-swimmingpool
R_t: <name/> caffe uno </name> is a very nice , expensive italian restaurant in the center of town . would you like a table there ? U_t: actually , *i change my mind* . i think i want to stick with british food after all . can you suggest any 1 thats in the centre of town ?	restaurant-name-clowns	restaurant-name-clowns	restaurant-name-<nm>
R_t: <name/> primavera </name> is a museum in the center of town . their address is 10 king s parade . what else can i help with ? U_t: oh , i made a mistake . i really need that table *for 16:15 , not 17:45* . can you change it , do you thing ?	restaurant-time-17:45	restaurant-time-17:45	restaurant-time-16:15
R_t: there are 5 museums in the west . i recommend *kettle 's yard* . would you like the address and phone ? U_t: yes , i would love the address . thank you so much !	attraction-name-cambridge punter	attraction-name-cambridge punter	attraction-name-kettles yard
R_t: you would like a second hotel , for which night and location ? U_t: i am sorry , i do not want a second hotel . i need a taxi between *the bed and breakfast* and the restaurant that arrives to the restaurant by the booked time .	taxi-departure-<nm>	taxi-departure-<nm>	taxi-departure-alexander bed and breakfast
R_t: to clarify you wanted me to book a table on friday ? U_t: i am sorry . my train was supposed to be for *tuesday* as well as my restaurant reservation .	train-day-<nm>	train-day-<nm>	train-day-tuesday
R_t: there are 5 choices . to narrow down you need to choose the side of town you prefer U_t: *area does not matter* , but it should be a guest house with a 4 star rating .	hotel-area-<nm>	hotel-area-<nm>	hotel-area-<dc>
R_t: the entrance fee is unknown . can i help you with anything else today ? U_t: i would also like a taxi to *arrive at the restaurant* on time . can i have the taxis phone number and vehicle type ?	taxi-destination-<nm>	taxi-destination-tajione restaurant and coffee bar	taxi-destination-stazione restaurant and coffee bar
R_t: okay ! they are at king's parade , cb21rl . their phone number is 01223338300 . what time would you like to depart in the taxi ? U_t: i need a taxi to *commute between the 2 place -s . i need to leave the restaurant* by 18:15 and need the contact # and car type	taxi-destination-<nm>	taxi-destination-saint catharine's college	taxi-destination-saint catharines college
R_t: i have got you a reservation for 6 at *hobson 's house* for 2 nights . your reference number is 4wngilmf . U_t: thank you so much ! that should be all i need .	hotel-name-<nm>	hotel-name-hobson's house	hotel-name-hobsons house
R_t: is there anything i can do for you ? U_t: i would like a taxi to the *cafe jello gallery* please .	taxi-destination-<nm>	taxi-destination-caffe jello gallery	taxi-destination-cafe jello gallery
R_t: <name/> *camboats* </name> is located at the plough , green end , fen ditton , in the east side of town U_t: ok ! thank you ! can you get me a taxi to cambots ?	taxi-destination-<nm>	taxi-destination-cambots	taxi-destination-camboats
R_t: the postcode is cb28rj for <name/> *bridge guest house* </name> . what time do you want to be *picked up at the guest house* or to arrive at eraina ? U_t: okay i need a taxi too .	taxi-destination-eraina	taxi-destination-eraina	taxi-destination-bridge guest house

Table 9: Examples of the amending generation. The key information in the dialogue is shown in blue.

What Went Wrong?
Explaining Overall Dialogue Quality through Utterance-Level Impacts

James D. Finch* Dept. of Computer Science Emory University Atlanta, GA, USA jdfinch@emory.edu

Sarah E. Finch* Dept. of Computer Science Emory University Atlanta, GA, USA sfillwo@emory.edu

Jinho D. Choi Dept. of Computer Science Emory University Atlanta, GA, USA jinho.choi@emory.edu

Abstract

Improving user experience of a dialogue system often requires intensive developer effort to read conversation logs, run statistical analyses, and intuit the relative importance of system shortcomings. This paper presents a novel approach to automated analysis of conversation logs that learns the relationship between user-system interactions and overall dialogue quality. Unlike prior work on utterance-level quality prediction, our approach learns the impact of each interaction from the overall user rating without utterance-level annotation, allowing resultant model conclusions to be derived on the basis of empirical evidence and at low cost. Our model identifies interactions that have a strong correlation with the overall dialogue quality in a chatbot setting. Experiments show that the automated analysis from our model agrees with expert judgments, making this work the first to show that such weakly-supervised learning of utterance-level quality prediction is highly achievable.

1 Introduction

A typical life cycle of a dialogue system involves many iterative updates where developers improve the system's language understanding capabilities and attempt to increase the overall user engagement. One of the most challenging aspects of executing these updates is to identify characteristics of the dialogue system that are impacting user experience the most. Doing so often involves manually crawling potentially thousands of system logs and designing statistical analyses, both of which are time consuming and unlikely to provide a holistic view of a system's shortcomings.

Inspired by this problem, the presented work investigates the extent to which it is possible to automatically distinguish turns within chat-oriented dialogues that have a negative effect on overall dialogue quality. The interpretation of dialogue quality is especially difficult in the chat-oriented dialogue setting due to its subjective and multi-faceted objectives. System misunderstandings and low user engagement are factors of low quality that are relatively easy to identify, but more subtle factors such as boring responses, awkward topic switches, and individual preferences can also have a substantial effect. Furthermore, the practical value of any approach to estimate the quality of individual dialogue turns is highly sensitive to the cost of collecting relevant data. Chatbots, and the settings they are placed in, can differ drastically in both their topics of conversation and interaction styles. And while conversation-level quality labels can be obtained relatively quickly by asking users to provide a rating at the end of a conversation, collecting data with turn-level labels that adequately characterizes a new chatbot or chat setting is an expensive process.

In this paper we present our dialogue analysis approach, which addresses these challenges by producing quality scores for each utterance in a given conversation dataset using only conversation-level quality ratings. Unlike other work that focuses on utterance-level quality prediction using labeled data, our approach involves training a neural model to learn explicit relationships between utterance-level features and conversation quality without the need for costly utterance-level annotations. We evaluate this approach on two conversation datasets and show high agreement between our model and experts for identifying problematic interactions. By developing an empirical technique that models the relationship between specific interactions and overall conversation quality, our work has the potential to remove much of the human effort and guesswork involved in dialogue system development.

2 Related Work

Related work has explored techniques for modelling dialogue quality on both the conversation and utterance level. Sandbank et al. (2018) present

Proceedings of the Third Workshop on Natural Language Processing for Conversational AI, pages 93–101
November 10, 2021.

an approach for classifying low-quality conversations in commercial conversational assistants. Liang et al. (2020) argued against the feasability of conversation-level quality prediction on a Likert-scale and present a pairwise comparison model instead using methods that compensated for the high noise in user scores. Choi et al. (2019) presents methods for both predicting user satisfaction and detecting conversation breakdowns at the turn level. Ghazarian et al. (2020)'s work is similar, predicting utterance-level user engagement.

Ghazarian et al. (2020) and Choi et al. (2019)'s work is similar to ours, as they build models targeted towards utterance-level quality outcomes. However, unlike our approach, these works are reliant on costly turn-level annotations: given conversations annotated for quality on the utterance level, their approach is to train a model that can predict utterance quality on unseen conversations within a similar conversation setting. This strategy incurs a substantial cost whenever the training data needs to be updated to fit a novel conversational setting or chatbot.

To avoid the cost of collecting turn-level labels, our approach is more in line with techniques such as multiple regression analysis, where fitting a model to a dataset is used to explain the relationship between features and some outcome, rather than to predict an outcome for unseen examples. In our case, our model can be fit to any dataset of conversations with conversation-level quality labels in order to estimate the quality impact of each utterance on the overall conversation quality. This approach has a couple advantages over existing work. First, collecting utterance-level annotations in a supervised setting is not necessary for our approach as it was for Choi et al. (2019) and Ghazarian et al. (2020). Second, our model learns empirically-derived relationships between the utterance level and conversation quality, rather than learning to mimic human judgements of utterance level quality irrespective of conversation-level impact. Given the unreliability of human judgements on conversation quality noted in prior work (Liang et al., 2020), it is possible that removing human estimations of the relationship between turn-level and conversation-level quality eliminates a source of bias in the model's training objective. To our knowledge, no previous work has presented an approach for utterance-level quality estimation that does not require data annotated on the turn level.

3 Aggregated Regression Analysis

We utilize a neural network model to accomplish this task of utterance-level quality inference. It learns to assign scores to utterances within a dialogue such that it maximizes its ability to produce correct dialogue-level quality scores from aggregation of these utterance scores.

Our Aggregated Regression Analysis (ARA) neural model takes as input the entire sequence of utterances for a single dialogue and outputs the predicted dialogue quality q on a continuous scale. Each utterance is first embedded into a continuous space vector representation, producing a sequence of embeddings $(u_1, ..., u_N)$. The rating r_i and weight w_i of each utterance embedding are then assigned through learned linear transformations of the embedding. The linear transformations are learned independently for the ratings and the weights:

$$r_i = u_i v_r^T + b_r \quad (1)$$

$$w_i = \sigma(u_i v_w^T + b_w) \quad (2)$$

where parameters v_r, b_r and v_w, b_w are learned weights and biases for the rating and weight calculations, respectively.

The final dialogue quality prediction q is then calculated as the weighted sum of the utterance ratings as follows, where N is the total number of utterances in a given dialogue:

$$q = \frac{\sum_{i=0}^{N} r_i w_i}{\sum_{i=0}^{N} w_i} \quad (3)$$

We also extend this approach to capture inter-utterance interactions by including an utterance contextualization step. The original utterance embeddings $(u_1, ..., u_N)$ are passed through a contextualization layer to generate a contextualized utterance embedding for each utterance i as h_i. The resultant rating and weight calculations follow Equations 1 and 2 with u_i replaced by h_i. This final architecture is shown in Figure 1.
Although our task is to quantify the relationship between individual utterances and conversation quality, our model is formulated as a conversation-level quality predictor in order to fit to datasets where conversation quality labels are available. Since the top layers of our architecture enforce

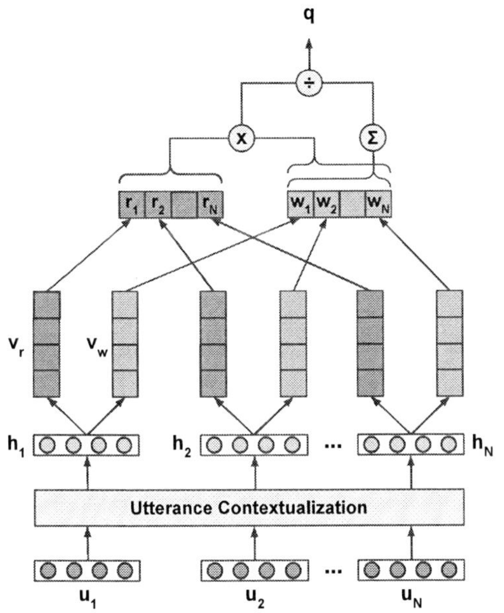

Figure 1: Model architecture for predicting dialogue quality by aggregating predicted utterance ratings and weights with contextualization.

this conversation-level prediction to be constructed from individual ratings and weights of each utterance in the conversation, this conversation quality prediction architecture can be applied to the model analysis task that is the focus of this paper. After fitting this model to a conversation dataset with quality labels, utterance-level effects on quality can be inferred by extracting the ratings and weights of each utterance from the model's intermediate output. The final inferred impact score s_i of each utterance u_i on the conversation quality is then simply given as a product of the rating and weight:

$$s_i = r_i * w_i \quad (4)$$

4 Experiment

4.1 Data

Our task requires dialogue datasets that contain dialogue-level quality ratings. However, to measure the success of inferring utterance-level impacts from these dialogue-level quality ratings, we need to evaluate any approach on this task against dialogues that also contain utterance-level ratings. To our knowledge, there are two publically available datasets that provide both dialogue-level and utterance-level quality ratings: Amazon's Topical-Chat (Gopalakrishnan et al., 2019) and the First Conversational Intelligence Challenge (ConvAI) (Burtsev et al., 2018).

Although Topical-Chat obtained human annotations on utterance quality, there are several limitations to these annotations that make them unsuitable as an evaluation dataset for our task. For one, the quality of the utterance-level annotations is questionable. Through a preliminary analysis of the dataset, we observed many cases where we could not justify the human annotator's ratings. In fact, 99% of the utterance-level annotations received a rating of 4 or 5, and annotators seemed likely to give such a rating with no regard to the coherence of the utterance in its context. Additionally, even if the annotation reliability was not in question, this dramatic bias towards a small subset of the rating classes also leads to the dataset containing a substantial lack of variety in utterance quality, which would make this dataset uninteresting as an evaluation method. For these reasons, we choose to exclude Topical-Chat from our evaluation.

On the other hand, ConvAI contains more distributed utterance-level ratings that did not raise the same quality concerns upon our preliminary analysis. As a result, we include ConvAI in the evaluation of this task. In addition, we augmented a subset of the dialogues collected through our participation in the 2019 Alexa Prize with utterance-level annotations. We use this augmented dataset for evaluation as well. More details on these included datasets are provided next.

ConvAI ConvAI was held as a Competition Workshop at NIPS 2017, where 10 teams submitted bots that were able to hold conversations with humans on short text news articles. During evaluation of the bots, humans provided a dialogue quality rating at the conclusion of their conversation, and also had the option of rating each of their conversational partner's turns using an online good/bad indicator. We heldout 200 conversations from the overall dataset as development and test splits. Table 1 shows statistics of the remaining ConvAI conversations (N=2,459) used for training and utterance-level evaluation.

AP19 AP19 consists of dialogues that we collected during the 2019 Amazon Alexa Prize Competition (Gabriel et al., 2020). These dialogues occurred between Amazon Alexa users and one socialbot from the 2019 competition. This socialbot

Rating	1	2	3	4	5
Dialogues	1100	537	345	308	169
Proportion	44.7	21.8	14.0	12.5	6.9
Avg. Turns	5.99	12.06	12.98	12.38	13.05
Good Turns	406	726	720	1262	783
Bad Turns	1371	1168	623	320	111

Table 1: Statistics for the ConvAI dataset.

was developed to hold in-depth chat-oriented conversations on a wide variety of topics with users, including sports, pets, work, and family. Dialogues were rated by the user at the conclusion of the dialogue on a voluntary basis by providing a numeric score between one and five in response to the question of how much they would want to talk to this socialbot again.

The AP19 dataset was collected between March and July of 2020. Dialogues with less than 5 utterances were excluded because we observed that such dialogues frequently occurred due to unintentional invocation of the Alexa Prize skill. We heldout 4873 conversations as development and test splits each. Table 2 shows statistics of the remaining AP19 conversations (N=38,693) used for training and utterance-level evaluation.

Rating	1	2	3	4	5
Dialogues	4785	4534	5965	8385	15024
Proportion	12.4	11.7	15.4	21.7	38.8
Avg. Turns	26.04	30.22	32.80	36.57	34.98

Table 2: Statistics for the AP19 dataset.

4.2 Models

We trained 3 variants of the ARA model presented in Section 3, including both the non-contextualized base version and two extensions using different contextualization methods:

Non-Contextualized This is the base ARA model from Section 3 that does not utilize contextualization of the utterance embeddings.

Order Driven Contextualization ARA-O extends the base model by using a bidirectional LSTM layer in order to target the importance of utterance order when determining utterance quality.

Attention Based Contextualization ARA-A extends the base model by using a self-attention layer to incorporate long-range cross-utterance relationships when determining utterance quality.

We also include an additional baseline model:

Non-Aggregated Regression Analysis NARA is trained on the task of directly predicting utterance scores, instead of a final dialogue score. It employs a heuristic for obtaining target scores for utterances, where each utterance score is equal to the dialogue score in which it occurs. This problem is treated as a sequence regression task, where the model takes as input a sequence of utterances for a given conversation and the utterances are first contextualized using a bidirectional LSTM layer before being passed through a fully connected layer to output the predicted score for each.

4.3 Model Configurations

Utterances are embedded using the DistilBERT version of Sentence-BERT (SBERT) by Reimers and Gurevych (2019). SBERT is a sentence encoder utilizing a siamese neural network architecture and BERT-based embeddings that has been shown to outperform other methods of encoding sentences on a variety of downstream NLP tasks.

For all ARA-derivative models, hyperparameters were chosen such that they yielded the best-performing models at predicting conversation quality according to Pearson's correlation on a development set of the data. For NARA, the decision was based on performance on utterance-level quality prediction instead. Details on the final configurations are provided in Appendix A.

4.4 Dialogue Quality Regression Results

Table 3 shows the performance of our models on predicting overall dialogue quality. Previous works have shown the difficulty of this task, the noisiness of user ratings, and the low agreement between independent human annotators on the same conversations (Liang et al., 2020; Finch and Choi, 2020). As noted in Section 4.3, we used the development performance for hyperparameter tuning only.

	AP19		ConvAI	
Model	Dev	Test	Dev	Test
ARA	0.34	0.33	0.29	0.27
ARA-O	0.37	0.36	0.44	0.39
ARA-A	0.36	0.35	0.34	0.25
NARA	0.36	0.35	0.40	0.20

Table 3: Pearson's r correlations achieved by each model on the dev/test data.

5 Evaluation

Evaluating our model is challenging because it requires human judgements about the magnitude and direction of effect of each utterance on the quality of the conversation it is a part of. Annotating quality on an utterance level is already a difficult task with much subjectivity involved (Higashinaka et al., 2016). Furthermore, asking humans to annotate quality using real numbered values results in arbitrary judgements of magnitude, further complicating a direct evaluation of our task. Nevertheless, a model that appropriately assigns utterance scores in a way that explains each utterance's relative impact to the conversation quality should agree substantially with judgements of human experts.

We address these challenges by presenting two evaluation procedures that approximate the ground truth of our task formulation while framing all human judgements as non-arbitrary decisions with high inter-annotator agreement. These evaluations focus especially on utterances that have a substantial negative effect on conversation quality, since this case is most in line with the main motivations of our work to automatically identify problematic interactions.

5.1 Human-Led Evaluation

Our first evaluation is motivated by the idea that a good model should score interactions with well-known issues lower than most other interactions. To measure this, human annotators provide binary judgements on the quality of each utterance. Given these human annotations, we evaluate our model by treating the binary utterance-level annotations as a partial ordering of the impact of each utterance on the conversation rating against which we can measure the agreement of the model's full ranking of utterances composed of their assigned scores. This agreement is represented by the C-Index as used by Steck et al. (2008), which measures the extent to which pairs of items in a predicted ranking agree with some ground-truth partial ranking.

ConvAI The ConvAI dataset was released with utterance-level ratings by human annotators. Human users provided a binary rating to utterances indicating whether it was good or bad on a voluntary basis. Thus, we use these ratings provided by the human users for the automatic evaluation of our proposed approach on the ConvAI dataset.

AP19 Although AP19 contains dialogue-level quality ratings from human users, it does not contain such ratings for utterances. To this end, we construct an evaluation dataset by asking experts to pick out issues within each dialogue that are likely to cause a lower user rating. We specifically investigate two types of issues: system misunderstandings and user dissatisfaction. These two issue types are prevalent in our AP19 data and are a frequent cause of conversation quality degradation.

Two of the authors annotated issues in these two categories on 100 randomly sampled dialogues from our AP19 dataset. Sampling was restricted to only select dialogues with less than a 5 quality rating, since high-rated conversations often have no major problems. The following guidelines were used to annotate each dialogue:

1. Out of the system utterances that signaled a misunderstanding, mark the one that was most likely to negatively impact the user rating.
2. Out of the user utterances that signaled dissatisfaction, mark the one that most strongly indicated that the user was dissatisfied.
3. If the severity of two or more system misunderstandings or user dissatisfaction signals cannot be discriminated, mark all of them.

All conversations in the sample were doubly annotated, with an interannotator agreement (Cohen's kappa) of 0.674 For evaluation purposes, we ignore utterances that the annotators did not agree on, with the final evaluation containing 158 issue utterances and 3020 non-issue utterances.

5.1.1 Human-Led Evaluation Results

Model	AP19	ConvAI
NARA	0.760	0.739
ARA	0.712	0.574
ARA-O	0.807	0.728
ARA-A	0.638	0.599

Table 4: Average model performance (C-Index) on ranking utterances with respect to human annotations.

Table 4 shows the performance of our proposed approach in predicting the correct quality ranking of utterances. These results are based on the average performance across three independent iterations of each model fitted on the datasets. Across all versions of the evaluation, our proposed approach using the order-driven contextualization (ARA-O) displays strong performance, achieving a C-Index of 0.807 on AP19 and 0.728 on ConvAI. For ConvAI, however, ARA-O is slightly outperformed by the NARA baseline. For AP19, the attention-based contextualization (ARA-A) configuration performs much worse, producing performance that is lower than either of the baselines, although it outperforms the base ARA for ConvAI. We observe that ARA-A is prone to significant overfitting which may account for this poor performance.

We also investigated the transferability of the best-performing model trained on one dataset (AP19) to another (ConvAI) shown in Table 5. On its own, the model performs poorly on the out-of-domain dialogues which we expected. When fine-tuned on ConvAI, its performance is comparable to a model trained only on the ConvAI dataset.

	ConvAI
AP19 ARA-O	0.506
+ Finetune	0.724

Table 5: Performance of model trained on AP19 when applied to ConvAI.

We include the C-Index scores of the annotators against each other (Table 6) in order to provide a strong comparison for our models. Although the difference between our best model and human performance is not too great, there is still a small gap in performance.

	Annot. 1	**Annot. 2**
Annot. 1	-	0.823
Annot. 2	0.853	-

Table 6: Human annotator's agreement (C-Index) on utterance-level issue scores for AP19.

5.2 Model-Led Evaluation

A major limitation of our human-led evaluation is the restriction to only two kinds of issues. Although humans seem capable of judging when well-known problems like misunderstandings and dissatisfaction impact the dialogue quality, there are a number of non-obvious factors that contribute to the user's experience as well. Data-driven models have a greater potential than humans to uncover these factors, since they can make inferences based on information aggregated across thousands of conversations rather than on biased intuition. However, given that such a model outputs some estimation of an utterance's impact on conversation quality, that output should be verifiable by a human and agree substantially with expert judgement.

To account for a broader spectrum of factors that may affect conversation quality, we conducted an additional evaluation that asks experts to judge pairs of interactions, where one interaction was assigned a low score by the model and one was assigned a high score. We choose the 5th percentile as a cutoff to distinguish issues (low-scored) from non-issues (high-scored), and randomly sample one utterance from each side of the distribution to construct pairs. Sampling is not done at uniform random, since we observed in a pilot evaluation that this results in many similar samples that are often paraphrases of one another. Instead, we run k-means clustering on the pretrained SBERT embeddings of the bottom 5%-scored utterances and restrict our sampling to the k utterances closest to the centroid of each cluster. We chose k to be 1% of the total number of issue utterances being clustered, $k = 683$. This procedure ensures a high degree of variety among chosen samples, increasing the robustness of the evaluation.

Each sampled issue from the clustering procedure is paired with a non-issue drawn uniform-randomly from the upper 95%-scored utterances. Each pair of utterances is then presented to the human judge with random intra-pair order, so the judge is blind to which utterance was scored lower by the model. We allow judges to see two preceding utterances and one following utterances from the full conversation when viewing each example. Providing a context window of this size was done in order to focus the judgement on a specific interaction of the dialogue, while still providing sufficient background to interpret the sampled utterance correctly. Given expert judgements on these pairs, model accuracy is calculated as the proportion of times expert judgements agreed with model score assignments. We retrieve 300 pairs for evaluation from our AP19 dataset and two of the authors performed the evaluation.

5.2.1 Model-Led Evaluation Results

We conducted the Model-Led Evaluation on ARA-O for our AP19 dataset, since it outperformed all other models in the initial Human-Led Evaluation. Table 7 presents the model's ability to discriminate quality ratings between utterances. Our model is able to achieve an accuracy of 0.775 on average.

6 Error Analysis

We conducted an error analysis to determine the frequently occurring mistakes of the proposed approach. To do this, we manually reviewed the 70 utterance pairs and their contexts that resulted in disagreement between the system and at least one

	Accuracy
Annot. 1	0.77
Annot. 2	0.78
Average	0.775

Table 7: Model accuracy at identifying low-quality utterances. **Annot #** is relative to individual annotators' selections. **Average** takes the average of the annotators' accuracy results.

Mistake Type	Frequency	Percentage
Both Issues	37	53%
Both Non-issues	24	34%
Flipped Assignment	9	13%

Table 8: Distribution of the three mistake types.

annotator in the System-Led Evaluation. We created 3 categories that captured the underlying problems that caused the disagreement. *Both Issues* contains cases where the non-issue selection was as problematic as its issue selection. *Both Non-issues* represents cases where the issue selection was not interpretable as a problematic conversation exchange. *Flipped Assignment* captures the cases where the non-issue selection was more problematic than the issue selection. Table 8 illustrates the distribution of identified mistake categories across the 70 pairs, with examples shown in Table 10.

Dialogue Pattern	Issue Prop.	Nonissue Prop.
Stop Request	20%	7%
Irrelevant Topic	16%	6%
Topic Switch Request	13%	3%
Unengaging Handoff	11%	3%

Table 9: Distribution of the dialogue patterns within system-selected issue contexts and nonissue contexts.

Upon closer analysis of these disagreed pairs, we observed some dialogue patterns that had high correlation with the system assigning a low score to an utterance as shown in Table 9. Using a context window of size 2 around the selected issue, we observed the following patterns:

Stop Request the selected issue was within one turn of the user requesting the conversation to be over.

Irrelevant Topic the selected issue occurred near the user sharing that they did not have a particular trait (e.g. not in school, no job, no pets, etc.).

Topic Switch Request the selected issue was within one turn of the user requesting a new topic.

Unengaging Handoff the selected issue was within one turn of the system transitioning out of one topic using one of three unengaging statements, such as *Ok well I find it inspiring that we have so many different types of music to listen to*.

The frequency of these dialogue patterns is shown in Table 9 and examples illustrating these dialogue patterns can be found in Table 10.

These dialogue patterns were present in many of the pairs in the *Both Non-issues* class. In isolation, the instances of these dialogue patterns do not seem indicative of a problematic conversational interaction; however, when taken as an emergent pattern, they begin to illuminate types of interactions that may be subtly indicative of poor user experience. For instance, there would be no reason to request a new topic or to end the conversation if the user was enjoying themselves, thus these actions are a good indication of the user being dissatisfied. Similarly, our socialbot was better equipped to talk about certain life traits, such as being in school or having a pet, and the analogous conversation for those users who did not fit those categories were not as strong. It could be the case that the model's selection of such utterances was not incorrect and rather it was reaching appropriate conclusions based on a large volume of information it was working with, whereas the human annotators were unaware of this, although it is impossible to verify this through our evaluation procedure.

On the other hand, for the *Stop Request* category, it could also be the case that the model is overrelying on the stop utterances as a negative signal. Knowing the end of the conversation provides the model with the opportunity to make any last-second corrections to achieve the dialogue quality it needs to assign for the current conversation.

7 Discussion

By achieving a C-Index score of 0.80 and 0.72 on the AP19 and ConvAI datasets respectively, our approach demonstrates the feasability of inferring utterance-level quality information from aggregation over a dataset of rated conversations. Since C-Index is a generalization of the AUC curve, random decision-making would result in a performance of 0.5, thus we obtain improvements of over 20% against random.

The success of our proposed approach on two datasets also demonstrates its applicability across different dialogue settings. A key difference be-

Example of system-chosen issue utterance:

System: Oh, that is unfortunate, you should definitely try it sometime, V R is slowly becoming the future of gaming. Another emerging area is augmented reality, or A R . what do you think of augmented reality?
User: i don't know what that is
System: *You don't have any ideas? That is ok. It is still a relatively new thing, so it may be hard to form an opinion. If you were to play a mobile game using A R, what would make it the most fun, do you think?*
User: what is a r.

Example of system-chosen issue utterance with *Topic Switch Request*:

System: Yeah. You know I hear the grocery stores in affected areas have lots of empty shelves right now. I'm not sure how necessary it is, but have you been stocking up on supplies?
User: yeah
System: *I guess you can never be too prepared. You know, sometimes I think, if everyone just stayed home and avoided public areas for a couple weeks, the whole thing could just blow over. But realistically, I think slowing the virus down so that everyone doesn't get sick at once is the best we can hope for.*
User: let's talk about the drivers

Example of system-chosen non-issue utterance to which annotators disagreed:

System: Yeah, that is true. There are probably many difficult pieces in the puzzle of teleportation, but we can leave that up to the scientists. I cannot seem to remember any movies that involve teleportation, can you?
User: i don't know
System: *Good one. I will have to remember that. Ok. tell me, what was the last movie you liked?*
User: i like joker

Table 10: Examples illustrating highlights and shortcomings of the proposed approach, where the utterances assigned a low quality are indicated by italics. These examples are similar to interactions seen in the Alexa Prize logs (conversations have been modified to protect customer privacy).

tween the AP19 and ConvAI datasets is their rating distributions: ConvAI was more right-skewed whereas AP19 was more left-skewed. In addition, the ConvAI dataset employs a text-based interface, includes both human-machine and human-human dialogues, and the dialogues were less socially-oriented. This suggests that our approach to utterance-level explainability is not constrained to only one dialogue system configuration.

It is worth noting that the NARA baseline slightly outperforms the presented approach on the ConvAI dataset. This suggests that parsing through all of the variability present in noisy quality ratings across users to determine utterance-level correlations is potentially challenging when given a small dataset. It may be more suitable to use the conversation rating as a heuristic utterance-level score target in these cases. However, the difference between the proposed approach and this baseline is not too great, so it is difficult to make a strong conclusion.

8 Conclusion

Our approach and evaluation results demonstrate the feasibility of an automatic approach for dialogue quality analysis. By training a model to learn the relationship between utterance-level features and conversation-level outcomes, it is possible to obtain an empirically-derived ranking of interactions based on whether they relate to positive or negative conversation quality. This work has obvious applications in dialogue system development, mitigating the high developer effort involved in manual analysis and human bias in determining the relative importance of system issues.

References

Mikhail Burtsev, Varvara Logacheva, Valentin Malykh, Iulian Vlad Serban, Ryan Lowe, Shrimai Prabhumoye, Alan W Black, Alexander Rudnicky, and Yoshua Bengio. 2018. The first conversational intelligence challenge. In *The NIPS'17 Competition: Building Intelligent Systems*, pages 25–46. Springer.

Jason Ingyu Choi, Ali Ahmadvand, and Eugene Agichtein. 2019. Offline and Online Satisfaction Prediction in Open-Domain Conversational Systems. In *Proceedings of the 28th ACM International Conference on Information and Knowledge Management*, CIKM '19, pages 1281–1290, Beijing, China. Association for Computing Machinery.

Sarah E. Finch and Jinho D. Choi. 2020. Towards unified dialogue system evaluation: A comprehensive analysis of current evaluation protocols. In *Proceedings of the 21st Annual Meeting of the Special Interest Group on Discourse and Dialogue*, pages 236–245, 1st virtual meeting. Association for Computational Linguistics.

Raefer Gabriel, Yang Liu, Anna Gottardi, Mihail Eric, Anju Khatri, Anjali Chadha, Qinlang Chen, Behnam Hedayatnia, Pankaj Rajan, Ali Binici, Shui Hu, Karthik Gopalakrishnan, Seokhwan Kim, Lauren

Stubel, Kate Bland, Arindam Mandal, and Dilek Hakkani-Tür. 2020. Further advances in open domain dialog systems in the third alexa prize socialbot grand challenge. *Alexa Prize 3 Proceedings*.

Sarik Ghazarian, Ralph Weischedel, Aram Galstyan, and Nanyun Peng. 2020. Predictive Engagement: An Efficient Metric For Automatic Evaluation of Open-Domain Dialogue Systems. *arXiv:1911.01456 [cs]*.

Karthik Gopalakrishnan, Behnam Hedayatnia, Qinglang Chen, Anna Gottardi, Sanjeev Kwatra, Anu Venkatesh, Raefer Gabriel, Dilek Hakkani-Tür, and Amazon Alexa AI. 2019. Topical-chat: Towards knowledge-grounded open-domain conversations. In *INTERSPEECH*, pages 1891–1895.

Ryuichiro Higashinaka, Kotaro Funakoshi, Yuka Kobayashi, and Michimasa Inaba. 2016. The dialogue breakdown detection challenge: Task description, datasets, and evaluation metrics. In *Proceedings of the Tenth International Conference on Language Resources and Evaluation (LREC'16)*, pages 3146–3150.

Weixin Liang, James Zou, and Zhou Yu. 2020. Beyond User Self-Reported Likert Scale Ratings: A Comparison Model for Automatic Dialog Evaluation. *ACL 2020*.

Nils Reimers and Iryna Gurevych. 2019. Sentence-bert: Sentence embeddings using siamese bert-networks. In *Proceedings of the 2019 Conference on Empirical Methods in Natural Language Processing and the 9th International Joint Conference on Natural Language Processing (EMNLP-IJCNLP)*, pages 3973–3983.

Tommy Sandbank, Michal Shmueli-Scheuer, Jonathan Herzig, David Konopnicki, John Richards, and David Piorkowski. 2018. Detecting Egregious Conversations between Customers and Virtual Agents. *Proceedings of NAACL-HLT*.

Harald Steck, Balaji Krishnapuram, Cary Dehing-Oberije, Philippe Lambin, and Vikas C Raykar. 2008. On ranking in survival analysis: Bounds on the concordance index. In *Advances in neural information processing systems*, pages 1209–1216.

A Data Preprocessing and Model Hyperparameters

AP19 All utterances in the AP19 dataset were preprocessed by removing all punctuation. All models were trained using the Adam optimizer with a learning rate of 0.00001 and Mean Squared Error loss function. All models had a dropout layer of 0.1 applied to the utterance embeddings. The *ARA-O* and *NARA* models had a hidden dimension of 200. The *ARA-A* had 1 layer with 1 head, hidden dimension 200, and dropout of 0.1 in the Transformer layer.

ConvAI All utterances in the ConvAI dataset were preprocessed by converting all symbols to a language representation (e.g. **>:(** to 'angry face', **lol** to 'laughing out loud', and so on) and then removing all remaining punctuation. In addition, multiple sequential utterances by the same speaker in a conversation were concatenated together into a single response.

All models were trained with the Adam optimizer with a learning rate of 0.00001 and Mean Squared Error loss function. All models had a dropout layer applied to the utterance embeddings (*ARA*: 0.2, *Others*: 0.1). The *ARA-O* and *NARA* models had a hidden dimension of 200. The *ARA-A* had 1 layer with 1 head, hidden dimension 100, and dropout of 0.1 in the Transformer layer.

XPersona: Evaluating Multilingual Personalized Chatbot

Zhaojiang Lin*, Zihan Liu*, Genta Indra Winata*, Samuel Cahyawijaya*, Andrea Madotto*, Yejin Bang, Etsuko Ishii, Pascale Fung
Center for Artificial Intelligence Research (CAiRE)
Department of Electronic and Computer Engineering
The Hong Kong University of Science and Technology, Clear Water Bay, Hong Kong
{zlinao,zliucr,giwinata,scahyawijaya,amadotto}@connect.ust.hk

Abstract

Personalized dialogue systems are an essential step toward better human-machine interaction. Existing personalized dialogue agents rely on properly designed conversational datasets, which are mostly monolingual (e.g., English), which greatly limits the usage of conversational agents in other languages. In this paper, we propose a multi-lingual extension of Persona-Chat (Zhang et al., 2018), namely XPersona. Our dataset includes persona conversations in six different languages other than English for evaluating multilingual personalized agents. We experiment with both multilingual and cross-lingual trained baselines, and evaluate them against monolingual and translation-pipeline models using both automatic and human evaluation. Experimental results show that the multilingual trained models outperform the translation-pipeline and that they are on par with the monolingual models, with the advantage of having a single model across multiple languages. On the other hand, the state-of-the-art cross-lingual trained models achieve inferior performance to the other models, showing that cross-lingual conversation modeling is a challenging task. We hope that our dataset and baselines [1] will accelerate research in multilingual dialogue systems.

1 Introduction

Personalized dialogue agents have been shown efficient in conducting human-like conversation. This progress has been catalyzed thanks to existing conversational dataset such as Persona-chat (Zhang et al., 2018; Dinan et al., 2019a). However, the training data are provided in a single language (e.g., English), and thus the resulting systems can perform conversations only in the training language. Commercial dialogue systems are required to handle a large number of languages since the smart home devices market is increasingly international (Etherington, 2019). Therefore, creating multilingual conversational benchmarks is essential, yet challenging since it is costly to perform human annotation of data in all languages.

A possible solution is to use translation systems before and after the model inference. This comes with three major problems: 1) amplification of translation errors since the current dialogue systems are far from perfect, especially with noisy input; 2) the three-stage pipeline system is significantly slower in terms of inference speed; and 3) high translation costs since the current state-of-the-art models, especially in low resources languages, are only available using costly APIs.

In this paper, we analyze two possible workarounds to alleviate the aforementioned challenges. The first is to build a cross-lingual transferable system by aligning cross-lingual representations, as in Conneau et al. (2018), in which the system is trained on one language and zero-shot to another language. The second is to learn a multilingual system directly from noisy multilingual data (e.g., translated data), thus getting rid of the translation system dependence at inference time.

To evaluate the aforementioned solutions, we propose a dataset called Multilingual Persona-Chat, or XPersona, by extending the Persona-Chat corpora (Dinan et al., 2019a) to six languages: Chinese, French, Indonesian, Italian, Korean, and Japanese. In XPersona, the training sets are automatically translated using translation APIs with several human-in-the-loop passes of mistake correction. In contrast, the validation and test sets are annotated by humans to facilitate both automatic and human evaluations in multiple languages.

Furthermore, we propose competitive baselines in two training settings, namely, cross-lingual and multilingual, and compare them with translation pipeline models. Our baselines leverage pre-

* Equal contributions. Listing order is random

[1] The code and dataset are available in https://github.com/HLTCHKUST/Xpersona.

Proceedings of the Third Workshop on Natural Language Processing for Conversational AI, pages 102–112
November 10, 2021.

Persona	I helped design the game starcraft. I am a famous twitch streamer..
En	**Sys:** do you know the game starcraft ? i helped designing it ! **Usr:** that s awesome , i m sure my ex boyfriend would like that game **Sys:** i usually stream the game on my twitch channel that s great , i also love twitch as well
It	**Sys:** conosci il gioco starcraft? ho aiutato a progettarlo! **Usr:** è fantastico, sono sicuro che al mio ex ragazzo gli piacerebbe **Sys:** di solito faccio streaming mentre gioco sul mio canale Twitch
Fr	**Sys:** connaissez-vous le jeu starcraft? j'ai aidé à le concevoir! **Usr:** c'est génial, je suis sûr que mon ex petit ami aimerait ce jeu **Sys:** Je diffuse généralement le jeu sur ma chaîne Twitch
Id	**Sys:** apakah anda tahu game starcraft? saya yang mendesainnya! **Usr:** itu luar biasa, saya yakin mantan pacar saya suka game itu. **Sys:** saya biasanya memainkan game itu di channel twitch saya.
Zh	**Sys:** 你知道游戏《星际争霸》吗？我帮忙设计了它！ **Usr:** 好厉害，我觉得我的前男友会喜欢那个游戏 **Sys:** 我经常在我的直播频道上直播游戏
Ko	**Sys:** 너 게임 스타크래프트를 아니? 나는 그것을 디자인하는 것을 도왔어! **Usr:** 멋진데, 내 전 남자친구가 그 게임을 좋아할 거라고 확신해. **Sys:** 나는 보통 내 트위치 채널로 그 게임을 스트리밍해.
Jp	**Sys:** ゲームのスタークラフトを知っていますか？私はそれを設計するのを助けました！ **Usr:** それはすごいです、私は私の元彼がそのゲームを好きになると確信しています **Sys:** 私は通常、twitchチャンネルでゲームをストリーミングします

Table 1: Multi-turn annotated dialogue samples from test set in seven languages. For simplicity, we only show three turns for each dialogue and the persona in English.

trained cross-lingual (Chi et al., 2019) and multilingual (Devlin et al., 2018) models.

An extensive automatic and human evaluation (Li et al., 2019) of our models shows that a multilingual system is able to outperform strong translation-based models and on par with or even improve the monolingual model. The cross-lingual performance is still lower than other models, which indicates that cross-lingual conversation modeling is very challenging. The main contributions of this paper are summarized as follows:

- We present the first multilingual non-goal-oriented dialogue benchmark for evaluating multilingual generative chatbots.
- We provide both cross-lingual and multilingual baselines and discuss their limitations to inspire future research.
- We show the potential of multilingual systems to understand the mixed language dialogue context and generate coherent responses.

2 Related Work

Dialogue Systems are categorized as goal-oriented and chit-chat. Interested readers may refer to Gao et al. (2018) for a general overview. In this paper, we focus on the latter, for which, in recent years, several tasks and datasets have been proposed to ground the conversation on knowledge (Dinan et al., 2019b; Gopalakrishnan et al., 2019; Fan et al., 2019; Reddy et al., 2019; Moon et al., 2019) such as Wiki-Articles, Reddit-Post, and CNN-Article. In this work, we focus on personalized dialogue agents where the dialogues are grounded on persona information.

Li et al. (2016a) was the first to introduce a persona-grounded dialogue dataset for improving response consistency. Later on, Zhang et al. (2018) and Dinan et al. (2019a) introduced Persona-chat, a multi-turn conversational dataset, where two speakers are paired, and a persona description (4–5 sentences) is randomly assigned to each of them. By conditioning the response generation on the persona descriptions, a chit-chat model is able to produce a more persona-consistent dialogue (Zhang et al., 2018). Several works have improved on the initial baselines with various methodologies, especially using large pre-trained models (Wolf et al., 2019).

Multilingual Extensive approaches have been introduced to construct multilingual systems, for example, multilingual semantic role labeling (Akbik et al., 2015), multilingual machine trans-

	Valid.				Test			
Lang	*#Dial.*	*#Utt.*	*Edit*	*BLEU*	*#Dial.*	*#Utt.*	*Edit*	*BLEU*
Fr	248	3868	21.23	94.45	249	3900	24.29	94.19
It	140	2160	83.01	80.45	140	2192	81.93	80.08
Id	484	7562	157.58	60.46	484	7540	156.19	60.66
Jp	275	4278	71.41	53.66	275	4322	75.83	49.56
Ko	299	4684	74.04	61.25	300	4678	70.96	62.49
Zh	222	3440	30.33	59.89	222	3458	33.07	64.61

Table 2: The statistics of the collected dataset. We report the number of dialogues (#Dial.) and utterances (#Utt.) of the validation and test set in six languages. Edit distance per dialogue (Edit) and BLEU score are computed to show the difference between the human-annotated dataset and auto-translated dataset (Training set is reported in Appendix A). The BLEU score also reflects the quality of machine translated dialogues.

lation (Johnson et al., 2017), and multilingual automatic speech recognition (Toshniwal et al., 2018). Multilingual deep contextualized model, such as Multilingual BERT (M-BERT) (Devlin et al., 2018), MT5 (Xue et al., 2021), MBART (Liu et al., 2020) have been commonly used to represent multiple languages and elevate the performance in many NLP applications, such as classification tasks (Pires et al., 2019), textual entailment, named entity recognition (K et al., 2020), and natural language understanding. Multilingual datasets have also been created for a number of NLP tasks, such as named entity recognition or linking (Pan et al., 2017; Aguilar et al., 2018), question answering (Liu et al., 2019; Lewis et al., 2019), dialogue state tracking (Mrkšić et al., 2017), and natural language understanding (Schuster et al., 2019). However, none of these datasets include the multilingual chit-chat task.

Cross-lingual Cross-lingual adaptation learns the inter-connections among languages and circumvents the requirement of extensive training data in target languages (Wisniewski et al., 2014; Zhang et al., 2016). Cross-lingual transfer learning methods have been applied to multiple NLP tasks, such as named entity recognition (Ni et al., 2017), dialogue state tracking (Chen et al., 2018), part-of-speech tagging (Wisniewski et al., 2014; Zhang et al., 2016; Kim et al., 2017), and dependency parsing (Ahmad et al., 2019). Meanwhile, Lample and Conneau (2019) and Conneau et al. (2019) proposed pre-trained cross-lingual language models to align multiple language representations, achieving state-of-the-art results in many cross-lingual classification tasks. The aforementioned tasks focused on classification and sequence labeling, while instead, Chi et al. (2019) proposed to pre-train both the encoder and decoder of a sequence-to-sequence model (XNLG) to conduct cross-lingual generation tasks, namely, question generation and abstractive summarization. The latter is the closest to our task since it focuses on language generation; however cross-lingual dialogue generation has not yet been explored.

3 Data Collection

The proposed XPersona dataset is an extension of the persona-chat dataset (Zhang et al., 2018; Dinan et al., 2019a). Specifically, we extend ConvAI2 (Dinan et al., 2019a) to six languages: Chinese, French, Indonesian, Italian, Korean, and Japanese. Since the test set of ConvAI2 is hidden, we split the original validation set into a new validation set and test sets. Then, we firstly automatically translate the training, validation, and test set using APIs (PapaGo for Korean, Google Translate for other languages). For each language, we hired native speaker annotators with at least a bachelor degree and a fluent level of English and asked them to revise the machine-translated dialogues and persona sentences in the validation set and test set according to original English dialogues. The main goal of human annotation is to ensure the revised conversations are coherent and fluent in target language despite the cultural discrepancy in different languages. Therefore, annotators are not restricted to translate the English dialogues. They are also **allowed** to customize dialogues and persona sentences. The annotated dialogues can deviate from original translation while **retain persona and conversation consistency**. The full annotation instructions are reported in Appendix A.

Compared to collecting new persona sentences and dialogues in each language, human-annotating

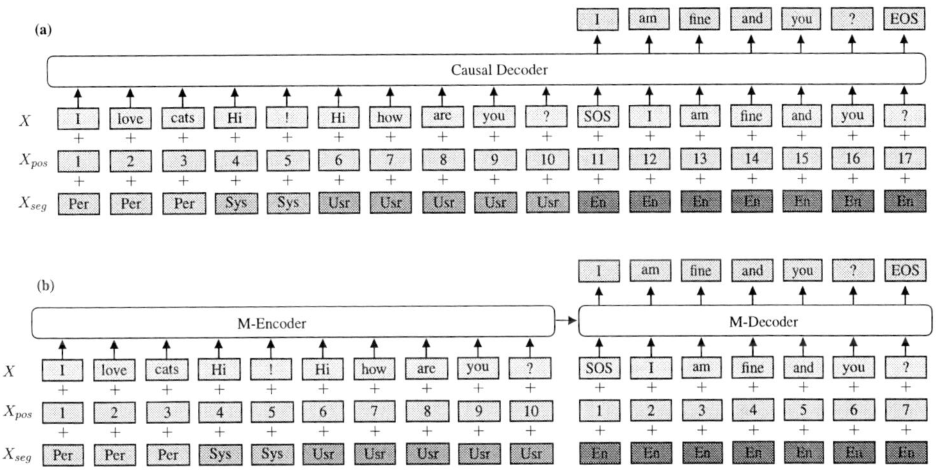

Figure 1: (a) Multilingual Causal Decoder model. (b) Multilingual Encoder-Decoder model.

the dialogues by leveraging translation APIs has multiple advantages. First, it increases the data distribution similarity across languages (Conneau et al., 2018), which can better examine the system's cross-lingual transferability. Second, revising the machine-translated dialogues based on the original English dialogue improves the data construction efficiency. Third, it leverages the well-constructed English persona conversations as a reference to ensure the dialogue quality without the need for training a new pool of workers to generate new samples (Conneau et al., 2018).

On the other hand, human-translating the entire training-set (~130K utterances) in six languages is expensive. Therefore, we propose an iterative method to improve the quality of the automatically translated training set. We firstly sample 200 dialogues from the training set (~2600 utterances) in each language, and we assign human annotators to list all frequent translation mistakes in the given dialogues. For example, daily colloquial English expressions such as "cool", "I see", and "lol" are usually literally translated. After that, we use a simple string matching to revise the inappropriate translations [2] in the whole training-set and return a revision log, which records all the revised utterances. Then, we assign human annotators to check all the revised utterances and list translation mistakes again. We repeat this process at least twice for each language. Finally, we summarize the statistics of the collected dataset in Table 2.

[2]The list of corrections and matching rules are reported in Appendix.

4 Multilingual Personalized Conversational Models

Let us define a dialogue $\mathcal{D} = \{U_1, S_1, U_2, S_2, \ldots, U_n, S_n\}$ as an alternating set of utterances from two speakers, where U and S represent the user and the system, respectively. Each speaker has its corresponding persona description that consists of a set of sentences $\mathcal{P} = \{P_1, \ldots, P_m\}$. Given the system persona sentences $\mathcal{P}_s$, dialogue history $U_{\leq k}$, $S_{<k}$, and response language l, we are interested in predicting the next system utterances S_k with model $f(\theta)$.

$$S_k = f(U_{\leq k}, S_{<k}, l; \theta) \quad (1)$$

4.1 Model Architecture

We explore both encoder-decoder and causal decoder architectures, and we leverage existing pre-trained contextualized multilingual language models as weights initialization. Hence, we firstly define the multilingual embedding layer and then the two multilingual models used in our experiments.

Embedding We define three embedding matrices: word embedding $E^W \in \mathbb{R}^{|V| \times d}$, positional embedding $E^P \in \mathbb{R}^{M \times d}$, and segmentation embedding $E^S \in \mathbb{R}^{|S| \times d}$, where $|.|$ denotes set cardinality, d is the embedding size, V denotes the vocabulary, M denotes the maximum sequence length, and S denotes the set of segmentation tokens. Segmentation embedding (Wolf et al., 2019) is used to indicate whether the current token is part of i) **Persona** sentences, ii) System (**Sys.**) utterances, iii) **User** utterances, iv) response in **Language** l. The language embedding l_{id} is used to inform the model which language to generate. Hence, given a sequence of tokens X, the embedding functions E are defined as:

$$E(X) = E^W(X) \oplus E^P(X_{pos}) \oplus E^S(X_{seg}), \quad (2)$$

where $\oplus$ denotes the positional sum, $X_{pos} = \{1, \ldots, |X|\}$ and X_{seg} is the sequence of segmentation tokens, as in Wolf et al. (2019). Figure 1 shows a visual representation of the embedding process. A more detailed illustration is reported in Appendix B.

Encoder-Decoder To model the response generation, we use a Transformer (Vaswani et al., 2017) based encoder-decoder (Vinyals and Le, 2015). As illustrated in Figure 1, we concatenate [3] the system persona $\mathcal{P}_s$ with the dialogue history $U_{\leq k}$, $S_{<k}$. Then we use the embedding layer E to finally pass it to the encoder. In short, we have:

$$H = \text{Encoder}(E([\mathcal{P}_s, U_{\leq k}, S_{<k}])), \quad (3)$$

where $H \in \mathbb{R}^{L \times d_{model}}$ is the hidden representation computed by the encoder, and L denotes the input sequence length. Then, the decoder attends to H and generates the system response S_k token by token. In the decoder, segmentation embedding is the language ID embedding (e.g., we look up the embedding for Italian to decode Italian). Thus:

$$S_k = \text{Decoder}(H, l), \quad (4)$$

Causal Decoder As an alternative to encoder-decoders, the causal-decoders (Radford et al., 2018, 2019; He et al., 2018) have been used to model conversational responses (Wolf et al., 2019; Zhang et al., 2019) by giving as a prefix the dialogue history. In our model, we concatenate the persona $\mathcal{P}_s$ and the dialogue history $U_{\leq k}$, $S_{<k}$ as the language model prefix, and autoregressively decode the system response S_k based on language embedding:

$$S_k = \text{Decoder}(E([\mathcal{P}_s, U_{\leq k}, S_{<k}]), l). \quad (5)$$

Figure 1 shows the conceptual differences between the encoder-decoder and casual decoder. Note that in both multilingual models, the dialogue history encoding process is language-agnostic, while decoding language is controlled by the language embedding. Such design allows the model to understand mixed-language dialogue contexts and to respond in the desired language (details in Section 5.3.2).

[3] $[a; b]$ denotes concatenating the vectors a and b

4.2 Training Strategy

We consider two training strategies to learn a multilingual conversational model: multilingual training and cross-lingual training.

Multilingual Training jointly learns personalized conversations in multiple languages. We follow a transfer learning approach (Wolf et al., 2019) by initializing our models with the weights of the large multilingual pretrained model M-Bert (Pires et al., 2019). For the causal decoder, we add the causal mask into self-attention layer to convert M-Bert encoder to decoder. For encoder-decoder model, we randomly initialize the cross encoder-decoder attention (Rothe et al., 2019). Then, we train the both models on the combined training set in all 7 languages using cross-entropy loss.

Cross-lingual Training transfers knowledge from the source language data to the target languages. In this setting, the model is trained on English (source language) conversational samples, and evaluated on the other 6 languages. Following the methodology proposed by Chi et al. (2019), we align the embedded representations of different languages into the same embedding space by applying cross-lingual pre-training to the encoder-decoder model. The pre-training procedure consists of two stages:

- pre-training the encoder and the decoder independently utilizing masked language modeling, as in Lample and Conneau (2019);
- jointly pre-training the encoder-decoder by using two objective functions: Cross-Lingual Auto-Encoding (XAE) and Denoising Auto-Encoding (DAE) (Chi et al., 2019).

For instance, DAE adds perturbations to the input sentence of encoder and tries to reconstructs the original sentence using the decoder, whereas, XAE uses parallel translation data to pre-train both the encoder and decoder with machine translation objective. As in the multilingual models, the language IDs are fed into the decoder to control the language of generated sentences. Both pre-training stages require both parallel and non-parallel data in the target language.

	Bert2Bert		M-Bert2Bert		CausalBert		M-CausalBert		XNLG	
	ppl.	*BLEU*	*ppl.*	*BLEU*	*ppl.*	*BLEU*	*ppl.*	*BLEU*	*ppl.*	*BLEU*
En	21.99	1.53	25.99	0.57	16.08	1.79	**15.62**	1.97	54.74*	**2.25***
Zh	21.35	3.36	13.24	1.25	**8.69**	5.51	9.27	**5.7**	3482.27	2.16
It	50.36	0.6	24.16	0.31	18.41	1.32	**15.12**	**1.3**	917.63	0.41
Jp	10.09	5.23	10.64	0.79	11.00	**6.74**	**7.13**	4.53	999.81	0.0
Ko	12.81	0.24	34.31	0.00	9.66	1.06	**9.56**	**1.08**	331.23	0.32
Id	21.37	0.11	22.83	0.22	14.77	**2.1**	**14.61**	1.92	844.98	0.15
Fr	13.22	0.35	15.58	0.50	**10.39**	1.97	10.59	**2.17**	640.33	0.09

Table 3: Results of automatic evaluation score on test set in seven languages. We compute the BLEU score and perplexity (ppl.) for monolingual, multilingual, and cross-lingual models.

After the two stages of pre-training, the model is fine-tuned using just the source language samples (i.e., English) with the same cross-entropy loss as for the multilingual training. However, as suggested in Chi et al. (2019), only the encoder parameters are updated with back-propagation and both the decoder and the word embedding layer remain frozen. This retains the decoders' ability to generate multilingual output while still being able to learn new tasks using only the target language.

5 Experiments

5.1 Evaluation Metrics

Evaluating open-domain chit-chat models is challenging, especially in multiple languages and at the dialogue-level. Hence, we evaluate our models using both automatic and human evaluation. In both cases, human-annotated dialogues are used, which show the importance of the provided dataset.

Automatic For each language, we evaluate responses generated by the models using perplexity (ppl.) and BLEU (Papineni et al., 2002) with reference to the human-annotated responses. Although these automatic measures are not perfect (Liu et al., 2016), they help to roughly estimate the performance of different models under the same test set. More recently, Adiwardana et al. (2020) has shown the correlation between perplexity and human judgment in open-domain chit-chat models.

Human Asking humans to evaluate the quality of a dialogue model is challenging, especially when multiple models have to be compared. The likert score (a.k.a. 1 to 5 scoring) has been widely used to evaluate the interactive experience with conversational models (Venkatesh et al., 2018; See et al., 2019; Zhang et al., 2018; Dinan et al., 2019a). In such evaluation, a human interacts with the systems for several turns, and then they assign a score from 1 to 5 based on three questions (Zhang et al., 2018) about fluency, engagingness, and consistency. This evaluation is both expensive to conduct and requires many samples to achieve statistically significant results (Li et al., 2019). To cope with these issues, Li et al. (2019) proposed ACUTE-EVAL, an evaluation for dialogue systems. The authors proposed two modes: human-model chats and self-chat (Li et al., 2016b; Ghandeharioun et al., 2019). In this work, we opt for the latter since it is cheaper to conduct and achieves similar results (Li et al., 2019) to the former. Another advantage of using this method is the ability to evaluate multi-turn conversations instead of single-turn responses.

Following ACUTE-EVAL, the annotator is provided with two full dialogues made by self-chat or human-dialogue. The annotator is asked to choose which of the two dialogues is better in terms of engagingness, interestingness, and humanness. For each comparison, we sample 60–100 conversations from both models. In Appendix C, we report the exact questions and instructions given to the annotators, and the user interface used in the evaluation. We hired at least 10 annotators for each considered language, the annotators are either native speakers or linguists in corresponding language. The annotators were different from the dataset collection annotators to avoid any possible bias.

5.2 Implementation Details

Multilingual Models We use the "BERT-Base, Multilingual Cased" checkpoint, and we denote the multilingual encoder-decoder model as **M-Bert2Bert** (~220M parameters) and causal decoder model as **M-CausalBert** (~110M parameters). We fine-tune both models in the combined

	Lang	*Engageness*			*Interestingness*			*Humanness*		
		Human	**Mono**	**Poly**	**Human**	**Mono**	**Poly**	**Human**	**Mono**	**Poly**
Multi Wins %	*En*	**23.33**	**68.57**	36.36	**23.33**	**64.29**	**32.73**	**30.00**	**62.86**	42.73
	Fr	32.00	55.17	42.86	**16.00**	53.45	48.21	**28.00**	50.00	44.64
	Id	**21.67**	51.67	**65.45**	**23.33**	46.67	55.45	**25.00**	46.67	**65.45**
	It	**35.00**	48.33	56.36	**30.00**	48.33	53.64	**30.00**	40.00	57.27
	Jp	**18.33**	50.00	**61.82**	**13.33**	43.33	45.45	**18.33**	51.67	59.09
	Ko	**30.00**	52.46	**62.39**	**26.67**	50.82	59.63	**28.33**	52.46	**64.22**
	Zh	**36.67**	55.00	**65.45**	**36.67**	60.00	**61.82**	**36.67**	55.00	**70.91**

Table 4: Results of ACUTE-EVAL human evaluation. Tests are conducted pairwise between M-CausalBert (Multi.) and other models (Human, Poly-encoder (Poly), Monolingual CausalBert (Mono)). **Numbers indicate the winning rate of M-CausalBert**. Numbers in bold are statistically significant ($p < 0.05$).

training set (English in Persona-chat (Zhang et al., 2018), six languages in Xpersona) for five epochs with AdamW optimizer and a learning rate of $6.25e$-5.

Monolingual Models To verify whether the multilingual agent will under-perform the monolingual agent in the monolingual conversational task, we build a monolingual encoder-decoder model and causal decoder model for each language. For a fair comparison, we initialize the monolingual models with a pre-trained monolingual BERT [4] (Devlin et al., 2018; Cui et al., 2019; Martin et al., 2019). We denote the monolingual encoder-decoder model as **Bert2Bert** ($\sim$220M parameters) and causal decoder model as **CausalBert** ($\sim$110M parameters). Then we fine-tune each model in each language independently for the same number of epoch and optimizer as the multilingual model. Our **CausalBert** model achieve 16.08 perplexity, which is similar to 17.51 of the GPT based models (Wolf et al., 2019).

Translation-based Models Another strong baseline we compare with is Poly-encoder (Humeau et al., 2019), a large-scale pre-trained retrieval model that **fine-tuned** on English Persona-chat, has shown state-of-the-art performance in the ConvAI dataset (Li et al., 2019; Humeau et al., 2019). We adapt this model to the other languages by using the Google Translate API to translate target languages (e.g., Chinese) query to English as the input to the model, then translate the English response back to the target language. Thus, the response generation flow is: target query $\rightarrow$ English query $\rightarrow$ English response $\rightarrow$ target response. We denote this model as **Poly**.

[4]The monolingual BERT pre-trained models are available in https://github.com/huggingface/transformers

Cross-lingual Models. In the first pre-training stage, we use the pre-trained weights from XLMR-base (Conneau et al., 2019). Then, we follow the second pre-training stage of XNLG (Chi et al., 2019) for pre-training Italian, Japanese, Korean, Indonesia cross-lingual transferable models. For Chinese and French, we directly apply the pre-trained XNLG (Chi et al., 2019) weights[5]. Then, the pre-trained models are fine-tune on English PersonaChat training set and early stop based on the perplexity on target language validation set.

5.3 Results and Discussion

5.3.1 Quantitative Analysis

Table 3 compares monolingual, multilingual, and cross-lingual models in terms of BLEU and perplexity in the human-translated test set. On both evaluation matrices, the causal decoder models outperform the encoder-decoder models. We observe that the encoder-decoder model tends to overlook dialogue context and generate digressive responses. (Generated samples are available in Appendix D) We hypothesize that this is because the one-to-many problem (Zhao et al., 2017) in open-domain conversation weakens the relation between encoder and decoder; thus the well pre-trained decoder (Bert) easily converges to a local optimum, and learns to ignore the dialogue context from the encoder and generate the response in an unconditional language model way. We leave the investigation of this problem to future work. On the other hand, M-CausalBert achieves a comparable or slightly better performance compared to CausalBert, which suggests that M-CausalBert leverages the data from other languages. As expected, we observe a significant gap between the cross-lingual model and

[5]Available in https://github.com/CZWin32768/XNLG

other models, which indicates that cross-lingual zero-shot conversation modeling is very challenging.

Table 4 shows the human evaluation result of comparing M-CausalBert (Multi) against the human, translation-based Poly-encoder (Poly), and monolingual CausalBert (Mono). The results illustrate that Multi outperforms Mono in English and Chinese, and is on par with Mono in other languages. On the other hand, Poly shows a strong performance in English as it was pre-trained with a large-scale English conversation corpus. In contrast, the performance of Poly drops in other languages, which indicates that the imperfect translation affects translation-based systems. We also conduct M-CausalBert against XNLG (cross) human evaluation, and Multi achieve nearly 100 percent winning rate.

5.3.2 Qualitative Analysis and Discussion

We randomly sample 7 self-chat dialogues for each baseline model in the seven languages and report them in Appendix D., And we summarize the generation of each model as follows:

Poly Poly-encoder, pretrained on 174 million Reddit data and fine tuned on English Persona-Chat, can accurately retrieve coherent and diverse responses in English. However, in the other six languages, some of the retrieved responses are digressive due to translation errors.

Monolingual & Multilingual We observe that both the monolingual and multilingual models can generate fluent responses. Compared to Bert2Bert and M-Bert2Bert, CausalBert and M-CausalBert can generate more on-topic responses but sometimes repeat through turns. CausalBert and M-CausalBert are on par with each other in monolingual conversational tasks, while M-CausalBert shows the advantage of handling a mixed-language context. For multilingual speakers, the conversation may involve multiple languages. Therefore, we test M-CausalBert with extra-Sentential code-switching context. Table 5 shows that M-CausalBert can understand the mixed-language context, and decode coherent responses. In Appendix C.1, we report more generation examples, and we also show that the response language of M-CausalBert can be control by language embeddings.

System Persona
My favorite activity is rock climbing.
I'm a mechanical engineer.
I like to go hiking in the spring.
I live in colorado.

Dialogue

Usr	studio inglese oggi e tu? (I am studying English today, you?)
Sys	just watching netflix with friends
Usr	我喜欢攀岩，你呢？ (I like rock climbing, what about you?)
Sys	nice, I enjoy it while in the summer. what are you up to?
Usr	saya ingin melakukan panjat tebing (I want to go to hike)
Sys	I'm going hiking the most time of year
Usr	スポーツがお好きなようですね (It seems you like sports)
Sys	I love the outdoors too, do you have any hobbies?
Usr	나는 티비 보는 것을 좋아해.(I like to watch tv)
Sys	i really like hiking and listening to music

Table 5: M-CausalBert handles extra-Sentential code-switching context without any language identifiers.

Cross-lingual. The current state-of-the-art cross-lingual generation approach XNLG (Chi et al., 2019) shows inferior performance on multi-turn dialogue tasks, and generates repetitive responses. Although cross-lingual dialogue generation is challenging, it reduces the human effort for data annotation in different languages. Therefore, the cross-language transfer is an important direction to investigate.

6 Conclusion

In this paper, we studied both cross-lingual and multilingual approaches in end to-end personalized dialogue modeling. We presented the XPersona dataset, a multilingual extension of Persona-Chat, for evaluating the multilingual personalized chatbots. We further provided both cross-lingual and multilingual baselines and compared them with the monolingual approach and two-stage translation approach. Extensive automatic evaluation and human evaluation were conducted to examine the models' performance. The experimental results showed that multilingual trained models, with a single model across multiple languages, can outperform the two-stage translation approach and is on par with monolingual models. On the other hand, the current state-of-the-art cross-lingual approach XNLG achieved lower performance than other baselines. In future work, we plan to research a more advanced cross-lingual generation approach and construct a mixed-language conversational benchmark for evaluating multilingual systems.

References

Daniel Adiwardana, Minh-Thang Luong, David R So, Jamie Hall, Noah Fiedel, Romal Thoppilan, Zi Yang, Apoorv Kulshreshtha, Gaurav Nemade, Yifeng Lu, et al. 2020. Towards a human-like open-domain chatbot. *arXiv preprint arXiv:2001.09977.*

Gustavo Aguilar, Fahad AlGhamdi, Victor Soto, Mona Diab, Julia Hirschberg, and Thamar Solorio. 2018. Named entity recognition on code-switched data: Overview of the calcs 2018 shared task. In *Proceedings of the Third Workshop on Computational Approaches to Linguistic Code-Switching*, pages 138–147.

Wasi Ahmad, Zhisong Zhang, Xuezhe Ma, Eduard Hovy, Kai-Wei Chang, and Nanyun Peng. 2019. On difficulties of cross-lingual transfer with order differences: A case study on dependency parsing. In *Proceedings of the 2019 Conference of the North American Chapter of the Association for Computational Linguistics: Human Language Technologies, Volume 1 (Long and Short Papers)*, pages 2440–2452.

Alan Akbik, Laura Chiticariu, Marina Danilevsky, Yunyao Li, Shivakumar Vaithyanathan, and Huaiyu Zhu. 2015. Generating high quality proposition banks for multilingual semantic role labeling. In *Proceedings of the 53rd Annual Meeting of the Association for Computational Linguistics and the 7th International Joint Conference on Natural Language Processing (Volume 1: Long Papers)*, pages 397–407.

Wenhu Chen, Jianshu Chen, Yu Su, Xin Wang, Dong Yu, Xifeng Yan, and William Yang Wang. 2018. Xl-nbt: A cross-lingual neural belief tracking framework. In *Proceedings of the 2018 Conference on Empirical Methods in Natural Language Processing*, pages 414–424.

Zewen Chi, Li Dong, Furu Wei, Wenhui Wang, Xian-Ling Mao, and Heyan Huang. 2019. Cross-lingual natural language generation via pre-training. *arXiv preprint arXiv:1909.10481.*

Alexis Conneau, Kartikay Khandelwal, Naman Goyal, Vishrav Chaudhary, Guillaume Wenzek, Francisco Guzmán, Edouard Grave, Myle Ott, Luke Zettlemoyer, and Veselin Stoyanov. 2019. Unsupervised cross-lingual representation learning at scale. *arXiv preprint arXiv:1911.02116.*

Alexis Conneau, Ruty Rinott, Guillaume Lample, Adina Williams, Samuel Bowman, Holger Schwenk, and Veselin Stoyanov. 2018. Xnli: Evaluating cross-lingual sentence representations. In *Proceedings of the 2018 Conference on Empirical Methods in Natural Language Processing*, pages 2475–2485.

Yiming Cui, Wanxiang Che, Ting Liu, Bing Qin, Ziqing Yang, Shijin Wang, and Guoping Hu. 2019. Pre-training with whole word masking for chinese bert. *arXiv preprint arXiv:1906.08101.*

Jacob Devlin, Ming-Wei Chang, Kenton Lee, and Kristina Toutanova. 2018. Bert: Pre-training of deep bidirectional transformers for language understanding. *arXiv preprint arXiv:1810.04805.*

Emily Dinan, Varvara Logacheva, Valentin Malykh, Alexander Miller, Kurt Shuster, Jack Urbanek, Douwe Kiela, Arthur Szlam, Iulian Serban, Ryan Lowe, et al. 2019a. The second conversational intelligence challenge (convai2). *arXiv preprint arXiv:1902.00098.*

Emily Dinan, Stephen Roller, Kurt Shuster, Angela Fan, Michael Auli, and Jason Weston. 2019b. Wizard of wikipedia: Knowledge-powered conversational agents. In *International Conference on Learning Representations.*

Darrell Etherington. 2019. Amazon launches multilingual mode for using alexa in multiple languages at once.

Angela Fan, Yacine Jernite, Ethan Perez, David Grangier, Jason Weston, and Michael Auli. 2019. Eli5: Long form question answering. *arXiv preprint arXiv:1907.09190.*

Jianfeng Gao, Michel Galley, and Lihong Li. 2018. Neural approaches to conversational ai. In *The 41st International ACM SIGIR Conference on Research & Development in Information Retrieval*, pages 1371–1374. ACM.

Asma Ghandeharioun, Judy Hanwen Shen, Natasha Jaques, Craig Ferguson, Noah Jones, Agata Lapedriza, and Rosalind Picard. 2019. Approximating interactive human evaluation with self-play for open-domain dialog systems. In *Advances in Neural Information Processing Systems*, pages 13658–13669.

Karthik Gopalakrishnan, Behnam Hedayatnia, Qinlang Chen, Anna Gottardi, Sanjeev Kwatra, Anu Venkatesh, Raefer Gabriel, Dilek Hakkani-Tür, and Amazon Alexa AI. 2019. Topical-chat: Towards knowledge-grounded open-domain conversations. *Proc. Interspeech 2019*, pages 1891–1895.

Tianyu He, Xu Tan, Yingce Xia, Di He, Tao Qin, Zhibo Chen, and Tie-Yan Liu. 2018. Layer-wise coordination between encoder and decoder for neural machine translation. In *Advances in Neural Information Processing Systems*, pages 7944–7954.

Samuel Humeau, Kurt Shuster, Marie-Anne Lachaux, and Jason Weston. 2019. Poly-encoders: Transformer architectures and pre-training strategies for fast and accurate multi-sentence scoring. *CoRR abs/1905.01969. External Links: Link Cited by*, 2:2–2.

Melvin Johnson, Mike Schuster, Quoc Le, Maxim Krikun, Yonghui Wu, Zhifeng Chen, Nikhil Thorat, Fernanda Viégas, Martin Wattenberg, Greg Corrado, et al. 2017. Google's multilingual neural machine translation system: Enabling zero-shot translation. *Transactions of the Association for Computational Linguistics*, 5:339–351.

Karthikeyan K, Zihan Wang, Stephen Mayhew, and Dan Roth. 2020. Cross-lingual ability of multilingual bert: An empirical study. In *International Conference on Learning Representations*.

Joo-Kyung Kim, Young-Bum Kim, Ruhi Sarikaya, and Eric Fosler-Lussier. 2017. Cross-lingual transfer learning for pos tagging without cross-lingual resources. In *Proceedings of the 2017 Conference on Empirical Methods in Natural Language Processing*, pages 2832–2838.

Guillaume Lample and Alexis Conneau. 2019. Cross-lingual language model pretraining. *arXiv preprint arXiv:1901.07291*.

Patrick Lewis, Barlas Oğuz, Ruty Rinott, Sebastian Riedel, and Holger Schwenk. 2019. Mlqa: Evaluating cross-lingual extractive question answering. *arXiv preprint arXiv:1910.07475*.

Jiwei Li, Michel Galley, Chris Brockett, Georgios Spithourakis, Jianfeng Gao, and Bill Dolan. 2016a. A persona-based neural conversation model. In *Proceedings of the 54th Annual Meeting of the Association for Computational Linguistics (Volume 1: Long Papers)*, volume 1, pages 994–1003.

Jiwei Li, Will Monroe, Alan Ritter, Michel Galley, Jianfeng Gao, and Dan Jurafsky. 2016b. Deep reinforcement learning for dialogue generation. *arXiv preprint arXiv:1606.01541*.

Margaret Li, Jason Weston, and Stephen Roller. 2019. Acute-eval: Improved dialogue evaluation with optimized questions and multi-turn comparisons. *arXiv preprint arXiv:1909.03087*.

Chia-Wei Liu, Ryan Lowe, Iulian Serban, Mike Noseworthy, Laurent Charlin, and Joelle Pineau. 2016. How not to evaluate your dialogue system: An empirical study of unsupervised evaluation metrics for dialogue response generation. In *Proceedings of the 2016 Conference on Empirical Methods in Natural Language Processing*, pages 2122–2132. Association for Computational Linguistics.

Jiahua Liu, Yankai Lin, Zhiyuan Liu, and Maosong Sun. 2019. Xqa: A cross-lingual open-domain question answering dataset. In *Proceedings of the 57th Annual Meeting of the Association for Computational Linguistics*, pages 2358–2368.

Yinhan Liu, Jiatao Gu, Naman Goyal, Xian Li, Sergey Edunov, Marjan Ghazvininejad, Mike Lewis, and Luke Zettlemoyer. 2020. Multilingual denoising pre-training for neural machine translation. *Transactions of the Association for Computational Linguistics*, 8:726–742.

Louis Martin, Benjamin Muller, Pedro Javier Ortiz Suárez, Yoann Dupont, Laurent Romary, Éric Villemonte de la Clergerie, Djamé Seddah, and Benoît Sagot. 2019. Camembert: a tasty french language model. *arXiv preprint arXiv:1911.03894*.

Seungwhan Moon, Pararth Shah, Anuj Kumar, and Rajen Subba. 2019. Opendialkg: Explainable conversational reasoning with attention-based walks over knowledge graphs. In *Proceedings of the 57th Annual Meeting of the Association for Computational Linguistics*, pages 845–854.

Nikola Mrkšić, Ivan Vulić, Diarmuid Ó Séaghdha, Ira Leviant, Roi Reichart, Milica Gašić, Anna Korhonen, and Steve Young. 2017. Semantic specialization of distributional word vector spaces using monolingual and cross-lingual constraints. *Transactions of the Association for Computational Linguistics*, 5:309–324.

Jian Ni, Georgiana Dinu, and Radu Florian. 2017. Weakly supervised cross-lingual named entity recognition via effective annotation and representation projection. In *Proceedings of the 55th Annual Meeting of the Association for Computational Linguistics (Volume 1: Long Papers)*, pages 1470–1480.

Xiaoman Pan, Boliang Zhang, Jonathan May, Joel Nothman, Kevin Knight, and Heng Ji. 2017. Cross-lingual name tagging and linking for 282 languages. In *Proceedings of the 55th Annual Meeting of the Association for Computational Linguistics (Volume 1: Long Papers)*, volume 1, pages 1946–1958.

Kishore Papineni, Salim Roukos, Todd Ward, and Wei-Jing Zhu. 2002. Bleu: a method for automatic evaluation of machine translation. In *Proceedings of the 40th annual meeting on association for computational linguistics*, pages 311–318. Association for Computational Linguistics.

Telmo Pires, Eva Schlinger, and Dan Garrette. 2019. How multilingual is multilingual bert? In *Proceedings of the 57th Annual Meeting of the Association for Computational Linguistics*, pages 4996–5001.

Alec Radford, Karthik Narasimhan, Time Salimans, and Ilya Sutskever. 2018. Improving language understanding with unsupervised learning. *Technical report, OpenAI.*

Alec Radford, Jeffrey Wu, Rewon Child, David Luan, Dario Amodei, and Ilya Sutskever. 2019. Language models are unsupervised multitask learners. *OpenAI Blog*, 1(8):9.

Siva Reddy, Danqi Chen, and Christopher D Manning. 2019. Coqa: A conversational question answering challenge. *Transactions of the Association for Computational Linguistics*, 7:249–266.

Sascha Rothe, Shashi Narayan, and Aliaksei Severyn. 2019. Leveraging pre-trained checkpoints for sequence generation tasks. *arXiv preprint arXiv:1907.12461*.

Sebastian Schuster, Sonal Gupta, Rushin Shah, and Mike Lewis. 2019. Cross-lingual transfer learning for multilingual task oriented dialog. In *Proceedings of the 2019 Conference of the North American Chapter of the Association for Computational Linguistics: Human Language Technologies, Volume 1 (Long and Short Papers)*, pages 3795–3805.

Abigail See, Stephen Roller, Douwe Kiela, and Jason Weston. 2019. What makes a good conversation? how controllable attributes affect human judgments. *arXiv preprint arXiv:1902.08654*.

Shubham Toshniwal, Tara N Sainath, Ron J Weiss, Bo Li, Pedro Moreno, Eugene Weinstein, and Kanishka Rao. 2018. Multilingual speech recognition with a single end-to-end model. In *2018 IEEE International Conference on Acoustics, Speech and Signal Processing (ICASSP)*, pages 4904–4908. IEEE.

Ashish Vaswani, Noam Shazeer, Niki Parmar, Jakob Uszkoreit, Llion Jones, Aidan N Gomez, Łukasz Kaiser, and Illia Polosukhin. 2017. Attention is all you need. In *Advances in neural information processing systems*, pages 5998–6008.

Anu Venkatesh, Chandra Khatri, Ashwin Ram, Fenfei Guo, Raefer Gabriel, Ashish Nagar, Rohit Prasad, Ming Cheng, Behnam Hedayatnia, Angeliki Metallinou, et al. 2018. On evaluating and comparing conversational agents. *arXiv preprint arXiv:1801.03625*, 4:60–68.

Oriol Vinyals and Quoc V Le. 2015. A neural conversational model. *arXiv preprint arXiv:1506.05869*.

Guillaume Wisniewski, Nicolas Pécheux, Souhir Gahbiche-Braham, and François Yvon. 2014. Cross-lingual part-of-speech tagging through ambiguous learning. In *Proceedings of the 2014 Conference on Empirical Methods in Natural Language Processing (EMNLP)*, pages 1779–1785.

Thomas Wolf, Victor Sanh, Julien Chaumond, and Clement Delangue. 2019. Transfertransfo: A transfer learning approach for neural network based conversational agents. *arXiv preprint arXiv:1901.08149*.

Linting Xue, Noah Constant, Adam Roberts, Mihir Kale, Rami Al-Rfou, Aditya Siddhant, Aditya Barua, and Colin Raffel. 2021. mt5: A massively multilingual pre-trained text-to-text transformer. In *Proceedings of the 2021 Conference of the North American Chapter of the Association for Computational Linguistics: Human Language Technologies*, pages 483–498.

Saizheng Zhang, Emily Dinan, Jack Urbanek, Arthur Szlam, Douwe Kiela, and Jason Weston. 2018. Personalizing dialogue agents: I have a dog, do you have pets too? In *Proceedings of the 56th Annual Meeting of the Association for Computational Linguistics (Volume 1: Long Papers)*, pages 2204–2213. Association for Computational Linguistics.

Yizhe Zhang, Siqi Sun, Michel Galley, Yen-Chun Chen, Chris Brockett, Xiang Gao, Jianfeng Gao, Jingjing Liu, and Bill Dolan. 2019. Dialogpt: Large-scale generative pre-training for conversational response generation. *arXiv preprint arXiv:1911.00536*.

Yuan Zhang, David Gaddy, Regina Barzilay, and Tommi Jaakkola. 2016. Ten pairs to tag–multilingual pos tagging via coarse mapping between embeddings. In *Proceedings of the 2016 Conference of the North American Chapter of the Association for Computational Linguistics: Human Language Technologies*, pages 1307–1317.

Tiancheng Zhao, Ran Zhao, and Maxine Eskenazi. 2017. Learning discourse-level diversity for neural dialog models using conditional variational autoencoders. In *Proceedings of the 55th Annual Meeting of the Association for Computational Linguistics (Volume 1: Long Papers)*, pages 654–664.

Collaborative Data Relabeling for Robust and Diverse Voice Apps Recommendation in Intelligent Personal Assistants

Qian Hu, Thahir Mohamed, Wei Xiao, Zheng Gao,
Xibin Gao, Radhika Arava, Xiyao Ma, Mohamed AbdelHady
Alexa AI
{huqia,thahirm,weixiaow,zhenggao,gxibin,aravar,maxiya,mbdeamz}@amazon.com

Abstract

Intelligent personal assistants (IPAs) such as Amazon Alexa, Google Assistant and Apple Siri extend their built-in capabilities by supporting voice apps developed by third-party developers. Sometimes the smart assistant is not able to successfully respond to user voice commands (aka utterances). There are many reasons including automatic speech recognition (ASR) error, natural language understanding (NLU) error, routing utterances to an irrelevant voice app or simply that the user is asking for a capability that is not supported yet. The failure to handle a voice command leads to customer frustration. In this paper, we introduce a fallback skill recommendation system to suggest a voice app to a customer for an unhandled voice command. One of the prominent challenges of developing a skill recommender system for IPAs is partial observation. To solve the partial observation problem, we propose collaborative data relabeling (CDR) method. In addition, CDR also improves the diversity of the recommended skills. We evaluate the proposed method both offline and online. The offline evaluation results show that the proposed system outperforms the baselines. The online A/B testing results show significant gain of customer experience metrics.

1 Introduction

Intelligent personal assistants such as Alexa, Siri, and Google Assistant have been becoming more and more popular and making people's daily lives convenient. IPAs can fulfill users' requests by answering questions ranging from weather to stock price. To enrich user experience, a large amount of third-party (3P) voice apps (aka skills) have been developed. These voice apps extend IPAs built-in capabilities to better serve customers. They can perform operations like ordering food, playing a game, or helping a user sleep by playing soothing sounds. The supported 3P skills can number up to hundreds of thousands.

IPAs understand user's request using spoken language understanding (SLU) system. The request goes through a series of components to get response, as illustrated in Figure 1. The first component is automatic speech recognition (ASR), which converts speech to its transcription also called utterance. At the second stage, the utterance is interpreted by NLU system. NLU as the critical component of SLU interprets the meaning of an utterance by using several NLP technologies including domain classifier (DC), intent classifier (IC), and named entity recognition (NER). After NLU, the arbiter is responsible to select the most relevant voice app (skill) for a given NLU interpretation. Sometimes the arbiter may fail to find a relevant skill that can handle the user request. It could be a system error such as automatic speech recognition (ASR) error, natural language understanding (NLU) error. Another reason could be that the feature requested by the user is not supported yet by the dialog system or the requested content is not found such as music, video, book, recipe, etc. To reduce customer friction and recover the conversation, we propose a skill recommender system which proactively suggests 3P skills to users for unhandled requests, even if the users are not aware of the skills.

The proposed skill recommender system is composed of two components: a shortlister, and a reranker. Figure 2 shows the system architecture. Given an utterance, the shortlister, also known as the candidate generator retrieves k most relevant skills out of the skill catalog. The retrieved skills are passed to the reranker that ranks the skill candidates by using skill specific information and the utterance. Finally, the top-1 skill is presented to the user. This system is not meant to replace the original NLU or arbiter components. It is specifically designed to serve as a fallback for utterances that are not handled by the existing system (i.e., unclaimed utterances) using the increasing catalog

Proceedings of the Third Workshop on Natural Language Processing for Conversational AI, pages 113–119
November 10, 2021.

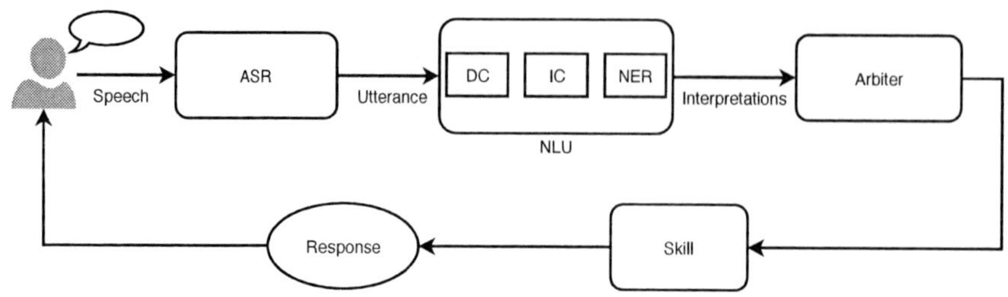

Figure 1: A high-level overview of an IPA.

of 3P skills.

Traditional recommender systems such as video recommendation recommend a ranked list of items to a user. The user scans the list and select the one he/she likes the most (Covington et al., 2016). The feedback from the user is treated as label (accept/reject) for learning a model. However, due to the limitation of voice user interface (VUI), we can only present the top-1 skill to users, as listening to the playback of a long list is tedious and can significantly degrade user experience (Cohen et al., 2004). This limitation results in partial observation problem. Namely, users cannot observe the full recommendation list and make a decision, which imposes difficulties in learning a ranking model. To solve partial observation problem, we propose a novel method called collaborative data relabeling (CDR). CDR mitigates the partial observation problem by trying to answer a counterfactual question, "what if we present another skill to the user?". CDR answers this question by matching a similar request and using feedback from that request to relabel the original ranked list. Recommender systems usually focus on optimizing the accuracy of predictions while ignoring the diversity of the recommended items, which can degrade user experience if similar items get recommended over and over again (Ekstrand et al., 2014; Castagnos et al., 2013; Knijnenburg et al., 2012; Ziegler et al., 2005; Willemsen et al., 2016). CDR improves the diversity of recommended skills by relabeling different skill candidates that serve the same intent. The relabeled skills force the model to learn to diversify their prediction distribution among multiple skill candidates.

At the beginning, we do not have data for training the model. To collect training data, we build a rule-based system. Similar to the proposed system, the rule-based system also has a two-stage architecture. We use the data collected from this system to train and evaluate our proposed model offline. The proposed model is put into production for online A/B testing after it has achieved satisfying offline results. Online experimental results show significant gains of user experience metrics such as higher volume of acceptances, lower friction rates, etc.

Overall, the contributions of this work are summarized as following:

- We propose a skill recommender system for IPAs to handle unclaimed utterances by exploiting the ever-increasing 3P voice apps.
- To mitigate partial observation issue, we propose collaborative data relabeling inspired by causal inference. Collaborative data relabeling also has the advantage of improving recommendation diversity and thus improving user satisfaction. Suggesting diverse skills to users can help them explore and discover more skills, which is also beneficial to third-party skill developers.
- We conduct offline and online experiments. Online experimental results show significant gains of user experience metrics.

2 Skill Recommender System

Our skill recommender system consists of two components, shortlister and reranker, as shown in Figure 2.

Given the input utterance text, shortlister selects top-k relevant skills from the skill catalog. We implement shortlister as a keyword-based search engine. To build the skill search engine, we index skill metadata including skill name, skill descriptions, example phrases, and invocation phrases. At retrieval time, the relevancy score between an utterance and a skill is computed as the sum of TF-IDF score (Rajaraman and Ullman, 2011) of every word in the utterance. The skills with top k relevancy scores are returned.

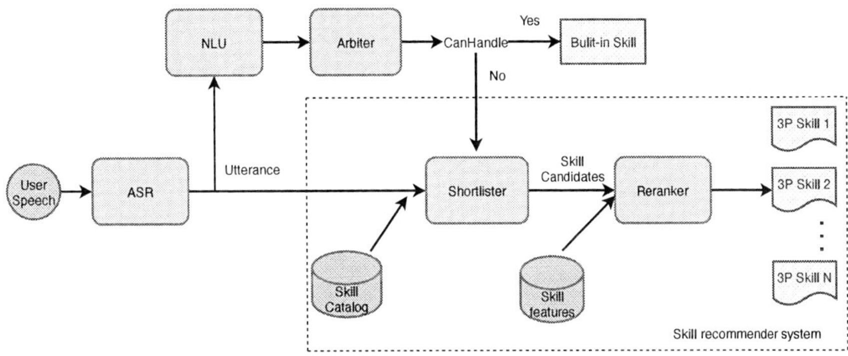

Figure 2: A overview of skill recommender system.

The reranker model takes in the skill candidates generated by shortlister and returns a ranked list of skills based on the utterance and skill specific information. The reranker is a deep learning model with a listwise ranking loss function. Figure 3 shows the reranker model architecture. The utterance is

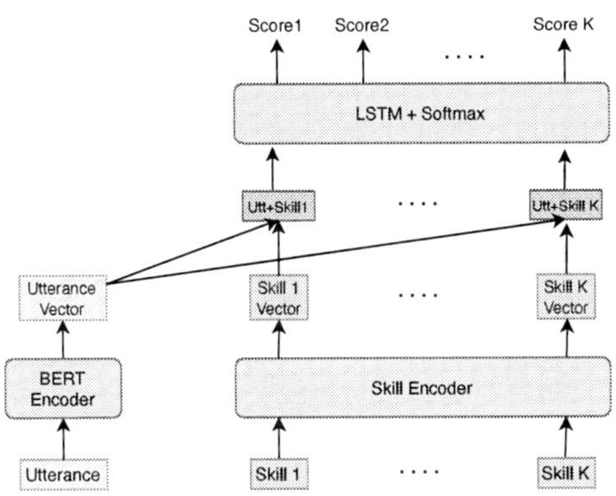

Figure 3: Model architecture of reranker.

encoded by a BERT encoder (Devlin et al., 2018). The features of skills include skill id, skill name, and skill score returned by shortlister. Skill id is represented using an embedding vector; skill name is encoded into an embedding vector by BERT. The skill score feature is converted into a bin and encoded as an embedding vector. The skill feature embedding vectors are concatenated to form a single embedding vector. The utterance embedding vector is concatenated with every skill embedding vector to form a sequence of utterance-skill embedding vectors. As the skill candidates returned by shortlister is ordered by relevance score, to capture such sequential information, these sequence of embedding vectors are put into a Bi-LSTM layer (Hochreiter and Schmidhuber, 1997). The outputs from the Bi-LSTM layer is converted to probability scores by using softmax function. Each skill has a corresponding probability score. The skills are reranked according to the predicted probability scores. For a list of skill candidates, the user feedback for the skill candidates is $\mathbf{y} = \{y_1, ..., y_k\}, y_i \in \{0, 1\}$ indicating whether the user accepts or rejects the skills and the predicted probabilities by the reranker model is $\mathbf{s} = \{s_1, ..., s_k\}$. We use listwise ranking objective function (Cao et al., 2007). The objective function is formulated as

$$L(\mathbf{y}, \mathbf{s}) = \frac{1}{k} \sum_{i=1}^{k} [-y_i \log(s_i) - (1 - y_i) \log(1 - s_i)]. \tag{1}$$

Due to the partial observation issue, the labels of the unobserved skills are treated as negative. However, this assumption is not realistic and can bias the model, because the missing values are not necessarily negative. In the next section, we introduce collaborative data relabeling to mitigate this issue.

3 Collaborative Data Relabeling

Compared to traditional recommender system such as video recommendation where users view the full recommended list and select the best one they like, the skill recommender system has its unique challenge. Limited by VUI, we can only present the top-1 ranked skill to user, which results in a partial observation problem. With partial observation, users have no chance to view and compare other skills in the list. We do not know if the user would like the other skills more than the top-1. Without comparing the top-1 skill with the other skills, it is hard to learn a ranking model, as ranking in essence is about comparing. To solve partial observation problem, we propose collaborative data relabeling (CDR) approach.

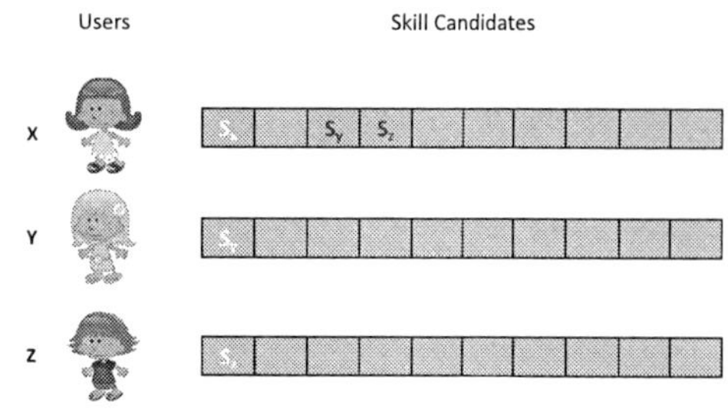

Figure 4: Illustration of collaborative data relabeling. In skill recommendation, only the top-1 skill is presented to users. Given a user x who invoked voice assistant with some utterance, to know her responses to skills s_y and s_z that were not presented to her, we found two users y and z who spoke similar utterances and were suggested with skills s_y and s_z, respectively and use their responses to relabel user x's feedback to skills s_y and s_z.

The intuition of CDR is to answer a counterfactual question, namely, "what if we had presented another skill to user?". To answer this question, we find k nearest neighbors of a user request (utterance) and use their feedback to relabel the original ranked list of skill candidates, which is inspired by matching method (Stuart, 2010) in causal inference. In causal inference, matching is an approach to estimate the treatment effect by comparing the treated units to non-treated units with similar characteristics. CDR has a similar working mechanism. Given a user utterance, to know the user's response to an unpresented skill, we find a similar utterance whose invoker has interacted with that skill and use his/her response to relabel it as either positive or negative, as illustrated in Figure 4. Usually, there are more than one neighbors that have interacted with the skill, in which case we use majority vote to decide the final label. As the final labels are decided by multiple neighbors, they are more reliable than those of just one user, which results in learning a more robust model.

Recommender systems are confronted with an over-fitting problem that only a small portion of items are recommended to users (Kunaver and Požrl, 2017), which can hurt user satisfaction as they can quickly get bored by always being suggested with similar types of items. This problem is especially relevant for skills that serve the same intent with different content. For example, when users ask to play a soothing sound to help them sleep, always suggesting the same sleep sound can get users bored, while there exist many types of sleep sounds in the skill store such as frog, ocean, rain, waterfall sleeping sound, etc. Suggesting diverse skills can improve user satisfaction (Castagnos et al., 2013). The proposed CDR method improves diversity by relabeling different skill candidates as positive, which forces the model's predictive distribution to be dispersed among more skills. Diversified suggestions can lead to drop in accuracy (McNee et al., 2006; Ziegler et al., 2005), which imposes difficulties in faithfully evaluating the real user satisfaction metrics. To evaluate how diversity can influence user satisfaction, we use manual annotation. The detail of manual annotation schema will be explained in Section 5.1.2.

To capture semantic meaning of utterances for similarity measurements, we use fine-tuned BERT encoder to encode utterances into embedding vectors. The BERT model is fine-tuned using data with a multi-task objective function, specifically, intent classification and named entity recognition. We also experiment with pre-trained BERT encoder and find that it does not work well for capturing semantics of an utterance, which has also been discovered by several works such as (Reimers and Gurevych, 2019) and (Li et al., 2020). We use the average pooling of the contextual embedding vectors in the last layer as the utterance embedding vector. We measure the similarity score between two utterances using cosine similarity between their embedding vectors.

4 Experiments

4.1 Data Collection

At the beginning, we do not have data to train and evaluate our system. To collect data, we build a rule-based system which has similar architecture as our proposed one. The rule-based system uses the same shortlister but a rule-based reranker. The rule-based reranker ranks the skill candidates by using their historical acceptance rates. The skill with the highest acceptance rate is selected. To ensure high quality of recommendation, we only suggest the top skill to customer if its acceptance rate is higher than 0.5. We collect two-month data from a commercial voice assistant traffic for model training and evaluation. The data of the last week is used for testing. The data of the second last week is used for validation. The remaining is used for training. The proportions of training, validation and testing data are around $80\%, 10\%, 10\%$, respectively. Each data sample is composed of an utterance u_t, forty skill candidates $s_{t,1}, ..., s_{t,40}$ generated by shortlister, and ground truth label y_t, denoted as $(u_t, (s_{t,1}, ..., s_{t,40}), y_t)$, where $y_t \in \{s_{t,1}, ..., s_{t,40}\} \cup \{N\}$, N is null which means all the skill candidates are rejected by the user. Note that for the sake of customer privacy, the data is de-identified and we are not able to know the identify of the user from the data.

4.2 Collaborative Data Relabeling

For CDR, the k-nearest neighbors of an utterance is found from the training data. And only the training data is relabeled. We keep the labels of the validation and testing data as it is. When relabeling the skill candidates of an utterance, we select up to 200 neighbors and keep those whose similarity score is above a certain threshold s. To avoid bringing noisy labels from neighbors, a skill candidate is relabeled if the number of its supportive neighbors are higher than n. The supportive neighbors of a skill are the neighboring utterances which relabel it as positive. The intuition is that if there are multiple neighbors confirming a skill candidate, the relabeled skill is reliable. We treat s and n as hyperparameter and choose the best value by using validation dataset.

4.3 Evaluation Metrics

To simulate the real application, we evaluate the model by selecting the top-1 skill with predicted probability higher than 0.5 and compare it with the ground truth label. The evaluation metrics are F1 scores, namely, $F1_1$ and $F1_2$ which are harmonic means of Recall and $Precision_1$, $Precision_2$, respectively. $Precision_1$ calculates the number of correct predictions over all the predictions, while $Precision_2$ means the number of correct predictions over all the non-empty predictions. Recall calculates the number of correct predictions over the number non-empty ground truth labels. Due to company policy, in this paper, we report relative performance numbers.

5 Experimental Results

5.1 Collaborative Data Relabeling

5.1.1 Comparative experimental results

Figure 5 shows the relative performance improvements of collaborative data relabeling method with the change of hyperparameters, the number of support n and similarity threshold s. The baseline model is listwise reranker model trained with the original training data. From the figures, we can see that with the increaseing of the number of support and similarity score, the F1 scores are becoming higher. With the increasing of s, the relabels we obtain are from closer neighbors which tend to bring cleaner labels. When the similarity score is lower, the two utterances are less similar, which even leads to wrong labels. With the increasing of n, we require more neighbors to confirm the relabeling of a skill candidate, which leads to higher quality of labels. Overall, the performance of the models trained on relabeled data is higher than that of the baseline model.

Table 1: Manual annotation results.

Model	Accuracy	Score	#suggestions
CDR-based model	+19.21%	+62.73%	+112.13%

5.1.2 Manual evaluation

To evaluate how CDR impacts the model performance, we manually compare the relabeled model against the baseline model. We randomly sampled 2500 samples and asked human annotators to check the suggested skills by relabeled and baseline models. We use two types of evaluation metrics. The first one is accuracy which is the number of correct predictions divided by the total number of predictions. As the model only makes a suggestion if the predicted probability is higher than 0.5, the model can reject to make a suggestion if it is not confident enough. To compare no suggestion with suggestion, we use score. A model gets a score by the following rules:

- If the model's prediction is correct, it gets a score.
- If the model doesn't make a suggestion: a) if the other model makes a wrong prediction, the current model gets a score; b) if the other model makes a correct prediction, the current model does not get a score. The intuition is that no suggestion is better than a wrong suggestion and a correct suggestion is better than no suggestion.

Table 1 shows the evaluation results based on manual annotation. The baseline model is the model trained on original data. From the results, we can see that the relabeled model has higher accuracy, which indicates higher user satisfaction. The relabeled model also gets higher score and make more suggestions.

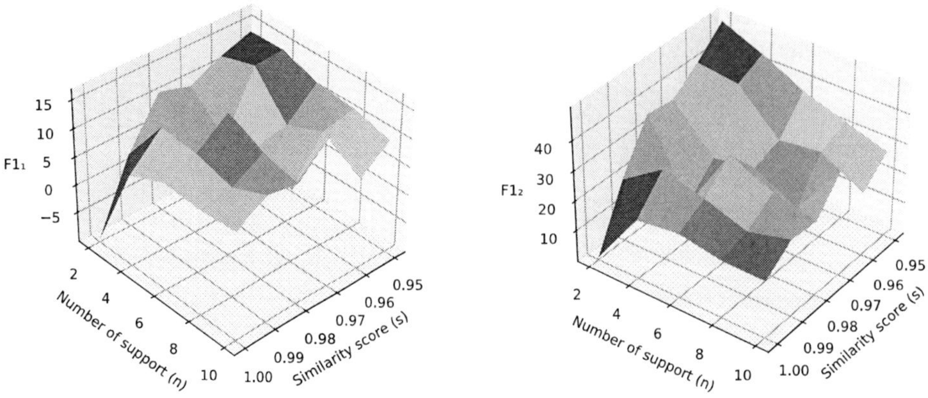

(a) $\mathrm{F1}_1$ (b) $\mathrm{F1}_2$

Figure 5: Experimental results of collaborative data relabeling method by varying the number of support and similarity threshold. The unit of vertical axis is percentage.

5.2 Online Experiments

After seeing performance gains in offline experiments, we put our model into online A/B testing. We compare it with the rule-based heuristic model. The online experiments show that the proposed model reduced friction rate by 0.35%. Friction means the circumstances where the voice assistant does not understand the user and cannot act on the user's request. The number of accepted skills increased by 5.86%. The average number of new skills enabled per customer increased by 0.98%. A skill has to be enabled before it can be used by the customer. In addition, the number of unique suggested and accepted skills increased by 233% and 98.75%, respectively, which indicates that the new model makes more diverse suggestions than the legacy system.

6 Conclusions and Future Work

In this work, we proposed a skill recommender system to suggest skills for unhandled voice commands in intelligent personal assistants that aims to reduce the user friction and recover the conversation. Compared to traditional recommender systems, the skill recommender system faces the challenge of partial observation. To resolve this challenge, we proposed collaborative data relabeling. In addition, it improves the diversity of recommended skills. Collaborative data relabeling as a simple and effective approach is especially useful for industrial deployment. We evaluated the proposed system offline before put it online for A/B testing. The online experimental results showed significant gains of user experience metrics. In the future, we will try contextual bandits and let the model learn to explore the under-exploited skills.

References

Zhe Cao, Tao Qin, Tie-Yan Liu, Ming-Feng Tsai, and Hang Li. 2007. Learning to rank: from pairwise approach to listwise approach. In *Proceedings of the 24th international conference on Machine learning*, pages 129–136.

Sylvain Castagnos, Armelle Brun, and Anne Boyer. 2013. When diversity is needed... but not expected!

Michael H Cohen, Michael Harris Cohen, James P Giangola, and Jennifer Balogh. 2004. *Voice user interface design*. Addison-Wesley Professional.

Paul Covington, Jay Adams, and Emre Sargin. 2016. Deep neural networks for youtube recommendations. In *Proceedings of the 10th ACM conference on recommender systems*, pages 191–198.

Jacob Devlin, Ming-Wei Chang, Kenton Lee, and Kristina Toutanova. 2018. Bert: Pre-training of deep bidirectional transformers for language understanding. *arXiv preprint arXiv:1810.04805*.

Michael D Ekstrand, F Maxwell Harper, Martijn C Willemsen, and Joseph A Konstan. 2014. User perception of differences in recommender algorithms. In *Proceedings of the 8th ACM Conference on Recommender systems*, pages 161–168.

Sepp Hochreiter and Jürgen Schmidhuber. 1997. Long short-term memory. *Neural computation*, 9(8):1735–1780.

Bart P Knijnenburg, Martijn C Willemsen, Zeno Gantner, Hakan Soncu, and Chris Newell. 2012. Explaining the user experience of recommender systems. *User Modeling and User-Adapted Interaction*, 22(4-5):441–504.

Matevž Kunaver and Tomaž Požrl. 2017. Diversity in recommender systems–a survey. *Knowledge-Based Systems*, 123:154–162.

Bohan Li, Hao Zhou, Junxian He, Mingxuan Wang, Yiming Yang, and Lei Li. 2020. On the sentence embeddings from pre-trained language models. *arXiv preprint arXiv:2011.05864*.

Sean M McNee, John Riedl, and Joseph A Konstan. 2006. Being accurate is not enough: how accuracy metrics have hurt recommender systems. In *CHI'06 extended abstracts on Human factors in computing systems*, pages 1097–1101.

Anand Rajaraman and Jeffrey David Ullman. 2011. *Mining of massive datasets*. Cambridge University Press.

Nils Reimers and Iryna Gurevych. 2019. Sentence-bert: Sentence embeddings using siamese bert-networks. *arXiv preprint arXiv:1908.10084*.

Elizabeth A Stuart. 2010. Matching methods for causal inference: A review and a look forward. *Statistical science: a review journal of the Institute of Mathematical Statistics*, 25(1):1.

Martijn C Willemsen, Mark P Graus, and Bart P Knijnenburg. 2016. Understanding the role of latent feature diversification on choice difficulty and satisfaction. *User Modeling and User-Adapted Interaction*, 26(4):347–389.

Cai-Nicolas Ziegler, Sean M McNee, Joseph A Konstan, and Georg Lausen. 2005. Improving recommendation lists through topic diversification. In *Proceedings of the 14th international conference on World Wide Web*, pages 22–32.

Semi-supervised Intent Discovery with Contrastive Learning

Xiang Shen   Yinge Sun   Yao Zhang   Mani Najmabadi
Expedia Group
{xianshen, yinsun, yaozhang, mnajmabadi}@expediagroup.com

Abstract

User intent discovery is a key step in developing a Natural Language Understanding (NLU) module at the core of any modern Conversational AI system. Typically, human experts review a representative sample of user input data to discover new intents, which is subjective, costly, and error-prone. In this work, we aim to assist the NLU developers by presenting a novel method for discovering new intents at scale given a corpus of utterances. Our method utilizes supervised contrastive learning to leverage information from a domain-relevant, already labeled dataset and identifies new intents in the corpus at hand using unsupervised K-means clustering. Our method outperforms the state-of-the-art by a large margin up to 2% and 13% on two benchmark datasets, measured by clustering accuracy. Furthermore, we apply our method on a large dataset from the travel domain to demonstrate its effectiveness on a real-world use case.

1 Introduction

Conversational AI systems such as chatbots and virtual assistants are widely used in a variety of applications to assist users. Natural Language Understanding (NLU), as an integral part of a conversational AI system, is the process of classifying the user's input into a set of pre-defined categories, generally referred to as intents. In most applications, the task of NLU is achieved by developing a supervised text classification model. Understanding and identifying user intents is key to developing intent classification models as it directly impacts the performance of the system.

Generally, the set of intents that can be recognized by the model is defined by human experts based on domain knowledge and business requirements. This process usually requires a significant amount of effort to manually review large-scale user input data. In addition, this task becomes increasingly complex as the number of potential intents in the dataset grows.

To address these challenges, intent discovery methods that aim to detect new user intents, either automatically or semi-automatically, from a large number of unlabeled utterances, have been developed in recent years.

A popular approach for intent discovery is based on unsupervised clustering algorithms. For instance, Shi et al. (2018) conduct hierarchical clustering on sentence representations from autoencoder based on a combination of word embeddings, POS tagging, keywords, and topic modeling. Vedula et al. (2019, 2020) establish a multi-stage procedure which detects out-of-domain utterances with a classification model and then group the text with unknown intents by clustering. Chatterjee and Sengupta (2020) extend DBSCAN (Ester et al., 1996) to discover intents in conversations based on sentence embeddings from universal sentence encoder (Cer et al., 2018). However, the unsupervised approaches often fail to produce highly accurate and granular intents. As such, researchers have developed semi-supervised methods to leverage existing domain-relevant labeled data in order to improve the intent discovery results. Zhang et al. (2021) propose deep aligned clustering (DAC) in a semi-supervised framework to leverage the prior information of known intents. DAC uses BERT to generate sentence representations. However, BERT has poor performance with respect to generating semantically meaningful sentence representations (Reimers and Gurevych, 2019; Li et al., 2020). Alternatively, Sahay et al. (2021) use sentence-BERT (SBERT) to learn sentence representations but fail to achieve significantly better results using the DAC algorithm without adjusting their training methods for SBERT.

Proceedings of the Third Workshop on Natural Language Processing for Conversational AI, pages 120–129
November 10, 2021.

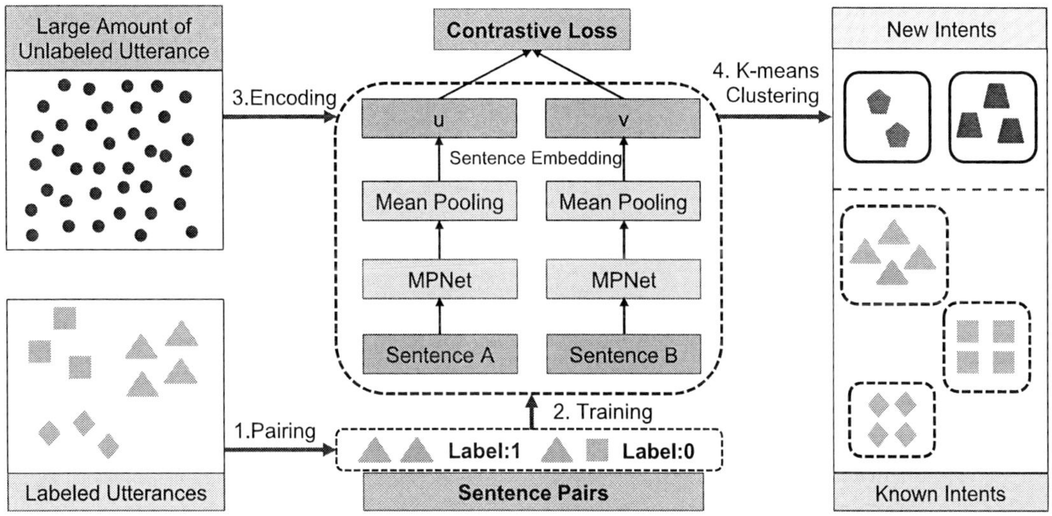

Figure 1: The architecture of the proposed method. First, we use labeled data to pair utterances based on their labels. Then, we train the sentence transformer, MPNet, in the Siamese Network structure with contrastive loss to learn sentence representations using sentence pairs in a supervised way. Next, we encode unlabeled data by the trained model. Finally, we estimate the optimal values of the number of clusters and perform K-means to discover new intents from identified clusters.

To address the limitations in the methods mentioned above and to further improve the results, we propose a novel semi-supervised method as illustrated in Figure 1. We use a Siamese Network (Reimers and Gurevych, 2019) to learn semantically meaningful sentence representations, in which a model is trained to differentiate pairs of sentences with the same intent and those with different intents. A pre-trained model that achieves the state-of-the-art performance among sentence transformers, MPNet (Song et al., 2020), is used in the Siamese Network structure combined with contrastive learning to learn similar and dissimilar representations for sentences with the same and different intents respectively. K-means algorithm is then applied to cluster the unlabeled utterances based on their sentence representations for discovering new intents at scale. In addition, we propose a novel way to determine the optimal number of clusters k based on the concept of clustering stability, where k selection solely depends on the dataset at hand as opposed to relying on any prior knowledge. Inspired by self-supervised learning with aligned pseudo labels introduced in DAC (Zhang et al., 2021), we further propose and experiment with four different pseudo label training (PLT) strategies in the setting of Siamese Network, and examine the impact of PLT in our experiments.

The contributions of our work are summarized as follows. First, we propose a novel semi-supervised framework that learns sentence representations effectively via supervised contrastive learning and discovers new intents at scale via unsupervised clustering. Second, we propose a simple and robust method based on clustering stability to determine the optimal number of clusters for K-means. Third, we conduct extensive experiments to show that our method achieves state-of-the-art performance on two public benchmark datasets, widely used for intent discovery. In addition, we successfully apply our methods to a real-world dataset from an application in the travel domain.

2 Related Work

In this section we review the previous work focused on the main components of the intent discovery process in more detail.

2.1 Sentence Representation

Sentence representation has a significant impact on the quality of the intent discovery results. A simple method is to employ mean pooling of word embeddings such as word2vec (Mikolov et al., 2013) and GloVe (Pennington et al., 2014), but it does not capture the information in the order of words. InferSent (Conneau et al., 2017) obtains sentence embeddings from pre-training bidirectional LSTM and max-pooling the output. Cer et al. (2018) introduce universal sentence encoder (USE) which trains a transformer network on multiple tasks and achieves great performance on tasks through transfer learning.

A common approach to generate sentence embeddings using pre-trained transformer networks such as BERT (Devlin et al., 2019) is to extract the embeddings of CLS token, a special token inserted at the beginning of the input, from the last layer. However, this approach leads to anisotropic semantic space and performs poorly on textual similarity tasks (Reimers and Gurevych, 2019). Reimers and Gurevych (2019) demonstrate that averaging over the embeddings of all tokens improves the performance and further present a fine-tuned BERT in Siamese network architecture (SBERT) pre-trained on sentence pairs. Li et al. (2020) tackle the anisotropy issue and transform the embeddings to Gaussian distribution through a normalizing flow. Su et al. (2021) provide an even simpler solution to boost the performance based on the whitening of embeddings from BERT.

2.2 Contrastive Learning

Contrastive learning has demonstrated its ability to learn effective representations primarily in the computer vision field. In recent years, several studies have explored constructing sentence embeddings using contrastive learning. The core idea of contrastive learning is to create positive and negative sentence pairs such that representations of positive pairs are pulled together while negative pairs are pushed apart. Different strategies have been proposed to achieve this goal. Fang et al. (2020) utilize back-translation to perform sentence augmentation. Giorgi et al. (2020) sample text segmentations within the same document to construct sentence pairs. Gao et al. (2021) create positive instances by simply adding dropout masks to the original sentences.

2.3 Clustering

Clustering as an essential part of the intent discovery process identifies and groups similar sentence representations in an unsupervised setting. Popular algorithms include density-based methods (e.g., DBSCAN (Ester et al., 1996)) and centroid-based methods (e.g., K-means (MacQueen et al., 1967; Arthur and Vassilvitskii, 2006)). DBSCAN is not scalable for large datasets and not efficient for high-dimensional data. In contrast, K-means is a fast and scalable algorithm. Therefore, it is more suitable for identifying clusters from large datasets (usually thousands of or even hundreds of thousands of utterances) with high dimensional sentence representations (e.g., 768).

The K-means algorithm requires the number of clusters (k) to be provided by the user. There are several methods proposed in the literature that aim to identify the optimal k. The elbow method (Thorndike, 1953), the silhouette method (Rousseeuw, 1987), and the information criterion methods, such as Akaike information criterion (Akaike, 1974) and Bayesian information criterion (Schwarz, 1978), use simple measures to select k based on the tightness or separation of clusters. Ben-David et al. (2007); Levine and Domany (2001) introduce the notion of clustering stability to determine k that produces the most stable clustering results. DAC (Zhang et al., 2021) selects k by eliminating low confidence clusters from K' (a large pre-determined value), however, this method produces unstable clustering results that are highly dependent on the pre-determined value.

3 Our Approach

In this section, we describe the proposed method in detail. As shown in Figure 1, we start by constructing the sentence pairs from our labeled dataset. Then, we train a binary classifier with contrastive loss in a Siamese network structure which uses a pre-trained MPNet model to identify if two utterances have the same intent or not. Next, we encode a large number of unlabeled utterances using the trained MPNet. Finally, we find the optimal k for K-means based on the concept of clustering stability and group the utterances using K-means to obtain new intents.

3.1 Sentence Representation

To construct effective sentence embeddings, we train a MPNet with contrastive loss as a binary encoder using the labeled data. MPNet is a transformer-based language model which improves the pre-trained BERT model by introducing masked and permuted language models. The new pre-training technique maintains the advantages of the masked language modeling (MLM) from BERT as well as the permuted language modeling (PLM) from XLNet (Yang et al., 2019). In this study, we employ a pretrained version of MPNet model 'paraphase-mpnet-base-v2' from Reimers and Gurevych (2019).

While feeding a sentence with m different tokens to BERT or MPNet, token embeddings are extracted from the last hidden layer as $[CLS, T_1, T_2, \cdot, T_m]$ where CLS is a special token and short for classification. Then the sentence representation is obtained by applying mean-pooling of the token embeddings with fixed length:

$$u = \text{mean-pooling}([CLS, T_1, T_2, \cdot, T_m])$$

A binary classifier is added on the top of a sentence pair with representation u and v obtained from the MPNet model with the same weights. The binary classifier identifies if two sentences have the same intent or not. We transform the labeled utterances into sentence pairs in a way that sentences with the same intent are labeled 1 and labeled as 0 otherwise. In this case, a total number of N labeled utterances will lead to $N(N-1)/2$ sentence pairs. The supervised contrastive learning objective is to minimize the contrastive loss:

$$L = y*(D(u,v))^2 + (1-y)*(max(0, m-D(u,v))^2$$

Where $D(u, v)$ is the distance of u and v. This supervised contrastive learning (SCL) method aims to pull together utterances with the same intent and push apart utterances with different intents.

In the next step, we feed unlabeled utterances into the trained MPNet to obtain sentence embeddings for K-means clustering.

3.2 K-means Clustering

We use K-means to group sentences with similar sentence embeddings into clusters. Each resulting cluster consists of sentences with the same intent (either known or unknown). However, a key hyperparameter in K-means, the number of clusters k, is often unknown in practice due to lack of information about the corpus, e.g., the total number of intents in the corpus in our case. Therefore, we propose a novel method to determine the optimal value of k.

Our selection of k is based on the concept of clustering stability inspired by Ben-David et al. (2007); Levine and Domany (2001). The stability refers to the robustness of a clustering model to small perturbations in the data. Intuitively, the optimal number of clusters should generate a clustering model with high stability. In other words, if we repeat a clustering algorithm on different samples of the data, then the clustering results on those samples with the optimal k should be similar. We measure the

Algorithm 1 Select the number of clusters k

1: Draw r random samples (without replacement) from the complete training data, each containing $\beta\%$ messages.
2: **for** k in k_{min} to k_{max} with increment of s **do**
3: Apply K-means with k clusters on the complete training data.
4: **for** i in 1 to r **do**
5: Apply K-means with k clusters on the ith sample.
6: Calculate ACC between the clustering labels from the complete training data and those from the ith sample.
7: Calculate stability score for k.
8: Fit s pairs of (k, stability score at k) to a Gaussian Process model M_{GP}.
9: **for** t in 1 to T **do**
10: Predict k_{new} by model M_{GP}.
11: Calculate stability score at k_{new} (step 3-7 with $k = k_{new}$).
12: Update model M_{GP} with (k_{new}, stability score at k_{new}).
13: Select k with the highest stability score.

similarity between a pair of different clustering results (taking one clustering result in the pair as the ground truth) by ACC, an unsupervised equivalent of classification accuracy. Given that different clustering results may have different labels for the same cluster, the Hungarian algorithm (Kuhn, 1955) is employed in the process of calculating ACC to map labels from one clustering to those from the other. We then define the stability score as the mean ACC across all pairs (the number of pairs is equal to the number of samples r), which is a function of k. The optimal value of k is estimated by the k with the highest stability score from a pre-defined range of $[k_{min}, k_{max}]$.

To further speed up the process of selecting the optimal value of k described above, we use Bayesian Optimization (BO), which is an efficient method to optimize functions of any forms and thus is suitable for hyperparameter tuning when the objective function is expensive to compute (Snoek et al., 2012). In BO, a surrogate model of the objective function is an easy-to-optimize probability model (commonly Gaussian Process) of hyperparameters. It is easy to find its extreme point (the hyperparameters that reach the minimum/maximum of the surrogate model) and then update the model with the value of objective function at the extreme point. Such BO process conducts optimization-update at each step and thus enables faster convergence. We adopt Discrete-BO proposed in Luong et al. (2019) as the hyperparameter, number of clusters k, is a discrete variable. More specifically, instead of calculating the stability score (i.e., the objective function) for each k in $[k_{min}, k_{max}]$, we only calculate at k from $[k_{min}, k_{max}]$ in increments of s and build a surrogate model based upon those calculated values. Then we repeat the optimization-update step for T times. The procedure (named Clustering Stability with Bayesian Optimization) is summarized in Algorithm 1.

4 Experimentation

4.1 Datasets

We conducted experiments using two benchmark datasets, CLINC (Larson et al., 2019) and BANKING (Casanueva et al., 2020), which are also used by Zhang et al. (2021) and Sahay et al. (2021).

For our use case in travel domain, we collected utterances sent by travelers to Expedia virtual assistant. We used a labeled dataset of 3082 utterances as the training set and 512 utterances as the validation set. A random sample of 100,000 English utterances from one month in 2021 was used for intent discovery. Those utterances are minimally preprocessed by removing invalid characters and lowercasing letters.

The detailed statistics of the datasets is shown in Table 1.

4.2 Evaluation Setup

To evaluate the effectiveness of SCL on two benchmark datasets, we split the datasets into training, validation, and test sets, and use different known intent class ratios of 25%, 50%, and 75% to compare the performance of different methods. For each known intent, 10% of training data is randomly sampled and used as labeled data. We use the labeled training set to train MPNet, and select the best model with the validation set. While Zhang et al. (2021) uses a validation set which is much larger than the labeled training set, our validation set is a smaller portion of the original validation set. More specifically, we use 30% of the original validation data within known intents to maintain the number of sentence pairs with a training validation ratio around 9:1. We use the trained MPNet to calculate sentence embeddings for the test set and evaluate K-means clustering performance on the test set. The number of clusters is fixed as the ground-truth number of intents for fair comparison. We report the average results over five runs of experiments with different random seeds.

In addition, to evaluate the performance of our proposed method on the selection of k, we set k_{min} to $0.5 \cdot k_{true}$ and k_{max} to $1.5 \cdot k_{true}$ to cover a wide range of possible values of k. We set the increment $s = 10$ in Algorithm 1 to reduce the number of times the stability score needs to be calculated to 10%. We set $T = 10$ as we observe 1 usually converges in a few steps. We try various numbers of random samples r (i.e., 10, 20, 30, 40, 50) and observe similar trends and peaks for the stability scores. Therefore, we set $r = 10$ for all experiments to reduce the computation cost. In each of the random samples, we set the sampling ratio, $\beta = 80$ to ensure each sample is representative of the entire dataset.

We also evaluate the effectiveness of pseudo label training (PLT) inspired by Zhang et al. (2021). In PLT, labels are updated at the end of each epoch to learn better sentence representations over the course of training. We compare different strategies for PLT with our proposed baseline SCL. More specifically, we experiment with 4 strategies.

- Inclusive pairing: pair up all sentences from the entire training data by pseudo labels from K-means to continue training.
- Exclusive pairing: pair up sentences from the labeled training set by true labels and pair up sentences from the unlabeled training set by pseudo labels to continue training.
- Alignment-A: align pseudo labels from K-means to the true labels of the labeled training set by maximizing ACC between pseudo labels and true labels, and then replace aligned pseudo labels of the labeled training set with true labels to pair up sentences and continue training.
- Alignment-C: align pseudo labels from K-means to the true labels of the labeled training set by minimizing cluster centroid distance between pseudo labels and true labels, and then replace aligned pseudo labels of the labeled training set with true labels to pair up sentences and continue training.

Dataset	#Classes	#Training	#Validation	#Test	Vocabulary	Length (mean/max)
CLINC	150	18,000	2,250	2,250	7,283	8.31/28
BANKING	77	9,003	1,000	3,080	5,028	11.91/79
TRAVEL	18	3,082	512	–	2,624	12.98/184

Table 1: Statistics of datasets.

		CLINC			BANKING		
	Method	ACC	ARI	NMI	ACC	ARI	NMI
25%	BERT	58.28	44.91	80.23	40.92	27.64	61.53
	DAC	**75.20**	**65.36**	**89.12**	47.58	35.49	68.88
	SMPNET	68.37	58.54	87.68	56.97	45.11	76.33
	SCL	71.23	62.02	88.30	**58.73**	**47.47**	**76.79**
50%	BERT	70.75	59.61	86.33	57.48	44.20	73.02
	DAC	**80.70**	**72.26**	**91.50**	59.44	47.07	76.14
	SMPNET	73.49	64.81	89.75	62.80	50.94	78.28
	SCL	78.36	70.71	91.38	**67.28**	**55.50**	**80.25**
75%	BERT	80.62	72.17	91.06	67.11	54.20	78.59
	DAC	86.40	79.56	93.92	63.68	52.11	78.77
	SMPNET	83.24	74.28	93.39	71.82	58.82	82.22
	SCL	**86.91**	**81.64**	**94.75**	**76.55**	**65.43**	**85.04**

Table 2: The clustering results on two datasets at known class ratio of 25%, 50% and 75%.

The difference between inclusive pairing and exclusive pairing is that the former does not utilize the information of true labels from the labeled training set while the latter does but it never pairs up sentences from the labeled training set with sentences from the unlabeled training set due to the mismatch between true labels and pseudo labels. In addition, alignment-A and alignment-C are two ways to tackle the mismatch problem and then leverage the true label information and to train with all pairs. We freeze the first 11 layers of MPNet to speed up the pseudo label training process and preserve universal features learned from SCL.

When applying our method to travel domain data, we first use the labeled data to train SCL. Then, we run our k selection algorithm on 100,000 unlabeled data to determine k. Finally, we apply K-means with the selected k to unlabeled data to get the intent clusters.

4.3 Evaluation Metrics

We employ three standard metrics for evaluating the performance of clustering: Clustering Accuracy (ACC), Normalized Mutual Information (NMI), and Adjusted Rand Index (ARI). To calculate ACC, Hungarian algorithm is used to map the clustering labels to the true labels.

For our travel domain data, we visualize the clustering results by t-SNE and manually review the utterances within each cluster to discover new intents.

5 Results and Discussion

5.1 Effectiveness of SCL

In this section, we compare our method SCL with three baseline methods, BERT, DAC and SMPNet. BERT refers to using the BERT model trained with labeled data to generate sentence representations on unlabeled data for K-means clustering. DAC is considered as the current state-of-the-art in the area of intent discovery. DAC uses pseudo labels generated by clustering to train BERT iteratively in a self-supervised learning way while BERT does not use clustering predictions for further training. SMPNet is simply trained by Siamese MPNet with sentence pairs using cosine similarity loss instead of contrastive loss used in SCL. SMPNet is included here to show the effectiveness of contrastive learning. We conduct experiments on two benchmark datasets described in Section 4.1. As shown in Table 2, our method consistently achieves better clustering performance compared to DAC by a large margin on the BANKING dataset across different known label ratios with respect to all 3 metrics. Our method also achieves comparable re-

	Method	CLINC (k = 150) $\hat{k}$	Error	ACC	ARI	NMI	BANKING (k = 77) $\hat{k}$	Error	ACC	ARI	NMI
25%	DAC	123	18.00	**67.22**	**59.28**	**87.50**	**63**	**18.18**	47.13	35.83	69.09
	SCL	**131**	**12.67**	66.05	57.86	87.09	47	38.96	**48.41**	**39.81**	**73.07**
50%	DAC	126	16.00	72.16	65.70	90.01	**64**	**16.88**	56.92	46.00	75.76
	SCL	**141**	**6.00**	**77.40**	**69.49**	**91.14**	60	22.08	**59.22**	**49.49**	**78.24**
75%	DAC	129	14.00	77.03	71.88	92.35	65	15.58	61.94	51.35	78.73
	SCL	**151**	**0.67**	**86.90**	**81.57**	**94.72**	**69**	**10.39**	**73.03**	**62.45**	**84.25**

Table 3: The results of k selection at known class ratio of 25%, 50% and 75%.

			CLINC			BANKING		
		PLT strategy	ACC	ARI	NMI	ACC	ARI	NMI
25%	SCL only	-	71.23	62.02	88.30	58.73	47.47	76.79
	SCL+PLT	Inclusive pairing	72.86	63.88	88.99	59.47	47.66	76.69
		Exclusive pairing	73.01	64.05	89.15	60.29	48.89	**77.26**
		Alignment-A	**73.77**	**64.78**	**89.31**	59.10	47.69	76.85
		Alignment-C	72.68	63.82	89.04	**61.09**	**48.91**	77.25
50%	SCL only	-	78.36	70.71	91.38	**67.28**	**55.50**	**80.25**
	SCL+PLT	Inclusive pairing	79.58	72.36	91.91	66.12	55.14	80.24
		Exclusive pairing	**80.59**	**73.25**	**92.21**	66.21	54.86	80.18
		Alignment-A	79.89	72.62	91.96	66.81	55.45	80.40
		Alignment-C	78.28	70.56	91.39	66.39	54.80	80.10
75%	SCL only	-	86.91	81.64	94.75	**76.55**	**65.43**	**85.04**
	SCL+PLT	Inclusive pairing	88.28	82.32	94.95	74.81	64.51	84.82
		Exclusive pairing	**88.68**	**83.44**	**95.25**	75.18	64.44	84.77
		Alignment-A	88.49	83.09	95.11	75.66	64.91	85.02
		Alignment-C	84.58	78.99	94.04	73.09	62.18	83.52

Table 4: The results of 4 different strategies for pseudo label training on two datasets at known class ratio of 25%, 50% and 75%.

sults on the CLINC dataset in which each intent has an equal number of utterances in training, validation, and test set. DAC performers slightly better on two settings in this experiment when the true k is provided. However, the advantages disappear when k is unknown, as demonstrated in the next subsection 5.2. In addition, it is to be noted that SCL significantly outperforms the baseline by 10% in ACC on the BANKING dataset, which is imbalanced and is more aligned with real-world cases. In comparison, the CLINC dataset has a perfect balance in terms of the number of data points for each intent. Our method, SCL, which utilizes information from each sentence pair provides more robust results when applied to imbalanced datasets.

We suppose the reasons for better results from our method include the following. First, constructing sentence pairs to train the Siamese network leverages the labeled data more effectively than only using individual sentences with labels to train a BERT classification model. Also, as the base model in our training, the pre-trained MPNet(i.e., 'paraphase-mpnet-base-v2') provides better sentence embedding performance than 'bert-base-uncased' with a similar model structure. Additionally, the contrastive loss function fits the training task better than the cosine similarity loss.

5.2 Selection of k

We compare the performance on the selection of k between our proposed method and DAC. More specifically, we calculate the error rate of the predicted k ($\hat{k}$) as well as ACC, ARI, and NMI for both methods at different known class ratios (25%, 50%, 75%) on the CLINC dataset and the BANKING dataset. Table 3 summarizes the average results over five runs of experiments with different random seeds. It shows our proposed method achieves significantly better results on estimating k than DAC by reducing the average error rate from 16.44%

to 10.36%, except for the BANKING dataset with 25% known classes. The reason that our method has a higher error rate on the BANKING dataset with 25% or 50% known classes is mainly due to the imbalance of the dataset in which small clusters with related intents tend to be grouped together as one large cluster. It is worth noting that the ACC, ARI, and NMI derived from our predicted k are much higher than those from DAC. In the case of 75% known class ratio, the results are comparable to those from the ground-truth k. That is compelling evidence that our proposed method works better in real-world cases when the number of intents is unknown.

5.3 Pseudo Label Training

Table 4 shows the results of SCL and PLT with 4 strategies at different known class ratios. The performance on the CLINC dataset across 3 known class ratios is further improved by PLT using the first 3 strategies. The fourth strategy, alignment-C, does not perform as well as the other methods. There are two reasons that could explain this performance drawback. First, matching by cluster centroids does not achieve a high alignment ACC. Second, the error induced by mismatching propagates along with training epochs. In addition, the performance on the BANKING dataset at 25% known class ratio is further improved by all PLT strategies.

5.4 Performance on Travel Domain Data

Figure 2: Visualization of the clustering result in 2D embeddings via t-SNE.

We apply our method to select k and obtain $k = 34$. In Figure 2, we further visualize the sentence representations of a large number of unlabeled utterances learned by SCL via t-SNE. Dots with different colors represent utterances in different clusters. Evidently, there is a clear margin between clusters captured by the 2D sentence representations learned by our model. We further analyze utterances within clusters and define new intents according to the business need. For confidentiality reasons, we do not disclose the details of new intents and example utterances.

6 Conclusion and Future Work

In this work, we propose a new semi-supervised framework to discover new intents by a sentence representation network via supervised contrastive learning followed by unsupervised K-means clustering. The method effectively leverages prior knowledge of existing intents to learn sentence representations and discovers new intents by grouping utterances with similar sentence representation. In the future, we will extend the work to discover intents with inherent hierarchy and automatically generate labels for new intents.

Acknowledgements

The authors wish to thank Matthew Fryer, Zoe Yang, and all members of the Conversational AI Team at Expedia Group for their support and review to this work. We also thank the anonymous reviewers for their valuable feedback.

References

Hirotugu Akaike. 1974. A new look at the statistical model identification. *IEEE transactions on automatic control*, 19(6):716–723.

David Arthur and Sergei Vassilvitskii. 2006. k-means++: The advantages of careful seeding. Technical report, Stanford.

Shai Ben-David, Dávid Pál, and Hans Ulrich Simon. 2007. Stability of k-means clustering. In *International conference on computational learning theory*, pages 20–34. Springer.

Iñigo Casanueva, Tadas Temčinas, Daniela Gerz, Matthew Henderson, and Ivan Vulić. 2020. Efficient intent detection with dual sentence encoders. In *Proceedings of the 2nd Workshop on Natural Language Processing for Conversational AI*, pages 38–45.

Daniel Cer, Yinfei Yang, Sheng-yi Kong, Nan Hua, Nicole Limtiaco, Rhomni St John, Noah Constant, Mario Guajardo-Céspedes, Steve Yuan, Chris Tar, et al. 2018. Universal sentence encoder. *arXiv preprint arXiv:1803.11175*.

Ajay Chatterjee and Shubhashis Sengupta. 2020. Intent mining from past conversations for conversational agent. In *Proceedings of the 28th International Conference on Computational Linguistics*, pages 4140–4152.

Alexis Conneau, Douwe Kiela, Holger Schwenk, Loïc Barrault, and Antoine Bordes. 2017. Supervised learning of universal sentence representations from natural language inference data. In *Proceedings of the 2017 Conference on Empirical Methods in Natural Language Processing*, pages 670–680.

Jacob Devlin, Ming-Wei Chang, Kenton Lee, and Kristina Toutanova. 2019. BERT: Pre-training of deep bidirectional transformers for language understanding. In *Proceedings of the 2019 Conference of the North American Chapter of the Association for Computational Linguistics: Human Language Technologies, Volume 1 (Long and Short Papers)*, pages 4171–4186, Minneapolis, Minnesota. Association for Computational Linguistics.

Martin Ester, Hans-Peter Kriegel, Jörg Sander, Xiaowei Xu, et al. 1996. A density-based algorithm for discovering clusters in large spatial databases with noise. In *Proceedings of the Second International Conference on Knowledge Discovery and Data Mining*, volume 96, pages 226–231.

Hongchao Fang, Sicheng Wang, Meng Zhou, Jiayuan Ding, and Pengtao Xie. 2020. Cert: Contrastive self-supervised learning for language understanding. *arXiv preprint arXiv:2005.12766*.

Tianyu Gao, Xingcheng Yao, and Danqi Chen. 2021. Simcse: Simple contrastive learning of sentence embeddings. *arXiv preprint arXiv:2104.08821*.

John M Giorgi, Osvald Nitski, Gary D. Bader, and Bo Wang. 2020. Declutr: Deep contrastive learning for unsupervised textual representations. *ArXiv*, abs/2006.03659.

Harold W Kuhn. 1955. The hungarian method for the assignment problem. *Naval research logistics quarterly*, 2(1-2):83–97.

Stefan Larson, Anish Mahendran, Joseph J. Peper, Christopher Clarke, Andrew Lee, Parker Hill, Jonathan K. Kummerfeld, Kevin Leach, Michael A. Laurenzano, Lingjia Tang, and Jason Mars. 2019. An evaluation dataset for intent classification and out-of-scope prediction. In *Proceedings of the 2019 Conference on Empirical Methods in Natural Language Processing and the 9th International Joint Conference on Natural Language Processing (EMNLP-IJCNLP)*.

Erel Levine and Eytan Domany. 2001. Resampling method for unsupervised estimation of cluster validity. *Neural computation*, 13(11):2573–2593.

Bohan Li, Hao Zhou, Junxian He, Mingxuan Wang, Yiming Yang, and Lei Li. 2020. On the sentence embeddings from pre-trained language models. In *Proceedings of the 2020 Conference on Empirical Methods in Natural Language Processing (EMNLP)*, pages 9119–9130.

Phuc Luong, Sunil Gupta, Dang Nguyen, Santu Rana, and Svetha Venkatesh. 2019. Bayesian optimization with discrete variables. In *Australasian Joint Conference on Artificial Intelligence*, pages 473–484. Springer.

James MacQueen et al. 1967. Some methods for classification and analysis of multivariate observations. In *Proceedings of the fifth Berkeley symposium on mathematical statistics and probability*, volume 1, pages 281–297. Oakland, CA, USA.

Tomas Mikolov, Kai Chen, Greg Corrado, and Jeffrey Dean. 2013. Efficient estimation of word representations in vector space. *arXiv preprint arXiv:1301.3781*.

Jeffrey Pennington, Richard Socher, and Christopher D Manning. 2014. Glove: Global vectors for word representation. In *Proceedings of the 2014 conference on empirical methods in natural language processing (EMNLP)*, pages 1532–1543.

Nils Reimers and Iryna Gurevych. 2019. Sentence-bert: Sentence embeddings using siamese bert-networks. In *Proceedings of the 2019 Conference on Empirical Methods in Natural Language Processing*. Association for Computational Linguistics.

Peter J Rousseeuw. 1987. Silhouettes: a graphical aid to the interpretation and validation of cluster analysis. *Journal of computational and applied mathematics*, 20:53–65.

Saurav Sahay, Eda Okur, Nagib Hakim, and Lama Nachman. 2021. Semi-supervised interactive intent labeling. In *Proceedings of the Second Workshop on Data Science with Human in the Loop: Language Advances*, pages 31–40.

Gideon Schwarz. 1978. Estimating the dimension of a model. *The annals of statistics*, pages 461–464.

Chen Shi, Qi Chen, Lei Sha, Sujian Li, Xu Sun, Houfeng Wang, and Lintao Zhang. 2018. Auto-dialabel: Labeling dialogue data with unsupervised learning. In *Proceedings of the 2018 conference on empirical methods in natural language processing*, pages 684–689.

Jasper Snoek, Hugo Larochelle, and Ryan P Adams. 2012. Practical bayesian optimization of machine learning algorithms. *Advances in neural information processing systems*, 25.

Kaitao Song, Xu Tan, Tao Qin, Jianfeng Lu, and Tie-Yan Liu. 2020. Mpnet: Masked and permuted pre-training for language understanding. *arXiv preprint arXiv:2004.09297*.

Jianlin Su, Jiarun Cao, Weijie Liu, and Yangyiwen Ou. 2021. Whitening sentence representations for better semantics and faster retrieval. *arXiv preprint arXiv:2103.15316*.

Robert L Thorndike. 1953. Who belongs in the family? *Psychometrika*, 18(4):267–276.

Nikhita Vedula, Rahul Gupta, Aman Alok, and Mukund Sridhar. 2020. Automatic discovery of novel intents & domains from text utterances. *arXiv preprint arXiv:2006.01208*.

Nikhita Vedula, Nedim Lipka, Pranav Maneriker, and Srinivasan Parthasarathy. 2019. Towards open intent discovery for conversational text. *arXiv preprint arXiv:1904.08524*.

Zhilin Yang, Zihang Dai, Yiming Yang, Jaime Carbonell, Russ R Salakhutdinov, and Quoc V Le. 2019. Xlnet: Generalized autoregressive pretraining for language understanding. *Advances in neural information processing systems*, 32.

Hanlei Zhang, Hua Xu, Ting-En Lin, and Rui Lyu. 2021. Discovering new intents with deep aligned clustering. In *Proceedings of the AAAI Conference on Artificial Intelligence*.

CS-BERT: a pretrained model for customer service dialogues

Peiyao Wang, Joyce Fang and **Julia Reinspach**
Amazon, Seattle, USA
peiyaow,joycfang,reinspac@amazon.com

Abstract

Large-scale pretrained transformer models have demonstrated state-of-the-art (SOTA) performance in a variety of NLP tasks. Nowadays, numerous pretrained models are available in different model flavors and different languages, and can be easily adapted to one's downstream task. However, only a limited number of models are available for dialogue tasks, and in particular, goal-oriented dialogue tasks. In addition, the available pretrained models are trained on general domain language, creating a mismatch between the pretraining language and the downstream domain launguage. In this contribution, we present CS-BERT, a BERT model pretrained on millions of dialogues in the customer service domain. We evaluate CS-BERT on several downstream customer service dialogue tasks, and demonstrate that our in-domain pretraining is advantageous compared to other pretrained models in both zero-shot experiments as well as in finetuning experiments, especially in a low-resource data setting.

1 Introduction

The introduction of large-scale pretrained transformers such has BERT and GPT-2 (1; 2) has led to SOTA results in a variety of NLP tasks, such as question answering (QA) (3; 4; 5), named-entity recognition (NER) (6), or text summarization (7). The pretraining of these models is performed on large unlabeled text datasets with self-supervised objective functions: auto-regressive language modeling (2; 5; 8), masked language modeling (1; 9), replaced token detection (10), or next sentence prediction (1; 11), to name a few. Afterwards, the pretrained model can be adapted to a specific task by finetuning on a much smaller, labeled, and task-specific dataset, thus eliminating the need for huge labeled datasets while still maintaining the power of large-scale transformer models.

Most of the published pretrained transformer encoders have been pretrained on large text corpora covering general topics and domains, such as the Wikipedia corpus or the books corpus. Hence, they do not represent the structure that is inherent to a dialogue, i.e., two or more speakers conversing on a topic, exchanging information, or working towards solving a problem. Recently, a few pretrained transformer encoders for dialogue tasks have been released, i.e., conversational-BERT (12) for chit-chat dialogues, and TOD-BERT (13) for goal-oriented dialogues. However, dialogue models for customer service are very domain-specific (e.g. check order status, request a refund), and as a result, even the few existing dialogue-specific pretrained models exhibit a language domain mismatch between the pretraining and the downstream task. This language mismatch leads to inefficiencies in the knowledge transfer from pretraining to finetuning, resulting in worse downstream task performance, and requiring larger amounts of labeled finetuning data.

In this work, we focus on developing retrieval-based task-oriented dialogue systems, which have been successfully deployed in real-world customer service applications (14; 15). In these systems, the dialogue model ranks a pre-defined pool of agent responses, given a customer's input and the conversation history. One of the biggest challenges of developing such models is the limited amount of training data (15): high-quality annotated dialogue data is needed, which is expensive to obtain. As one of the most effective solutions, in-domain pretraining has been shown to lead to performance gains under the low-resource setting (16; 17). More specifically, for customer service dialogue modeling, (15) showed that pretraining on a large, unannotated and noisy dataset with subsequent finetuning on a small, high-quality labeled dataset yields improved performance as compared to only training with the small labeled dataset from scratch. However, the authors only evaluated their pretraining-finetuning approach using a rather small pretraining dataset of ca. 380K dialogues, and using a small-scale transformer architecture. In addition, they did not consider advanced pretraining objectives such as masked language modeling (MLM) used in BERT,

Proceedings of the Third Workshop on Natural Language Processing for Conversational AI, pages 130–142
November 10, 2021. ©2021 Association for Computational Linguistics

but their pretraining was done using the same training objective as the downstream task.

In this paper, we present CS-BERT, a BERT model pretrained on customer service dialogues, which efficiently reduces the need for expensive high-quality labeled dialogue task training data. In particular, we present the following novelties:

1. We develop CS-BERT, the first customer service domain-specific dialogue BERT model.
2. We present two novel BERT pretraining strategies specific for dialogue tasks, i.e., "masked speaker prediction" and "segment embeddings by speaker roles", which outperform models pretrained on the original BERT objectives (i.e., MLM and next sentence prediction).
3. We evaluate CS-BERT on several downstream tasks, and show that CS-BERT yields superior performance compared to BERT, conversational-BERT and TOD-BERT, in both a zero-shot setting as well as after finetuning, especially in a low-resource data setting.

The paper is structured as follows: Section 2 provides a literature overview of BERT and other available pretrained encoders. Section 3 describes the pretraining strategies that we used to develop CS-BERT. In Section 4 we describe the datasets and model training details for pretraining, as well as for finetuning on three specific downstream tasks. Section 5 follows with experimental results and discussions. We conclude the paper with a summary in Section 6.

2 Related literature

In this section, we review related literature. We first introduce BERT, then we discuss BERT variations that were developed to improve the original model. Lastly, we present the available pretrained models for dialogue tasks.

2.1 Pretrained transformer encoders: BERT

The original BERT model (1) has two self-supervised pretraining objectives: MLM and next sentence prediction (NSP). For the MLM objective, a small percentage ($\sim$15%) of the input subword tokens (18) are randomly masked, and the training objective is to predict the original token. For the NSP objective, 50% of the last sentences in an input document are replaced with a random sentence, and the training objective is to predict whether the last sentence belongs to the document or not. The last sentence is highlighted by a special separator in the input text, and by segment embeddings (segment A for the first part of the document, segment B for the last sentence).

2.2 Pretrained encoder flavors

After the initial publication of BERT, several pretrained transformer encoder flavors have been released. For example, RoBERTa (9) demonstrates improved performance by using a 10x larger pretraining dataset, and by optimizing training hyperparameters more carefully. ELECTRA (10) improves performance and pretraining time by a more efficient pretraining objective: instead of MLM, they introduce the "replaced token detection" task, thus making use of all the tokens in the input sequence. ALBERT (19) reduces model memory footprint by reducing the vocabulary embedding size and by parameter sharing. In addition, instead of using BERT's NSP task, ALBERT introduces a new and more difficult pretraining objective, i.e., "inter-sentence coherence loss", which helps model performance. Several works addressed BERT's issue of both long pretraining and inference time by reducing its quadratic computational complexity in the self-attention module, e.g., SqueezeBERT, Reformer, Performer and Longformer (11; 20; 21; 22). Other publications focus on reducing BERT's large memory footprint by model distillation, e.g., DistilBERT or DistilRoBERTa (23), which can benefit applications with limited computational resources.

2.3 Pretrained encoders for dialogue models

Most pretrained transformer encoders are pretrained on text corpora such as Wikipedia, News or Books. Thus, none of these represents the structure that is inherent to a dialogue, i.e., two or more speakers conversing on a topic, exchanging information, or working towards solving a problem. In the following, we briefly review the publicly available pretrained models that have been adapted for dialogue tasks.

Conversational-BERT (12) is a BERT model that was trained on several chit-chat type dialogue corpora, e.g., Twitter, Reddit, and Facebook News. The authors start from a cased BERT-base checkpoint, and then use BERT's standard objectives (MLM and NSP) for further pretraining on the dialogue data. Thus, while conversational-BERT is trained on dialogue-type datasets, it is neither trained on task-oriented dialogues, nor specific to any domain.

TOD-BERT (13) is a BERT model explicitly pretrained on goal-oriented datasets only. As in conversational-BERT, the authors start from an existing BERT-base checkpoint, and then pretrain TOD-BERT in a bi-encoder architecture, using a response contrastive loss in addition to the MLM objective. In addition, the authors also introduce two additional special tokens to indicate whether a user or system generated the text, i.e., "[USR]" and "[SYS]". While TOD-BERT was trained on task-oriented dialogues, it is also not specific to any domain.

In addition to the above mentioned dialogue transformer encoders, there also exist few pretrained generative models for open-domain conversations. Blenderbot (24) is an encoder-decoder architecture pretrained on Reddit data, while DialoGPT (25) is a decoder-only transformer model pretrained on Reddit data. However, in order to provide a fair comparison, we do not consider DialoGPT (25) or Blenderbot (24) for this work, since these are not transformer encoders.

3 CS-BERT pretraining strategies

In this section, we review the different pretraining strategies that we use to train CS-BERT. In particular, we use three pretraining strategies: (1) we use the same pretraining objectives as BERT, i.e., MLM and NSP/NTP (denoted as CS-BERT), (2) we add an additional objective, i.e., masked speaker prediction (MSP), to BERT's original pretraining objectives (denoted as CS-BERT-MSP), and (3) we use the same pretraining objectives as BERT, but use a different segment embedding strategy (denoted as CS-BERT-SSR).

3.1 Masked language modeling (MLM)

As in the original BERT paper, we pick 15% of tokens at random. We then replace 80% of these tokens with "[MASK]", 10% with another random token, and we keep 10% of the tokens unchanged. Then we compute the cross-entropy loss to predict the original token.

3.2 Next turn prediction (NTP)

Similar to the NSP task used in BERT, where the goal is to predict the next consecutive sentence following the context, the NTP task aims to predict the next consecutive agent turn following the dialogue context. We keep the actual agent turn following a dialogue history as a positive context-response pair, and we randomly sample one agent response from the pool of all available agent responses as a negative context-response pair.

3.3 Masked speaker prediction (MSP)

To enhance the model's ability to capture different roles from the dialogue, we incorporate the objective of MSP, which can be considered a special case of MLM applied to the three special dialogue tokens that indicate the speaker roles, i.e., "INITIALQUESTION", "AGENTSTART" and "CUSTOMERSTART" (see Table 1 for an illustration of the input format). During the training data generation, we randomly select 50% of these three tokens. We then replace 80% of them with "[MASK]", we replace 10% with another special dialogue token, and we keep 10% unchanged. The model then predicts whether the selected token is from the customer (i.e., if the original token is either "INITIALQUESTION" or "CUSTOMERSTART") or from the agent (i.e., if the original token is "AGENTSTART"). Binary cross-entropy loss is used for each masked token.

3.4 Segment embedding by speaker roles (SSR)

BERT uses binary segment embeddings to help the model distinguish between parts of the input sequence. Using BERT's default approach, the segment embeddings for the dialogue context are 0s, while the segment embeddings for the agent response (i.e., last turn in the dialogue) are 1s. For SSR, we develop a different segment embedding strategy motivated by the fact that in a dialogue there are alternating roles of customer and agent. In particular, we set the segment embeddings of all agent turns to 1s, and the segment embeddings of all customer turns to 0s. Compared to the standard segment embedding strategy, SSR focuses less on the NTP task, and more on the global contextual understanding of the dialogue.

4 Experiment setup

For all experiments in this paper, we use dialogues collected from the customer service of a large e-commerce company. We only use "chat" dialogues, i.e., written interactions between customer service agents and customers (as opposed to email conversations or transcribed spoken interactions, e.g., via phone support). We will distinguish between two dialogue datasets types:"non-annotated" dialogues and "annotated" dialogues. "Non-annotated" dialogues are free text conversations between a customer and an agent, and are inherently noisy. "Annotated" dialogues are conversations between customers and specialized agents, who provide annotations and only use a limited pool of approved agent responses (15). These annotated dialogues are of higher quality and are less noisy, and thus make it easier for a model to learn from. However, they are also more expensive to obtain.

4.1 CS-BERT pretraining

4.1.1 Pretraining dataset

As pretraining dataset, we use roughly 40,000,000 non-annotated customer-agent dialogues in English language. These dialogues come from all available customer service intents. The dialogues were filtered to have a minimum length of 1,000 words, and a maximum length of 80,000 words.

After splitting the dialogues in train and dev sets, we create turn-level training data: for each agent turn and its corresponding dialogue history (context), we use the actual agent turn as a positive example for the NTP task, and use randomly sampled agent responses as negative examples. For the dev dataset, we do not use all turns in the dialogues, but randomly sample a smaller subset of turns. This makes hyperparameter tuning and model evaluation more computationally efficient. Table 1 provides an example of a positive context-response pair that was created for pretraining CS-BERT. The pretraining dataset statistics are described in Table A.1 in the Appendix.

4.1.2 CS-BERT model training

To leverage the useful knowledge from the pretrained BERT, we do not train CS-BERT from scratch, but start from the pretrained BERT-base checkpoint. As in (1), we train with a total batch size of 256 sequences for 1,000,000 steps. However, we use a maximum sequence length of 256 throughout the whole process. We use the same Adam optimizer as in (1) with learning rate of 1e−4, $\beta_1 = 0.9, \beta_2 = 0.999$, L_2 weight decay of 0.01, learning rate warmup over the first 10,000 steps, and linear decay of the learning rate. All our CS-BERT models were trained on 8 GPUs, and the total training time is around 14 days.

4.2 Response ranking

The first downstream task we evaluate is dialogue response ranking, the objective of which is to predict the most likely agent response from a predefined pool of agent responses, given the dialogue history (context) and (optionally) other dialogue metadata or features. The response ranking model is finetuned as a binary classification model, i.e., given a dialogue history and features, the model needs to predict whether the response is a valid next turn or not. During inference, the scores of all responses in the response pool are calculated, and then ranked to determine the most likely agent response.

4.2.1 Datasets for response ranking

While the non-annotated pretraining dataset described in Section 4.1.1 made use of all available customer service intents, in practice, we develop separate downstream models for specific intents. For this work, we use datasets from three different intents, i.e., "item-in-transit" (in-transit), "item-delivered-not-received" (DNR), and "start-return" (SR). For all intents, we use two types of dialogue data, as described below.

Annotated finetuning response ranking data We obtain high-quality labeled datasets for finetuning from conversations and annotations created by a pool of specialized, highly trained customer service agents (15). For all three intents, we collect these annotated dialogues for a ca. 3 month period (that is non-overlapping with the CS-BERT pre-training data time period), and then split the dataset into train and dev sets. We then further collect several weeks of annotated data to create a non-overlapping test dataset, which will be used for model evaluation. As for the pretaining data, we only use dialogues in English language.

After collecting the dialogues for the train/dev/test distributions, we create turn-level training data for the response ranking task. For each agent turn and its corresponding dialogue history (context), we use the actual agent turn a positive example. As a negative example, we randomly sample from the pool of available agent responses (i.e., the pool of responses that the model has available during inference). For the sake of computational efficiency, during hyperparameter tuning, we do not use all turns in the dialogue for the dev sets, but sample a subset of turns. For the test set that we use for

context	agent response
INITIALQUESTION Tracking says that my package may be lost. It was supposed to arrive on UCI_TOKEN. AGENTSTART Can you confirm the shipping address of the order? CUSTOMERSTART UCI_TOKEN	As I see, both the UCI_TOKEN and UCI_TOKEN are sold by our partner sellers and are shipped by Fedex so as much as I would love to send replacements for you, I don't have the option for that since we don't have the direct inventory of the items.

Table 1: An example of a positive context-response pair we use for pretraining. In particular, in the context, "INITIALQUESTION" is always added at the beginning of the dialogue to mark the customer's first utterance. "AGENTSTART" is always added before an agent's utterance; "CUSTOMERSTART" is always added before a customer's utterance (unless it's the customer's first utterance). Sensitive customer informations in the dialogue text are replaced by "UCI_TOKEN" to protect customer privacy.

model evaluation, we keep all turns in a dialogue.

For the response ranking finetuning data, we also collect metadata. Metadata are specific to each intent, and can be helpful for the model to predict the correct response. Table A.2 illustrates a positive context-response pair of the finetuning response ranking dataset, including metadata. The dataset statistics for the three intents can be found in Table A.3 in the Appendix.

Non-annotated finetuning response ranking data In addition to the annotated finetuning datasets, we also use general customer-agent dialogues for finetuning (i.e., dialogues from general customer service agents). We do that because we found that adding this data to the annotated finetuning data improves the response ranking model's generalization and performance. Please note that this is the same dialogue data type as used for CS-BERT pretraining. However, we filter by intent to match the intent of the annotated data[1]. The processing for this dataset is the same as the processing for the CS-BERT pretraining dataset (see Table A.4 in the Appendix for the dataset statistics). Since the non-annotated datasets are used for regularization purposes only, we do not report metrics on these.

4.2.2 Response ranking finetuning details

We finetune all response ranking downstream tasks on a 1:1 mixture of annotated:non-annotated data. We adopt the same cross-encoder architecture as in pretraining and use the NSP head for response ranking. We use the Adam optimizer with learning rate of 2e−5, a linear learning rate warmup for the first 1,000 steps, and then linear decay. All the other parameters are the same as in pretraining. We finetune with a batch size of 176 for 5 epochs, and we pick the model that yields the highest Recall@1 on the dev dataset to perform the evaluation on the test set.

4.3 Dialogue failure detection

Another downstream task we evaluate is the dialogue failure detection task. The goal of failure detection is to detect when the goal-oriented chatbot is not able to solve a customer's issue, given the limited number of agent responses in the predefined response pool. When a failure happens, the chatbot exits the conversation and transfers the customer to a general customer service agent. The failure detection model and the response ranking model work in combination to create a real-world dialogue system for customer service.

We also approach failure detection as a binary classification task, i.e., given a dialogue history and metadata, we aim to predict whether the dialogue is a failure or not. During real-world inference, we call the failure detection model at each turn in the conversation, and transfer the customer to a human agent in the case of failure.

4.3.1 Dialogue failure detection data

We obtain the failure detection labels from the annotated response ranking finetuning data. Each turn in the conversation is labeled as non-failure if the conversation continues, and as failure if the conversation should be transferred to a human agent. To avoid target leakage, we only use the dialogue context to model failure detection, and exclude the selected response. See Table A.5 in the Appendix for an illustration of the model input. The full dataset statistics can be found in Table A.6 in the Appendix.

4.3.2 Failure detection finetuning details

We adopt the same cross-encoder architecture and its optimization setup as for the response ranking

[1]Noisy intent labels for this dataset were obtained by an intent classifier on the initial customer utterance.

model described in Section 4.2.2. The failure detection model is finetuned for up to 5 epochs, with a batch size of 80. We evaluate all the models on the test sets at the epoch that yields the smallest loss on the dev set.

4.4 NER

We investigate the CS-BERT models for a NER downstream task. In particular, we build a NER model to identify personally identifiable information (PII) in customer and agent turns, which helps to protect the privacy information of our customers. We approach this as a token classification task. Given a turn from a customer or an agent, we finetune the NER model to predict the PII tokens within each turn. This is a multi-label classification task where we define a total of 14 PII entities.

4.4.1 NER data

The NER datasets are randomly sampled utterances from customer-agent chat dialogues that were labeled with PII entities by human annotators. We use $50,000$ agent or customer turns, where 12.2% of these contains at least one PII entity. Although we define 14 PII entities in the annotation task, the data is highly skewed toward common entities, such as name, phone number, email, physical address, and some of the entities are not even observed in the 50,000 turns. We split 70% of the data for training and validation, and the remaining 30% are used as test set for evaluation. Table A.7 in the Appendix shows the entity distribution of the NER dataset. We preprocess the data to inside, outside, beginning (IOB) format (26) before finetuning. Table 2 shows an example model input and corresponding output IOB labels.

4.4.2 NER finetuning details

The NER model uses each pretrained model with an additional linear layer and softmax activation for final token classification. We use the Adam optimizer for finetuning where the learning rate is 4e-5, $\beta = (0.9, 0.999)$, $\epsilon = 1e{-8}$, and the training batch size = 64. For each pretrained model we train the NER task for 5 epochs, and the model of the epoch with the highest F1 score on the validation set is selected for evaluation on the test set.

5 Results and discussion

5.1 Response ranking results

Throughout this paper the metrics we use for response ranking evaluation are mean reciprocal rank (MRR), recall@1 and recall@5. We evaluate model performance on the test set of the high-quality annotated response ranking dataset here. For completeness, we also report test results on the non-annotated response ranking datasets in the Appendix.

5.1.1 Response ranking zero-shot results

We first evaluate the pretrained models' performance on the high-quality annotated test sets for the three intents. We consider this a zero-shot inference task across all pretrained models, since none of them were pretrained using finetuning type training data.

To perform the zero-shot evaluation on the CS-BERT models, we use the NSP prediction head inherited from pretraining. For BERT, we use the NSP head inherited from the pretrained BERT model. For TOD-BERT we use the bi-encoder architecture, since this is how it was pretrained. We modify their original response contrastive loss head into a softmax cross entropy head to compute the scores for response ranking evaluation. For conversational-BERT, we use an NSP head as in the CS-BERT/BERT models, but with weights randomly initialized, because the authors did not release the model weights of the NSP head.

The results from the six pretrained models are summarized in Table 3. The CS-BERT pretrained models are consistently better than the non-CS-BERT models for all three intents. In particular, for in-transit and DNR, the MRR and recall@1 from CS-BERT-MSP evaluated on the test data are much better than those from the other two CS-BERT models. This demonstrates the usefulness of adding the MSP task into pretraining for dialogue downstream tasks.

5.1.2 Response ranking finetuning results

High-quality annotated finetuning data is time-consuming and expensive to obtain. Hence, we experiment with the low-resource data setup to evaluate the data efficiency of different pretrained models on the downstream response ranking task. In particular, we finetune the response ranking models with 5%, 10%, 20%, 50% and 100% of the available annotated finetuning data. The full results can be found in Table A.8 in the Appendix.

For illustration, in Figure 1, we plot MRR and recall@1 evaluated on the annotated finetuning test

context	IOB label
CUSTOMERSTART My name is Jane Doe.	O O O O B-NAME I-NAME O
I have an item delivered to Seattle WA.	O O O O O O B-ADDRESS I-ADDRESS O

Table 2: An example of the model input and label output for the finetuning NER task. The input to the model is one turn and the output are the entities in IOB format.

pretrained encoder	MRR	Recall@1	Recall@5	MRR	Recall@1	Recall@5	MRR	Recall@1	Recall@5
		in-transit			DNR			SR	
BERT	10.00%	0.60%	17.20%	5.50%	0.00%	1.20%	6.43%	1.31%	5.63%
Tod-BERT	13.30%	2.30%	18.40%	11.10%	1.60%	17.70%	9.19%	2.55%	10.56%
conversational-BERT	11.70%	4.90%	9.90%	8.00%	1.30%	10.00%	10.14%	3.68%	11.27%
CS-BERT	26.00%	6.00%	55.80%	33.40%	14.20%	**54.60%**	50.15%	30.97%	**75.62%**
CS-BERT-SSR	29.70%	6.50%	**58.80%**	31.30%	11.50%	51.10%	**50.41%**	**31.46%**	75.58%
CS-BERT-MSP	**33.10%**	**12.10%**	58.10%	**35.00%**	**19.70%**	52.90%	49.63%	30.95%	74.04%

Table 3: Zero-shot inference results from pretrained models on the annotated response ranking finetuning test sets.

	Entity level			Word level		
	Precision	Recall	F1 score	Precision	Recall	F1 score
BERT	87.73%	93.02%	90.30%	89.63%	92.06%	90.83%
Tod-BERT	90.52%	89.36%	89.94%	91.94%	87.89%	89.87%
conversational-BERT	91.13%	89.79%	90.46%	93.13%	87.97%	90.48%
CS-BERT	87.84%	93.64%	90.65%	88.39%	91.90%	90.11%
CS-BERT-MSP	89.10%	93.11%	**91.06%**	89.88%	91.82%	**90.84%**

Table 4: NER result

set as a function of data percentages used to finetune the response ranking models. For clarity, we only pick one CS-BERT model for these figures, since the curves for all three CS-BERT models are very similar. The plots clearly show that the CS-BERT model consistently outperforms the other three models in the low-resource data setting across three intents. This indicates a more efficient knowledge transfer from CS-BERT pretraining. As the amount of finetuning data gets larger, the metrics from different models start to converge. For SR, the conversational-BERT also achieves certain improvements over BERT and TOD-BERT, which illustrates that pretraining on general dialogues itself can help dialogue related downstream tasks. Even though TOD-BERT was pretrained using goal-oriented dialogues, it does not demonstrate a powerful knowledge transfer, probably due to the pretraining-finetuning model architecture mismatch.

5.2 Failure detection finetuning results

We run the same data efficiency experiments described in Section 5.1.2 for the failure detection task. As metrics we use area under precision-recall curve (AUC) scores. The full results can be found in Table A.9 in the Appendix.

For illustration, in Figure 2, we plot AUC evaluated on the failure detection test set as a function of data percentages used to finetune the failure detection models. For conciseness, we only plot one curve from CS-BERT for all three CS-BERT models. The CS-BERT model clearly outperforms the other three models, especially in the low-resource data setting. In particular, when using only 50% of annotated data or less, the CS-BERT demonstrates higher AUC than the non-CS-BERT models trained on 100% of the available annotated data, demonstrating the usefulness of in-domain pretraining. Moreover, TOD-BERT and conversational-BERT outperform BERT in the low-resource setting, which further agrees with our assumption that pretraining on general dialogues yields better performance on dialogue related downstream tasks.

5.3 NER finetuning results

We evaluate two CS-BERT models versus BERT, Tod-BERT and conversational-BERT for the NER task. We measure the model performance on both entity level and token level. For entity level evaluation, we count a true positive when the model correctly predicts the entire entity (i.e. the beginning and end of an entity). For word level evaluation, we count a true positive if a word is correctly labeled as its entity type, where we separate a sentence into words using spaces. Note that CS-BERT-SSR is not included in this experiment. Our NER data is single utterance-level, and thus is not expected to

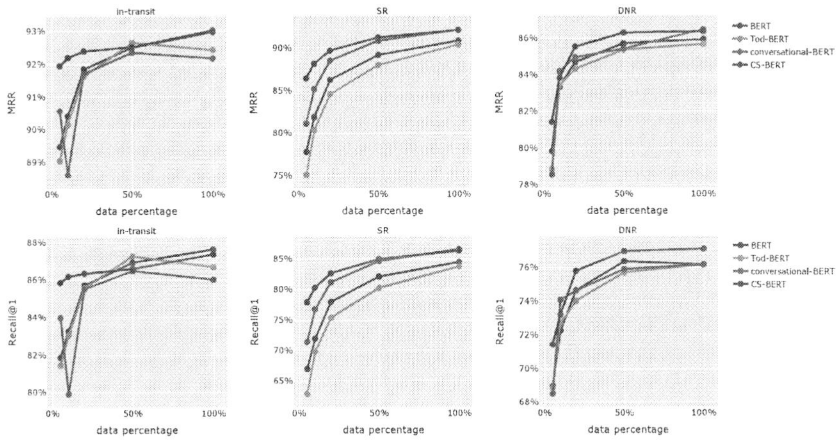

Figure 1: Recall@1 and MRR as a function of finetuning dataset percentage, evaluated on the response ranking task.

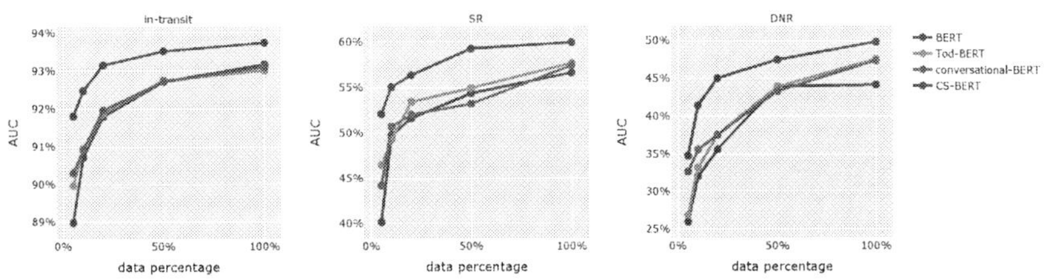

Figure 2: AUC as a function of finetuning dataset percentage, evaluated on the failure detection task.

benefit from the SSR embedding strategy.

Table 4 shows that CS-BERT-MSP performs slightly better than other models on entity and word level F1 score. However, we do not see significant difference in between the different pretrained models. We believe the reasons for this could be: (1) The NER annotated data are turn-level while the CS-BERT models are trained at the conversation level. (2) All pretrained models are sufficient enough to initialize the NER model, resulting in similar performance after finetuning. (3) Our human annotated data is noisy. We estimate that human level entity and word level F1 score are around 91.9% and 92.1%, respectively, based on 5,000 double labeled samples. Thus, we can see all models are reasonably close to human level performance. As a future work, we will improve our data quality by aggregating multiple annotations, and we plan to extend from turn level annotations to conversation level annotations.

6 Summary

In this work, we present three CS-BERT models pretrained on real-world customer service dialogues. We show that in zero-shot response ranking tasks, the CS-BERT models are superior to publicly available pretrained models, and benefit from our dialogue-specific objective function MSP.

We evaluate CS-BERT on three different downstream tasks, and demonstrate that CS-BERT consistently outperforms other non-CS-BERT models on the response ranking and failure detection task, especially in a low-resource data setting. We observe that CS-BERT is superior compared to BERT, as well as compared to two models pretrained on dialogue data, i.e., conversational-BERT and TOD-BERT, thus demonstrating the advantage of in-domain pretraining. However we also observe that the performance gains diminish with the size of the finetuning datasets, with some models reaching parity with CS-BERT when using all available finetuning data.

Due to customer data privacy concerns, we will not publicly release our CS-BERT models nor the datasets used in this work. However, we hope to inspire other researchers to experiment with pretraining their own, domain-specific BERT models. Our experiments demonstrate that these domain-specific pretrained models can improve performance on in-domain downstream tasks and can reduce the need for large amounts of expensive labeled datasets.

References

[1] Devlin, J., Chang, M.-W., Lee, K., et al. Bert: Pre-training of deep bidirectional transformers for language understanding. In *NAACL-HLT*. 2019.

[2] Radford, A., Wu, J., Child, R., et al. Language models are unsupervised multitask learners. 2019.

[3] Reimers, N., Gurevych, I. Sentence-bert: Sentence embeddings using siamese bert-networks. In *EMNLP/IJCNLP*. 2019.

[4] Garg, S., Vu, T., Moschitti, A. Tanda: Transfer and adapt pre-trained transformer models for answer sentence selection. *ArXiv*, abs/1911.04118, 2020.

[5] Yang, Z., Dai, Z., Yang, Y., et al. Xlnet: Generalized autoregressive pretraining for language understanding. In *NeurIPS*. 2019.

[6] Li, J., Sun, A., Han, J., et al. A survey on deep learning for named entity recognition. *IEEE Transactions on Knowledge and Data Engineering*, 2020.

[7] Liu, Y., Lapata, M. Text summarization with pretrained encoders. In *EMNLP/IJCNLP*. 2019.

[8] Radford, A., Narasimhan, K. Improving language understanding by generative pre-training. 2018.

[9] Liu, Y., Ott, M., Goyal, N., et al. Roberta: A robustly optimized bert pretraining approach. *ArXiv*, abs/1907.11692, 2019.

[10] Clark, K., Luong, M.-T., Le, Q. V., et al. Electra: Pre-training text encoders as discriminators rather than generators. *ArXiv*, abs/2003.10555, 2020.

[11] Iandola, F. N., Shaw, A. E., Krishna, R., et al. Squeezebert: What can computer vision teach nlp about efficient neural networks? *ArXiv*, abs/2006.11316, 2020.

[12] https://huggingface.co/DeepPavlov/bert-base-cased- conversational.

[13] Wu, C.-S., Hoi, S., Socher, R., et al. Tod-bert: Pre-trained natural language understanding for task-oriented dialogue. In *EMNLP*. 2020.

[14] Lu, Y., Srivastava, M., Kramer, J., et al. Goal-oriented end-to-end conversational models with profile features in a real-world setting. In *NAACL-HLT*. 2019.

[15] Srivastava, M., Lu, Y., Peschon, R., et al. Pretrain-finetune based training of task-oriented dialogue systems in a real-world setting. In *NAACL*. 2021.

[16] Howard, J., Ruder, S. Universal language model fine-tuning for text classification. *arXiv preprint arXiv:1801.06146*, 2018.

[17] Gururangan, S., Marasović, A., Swayamdipta, S., et al. Don't stop pretraining: adapt language models to domains and tasks. *arXiv preprint arXiv:2004.10964*, 2020.

[18] Wu, Y., Schuster, M., Chen, Z., et al. Google's neural machine translation system: Bridging the gap between human and machine translation. *ArXiv*, abs/1609.08144, 2016.

[19] Lan, Z., Chen, M., Goodman, S., et al. Albert: A lite bert for self-supervised learning of language representations. *ArXiv*, abs/1909.11942, 2020.

[20] Kitaev, N., Kaiser, L., Levskaya, A. Reformer: The efficient transformer. *ArXiv*, abs/2001.04451, 2020.

[21] Choromanski, K., Likhosherstov, V., Dohan, D., et al. Rethinking attention with performers. *ArXiv*, abs/2009.14794, 2020.

[22] Beltagy, I., Peters, M. E., Cohan, A. Longformer: The long-document transformer. *ArXiv*, abs/2004.05150, 2020.

[23] Sanh, V., Debut, L., Chaumond, J., et al. Distilbert, a distilled version of bert: smaller, faster, cheaper and lighter. *ArXiv*, abs/1910.01108, 2019.

[24] Roller, S., Dinan, E., Goyal, N., et al. Recipes for building an open-domain chatbot. In *EACL*. 2021.

[25] Zhang, Y., Sun, S., Galley, M., et al. Dialogpt: Large-scale generative pre-training for conversational response generation. In *ACL*. 2020.

[26] Kudo, T., Matsumoto, Y. Chunking with support vector machines. In *Second Meeting of the North American Chapter of the Association for Computational Linguistics*. 2001.

A Appendix

dataset	dialogues	# turns
train	40,505,050	317,093,459
dev	151,960	250,423

Table A.1: Pretraining dataset.

context	response
INITIALQUESTION AGENTSTART Can you describe in a few words how I can help you with your recent order? CUSTOMERSTART want to return CUSTOMERSTART but hasn't been delivered yet PROFILESTART paymentmethod_credit_card shippingstatus_delayed carrier_usps	Ok, give me a minute to look into this.

Table A.2: An example of a positive context-response pair created of the annotated response ranking finetuning dataset. Unlike the non-annotated pretraining data, we also use metadata for finetuning. We add "PROFILESTART" into the context as a separator between the dialogue history and the metadata. Each key-value pair in the metadata is concatenated by "_".

dataset	intent	dialogues	# turns
train	in-transit	58,515	174,434
dev	in-transit	4,815	5,000
test	in-transit	6,210	35,794
train	DNR	29,755	123,956
dev	DNR	4,674	5,000
test	DNR	3,104	19,828
train	SR	29,697	295,788
dev	SR	4,636	5,000
test	SR	7,473	95,879

Table A.3: High-quality annotated response ranking finetuning datasets for the intents "item-in-transit" (in-transit), "item-delivered-not-received" (DNR), and "start-return" (SR).

dataset	intent	# dialogues	# turns
train	in-transit	2,928,223	16,661,901
dev	in-transit	9,986	10,000
test	in-transit	9983	10,000
train	DNR	285,520	1,496,534
dev	DNR	9,876	10,000
test	DNR	9,833	10,000
train	SR	328,841	2,024,866
dev	SR	9,872	10,000
test	SR	9,871	10,000

Table A.4: Non-annotated response ranking finetuning dataset that was used to supplement the annotated dataset, for the intents "item-in-transit" (in-transit), "item-delivered-not-received" (DNR), and "start-return" (SR).

context	Failure label
INITIALQUESTION I'm still waiting for a pick up AGENTSTART Can you describe in a few words how I can help you with your recent order? CUSTOMERSTART I'm still waiting for pick up of the return item PROFILESTART membership_active shippingstatus_delivered carrier_fedex	1

Table A.5: An example of the model input we use for finetuning the failure detection task. The model's response pool was not able to handle this customer's problem and thus this conversation turn was labeled as failure. We do not use the predicted response as model input to prevent target leakage.

dataset	intent	# dialogues	# turns
train	in-transit	58,515	282,348
dev	in-transit	4,815	5,000
test	in-transit	6,210	35,794
train	DNR	29,755	164,919
dev	DNR	4,674	5,000
test	DNR	3,104	19,828
train	SR	29,697	391,052
dev	SR	4,636	5,000
test	SR	7,473	95,879

Table A.6: Annotated failure detection finetuning dataset for the intents "item-in-transit" (in-transit), "item-delivered-not-received" (DNR), and "start-return" (SR).

Label	# of entities	Percentage
Name	6304	89.2%
Physical address	168	2.4%
Phone fax	161	2.3%
URL	152	2.2%
Email	128	1.8%
Credit card number	92	1.3%
Unknown PII	47	0.7%
Membership ID	8	0.1%
CVC code	3	0.0%
Bank account	2	0.0%
Date of birth	2	0.0%

Table A.7: NER dataset entity distribution.

pretrained encoder	in-transit					DNR					SR				
	epoch	Accuracy	MRR	Recall@1	Recall@5	epoch	Accuracy	MRR	Recall@1	Recall@5	epoch	Accuracy	MRR	Recall@1	Recall@5
5%															
BERT	3	98.43%	89.47%	81.86%	98.78%	3	97.86%	79.83%	68.97%	96.09%	3	98.04%	77.76%	66.96%	91.40%
TOD-BERT	3	98.28%	89.04%	81.45%	98.33%	3	97.61%	78.85%	68.84%	95.67%	3	97.27%	75.08%	62.82%	90.85%
conversational-BERT	3	98.67%	90.56%	83.97%	98.93%	3	98.07%	78.56%	68.50%	95.86%	3	98.23%	81.11%	71.40%	93.35%
CS-BERT	2	98.80%	91.94%	85.84%	99.41%	3	98.10%	81.42%	71.43%	97.65%	3	98.65%	86.43%	77.85%	97.18%
CS-BERT-SSR	2	98.71%	91.97%	86.01%	99.37%	3	98.21%	81.26%	71.18%	97.78%	3	98.61%	86.29%	77.62%	97.18%
CS-BERT-MSP	2	98.76%	92.18%	86.33%	99.41%	3	98.18%	81.29%	71.02%	97.40%	2	98.56%	86.21%	77.43%	97.30%
10%															
BERT	3	98.58%	90.40%	83.25%	99.15%	3	98.24%	83.35%	72.26%	96.59%	3	98.24%	81.87%	71.94%	94.41%
TOD-BERT	3	98.51%	90.14%	83.02%	98.98%	3	98.05%	83.42%	72.69%	97.34%	3	97.74%	80.34%	69.82%	93.92%
conversational-BERT	3	98.47%	88.61%	79.90%	99.01%	3	98.33%	84.19%	74.08%	97.73%	3	98.67%	85.18%	76.75%	95.83%
CS-BERT	3	98.86%	92.19%	86.16%	99.50%	3	98.26%	83.84%	73.21%	98.42%	3	98.83%	88.14%	80.29%	97.86%
CS-BERT-SSR	3	98.80%	92.00%	85.79%	99.51%	3	98.26%	84.67%	74.57%	98.27%	2	98.73%	87.91%	79.87%	97.94%
CS-BERT-MSP	3	98.81%	92.15%	86.13%	99.51%	3	98.24%	82.93%	71.21%	98.36%	3	98.86%	88.29%	80.54%	97.86%
20%															
BERT	3	98.73%	91.84%	85.70%	99.31%	3	98.51%	84.69%	74.63%	97.29%	3	98.60%	86.26%	77.95%	96.61%
TOD-BERT	3	98.69%	91.62%	85.56%	99.21%	3	98.29%	84.32%	74.01%	97.22%	3	98.48%	84.56%	75.36%	96.18%
conversational-BERT	3	98.83%	91.70%	85.50%	99.36%	3	98.45%	84.95%	74.62%	97.86%	3	98.83%	88.51%	81.15%	97.66%
CS-BERT	3	98.89%	92.39%	86.33%	99.66%	3	98.59%	85.53%	75.79%	98.09%	3	98.91%	89.70%	82.64%	98.42%
CS-BERT-SSR	3	98.87%	92.35%	86.34%	99.65%	3	98.61%	85.95%	76.14%	98.20%	3	98.77%	89.20%	81.78%	98.37%
CS-BERT-MSP	3	98.82%	92.43%	86.50%	99.62%	3	98.52%	85.60%	75.83%	98.13%	2	98.94%	89.54%	82.33%	98.37%
50%															
BERT	3	98.81%	92.50%	86.91%	99.49%	3	98.66%	85.71%	76.36%	98.25%	3	98.92%	89.16%	82.06%	97.94%
TOD-BERT	3	98.82%	92.65%	87.24%	99.45%	3	98.61%	85.36%	75.70%	98.35%	3	98.63%	87.99%	80.20%	97.72%
conversational-BERT	3	98.84%	92.35%	86.47%	99.57%	3	98.63%	85.42%	75.89%	98.37%	3	99.08%	90.84%	84.62%	98.47%
CS-BERT	3	98.90%	92.52%	86.58%	99.64%	3	98.72%	86.29%	76.95%	98.65%	3	99.04%	91.23%	84.94%	98.84%
CS-BERT-SSR	3	98.87%	92.94%	87.44%	99.68%	3	98.74%	86.08%	76.85%	98.73%	3	99.03%	91.08%	84.72%	98.80%
CS-BERT-MSP	3	98.83%	92.23%	86.06%	99.67%	3	98.71%	86.15%	76.86%	98.66%	3	99.07%	91.07%	84.70%	98.81%
100%															
BERT	3	98.83%	92.97%	87.60%	99.57%	3	98.66%	85.93%	76.17%	98.34%	3	99.02%	90.84%	84.46%	98.62%
TOD-BERT	3	98.83%	92.43%	86.66%	99.50%	2	98.60%	85.66%	76.15%	98.33%	3	98.93%	90.37%	83.72%	98.45%
conversational-BERT	2	98.78%	92.17%	86.00%	99.58%	3	98.71%	86.46%	76.16%	98.12%	3	99.17%	92.11%	86.55%	98.89%
CS-BERT	3	98.98%	93.03%	87.34%	99.70%	2	98.75%	86.36%	77.09%	98.68%	3	99.14%	92.11%	86.31%	99.10%
CS-BERT-SSR	3	98.93%	92.29%	86.09%	99.70%	2	98.70%	86.41%	76.84%	98.67%	3	99.12%	92.15%	86.39%	99.11%
CS-BERT-MSP	3	98.96%	92.93%	87.17%	99.74%	3	98.70%	86.46%	76.63%	98.65%	3	99.08%	92.07%	86.27%	99.07%

Table A.8: Full results from finetuning the response ranking task on the six pretrained models at different dataset percentage levels, evaluated on the annotated response ranking test sets.

pretrained encoder	in-transit		DNR		SR	
	epoch	**AUC**	**epoch**	**AUC**	**epoch**	**AUC**
5%						
BERT	3	88.98%	4	25.97%	2	40.13%
Tod-BERT	3	89.96%	4	26.90%	3	46.45%
conversational-BERT	3	90.30%	4	32.64%	2	44.18%
CS-BERT	3	91.80%	4	34.76%	3	52.08%
CS-BERT-SSR	3	91.90%	4	38.85%	2	51.97%
CS-BERT-MSP	3	92.08%	4	40.47%	3	52.55%
10%						
BERT	2	90.72%	3	31.99%	3	49.74%
Tod-BERT	2	90.94%	3	33.20%	3	49.31%
conversational-BERT	2	90.92%	3	35.58%	3	50.69%
CS-BERT	2	92.47%	3	41.43%	3	55.02%
CS-BERT-SSR	2	92.65%	3	40.88%	3	56.67%
CS-BERT-MSP	2	92.54%	3	42.81%	3	53.95%
20%						
BERT	2	91.79%	2	35.60%	2	51.62%
Tod-BERT	2	91.86%	2	37.51%	2	53.40%
conversational-BERT	2	91.96%	2	37.51%	2	51.99%
CS-BERT	2	93.15%	2	45.01%	2	56.35%
CS-BERT-SSR	2	92.90%	2	45.75%	2	56.67%
CS-BERT-MSP	2	92.92%	2	45.65%	2	56.13%
50%						
BERT	2	92.71%	2	43.90%	2	54.35%
Tod-BERT	2	92.75%	2	43.90%	2	54.91%
conversational-BERT	2	92.71%	2	43.29%	2	53.19%
CS-BERT	2	93.52%	2	47.43%	2	59.25%
CS-BERT-SSR	2	93.59%	2	47.70%	2	59.48%
CS-BERT-MSP	2	93.53%	2	48.60%	2	58.94%
100%						
BERT	2	93.17%	1	44.13%	2	56.60%
Tod-BERT	2	93.01%	2	47.50%	2	57.65%
conversational-BERT	2	93.10%	2	47.30%	2	57.40%
CS-BERT	2	93.74%	1	49.79%	2	59.94%
CS-BERT-SSR	2	93.79%	1	49.26%	2	59.95%
CS-BERT-MSP	2	93.77%	1	48.76%	2	60.32%

Table A.9: Full results from finetuning the failure detection task on the six pretrained models at different dataset percentage levels, evaluated on the failure detection test set.

PLATO-KAG: Unsupervised Knowledge-Grounded Conversation via Joint Modeling

Xinxian Huang, Huang He, Siqi Bao, Fan Wang, Hua Wu, Haifeng Wang
Baidu Inc., China
{huangxinxian01,hehuang,baosiqi,wang.fan,
wu_hua,wanghaifeng}@baidu.com

Abstract

Large-scale conversation models are turning to leveraging external knowledge to improve the factual accuracy in response generation. Considering the infeasibility to annotate the external knowledge for large-scale dialogue corpora, it is desirable to learn the knowledge selection and response generation in an unsupervised manner. In this paper, we propose PLATO-KAG (**K**nowledge-**A**ugmented **G**eneration), an unsupervised learning approach for end-to-end knowledge-grounded conversation modeling. For each dialogue context, the top-k relevant knowledge elements are selected and then employed in knowledge-grounded response generation. The two components of knowledge selection and response generation are optimized jointly and effectively under a balanced objective. Experimental results on two publicly available datasets validate the superiority of PLATO-KAG.

1 Introduction

Recently, the capability of large-scale pre-trained models has been verified in open-domain dialogue generation, including Meena (Adiwardana et al., 2020), Blender (Roller et al., 2021), and PLATO-2 (Bao et al., 2020). Without introducing explicit knowledge in learning process, substantive knowledge is implicitly embedded into parameters from the training corpus. However, these models are found to suffer from knowledge hallucinations (Roller et al., 2021; Marcus, 2020), producing plausible statements with factual errors. To boost the generation accuracy, there is a trend to leverage external knowledge in addition to the parameters of large-scale pre-trained models (Guu et al., 2020; Lewis et al., 2020).

In knowledge-grounded conversation, several datasets have been collected through crowd-sourcing (Dinan et al., 2019; Gopalakrishnan et al., 2019; Komeili et al., 2021). Given that manual annotation is expensive and time-consuming, it is not feasible to annotate the corresponding knowledge for each response on a large scale. Therefore, it is desirable to develop knowledge-grounded dialogue generation models without reliance on explicit knowledge labels.

Some attempts have been made to learn the unsupervised retrieval of external knowledge based on semantic similarity (Ghazvininejad et al., 2018; Dinan et al., 2019). Whereas, there exists the one-to-many phenomenon in knowledge-grounded conversation (Kim et al., 2019), where multiple knowledge elements can be appropriate to reply a given context. The prior top-1 knowledge selection employed by these approaches (Ghazvininejad et al., 2018; Dinan et al., 2019) has difficulties to hit the knowledge contained in the target response, deteriorating the learning of knowledge utilization. As an improvement, PostKS (Lian et al., 2019) and KnowledGPT (Zhao et al., 2020) rely on the target response to identify the grounded knowledge. However, involving the posterior knowledge selection will inevitably cause discrepancy between the training and inference stages (Zhao et al., 2019).

In this paper, we propose an unsupervised approach for end-to-end knowledge-grounded conversation modeling, namely PLATO-KAG (**K**nowledge-**A**ugmented **G**eneration). As shown in Figure 1, given each dialogue context, the top-k relevant knowledge elements are selected for the subsequent response generation. Then, the model learns to generate the target response grounded on each of the selected knowledge. The generation probability can in turn provide back-propagating signal for the precedent knowledge selection. These two components of knowledge selection and response generation are optimized jointly.

Two essential ingredients contribute to the performance of PLATO-KAG: top-k knowledge selection and balanced joint training. Firstly, in comparison to the conventional top-1 selection, top-k

Proceedings of the Third Workshop on Natural Language Processing for Conversational AI, pages 143–154
November 10, 2021.

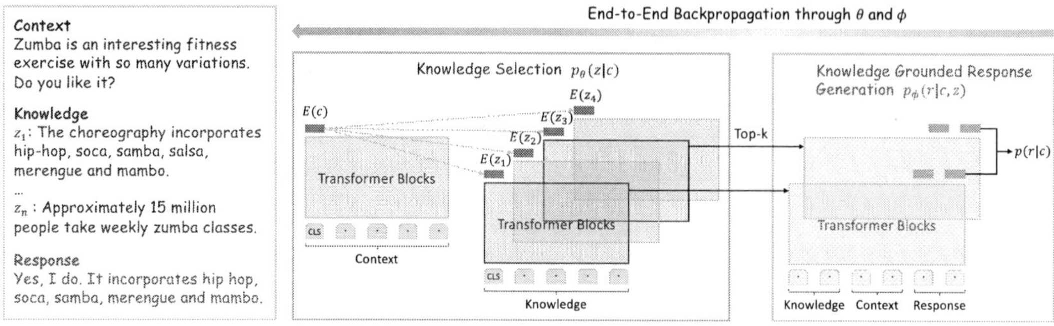

Figure 1: An overview of joint training in PLATO-KAG. For each dialogue context, top-k relevant knowledge elements are selected and employed in response generation. The generation probability can reflect the quality of the precedent knowledge selection. These two components of knowledge selection θ and response generation ϕ are optimized jointly in an unsupervised manner.

selection remarkably increases the chance to hit the grounded knowledge and improves the effectiveness of prior knowledge selection. Without the interlude of posterior knowledge selection, we manage to avoid the discrepancy between training and inference stages. Secondly, considering the difference of knowledge selection and response generation, balanced training is further designed for their effective joint optimization. To evaluate the performance of the proposed method, comprehensive experiments have been carried out on two publicly available datasets. Experimental results demonstrate that our method achieves better performance as compared with other state-of-the-art unsupervised approaches.[1]

2 Methodology

There are two main components in PLATO-KAG: knowledge selection and knowledge-grounded response generation.

2.1 Knowledge Selection

As shown in Figure 1, a dual encoder with shared parameters (Siamese network) (Bromley et al., 1993) is employed in knowledge selection, where the semantic representations of the dialogue context and knowledge are extracted independently. Then the relevance between the dialogue context c and each piece of knowledge z is estimated by:

$$f(c, z) = (W_c E(c))^{\mathrm{T}} (W_z E(z)) \quad (1)$$

where $E(\cdot)$ is the encoder's output on the [CLS] token, corresponding to the input's pooled representation. W_c and W_z denotes the linear projection matrix for the dialogue context and knowledge, respectively. The relevance function f calculates the inner product of these two projected embeddings.

For the subsequent response generation, the top-k knowledge elements with highest relevance scores are selected. The prior selection probability is further normalized as:

$$p_\theta(z|c) = \frac{\exp(f(c, z))}{\sum_{z'} \exp(f(c, z'))} \quad (2)$$

where z' is one element from the top-k relevant knowledge. The benefits brought by the top-k knowledge selection are two-fold. First, top-k selection significantly increases the robustness of prior knowledge selection, as compared with the widely adopted top-1 knowledge selection (Dinan et al., 2019). As mentioned before, there exists the one-to-many problem in knowledge-grounded conversation (Kim et al., 2019). The top-k selection remarkably increases the chance to hit the knowledge and facilitates the training of generation model grounded on appropriate knowledge. Second, for the generation of one response, it is computational intractable to marginalize over the whole knowledge set. The top-k selection is an effective approximation, as most knowledge elements are not relevant with the current dialogue context.

2.2 Knowledge-Grounded Response Generation

The overall probability of generating the target response is estimated as follows:

$$p(r|c) = \sum_z p_\theta(z|c) p_\phi(r|c, z) \quad (3)$$

[1]Our training code and models will be released at https://github.com/PaddlePaddle/Knover/tree/develop/projects/PLATO-KAG.

where the summation is running over the top-k selected knowledge elements. The second part of knowledge-grounded response generation can be further decomposed into the following form, if conditioned on one piece of knowledge:

$$p_\phi(r|c,z) = \prod_t^T p_\phi(r_t|c,z,r_{<t}) \tag{4}$$

where $r_{<t} = r_1, ..., r_{t-1}$. In fact, the above generation probability is dependent on the quality of knowledge selection. If the selected knowledge is coherent to the context and relevant to the target response, it is able to benefit the prediction of the target response and lead to a higher generative probability. Otherwise, it leads to a lower probability. As such, the generative probability given by Equation (4) can in turn provide learning signal for the precedent knowledge selection.

2.3 Balanced Joint Training

In PLATO-KAG, the knowledge selection and response generation are optimized jointly. Depending on the marginalization strategy over knowledge (Lewis et al., 2020), the objective in Equation (3) can be expanded in the following two ways:

$$p_{\text{seq}}(r|c) = \sum_z p_\theta(z|c) \prod_t^T p_\phi(r_t|c,z,r_{<t}) \tag{5a}$$

$$p_{\text{tok}}(r|c) = \prod_t^T \sum_z p_\theta(z|c) p_\phi(r_t|c,z,r_{<t}) \tag{5b}$$

In the sequence form of Equation (5a), it relies on one knowledge element to predict the whole sequence of the target response. In the token form of Equation (5b), the generative process can rely on different knowledge elements independently for each token.

With the sequence form, the selection of knowledge just weight like the generation of one response token. Given the long responses in knowledge-grounded conversation[2], the module of knowledge selection is at a distinct disadvantage during joint optimization. With the token form, the weight of knowledge selection becomes identical as that of response generation. However, in the preliminary experiments, some of its generated responses exhibit some degree of knowledge misuse, where knowledge fragments are mixed inappropriately.

[2]For example, the dialogue response has 18.431 words on average in the Wizard of Wikipedia dataset.

The proposed method combines the merits of these two forms and introduces the following joint training objective for knowledge-grounded dialogue generation:

$$p(r|c) \propto \sum_z p_\theta(z|c) \Big(\prod_t^T p_\phi(r_t|c,z,r_{<t}) \Big)^\alpha \tag{6}$$

where $\alpha > 0$ is a variable controlling the weight of knowledge selection and response generation. The sequence form is preserved for the sake of generation accuracy. It is worth noting that these two components are complementary to each other. A too small or too large value of α can lead to biased and ineffective optimization. When α is close to 0, the optimization focuses on knowledge selection, neglecting the signals from response generation. When α approaches positive infinity, the optimization focuses on response generation, ignoring the effects of knowledge selection. Therefore, it is crucial to keep the balance during the joint optimization. In PLATO-KAG, α is set to $1/T$, where T is the length of target response. Through the adaptive normalization on the second term, our method successfully maintains the balance between knowledge selection and knowledge-grounded response generation. More analyses on the component weight are included in the experiments.

3 Experiments

3.1 Settings

3.1.1 Datasets

We conducted experiments on two knowledge-grounded conversation datasets: Wizard of Wikipedia (WoW) (Dinan et al., 2019) and Holl-E (Moghe et al., 2018).

In **Wizard of Wikipedia**, two participants conduct in-depth discussion on a chosen beginning topic. One of the participants has access to relevant knowledge and plays the role of an expert (*wizard*). The other one acts as a curious learner (*apprentice*). There are 18,430/1,948/1,933 dialogues in the training/validation/test set. Validation and test sets are further split into seen and unseen parts, where the latter one is about new topics outside the training set.

In **Holl-E**, a single document about a specific movie is given as external knowledge for two participants to discuss in the conversation. There are 7,228/930/913 dialogues in the training/validation/test set. To facilitate the evaluation, the test set includes multiple reference responses for each dialogue context. We use the scripts provided by Kim et al. (2019) to process this dataset.[3]

As these two datasets have annotated the ground truth knowledge used by participants to ground their conversation responses, both components of knowledge selection and knowledge-grounded response generation can be evaluated thoroughly in the experiments.

3.1.2 Baselines

We compared the proposed method with the following approaches.

Transformer Memory Network (TMN) is a classical knowledge-grounded dialogue generation method (Dinan et al., 2019). Its training can be carried out in a supervised or unsupervised way, depending on whether the ground truth knowledge label is involved or not. In our experiments, we also included the supervised TMN as the performance upper bound of unsupervised models for reference.

PostKS is an unsupervised approach, which employs the target response to estimate the posterior distribution over knowledge (Lian et al., 2019). During training, the KL divergence is employed to reduce the gap between prior and posterior distributions. During inference, it will rely on the prior distribution to select knowledge for response generation.

KnowledGPT employs a cross encoder for knowledge selection(Zhao et al., 2020). It constructs pseudo knowledge labels based on word overlaps and uses them as weak supervision signals to warm up the models. The knowledge selection is then optimized using reinforcement learning with the rewards from generated responses. The response generation is learned gradually conditioned on knowledge selected from pseudo label to the prior distribution. They are optimized iteratively under their corresponding training objectives.

3.1.3 Implementation Details

We initialized the model parameters of knowledge selection and response generation with pre-trained dialogue generation models (Bao et al., 2020). There are 24 transformer blocks and 16 attention heads, with the embedding dimension of 1024. The maximum sequence length of context, knowledge and response is set to 256, 128 and 128, respectively. We used Adam optimizer (Kingma and Ba, 2015) with a learning rate of $2e-5$ and a batch size of 64. The number of relevant knowledge elements (top-k) was set to 8 during training. Detailed explorations of top-k settings on the validation sets are included in the Appendix. The training process was carried out on 8 Nvidia Tesla V100 32G GPU cards. Following the convention in knowledge-grounded conversation, only the most relevant knowledge was selected for response generation during inference.

Since the original TMN and PostKS are developed on shallow networks, for the sake of fair comparison, we re-implemented them and initialized the model parameters in the way as the proposed method. For KnowledGPT, we used its open-sourced checkpoint[4] in our experiments.

3.1.4 Evaluation Metrics

In the automatic evaluation, Perplexity (PPL) and Unigram F1 of ground truth responses (Dinan et al., 2019) are adopted to assess the response quality. Recall@1 (top-1 knowledge accuracy) is used to evaluate the performance of knowledge selection. We used the evaluation scripts provided by Dinan et al. (2019).[5]

In the human evaluation, we randomly sampled 100 examples from WoW seen and unseen test set, respectively. Each sample was distributed to three annotators and evaluated on the four aspects:

- **Coherence** evaluates whether the response is consistent and relevant with the context.
- **Informativeness** assesses whether the response contains appropriate information.
- **Engagingness** measures the annotator's willingness to discuss with the speaker for a long conversation.
- **Hallucination** estimates the factual correctness in the response.

Coherence, informativeness and engagingness are scored on a range of [0, 1, 2], with the higher value, the better. Hallucination is evaluated on a range of [0, 1], where 0 means the response is factually correct and 1 means the response contains factual errors. The scoring criteria are provided in the Appendix. The final score of each sample was determined through majority voting.

[3] https://github.com/bckim92/sequential-knowledge-transformer/blob/master/data/holle.py

[4] https://github.com/zhaoxlpku/KnowledGPT

[5] https://github.com/facebookresearch/ParlAI

WoW Seen Test Model	Knowledge Label	Automatic Evaluation			Human Evaluation			
		PPL↓	Recall@1	Unigram F1	Coherence	Informativeness	Engagingness	Hallucination↓
TMN	N	10.136	0.041	0.168	1.27	1.10	1.13	0.34
PostKS	N	11.577	0.224	0.187	1.33	1.28	1.30	0.21
KnowledGPT	N	19.600*	**0.262+**	0.183	1.16	1.16	1.12	0.28
PLATO-KAG	N	**9.767**	0.253	**0.188**	**1.54**	**1.44**	**1.40**	**0.17**
TMN	Y	9.633	0.265	0.188	1.51	1.39	1.38	0.17

WoW Unseen Test Model	Knowledge Label	Automatic Evaluation			Human Evaluation			
		PPL↓	Recall@1	Unigram F1	Coherence	Informativeness	Engagingness	Hallucination↓
TMN	N	12.910	0.042	0.156	1.33	1.07	1.12	0.40
PostKS	N	13.668	0.199	0.176	1.33	1.29	1.28	0.28
KnowledGPT	N	22.849*	0.238+	0.173	1.16	1.11	1.03	0.31
PLATO-KAG	N	**11.458**	**0.253**	**0.181**	**1.50**	**1.34**	**1.41**	**0.24**
TMN	Y	11.362	0.260	0.180	1.50	1.40	1.42	0.19

Table 1: Evaluation results on the WoW seen and unseen test sets. The second column indicates whether the model is trained using knowledge labels (supervised) or not (unsupervised). * Not comparable to the rest models due to the different vocabulary. + Not comparable to the rest models due to the cross encoder in knowledge selection.

3.2 Experimental Results

The evaluation results on the WoW test sets are summarized in Table 1. Besides the unsupervised models, the supervised TMN with reliance on knowledge labels during training was also included in the experiments for reference. The automatic and human evaluation results demonstrate that PLATO-KAG achieves better performance as compared with other state-of-the-art unsupervised approaches, even on par with the supervised approach. Based on appropriate knowledge selection, PLATO-KAG produces high-quality responses that are coherent, informative and engaging. Moreover, it alleviates the problem of knowledge hallucinations and generates more factual accurate responses.

As shown in the Table 1, unsupervised TMN generates less informative responses and suffers from a higher degree of hallucination. As for PostKS, based on inferior prior knowledge selection, it generates less coherent responses. Since KnowledGPT employs a cross encoder in the knowledge selection, it achieves a higher value of Recall@1. While cross encoder is hardly feasible for practical deployment given its expensive computation cost. Another factor that attributes to the weak performance of KnowledGPT might be the pre-training models used for initialization[6]. The average Fleiss's kappa (Fleiss, 1971) in human evaluation is 0.502, indicating that annotators have reached moderate agreement.

The evaluation results on the Holl-E test set are summarized in Table 2. In the evaluation on the multiple reference test set, we took the best score over multiple reference responses for each dialogue context. The results demonstrate that PLATO-KAG also achieves competitive results in Holl-E. PostKS obtains a slightly higher value on Unigram F1 than PLATO-KAG and supervised TMN. While the values on Distinct-1/2 (Li et al., 2016) indicate the PLATO-KAG and supervised TMN might have better capacity on lexical diversity.

3.3 Discussions

3.3.1 Case Analysis

For further qualitative analysis, two examples of generated responses from the WoW test set are provided in Table 3. It can be observed that unsupervised TMN suffers from low-quality response generation, such as generic replies with little information or statements with factual errors. In comparison, PostKS and KnowledGPT are able to generate much more informative responses, depicting contents from the selected knowledge. However, the responses fail to be coherent with the dialogue context due to the inferior knowledge selection. Among these unsupervised approaches, PLATO-KAG achieves better performance, producing coherent and informative responses.

The above analysis is also validated by the re-

[6]The released checkpoint of KnowledGPT is developed on the general language model GPT-2, while the rest models are developed on dialogue pre-training models.

Holl-E Test Model	Knowledge Label	Distinct-1/2	Single Reference			Multiple References		
			PPL↓	Recall@1	Unigram F1	PPL↓	Recall@1	Unigram F1
TMN	N	0.091 / 0.292	16.693	0.035	0.169	14.100	0.044	0.223
PostKS	N	0.120 / 0.379	16.808	0.238	**0.308**	11.790	0.343	**0.376**
PLATO-KAG	N	**0.128** / **0.416**	**10.222**	**0.271**	0.300	**7.724**	**0.371**	0.368
TMN	Y	0.126 / 0.400	10.081	0.296	0.300	7.964	0.394	0.363

Table 2: Automatic evaluation results on the Holl-E test set.

Context	[Topic] zumba [Wizard] hello dear, have you hard of zumba? is an exercise fitness program created by colombian dancer [Apprentice] i have! my best friend and i occasionally take classes! [Wizard] do you know that zumba is a trademark owned by zumba fitness, . [Apprentice] i didn't know that. it's interesting because there seem to be so many variations. do you like it?
Unsupervised TMN	yes i have tried it and i like it a lot.
PostKS	approximately 15 million people take weekly zumba classes in over 200,000 locations across 180 countries.
KnowledGPT	its an exercise fitness program created by colombian dancer and cyclist/choreographer alberto "beto" "power pedal"
PLATO-KAG	yes. it incorporates hip hop, soca, samba, merengue and mambo.
Supervised TMN	yes i do. it includes hip-hop and samba, socal, salsa, choreography, mambo.
Ground Truth	yes, zumba fitness ambassador is abrazilian pop singer claudia leitte

Context	[Topic] elvis presley [Wizard] do you like elvis presley? he was a famous american singer [Apprentice] he is pretty good, i am from nashville, so i've even been to graceland. [Wizard] presley was born in tupelo, mississippi, and then to memphis [Apprentice] what was elvis's most popular songs?
Unsupervised TMN	his first big hit was "favorite song"
PostKS	he had a series of successful netflix appearances and chart-topping records
KnowledGPT	he became the leading figure of the new popular rock group, the new sound of rock and roll. he was very popular.
PLATO-KAG	his first rca single was "heartbreak hotel" and became a number one hit in the united states
Supervised TMN	his first rca single, "heartbreak hotel" was released in 1956 and became a number one hit in the us
Ground Truth	heartbreak hotel was a number one hit in the usa

Table 3: Examples of the generated responses on the WoW seen (upper) and unseen (bottom) test sets.

	WoW Seen Test	WoW Unseen Test
Unsupervised TMN	0.107	0.106
PostKS	0.443	0.430
KnowledGPT	0.385	0.375
PLATO-KAG	0.347	0.340
Supervised TMN	0.314	0.306
Ground Truth	0.334	0.335

Table 4: Knowledge F1 on the WoW test set.

sults on knowledge dependency. Knowledge F1 (Lian et al., 2019), which is defined as the unigram F1 between the generated response and the selected knowledge, can measure the degree of knowledge dependency. A too low Knowledge F1 value means the models hardly reference the knowledge when generating responses. A too high value indicates the models "copy" the knowledge too much, which might cause unnatural responses. The values of

	Hallucination		
	PLATO-KAG Win	Tie	PLATO-KAG w/o EK Win
WoW Seen	13	78	9
WoW Unseen	26	67	7

	Informativeness		
	PLATO-KAG Win	Tie	PLATO-KAG w/o EK Win
WoW Seen	23	61	16
WoW Unseen	35	46	19

Table 5: Comparison of hallucination and informativeness between PLATO-KAG and PLATO-KAG w/o EK on the WoW test sets.

Knowledge F1 are reported in Table 4. The results indicate that unsupervised TMN suffers from poor knowledge utilization. As for PostKS and KnowledGPT, since posterior knowledge selection

Context	[Topic] harry potter [Apprentice] everyone has seen harry potter except me. have you ever read the books or watched the movies? [Wizard] yes i am a big fan of it actually. i love reading about chronicles of the life of a young wizard [Apprentice] was he born a wizard? [Wizard] as far as the main story arc concerns, he was and he went to wizard school to improve himself. [Apprentice] who wrote these stories?
PLATO-KAG w/o EK	it was written by j.k. rowling. and it was published *in 1977 by hermione granger.*
PLATO-KAG	harry potter is a series of fantasy novels written by british author j. k. rowling.

Context	[Topic] bowling [Apprentice] i used to be really into bowling. ... [Wizard] you aim to knock over the pins at the end [Apprentice] yup, though it can be hard at times haha.
PLATO-KAG w/o EK	the most common way to bowl is to use *a rectangular ball!*
PLATO-KAG	the max score is 300 which is achieved by getting 12 strikes in a row

Table 6: Examples of PLATO-KAG and PLATO-KAG w/o EK on the WoW seen and unseen test sets. Italic blocks are contents with factually errors.

is involved in their training process, their generation models learn to rely heavily on the provided knowledge, resulting in very high Knowledge F1 values. During inference with their inferior prior knowledge selection, this kind of strong dependency will lead to unrelated and unnatural response generation. Our method gets exempt from this discrepancy with end-to-end modeling and optimization. The close values of PLATO-KAG and the ground truth (0.347/0.334 on seen and 0.340/0.335 on unseen) indicates our method achieves a natural degree of knowledge utilization.

3.3.2 External Knowledge Effects on Response Quality

As discussed in the introduction, conversation models are turning to leveraging external knowledge explicitly to boost generation accuracy. To quantitatively analyze the performance, one dialogue generation model was trained on the WoW dataset without grounding on external knowledge, denoted as PLATO-KAG w/o EK. We asked annotators to compare the hallucination and informativeness between our method and PLATO-KAG w/o EK, with results summarized in Table 5. It is notable that the tie score of hallucination from PLATO-KAG w/o EK is a little inflated. This is because the model generates less informative responses, which helps keep the factual correctness (less talk, less mistake). With access to external knowledge, our method achieves better performance consistently. Moreover, the performance gaps on both metrics get enlarged from the seen to unseen test set. PLATO-KAG w/o EK produces plausible statements with factual errors more easily under unseen topics.

Two examples of generated responses by these two models are shown in Table 6, where the contents with factual errors are displayed in italic blocks. It reveals that PLATO-KAG w/o EK has difficulties to memorize and describe the knowledge details precisely. In fact, the initial publication of Harry Potter is in 1997 and Hermione Granger is one representative character in the book instead of a publisher. Sometimes, PLATO-KAG w/o EK produces statements that are obviously problematic and against the common sense, like "a rectangular ball". By leveraging external knowledge, PLATO-KAG can generate more accurate and informative responses.

Marginalization Strategy	Component Weight	WoW Seen	WoW Unseen	Holl-E
Sequence Form	$\alpha = T$	11.455	12.926	12.043
	$\alpha = 1$	10.965	11.962	11.089
	$\alpha = 1/T$ (PLATO-KAG)	**9.863**	**11.387**	**10.148**
	$\alpha = 1/T^2$	10.399	11.787	12.551
Token Form	-	11.841	13.099	12.679

Table 7: Perplexity under different marginalization strategies and component weights on the WoW and Holl-E validation sets.

3.3.3 Impacts of Marginalization Strategies and Component Weight

As discussed in Section 2.3, the quality of joint optimization is effected by the marginalization strategies and component weight. Explorations on these settings have been carried out on the validation sets, with the perplexity results summarized in Table 7. For the marginalization strategy, the token form (Equation (5b)), which depends on various knowledge elements to predict one response token, obtains relatively poor results. Under this training paradigm, the model tends to mix information from various knowledge fragments and is prone to generate low-quality responses. Two more examples are included in the Appendix to illustrate this phenomenon.

As comparison, with the marginalization strategy in sequence form (Equation (6)), the models achieve relatively better performance on perplexity. For the sequence form, one crucial factor affecting the performance is the component weight α between knowledge selection and knowledge-grounded response generation. Under the straightforward setting ($\alpha = 1$), knowledge selection weighs like one single response token. In PLATO-KAG ($\alpha = 1/T$, where T is the length of target response), the weight of knowledge selection becomes identical to that of the whole response generation. The results indicate PLATO-KAG achieves better performance with the help of balanced training. A too large or too small weight value (such as $\alpha = T$ or $\alpha = 1/T^2$) will lead to ineffective optimization and performance degradation.

4 Related Work

Knowledge-grounded conversation is becoming a more important and popular topic, with several datasets (Zhang et al., 2018; Moghe et al., 2018; Zhou et al., 2018; Dinan et al., 2019; Gopalakrishnan et al., 2019; Komeili et al., 2021) collected to study it. Besides interactive dialogues, some of these datasets have annotated the corresponding knowledge for each response, aiming to ease the learning difficulty of knowledge-grounded conversation. However, given that manual annotation is expensive and time-consuming, it is not feasible to carry out the knowledge labelling on a large scale.

Unsupervised approaches have been introduced to model knowledge-grounded conversation. Some of these such as Li et al. (2019); Yavuz et al. (2019); Lin et al. (2020) perform implicit soft fusion over provided knowledge elements and do not select knowledge explicitly. Some attempts have been made to learn the unsupervised selection of external knowledge based on semantic similarity (Ghazvininejad et al., 2018; Dinan et al., 2019). Due to the one-to-many problem in knowledge-grounded conversation (Kim et al., 2019), the prior top-1 knowledge selection employed by these approaches has difficulties to hit the knowledge contained in the target response, and deteriorates the learning of knowledge utilization. Our top-k selection improves the robustness of prior knowledge selection. Some other works (Lian et al., 2019; Zhao et al., 2020; Ren et al., 2020) employ the target response to identify the grounded knowledge. Since the posterior knowledge selection is involved, it will inevitably cause discrepancy between the training and inference stages (Zhao et al., 2019). With end-to-end modeling and optimization, PLATO-KAG gets exempt from this discrepancy. KIF (Fan et al., 2021) explicitly selects external knowledge through a retrieval module, and fuses into one integrated representation to assist dialogue generation. While some knowledge details might be obscured with this fusion. As comparison, the knowledge keeps its independence and integrity in our response generation, which helps reduce the hallucination.

More recently, Shuster et al. (2021) attempts to utilize the pre-trained retriever DPR (Karpukhin et al., 2020). DPR has been trained on Wikipedia which includes the knowledge sets of WoW and Holl-E. Due to the concern of potential data contamination, we choosed to initialize our knowledge selection module with a general dialogue model which is pre-trained on Reddit. Thus, we facilitated an unbiased setting for our experiments and the analysis of framework generalization.

5 Conclusion

In this paper, an unsupervised approach is proposed for end-to-end knowledge grounded conversation modeling. There are two main components in our method: knowledge selection and response generation. Given a dialogue context, top-k relevant knowledge elements are selected and utilized for response generation. The generation probability can in turn provide training signal for the precedent knowledge selection. Joint balanced training is further introduced for the effective optimization of these two components. Comprehensive experiments have been carried out on WoW and Holl-E, verifying the effectiveness and superiority of the proposed method.

Acknowledgements

We would like to thank the anonymous reviewers for their constructive suggestions and Yunyi Yang for the helpful discussions. This work was supported by the Natural Key Research and Development Project of China (No. 2018AAA0101900).

References

Daniel Adiwardana, Minh-Thang Luong, David R So, Jamie Hall, Noah Fiedel, Romal Thoppilan, Zi Yang, Apoorv Kulshreshtha, Gaurav Nemade, Yifeng Lu, and Quoc V. Le. 2020. Towards a human-like open-domain chatbot. *arXiv preprint arXiv:2001.09977.*

Siqi Bao, Huang He, Fan Wang, Hua Wu, Haifeng Wang, Wenquan Wu, Zhen Guo, Zhibin Liu, and Xinchao Xu. 2020. Plato-2: Towards building an open-domain chatbot via curriculum learning. *arXiv preprint arXiv:2006.16779.*

Jane Bromley, Isabelle Guyon, Yann LeCun, Eduard Säckinger, and Roopak Shah. 1993. Signature verification using a" siamese" time delay neural network. *Advances in neural information processing systems*, 6:737–744.

Emily Dinan, Stephen Roller, Kurt Shuster, Angela Fan, Michael Auli, and Jason Weston. 2019. Wizard of wikipedia: Knowledge-powered conversational agents. *International Conference on Learning Representations.*

Angela Fan, Claire Gardent, Chloé Braud, and Antoine Bordes. 2021. Augmenting transformers with knn-based composite memory for dialog. *Transactions of the Association for Computational Linguistics*, 9:82–99.

Joseph L Fleiss. 1971. Measuring nominal scale agreement among many raters. *Psychological bulletin*, 76(5):378.

Marjan Ghazvininejad, Chris Brockett, Ming-Wei Chang, Bill Dolan, Jianfeng Gao, Wen-tau Yih, and Michel Galley. 2018. A knowledge-grounded neural conversation model. In *Proceedings of the AAAI Conference on Artificial Intelligence.*

Karthik Gopalakrishnan, Behnam Hedayatnia, Qinglang Chen, Anna Gottardi, Sanjeev Kwatra, Anu Venkatesh, Raefer Gabriel, Dilek Hakkani-Tür, and Amazon Alexa AI. 2019. Topical-chat: Towards knowledge-grounded open-domain conversations. In *Interspeech*, pages 1891–1895.

Kelvin Guu, Kenton Lee, Zora Tung, Panupong Pasupat, and Ming-Wei Chang. 2020. Realm: Retrieval-augmented language model pre-training. In *Proceedings of the 37th Annual International Conference on Machine Learning*, pages 3929–3938.

Vladimir Karpukhin, Barlas Oguz, Sewon Min, Patrick Lewis, Ledell Wu, Sergey Edunov, Danqi Chen, and Wen-tau Yih. 2020. Dense passage retrieval for open-domain question answering. In *Proceedings of the 2020 Conference on Empirical Methods in Natural Language Processing (EMNLP)*, pages 6769–6781.

Byeongchang Kim, Jaewoo Ahn, and Gunhee Kim. 2019. Sequential latent knowledge selection for knowledge-grounded dialogue. In *International Conference on Learning Representations.*

Diederik P Kingma and Jimmy Ba. 2015. Adam: A method for stochastic optimization. In *International Conference on Learning Representations.*

Mojtaba Komeili, Kurt Shuster, and Jason Weston. 2021. Internet-augmented dialogue generation. *arXiv preprint arXiv:2107.07566.*

Patrick Lewis, Ethan Perez, Aleksandara Piktus, Fabio Petroni, Vladimir Karpukhin, Naman Goyal, Heinrich Küttler, Mike Lewis, Wen-tau Yih, Tim Rocktäschel, et al. 2020. Retrieval-augmented generation for knowledge-intensive nlp tasks. In *Advances in Neural Information Processing Systems*, pages 9459–9474.

Jiwei Li, Michel Galley, Chris Brockett, Jianfeng Gao, and William B Dolan. 2016. A diversity-promoting objective function for neural conversation models. In *Proceedings of the 2016 Conference of the North American Chapter of the Association for Computational Linguistics: Human Language Technologies*, pages 110–119.

Zekang Li, Cheng Niu, Fandong Meng, Yang Feng, Qian Li, and Jie Zhou. 2019. Incremental transformer with deliberation decoder for document grounded conversations. In *Proceedings of the 57th Annual Meeting of the Association for Computational Linguistics*, pages 12–21.

Rongzhong Lian, Min Xie, Fan Wang, Jinhua Peng, and Hua Wu. 2019. Learning to select knowledge for response generation in dialog systems. In *Proceedings of the 28th International Joint Conference on Artificial Intelligence*, pages 5081–5087.

Xiexiong Lin, Weiyu Jian, Jianshan He, Taifeng Wang, and Wei Chu. 2020. Generating informative conversational response using recurrent knowledge-interaction and knowledge-copy. In *Proceedings of the 58th Annual Meeting of the Association for Computational Linguistics*, pages 41–52.

Gary Marcus. 2020. The next decade in ai: four steps towards robust artificial intelligence. *arXiv preprint arXiv:2002.06177.*

Nikita Moghe, Siddhartha Arora, Suman Banerjee, and Mitesh M Khapra. 2018. Towards exploiting background knowledge for building conversation systems. In *Proceedings of the 2018 Conference on Empirical Methods in Natural Language Processing*, pages 2322–2332.

Pengjie Ren, Zhumin Chen, Christof Monz, Jun Ma, and Maarten de Rijke. 2020. Thinking globally, acting locally: Distantly supervised global-to-local knowledge selection for background based conversation. In *Proceedings of the AAAI Conference on Artificial Intelligence*, volume 34, pages 8697–8704.

Stephen Roller, Emily Dinan, Naman Goyal, Da Ju, Mary Williamson, Yinhan Liu, Jing Xu, Myle Ott, Kurt Shuster, Eric M Smith, et al. 2021. Recipes for building an open-domain chatbot. In *Proceedings of the 16th Conference of the European Chapter of the Association for Computational Linguistics*, page 300–325.

Kurt Shuster, Spencer Poff, Moya Chen, Douwe Kiela, and Jason Weston. 2021. Retrieval augmentation reduces hallucination in conversation. *arXiv preprint arXiv:2104.07567*.

Semih Yavuz, Abhinav Rastogi, Guan-Lin Chao, and Dilek Hakkani-Tur. 2019. Deepcopy: Grounded response generation with hierarchical pointer networks. In *Proceedings of the 20th Annual SIGdial Meeting on Discourse and Dialogue*, pages 122–132.

Saizheng Zhang, Emily Dinan, Jack Urbanek, Arthur Szlam, Douwe Kiela, and Jason Weston. 2018. Personalizing dialogue agents: I have a dog, do you have pets too? In *Proceedings of the 56th Annual Meeting of the Association for Computational Linguistics*, pages 2204–2213.

Tiancheng Zhao, Kaige Xie, and Maxine Eskenazi. 2019. Rethinking action spaces for reinforcement learning in end-to-end dialog agents with latent variable models. In *Proceedings of the 2019 Conference of the North American Chapter of the Association for Computational Linguistics: Human Language Technologies*, pages 1208–1218.

Xueliang Zhao, Wei Wu, Can Xu, Chongyang Tao, Dongyan Zhao, and Rui Yan. 2020. Knowledge-grounded dialogue generation with pre-trained language models. In *Proceedings of the 2020 Conference on Empirical Methods in Natural Language Processing*, pages 3377–3390.

Kangyan Zhou, Shrimai Prabhumoye, and Alan W Black. 2018. A dataset for document grounded conversations. In *Proceedings of the 2018 Conference on Empirical Methods in Natural Language Processing*, pages 708–713.

A Human Evaluation Scoring Criteria

The detailed criteria used in human evaluation are provided in Table 8. To evaluate the criteria of hallucination, the human annotators were provided with referenced knowledge and allowed to use search engine to check the factual correctness.

Score	Coherence
0	• The response is irrelated with the context. • The response simply repeats the context. • The response has obvious conflicts with the context. • There are serious logic conflicts within the response.
1	• The response is less coherent with the context. • There are minor logic conflicts within the response.
2	• The response is consistent and relevant with the context.

Score	Informativeness
0	• The response contains no information. • The response simply repeats the context and contains no additional information. • Since coherence score is 0, the information is invalid.
1	• The response contains a little additional information.
2	• The response has appropriate information.

Score	Engagingness
0	• I am not willing to talk with the speaker.
1	• It is a bit boring, but still ok to go on talking with this speaker.
2	• I would like to talk with the speaker for a long conversation.

Score	Hallucination
0	• The response is factually correct.
1	• Some details in the response are factually incorrect.

Table 8: Scoring criteria of four metrics in human evaluation.

B Knowledge Hallucination with Token Form Marginalization Strategy

In our preliminary experiments, the model trained with token form marginalization strategy exhibits a certain degree of knowledge misuse. Some examples are provided in Table 9. In the upper case, the fragments from the reference knowledge "in his spare time" and "selling pharmaceuticals" are mixed to "selling his spare time to a pharmacist" in the generated response. The bottom case also exhibits a low level of fidelity to the selected knowledge. One hypothesis to this phenomenon is that under the objective of token form (Equation (5b)), the model learns to blend information across various knowledge fragments to predict one response token. Under this training paradigm, the learned model is prone to hallucinate knowledge, mixing knowledge fragments inappropriately.

Context	[Topic] nicholas sparks [Apprentice] i've heard nicholas sparks is a great writer but i'm not sure if i've ever read any of his books ... [Wizard] yes it was called the passing, though his first published work didn't come until 1990. [Apprentice] what was the passing about?
Referenced Knowledge	in 1993, sparks wrote his breakthrough novel the notebook **in his spare time while selling pharmaceuticals** in washington, d.c.. two years later, his novel was discovered by literary agent theresa park who offered to represent him.
Generated Response	i believe it was about him *selling his spare time to a pharmacist* who helped him sell his notebook in 1994.

Context	[Topic] john grisham [Apprentice] did you know john grisham is a popular author? [Wizard] yes, his first bestseller "the firm" sold more than 7 million copies! ... [Apprentice] do you know any other movies that were made into movies from his books?
Referenced Knowledge	eight of his other novels have also been **adapted into films**: "the chamber", **"the client"**, "a painted house", "the pelican brief", "the rainmaker", "the runaway jury", **"skipping christmas"**, and "a time to kill".
Generated Response	yes, "the runaway jury" has also been *adapted into other novels "the client of christmas", "children of men"* and "a time to kill"

Table 9: Examples of knowledge misuse under token form marginalization strategy on the WoW seen and unseen test sets. Referenced knowledge is the model selected to ground response generation. Italic blocks are contents with factually errors.

C Explorations of Top-k Settings in Knowledge Selection

Top-k	WoW Seen		WoW Unseen		Holl-E	
	PPL↓	Recall @1	PPL↓	Recall @1	PPL↓	Recall @1
1	10.583	0.064	12.842	0.061	16.720	0.031
2	9.897	0.250	11.344	0.228	10.634	0.251
4	9.865	**0.258**	11.339	0.228	10.359	0.262
8	**9.863**	0.257	11.325	**0.231**	**10.246**	**0.266**
16	9.871	0.256	**11.321**	**0.231**	10.309	0.263

Table 10: Perplexity and Recall@1 under different top-k settings on the WoW and Holl-E validation sets.

To decide the proper number of relevant knowledge elements (top-k) for the training process, we conducted 3 runs of experiments for each top-k setting (k = 1, 2, 4, 8, 16). The median results on the validation sets are reported in Table 10. As discussed in the introduction, the prior top-1 knowledge selection hardly hits the grounded knowledge and suffers from relatively poor results. It also reveals a trend that models with larger k values can achieve better performance. It reaches stable states around k = 8. To balance the efficiency and performance, we set k = 8 in our experiments.

Improving Dialogue State Tracking by Joint Slot Modeling

Ting-Rui Chiang and **Yi-Ting Yeh**
Carnegie Mellon University
{tingruic,yitingye}@andrew.cmu.edu

Abstract

Dialogue state tracking models play an important role in a task-oriented dialogue system. However, most of them model the slot types conditionally independently given the input. We discover that it may cause the model to be confused by slot types that share the same data type. To mitigate this issue, we propose TripPy-MRF and TripPy-LSTM that models the slots jointly. Our results show that they are able to alleviate the confusion mentioned above, and they push the state-of-the-art on dataset MultiWoZ 2.1 from 58.7 to 61.3. Our implementation is available at https://github.com/CTinRay/Trippy-Joint.

1 Introduction

Multi-domain dialogue state tracking (DST) has been an important challenge of conversational artificial intelligence (Ram et al., 2018). Compared to single-domain DST, the belief state of a multi-domain DST contains slot types across multiple domains. It causes difficulty to the traditional DST models that assume the complete ontology is available because a complete ontology becomes hard to obtain (Wu et al., 2019b) when there are many domains,

To tackle these challenges, many of the mainstream approaches for DST formulate this as a span prediction task (Xu and Hu, 2018; Wu et al., 2019a; Kumar et al., 2020). Instead of predicting a predefined value in the ontology, the span-based DST models predict slot values by extracting a span from the conversation between the user and the system. By directly extracting spans as slot values, the DST models are able to handle unseen slot values and are potentially transferable to different domains. However, the span-based DST models can only deal with the slot values that are explicitly expressed as a sequence of tokens and fall short in dealing with coreference ("I'd like a restaurant in the same area") and implicit choice ("Any of those is ok") The current state-of-the-art DST model TripPy (Heck et al., 2020) is designed to deal with these problems. In addition to extracting values directly from the user utterance, TripPy maintains two additional memories on the fly and uses them to deal with the coreference and implicit choice challenges. The design details of TripPy will be further illustrated in Section 2.2

Despite the success of these span-based models, one concern is that they often consider the slots conditionally independently. For example, in TripPy, the conversation is first encoded by BERT (Devlin et al., 2019), and then the extracted features are used by n modules for the n slot types independently. That implies, conditioning the features extracted by BERT, the slots are predicted independently. This may increase the difficulty of this task because these slot types are indeed not independent of each other. If the value of one slot type in a domain is present in an utterance, then it is more likely that the value of another slot type of the same domain is present.

In particular, in this work, we focus on the cases where modeling the joint probability of the slots could possibly be helpful. We notice that there are some slot types that share the same data type. The data types of both the slot type "hotel-people" and the slot type "restaurant-book people" are both integers. Therefore, when an integer is present in an utterance, a DST model needs to predict which slot(s) this integer is for. Given the fact that some slots co-occur more often than others, modeling the slot types jointly may be helpful when making this kind of prediction. Based on this intuition, we group the slot types into 4 groups by their data type: time, place name, integer. We then analyze the current state-of-the-art model TripPy (Heck et al., 2020; Mehri et al., 2020). Our analysis shows that TripPy is indeed often confused with slot types in the same group.

Proceedings of the Third Workshop on Natural Language Processing for Conversational AI, pages 155–162
November 10, 2021. ©2021 Association for Computational Linguistics

We then investigate whether modeling the relation between slot types explicitly can alleviate this problem. By modeling the slot types jointly, information from the slots that the model is more confident with may reduce the confusion for the other slots. Specifically, to achieve this goal, we propose to model the joint probability of slots with MRF and LSTM models. They can be plugged into any DST model that models the slots conditionally independently. In this work, we choose the current state-of-the-art DST model, TripPy pretrained with DialoGLUE (Mehri et al., 2020). We experiment on the most widely used multi-domain DST dataset MultiWoZ 2.1 (Zang et al., 2020b; Eric et al., 2019). The results show that both the MRF and the LSTM models are able to mitigate the confusion, and can improve the performance consistently. We push the state-of-the-art performance on MultiWoZ 2.1 from 58.7 to 61.3.

2 Background

2.1 Problem Formulation

The dialogue state tracking (DST) task is to predict values of slot types for each turn in task-oriented dialogue. Specifically, dialogue consists of a sequence of user and system utterances. The input of the task is a dialogue $X = \{(U_1, M_1), \cdots, (U_T, M_T)\}$, where U_t and M_t are utterances by user and system respectively, and T is the total number of turns in this dialogue. The output of the task is the dialogue state at each time step. A dialogues state consists of N slot types. The goal of a DST task is to predict the slot values of those N slot types at each time step. The slot value $S_s^{(t)}$ of the s-th slot type at time step t might be a span in the previous conversation of simply *none*. We denote the state at time step t as $S^{(t)} = \{S_1^{(t)}, S_2^{(t)}, \cdots, S_N^{(t)}\}$.

2.2 TripPy: Triple Copy Strategy for DST

As described in Section 1, in addition to extract values from the user utterance, TripPy maintains two memories to tackle the coreference and the implicit choice problems in the span-based DST model. Specifically, we use *system inform memory* to remember the slots which the model previously informed, and *DS memory* to store the seen slots in the dialogue history. At dialogue turn t, TripPy predicts the belief state $S^{(t)}$ with the following steps: 1) The model first uses a pretrained BERT model to encode the dialogue history until the current time step t. 2) For each slot type s, it uses a classifier to predict the *slot class* $C_s^{(t)}$. For slot types whose possible values are "yes" or "no", possible values of $C_s^{(t)}$ are $\{$*none*, *dontcare*, *yes*, *no*$\}$. For the other slot types, possible values of $C_s^{(t)}$ are $\{$*none*, *dontcare*, *span*, *inform*, *refer*$\}$. These slot classes determine which source the slot value should be copied from. 3) The first two slot classes express special cases. *none* denotes that the slot does not take a value in this turn, and *dontcare* states that any value is acceptable for this slot. If $C_s^{(t)}$ is *span*, then TripPy uses a span prediction model to copy a span of text from the dialogue history as the prediction of a slot type. On the other hands, if C_s^t is *inform* and *refer*, the model will instead copy the value from *system inform memory* and *DS memory* respectively. The *system inform memory* allows the model to solve the implicit choice issue and the *DS memory* helps the model solve coreference problems.

2.3 Experimental Setup

We train and test our model on MultiWoZ 2.1 (Eric et al., 2019), which is the most challenging dataset for DST and is widely used for the evaluation of multi-domain DST models. MultiWoZ 2.1 is comprised of over 10000 dialogues in 5 domains and has 30 different slots with over 45000 possible values. We compute the joint goal accuracy (JGA) on all test samples to evaluate our models. The JGA is the ratio of dialog turns in the dataset for which all slots have been filled with the correct value according to the ground truth. Our baseline is the TripPy model in (Mehri et al., 2020), which is additionally pretrained with more dialogue tasks. To reproduce their result, we follow the setting of their hyperparameters and successfully achieve JGA 58.0, which is close to the reported result of 58.7 in the paper.

3 Analysis

3.1 Accuracy per Copy Class

We analyze the accuracy of each slot by the ground truth copy strategy to use on the validation set. For each slot type, we also calculate the joint goal accuracy presuming it is predicted correctly. From the results in Table 1 we can have a few observations. 1) The class *none* takes most of the cases. Therefore, it is important to predict whether the value is *none* correctly. 2) On the other hand, improving other classes may be less effective, since the number of mistakes is much smaller.

Slot Type	none	don't care	span	inform	refer	true	false	Oracle	Δ
taxi-leaveAt	.99 (7218)	- (0)	.88 (131)	.91 (23)	.00 (2)	. - (0)	. - (0)	.581	.001
taxi-destination	.98 (7159)	- (0)	.98 (108)	.94 (18)	.61 (89)	. - (0)	. - (0)	.587	.007
taxi-departure	.98 (7169)	- (0)	.89 (100)	1.0 (21)	.60 (84)	. - (0)	. - (0)	.587	.007
taxi-arriveBy	.99 (7278)	.50 (2)	.85 (55)	1.0 (10)	.76 (29)	. - (0)	. - (0)	.581	.001
restaurant-book_people	.99 (7001)	- (0)	.99 (319)	1.0 (41)	.85 (13)	. - (0)	. - (0)	.583	.002
restaurant-book_day	1.0 (7011)	- (0)	.99 (286)	1.0 (53)	.92 (24)	. - (0)	. - (0)	.581	.001
restaurant-book_time	.99 (6979)	- (0)	.98 (328)	1.0 (67)	. - (0)	. - (0)	. - (0)	.583	.003
restaurant-food	.99 (6801)	.45 (20)	1.0 (422)	.98 (131)	. - (0)	. - (0)	. - (0)	.593	.013
restaurant-pricerange	.99 (6906)	.78 (9)	.98 (343)	.98 (113)	1.0 (3)	. - (0)	. - (0)	.587	.006
restaurant-name	.96 (6926)	.00 (2)	.93 (162)	1.0 (283)	.00 (1)	. - (0)	. - (0)	.598	.018
restaurant-area	.98 (6881)	.71 (17)	.97 (314)	.96 (137)	.88 (25)	. - (0)	. - (0)	.594	.014
hotel-book_people	.99 (7031)	- (0)	.99 (300)	.97 (35)	.62 (8)	. - (0)	. - (0)	.581	.001
hotel-book_day	1.0 (7035)	- (0)	.98 (289)	1.0 (40)	.70 (10)	. - (0)	. - (0)	.582	.002
hotel-book_stay	.99 (7015)	- (0)	.99 (314)	1.0 (45)	. - (0)	. - (0)	. - (0)	.582	.001
hotel-name	.96 (6884)	.00 (1)	.98 (170)	1.0 (319)	. - (0)	. - (0)	. - (0)	.59	.009
hotel-area	.97 (7028)	.45 (29)	1.0 (205)	.98 (92)	.65 (20)	. - (0)	. - (0)	.595	.014
hotel-parking	.97 (7204)	.33 (6)	. - (0)	. - (0)	. - (0)	.86 (154)	.50 (10)	.587	.007
hotel-pricerange	.98 (6986)	.67 (21)	.97 (271)	1.0 (91)	.60 (5)	. - (0)	. - (0)	.59	.01
hotel-stars	.99 (7094)	.50 (6)	.98 (210)	.91 (64)	. - (0)	. - (0)	. - (0)	.584	.004
hotel-internet	.98 (7200)	1.0 (2)	. - (0)	. - (0)	. - (0)	.89 (169)	.67 (3)	.588	.007
hotel-type	.93 (7135)	.00 (5)	. - (0)	. - (0)	. - (0)	.59 (80)	.85 (154)	.612	.031
attraction-type	.98 (6835)	.38 (8)	.98 (430)	1.0 (101)	. - (0)	. - (0)	. - (0)	.595	.015
attraction-name	.98 (7006)	.00 (2)	.97 (137)	1.0 (229)	. - (0)	. - (0)	. - (0)	.59	.01
attraction-area	.98 (6946)	.39 (18)	.98 (248)	.96 (135)	.93 (27)	. - (0)	. - (0)	.593	.013
train-book_people	.98 (7040)	- (0)	.96 (314)	1.0 (8)	.42 (12)	. - (0)	. - (0)	.591	.011
train-leaveAt	.97 (7125)	.50 (2)	.96 (228)	.68 (19)	. - (0)	. - (0)	. - (0)	.612	.032
train-destination	.98 (6693)	- (0)	.99 (503)	1.0 (176)	.00 (2)	. - (0)	. - (0)	.586	.006
train-day	.99 (6791)	- (0)	1.0 (481)	1.0 (86)	.94 (16)	. - (0)	. - (0)	.585	.005
train-arriveBy	.99 (7034)	.75 (4)	.98 (322)	.75 (12)	.00 (2)	. - (0)	. - (0)	.592	.012
train-departure	.98 (6749)	- (0)	.99 (478)	1.0 (146)	.00 (1)	. - (0)	. - (0)	.587	.007
sum	3928	77	168	73	29	116	37		

Table 1: Accuracy of each slot type by ground truth class. The number in the parenthesis is the number of occurrence of the class for the slot type. The oracle column is the performance calculated when presuming the slot value is predicted correctly.

The above results encourage us to inspect the prediction of the class *none* more closely. Here we focus on the cases where the model is to decide whether it is going to give a value to a slot type. We ignore cases where the value of the slot type in the previous turn is not none. We calculate the number of incorrect value predictions when *none* is predicted incorrectly. From Table 2, we can see that many incorrect predictions are resulted from incorrect *none* prediction.

3.2 Relation Between Slots

We further examine the model's behavior when *none* is not predicted correctly. We check the frequency of the following cases of incorrect prediction: 1) p_1: when the ground truth class is *none*, the cases where the predicted slot value is the ground truth value of another slot type. 2) p_2: when the predicted class is *none*, cases of the slot value that is the ground truth value of another slot type. We plot the frequency $p_1 + p_2$ in Figure 1. From the figure, we can see that the model is often confused by similar slot types. For example, the value of the slot type "taxi-departure" and the value of the slot type "taxi-ariveBy" is time. It may be the reason why the model often fails to give non-*none* value to the correct slot type.

4 Proposed Method

We conjecture some mistakes made by TripPy maybe because it models the slots conditionally independently. Based on Table 2, the model does not predict *none* very accurately, and Figure 1 indicates that it is because the model is often confused by similar slot types. In the original design, given a dialogue X, TripPy models the class prediction independently as follow:

$$P(C_1^{(t)}, C_2^{(t)}, \cdots, C_N^{(t)}|X) = \prod_{s=1}^{N} P(C_s^{(t)}|X). \tag{1}$$

TripPy ignores the potential correlation between different slots. Thus, for all s, $P(C_s^{(t)}|X)$ needs to predict the class correctly at the same time. It may be difficult since there are numerous slots.

To alleviate this problem, we propose to directly model the joint probability $P(C_1^{(t)}, C_2^{(t)}, \cdots, C_N^{(t)}|X)$. If $c_1, c_2, \cdots, c_N$ are the correct classes, modeling the joint probability does not require $P(C_s^{(t)} = c_s) > P(C_s^{(t)} = c_s')$ for all s and all incorrect assignments $\{c_s'\}_{s=1}^{N}$. Instead, to predict the belief state correctly, the model is only required to ensure $P(C_1^{(t)} = c_1, C_2^{(t)} = c_2, \cdots, C_N^{(t)} = c_N|X) > P(C_1^{(t)} = c_1', C_2^{(t)} = c_2', \cdots, C_N^{(t)} = c_N'|X)$. In this way, information from the other states

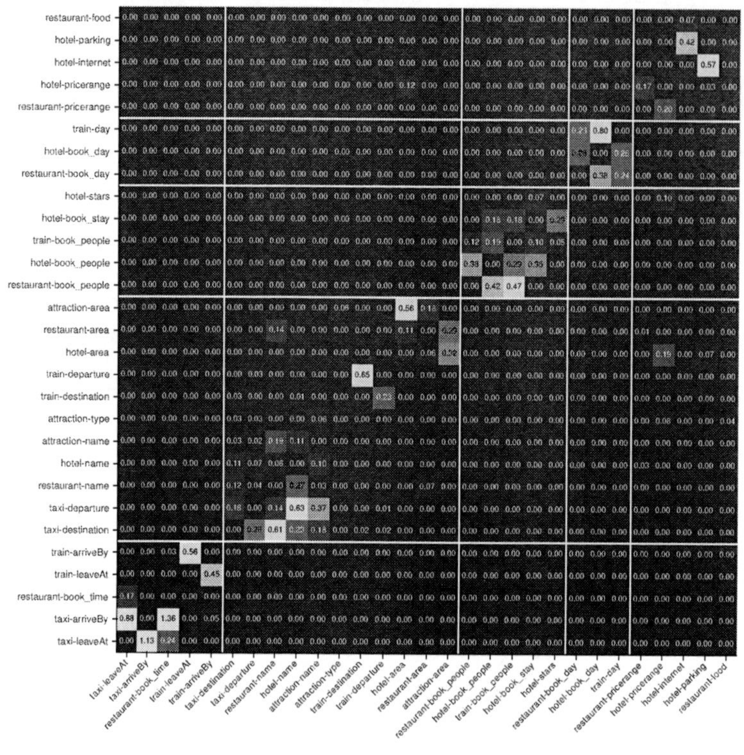

Figure 1: The value of $p_1 + p_2$ as described in section 3.2.

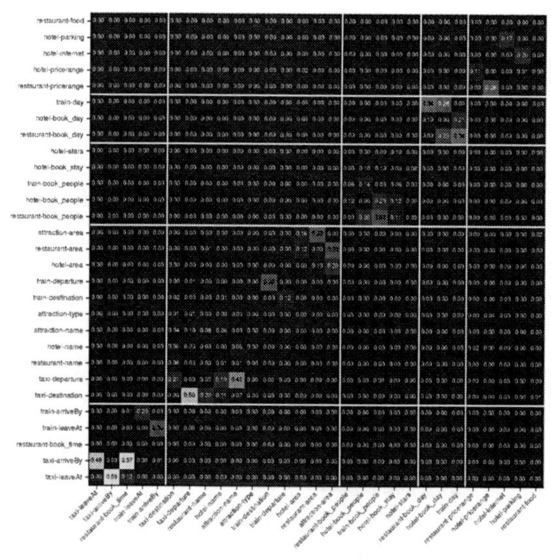

Figure 2: The value of $p_1 + p_2$ (Section 3.2) predicted by the TripPy + MRF model.

could possibly help the prediction of difficult slot types. For example, if the model has high confidence that the utterance contains the value of slot "restaurant-name", the number in the utterance is more likely the value of slot "restaurant-book people". Therefore, confusion shown in Figure 1 could possibly be alleviated.

4.1 Modeling the Joint Probability with Graphical Models

One approach that models the joint probability is to use a Markov random field (MRF). This approach

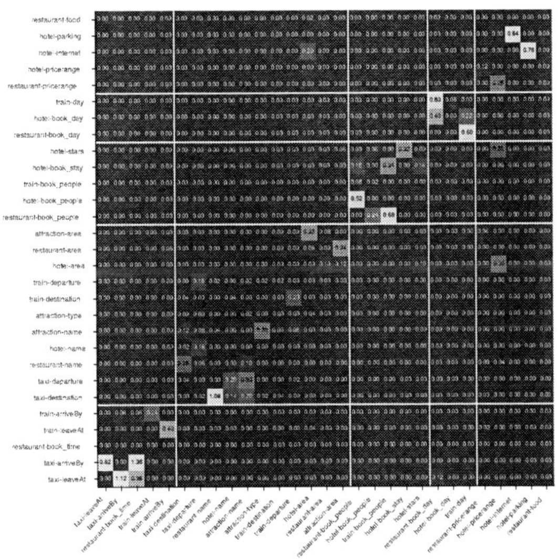

Figure 3: The value of $p_1 + p_2$ (Section 3.2) predicted by the TripPy + LSTM model.

is parameter-efficient and incurs little computation overhead for inference. However, having a large number of vertices in an MRF makes training intractable. Therefore, we follow the intuition above, grouping the slots by their domains, and model the joint distribution within each group respectively. Since a large portion of the mistakes made by the original TripPy model is due to the incorrect prediction of whether a slot value is present in an utterance, we further decompose the probability of a class as

$$P(C_s^{(t)} = c) = P(C_s^{(t)} = c | C_s^{(t)} \neq \text{"}none\text{"}) P(C_s^{(t)} \neq \text{"}none\text{"}) \quad (2)$$

Let $C_s'^{(t)}$ be the random variable indicating whether $C_s^{(t)} = \text{"}none\text{"}$. Modeling only the $P(\{C_s'^{(t)}\}_{s=1}^{N})$ part jointly makes the training and inference of the MRF model feasible: given input x, for each domain d and the assignment of slots $c_1, c_2, \cdots, c_N$ for the N slots in d, the probability of the assignment is

$$\begin{aligned} &P(c_1, c_2, \cdots, c_N | x) \\ &= \frac{1}{Z(x)} \Phi_d(\{C_s'^{(t)} = c_s'\}_{s=1}^{N}) \\ &\prod_{s=1}^{N} \Phi_s(c_s, x) P(C_s^{(t)} = c_s | C_s'^{(t)} = c_s'), \end{aligned} \quad (3)$$

where Φ_d map each assignment $c_1', c_2', \cdots, c_N'$ to a learnable scalar, and $\Phi_s(c_s', x)$ is a scalar resulted from applying a linear layer over the pooled BERT output. Since the number of slot types in a domain is at most 10, and all of the variables are binary, the partition function $Z_i(x)$ can be calculated by enumerating all the possible assignments of $c_1', c_2', \cdots, c_N'$. Therefore, we can train this model with the plain MLE loss.

4.2 Modeling with LSTM models

Another approach we explore is to use the LSTM model (Schmidhuber and Hochreiter, 1997). Similar to language modeling, we model the joint probability by predicting the value of each slot sequentially:

$$\begin{aligned} &P(C_1^{(t)}, C_2^{(t)}, \cdots, C_N^{(t)} | X) \\ &= \prod_{s=1}^{N} P(C_s^{(t)} | X, C_1^t, \ldots, C_{s-1}^t), \end{aligned} \quad (4)$$

For the implementation of this model, we first encode the dialogue history X with BERT and extract its CLS token representation h_X. The original TripPy model will feed h_X into a linear layer f_s to predict slot class for each slot.

$$P(C_s^{(t)} | X) = Softmax(f_s(h_X)) \quad (5)$$

Here, for all s, we additionally train another linear layer f_s^{lstm} to transform h_X and feed it into a LSTM layer:

$$h_s = LSTM(f_s^{lstm}(h_X), h_{s-1}) \quad (6)$$

	Other	FN	FP
taxi-leaveAt	13	7	25
taxi-destination	10	32	13
taxi-departure	14	37	13
taxi-arriveBy	1	15	19
restaurant-book_people	1	5	37
restaurant-book_day	1	3	16
restaurant-book_time	3	4	12
restaurant-food	3	13	48
restaurant-pricerange	4	8	57
restaurant-name	9	7	45
restaurant-area	3	19	57
hotel-book_people	2	6	34
hotel-book_day	1	7	8
hotel-book_stay	2	2	17
hotel-name	6	3	72
hotel-area	2	24	94
hotel-parking	11	20	88
hotel-pricerange	5	13	38
hotel-stars	4	10	24
hotel-internet	1	18	85
hotel-type	12	49	220
attraction-type	2	11	104
attraction-name	21	5	31
attraction-area	0	25	53
train-book_people	1	19	37
train-leaveAt	3	14	57
train-destination	6	4	12
train-day	1	2	17
train-arriveBy	3	9	24
train-departure	3	6	8
	148	397	1365

Table 2: Number of incorrect slot value predictions in different cases of *none* prediction. FN (false negative)/FP (false positive) means that the ground truth class is *none*/is not *none*, but the model predicts the class incorrectly.

Model	Dev.	Test
TripPy (Mehri et al., 2020)		58.7
TripPy (reproduced)	61.3	58.0
+ MRF	59.3	60.1
+ LSTM	62.8	61.3

Table 3: Joint goal accuracy on MultiWoZ 2.1.

We then concatenate h_s and h_x to model the conditional probability:

$$P(C_s^{(t)}|X, C_1^{(t)}, \ldots, C_{s-1}^{(t)}) = f_s([h_X; h_s]) \quad (7)$$

where $[x; y]$ denotes the concatenation of vectors x and y. We name this model TripPy+LSTM.

5 Results and Discussion

Our main results are shown in Table 3. Both MRF and LSTM modules have a consistent improvement over the baseline model on the test set of MultiWoZ 2.1, which proves the effectiveness of our proposed approaches.

As a more fine-grained analysis, we plot the frequency of incorrect prediction as described in Section 3.2. Compared to Figure 1, Figure 2 and Figure 3 show that both TripPy+MRF and TripPy+LSTM can relieve the confusion between slot types that have the same data type. This is coherent to our intuition for modeling the slot types jointly.

The results also show that TripPy+LSTM performs better than TripPy+MRF. It may be because TripPy+LSTM models all the assignment $\{C_s\}_{s=1}^N$ of the classes jointly, while TripPy+MRF only models $\{C'_s\}_{s=1}^N$ jointly. Also, TripPy+LSTM has the potential to model the joint distribution across the domains. However, this also sacrifices efficiency. Since TripPy+LSTM predicts the slots sequentially, it cannot predict the slots in parallel. TripPy+MRF could be a better choice when latency is an important issue.

6 Related Work

Williams et al. (2013) is the first benchmark for DST models. After that, Henderson et al. (2014) proposed the DSTC2 dataset which includes more linguistic phenomena. Ramadan et al. (2018a) proposed MultiWoZ, which is the first large-scale human-human multi-domain task-oriented DST dataset. Its successive versions (Eric et al., 2019;

Zang et al., 2020a) cleanse the noisy conversations in it. Since then, it has become the standard DST benchmark dataset.

Early approaches for DST rely on a list candidate slot values (Mrkšić et al., 2017; Liu and Lane, 2017; Ramadan et al., 2018b; Rastogi et al., 2017). Some recent approaches formulate it as a sequence generation task. TRADE (Wu et al., 2019a) and MA-DST (Kumar et al., 2020) generates slot values with a pointer generator with a copy mechanism. SOM-DST (Kim et al., 2020) uses a BERT model to encode the dialogue. To improve the efficiency, the state from the previous turn instead of the whole dialogue history is fed into the model. SUMBT (Lee et al., 2019) utilizes a BERT model (Devlin et al., 2019) to encode both the dialogue history and candidate slot values. In Gao et al. (2019) they formulate DST as a question answering task. DS-DST (Zhang et al., 2020) adopts a dual strategy: they predict slot values from candidates but also predict slot values by copying from the dialogue. TripPy (Heck et al., 2020) predicts slot values by copying text span from three different sources. In Mehri et al. (2020), they improve the performance of TripPy by pre-training the BERT with multiple dialogue tasks. Simple-TOD (Hosseini-Asl et al., 2020) and SOLOIST (Peng et al., 2020) utilize GPT-2 for end-to-end slot value and response generation. In Li et al. (2020), they investigate the generalization capability of DST models for unseen slot values. MinTL (Lin et al., 2020) augments data by substituting slot values in the utterances and modifying the syntax structure.

7 Conclusion

In this work, we explore the relation between slot types. Our contributions are two-fold. 1) We identify a problem with the current state-of-the-art model TripPy. We observe that it is often confused by slots that share the same type of value. 2) We propose TripPy+MRF and TripPy+LSTM that aim at mitigating this problem. One can choose one of them based on the trade-off between efficiency and accuracy. Our preliminary results show that both of them are able to alleviate the confusion. Our findings in this work lead future researchers in a promising direction to improve the performance of multi-domain DST.

Acknowledgments

We would like to thank Graham Neubig for his in-depth discussions. We are also thankful to the anonymous reviewers for their comments on the paper.

References

Jacob Devlin, Ming-Wei Chang, Kenton Lee, and Kristina Toutanova. 2019. BERT: Pre-training of deep bidirectional transformers for language understanding. In *Proceedings of the 2019 Conference of the North American Chapter of the Association for Computational Linguistics: Human Language Technologies, Volume 1 (Long and Short Papers)*, pages 4171–4186, Minneapolis, Minnesota. Association for Computational Linguistics.

Mihail Eric, Rahul Goel, Shachi Paul, Adarsh Kumar, Abhishek Sethi, Peter Ku, Anuj Kumar Goyal, Sanchit Agarwal, Shuyang Gao, and Dilek Hakkani-Tur. 2019. Multiwoz 2.1: A consolidated multi-domain dialogue dataset with state corrections and state tracking baselines. *arXiv preprint arXiv:1907.01669*.

Shuyang Gao, Abhishek Sethi, Sanchit Agarwal, Tagyoung Chung, and Dilek Hakkani-Tur. 2019. Dialog state tracking: A neural reading comprehension approach. In *Proceedings of the 20th Annual SIGdial Meeting on Discourse and Dialogue*, pages 264–273, Stockholm, Sweden. Association for Computational Linguistics.

Michael Heck, Carel van Niekerk, Nurul Lubis, Christian Geishauser, Hsien-Chin Lin, Marco Moresi, and Milica Gasic. 2020. TripPy: A triple copy strategy for value independent neural dialog state tracking. In *Proceedings of the 21th Annual Meeting of the Special Interest Group on Discourse and Dialogue*, pages 35–44, 1st virtual meeting. Association for Computational Linguistics.

Matthew Henderson, Blaise Thomson, and Jason D. Williams. 2014. The second dialog state tracking challenge. In *Proceedings of the 15th Annual Meeting of the Special Interest Group on Discourse and Dialogue (SIGDIAL)*, pages 263–272, Philadelphia, PA, U.S.A. Association for Computational Linguistics.

Ehsan Hosseini-Asl, Bryan McCann, Chien-Sheng Wu, Semih Yavuz, and Richard Socher. 2020. A simple language model for task-oriented dialogue. *arXiv preprint arXiv:2005.00796*.

Sungdong Kim, Sohee Yang, Gyuwan Kim, and Sang-Woo Lee. 2020. Efficient dialogue state tracking by selectively overwriting memory. In *Proceedings of the 58th Annual Meeting of the Association for Computational Linguistics*, pages 567–582, Online. Association for Computational Linguistics.

Adarsh Kumar, Peter Ku, Anuj Goyal, Angeliki Metallinou, and Dilek Hakkani-Tur. 2020. Ma-dst: Multi-attention-based scalable dialog state tracking. In *Proceedings of the AAAI Conference on Artificial Intelligence*, volume 34, pages 8107–8114.

Hwaran Lee, Jinsik Lee, and Tae-Yoon Kim. 2019. SUMBT: Slot-utterance matching for universal and scalable belief tracking. In *Proceedings of the 57th Annual Meeting of the Association for Computational Linguistics*, pages 5478–5483, Florence, Italy. Association for Computational Linguistics.

Shiyang Li, Semih Yavuz, Kazuma Hashimoto, Jia Li, Tong Niu, Nazneen Rajani, Xifeng Yan, Yingbo Zhou, and Caiming Xiong. 2020. Coco: Controllable counterfactuals for evaluating dialogue state trackers. *ArXiv*, abs/2010.12850.

Zhaojiang Lin, Andrea Madotto, Genta Indra Winata, and Pascale Fung. 2020. Mintl: Minimalist transfer learning for task-oriented dialogue systems. *arXiv preprint arXiv:2009.12005*.

Bing Liu and Ian Lane. 2017. An end-to-end trainable neural network model with belief tracking for task-oriented dialog. In *Proc. Interspeech 2017*, pages 2506–2510.

S. Mehri, M. Eric, and D. Hakkani-Tur. 2020. Dialoglue: A natural language understanding benchmark for task-oriented dialogue. *ArXiv*, abs/2009.13570.

Nikola Mrkšić, Diarmuid Ó Séaghdha, Tsung-Hsien Wen, Blaise Thomson, and Steve Young. 2017. Neural belief tracker: Data-driven dialogue state tracking. In *Proceedings of the 55th Annual Meeting of the Association for Computational Linguistics (Volume 1: Long Papers)*, pages 1777–1788, Vancouver, Canada. Association for Computational Linguistics.

Baolin Peng, Chunyuan Li, Jinchao Li, Shahin Shayandeh, Lars Liden, and Jianfeng Gao. 2020. Soloist: Few-shot task-oriented dialog with a single pretrained auto-regressive model. *arXiv preprint arXiv:2005.05298*.

Ashwin Ram, Rohit Prasad, Chandra Khatri, Anu Venkatesh, Raefer Gabriel, Qing Liu, Jeff Nunn, Behnam Hedayatnia, Ming Cheng, Ashish Nagar, et al. 2018. Conversational ai: The science behind the alexa prize. *arXiv preprint arXiv:1801.03604*.

Osman Ramadan, Paweł Budzianowski, and Milica Gasic. 2018a. Large-scale multi-domain belief tracking with knowledge sharing. In *Proceedings of the 56th Annual Meeting of the Association for Computational Linguistics*, volume 2, pages 432–437.

Osman Ramadan, Paweł Budzianowski, and Milica Gašić. 2018b. Large-scale multi-domain belief tracking with knowledge sharing. In *Proceedings of the 56th Annual Meeting of the Association for Computational Linguistics (Volume 2: Short Papers)*, pages 432–437, Melbourne, Australia. Association for Computational Linguistics.

Abhinav Rastogi, Dilek Hakkani-Tür, and Larry Heck. 2017. Scalable multi-domain dialogue state tracking. In *2017 IEEE Automatic Speech Recognition and Understanding Workshop (ASRU)*, pages 561–568. IEEE.

Jürgen Schmidhuber and Sepp Hochreiter. 1997. Long short-term memory. *Neural Comput*, 9(8):1735–1780.

Jason Williams, Antoine Raux, Deepak Ramachandran, and Alan Black. 2013. The dialog state tracking challenge. In *Proceedings of the SIGDIAL 2013 Conference*, pages 404–413, Metz, France. Association for Computational Linguistics.

Chien-Sheng Wu, Andrea Madotto, Ehsan Hosseini-Asl, Caiming Xiong, Richard Socher, and Pascale Fung. 2019a. Transferable multi-domain state generator for task-oriented dialogue systems. In *Proceedings of the 57th Annual Meeting of the Association for Computational Linguistics*, pages 808–819, Florence, Italy. Association for Computational Linguistics.

Chien-Sheng Wu, Richard Socher, and Caiming Xiong. 2019b. Global-to-local memory pointer networks for task-oriented dialogue. *arXiv preprint arXiv:1901.04713*.

Puyang Xu and Qi Hu. 2018. An end-to-end approach for handling unknown slot values in dialogue state tracking. In *Proceedings of the 56th Annual Meeting of the Association for Computational Linguistics (Volume 1: Long Papers)*, pages 1448–1457, Melbourne, Australia. Association for Computational Linguistics.

Xiaoxue Zang, Abhinav Rastogi, Srinivas Sunkara, Raghav Gupta, Jianguo Zhang, and Jindong Chen. 2020a. MultiWOZ 2.2 : A dialogue dataset with additional annotation corrections and state tracking baselines. In *Proceedings of the 2nd Workshop on Natural Language Processing for Conversational AI*, pages 109–117, Online. Association for Computational Linguistics.

Xiaoxue Zang, Abhinav Rastogi, Srinivas Sunkara, Raghav Gupta, Jianguo Zhang, and Jindong Chen. 2020b. Multiwoz 2.2: A dialogue dataset with additional annotation corrections and state tracking baselines. In *Proceedings of the 2nd Workshop on Natural Language Processing for Conversational AI, ACL 2020*, pages 109–117.

Jianguo Zhang, Kazuma Hashimoto, Chien-Sheng Wu, Yao Wang, Philip Yu, Richard Socher, and Caiming Xiong. 2020. Find or classify? dual strategy for slot-value predictions on multi-domain dialog state tracking. In *Proceedings of the Ninth Joint Conference on Lexical and Computational Semantics*, pages 154–167, Barcelona, Spain (Online). Association for Computational Linguistics.

Learning to Learn End-to-End Goal-Oriented Dialog From Related Dialog Tasks

Janarthanan Rajendran
University of Michigan
rjana@umich.edu

Jonathan K. Kummerfeld
University of Michigan
jkummerf@umich.edu

Satinder Singh
University of Michigan
baveja@umich.edu

Abstract

For each goal-oriented dialog task of interest, large amounts of data need to be collected for end-to-end learning of a neural dialog system. Collecting that data is a costly and time-consuming process. Instead, we show that we can use only a small amount of data, supplemented with data from a related dialog task. Naively learning from related data fails to improve performance as the related data can be inconsistent with the target task. We describe a meta-learning based method that selectively learns from the related dialog task data. Our approach leads to significant accuracy improvements in an example dialog task.

1 Introduction

One key benefit of goal-oriented dialog systems that are trained end-to-end is that they only require examples of dialog for training. Avoiding the modular structure of pipeline methods removes the human effort involved in creating intermediate annotations for data to train the modules. The end-to-end structure also enables automatic adaptation of the system, with different components of the model changing together. This flexibility is particularly valuable when applying the system to a new domain.

However, end-to-end systems currently require significantly more data, increasing the human effort in data collection. The most common method for training is Supervised Learning (SL) using a dataset of dialogs of human agents performing the task of interest (Bordes et al., 2017; Eric and Manning, 2017; Wen et al., 2017). To produce an effective model, the dataset needs to be large, high quality, and in the target domain. That means for each new dialog task of interest large amounts of new data has to be collected. The time and money involved in that collection process limits the potential application of these systems.

We propose a way to reduce this cost by selectively learning from data from related dialog tasks: tasks that have parts/subtasks that are similar to the new task of interest. Specifically, we describe a method for learning which related task examples to learn from. Our approach uses meta-gradients to automatically meta-learn a scalar weight $\in (0, 1)$ for each of the related task data points, such that learning from the weighted related task data points improves the performance of the dialog system on the new task of interest. These weights are dynamically adjusted over the course of training in order to learn most effectively. We still learn from data for the target task, but do not need as much to achieve the same results.

To demonstrate this idea, we considered two experiments. First, we confirmed that the method can work in an ideal setting. We constructed a classification task where the related task data is actually from the same task, but with the incorrect label for 75% of examples, and there is an input feature that indicates whether the label is correct or not. Our approach is able to learn to ignore the misleading data, achieving close to the performance of a model trained only on the correct examples.

Second, we evaluated the approach on a personalized restaurant reservation task with limited training data. Here, the related task is also restaurant reservation, but without personalization and with additional types of interactions. We compare our approach to several standard alternatives, including multi-task learning and using the related data for pre-training only. Our approach is consistently the best, indicating its potential to effectively learn which parts of the related data to learn from and which to ignore. Successfully learning from available related task data can allow us to build end-to-end goal-oriented dialog systems for new tasks faster with reduced cost and human effort in data collection.

Proceedings of the Third Workshop on Natural Language Processing for Conversational AI, pages 163–178
November 10, 2021.

2 Related Work

The large cost of collecting data for every new dialog task has been widely acknowledged, motivating a range of efforts. One approach is to transfer knowledge from other data to cope with limited availability of training dialog data for the new task of interest. For example Zhao et al. (2020) split the dialog model such that most of the model can be learned using ungrounded dialogs and plain text. Only a small part of the dialog model with a small number of parameters is trained with the dialog data available for the task of interest. In contrast, we explore how to learn from related grounded dialogs, and also without any specific constraints on the structure of the end-to-end dialog system architecture. Wen et al. (2016) pre-train the model with data automatically generated from different tasks and Lin et al. (2020) use pre-trained language models as initialization and then fine-tune the dialog model with data from the task of interest. These ideas are complementary to our approach as we make no assumptions about how the model was pre-trained.

Recently, there has been work that explored ways to automatically learn certain aspects of the transfer process using meta-learning. Xu et al. (2020) look at the problem of learning a joint dialog policy using Reinforcement Learning (RL) in a multi-domain setting which can then be transferred to a new domain. They decomposed the state and action representation into features that correspond to low level components that are shared across domains, facilitating cross-domain transfer. They also proposed a Model Agnostic Meta Learning (MAML Finn et al., 2017) based extension that learns to adapt faster to a new domain. Madotto et al. (2019), Mi et al. (2019), Qian and Yu (2019) and Dai et al. (2020) also look at multi-domain settings. They use MAML based meta-learning methods to learn an initialization that adapts fast with few dialog samples from a new task.

All of the papers above consider settings where there is access to a large set of training tasks. The meta-learning systems learn to transfer knowledge to a new test task by learning how to do transfer on different training tasks. While each task only has a limited amount of dialog data, they need a lot of tasks during training. In contrast, we look at a setting where the task from which we want to transfer knowledge from and the task that we want to transfer knowledge to are the only tasks that we have access to at training time. Any learning about how to transfer knowledge has to happen from just these two tasks. None of the above methods are applicable to this setting.

Learning a task, while simultaneously meta-learning certain aspects of the learning process has been done successfully in some SL and RL settings recently. Wu et al. (2018); Wichrowska et al. (2017) use meta-learning to adapt hyperparemeters such as learning rate and and even learn entire optimizers themselves during training for SL tasks such as image classification. Given a single task, Zheng et al. (2018) successfully meta-learn intrinsic rewards that help the agent perform well on that task. Xu et al. (2018) use meta-gradients to learn RL training hyperparameters such as the discount factor and bootstrapping parameters. The meta-gradient technique used in our proposed method is closely related to Rajendran et al. (2020). They learn intrinsic rewards for an RL agent acting in given domain, such that learning with those intrinsic rewards improves the performance of the agent in the task of interest in a different domain.

While we use a meta-learning based method for learning the weights for the related task data points in this work, there are other techniques in the machine learning literature, especially in the computer vision literature, that can potentially be used to learn the weights. A large section of these recent techniques are based on learning an adversarially trained discriminator for estimating the weights of related image classification task data points (Zhao et al., 2018; Cao et al., 2018; Sankaranarayanan et al., 2018; Wang et al., 2019). Jiang and Zhai (2007) use a combination of several domain adaptation heuristics to assign weights and evaluate on NLP tasks. Moon and Carbonell (2017) cluster the related task data points and learn attention weights for the clusters. An interesting future direction would be to study which weighting methods are best suited for end-to-end learning of neural goal-oriented dialog systems using related tasks and under what conditions.

3 Proposed Method

3.1 Intuition

Consider a scenario where we are building a restaurant reservation dialog system and have data collected in the past for a hotel reservation dialog system. The hotel reservation data could have parts that might be useful to learn from, e.g., greeting and obtaining a user's name/contact information. The data could also have parts that are inconsistent with the needs of the restaurant reservation system, e.g., hotel reservation might require the dialog system to ask for the user's duration of stay while the restaurant reservation might require the dialog system to ask for the particular day and time of table reservation. There could also be a lot of irrelevant information in the data that would be best to ignore for a learning system with limited capacity, e.g., answering questions about fitness facilities and the pool in a hotel.

Another type of scenario is when the new task is a modified version of a previous task. In this case, the previous task is an excellent source of related data, but will have critical differences. For example, the new system may need to ask users for their email address rather than a mailing address. To use the data effectively, the model needs to learn what to use and what to ignore.

Data from the related tasks could also provide rich information about different user behaviors and natural language in general of both users and agents. Tapping into and learning from the related tasks' data that is already available can potentially allow us to build dialog systems with improved performance on the new task of interest with only a limited amount of data collected, saving us time, effort and money in data collection.

3.2 Algorithm

Let T^P be the new task of interest (primary task) for which we have collected a limited amount of training data. Let T^R be the related task for which we have relatively large amounts of data already available. We are interested in building a dialog system for the task T^P. The data points are pairs of the form context (c) and dialog system's next utterance (a), where the context has the history of the dialog so far, ending with the most recent user utterance. We learn a dialog model M parameterized by θ that takes as input the context c and predicts the next dialog system utterance a.

Each iteration of training is comprised of the following three major steps. 1) The dialog model is updated using a batch of data points from the primary task. 2) The dialog model is updated using a batch of data points from the related task, where each related task data point's training loss is weighted between $(0, 1)$. 3) The related task data points' weights are updated. These three steps are repeated at each training iteration. We describe each step in detail below.

1) Updating the dialog model using primary task data points. We sample a batch of data points $\{\ldots,(c_i^P, a_i^P),\ldots\}$ from the primary task T^P. Let $L(M_\theta(c_i), a_i)$ represent the supervised learning prediction loss between $M_\theta(c_i)$: the next utterance predicted by the dialog model and a_i: the ground truth next utterance. Model M_θ is updated using the supervised learning prediction loss of the primary task data points L^P as shown below:

$$L^P(\theta) = \sum_i L\left(M_\theta(c_i^P), a_i^P\right) \quad (1)$$

$$\theta \leftarrow \theta - \alpha \nabla_\theta L^P(\theta), \quad (2)$$

where α is the learning rate and $\nabla_\theta L^P(\theta)$ is the gradient of the loss $L^P(\theta)$ with respect to θ.

2) Updating the dialog model using weighted related task data points. We sample a batch of data points $\{\ldots,(c_i^R, a_i^R),\ldots\}$ from the related task T^R. The supervised learning prediction loss $L(M_\theta(c_i), a_i)$ for each data point in the batch is weighed by a scalar weight $w_i \in (0, 1)$ corresponding to each of the data points. The scalar weight for each of the related task data point is obtained as a function of that particular data point. Let P parameterized by η be the module that outputs the weights. The weight for a related task data point is calculated as shown below:

$$w_i(\eta) = \sigma(P_\eta(c_i^R, a_i^R)), \quad (3)$$

where σ is a sigmoid function used to normalize the output of P to $(0, 1)$. Model M_θ is updated using the weighted prediction loss of related task data points L^R as shown below:

$$L^R(\theta, \eta) = \sum_i w_i(\eta) L\left(M_\theta(c_i^R), a_i^R\right) \quad (4)$$

$$\theta \leftarrow \theta - \beta \nabla_\theta L^R(\theta, \eta), \quad (5)$$

where β is the learning rate and $\nabla_\theta L^R(\theta, \eta)$ represents the gradient of the loss $L^R(\theta, \eta)$ with respect to θ. The weights w_i allow for selectively using data points from the related task data for updating the dialog model.

3) Updating the related task data points' weights. In this key step of our proposed method, we update the related task data points' weights

$w_i(\eta)$. The update increases the weights of related task data points that improve the dialog model's performance on the primary task when learned from and decreases the weights of those that degrade the dialog model's performance on the primary task.

We first sample a batch of related task data points and simulate how the model parameters θ would change if we update the model with a batch of related task data points with the current assignment of weights provided by P_η:

$$L^R(\theta, \eta) = \sum_i w_i(\eta) L\left(M_\theta(c_i^R), a_i^R\right) \quad (6)$$

$$\theta' = \theta - \beta \nabla_\theta L^R(\theta, \eta). \quad (7)$$

We then evaluate how the updated model $M_{\theta'}$ performs on the primary task to decide how to change P_η that assigned weights to the related task data points that resulted in $M_{\theta'}$:

$$L^P(\theta') = \sum_i L\left(M_{\theta'}(c_i^P), a_i^P\right), \quad (8)$$

where $L^P(\theta')$ is the supervised learning loss of the updated model $M_{\theta'}$ on a new batch of data points sampled from the primary task. The parameters of P_η are updated as shown below:

$$\begin{aligned} \eta \leftarrow & \eta - \gamma \nabla_\eta L^P(\theta') && (9) \\ = & \eta - \gamma \nabla_\eta \theta' \nabla_{\theta'} L^P(\theta'), && (10) \end{aligned}$$

where γ is the learning rate and $\nabla_\eta L^P(\theta')$ represents the gradient of the loss $L^P(\theta')$ with respect to η. The gradient, $\nabla_\eta L^P(\theta')$ is split into products of two gradients $\nabla_\eta \theta'$ and $\nabla_{\theta'} L^P(\theta')$ using the chain rule. $\nabla_\eta \theta'$ can be calculated using meta-gradients as follows:

$$\begin{aligned} \nabla_\eta \theta' = & \nabla_\eta(\theta - \beta \nabla_\theta L^R(\theta, \eta)) && (11) \\ = & \nabla_\eta \left(\beta \nabla_\theta L^R(\theta, \eta)\right) && (12) \\ = & \nabla_\eta \left(\beta \nabla_\theta \left(\sum_i w_i(\eta) L(M_\theta(c_i^R), a_i^R)\right)\right) && (13) \\ = & \beta \sum_i \nabla_\eta w_i(\eta) \nabla_\theta L(M_\theta(c_i^R), a_i^R). && (14) \end{aligned}$$

3.3 Discussion

The proposed method learns a dialog model from the primary task data points and also selectively from the related task data points. The proposed method meta-learns, at different points in training of the dialog model, which related task data points to learn from (and also to what degree $(0, 1)$). The weight assigned to a particular related task data point can therefore vary across training.

For simplicity, we described our proposed method with one update each using primary task data points, using weighted related task data points, and of related task data points' weights in each training iteration. But in practice, we make multiple updates to the related task data points' weights (η parameters) within each iteration. Also, for each η update we simulate how the model parameters θ change over multiple gradient updates (instead of just one as described in equations 6 and 7). This allows for a better estimate of how the updates using related task data points with the current parameters η affect the updated dialog model's performance on the primary task. Note that our proposed method is agnostic to the exact architecture of the model M and weight module P. Also, while we focus on settings with a single related task, the proposed method naturally extends to settings with more than one related task.

4 Experiments and Results

We first illustrate our proposed method on a simple image classification task with a hand designed related task that allows us to verify if the proposed method can learn meaningful weights. We then evaluate our proposed method on the task of personalized restaurant reservation.

4.1 MNIST Image Classification

This experiment illustrates in a very simple setting how our proposed method works. We set up the experiment with a clear indication of which related task data points should have high weights and which should have low weights. The primary task is the classification of hand-written digits from the MNIST dataset (LeCun et al., 2010). The related task is created by taking the primary task data and changing the label to an incorrect one for 75% of the training data. This means that of the 50,000 related task data points, 25% (12,500 data points) are useful for the primary task while 75% (37,500 data points) are not. We also add an input feature to every related task data point that indicates whether that data point's label is correct or not.

In this experiment, to focus on the effect of our

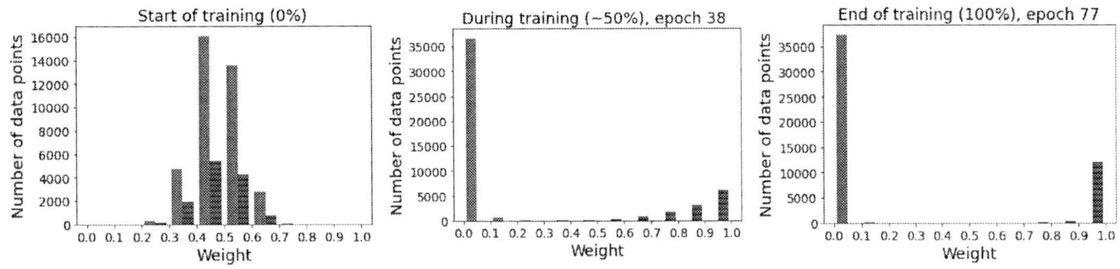

Figure 1: Distributions of learned weights for data points at different points during training on the image classification task. The histograms in red (plain) and blue (stripped) correspond to the related task data points with incorrect and correct labels respectively. Our method successfully uses the indicator feature to assign weights that ignore incorrect points and learn from correct points.

learned related task data point weights on performance, we perform only the last two steps (steps 2 and 3) of the algorithm. In other words, no updates are made to the model using the primary task data, we only update the model using the weighted related task data and then update the weights of the related task data points. However, primary task data is still used in the calculation of the meta-gradients for updating the weights of the related task data points. In order for the dialog model to perform well on the primary task, the data points with incorrect labels in the related task data need to be assigned weights lower than the data points that have the correct label.

We use logistic regression as our classification model (M_θ) and a perceptron with a sigmoid nonlinearity at the output for the weight generation module (P_η). The weight generation module takes as input the image, its label and a binary feature that indicates if that label is correct or not for that image, and produces a scalar weight between 0 and 1 as the output. Refer to Appendix A for more details of the architecture and training.

4.1.1 Results

Figure 1 shows the distribution of data points over the range of weights. The histogram in red (plain) and blue (striped) correspond to the related task data points with incorrect and correct labels respectively. Refer to Figures 3 and 4 in Appendix A for visualization of weights at other intermediate stages of training. Our proposed method with the meta-gradient based update to the weight generation module learns to give high weights to the data points with correct labels and low weights to the data points with incorrect labels. We observed similar weight assignment over multiple runs with different random seeds. In the last epoch of training, the average weight given to the related task data points with correct labels is 0.9747 ± 0.0004 and the average weight given to those with incorrect labels is 0.0074 ± 0.0002 (mean and standard deviation over 5 runs). Note that the method starts with random weights and updates the weights during training. The average weight across all the training epochs, given to the related task data points with correct labels is 0.8558 ± 0.0020 and to the related task data points with incorrect labels is 0.1508 ± 0.0041.

Weighting Method	Accuracy (%)
1 for All	21.63 ± 3.81
Random-Fixed	20.81 ± 4.46
Random-Changing	20.40 ± 4.42
Learned (Proposed Method)	87.86 ± 0.17
Oracle	90.32 ± 0.33

Table 1: MNIST Test results when using our constructed related task data in various ways, including an oracle method that only learns from correct related data. Mean and standard deviation are over 5 runs. Our approach effectively learns to use the related data, ignoring the examples with incorrect labels.

Table 1 shows the performance of the classification model with different types of weighting for the related task data points. We compare with:

1 for All: Use all related task data equally.

Random-Fixed: Assign a random weight to each related task data point at the start of the training.

Random-Changing: Each time a related task data point is sampled, use a new random weight.

Oracle: From the start, use a weight of 1 for correct data points and 0 for incorrect data points.

From the results, we observe that selectively learning from the related task data points with learned weights (row 4) performs much better than the methods that use all the data points uniformly (row 1) or assign random weights to the data points (rows 2 and 3). The proposed method's performance is very close to the oracle method that has access to the perfect weights for the related task data points from the start (row 5) and throughout training. We attribute this small gap mainly to the lingering effects of incorrect weights used for learning from the related task data points in the early stages of training in the proposed method. The visualization of the weights and the resulting performance indicate that the proposed method can indeed learn suitable weights using the meta-gradient update in this setting and lead to a performance very close to the best performance possible with perfect weights.

4.2 Personalized Restaurant Reservation

Personalizing dialog system responses based on the user that the dialog system is interacting with will be a key step in seamless integration of dialog systems into our everyday lives. Recognizing this, Joshi et al. (2017) proposed the first open dataset for training end-to-end dialog systems where the dialog system responses are based on the profile of the user. Their dataset is set in the domain of restaurant reservation, built as an extension of the bAbI dialog tasks from Bordes et al. (2017).

The bAbI dialog tasks are a testbed to evaluate the strengths and shortcomings of end-to-end dialog systems in goal-oriented applications. The dataset is generated by a restaurant reservation simulation where the final goal is to book a table. The simulator uses a Knowledge Base (KB) which contains information about restaurants. There are five tasks: Task 1 (Issuing API calls; by collecting relevant information from the user), Task 2 (Updating API calls; based on the information that the user wants to change), Task 3 (Displaying options; from the restaurants retrieved by the API call, suggesting restaurants in the order of their ratings), Task 4 (Providing extra information; if asked, providing the directions and/or contact information of the restaurant selected by the user) and Task 5 (Conducting full dialogs; combining tasks 1,2,3 and 4). Figure 5 (Left) in Appendix B shows an example of Task 5 from the bAbI dialog tasks.

In Joshi et al. (2017)'s extension of the bAbI dialog tasks (referred to as personalized-bAbI from here on), in addition to the goal of the bAbI dialog tasks, the dialog system should also use the additional user profile information provided, to personalize the response styles and reasoning over the Knowledge Base (KB). The user profile consists of the user's age (young, middle-aged, elderly), gender (male, female), dietary preference (vegetarian, non-vegetarian) and favorite food item (Fish and Chips, Biryani, etc). The style of the dialog system's response depends on the age and the gender of the user. In Task 3, from the restaurants retrieved through the API call, the dialog system now has to sort and suggest restaurants based not just on the restaurant's rating, but also based on the user's dietary preference and favorite food item. For this, the personalized-bAbI dialog task KB has additional information about restaurant type (vegetarian or non-vegetarian) and speciality (Fish and Chips, Biryani, etc). Figure 5 (Right) in Appendix B shows an example of Task 3 from the personalized-bAbI dialog tasks.

We use Task 3 from the personalized-bAbI dialog tasks as our primary task, and Task 5 of the bAbI dialog tasks as the related task. 100% (1000 dialogs) of the training dialogs of bAbI dialog Task 5 are available as the related task data. For the primary task, we simulate limited data availability by decreasing the number of training and validation dialogs. We look at three data settings: 5% (50 dialogs), 10% (100 dialogs) and 15% (150 dialogs) of the primary task training and validation dialogs. For testing, we use 100% (1000 dialogs) of the test dialogs from the personalized-bAbI dataset.

Let us look at the similarities and differences between the related task and the primary task. The related task has parts in its dialog, such as the greetings and getting information from the user, that are semantically similar to that of the primary task. They are not exactly the same due to the differences in response style (the style differs based on the user profile in the primary task). Due to the presence of different response styles, the vocabulary of the primary task is also much larger and different than that of the related task. The related task also has some parts that involve different output choices, such as the ordering of the restaurants to suggest to the user. In the primary task the ordering should be based on the restaurant's rating, user's dietary pref-

Method	Number of primary task dialogs 50	100	150
Primary	54.7 ± 1.3	59.3 ± 0.5	61.1 ± 0.5
Primary + Related Pre-Training	32.8 ± 3.5	42.1 ± 4.7	47.8 ± 0.8
Primary + Related	37.1 ± 4.1	50.9 ± 1.7	58.6 ± 0.7
Primary + Auxiliary Related (Multi-Task)	51.2 ± 2.4	58.2 ± 1.2	60.6 ± 0.7
Primary + Weighted Auxiliary Related:			
Proposed Method	$\mathbf{57.7 \pm 1.6}$	$\mathbf{64.6 \pm 0.8}$	$\mathbf{67.1 \pm 0.6}$
Random-Fixed	50.7 ± 2.0	58.7 ± 0.8	61.2 ± 1.0
Random-Changing	52.3 ± 0.9	58.7 ± 1.0	59.8 ± 0.8

Table 2: Test results, % Per-turn retrieval accuracy (mean and standard deviation over 5 runs) in predicting the next dialog system utterance.

erence and favorite food, while in the related task it is based on only the restaurant's rating. There are also parts of the related task that are not relevant to the primary task. These includes the parts corresponding to Task 2 (updating API calls) and Task 4 (providing extra information such as the restaurant's direction or contact information) of the related task.

As noted earlier, our proposed method is agnostic to the dialog model architecture. In our experiments we use the same dialog model architecture as used in Joshi et al. (2017), end-to-end memory networks (Sukhbaatar et al., 2015), for both the dialog model M_θ and the weight generation module P_η. In the dialog model, the internal dialog state generated after attending over the dialog history is used to select the candidate response from the list of candidates. For the weight generation module, the internal dialog state generated after attending over the dialog history is used to generate the scalar $(0, 1)$ weight. Refer to Appendix B for more details of the architecture and training.

4.2.1 Results

Table 2 shows the performance of our proposed method along with several other methods:

Primary: Trained using only the primary task data.

Primary + Related Pre-Training: Pre-trained with related task data and then fine-tuned with primary task data.

Primary + Related: Trained using related task and primary task data points together.

Primary + Auxiliary Related (Multi-Task): The dialog model has two prediction heads, one for the primary task, and one for the related task, with a shared end-to-end memory network body that generates the internal dialog state used for selecting the candidate response. This is similar to the conventional way of performing multi-task learning. This can also be interpreted as using related task prediction as an auxiliary task.

Proposed Method: Primary + Weighted Auxiliary Related : Identical to the previous approach, except that the prediction loss of the related task is weighted by the weights learned by our proposed method. We also show results for two variations with random weighting methods.

Table 2 shows that in all the three data settings the conventional methods of using the related task data (rows 2,3,4) lead to a reduction in performance (negative transfer) compared to not using the related task data points at all (row 1: Primary).

The closest conventional method is row four, learning from both the primary task data and related task data simultaneously with a shared network body and separate prediction heads. The worst result is the second row, pre-training with the related task data points. We hypothesise that, due to the differences (vocabulary, contradictory and irrelevant sub-tasks) in the primary and related task, starting from the pre-trained network weights obtained using related task data leads to a worse local minimum during fine-tuning compared to starting from a randomly initialized network weights and training with primary task data alone.

The best result is our proposed method (row 5: Primary + Weighted Auxiliary Related), which

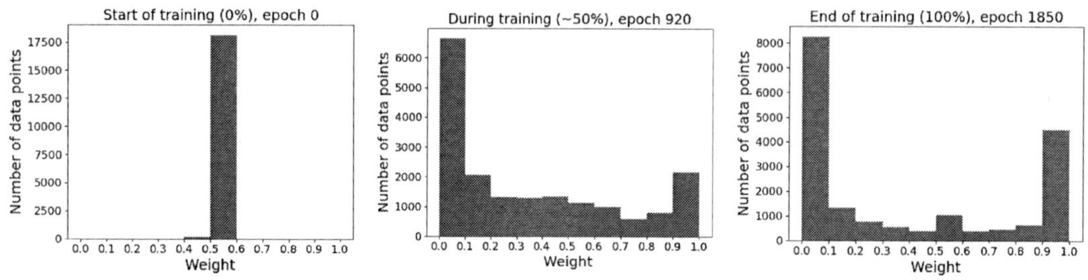

Figure 2: Personalized Restaurant Reservation. Histograms of the number of related task data points in the different interval of weights.

weights the auxiliary related task update between $(0, 1)$ and selectively learns from them. Our method scores $\approx$ 6.5% higher than the standard multi-task learning approach (row 4). We avoid negative transfer, improving over the first row by 3-6% depending on the amount of primary data available. The improvement is larger as more primary task data is available, indicating that the related task data (fixed in size) can be utilised better with more primary task data. While selectively learning can always help with avoiding negative transfer by lowering the weights for data points that lead to negative transfer, the improvement in performance (compared to not using related task data) possible by using the related task data points will depend on the relationship between the primary task and the related task.

To verify that our learned weights are meaningful, we also consider random weights. The last three rows compare the performance with different types of weighting for the related task data points. It is clear that random weighting does not lead to the improvement in performance that we observe when we learn the weights using our proposed method.

Figure 2 shows histograms of the data points based on the assigned weights. Unlike the simple MNIST image classification (Section 4.1), here we do not know which related task data points should have high weights and which data points should not. The optimal weights for the related task data points at any given stage of training can be different from the optimal weights for them at a different stage of training, i.e., the optimal weights for the related task data points are non-stationary, as they depend on the current state (parameters of the dialog model) of the dialog system. For example, some data points of the related task which are quite different from the primary task might still be useful to learn from at the early stages of training to help with learning better representations for the vocabulary, and some data points that the dialog system has already learned from might get lower weights at later stages of learning so as to avoid overfitting and thereby helping with the prediction of other data points. For visualization of weights at more intermediate stages of training see Figures 6 and 7 in Appendix B.

5 Conclusion

End-to-end learning of neural goal-oriented dialog systems requires large amounts of data for training. Collecting data is a costly and time consuming process. In this work we showed on an example dialog task we can utilise a related task's data to improve the performance of a new task of interest with only a limited amount of data. Our proposed method uses meta-learning to automatically learn which of the related task data points to selectively learn from. An important future work is to evaluate/extend the proposed method to more challenging and complex dialog datasets/tasks.

Data useful for a dialog task of interest (related data) could be present in different formats. The related data could include, for example, natural language instructions on how to perform the task of interest, or a description of how the new dialog task of interest is different from a related dialog task. An interesting future direction is to investigate methods to successfully utilise such related data.

References

Antoine Bordes, Y-Lan Boureau, and Jason Weston. 2017. Learning end-to-end goal-oriented dialog. *International Conference on Learning Representations (ICLR)*.

Zhangjie Cao, Lijia Ma, Mingsheng Long, and Jianmin Wang. 2018. Partial adversarial domain adaptation. In *Proceedings of the European Conference on Computer Vision (ECCV)*.

Yinpei Dai, Hangyu Li, Chengguang Tang, Yongbin Li, Jian Sun, and Xiaodan Zhu. 2020. Learning low-resource end-to-end goal-oriented dialog for fast and reliable system deployment. In *Proceedings of the 58th Annual Meeting of the Association for Computational Linguistics (ACL)*.

Mihail Eric and Christopher D Manning. 2017. Key-value retrieval networks for task-oriented dialogue. *Proceedings of the 18th Annual Meeting of the Special Interest Group on Discourse and Dialogue (SIGDIAL)*.

Chelsea Finn, Pieter Abbeel, and Sergey Levine. 2017. Model-agnostic meta-learning for fast adaptation of deep networks. In *Proceedings of International Conference on Machine Learning (ICML)*.

Jing Jiang and ChengXiang Zhai. 2007. Instance weighting for domain adaptation in NLP. In *Proceedings of the 45th Annual Meeting of the Association of Computational Linguistics (ACL)*.

Chaitanya K. Joshi, Fei Mi, and Boi Faltings. 2017. Personalization in goal-oriented dialog. *Workshop on Conversational AI, Advances in Neural Information Processing Systems (NeurIPS)*.

Yann LeCun, Corinna Cortes, and CJ Burges. 2010. Mnist handwritten digit database. *ATT Labs [Online]. Available: http://yann.lecun.com/exdb/mnist*.

Zhaojiang Lin, Andrea Madotto, Genta Indra Winata, and Pascale Fung. 2020. MinTL: Minimalist transfer learning for task-oriented dialogue systems. In *Proceedings of the 2020 Conference on Empirical Methods in Natural Language Processing (EMNLP)*.

Andrea Madotto, Zhaojiang Lin, Chien-Sheng Wu, and Pascale Fung. 2019. Personalizing dialogue agents via meta-learning. In *Proceedings of the 57th Annual Meeting of the Association for Computational Linguistics (ACL)*.

Fei Mi, Minlie Huang, Jiyong Zhang, and Boi Faltings. 2019. Meta-learning for low-resource natural language generation in task-oriented dialogue systems. In *Proceedings of the 28th International Joint Conference on Artificial Intelligence, (IJCAI)*.

Seungwhan Moon and Jaime Carbonell. 2017. Completely heterogeneous transfer learning with attention - what and what not to transfer. In *Proceedings of the 26th International Joint Conference on Artificial Intelligence (IJCAI)*.

Kun Qian and Zhou Yu. 2019. Domain adaptive dialog generation via meta learning. In *Proceedings of the 57th Annual Meeting of the Association for Computational Linguistics (ACL)*.

Janarthanan Rajendran, Richard Lewis, Vivek Veeriah, Honglak Lee, and Satinder Singh. 2020. How should an agent practice? In *Proceedings of 34th AAAI Conference on Artificial Intelligence (AAAI)*.

S. Sankaranarayanan, Y. Balaji, C. D. Castillo, and R. Chellappa. 2018. Generate to adapt: Aligning domains using generative adversarial networks. In *IEEE/CVF Conference on Computer Vision and Pattern Recognition (CVPR)*.

Sainbayar Sukhbaatar, arthur szlam, Jason Weston, and Rob Fergus. 2015. End-to-end memory networks. In *Advances in Neural Information Processing Systems (NeurIPS)*.

Z. Wang, Z. Dai, B. Póczos, and J. Carbonell. 2019. Characterizing and avoiding negative transfer. In *IEEE/CVF Conference on Computer Vision and Pattern Recognition (CVPR)*.

Tsung-Hsien Wen, Milica Gašić, Nikola Mrkšić, Lina M. Rojas-Barahona, Pei-Hao Su, David Vandyke, and Steve Young. 2016. Multi-domain neural network language generation for spoken dialogue systems. In *Proceedings of the Conference of the North American Chapter of the Association for Computational Linguistics: Human Language Technologies (NAACL-HLT)*.

Tsung-Hsien Wen, David Vandyke, Nikola Mrkšić, Milica Gasic, Lina M. Rojas Barahona, Pei-Hao Su, Stefan Ultes, and Steve Young. 2017. A network-based end-to-end trainable task-oriented dialogue system. In *Proceedings of the 15th Conference of the European Chapter of the Association for Computational Linguistics (EACL)*.

Olga Wichrowska, Niru Maheswaranathan, Matthew W. Hoffman, Sergio Gómez Colmenarejo, Misha Denil, Nando de Freitas, and Jascha Sohl-Dickstein. 2017. Learned optimizers that scale and generalize. In *Proceedings of the International Conference on Machine Learning (ICML)*.

Yuhuai Wu, Mengye Ren, Renjie Liao, and Roger Grosse. 2018. Understanding short-horizon bias in stochastic meta-optimization. In *International Conference on Learning Representations (ICLR)*.

Yumo Xu, Chenguang Zhu, Baolin Peng, and Michael Zeng. 2020. Meta dialogue policy learning. *arXiv preprint arXiv:2006.02588*.

Zhongwen Xu, Hado P van Hasselt, and David Silver. 2018. Meta-gradient reinforcement learning. In *Advances in Neural Information Processing Systems (NeurIPS)*.

Han Zhao, Shanghang Zhang, Guanhang Wu, José M. F. Moura, Joao P Costeira, and Geoffrey J Gordon. 2018. Adversarial multiple source domain adaptation. In *Advances in Neural Information Processing Systems (NeurIPS)*.

Xueliang Zhao, Wei Wu, Chongyang Tao, Can Xu, Dongyan Zhao, and Rui Yan. 2020. Low-resource knowledge-grounded dialogue generation. In *International Conference on Learning Representations (ICLR)*.

Zeyu Zheng, Junhyuk Oh, and Satinder Singh. 2018. On learning intrinsic rewards for policy gradient methods. In *Advances in Neural Information Processing Systems (NeurIPS)*.

A MNIST Image Classification

A.1 Architecture and Training Details

The MNIST dataset contains 60,000 training images and 10,000 testing images. Among the training images, we use 50,000 for training and 10,000 for validation. The primary task is the classification of hand-written digits from the MNIST dataset (LeCun et al., 2010). The related task is created by taking the primary task data and changing the label to an incorrect one for 75% of the training data. This means that of the 50,000 related task data points, 25% (12,500 data points) are useful for the primary task while 75% (37,500 data points) are not. The MNIST hand-written digit images are resized to 28 x 28 images and the pixel values are normalized to [0, 1]. The images are flattened to a 1-D array of 784 features (28 x 28). We use a logistic regression as our classification model (M_θ) and a perceptron with sigmoid non-linearity at the output for the weight generation module (P_η). The weight generation module takes as input the image, its label and the indicator that tells if that label is correct or not for that image, and produces a scalar weight between $(0, 1)$ as the output. The classification model has 7850 ((784(image) x 10(output label)) + 10(bias)) parameters and the weight generation module has 797(((784(image) + 10(label) + 2(indicator)) x 1(output weight)) + 1(bias)) parameters.

At each iteration of training, we make one update to the classification model using weighted related task data and one update to the related task data points' weights using meta-gradients. For each of the meta-gradient update we simulate how the model parameters θ changes over one gradient update step using weighted related task data points. The training uses a batch size of 256, with Adam optimizer (learning rate = 0.001, epsilon = 1e-8). The training is run for a maximum of 15000 iterations and the validation data is used for model selection for testing. These experiments were run on a CPU laptop with 2.5 GHz Intel Core i5 processor and 8 GB RAM. It takes approximately 1 hour for each training run.

A.2 Visualization of learned related task data points' weights

Figure 3 (left) and Figure 4 (left) shows the weights assigned for the different related task data points by our proposed method during different stages of training. The points in red (cross) and blue (dots) correspond to the weights of data points that have incorrect and correct labels respectively. Figure 3 (right) and Figure 4 (right) shows the histograms of number of data points in the different interval of weights. The histogram in red (plain) and blue (striped) correspond to the related task data points with incorrect and correct labels respectively.

B Personalized Restaurant Reservation

B.1 Example dialogs

Figure 5 (Left) shows a simplified example of Task 5 from the bAbI dialog tasks, which is our related task. Figure 5 (Right) shows a simplified example of Task 3 from the personalized-bAbI dialog tasks, our primary task of interest.

B.2 Architecture and Training Details

In this experiment, we use Task 3 from the personalized-bAbI dialog tasks as our primary task, and Task 5 of the bAbI dialog tasks as the related task. 100% (1000 dialogs) of the training dialogs of bAbI dialog Task 5 are available as the related task data. For the primary task, we simulate limited data availability by decreasing the number of training and validation dialogs. We look at three data settings: 5% (50 dialogs), 10% (100 dialogs) and 15% (150 dialogs) of the primary task training and validation dialogs. For testing, we use 100% (1000 dialogs) of the test dialogs from the personalized-bAbI dataset.

In this experiment we use the same dialog model architecture as used in Joshi et al. (2017), end-to-end memory networks (Sukhbaatar et al., 2015). The sentences in the dialog are encoded using Bag of Words encoding. The encoded sentences, which are part of the dialog history, are stored in the memory and the query (last user utterance) embedding is used to attend over the memory (3 times) to get relevant information from the memory. The generated internal state is used to select the candidate response from the list of candidates. The entire network is trained end-to-end using cross-entropy loss of the candidate selection. We use an end-to-end memory network for the module P_η (that produces the weights for each of the related task data points) as well. In this case, the internal state generated after attending over the memory is used to generate the scalar $(0, 1)$ weight.

At each iteration of training, we make one update to the dialog model using primary task data, one update to the dialog model using weighted related task data and 10 updates to the related task data points' weights using meta-gradients. For each of the meta-gradient update we simulate how the model parameters θ changes over 5 gradient updates of weighted related task data points. We use the same hyper-parameters used by Joshi et al. (2017) for both our end-to-end memory networks: embedding size = 20, batch size = 32, optimizer = Adam (learning rate = 0.001, epsilon = 1e-8).

The parameters of the dialog model are made up of a word embedding matrix of size |Vocab| x 20 that encodes the dialog history and the current user utterance, a matrix of size 20 x 20 that transforms the selected memory embeddings to generate the internal dialog state, and a word embedding matrix of size |Vocab| x 20 for encoding the candidate responses. The parameters of the weight generation module are made up of a word embedding matrix of size |Vocab| x 20 that encodes the dialog history, the current user utterance, and the next dialog system utterance, a matrix of size 20 x 20 that transforms the selected memory embeddings to generate the internal dialog state, and a matrix of size 20 x 1 and a bias term of size 1 for transforming the internal dialog state to a scalar weight. The size of the vocabulary |Vocab| for different primary task data settings of 5%, 10% and 15% are 4129, 4657, and 4981 respectively. The training is run for 4000 epochs (of the related task data points) and the primary task validation dataset is used for model selection for testing. These experiments were run using GeForce GTX 1080 Ti GPUs. It takes approximately 15 hours for each training run.

B.3 Visualization of learned related task data points' weights

Figure 6 (left) and Figure 7 (left) show the weights assigned for the different related task data points by our proposed method during different stages of training. Figure 6 (right) and Figure 7 (right) shows the histograms of number of data points in the different interval of weights.

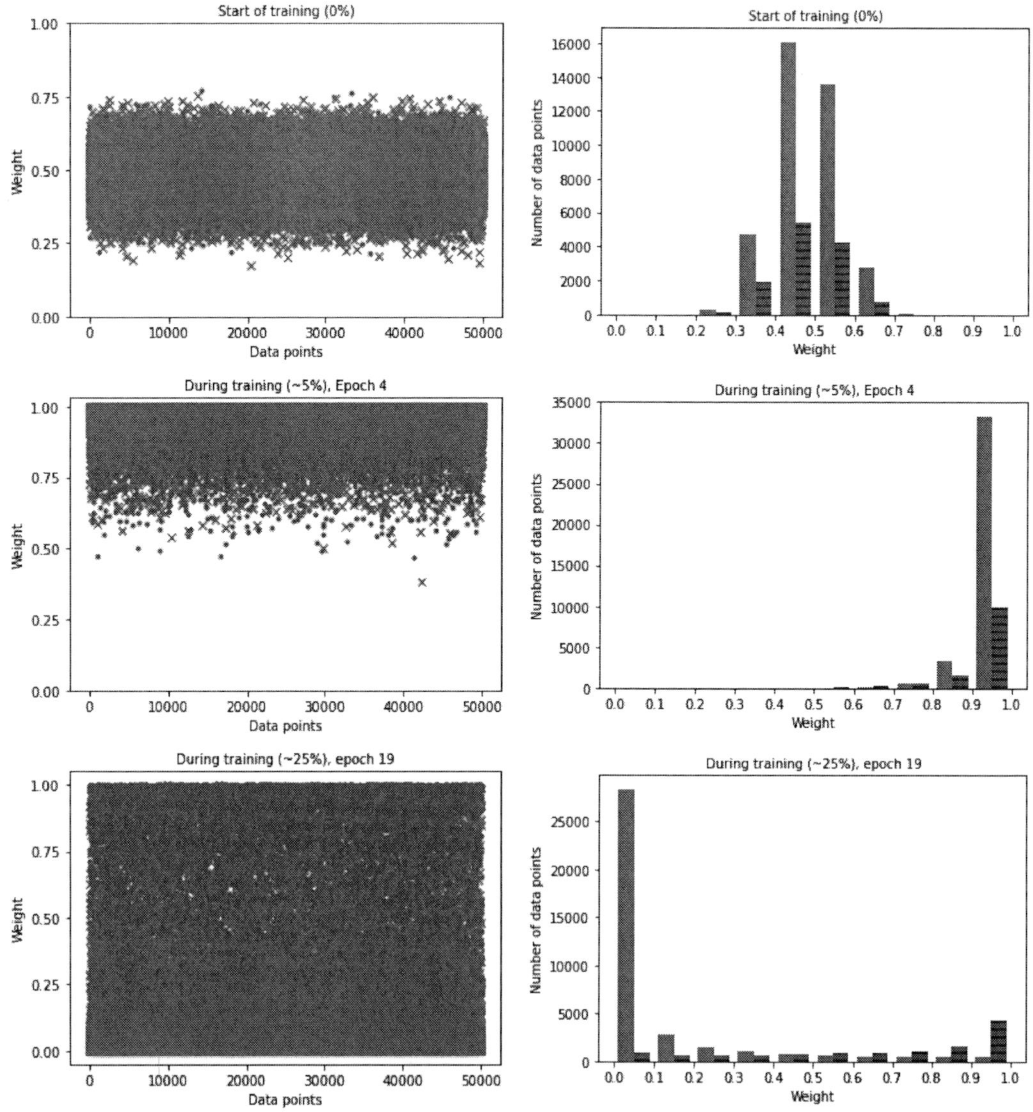

Figure 3: (Part 1/2) MNIST image classification. *Left*: The weights assigned for the different related task data points by our proposed method during different stages of training. The points in red (cross) and blue (dots) correspond to the weights of the related task data points that have incorrect and correct labels respectively. *Right*: Histograms of the number of data points in the different interval of weights. The histograms in red (plain) and blue (striped) correspond to the related task data points with incorrect and correct labels respectively. Refer to Figure 4 for Part 2/2.

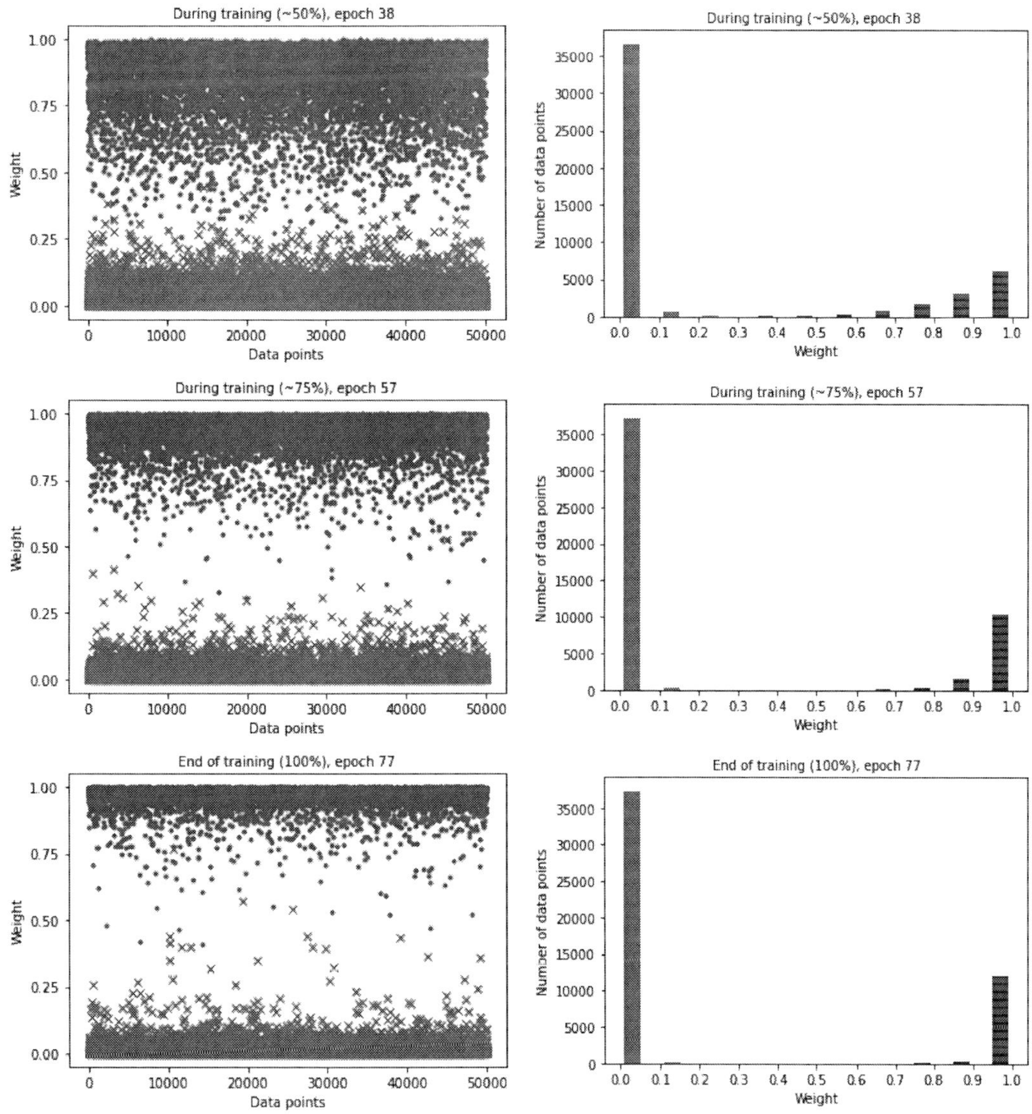

Figure 4: (Part 2/2) MNIST image classification. *Left*: The weights assigned for the different related task data points by our proposed method during different stages of training. The points in red (cross) and blue (dots) correspond to the weights of the related task data points that have incorrect and correct labels respectively. *Right*: Histograms of the number of data points in the different interval of weights. The histograms in red (plain) and blue (striped) correspond to the related task data points with incorrect and correct labels respectively. Refer to Figure 3 for Part 1/2.

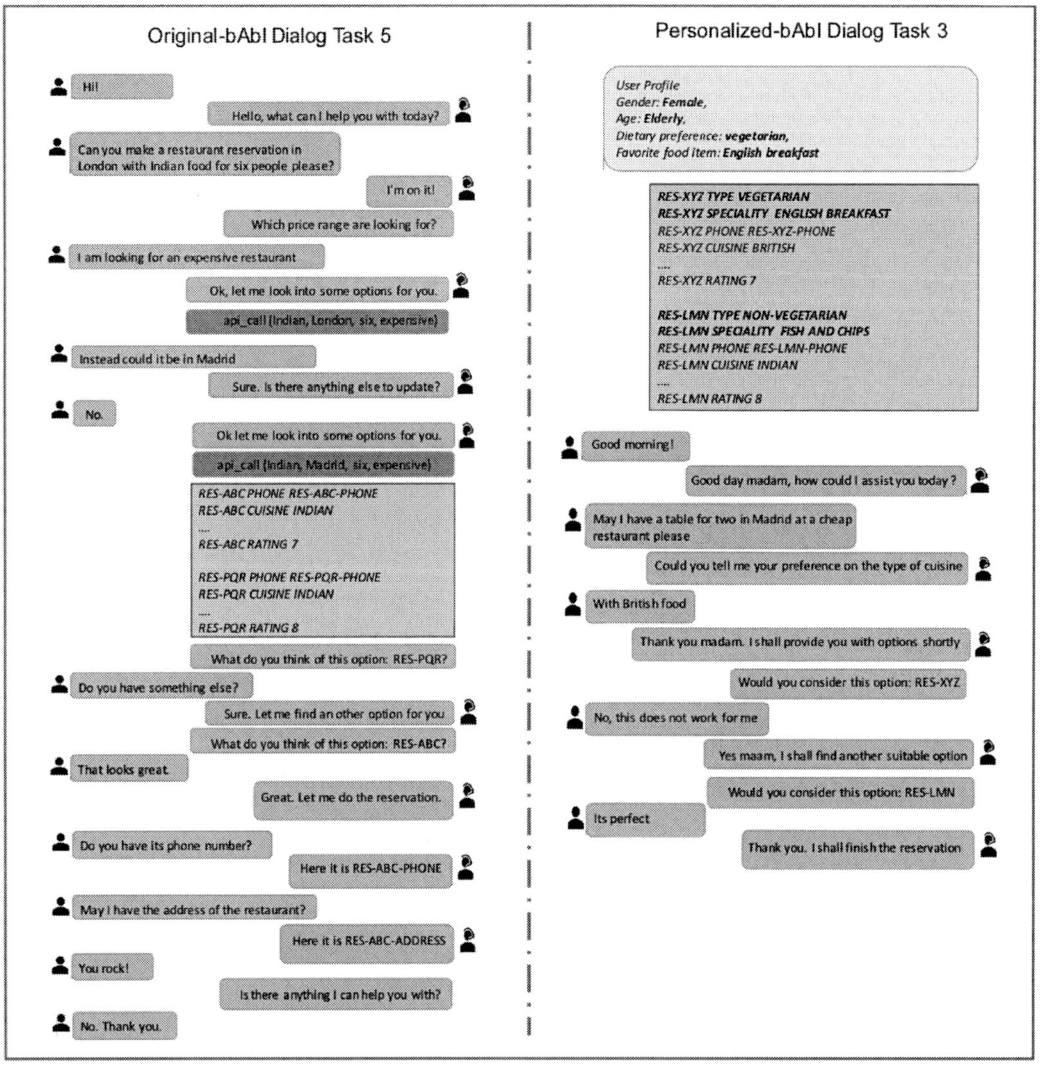

Figure 5: A user (in green) chats with a dialog system (in blue) to book a table at a restaurant. *Left*: (Related Task) An example dialog from bAbI dialog Task 5. *Right*: (Primary Task) An example dialog from Personalized-bAbI dialog Task 3.

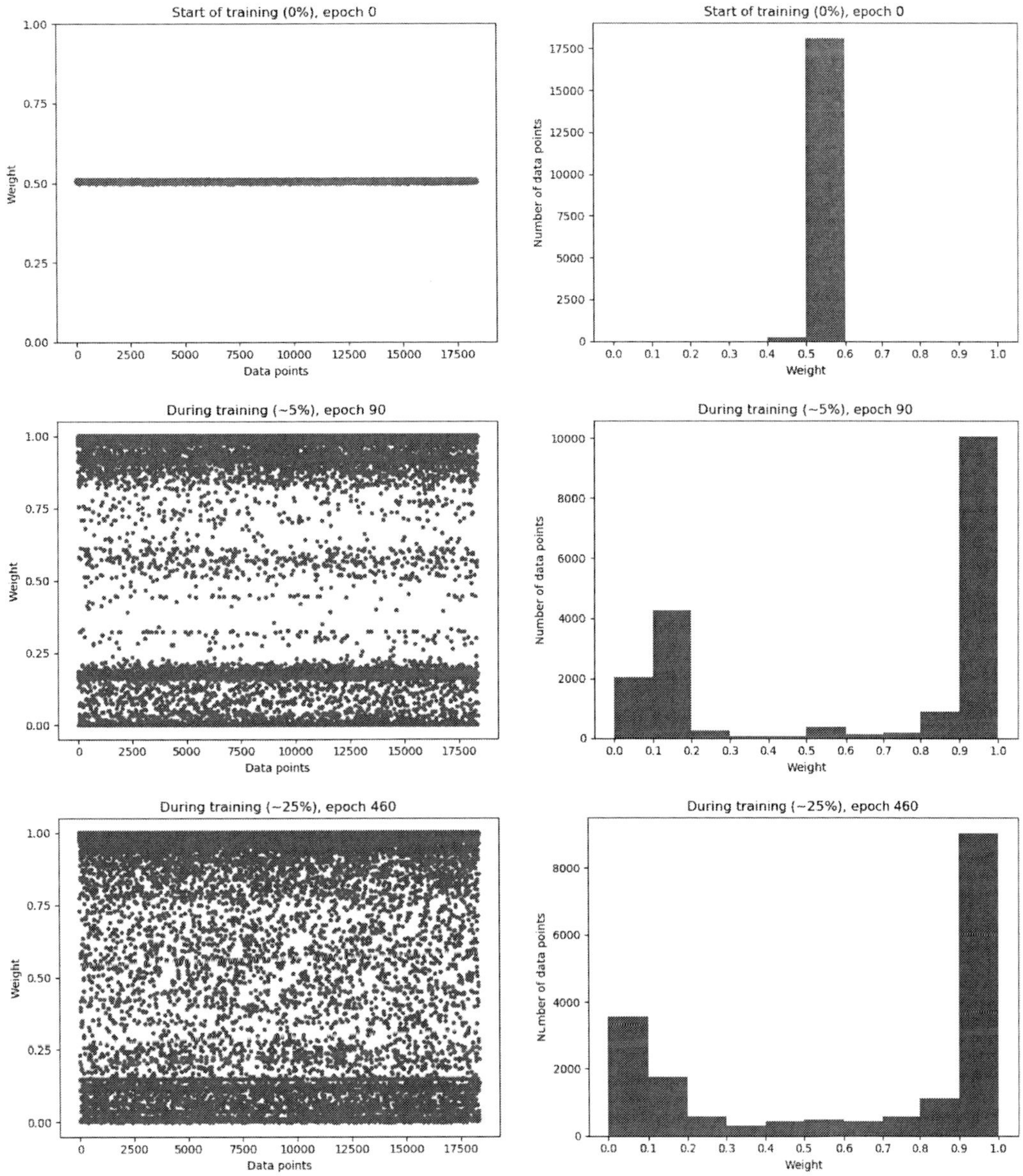

Figure 6: (Part 1/2) Personalized Restaurant Reservation. *Left*: The weights assigned for the different related task data points by our proposed method during different stages of training. *Right*: Histograms of the number of data points in the different interval of weights. Refer to Figure 7 for Part 2/2.

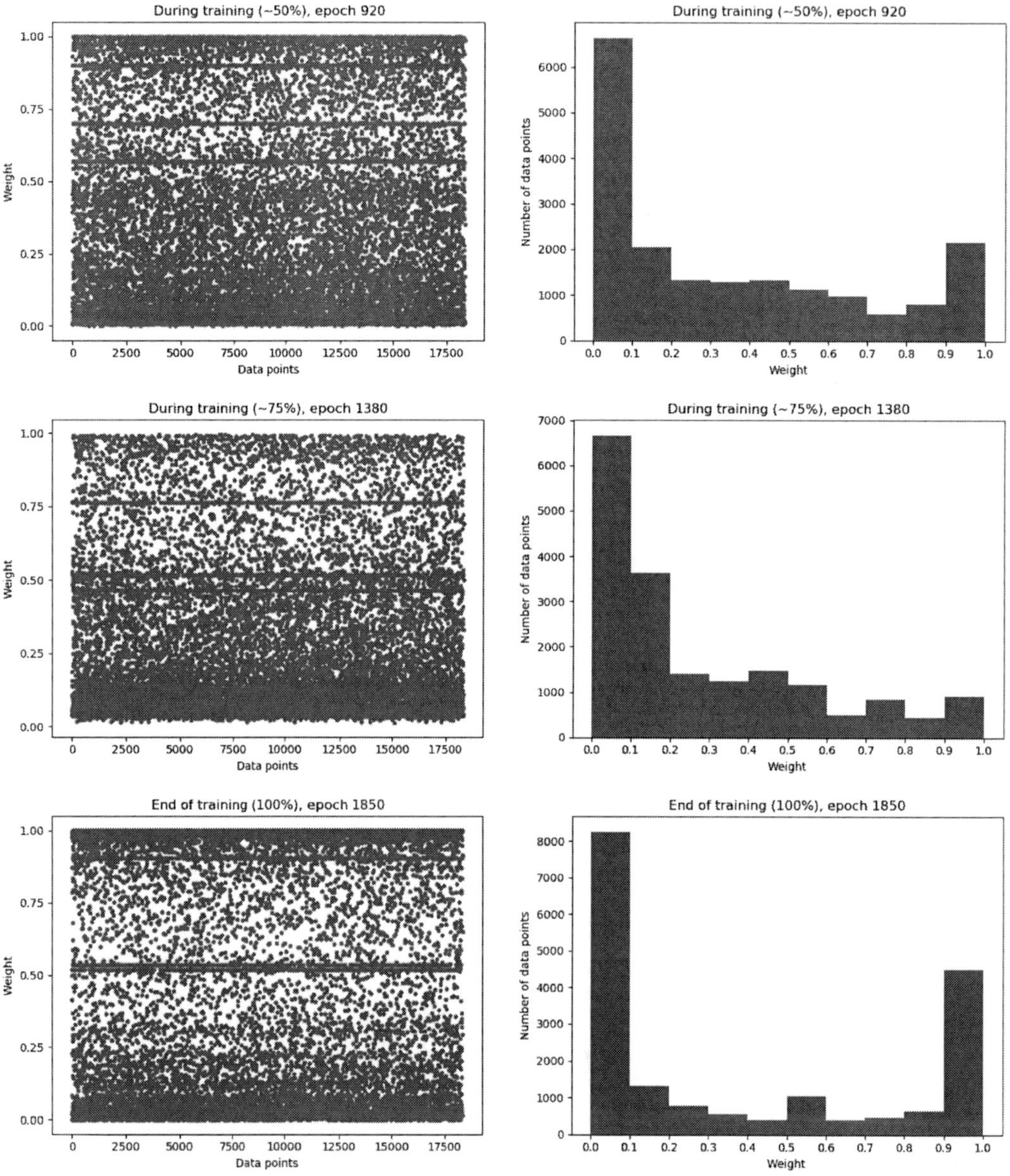

Figure 7: (Part 2/2) Personalized Restaurant Reservation. *Left*: The weights assigned for the different related task data points by our proposed method during different stages of training. *Right*: Histograms of the number of data points in the different interval of weights. Refer to Figure 6 for Part 1/2.

Personalized Search-based Query Rewrite System for Conversational AI

Eunah Cho **Ziyan Jiang** **Jie Hao** **Zheng Chen**
Saurabh Gupta **Xing Fan** **Chenlei Guo**

Amazon Alexa AI
{eunahch, ziyjiang, jieha, zgchen,
gsaur, fanxing, guochenl}@amazon.com

Abstract

Query rewrite (QR) is an emerging component in conversational AI systems, reducing user defect. User defect is caused by various reasons, such as errors in the spoken dialogue system, users' slips of the tongue or their abridged language. Many of the user defects stem from personalized factors, such as user's speech pattern, dialect, or preferences. In this work, we propose a personalized search-based QR framework, which focuses on automatic reduction of user defect. We build a personalized index for each user, which encompasses diverse affinity layers to reflect personal preferences for each user in the conversational AI. Our personalized QR system contains retrieval and ranking layers. Supported by user feedback based learning, training our models does not require hand-annotated data. Experiments on personalized test set showed that our personalized QR system is able to correct systematic and user errors by utilizing phonetic and semantic inputs.

1 Introduction

With the increased popularity of virtual assistant agents such as Alexa, Cortana and Siri, millions of users interact with spoken dialog system on daily basis. Some of the user interactions lead to *defect* experiences, where users do not get what they requested for, or the AI agent has to engage with the user again to clarify the user request. Such errors originate either from the spoken dialogue system itself (e.g. automatic speech recognition (ASR) error, natural language understanding (NLU) error, etc.) or the user. For example, an ASR error can lead to "play son in dance" instead of the correct query "play stolen dance". Often users' slips of the tongue can lead to the similar issue. It can be also the case that a partial song name is used in the request, or lyrics instead of the song name. The goal of QR component is to automatically recover from the defect and achieve better user experience.

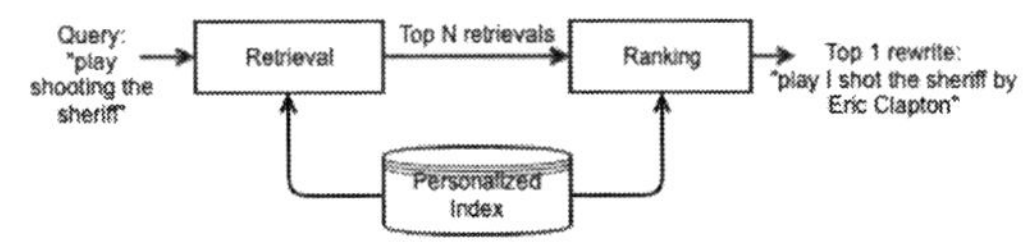

Figure 1: Search-based personalized rewrite framework

In production spoken dialogue systems, QR component is often triggered when the conversational AI cannot process user requests with a good confidence. For example, if ASR confidence score is low or named entity tagger (NER) confidence score for NLU is low, QR component can be triggered to automatically map a user query to another form, so that the dialog system can be more robust.

A crucial nature of QR is that often it needs to reflect personal preference or personalized error types to recover from the defect. While certain generic defect patterns may occur globally for many users, personalized error recovery is often expected to correctly fulfill each individual user's request. For example, a query "turn on the moon" might be a mis-recognized utterance requesting for the Moonlight Sonata. For other users who have a smart light device called "the moon lamp", this might be a request to turn on the lamp. Personalized QR can be leveraged for such scenario, providing rewrites such as "turn on the moonlight sonata" or "turn on the moon lamp".

Inspired by Fan et al. (2021), we approach the personalized QR task here with a search-based solution. A search system mainly comprises of two stacks operating sequentially: retrieval and ranking. Figure 1 shows the overall framework of our search-based personalized rewrite system. Personalized index contains successful utterances from each user. Given the user query, retrieval model first retrieves top N candidates from the user's personalized index. In the retrieval stage, we aim to obtain the most relevant rewrite candidates with a

Proceedings of the Third Workshop on Natural Language Processing for Conversational AI, pages 179–188
November 10, 2021.

good recall. The retrived candidates are ranked by the ranking model, utilizing personalized features extracted from personalized index. Top 1 ranked candidate is returned as a final rewrite for the query. In the example shown in Figure 1, we observe that the rewrite does not only correct the song name, but also finds the correct artist name based on the personalization for the user.

We utilize semi-supervised learning to obtain data and create the personalized index for each user in the conversational AI system. The personalized index primarily serves as a search pool for each user in the retrieval component. In our work, the index encompasses diverse affinity layers, which are utilized further as features in the ranking process. In Section 3, we describe how the documents are constructed for personalization index. In Section 4, we present the retrieval models we explored. Section 5 describes the ranker model and its diverse set of features.

2 Related Work

Many previous work focused on solving the QR problem in a non-personalized use case. In Ponnusamy et al. (2020), authors proposed a markov chain model as a collaborative filtering mechanism to mine users' reformulation patterns. Once the patterns are discovered, rewrite pairs are extracted (i.e. ASR recognition of defect query - detected reformulation interaction). At runtime, if a query is an exact text match with a defect query, a rewrite will be triggered using the offline mined pairs. Different from the Markov chain model, Chen et al. (2020) proposed a retrieval model for QR task, utilizing a query encoder that incorporates contextual language modeling pre-training.

At the same time, QR problem has been explored for other tasks as well. In Bonadiman et al. (2019), authors explored paraphrase retrieval for defect reduction on question answering task. A machine translation based method (Riezler and Liu, 2010) was explored for a QR problem in a search engine.

Fan et al. (2021) further extended previous work on search-based QR in spoken dialogue system to both global layer (serving non-personalized, generic rewrites) and personalized layer. They utilize the search based methods and metrics such as similarity measures. Compared to the markov chain model (Ponnusamy et al., 2020), this work provided a further flexibility to generalize over unseen input queries. For global layer, authors explore the importance of a ranking layer leveraging a neural feature extractor and a tree model. In Roshan-Ghias et al. (2020), authors present a retrieval model compared with a pointer-generator network with hierarchical attention to perform personalized rewrites within smart home domain. In our work, we focus on the search-based QR system that utilizes retrieval and ranking components. One strength of the search-based QR is that as the rewrite candidate pool is defined in the index, rewrite quality can be tightly controlled. Compared to generation-based methods, which may provide enhanced flexibility and diversity of the rewrites, this provides an advantage for system stability, especially for a task like QR which is strongly relevant with runtime production setup.

Our work distinguishes itself from previous work from the following aspects. First, we significantly extend the personalized index to incorporate diverse affinities and associated personal preferences. Our QR system is not limited to certain domains or usage, but capable of providing rewrites across all domains and functionalities within the spoken dialogue system (e.g. playing music, reading books, weather forecast, handling smart home devices, etc.). The retrieval component is further extended so that not only it utilizes the utterance information, but it incorporates phonetic information as well as ASR n-best information. While personalized search-based QR system in Fan et al. (2021) only leveraged a retrieval component, we introduce a ranking model with personalized features.

3 Personalized Index

In order to support personalized rewrites, we build an index for each user, leveraging individual interaction history. Personalized index reflects non-defect experiences for each user[1] observed within last 30 days of time window. We utilize a defect detection model such as Ling et al. (2020); Gupta et al. (2021) as well as rule-based criteria to obtain non-defect turns. The rule-based criteria utilizes both users' response (if user barged in or stopped agent's response, the turn is defect) as well as agent's response (if agent responds as "sorry, I do not know that" or similar, the turn is defect). To better define the search space and consider runtime aspects, we limit the personalized index size, by selecting top l history utterances based on utterance count and recency from the user. In order to control runtime

[1] All user information is in a de-identified format.

latency, we use $l = 100$ in this work.

Our personalized index contains different layers to represent fine-grained affinities; utterance (with NLU hypothesis), entity, intent, and template. The utterance layer directly serves as the search space for the personalized retrieval. The other layers provide personalized features utilized for ranking process. In the following sections, we describe each of them in detail.

3.1 Utterance Layer

As mentioned, personalized index is constructed for each user of the conversational AI system. Utterance layer can be considered as an entry point, where we trace non-defect utterances spoken by each user. Figure 2 shows an example personalized index.

The documents in the index are constructed using NLU hypothesis information. Using NLU hypothesis information, we aim to represent a group of queries sharing a similar goal in a dialogue system. NLU hypothesis is generated from the NLU component in the spoken dialog system, and can be represented in the following format "domain | intent | slot_type:slot_value". For example, given a query "put on cocomelon", we have an NLU hypothesis of "Music | PlayMusicIntent | ArtistName:cocomelon". The *domain* is the general topic of a query, e.g. "Music", "Weather". The *intent* reflects the action the user wants to take, e.g. "PlayRadio", "WeatherInfo"; The *slot-types/values* are results of entity labeling task. In the example, we can see that two queries spoken by the user "play cocomelon" and "put on cocomelon" are grouped together as they led to the same NLU hypothesis. For each NLU hypothesis and query, we trace how often the user has used this (*user count*) as well as how often this led to a defect experience (*user defect*).

3.2 Entity Layer

We further expand the affinity to include entity information so that the entity affinity information can be used during the ranking process. By *entity*, we refer to the slot values that we can observe in the NLU hypothesis. In the example index shown in Figure 2, we can extract the information that the user uses the entity "cocomelon" 30 times within the time window, and among them the defect experience was 3 times. To obtain an index with fine-grained affinity representation, we further gather the information on the joint occurrences between the slot types and the entity. Using this, we can reflect different usage pattern from each user. For example, for the users who frequently listen to "cocomelon" using an audio device, the entity would appear more frequently with ArtistName slot type. On the other hand, for the users who frequently watch videos of "cocomelon", the entity would appear more frequently as a VideoName enity. Such fine-grained usage pattern is leveraged as personalized features in the ranking layer (Section 5).

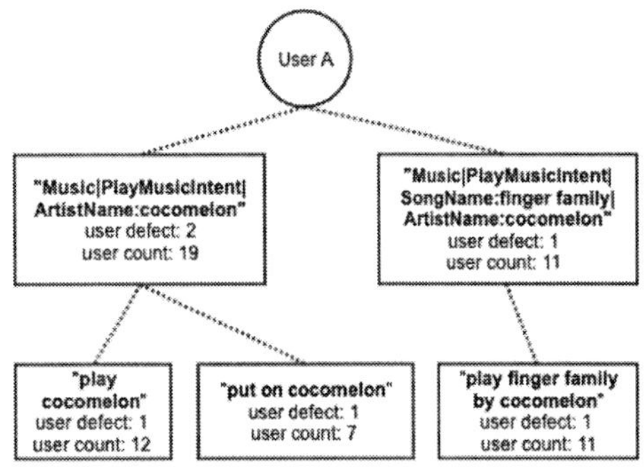

Figure 2: Example of utterance layer in personalized index

3.3 Intent Layer

Similarly to entity layer, we extract intent usage information. For each intent used by each user (e.g. "PlayMusic", "PlayVideo"), we trace user count as well as defect information.

3.4 Template Layer

By *template*, we refer to the utterance structure. For example, for a same-goal request, certain users may say "In my kitchen put John Lennon's song Imagine" while others may say "play Imagine by John Lennon on my kitchen device". We find those syntactic differences another way to represent user affinity and introduce the template layer. For template, entities are replaced to their slot-type and we only utilize the carrier phrase (e.g. "play SongName by ArtistName on my DeviceLocation device"). For each template, same as other affinity layers, we trace user count and user defect information.

4 Retrieval Component

In a search system, retrieval layer aims to retrieve a set of relevant documents from a great amount of documents. The goal is to retrieve them with good recall, with low latency and computational cost.

Following the work in Chen et al. (2020); Fan et al. (2021), we use a Deep Structured Semantic Models (DSSM) (Huang et al., 2013) based embedder. The learning objective is to project the embedding of input query (e.g. "turn on tape timer") and that of target rewrite (e.g. "turn on tea timer") closely.

4.1 Training Data Selection

For training data, as a baseline, we use weak-labeled data similar to Fan et al. (2021). We first find two consecutive user utterances, where the first turn was defect, but the second turn was successful. We utilized a DNN-based defect detection model such as Ling et al. (2020). In order to decrease potential noise in the data and find the pairs where the second utterance is indeed a rephrase of the first utterance, we further apply filters based on edit-distance and ASR n-best. For edit-distance based rephrases, we filter so that the utterance pairs have an edit distance smaller than d, and the time gap between the two utterances are shorter than t seconds. Additionally, we harvest ASR n-best-based rephrases. Two consecutive user utterances whose time gap is shorter than t seconds, if the first turn's ASR n-best ($n > 1$) is same as the following second turn's ASR 1-best, we consider them as rephrase as well. After preliminary experiments to control the trade-off between noise level and training data size, we chose $t = 45$ and $d = 5$. Maximum size for n is 5.

In order to decrease potential noise in above data, we apply another data selection method by adding a constraint on transitioning probability. From interaction history of each user, we calculate the probability of two utterances occurring one after another. We then apply a constraint so that $P(u_2|u_1) > p$, where u_1 denotes the first turn, and u_2 denotes the following turn. This helps to clean up the data further and filter out noise introduced in the training data for the personalized model. This way of data selection led to a smaller amount (60%) of rephrases as training data, compared to the baseline approach. In our experiments, we empirically set the $d = 7$ and $p = 0.5$.

4.2 Phonetic Information into Retrieval

We observe that user defects often stem from ASR error as well as users' slip of the tongue. For example, a query "did humidifier on" is an ASR error of "dehumidifier on". Another example includes an erroneous recognition "can you play alien bridges",

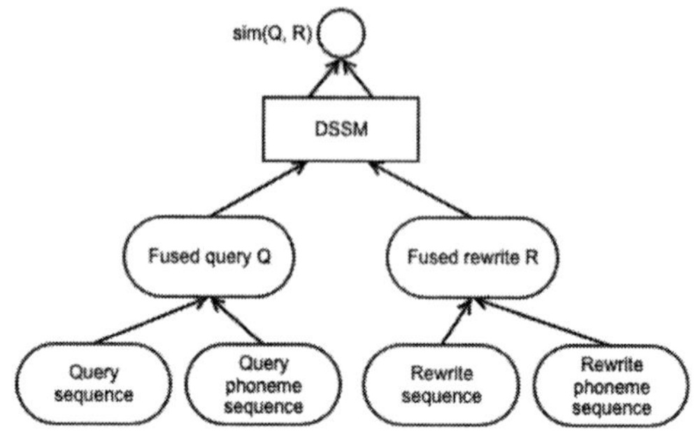

Figure 3: Illustration of DSSM model with phoneme sequence

which was rephrased by the user into "can you play leon bridges". While the baseline retrieval model (Fan et al., 2021) utilizes surface form representation of user utterances and their embedding space, we aim to further expand this to also incorporate phonetic information.

In order to obtain the phoneme sequence of each utterance, we utilize a grapheme to phoneme (G2P) model based on the Transformer (Vaswani et al., 2017)[2]. Baseline DSSM model uses the textual representation of the query (e.g. "did humidifier on") and the target rewrite (e.g. "dehumidifier on"). While still utilizing the DSSM structure, we introduce another layer to fuse textual input representation and the phonetic sequence representation (e.g. "d I d h j u m I d @ f aI @' A n"), for both query and target rewrite. Standard G2P outputs phoneme sequence in their monophone sequence. Our preliminary experiment showed that augmenting word boundaries in phoneme sequences (e.g. "dId hjumId@faI@' An"), making the phoneme sequence more comparable to the utterance sequence length, leads to better performance. Figure 3 depicts how the phoneme sequence is incorporated into the DSSM model.

The neural encoder, thus, learns to capture latent syntactic, semantic and phonetic information for the query and the rewrite candidates. For the final similarity comparison, we use the scoring function shown in Eq. 1, where *cos* represents cosine distance.

$$S(x, y) = cos(\mathbf{h}, \mathbf{r}) \quad (1)$$

$\mathbf{h}$ is the embedding of input query x and $\mathbf{r}$ is the embedding of the rewrite candidate y, generated by passing them through the neural encoder respectively.

[2]We utilized Sockeye package (Hieber et al., 2017)

We calculate the score S given the input query and rewrite candidates (utterances) from personalized index. Top N candidates are chosen by their score S and passed down to the ranker component.

4.3 Utilizing ASR n-best

The QR system is triggered when the conversational AI cannot process user queries with a good confidence. Many previous designs for QR component, such as Fan et al. (2021); Chen et al. (2020), consume ASR 1-best as an input query to the QR system. Instead of consuming only ASR 1-best to our QR system, in this work, we expand our retrieval component to also consume the full ASR n-best list. By expanding the input query to a list of ASR hypotheses, we aim to boost the recall in the retrieval layer. For example, for a query (ASR 1-best) "turn on prayer lights", considering its ASR n-best such as "turn on foyer lights" in addition might be helpful to retrieve the correct rewrite "turn on party lights".

We expand the scoring function to consider input query's ASR n-best, x_0, x_1, ..., x_{n-1}. Rewrite candidates are retrieved based on the maximum score S obtained between them and any of the input ASR n-best. In order to consider runtime latency, we limit the n to 5.

4.4 Model Training

The neural encoder in the retrieval layer takes character-level trigram and word-level as input. We sum the embeddings of all tokens and pass through three layers of fully connected MLP with 512 hidden layer size. The final embedding size is 300. The experiments are performed using AllenNLP[3].

5 Ranking Model

Given retrieved rewrite candidates, ranking layer aims to rank the most desired rewrite to the top. Thus, precision is critical in the ranking layer. In this work, we build a gradient boosting model that utilizes both global level features as well as personalized features.

In our personalized QR system, we retrieve top 10 rewrite candidates in the retrieval component and pass them down to the ranking component. The top 1 rewrite whose ranking score is higher than an empirically chosen θ is selected as the final rewrite.

[3]https://github.com/allenai/allennlp

5.1 Global Features

By *global* features, we refer to non-personalized, generic features that we can consider for a rewrite ranking model. Even though the major use case of the model is for personalization, our intuition is that there are generic features that the model can learn to boost good rewrites (e.g. how similar query and rewrite utterances are).

Global features include the followings. **Global IR features** includes many of traditional information retrieval (IR) features, including TF-IDF, BM25 (Robertson et al., 1995), (weighted) number of queries, (weighted) number of tokens and n-gram probability. To extract global IR features, we utilize a document aggregated in global level, similarly to Fan et al. (2021). Per each NLU hypothesis, we aggregate relevant queries, their frequency and defect information. To obtain **embedding features**, we use two utterance encoders; one based on utterance string, another based on phonetic sequence. Each model is used to represent utterance strings (query and rewrite candidate) in their embedding space. We then obtain similarity metrics between the query and the rewrite candidate, such as cosine distance, Euclidean distance, Manhattan distance, etc. The utterance encoder follows the DNN-based baseline retrieval model (Huang et al., 2013; Fan et al., 2021). Phonetic sequence encoder follows the model described in Section 4.2 but CNN-based (Shen et al., 2014). For both encoders, we use three layers of fully connected MLP with 512 hidden layer size. The final embedding size for both DNN and CNN is 300.

To obtain **phonetic features**, we first represent query and rewrite candidates in their phonetic sequence. Similar as in Section 4.2, we use G2P model to translate the utterance sequence to their phonetic sequence. Their textual similarity is calculated in Jaccard distance, edit-distance, as well as BLEU (Papineni et al., 2002). In addition, we utilize **utterance popularity** information as one of the global features. For this, we look into the number of users who spoke the utterance in a time window (i.e. 30 days).

Finally, **defect features** trace defect metrics for query and rewrite candidate. In order to build defect metrics, we observe production traffic utterances within a certain time window (i.e. 30 days) and obtain average defect metrics per utterance. Defect metrics consists rule-based ones (e.g. average *termination*, representing how often users follow up with "stop" or such after the query, average *barge-in*, representing how often users barged in right after they make a query, etc.) and model-based ones. Model-based ones include *rephrase* score from a rephrase detection model, indicating whether the query has been rephrased by the next turn. Rephrase detection model is a BERT (Devlin et al., 2018) based model, fine-tuned with human annotated rephrase pairs, and outputs the probability that the second query is a rephrase of the first query. Another model-based metric is *defect* score obtained from a DNN model for estimating dialogue quality (Ling et al., 2020).

5.2 Personalized Features

The ranker further utilizes rich personalized features. For **user affinity features**, we extensively used the affinity layer information from the personalized index (Section 3). For example, utilizing the entity layer in the personalized index, we extract user count and user defect information for an entity within the rewrite candidate. Intent and template layers are utilized in the similar manner. Intuition is that if the user hardly uses "PlayVideo" relevant intents but "PlayMusic" relevant intents more frequently with a certain entity (e.g. "cocomelon"), the ranker should be able to leverage this information to further promote the correct rewrite candidate. **User embedding** is obtained by utilizing personalized index described in Section 3, specifically utterance layer. We use the DNN based utterance encoder and obtain utterance embedding of 300 dimension for each utterance in user's personalized index. Each utterance embedding is weighted by user's utterance count and averaged. The averaged utterance embedding is used as the user's embedding. The intuition is that users' utterance usage will be reflected to the averaged embeddings. Similarly to the global features, we also construct **user IR features** by building a document for each user, extracting utterance frequency and defect information. Utilizing the document, we extracted the IR features comparable to the global IR features, such as TF-IDF, BM25, etc.

5.3 Training Data and Model Training

For model training, we obtained an adequate amount of rephrases from production traffic[4], following the methods described in Section 4. We run each rephrase through the personalized retrieval layer (Section 4) and obtain top 10 retrievals. If the retrieval matches rewrite label, it will serve as a positive label during the training. If not, the retrieval becomes a negative example.

[4] all user data is processed to be de-identified.

Table 1: Retrieval model performance in precision and trigger rate. All performance is reported in relative improvement compared to the Baseline.

No.	System	Precision	Trigger Rt.
1.	Data Selection	+3.35%	+18.88%
2.	+ Phoneme	+6.56%	+55.94%
3.	+ ASR n-best	+6.32%	+119.85%

In addition, we run the rephrases through a global retrieval model and obtain top 10 retrievals as well. Global index building follows the work in Fan et al. (2021), and we use the baseline retrieval model described in Section 4. By incorporating retrievals from both personalized and global layer, we aim to enhance model robustness. As personalized index reflects each user's preference and usage pattern, the retrievals are already rather distinctive for each other, leading to a relatively easier ranking problem. On the other hand, a global index contains documents aggregated from many users and can provide a relatively more challenging ranking problem. For example, given an input query "play shooting the sheriff", personalized index may have one strong rewrite candidate "play I shot the sheriff by Eric Clapton", reflecting user's previously shown preferences. However, global index can provide multiple relevant candidates, such as "play I shot the sheriff by Bob Marley" or "play sheriff". The global and personalized features together reach $\sim$730 dimensions of feature vector.

The ranker is trained using LightGBM (Ke et al., 2017) with DART (Vinayak and Gilad-Bachrach, 2015), where we set the max tree depth to be 20, learning rate to be 0.1, and the number of leaves to be 300.

6 Experiments and Results

In order to build the test set, we first find potential rephrase pairs that fulfill the following conditions: a) for the two consecutive utterances, the second turn utterance y is followed by the first turn utterance x within a short time window (i.e. 45 seconds) and their minimum edit distance is below an empirically chosen threshold, b) we can observe y in the user's personalized index with successful interaction indicated by the defect detection model. These

Table 2: Top 1 retrieval from retrieval model. "Retrieval sys." denotes the systems in Table 1.

Query	Top 1 retrieved rewrite	Retrieval sys.
Play my first **hertz** playlist	Play my first **church** playlist	1, 2, 3
Play 104 **WKQR**	Play 104.1 **WTQR**	2, 3
What's the weather in **Wharton beach**	What's the weather in **Boynton beach**	2, 3
Turn on **huel**	Turn on **newel**	3

samples are further annotated by human annotators to only select the true rephrases. After each test case is annotated by three human annotators, we have 6k test cases with the annotator agreement.

6.1 Evaluation Metrics

Evaluation is performed on the NLU hypothesis level, in precision and trigger rate. The precision here measures how often the triggered top 1 rewrite's NLU hypothesis matches the correct rewrite y's NLU hypothesis. Since our test set represents personalization opportunity, we also measure trigger rate, the ratio between rewrite-triggered test cases and all test cases. The QR component is triggered when the prediction score of the top 1 rewrite score is above an empirically chosen threshold. Trigger rate represents how often we can trigger the rewrite given personalization opportunities.

In this paper, performance is reported in terms of relative improvement over baseline. For example, given the precision of baseline system, we calculate the relative precision performance changes and report this in %. It is calculated as $100 \times (p_c - p_b)/p_b - 100$, where p_b is the baseline precision, and p_c denotes any comparing system's precision.

6.2 Results and Analysis

Table 1 shows the retrieval component performance on the personalized test set. To evaluate the performance of retrieval component, we take the top 1 retrieved candidate whose score exceeds a threshold θ, same as Fan et al. (2021). The threshold is carefully chosen empirically to avoid bad rewrites in production system. Thus, Table 1 represents the scenario where only the retrieval component is available for the personalized QR task.

For baseline, we utilize the utterance-based retrieval model following the weak-labelled training data selection described in Fan et al. (2021). As described, all performance is reported as relative performance against the baseline.

We can see that utilizing the utterance-based

Table 3: Ranking model performance. Baseline is best performant retrieval system's top 1 retrieval.

	Precision	Trigger Rt.
Ranker: global features	-1.17%	+7.39%
Ranker: all features	+7.60%	+19.10%

Table 4: Final top 1 rewrite examples.

Query	Final rewrite
Show me news room	Show me Indee's room
Burns office on	Marin's office on
Olana soundtrack	Play Moana soundtrack
Start my working	Start my work day
Lights sports show	Lights for show

retrieval model with data selection based on transition probability (row 1 in Table 1) improves both precision and trigger rate, even though the model is trained with a smaller amount of training data. Further significant improvement is achieved utilizing phoneme sequence on top of utterance sequence (row 2), and ASR n-best extension of input queries (row 3). It is especially noticeable that the baseline retrieval system's trigger rate is relatively low for the personalized test set. With all advancements (row 3), we can significantly improve the overall triggering rate with improved precision.

Table 2 shows examples of the top 1 retrieval from the retrieval component. We clarify which retrieval system achieved the rewrite by showing the system number corresponding to Table 1. We observe that the advancements in the retrieval component (data selection, phoneme sequence, and ASR n-best) led to the retrieval of personalized rewrites with a good confidence for many test cases. We can recover errors in user's playlist (hertz to church), frequently used radio station 104 WKQR to 104.1 WTQR). Other examples show that the retrieval system can correctly retrieve user's weather location (Boynton beach, Florida) for a mis-recognized location (Wharton beach, Australia).

Table 3 shows the ranking component performance. As Baseline, we took the best performing retrieval component configuration (last row system in Table 1). When utilizing ranker with only global features, we observe a slight degradation in precision, but a great improvement in trigger rate. Utilizing both global and personalized features, both precision and trigger rates are significantly improved. Examples of top 1 ranked rewrites are shown in Table 4. In this table, we show the examples where the retrieval component could not trigger a rewrite with a good confidence score, but the ranking component can trigger the final rewrite. In addition to correcting errors in user's smart device setups (e.g. room name, device name), it is also noticeable that the personalized QR corrects errors in users' routine setups (last two examples in Table 4). Many conversational AI systems support such routine phrase setups, where user can preset certain phrases (e.g. "start my work day") for specific actions from the agent (e.g. turning on lights and fans in user's office). During our analysis, we observe many of such corrections on routine phrases. The examples showcase that personalized QR system can enable AI agents to perform desired actions upon corrected utterances, rather than causing defect for the users (e.g. "Sorry, I don't know that. Can you repeat?").

We further looked into feature weight and analyzed the feature importance in the ranker model (See Appendix). We learned that 40% of user affinity features are ranked in the top 50 important features. Global features had shown importance as well. For example, 80% of defect features made into the top 50 important features out of all features, showing that the generic, non-personalized defect information is still required for the ranking process.

7 Conclusions

In this paper, we introduced a personalized search-based query rewrite system for conversational AI system. In order to fulfill personalization, the individualized index tracks each user's successful interaction history and is further expanded to reflect diverse affinities. Retrieval model leverages both utterance and phoneme information, and retrieves top 10 rewrite candidates. The candidates are ranked by the ranking model, utilizing highly personalized features based on the affinity layers as well as generic features for the query rewrite task. Experiments demonstrated that the search-based QR system with personalization advancements brings a significant improvement on both precision and trigger rate on the personalized rewrite test set.

For future work, we will focus on improving the model components further, including incorporation of richer prior information into the system (e.g. pre-trained contextual language modeling). Another future direction is to include richer contextual and personalized information into the retrieval process. The goal is to utilize contextual, cohort information and expand the QR experience to the functionalities that the user has not explored yet. Also, we will explore including external common knowledge into the ranking process.

References

Daniele Bonadiman, Anjishnu Kumar, and Arpit Mittal. 2019. Large scale question paraphrase retrieval with smoothed deep metric learning. In *EMNLP 2019, W-NUT*.

Zheng Chen, Xing Fan, Yuan Ling, Lambert Mathias, and Chenlei Guo. 2020. Pre-training for query rewriting in a spoken language understanding system. In *ICASSP*.

Jacob Devlin, Ming-Wei Chang, Kenton Lee, and Kristina Toutanova. 2018. Bert: Pre-training of deep bidirectional transformers for language understanding. *arXiv preprint arXiv:1810.04805*.

Xing Fan, Eunah Cho, Xiaojiang Huang, and Chenlei Guo. 2021. Search based self-learning query rewrite system in conversational ai. In *2nd International Workshop on Data-Efficient Machine Learning (DeMaL)*.

Saurabh Gupta, Xing Fan, Derek Liu, Benjamin Yao, Yuan Ling, Kun Zhou, Tuan-Hung Pham, and Chenlei Guo. 2021. Robertaiq: An efficient framework for automatic interaction quality estimation of dialogue systems. *2nd International Workshop on Data-Efficient Machine Learning (DeMaL)*.

Felix Hieber, Tobias Domhan, Michael Denkowski, David Vilar, Artem Sokolov, Ann Clifton, and Matt Post. 2017. Sockeye: A toolkit for neural machine translation. *arXiv preprint arXiv:1712.05690*.

Po-Sen Huang, Xiaodong He, Jianfeng Gao, Li Deng, Alex Acero, and Larry Heck. 2013. Learning deep structured semantic models for web search using clickthrough data.

Guolin Ke, Qi Meng, Thomas Finley, Taifeng Wang, Wei Chen, Weidong Ma, Qiwei Ye, and Tie-Yan Liu. 2017. Lightgbm: A highly efficient gradient boosting decision tree. *Advances in neural information processing systems*, 30:3146–3154.

Yuan Ling, Benjamin Yao, Guneet Kohli, Tuan-Hung Pham, and Chenlei Guo. 2020. Iq-net: A DNN model for estimating interaction-level dialogue quality with conversational agents. In *Proceedings of the KDD 2020 Workshop on Conversational Systems Towards Mainstream Adoption co-located with the 26TH ACM SIGKDD Conference on Knowledge Discovery and Data Mining (SIGKDD 2020), Virtual Workshop, August 24, 2020*, volume 2666 of *CEUR Workshop Proceedings*. CEUR-WS.org.

Kishore Papineni, Salim Roukos, Todd Ward, and Wei-Jing Zhu. 2002. Bleu: a method for automatic evaluation of machine translation. In *Proceedings of the 40th annual meeting of the Association for Computational Linguistics*, pages 311–318.

Pragaash Ponnusamy, Alireza Roshan-Ghias, Chenlei Guo, and Ruhi Sarikaya. 2020. Feedback-based self-learning in large-scale conversational ai agents. In *The Thirty-Second Annual Conference on Innovative Applications of Artificial Intelligence*.

Stefan Riezler and Yi Liu. 2010. Query rewriting using monolingual statistical machine translation. *Computational Linguistics*, 36(3):569–582.

Stephen E Robertson, Steve Walker, Susan Jones, Micheline M Hancock-Beaulieu, Mike Gatford, et al. 1995. Okapi at trec-3. *Nist Special Publication Sp*, 109:109.

Alireza Roshan-Ghias, Clint Solomon Mathialagan, Pragaash Ponnusamy, Lambert Mathias, and Chenlei Guo. 2020. Personalized query rewriting in conversational ai agents. *arXiv preprint arXiv:2011.04748*.

Yelong Shen, Xiaodong He, Jianfeng Gao, Li Deng, and Gregoire Mesnil. 2014. A convolutional latent semantic model for web search.

Ashish Vaswani, Noam Shazeer, Niki Parmar, Jakob Uszkoreit, Llion Jones, Aidan N Gomez, Łukasz Kaiser, and Illia Polosukhin. 2017. Attention is all you need. In *Advances in neural information processing systems*, pages 5998–6008.

Rashmi Korlakai Vinayak and Ran Gilad-Bachrach. 2015. Dart: Dropouts meet multiple additive regression trees. In *Artificial Intelligence and Statistics*, pages 489–497. PMLR.

A Appendix

Ranker model utilizes $\sim$ 730 dimensions of features. Among them, Table 5 lists the most important features, sorted by their feature weight.

Table 5: List of important ranker features, sorted by importance.

Category	Feature description
Global IR	Number of character changes between query and rewrite candidate
Global IR	Number of NLU slot types in rewrite candidate
Utterance popularity	Number of users who spoke query
Utterance popularity	Number of users who spoke rewrite candidate
Defect	Average defect score for rewrite candidate
Global IR	Character level BLEU score between query and rewrite candidate
Global IR	TF-IDF
User affinity	User count for the rewrite candidate
Phonetic	Edit-distance on phoneme sequence of query and rewrite candidate
User affinity	User count for the NLU slot type and entity combination
Global IR	Entity overlap between query and rewrite candidate
Defect	Global count for rewrite candidate
Defect	How often users barged-in for the rewrite candidate
User affinity	User count for the NLU intent for the rewrite candidate
Defect	How often users rephrased for the rewrite candidate
User IR	TF-IDF based on user document
Global IR	Unigram jaccard distance between query and rewrite candidate
User affinity	Template user count for the rewrite candidate
Phonetic	Character level BLEU score for phonetic sequences of query and rewrite candidate
Global IR	Bi-gram jaccard distance between query and rewrite candidate
Defect	How often the rewrite candidate was not actionable by the agent
Embedding	DNN-based Euclidean distance between query and rewrite candidate
Embedding	DNN-based Manhattan distance between query and rewrite candidate
Defect	How often users rephrased for the query
User affinity	Whether user's frequently used entity is in the query
Global IR	Bi-gram edit-distance between query and rewrite candidate
Defect	Average defect score for query
User affinity	User count for the entity in the rewrite candidate
User affinity	User count for the entity in the query
Global IR	BM25
User IR	Normalized defect score for the user utterance
User IR	BM25 based on user document

Dialogue Response Generation via Contrastive Latent Representation Learning

Shuyang Dai[1] **Guoyin Wang**[1] **Sunghyun Park**[1] **Sungjin Lee**[1]
[1]Amazon Alexa AI, Seattle, WA, USA
{shuyadai, guoyiwan, sunghyu, sungjinl}@amazon.com

Abstract

Large-scale auto-regressive models have achieved great success in dialogue response generation, with the help of Transformer layers. However, these models do not learn a representative latent space of the sentence distribution, making it hard to control the generation. Recent works have tried to learn sentence representations using Transformer-based framework, but do not model the context-response relationship embedded in the dialogue datasets. In this work, we aim to construct a robust sentence representation learning model, that is specifically designed for dialogue response generation, with Transformer-based encoder-decoder structure. An utterance-level contrastive learning is proposed, encoding predictive information in each context representation for its corresponding response. Extensive experiments are conducted to verify the robustness of the proposed representation learning mechanism. By using both reference-based and reference-free evaluation metrics, we provide detailed analysis on the generated sentences, demonstrating the effectiveness of our proposed model.

1 Introduction

Large-scale pretrained language models with Transformer-based architecture (Radford et al., 2019; Raffel et al., 2019; Zhang et al., 2019) have achieved state-of-the-art performance across a variety of natural language processing (NLP) tasks, including open-domain dialogue response generation. The majority of these models are auto-regressive (AR) language models, creating a matching mechanism between the input context and the generated response. However, such an approach often ignores the semantic meaning shared among sentences from an abstract level (Li et al., 2020), generating responses that have matching components with the context, but are not logically sound. Figure 1 demonstrates this potential problem by using some generated samples, where the response generation model generates similar patterns to the context but fail to predict semantically reasonable responses to continue the conversation.

Context (Dialogue History)
A: Hello, Miao Li, where are you going?
B: Hello, I am going to the store to buy some fruit.

Ground Truth Response
A: Oh, would you do me a favor?

Model Generated Examples
A: Oh, I see. Where are you going?
A: Hello! My name is Lin Ping, am I going to buy a beer?
A: Do you have any fruit?

Figure 1: Faulty generated sentences based on given context, via AR-based models. The provided dialogue is based on speakers 'A' and 'B'. Three model generated samples are given. Each pair of matching words/components are marked in the same color. The Ground Truth Response is provided for comparison.

In comparison, variational autoencoders (VAEs) (Kingma and Welling, 2013; Zhao et al., 2017; Gu et al., 2018) are able to explicitly model sentences in a representation space, providing control on the generated responses. While most VAE-based language models adopt shallow network such as LSTMs, it is straightforward to construct such a latent representation learning with a Transformer framework. Recent works (Li et al., 2020) aim to build a pretrained language model that uses a sentence-level VAE objective with a BERT (Devlin et al., 2018) encoder and a GPT-2 (Radford et al., 2019) decoder. Nevertheless, being designed for multiple language understanding and generation tasks, they do not utilize the enriched context-response relationship in the dialogue response generation task. (Maybe change to something like this: Nevertheless, these models are unable to utilize the enriched context-response relationship in the dialogue. This limits the model ability to capture predictive

Proceedings of the Third Workshop on Natural Language Processing for Conversational AI, pages 189–197
November 10, 2021.

relationship between context and response latent representations and hence constrains the response generation quality.)

In this work, we aim to design a dialogue response understanding and generation framework, that combines a higher-level sentence representation learning with a Transformer-based encoder-decoder architecture, yielding controllable response generation from an abstract level, while achieving top-tier generation quality. We adopt the approach that uses a BERT encoder and a GPT-2 decoder as the model backbone, and enrich the underlying information in the learned representation by performing utterance-level contrastive learning. Specifically, the latent representation of the context input (one or multiple utterances) is used to predict that of the response input (a single utterance). Note that our proposed contrastive loss is built based upon utterances, while the entire context input is encoded by a single context encoder.

To benefit the contrastive learning of the latent representation, we propose to use the hard negative sampling mechanism. Such an approach has been used in the computer vision domain (Robinson et al., 2020), guiding a learning method to correct its mistakes more quickly. In our case, we select the negative samples by using a pretrained context-response matching model (Cai et al., 2020). Given a context input, the responses with the top matching scores would be considered as the negative samples, and used for the contrastive objective. In terms of model architecture, we select conditional variational autoencoder (CVAE) (Zhao et al., 2017). This provides an encoder-decoder structure, in which the BERT-GPT backbone can be applied.

2 Preliminary

2.1 Contrastive Predictive Coding

The key idea of contrastive predictive coding (CPC) (Oord et al., 2018) is to learn representations that encode the underlying shared information between different parts of the high-dimensional signal, with the help of next step prediction. Given a sequence of inputs $\{x_1, x_2, \cdots, x_t, \cdots, x_T\}$ (*e.g.*, speech signal input), we obtain the latent representations $h_t = g_{\text{enc}}(x_t)$ for each x_t. A context representation $z_t = g_{\text{AR}}(h_{\leq t})$ summarizes all $\{h_1, h_2, \cdots, h_t\}$ using an auto-regressive model g_{AR}. To predict the future observations x_{t+k}, the following positive real score is considered.

$$f_k(x_{t+k}, z_t) = \exp(h_{t+k}^T W_k z_t), \quad (1)$$

where W_k is linear transformation for step k. To train the predictive model, a negative contrastive estimation (NCE) objective is used.

$$\mathcal{L}_{\text{CPC}} = -\mathbb{E}_X [\log \frac{f_k(x_{t+k}, z_t)}{\sum_{x_j \in X} f_k(x_j, z_t)}], \quad (2)$$

where $X = \{x_1, \cdots, x_N\}$ is a set of N random samples containing the positive sample x_{t+k} and $N - 1$ negative samples from some distribution $p(x_{t+k})$. The negative samples aim to provide guiding on learning predictive information in the latent representations of the context inputs.

2.2 Conditional VAE

The conditional VAE (CVAE) (Zhao et al., 2017) provides a way to utilize the context feature as a conditional input to the VAE framework. Originally, VAE contains an encoder $q_{\boldsymbol{\phi}}(\boldsymbol{z}|\boldsymbol{x})$ and a decoder $p_{\boldsymbol{\theta}}(\boldsymbol{x}|\boldsymbol{z})$, where $\boldsymbol{x}$ is the input data and $\boldsymbol{z}$ is the latent representation. It assumes a Gaussian prior distribution $p(\boldsymbol{z})$, and by using the following objective, it approximates the expected log-likelihood.

$$\begin{aligned}\mathcal{L}_{\text{VAE}}(\boldsymbol{x}; \boldsymbol{\theta}, \boldsymbol{\phi}) = \mathbb{E}_{\boldsymbol{z} \sim q_{\boldsymbol{\phi}}(\boldsymbol{z}|\boldsymbol{x})} [\log p_{\boldsymbol{\theta}}(\boldsymbol{x}|\boldsymbol{z})] \\ - \mathbb{D}_{\text{KL}}(q_{\boldsymbol{\phi}}(\boldsymbol{z}|\boldsymbol{x}) \parallel p(\boldsymbol{z})), \quad (3)\end{aligned}$$

where the conditional likelihood term (first) and the KL term (second) characterize reconstruction and generalization capabilities, respectively. In practice, reparameterization trick is used, in order to achieve Gaussian posterior distribution and compute the KL term in (3). Specifically, the encoder yields mean $\boldsymbol{\mu}$ and standard deviation $\boldsymbol{\sigma}$, and we can sample from such Gaussian distribution:

$$\boldsymbol{z} = \boldsymbol{\mu} + \boldsymbol{\sigma} \odot \boldsymbol{\epsilon}, \quad (4)$$

where $\boldsymbol{\epsilon} \sim \mathcal{N}(\boldsymbol{0}, \boldsymbol{I})$. The CVAE, in comparison, has an additional condition input $\boldsymbol{c}$. In the dialogue response problem setup, the condition $\boldsymbol{c}$ corresponds to the context input, while $\boldsymbol{x}$ is the response input. Both the encoder and the decoder take an extra input $\boldsymbol{c}$, denoted as $q_{\boldsymbol{\phi}}(\boldsymbol{z}|\boldsymbol{x}, \boldsymbol{c})$ and $p_{\boldsymbol{\theta}}(\boldsymbol{x}|\boldsymbol{z}, \boldsymbol{c})$, respectively. For the prior, a prior network $p_{\boldsymbol{\psi}}(\boldsymbol{z}|\boldsymbol{c})$ is required, resulting in the updated objective as follow.

$$\begin{aligned}\mathcal{L}_{\text{CVAE}}(\boldsymbol{x}; \boldsymbol{\theta}, \boldsymbol{\phi}, \boldsymbol{\psi}) = \mathbb{E}_{\boldsymbol{z} \sim q_{\boldsymbol{\phi}}(\boldsymbol{z}|\boldsymbol{x}, \boldsymbol{c})} [\log p_{\boldsymbol{\theta}}(\boldsymbol{x}|\boldsymbol{z}, \boldsymbol{c})] \\ - \mathbb{D}_{\text{KL}}(q_{\boldsymbol{\phi}}(\boldsymbol{z}|\boldsymbol{x}, \boldsymbol{c}) \parallel p_{\boldsymbol{\psi}}(\boldsymbol{z}|\boldsymbol{c})). \quad (5)\end{aligned}$$

During inference, we sample $\boldsymbol{z} \sim p_{\boldsymbol{\psi}}(\boldsymbol{z}|\boldsymbol{c})$ and generate using the decoder $p_{\boldsymbol{\theta}}(\boldsymbol{x}|\boldsymbol{z}, \boldsymbol{c})$, while the

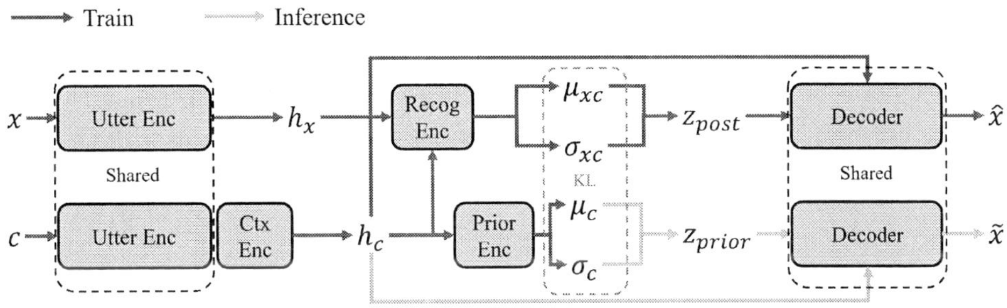

Figure 2: Conditional VAE Framework for Dialogue Response Generation with BERT Encoder and GPT-2 Decoder. The Training Flow is in Blue and the Inference Flow is in Orange.

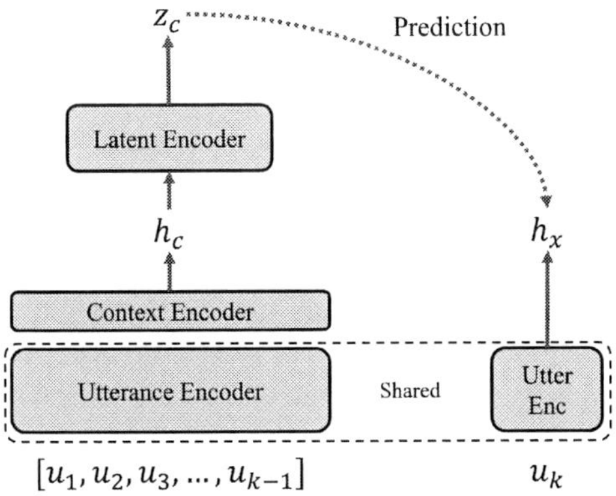

Figure 3: Applying Contrastive Learning on the Representation Framwork for Multi-turn Dialogue Response Generation Task.

response input $\boldsymbol{x}$ is not used. Similar to VAE, the reparameterization trick is used accordingly on both the posterior and prior networks.

3 Method

We include detailed model design in the following section. By introducing the utterance-level contrastive learning, our proposed model learns sentence representations that are capable of predicting future utterances. CVAE is considered as our main model architecture, where we use a BERT encoder and a GPT-2 decoder.

3.1 Representation Learning with a Transformer-Based Framework

We first introduce our model backbone, which is basically a CVAE model with a BERT encoder and a GPT-2 decoder. When encoding, we consider $\boldsymbol{h}_{[\text{CLS}]}$, the output of the special token $[CLS]$ of the last-layer, as the sentence-level representation, and obtain the latent representation by a linear mapping $e(\cdot)$ parameterized as $\boldsymbol{z} = \boldsymbol{W}_E \boldsymbol{h}_{[\text{CLS}]}$. In the CVAE framework, since we have the posterior and prior networks, we denote the former as the utterance encoder $f_u(\cdot)$, and define the latter as a combination of two encoders $f_c(f_u(\cdot))$, both of which are BERT encoders with outputs $\boldsymbol{h}_x$ and $\boldsymbol{h}_c$, respectively. Correspondingly, we have $e_r(\cdot)$ and $e_c(\cdot)$ as recognition encoder and prior encoder (*i.e.*, linear mappings), that take (h_x, h_c) and h_c as input, respectively. The outputs of the two encoder are $\boldsymbol{z}_{\text{post}} \sim q_\phi(\boldsymbol{z}|\boldsymbol{x}, \boldsymbol{c})$ and $\boldsymbol{z}_{\text{prior}} \sim p_\psi(\boldsymbol{z}|\boldsymbol{c})$, respectively.

When decoding, we follow the Memory approach in Optimus (Li et al., 2020). Specifically, we first compute $\boldsymbol{h}_M = \boldsymbol{W}_M \boldsymbol{z}$, where $\boldsymbol{W}_M \in \mathbb{R}^{LH}$ is a weight matrix. The output $\boldsymbol{h}_M \in \mathbb{R}^{LH}$ is separated into L vectors of length H, each of which is attended by one layer of the GPT-2 decoder $g(\cdot)$. Figure 2 shows the CVAE framework for both training and inference. Note that the outputs of the recognition encoder and the prior encoder are $\boldsymbol{\mu}$ and $\boldsymbol{\sigma}$, as the mean and standard deviation of the learnt $q_{\boldsymbol{\theta}}(\boldsymbol{z}|\boldsymbol{x}, \boldsymbol{c})$ and $p_\psi(\boldsymbol{z}|\boldsymbol{c})$, respectively. As discussed in Sec 2.2, such a reparameterization trick is often used in VAE framework, where $\boldsymbol{z} = \boldsymbol{\mu} + \boldsymbol{\sigma} \odot \boldsymbol{\epsilon}$ for some $\boldsymbol{\epsilon} \sim \mathcal{N}(\boldsymbol{0}, \boldsymbol{I})$.

3.2 Utterance Level Contrastive Learning

With latent representation learnt, it is straightforward to adapt the contrastive learning in our model backbone. Different from speech signal data on which the original CPC objective is applied, dialogue datasets contain multi-turn utterances between two speakers for each conversation input. In this case, we consider encoding $\boldsymbol{c} = \{\boldsymbol{u}_1, \boldsymbol{u}_2, \cdots, \boldsymbol{u}_{k-1}\}$ as a concatenation of all utterances in the context history. The output $\boldsymbol{h}_c$ is then sent to the latent encoder $e(\cdot)$, with an output $\boldsymbol{z} = e(\boldsymbol{h}_c)$ that is used to predict the sentence representation $\boldsymbol{h}_x$ of the next time step utterance $\boldsymbol{x} = \boldsymbol{u}_k$.

Figure 3 summarizes the utterance level contrastive learning procedure, with a training objective defined as follow.

$$\mathcal{L}_{\text{CL}} = -\mathbb{E}[\log \frac{\exp(\boldsymbol{h}_x \boldsymbol{W}_k \boldsymbol{z}_c)}{\sum_{\boldsymbol{x}_j \in X} \exp(\boldsymbol{h}_j \boldsymbol{W}_k \boldsymbol{z}_c)}], \quad (6)$$

where $\boldsymbol{W}_k$ is the weight matrix. Note that the proposed contrastive learning procedure can be directly applied to the CVAE model, in which $\boldsymbol{z}_c$ is basically the representation learnt by the prior encoder $e_c(\cdot)$. By combing the CVAE objective and the contrastive loss, we defined the final objective of our proposed model,

$$\mathcal{L} = \mathcal{L}_{\text{CVAE}} - \lambda \mathbb{E}_{\boldsymbol{z} \sim p_\psi(\boldsymbol{z}|\boldsymbol{c})}[\log \frac{\exp(\boldsymbol{h}_x \boldsymbol{W}_k \boldsymbol{z})}{\sum_{\boldsymbol{x}_j \in X} \exp(\boldsymbol{h}_j \boldsymbol{W}_k \boldsymbol{z})}], \quad (7)$$

where λ is the hyper-parameter.

3.3 Improved CL with Hard Negative Sampling

We further improve our contrastive learning (CL) procedure by introducing hard negative sampling. The traditional CL usually uniformly selects negative samples from the data distribution. In the dialogue setup, this would be sampling random response samples $\boldsymbol{x}_j$ for a given context input $\boldsymbol{c}$. However, it is known in the computer vision domain that using negative samples, which look similar to the positive sample, would help correct the mistakes made by the encoder and learn useful information much more quickly (Robinson et al., 2020). For image datasets, one may consider adding noisy pixels, or rotating the positive images to obtain the negative ones. Similar approaches can be done in the natural language domain by using word permutation.

In our case, the multi-turn dialogue data setup allows us to further utilize the context-response relationship, and conduct hard negative sampling by using context-response matching models. Following (Cai et al., 2020), we consider training a Multi-hop Selector Network (MSN) (Yuan et al., 2019) which provides matching scores between the context and response inputs. Specifically, we construct a dialogue dataset, in which each context input $\boldsymbol{c}$ is paired with one positive response sample $\boldsymbol{x}$, and multiple randomly sample distrator response samples $\boldsymbol{x}_j$. The model is trained to predict whether a given context-response pair is positive or negative. When training our proposed CVAE model, the hard negative samples are selected based on higher matching scores, provided by the MSN model.

4 Related Work

Transformer-based representation learning for text generation. Transformer layers have been applied in various language models and achnce engaged in such a framework, it aims to generate novel ieved great results (Devlin et al., 2018; Yang et al., 2019; Keskar et al., 2019). Many are pretrained models and can be fine-tuned to adapt to various downstream tasks (Le and Mikolov, 2014; Dai and Le, 2015; Kiros et al., 2015). Recent works try to learn an interpretable representation space for the sentence encoding, using Transformer-based encoders and decoders. OPTIMUS (Li et al., 2020) provides a pretrained language model with a BERT encoder and a GPT-2 decoder. With variational inferesentences by learning a universal latent space through the pretraining. PLATO (Bao et al., 2019) also adopts BERT framework. It is specifically designed for dialogue generation, while learning a discrete latent variable for action recognition, upon which the generation is based.

Contrastive learning in NLP. Contrastive learning has been widely used with applications on various computer vision (Chopra et al., 2005; Schroff et al., 2015) and NLP problems (Mikolov et al., 2013; Logeswaran and Lee, 2018). It aims to learn a latent representation by contrasting positive and negative pairs in different setups. In the NLP domain, contrastive learning is applied in Word2Vec (Mikolov et al., 2013), a word embedding model, in which neighbouring words are predicted from context. Other than that, it is also used for sentence representation, where the positive and negative pairs are sampled as two contiguous sentences and sentences from other document, respectively (Logeswaran and Lee, 2018). CLAPS (Lee et al., 2020) is proposed recently for conditional text generation, sampling positive and negative sentences by adding perturbations to the input sequence. Being seq2seq model, CLAPS focuses on machine translation and text summarization, while our model tackles dialogue response generation, contrasting each utterance against other matching responses from the dialogue dataset.

5 Experiments

In this section, we present the experiment results of the proposed model, with comparison to sev-

	BLEU			BOW			Intra		Inter	
	R	P	F1	A	E	G	dist1	dist2	dist1	dist2
GPT-2	0.467	0.14	0.215	0.891	0.637	0.58	0.871	0.946	0.499	0.867
PLATO	0.331	0.174	0.228	0.929	0.623	0.747	0.957	0.989	0.412	0.626
iVAE	0.425	**0.248**	0.313	0.923	**0.641**	**0.784**	0.837	0.879	0.413	0.749
CVAE	0.489	0.226	0.309	0.928	0.607	0.626	**0.972**	**0.998**	**0.695**	**0.975**
CVAE + CL	**0.498**	0.239	**0.323**	**0.937**	0.621	0.64	0.936	0.972	0.661	0.948

Table 1: Reference-based Results on DailyDialog. (P: precision, R: recall, A: average, E: extreme, G: greedy). Higher BLEU and BOW Embedding indicate better quality of generated responses. Higher intra/inter-dist means better generation diversity.

	BLEU			BOW			Intra		Inter	
	R	P	F1	A	E	G	dist1	dist2	dist1	dist2
GPT-2	0.372	0.203	0.263	0.924	0.571	0.737	0.823	0.852	0.517	0.894
PLATO	0.382	0.237	0.293	0.934	**0.593**	**0.768**	0.852	0.903	0.431	0.88
GLC	**0.433**	0.243	0.311	0.928	0.543	0.717	0.774	0.879	-	-
CVAE	0.415	0.256	0.317	0.949	0.584	0.757	**0.947**	**0.995**	0.617	0.932
CVAE + CL	0.419	**0.267**	**0.326**	**0.95**	0.583	0.761	0.943	0.993	**0.618**	**0.938**

Table 2: Reference-based Results on PersonaChat.

eral baseline models across different dialogue response datasets. Detailed experimental setups are included, with analysis on both reference-based and reference-free evaluation.

5.1 Implementation Details

We implement our proposed model based on the CVAE model backbone. As discussed in Section 3.1, we apply the contrastive learning procedure (Section 3.2) on the CVAE framework, in which the context latent representation z_c is used to predict the response hidden state h_x, with negative samples selected by the pretrained MSN model. Our model uses BERT encoder (12 transformer layers with hidden size 768 and self-attention heads 12), and GPT-2 decoder (12 transformer layers with hidden size 768 and self-attention heads 12).

5.2 Datasets

We mainly evaluate our model on two benchmark datasets, namely the DailyDialog dataset (Li et al., 2017) and the PersonaChat dataset (Zhang et al., 2018). The former contains 13K daily conversations for a English learner, with an average number of turns in a conversation as 8.5. The latter is a knowledge grounded conversation dataset where two participants chat naturally and try to get to know each other. A total of 11K dialogues are contained in PersonaChat with an average number of turns per conversation as 15. For both datasets, we process each utterance as the response of the previous context utterances from both speakers. Both datasets are separated into train, validation, and test subsets, with a separation ratio of 10:1:1 for DailyDialog, and 9:1:1 for PersonaChat.

5.3 Baseline Models

We select State-Of-The-Art (SOTA) models from different model categories as our baseline models. For auto-regressive model, we consider DialogGPT (Zhang et al., 2019), which is a GPT-2 based model that is specifically designed for dialogue response generation. For dialogue response generation model that uses contrastive learning, we include group-wise contrastive learning (GCL) (Cai et al., 2020), which conduct CL between target dialogue model and a pretrained reference model. PLATO (Bao et al., 2019) is another model that uses transformer-based model architecture while including a discrete latent variable to tackle the one-to-many mapping problem. Last but not the least, we compare our model to the SOTA VAE model on text generation, the implicit VAE (iVAE) (Fang et al., 2019), in which the original Gaussian assumption is replaced by an implicit distribution, learnt in an adversarial fashion.

5.4 Evaluation Metrics

In our work, we consider the traditional reference-based, as well as several newly proposed reference-

	DialogRPT				RoBERTa Eval
	updown	depth	width	score	
Grount Truth	0.403	0.537	0.591	0.319	2.812
GPT-2	0.311	0.414	0.437	0.243	**2.739**
PLATO	0.314	0.453	0.468	0.255	2.132
CVAE	0.392	0.496	0.547	0.301	1.931
CVAE + CL	**0.407**	**0.519**	**0.563**	**0.313**	2.106

Table 3: Reference-free Results on Dailydialog (H vs R: Human vs Random; H vs M: Human vs Machine). Higher scores indicate better generation quality in the corresponding categories.

	DialogRPT				RoBERTa Eval
	updown	depth	width	score	
GPT-2	0.339	0.523	0.625	0.301	1.383
PLATO	0.358	0.574	0.641	0.318	1.582
GLC	0.361	0.577	0.639	0.319	1.607
CVAE	0.367	0.577	0.647	0.322	1.678
CVAE + CL	**0.372**	**0.583**	**0.669**	**0.329**	**1.702**

Table 4: Reference-free Results on PersonaChat.

free evaluation metrics. The former basically measures the relevance between the reference response data (ground truth) and the generated response samples. In comparison, the reference-free evaluators do not need the reference responses, while computing the score based on a trained evaluation model.

We mainly consider three reference-based evaluation metrics: 1) BLEU score measures how many n-gram ($n = 4$ in our experiments) from generated response overlaps with the references. We sample 10 responses; BLEU-precision and BLEU-recall are defined as average and maximum scores. 2) Cosine similarity of bag-of-words (BOW) embedding between the generated response and the reference is considered (*e.g.*, 3 types of embedding including greedy, average, and extreme). 3) Distinct evaluates the diversity of the generation; dist-n is the ratio of unique n-grams ($n = 1, 2$) over all n-grams in the generated responses. We evaluate both within each sampled response and among all responses as intra-dist and inter-dist, respectively.

For reference-free evaluators, we consider the following two metrics. The first one is DialogRPT (Gao et al., 2020), which provides ranking scores of responses based on human evaluation on $i)$ Width: the number of dialogues after the current turn $(\boldsymbol{c}, \boldsymbol{x})$; $ii)$ Depth: the maximum length of the dialogue after the current turn; and $iii)$ Updown: the number of up votes minus the number of down votes (by human raters). Another one is the RoBERTa Evaluator (Zhao et al., 2020), which is first trained on next-sentence-prediction task in an unsupervised manner, and then trained on prediciting human annotated data in a semi-supervised setup. The model is trained using the RoBERTa encoder (Liu et al., 2019), on the concatenation of the input context $\boldsymbol{c}$ and the generated response $\tilde{\boldsymbol{x}}$, with output rescaled to the human rating scale.

5.5 Results

Table 1 and 2 show the reference-based results on DailyDialog and PersonaChat datasets, respectively. In terms of BLEU score, our proposed CVAE/CVAE+CL achieves better performance than the other Transformer-based models. By adding the proposed utterance level contrastive learning (CL) to CVAE, the BLEU score is improved from 0.309 to 0.318, outperforming GPT-2 and PLATO, while being comparable to iVAE. Meanwhile, CVAE-based models provide much higher generation diversity in both inter and intra-dist. Note that adding contrastive learning does slightly drop the generation diversity of CVAE, which is likely due to the additional predictive information learnt in the representation of context inputs. Overall, our proposed model CVAE+CL achieves top-tier performance in the majority of the evaluation categories, across both datasets.

Table 3 and 4 present the reference-free results on DailyDialog and PersonaChat, respectively. For

Models	Recall	Precision	F1
Proposed Model	0.498	0.239	0.323
- HNS	0.49	0.235	0.317
- CL	0.489	0.226	0.309
- TF	0.265	0.222	0.242

Table 5: Ablation Study on DailyDialog via Reference-based Evaluation Metrics.

Objective	λ	Recall	Precision	F1
$\mathcal{L}_{\text{CVAE}} + \lambda\mathcal{L}_{\text{CL}}$	0.0	0.489	0.226	0.309
	0.1	0.489	0.232	0.315
	0.2	0.493	0.232	0.316
	0.5	0.498	0.239	0.323
	1.0	0.496	0.24	0.323
	2.0	0.492	0.235	0.318

Table 6: Sensitiveness of Contrastive Learning Objective against Hyper-parameter λ. Results on DailyDialog via Reference-based Evaluation Metrics.

DailyDialog, CVAE provides better overall DialogRPT scores than the other baseline models. However, since responses are generated based on the context latent representations (instead of direct sentence inputs), CVAE does not provide matching words across context and response, reducing the RoBERTa score for the DailyDialog dataset. For PersonaChat, CVAE outperforms the other baseline models in both evaluation metrics. Overall, we see the effectiveness of adding CL to the CVAE framework, improving both DialogRPT and RoBERTa scores across the two datasets.

Ablation study is conducted based on each components in the proposed CVAE. Table 5 shows the BLEU score (*i.e.*, recall, precision, and F1) of our model on the DailyDialog dataset, in which we gradually remove one component at a time to demonstrate the effectiveness from each of them. We first remove hard negative sampling (HNS) and use random negative samples (from the same training mini batch) instead. The contrastive learning (CL) objective is then removed, where we notice a drop of 0.014 (from 0.323 to 0.309) in F1. Finally, the model performance drops drastically when we replace the transformer layers (TF) in the CVAE with LSTM (*i.e.*, original CVAE framework); F1 decreeases from 0.309 to 0.242.

We further show the sensitiveness of our proposed utterance-based contrastive loss against different values of hyper-parameter λ. By tuning λ from 0.0 to 2.0, we report the BLEU scores of each training objectives. As shown in Table 6, the model with $\lambda = 0.5$ and $\lambda = 1.0$ achieves the best overall performance, while the models with the other values of λ also provide competitive results. This demonstrates that our model is relatively insensitive to the hyper-parameter for contrastive learning objective. Meanwhile, we can see that adding the contrastive loss is improving the performance (regardless of different values of λ) when comparing the baseline CVAE (*i.e.*, $\lambda = 0.0$).

Context: - Say, Jim, how about going for a few beers after dinner?
Response: You know that is tempting but is really not good for our fitness.
All right. I'll cook for you.
I do like Thai food. Did you see much of Bangkok?
I'm so thirsty.

Context: - Are you all right? - I will be all right soon. I was terrified when I watched them fall from the wire.
Response: Don't worry. He is an acrobat.
That's all right.
And do you feel anything when I do this?
And do you have any questions?

Context: - Can you do push-ups? - Of course I can. It's a piece of cake! Believe it or not, I can do 30 push-ups a minute. - Really? I think that's impossible! - You mean 30 push-ups? - Yeah!
Response: It's easy. If you do exercise everyday, you can make it, too.
Believe me, he is the first-class.
Yeah. I'm going with Jennie.
Don't worry, Shan always screws up free throws.

Figure 4: Examples of Hard Negative Sampling. Blue Ones are Ground Truth Reference, and Red Ones are Negative Samples Selected by MSN.

Figure 4 provides examples of hard negative sentences selected by MSN. Each example case includes context sentence(s), a ground truth response sentence (reference), as well as 3 selected hard negative samples. As can be seen, the negative sentences share relevant words and contents with the input context, which provides a more efficient training for our model.

6 Conclusion

In this work, we propose a dialogue response generation model that combines the controllability of representation learning models and SOTA performance of AR-based frameworks. An efficient utterance level contrastive learning is introduced to enrich the information learned in the latent representations (*i.e.*, predictive information of utterance in the next time step). Our proposed model achieves competitive performance comparing to the SOTA models in different benchmark datasets.

References

Siqi Bao, Huang He, Fan Wang, Hua Wu, and Haifeng Wang. 2019. Plato: Pre-trained dialogue generation model with discrete latent variable. *arXiv preprint arXiv:1910.07931*.

Hengyi Cai, Hongshen Chen, Yonghao Song, Zhuoye Ding, Yongjun Bao, Weipeng Yan, and Xiaofang Zhao. 2020. Group-wise contrastive learning for neural dialogue generation. *arXiv preprint arXiv:2009.07543*.

Sumit Chopra, Raia Hadsell, and Yann LeCun. 2005. Learning a similarity metric discriminatively, with application to face verification. In *2005 IEEE Computer Society Conference on Computer Vision and Pattern Recognition (CVPR'05)*, volume 1, pages 539–546. IEEE.

Andrew M Dai and Quoc V Le. 2015. Semi-supervised sequence learning. *Advances in neural information processing systems*, 28:3079–3087.

Jacob Devlin, Ming-Wei Chang, Kenton Lee, and Kristina Toutanova. 2018. Bert: Pre-training of deep bidirectional transformers for language understanding. *arXiv preprint arXiv:1810.04805*.

Le Fang, Chunyuan Li, Jianfeng Gao, Wen Dong, and Changyou Chen. 2019. Implicit deep latent variable models for text generation. *arXiv preprint arXiv:1908.11527*.

Xiang Gao, Yizhe Zhang, Michel Galley, Chris Brockett, and Bill Dolan. 2020. Dialogue response ranking training with large-scale human feedback data. *arXiv preprint arXiv:2009.06978*.

Xiaodong Gu, Kyunghyun Cho, Jung-Woo Ha, and Sunghun Kim. 2018. Dialogwae: Multimodal response generation with conditional wasserstein autoencoder. *arXiv preprint arXiv:1805.12352*.

Nitish Shirish Keskar, Bryan McCann, Lav R Varshney, Caiming Xiong, and Richard Socher. 2019. Ctrl: A conditional transformer language model for controllable generation. *arXiv preprint arXiv:1909.05858*.

Diederik P Kingma and Max Welling. 2013. Auto-encoding variational bayes. *arXiv preprint arXiv:1312.6114*.

Ryan Kiros, Yukun Zhu, Russ R Salakhutdinov, Richard Zemel, Raquel Urtasun, Antonio Torralba, and Sanja Fidler. 2015. Skip-thought vectors. In *Advances in neural information processing systems*, pages 3294–3302.

Quoc Le and Tomas Mikolov. 2014. Distributed representations of sentences and documents. In *International conference on machine learning*, pages 1188–1196. PMLR.

Seanie Lee, Dong Bok Lee, and Sung Ju Hwang. 2020. Contrastive learning with adversarial perturbations for conditional text generation. *arXiv preprint arXiv:2012.07280*.

Chunyuan Li, Xiang Gao, Yuan Li, Baolin Peng, Xiujun Li, Yizhe Zhang, and Jianfeng Gao. 2020. Optimus: Organizing sentences via pre-trained modeling of a latent space. *arXiv preprint arXiv:2004.04092*.

Yanran Li, Hui Su, Xiaoyu Shen, Wenjie Li, Ziqiang Cao, and Shuzi Niu. 2017. Dailydialog: A manually labelled multi-turn dialogue dataset. *arXiv preprint arXiv:1710.03957*.

Yinhan Liu, Myle Ott, Naman Goyal, Jingfei Du, Mandar Joshi, Danqi Chen, Omer Levy, Mike Lewis, Luke Zettlemoyer, and Veselin Stoyanov. 2019. Roberta: A robustly optimized bert pretraining approach. *arXiv preprint arXiv:1907.11692*.

Lajanugen Logeswaran and Honglak Lee. 2018. An efficient framework for learning sentence representations. *arXiv preprint arXiv:1803.02893*.

Tomas Mikolov, Ilya Sutskever, Kai Chen, Greg S Corrado, and Jeff Dean. 2013. Distributed representations of words and phrases and their compositionality. In *Advances in neural information processing systems*, pages 3111–3119.

Aaron van den Oord, Yazhe Li, and Oriol Vinyals. 2018. Representation learning with contrastive predictive coding. *arXiv preprint arXiv:1807.03748*.

Alec Radford, Jeffrey Wu, Rewon Child, David Luan, Dario Amodei, and Ilya Sutskever. 2019. Language models are unsupervised multitask learners. *OpenAI blog*, 1(8):9.

Colin Raffel, Noam Shazeer, Adam Roberts, Katherine Lee, Sharan Narang, Michael Matena, Yanqi Zhou, Wei Li, and Peter J Liu. 2019. Exploring the limits of transfer learning with a unified text-to-text transformer. *arXiv preprint arXiv:1910.10683*.

Joshua Robinson, Ching-Yao Chuang, Suvrit Sra, and Stefanie Jegelka. 2020. Contrastive learning with hard negative samples. *arXiv preprint arXiv:2010.04592*.

Florian Schroff, Dmitry Kalenichenko, and James Philbin. 2015. Facenet: A unified embedding for face recognition and clustering. In *Proceedings of the IEEE conference on computer vision and pattern recognition*, pages 815–823.

Zhilin Yang, Zihang Dai, Yiming Yang, Jaime Carbonell, Russ R Salakhutdinov, and Quoc V Le. 2019. Xlnet: Generalized autoregressive pretraining for language understanding. *Advances in neural information processing systems*, 32.

Chunyuan Yuan, Wei Zhou, Mingming Li, Shangwen Lv, Fuqing Zhu, Jizhong Han, and Songlin Hu. 2019. Multi-hop selector network for multi-turn response selection in retrieval-based chatbots. In *Proceedings of the 2019 Conference on Empirical Methods in Natural Language Processing and the 9th International Joint Conference on Natural Language Processing (EMNLP-IJCNLP)*, pages 111–120.

Saizheng Zhang, Emily Dinan, Jack Urbanek, Arthur Szlam, Douwe Kiela, and Jason Weston. 2018. Personalizing dialogue agents: I have a dog, do you have pets too? *arXiv preprint arXiv:1801.07243*.

Yizhe Zhang, Siqi Sun, Michel Galley, Yen-Chun Chen, Chris Brockett, Xiang Gao, Jianfeng Gao, Jingjing Liu, and Bill Dolan. 2019. Dialogpt: Large-scale generative pre-training for conversational response generation. *arXiv preprint arXiv:1911.00536*.

Tiancheng Zhao, Ran Zhao, and Maxine Eskenazi. 2017. Learning discourse-level diversity for neural dialog models using conditional variational autoencoders. *arXiv preprint arXiv:1703.10960*.

Tianyu Zhao, Divesh Lala, and Tatsuya Kawahara. 2020. Designing precise and robust dialogue response evaluators. *arXiv preprint arXiv:2004.04908*.

AuGPT: Auxiliary Tasks and Data Augmentation for End-To-End Dialogue with Pre-Trained Language Models

Jonáš Kulhánek,[1,2,3] **Vojtěch Hudeček,**[1] **Tomáš Nekvinda**[1] and **Ondřej Dušek**[1]
[1]Charles University, Faculty of Mathematics and Physics, Prague, Czechia
[2]Czech Technical University in Prague, Czech Institute of Informatics, Robotics and Cybernetics
[3]Czech Technical University in Prague, Faculty of Electrical Engineering
jonas.kulhanek@cvut.cz, {hudecek,nekvinda,odusek}@ufal.mff.cuni.cz

Abstract

Attention-based pre-trained language models such as GPT-2 brought considerable progress to end-to-end dialogue modelling. However, they also present considerable risks for task-oriented dialogue, such as lack of knowledge grounding or diversity. To address these issues, we introduce modified training objectives for language model finetuning, and we employ massive data augmentation via back-translation to increase the diversity of the training data. We further examine the possibilities of combining data from multiples sources to improve performance on the target dataset. We carefully evaluate our contributions with both human and automatic methods. Our model substantially outperforms the baseline on the MultiWOZ data and shows competitive performance with state of the art in both automatic and human evaluation.

1 Introduction

Unlike traditional task-oriented systems based on modularized pipelines (Young et al., 2013; Gao et al., 2019), end-to-end dialogue systems integrate nearly all functionality required to hold a dialogue into a single neural network (Wen et al., 2017; Eric et al., 2017; Lei et al., 2018), reducing error-propagation and data annotation requirements. While these systems are not yet ready for production use, they made considerable progress in recent years, especially with the advent of pre-trained neural language models (LMs) (Devlin et al., 2019; Radford et al., 2019; Zhang et al., 2020c). Systems such as GPT-2 finetuned by Budzianowski and Vulić (2019) show that with an LM pre-trained on a large number of general-domain dialogues without annotation, only small amounts of data are required to perform well in a given task-oriented domain.

On the other hand, the pre-trained LMs run enormous risks. First, solely training for response generation may result in a lack of grounding for the responses, where the LM hallucinates words without any relation to the database. This has been addressed by multi-task training and auxiliary training objectives (Peng et al., 2021) to an extent. Second, finetuning on small datasets may reduce response diversity and fluency due to neural networks' known propensity for catastrophic forgetting (Greco et al., 2019) – the model overfits the finetuning dataset too tightly, "forgetting" the pre-trained language modeling capabilities.

This paper presents an end-to-end model for multi-domain task-oriented response generation on the MultiWOZ data (Budzianowski et al., 2018),[1] where we address the above problems with pre-trained LMs. AuGPT is based on the GPT-2 LM and Peng et al. (2021)'s basic approach. Our contributions can be summarized as follows:

- We introduce a new dialogue consistency classification task based on subtle changes to the dialogue state (instead of fully random resampling) used as an auxiliary training objective, and we demonstrate its performance improvements.
- We present a novel application of token unlikelihood loss (Welleck et al., 2020) in task-oriented dialogue to further improve diversity of our model's responses.
- We apply pre-training on additional datasets and massive data augmentation using back-translation via multiple languages (Sennrich et al., 2016) and demonstrate that both markedly improve task-oriented dialogue performance.
- We compare our model to multiple baselines on MultiWOZ in a corpus-based and simulated evaluation. We also include human evaluation results from a shared task competition, as well as detailed manual error analysis.

We publish our augmented training data, source code, and pre-trained models on GitHub.[2]

[1]https://convlab.github.io
[2]https://github.com/ufal/augpt

Proceedings of the Third Workshop on Natural Language Processing for Conversational AI, pages 198–210
November 10, 2021.

2 Related Work

While the first attempts to build generative end-to-end task-oriented systems mimicked the traditional dialogue system components (Wen et al., 2017), the task was soon recast as a sequence prediction problem in a two-stage setup. A sequence-to-sequence (seq2seq) model first generates the belief state based on dialogue context, then generates the system response based on the context and the belief state (Sequicity; Lei et al., 2018).

Recently, large-scale multi-domain task-oriented datasets were proposed (Budzianowski et al., 2018; Byrne et al., 2019; Rastogi et al., 2020). To address multiple domains, Zhang et al. (2020a) introduce the LABES-S2S model that – in addition to a two-stage seq2seq approach – models belief states as discrete latent variables. Zhang et al. (2020b) present DAMD, a three-stage seq2seq architecture which explicitly decodes the system action. They optimize for multiple good actions given a single belief state. Qin et al. (2020) investigate sharing of domain knowledge and performance on unseen domains. Lubis et al. (2020)'s LAVA model employs reinforcement learning over latent system actions initialized using a variational autoencoder.

The line of research closest to our work makes use of large pre-trained LMs based on the transformer architecture (Vaswani et al., 2017) such as GPT-2 (Radford et al., 2019) or BERT (Devlin et al., 2019). For example, Wu et al. (2020) propose finetuning BERT (Devlin et al., 2019) for task-oriented dialogue, Zhang et al. (2020c) extended the GPT-2 LM to model open-domain chit-chat.

We follow research initiated by Budzianowski and Vulić (2019), who use GPT-2 to model multi-domain task-oriented dialogues. Recently, three similar modifications to their model were proposed, namely SOLOIST (Peng et al., 2021), SimpleTOD (Hosseini-Asl et al., 2020), and the approach by Ham et al. (2020). Our work extends these models and proposes a novel training approach and data augmentation strategies based on back-translation (Edunov et al., 2018; Federmann et al., 2019). Earlier works used a single pivot language (Jin et al., 2018; Einolghozati et al., 2019), whereas our work applies 10 languages to increase variability.

3 Method

The task-oriented setting requires the dialogue system to respond adequately to the user's input and fulfill its goal, e.g., booking a train or requesting restaurant details. The system must process the user's input, keep track of the belief state (user preferences regarding individual slots, i.e., in-domain attributes) and generate a relevant response in natural language. It must also interact with a database to incorporate external information into its responses (see Figure 1 for an example). Following Budzianowski and Vulić (2019), we choose the GPT-2 LM as our backbone and use the LM to model both the belief state and the response.

3.1 Model Representation

The training instances for an LM-based task-oriented dialogue system can be considered as tuples (c, b, d, r), where c is the context (i.e., a concatenation of all previous utterances in the dialogue – both system's and user's), b is the system's belief state (used to query the database), d are the database results, and r is the system's response.

In our case, the dialogue system handles multiple domains and the belief state is a set of pairs (*domain name*, *domain belief*), where the *domain belief* is an assignment of values into slots, i.e., a set of pairs (*slot name*, *value*) (see Example 1). Similarly, the database results d are a set of pairs (*domain name*, *domain database results*), where the *domain database results* are an ordered list of entities returned by the database. We further define the *database result counts* d_c denoting the number of results in d for each domain.

Ideally, we would like our system to model the probability distribution over possible responses conditioned on the context $p(r|c)$. To simplify computation and model external database queries, we factorize this distribution as follows:

$$\begin{aligned} p(r|c) &= \sum_d p(r|d,c)p(d|c) \\ &= \sum_d \sum_b p(r|d,b,c)p(d|b)p(b|c) \\ &= \sum_b p(r|Query(b),b,c)p(b|c), \end{aligned} \quad (1)$$

where $p(d|b)$ is a deterministic distribution over the database results, and *Query* is a function returning database results.

Using this factorization allows the model to process the context, query the database and generate a response based on database results. However, generating responses directly would result in data sparsity issues with rare tokens (e.g., venue names or reference numbers). To maximally reuse the training samples, we choose to train our model

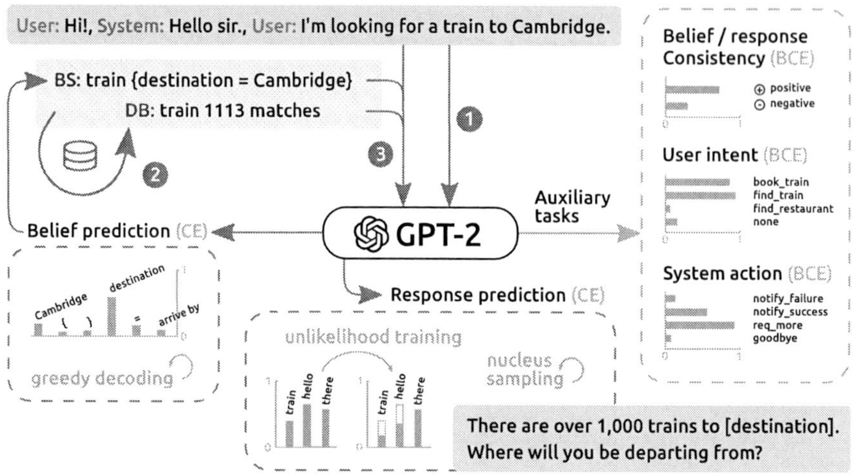

Figure 1: The architecture of AuGPT. The pipeline runs in two stages. First, a finetuned GPT-2 LM is used to predict a belief. Then the database results are obtained and everything is passed to the GPT-2 again to predict a final delexicalized response, along with possible auxiliary tasks (belief consistency, intent classification, system action classification). Unlikelihood loss is used for response prediction training.

on *delexicalized responses* denoted $\bar{r}$, where slot values are replaced with placeholders (Wen et al., 2015). During inference, the responses are lexicalized back deterministically using the belief state and the database results. We assume perfect lexicalization, i.e., always being able to lexicalize the response $\bar{r}$ back based on d and b.[3]

Both the database lookup and the lexicalization are deterministic, and the delexicalized response $\bar{r}$ does not depend on the database results d, but only on their counts d_c. Therefore, the distribution $p(r|d,b,c)$ is equal to the distribution $p(\bar{r}|d_c,b,c)$, and by maximizing its likelihood we are achieving the goal of maximizing the likelihood of $p(r|c)$.

We use the same language model $\hat{p}$ to model the belief state and to generate the delexicalized prediction. That is,

$$p(\bar{r}|d_c,b,c) \approx \hat{p}(\bar{r}|d_c,b,c,\theta) \quad (2)$$
$$p(b|c) \approx \hat{p}(b|\emptyset,\emptyset,c,\theta), \quad (3)$$

where we denote the model's parameters as θ.

In the MultiWOZ dataset (Budzianowski et al., 2018; Eric et al., 2020, see Section 4), responses are delexicalized by replacing concrete values with placeholder tokens of the form *domain_slot*. For better generalization across domains, we chose to only use *slot* instead as responses rarely involve more than one domain. We train our model to predict the *active domain* by outputting it first in the belief state (remaining domains follow in lexicographical order). The predicted active domain is then used during lexicalization.[4]

```
Belief state: train { leave at=15:30,
  arrive by=17:15 },
  hotel { price range = cheap }
DB: train 23 matches, hotel no match
```

Example 1: String format for AuGPT's belief state and database result count.

To fully exploit natural language pre-training of our LM, we represent the belief state and database result counts as strings containing as few special tokens as possible (see Example 1).

3.2 Model Training

Although parameters are shared for the belief state predictor and the delexicalized response predictor, the training objectives differ slightly. We use cross-entropy loss for both; response prediction uses unlikelihood loss (Welleck et al., 2020; Li et al., 2020) as an additional objective. Unlikelihood loss penalizes repeated tokens, which helps the model avoid repetitions and increases output diversity.

To help the model learn a better internal representation from the data, we employ additional auxiliary tasks. Similarly to Devlin et al. (2019)

[3]We found in our experiments on the MultiWOZ data (see Section 4) that this assumption was almost always fulfilled.

[4]A disadvantage of this approach is that we cannot determine the active domain if the belief state is empty. However, in such a case the lexicalization would fail anyway, so the system's performance is not affected by this decision.

and Peng et al. (2021), we train a binary classifier to detect dialogue inconsistencies. In each training batch, we corrupt half of the samples by randomly applying one or more of the following changes with the same probability:

1. We replace the belief state b with another belief state, sampled uniformly randomly from the training data.
2. We replace the delexicalized response $\bar{r}$ with a different randomly chosen one. If this change is applied in combination with the first one, the delexicalized response and the belief state are taken from the same random sample.
3. A different valid value is uniformly sampled for each slot in the belief state. In this case, the domain names and domain order are unchanged (i.e., the active domain is the same).

The first two changes are identical to Peng et al. (2021). The third one is a new one which we find very useful – it is much more challenging to detect if the belief state was changed when the domain stays the same. Consistency detection employs an affine binary classifier on top of last response token logits, trained using binary cross-entropy (BCE).

We also experiment with additional two classifiers predicting the user intent and the system action. These are implemented as two fully-connected layers attached to the last context token and the last database result token logits, respectively. However, based on our experimental results (see Table 4), we decided not to use these tasks in the final model.

We train the whole pipeline by optimizing the non-weighted sum of individual component losses, i.e., cross-entropy for belief state and response prediction, unlikelihood loss for the response, and BCE for consistency detection.

3.3 Response Generation

For each user input, the system goes through several stages (see Figure 1): (1) Previous dialogue context is passed to the LM, which greedily generates the string representation of the belief state. (2) The belief state is parsed and passed to the database handler. (3) The database handler returns a set of results for each domain. (4) A string representation of database result counts is created (see Example 1). (5) The context, belief state and database results are concatenated and passed again to the LM. We use nucleus sampling (Holtzman et al., 2020) to generate the delexicalized response.[5] (6) Placeholders in the delexicalized response are replaced by values from the database results and the belief state.

3.4 Data Augmentation

Following its successful usage in other NLP tasks, (Konstas et al., 2017; Elder et al., 2020), we experiment with data augmentation using paraphrases. In our setup, we generate multiple paraphrases for each training utterance and use them to augment the training data. This way, we effectively increase the variability of the data.

Various data-driven approaches for paraphrasing were proposed, the majority of them corpora-based (Madnani and Dorr, 2010). Recently, machine translation systems showed strong performance in generating paraphrases using back-translation (Sennrich et al., 2016; Edunov et al., 2018; Federmann et al., 2019), i.e., translating an English text into an intermediate language and then translating the result back into English. We use two different Transformer-based machine translation systems to paraphrase our data. We used Edunov et al. (2018)'s system with French and the system of Macháček et al. (2020); Zouhar et al. (2021) with additional 40 pivot languages. Based on empirical analysis of translation quality, we chose 10 pivot languages for our data – we obtain 10 different paraphrases for each input utterance.[6] When training, we choose the input user utterance uniformly at random from the set of all 10+1 variants of the utterance (backtranslation outputs and the original one).

4 Experiments

4.1 Datasets

As our primary dataset, we use MultiWOZ 2.1, a de-noised version of MultiWOZ 2.0 (Budzianowski et al., 2018). We also used the 2.0 version to compare to previous works. The dataset contains 7 distinct domains (all related to tourist information, e.g., hotels, restaurants) and 10,438 dialogues, 7,032 of which are multi-domain.

We experiment with pre-training our model on additional datasets. For the pre-training phase, we use Taskmaster-1 (Byrne et al., 2019) and Schema-

[5]We found nucleus sampling useful for generating the response since it increases diversity, but we prefer greedy decoding for the belief state with a fixed structure.

[6]Pivot languages used: Albanian, Arabic, Bulgarian, Bosnian, French, German, Russian, Spanish, Slovak, Swedish.

method	MultiWOZ 2.0 inform	success	BLEU	MultiWOZ 2.1 inform	success	BLEU
Human	91.0	82.7	–	86.3	79.1	–
AuGPT	83.1	70.1	17.2	83.5	67.3	17.2
SOLOIST (Peng et al., 2021)	85.5	72.9	16.5	–	–	–
SimpleTOD (Hosseini-Asl et al., 2020)	84.4	70.1	15.1	85.0	70.5	15.2
LABES-S2S (Zhang et al., 2020a)	–	–	–	78.1	67.1	18.3
DAMD (Zhang et al., 2020b)	76.3	60.4	16.6	–	–	–
MD-Sequicity (Zhang et al., 2020b)	86.6	71.6	16.8	–	–	–
LAVA (Lubis et al., 2020)	91.8	81.8	12.0	–	–	–

Table 1: Comparison with previous works on the MultiWOZ dataset (see Section 4.4 for a description of the metrics). *MD-Sequicity* is a variant of Lei et al. (2018)'s model, extended for a multi-domain setting.

method	complete	success	book	inform P	inform R	inform F1	turn succ	turn all
AuGPT	89.4	60.1	85.7	64.5	82.1	70.3	12.7	14.6
DAMD (Zhang et al., 2020b)	39.5	34.3	51.4	60.4	59.8	56.3	15.8	29.8
Sequicity (Lei et al., 2018)	23.1	9.8	4.1	33.0	32.7	29.9	12.2	32.6

Table 2: ConvLab evaluation comparison with other works (see Section 4.5 for a description of the metrics).

Guided Dialogue (Rastogi et al., 2020).[7] Both Taskmaster-1 and Schema-Guided Dialogue are multi-domain, task-oriented, large dialogue corpora consisting of 12,215 and 22,825 dialogues, respectively. Taskmaster-1 was obtained using the Wizard-of-Oz and self-dialogue methods, while the collection of Schema-Guided Dialogue is somewhat artificial – humans are only employed to paraphrase machine-generated utterances.

4.2 Data Preprocessing

Although the MultiWOZ 2.1 dataset was collected by humans, it contains a lot of inconsistencies. We hypothesize that when using only *clean* samples which are consistent with the database, the benefit of using higher quality training data outweighs the decrease in the number of training samples. This claim is further supported by experiments (see Section 6). To filter the training data, we choose only those dialogues where the annotated dialogue goal corresponds with the turn-level annotated data. When using the *clean* samples, we omit about 30% of the training data.

To effectively combine all our datasets, we unified the data ontologies. Since the datasets use different naming conventions (e.g., `leaveAt` vs. `leave_at`) and different domain and slot names to describe the same concepts (e.g., `restaurant-food` vs. `restaurant-type`), we manually designed a mapping between domain and slot names. Notably, we decided to rename some slots so they use natural language tokens, as we base our model on the GPT-2 LM which is pre-trained on natural language texts (e.g. "`leaveAt`" → "`leave at`"). Our final ontology that unifies all three datasets contains 22 domains and 135 slots.

We use our own implementation of delexicalization, which directly produces our belief state string representation (see Section 3.1 and Example 1).

4.3 Training Details

We implement our model in PyTorch (Paszke et al., 2019), based on GPT-2-*small*. It uses 12 layers with a size of 768. For all auxiliary tasks, we use a dropout of 0.1 with label smoothing 0.1. We use the AdamW optimizer (Loshchilov and Hutter, 2019). The finetuning runs for 8 epochs on the MultiWOZ 2.1 data when all the training examples are used, and for the same number of minibatches when using only *clean* samples. The training takes less than one day when using 4 GPUs.

4.4 Corpus-based Evaluation

To compare with previous results on MultiWOZ, we evaluate the model performance with a set of corpus-based intrinsic metrics on both versions of the data. For MultiWOZ 2.0, we use the original delexicalization used by compared baselines (Peng et al., 2021; Hosseini-Asl et al., 2020; Zhang et al., 2020b). For MultiWOZ 2.1, we use our own delexicalization. We employ the original evalua-

[7]There are also other large-sized task-oriented datasets such as MetalWOZ (Lee et al., 2019), however, their annotation is not detailed enough for our setup.

Method	Average Success	Success w/ DB	Success w/o DB	NLU score	Response appropriateness	Turns
Baseline	69.6	56.8	82.4	4.34	4.18	18.5
Winner	**74.8**	**70.2**	79.4	**4.54**	**4.47**	18.5
Our submission	72.3	62.0	**82.6**	4.53	4.41	**17.1**

Table 3: Human evaluation results obtained during the DSTC9 shared task using Amazon Mechanical Turk. Note that only 4 out of 10 submissions outperformed the Baseline according to the average success metric.

tion scheme by Budzianowski et al. (2018), which provides two metrics – the *inform rate* and the *success rate*. The *inform rate* is the percentage of dialogues in which the system mentioned a name or ID of an entity which does not contradict the current dialogue state and the user's goal, whereas the *success rate* is the percentage of dialogues in which the system outputted all the requested information. Moreover, we compute BLEU (Papineni et al., 2002) between the generated system utterances and the ground truth to get an approximation of the output fluency.

4.5 ConvLab 2 Evaluation

We use the ConvLab 2 platform (Zhu et al., 2020) for automatic evaluation with a simulated user agent. We run the evaluation component 1,000 times, i.e. on 1,000 simulated conversations. The agent mimics user behavior, interacts with the system under evaluation, and computes multiple metrics: The *complete rate* reflects the ratio of dialogues that are completed, i.e. all the user requests have been met. The *success rate* computes the percentage of dialogues which are successful, meaning the system captures correct informed entities and provides a valid booking if requested. Finally, the *book rate* is the proportion of dialogues where the system was able to book the correct entity (hotel, restaurant, train) if it was asked to. We also compute *precision, recall* and *F1 score* for the informed entities and the average number of turns in the dialogue.

4.6 Human Evaluation and Error Analysis

Thanks to our participation in the DSTC9 task-oriented dialogue shared task (Gunasekara et al., 2020; Li et al., 2021), a variant of our model (without pre-training on additional dialogue datasets, see Table 4) was selected for evaluation by human judges on the Amazon Mechanical Turk platform.[8] The judges communicated with the agent in natural language and rated the system afterward with respect to the success/failure of the dialogue, language understanding score, and response appropriateness. Information provided by the system was additionally checked for consistency with the database, and the average of success rates given by the judges and by database grounding is used as the main metric.

In addition to the crowdsourced evaluation, we perform a detailed in-house error analysis based on human interactions with our final system. Expert annotators followed randomly chosen dialogue goals accompanying the MultiWOZ test set and recorded any incorrect system behavior.

5 Results

We first discuss quantitative results for both corpus-based and crowdsourced human evaluation, then include a qualitative analysis of the model behavior.

5.1 Corpus-based Evaluation on MultiWOZ

Table 1 shows a comparison between our methods and current state-of-the-art systems (cf. Section 2). Since some of the compared methods do not provide results with on MultiWOZ 2.1, we report results on both MultiWOZ 2.0 and MultiWOZ 2.1. As we can see, AuGPT compares favorably to other approaches. The chosen variant of our model is not the best-scoring variant on corpus-based metrics (see Table 4). It was chosen based on the ConvLab evaluation, which may not be optimal for corpus-based evaluation. LABES-S2S produces higher BLEU scores, which would indicate a better fluency of the model, but scores lower on inform and success rates. LAVA, SOLOIST, SimpleTOD, and MD-Sequicity, on the other hand, provide slightly higher inform and success scores while doing worse in terms of fluency.

Table 2 shows a comparison with two other models in the ConvLab evaluation scheme with a simulated user. The compared systems were chosen

[8] The selection was done based on ConvLab 2 performance, but probably used a different version of the tool and thus arrived at different results – the chosen variant is not the best one according to our own measurements.

[...]
user: *I want to make a booking at sitar tandoori*
belief: restaurant {name = sitar tandoori}
train {arrive by = 18:00, day = sunday, departure = cambridge, destination = london liverpool street, people = 1}
system: What day would you like the booking for?
user: *the same day, 13:30*
belief: restaurant {day = sunday, name = sitar tandoori, people = 1, time = 13:30}
train {arrive by = 18:00, day = sunday, departure = cambridge, destination = london liverpool street, people = 1}
system: Booking was successful. The table will be reserved for 15 minutes. Reference number is: 00000200.

Example 2: A dialogue where the system did not ask for necessary information. The user previously booked a train trip for one person (cf. the belief state in the first turn shown). When they went on to book a restaurant, the system took over the number of persons from the train ride and did not ask again.

because they both implement fully trainable end-to-end methods. Our system outperforms both compared systems by a wide margin. Our model is able to perform well not just in a single-turn response generation scenario, but over the course of the whole dialogue. As the example of DAMD shows, this is not always guaranteed.

5.2 Human Evaluation

We show the DSTC9 human evaluation results in Table 3. Our model outperformed the baseline on the main average success metric (along with only 3 other submissions out of 10). We did not match the winning submission on average success, but we achieved the best overall success rate based on human judgments (without checking consistency with the database). This suggests that the main drawback of our model lies in database grounding. This could have been caused by our new delexicalization (Section 4.2). Finally, our model needed the smallest number of turns on average to complete the dialogues.

Note that the model variant chosen for human evaluation did not include pre-training on additional data (cf. Section 4.6 and Footnote 8), which could improve performance in human evaluation.

5.3 Error Analysis

Our expert annotators evaluated 130 dialogues in total, 50 of which contained at least one error. However, in most cases, the system was able to recover from the errors, resulting in an overall success rate

user : I am looking for a cheap *chinse* restaurant.
belief: restaurant {food = chinese, price range = cheap}
system: I have 4 cheap chinese restaurants. What area of town would you like to dine in?
user: downtown
belief: restaurant {area = centre, food = chinese, price range = cheap}
system: I have 3 cheap chinese restaurants in the centre. Would you like to book at Charlie Chan?
...

Example 3: A snippet from a challenging but successful dialogue. The system deals with input noise ("chinse") as well as with paraphrases ("downtown").

of 86.9% (i.e., 17 unsuccessful dialogues). The purpose of this analysis was to identify different types of errors occurring during full dialogues.

By far the most common error (21 counts) were *hallucinated values*, i.e., lack of grounding for some of the information provided (see the end of Example 2). Another frequent error type is *missing information* (5 counts), i.e., not asking for information that is required (and e.g. reusing information from a different domain without user confirmation). Example 2 also demonstrates another common error type, which is *bad domain* (4 counts). Here, the system does not react to the user's request for a different search (hotels instead of attractions in the example). This might be caused by a less frequent wording of the request in the given context, and usually gets resolved by rephrasing the request.

The analysis also found many examples of correct system behavior in non-trivial cases. As illustrated in Example 3, the model is able to deal with paraphrases and is robust to a certain amount of noise in the data. Specifically, it handles typos, various time formats, etc. Interaction between domains is also successful in most cases – the system is able to resolve references to another domain's belief state (e.g., make a booking for the same group of people as done before in a different venue).

6 Ablation Study

We tested many variants of our method with different combinations of components to evaluate their contributions. The results are presented in Table 4. Namely, we are interested in the following components: **(1)** unlikelihood loss, **(2)** auxiliary tasks, **(3)** data augmentation, **(4)** modified consistency task and **(5)** unclean data filtering.

We can see that all proposed contributions which are a part of our final system, except for the unlikelihood training, have a positive effect on the

	MultiWOZ 2.1			ConvLab 2						
							inform			
method	inf	suc	BLEU	comp	suc	book	P	R	F1	turns
AuGPT	83.5	67.3	17.2	**89.4**	**60.1**	85.7	64.5	**82.1**	70.3	14.6
w/o. unlikelihood	84.1	66.9	17.1	89.2	59.3	**90.8**	63.9	81.6	69.5	14.6
w/o. clean	81.9	64.0	15.8	85.0	57.7	85.6	65.6	79.1	69.6	14.5
w/o. unlikelihood, w/o. clean	**86.5**	**69.1**	**17.5**	85.9	58.4	81.3	62.2	79.8	67.5	**14.1**
w. all auxiliary	83.1	66.2	17.0	88.7	59.2	86.0	64.6	81.1	69.9	14.4
w/o. pre-training	81.0	62.7	15.1	88.1	59.8	83.7	**68.1**	80.9	72.1	15.6
w/o. back-translations	79.8	61.7	15.2	88.9	58.2	87.4	68.0	81.6	**72.2**	14.9
w. old consistency	81.4	65.8	17.0	85.5	57.8	86.0	65.2	80.0	69.8	14.6
w/o. consistency	81.9	64.5	16.3	86.4	57.1	84.1	66.3	81.2	70.9	14.6

Table 4: Ablation study (inf = inform, suc = success, book = book rate; see Section 4.4). The model version with the best ConvLab 2 success rate is chosen as our best model. Variants are denoted with their respective modifications compared to the default: "w/o. unlikelihood" = unlikelihood loss was not used; "w/o. clean" uses all training samples as opposed to using only the ones consistent with the database; "w/o. pre-training" = Taskmaster-1 and Schema-Guided datasets were not used for training (this variant was selected for human evaluation); "all auxiliary" = using two additional auxiliary tasks (see the Method section); "w/o. consistency" = dialogue consistency task is not used; "old consistency" refers to the consistency task by Peng et al. (2021) (see the Section 3.2).

system performance. In the ConvLab evaluation, our final system performs best. Removing either pre-training or back-translations decreases BLEU, inform and success rates substantially. Furthermore, we notice the positive effect of using our improved consistency detection task over the one used in SOLOIST (Peng et al., 2021), which in turn scores better than no consistency detection.

Training on all data as opposed to using only "clean" samples clearly reduces performance. On the other hand, unlikelihood training improves performance only in ConvLab while causing a performance drop in corpus-based metrics. This can be caused by the fact that the unlikelihood training promotes diversity and reduces repetitions on the token level, and thus does not play well with corpus-based evaluation. We did not notice any increase in performance when the user intent prediction and system action prediction auxiliary tasks were used (cf. Section 3.2). The reason for this behavior could be that the model learns to represent the actions well enough implicitly, without the need for these additional objectives. Therefore, these tasks are not a part of our final model.

7 Conclusions & Future Work

We present a dialogue modeling pipeline based on the pre-trained GPT-2 language model. AuGPT uses modified training objectives and employs data augmentation to increase the diversity of generated utterances. Our experiments show that the proposed approach outperforms baselines and is competitive with state of the art on the MultiWOZ dataset. We also run a series of ablation experiments to assess the individual contributions of the modifications. According to our detailed ablation study, training data augmentation using back-translation via multiple languages and a modified auxiliary training objective for dialogue consistency detection are the features that contribute most to our system's performance. Additionally, we perform a qualitative analysis of the outputs to give a better insight into our model behavior.

In the future, we plan to construct a latent representation of the belief state and optimize it jointly with the language model. We will replace the deterministic lexicalization with a trainable alternative, and possibly even integrate the database module into the model. To improve the transfer to new domains, we will learn a domain embedding and optimize it jointly with the model, unifying all datasets.

Acknowledgments

This work was supported by the Charles University GAUK grant No. 302120, the SVV project No. 260575, and the Charles University project PRIMUS/19/SCI/10. Jonáš Kulhánek was supported by the European Regional Development Fund under the project Robotics for Industry 4.0 (reg. no. CZ.02.1.01/0.0/0.0/15_003/0000470). Additional computational resources were supplied by the project "e-Infrastruktura CZ" (e-INFRA LM2018140) provided within the program Projects of Large Research, Development and Innovations Infrastructures.

References

Paweł Budzianowski and Ivan Vulić. 2019. Hello, it's GPT-2 - how can I help you? Towards the use of pretrained language models for task-oriented dialogue systems. In *Proceedings of the 3rd Workshop on Neural Generation and Translation*, pages 15–22, Hong Kong.

Paweł Budzianowski, Tsung-Hsien Wen, Bo-Hsiang Tseng, Iñigo Casanueva, Stefan Ultes, Osman Ramadan, and Milica Gašić. 2018. MultiWOZ - a large-scale multi-domain Wizard-of-Oz dataset for task-oriented dialogue modelling. In *Proceedings of the 2018 Conference on Empirical Methods in Natural Language Processing*, pages 5016–5026, Brussels, Belgium.

Bill Byrne, Karthik Krishnamoorthi, Chinnadhurai Sankar, Arvind Neelakantan, Ben Goodrich, Daniel Duckworth, Semih Yavuz, Amit Dubey, Kyu-Young Kim, and Andy Cedilnik. 2019. Taskmaster-1: Toward a realistic and diverse dialog dataset. In *Proceedings of the 2019 Conference on Empirical Methods in Natural Language Processing and the 9th International Joint Conference on Natural Language Processing (EMNLP-IJCNLP)*, pages 4516–4525, Hong Kong, China.

Jacob Devlin, Ming-Wei Chang, Kenton Lee, and Kristina Toutanova. 2019. BERT: Pre-training of deep bidirectional transformers for language understanding. In *Proceedings of the 2019 Conference of the North American Chapter of the Association for Computational Linguistics: Human Language Technologies, Volume 1 (Long and Short Papers)*, pages 4171–4186, Minneapolis, Minnesota.

Sergey Edunov, Myle Ott, Michael Auli, and David Grangier. 2018. Understanding back-translation at scale. In *Proceedings of the 2018 Conference on Empirical Methods in Natural Language Processing*, pages 489–500, Brussels, Belgium.

Arash Einolghozati, Sonal Gupta, Mrinal Mohit, and Rushin Shah. 2019. Improving robustness of task oriented dialog systems. In *3rd Conversational AI Workshop at 33rd Conference on Neural Information Processing Systems (NeurIPS 2019)*.

Henry Elder, Robert Burke, Alexander O'Connor, and Jennifer Foster. 2020. Shape of synth to come: Why we should use synthetic data for English surface realization. In *Proceedings of the 58th Annual Meeting of the Association for Computational Linguistics*, pages 7465–7471, Online.

Mihail Eric, Rahul Goel, Shachi Paul, Abhishek Sethi, Sanchit Agarwal, Shuyang Gao, Adarsh Kumar, Anuj Goyal, Peter Ku, and Dilek Hakkani-Tur. 2020. MultiWOZ 2.1: A consolidated multi-domain dialogue dataset with state corrections and state tracking baselines. In *Proceedings of the 12th Language Resources and Evaluation Conference*, pages 422–428, Marseille, France.

Mihail Eric, Lakshmi Krishnan, Francois Charette, and Christopher D. Manning. 2017. Key-value retrieval networks for task-oriented dialogue. In *Proceedings of the 18th Annual SIGdial Meeting on Discourse and Dialogue*, pages 37–49, Saarbrücken, Germany.

Christian Federmann, Oussama Elachqar, and Chris Quirk. 2019. Multilingual whispers: Generating paraphrases with translation. In *Proceedings of the 5th Workshop on Noisy User-generated Text (W-NUT 2019)*, pages 17–26, Hong Kong, China.

Jianfeng Gao, Michel Galley, and Lihong Li. 2019. Neural approaches to conversational AI: Question answering, task-oriented dialogues and social chatbots. volume 13 of *Foundations and Trends in Information Retrieval*.

Claudio Greco, Barbara Plank, Raquel Fernández, and Raffaella Bernardi. 2019. Psycholinguistics meets continual learning: Measuring catastrophic forgetting in visual question answering. In *Proceedings of the 57th Annual Meeting of the Association for Computational Linguistics*, pages 3601–3605, Florence, Italy.

Chulaka Gunasekara, Seokhwan Kim, Luis Fernando D'Haro, Abhinav Rastogi, Yun-Nung Chen, Mihail Eric, Behnam Hedayatnia, Karthik Gopalakrishnan, Yang Liu, Chao-Wei Huang, Dilek Hakkani-Tür, Jinchao Li, Qi Zhu, Lingxiao Luo, Lars Liden, Kaili Huang, Shahin Shayandeh, Runze Liang, Baolin Peng, Zheng Zhang, Swadheen Shukla, Minlie Huang, Jianfeng Gao, Shikib Mehri, Yulan Feng, Carla Gordon, Seyed Hossein Alavi, David Traum, Maxine Eskenazi, Ahmad Beirami, Eunjoon, Cho, Paul A. Crook, Ankita De, Alborz Geramifard, Satwik Kottur, Seungwhan Moon, Shivani Poddar, and Rajen Subba. 2020. Overview of the ninth dialog system technology challenge: DSTC9. *arXiv preprint arXiv:2011.06486*.

Donghoon Ham, Jeong-Gwan Lee, Youngsoo Jang, and Kee-Eung Kim. 2020. End-to-end neural pipeline for goal-oriented dialogue systems using GPT-2. In *Proceedings of the 58th Annual Meeting of the Association for Computational Linguistics*, pages 583–592, Online.

Ari Holtzman, Jan Buys, Li Du, Maxwell Forbes, and Yejin Choi. 2020. The curious case of neural text degeneration. In *8th International Conference on Learning Representations, ICLR 2020, Addis Ababa, Ethiopia, April 26-30, 2020*.

Ehsan Hosseini-Asl, Bryan McCann, Chien-Sheng Wu, Semih Yavuz, and Richard Socher. 2020. A simple language model for task-oriented dialogue. In *Advances in Neural Information Processing Systems 33: Annual Conference on Neural Information Processing Systems 2020, NeurIPS 2020, December 6-12, 2020, virtual*.

Lifeng Jin, David King, Amad Hussein, Michael White, and Douglas Danforth. 2018. Using paraphrasing and memory-augmented models to combat data sparsity in question interpretation with a virtual patient dialogue system. In *Proceedings of the Thirteenth Workshop on Innovative Use of NLP for Building Educational Applications*, pages 13–23, New Orleans, Louisiana.

Ioannis Konstas, Srinivasan Iyer, Mark Yatskar, Yejin Choi, and Luke Zettlemoyer. 2017. Neural AMR: Sequence-to-sequence models for parsing and generation. In *Proceedings of the 55th Annual Meeting of the Association for Computational Linguistics (Volume 1: Long Papers)*, pages 146–157, Vancouver, Canada.

Sungjin Lee, Hannes Schulz, Adam Atkinson, Jianfeng Gao, Kaheer Suleman, Layla El Asri, Mahmoud Adada, Minlie Huang, Shikhar Sharma, Wendy Tay, and Xiujun Li. 2019. Multi-domain task-completion dialog challenge.

Wenqiang Lei, Xisen Jin, Min-Yen Kan, Zhaochun Ren, Xiangnan He, and Dawei Yin. 2018. Sequicity: Simplifying task-oriented dialogue systems with single sequence-to-sequence architectures. In *Proceedings of the 56th Annual Meeting of the Association for Computational Linguistics (Volume 1: Long Papers)*, pages 1437–1447, Melbourne, Australia.

Jinchao Li, Qi Zhu, Lingxiao Luo, Lars Liden, Kaili Huang, Shahin Shayandeh, Runze Liang, Baolin Peng, Zheng Zhang, Swadheen Shukla, Ryuichi Takanobu, Minlie Huang, and Jianfeng Gao. 2021. Multi-domain task completion dialog challenge II at DSTC9. In *DSTC9 Workshop at AAAI*, Online.

Margaret Li, Stephen Roller, Ilia Kulikov, Sean Welleck, Y-Lan Boureau, Kyunghyun Cho, and Jason Weston. 2020. Don't say that! Making inconsistent dialogue unlikely with unlikelihood training. In *Proceedings of the 58th Annual Meeting of the Association for Computational Linguistics*, pages 4715–4728, Online.

Chin-Yew Lin. 2004. Rouge: A package for automatic evaluation of summaries. In *Text Summarization Branches Out*, pages 74–81, Barcelona, Spain.

Ilya Loshchilov and Frank Hutter. 2019. Decoupled weight decay regularization. In *7th International Conference on Learning Representations, ICLR 2019, New Orleans, LA, USA, May 6-9, 2019*.

Nurul Lubis, Christian Geishauser, Michael Heck, Hsien-chin Lin, Marco Moresi, Carel van Niekerk, and Milica Gasic. 2020. LAVA: Latent action spaces via variational auto-encoding for dialogue policy optimization. In *Proceedings of the 28th International Conference on Computational Linguistics*, pages 465–479, Barcelona, Spain (Online).

Dominik Macháček, Jonáš Kratochvíl, Sangeet Sagar, Matúš Žilinec, Ondřej Bojar, Thai-Son Nguyen, Felix Schneider, Philip Williams, and Yuekun Yao. 2020. ELITR non-native speech translation at IWSLT 2020. In *Proceedings of the 17th International Conference on Spoken Language Translation*, pages 200–208, Online.

Nitin Madnani and Bonnie J. Dorr. 2010. Generating phrasal and sentential paraphrases: A survey of data-driven methods. *Computational Linguistics*, 36(3):341–387.

Kishore Papineni, Salim Roukos, Todd Ward, and Wei-Jing Zhu. 2002. BLEU: a method for automatic evaluation of machine translation. In *Proceedings of the 40th Annual Meeting of the Association for Computational Linguistics*, pages 311–318, Philadelphia, Pennsylvania, USA.

Adam Paszke, Sam Gross, Francisco Massa, Adam Lerer, James Bradbury, Gregory Chanan, Trevor Killeen, Zeming Lin, Natalia Gimelshein, Luca Antiga, Alban Desmaison, Andreas Köpf, Edward Yang, Zachary DeVito, Martin Raison, Alykhan Tejani, Sasank Chilamkurthy, Benoit Steiner, Lu Fang, Junjie Bai, and Soumith Chintala. 2019. PyTorch: An imperative style, high-performance deep learning library. In *Advances in Neural Information Processing Systems 32: Annual Conference on Neural Information Processing Systems 2019, NeurIPS 2019, December 8-14, 2019, Vancouver, BC, Canada*, pages 8024–8035.

Baolin Peng, Chunyuan Li, Jinchao Li, Shahin Shayandeh, Lars Liden, and Jianfeng Gao. 2021. Soloist: Building task bots at scale with transfer learning and machine teaching. *Transactions of the Association for Computational Linguistics*, 9:807–824.

Libo Qin, Xiao Xu, Wanxiang Che, Yue Zhang, and Ting Liu. 2020. Dynamic fusion network for multi-domain end-to-end task-oriented dialog. In *Proceedings of the 58th Annual Meeting of the Association for Computational Linguistics*, pages 6344–6354, Online.

Alec Radford, Jeffrey Wu, Rewon Child, David Luan, Dario Amodei, and Ilya Sutskever. 2019. Language models are unsupervised multitask learners. Technical report, OpenAI.

Abhinav Rastogi, Xiaoxue Zang, Srinivas Sunkara, Raghav Gupta, and Pranav Khaitan. 2020. Towards scalable multi-domain conversational agents: The schema-guided dialogue dataset. In *Proceedings of the AAAI Conference on Artificial Intelligence*, pages 8689–8696, New York, NY, USA.

Rico Sennrich, Barry Haddow, and Alexandra Birch. 2016. Improving neural machine translation models with monolingual data. In *Proceedings of the 54th Annual Meeting of the Association for Computational Linguistics (Volume 1: Long Papers)*, pages 86–96, Berlin, Germany.

Ashish Vaswani, Noam Shazeer, Niki Parmar, Jakob Uszkoreit, Llion Jones, Aidan N. Gomez, Lukasz Kaiser, and Illia Polosukhin. 2017. Attention is all you need. In *Advances in Neural Information Processing Systems 30: Annual Conference on Neural Information Processing Systems 2017, December 4-9, 2017, Long Beach, CA, USA*, pages 5998–6008.

Sean Welleck, Ilia Kulikov, Stephen Roller, Emily Dinan, Kyunghyun Cho, and Jason Weston. 2020. Neural text generation with unlikelihood training. In *8th International Conference on Learning Representations, ICLR 2020, Addis Ababa, Ethiopia, April 26-30, 2020.*

Tsung-Hsien Wen, Milica Gašić, Dongho Kim, Nikola Mrkšić, Pei-Hao Su, David Vandyke, and Steve Young. 2015. Stochastic language generation in dialogue using recurrent neural networks with convolutional sentence reranking. In *Proceedings of the 16th Annual Meeting of the Special Interest Group on Discourse and Dialogue*, pages 275–284, Prague, Czech Republic.

Tsung-Hsien Wen, David Vandyke, Nikola Mrkšić, Milica Gašić, Lina M. Rojas-Barahona, Pei-Hao Su, Stefan Ultes, and Steve Young. 2017. A network-based end-to-end trainable task-oriented dialogue system. In *Proceedings of the 15th Conference of the European Chapter of the Association for Computational Linguistics: Volume 1, Long Papers*, pages 438–449, Valencia, Spain.

Chien-Sheng Wu, Steven Hoi, Richard Socher, and Caiming Xiong. 2020. ToD-BERT: Pre-trained natural language understanding for task-oriented dialogues. In *Proceedings of the 2020 Conference on Empirical Methods in Natural Language Processing (EMNLP)*, page 917–929, Online.

S. Young, M. Gašić, B. Thomson, and J. D. Williams. 2013. POMDP-based statistical spoken dialog systems: A review. *Proceedings of the IEEE*, 101(5):1160–1179.

Yichi Zhang, Zhijian Ou, Min Hu, and Junlan Feng. 2020a. A probabilistic end-to-end task-oriented dialog model with latent belief states towards semi-supervised learning. In *Proceedings of the 2020 Conference on Empirical Methods in Natural Language Processing (EMNLP)*, pages 9207–9219, Online.

Yichi Zhang, Zhijian Ou, and Zhou Yu. 2020b. Task-oriented dialog systems that consider multiple appropriate responses under the same context. In *Proceedings of the AAAI Conference on Artificial Intelligence*, pages 9604–9611, New York, NY, USA.

Yizhe Zhang, Siqi Sun, Michel Galley, Yen-Chun Chen, Chris Brockett, Xiang Gao, Jianfeng Gao, Jingjing Liu, and Bill Dolan. 2020c. DIALOGPT : Large-scale generative pre-training for conversational response generation. In *Proceedings of the 58th Annual Meeting of the Association for Computational Linguistics: System Demonstrations*, pages 270–278, Online.

Qi Zhu, Zheng Zhang, Yan Fang, Xiang Li, Ryuichi Takanobu, Jinchao Li, Baolin Peng, Jianfeng Gao, Xiaoyan Zhu, and Minlie Huang. 2020. ConvLab-2: An open-source toolkit for building, evaluating, and diagnosing dialogue systems. In *Proceedings of the 58th Annual Meeting of the Association for Computational Linguistics: System Demonstrations*, pages 142–149, Online.

Vilém Zouhar, Michal Novák, Matúš Žilinec, Ondřej Bojar, Mateo Obregón, Robin L. Hill, Frédéric Blain, Marina Fomicheva, Lucia Specia, and Lisa Yankovskaya. 2021. Backtranslation feedback improves user confidence in MT, not quality. In *Proceedings of the 2021 Conference of the North American Chapter of the Association for Computational Linguistics: Human Language Technologies*, pages 151–161, Online.

A Additional Results

A.1 Detailed Error Analysis

Our expert annotators evaluated 130 dialogues in total, 50 of which contained at least one error. However, in most cases, the system was able to recover from the errors, resulting in an overall success rate of 86.9% (i.e., 17 unsuccessful dialogues). The purpose of this analysis was to identify different types of errors occurring during full dialogues. The annotators were familiar with the model architecture and were instructed to categorize the errors according to the cause of the problem. Specifically, they identified which component caused the respective error and annotators categorized the errors into more specific types.

The overall results are given in Table 5. We observe that the most common reason for a failed dialogue is an error related to the belief state (30 errors, 10 failed dialogues). Also, although policy errors happen relatively often (21x), they rarely cause the whole dialogue to fail (2 dialogues). We observe that we have a slightly higher number of successful dialogues compared to the 82.6% success rate (without checking database consistency) found in human evaluation (cf. Table 3). The most likely cause is that our expert annotators were more motivated to recover from erroneous system behavior and finish the dialogue.

Fine-grained error types identified by annotators are given in Table 6 and Examples 2, 4 and 3. To extend the analysis from Section 5.3, we include another frequent error type – *missing information* (5 counts), i.e., not asking for information that is required (Example 4). In this case, the system uses information from a different domain without the user explicitly confirming this. A most probable cause of this is that most instances of the training data carry over the information.

A.2 Individual Component Analysis

We have conducted additional tests to obtain a deeper insight into each component's performance – DST and NLG. We have evaluated the accuracy of the generated belief states. Joint accuracy, slot accuracy, and F1 score were used. Joint accuracy gives the percentage of successfully generated belief states – with no error. Slot accuracy, on the other hand, is the average accuracy of correctly predicting the value for a domain-slot pair. To evaluate NLG, we compared the end-to-end system where the generated belief state is used to query the database and generate the response with a variant of the pipeline, where the ground-truth belief state and/or ground-truth database result counts were used. The BLEU (Papineni et al., 2002) and ROUGE-L (Lin, 2004) scores were used for evaluation.

In Table 7, we can see the performance of each individual component of the system. One can notice that the performance of NLG is not decreased when we use the generated belief state instead of the oracle belief state. Since the belief state prediction is not perfect, this suggests that the model does not actually need belief states for generating the delexicalized response. However, when the real database result counts are used instead of oracle database result counts, the performance decreases, which implies that the database result counts are important for NLG.

user:	*I'm looking for a theatre in Cambridge*
belief:	attraction {type = theatre}
system:	There are 5 theatres in Cambridge. Is there an area of town you prefer?
user:	*no I don't care*
belief:	attraction {type = theatre}
system:	I recommend Adc Theatre in the centre. Would you like more information?
user:	*no, I'm also looking for some place to stay*
belief:	attraction {type = theatre}
system:	I have 5 theatres in the centre. Do you have a price range?
user:	*I'm looking for a place to stay*
belief:	attraction {type = theatre}
system:	There are 5 theatres in the centre. Do you have a preference for area?
user:	*I'm looking for a hotel*
belief:	hotel {type = hotel} attraction {type = theatre}
system:	*There are 9 hotels in the north. Do you have a price range?*

Example 4: Dialogue sample with a bad domain focus and a hallucination. First, the system ignores that the user switched from searching for a theater to searching for a hotel. After accepting the new domain, the system replies with hotels "in the north" even though the user did not specify.

	Erroneous Dialogues	BS Error	DB Error	Policy Error	Other Error
All dialogues	50	30	4	21	6
Unsuccessful dialogues	17	10	3	2	2

Table 5: Interactive analysis performed by human evaluators using 130 prepared dialogue goals. 17 of these dialogues contained an error that caused the dialogue to fail. We show summary statistics regarding the number of respective error sources (BS = belief state, DB = database). Note that some of the dialogues contain more than one error.

Type	Count	Source	Description
Hallucinated values	21	BS/Policy	Used a slot value in the reply that is not grounded in the DB nor in the context
Wrong lexicalization	6	Policy	Repeats the same value in a list of choices during lexicalization
Missing information	5	Policy	Makes booking while not all information is specified
Ignored input	5	BS	Keeps asking for information that was provided
Bad domain	4	BS	Fails to focus on the correct domain
False response	4	Policy	States a different value of a slot than the value stored in DB
Repeated output	3	Policy	Repeats the same slot twice on the output
Failed booking	3	DB/Policy	Booking was unsuccessful due to DB mismatch
Other	10	BS/DB/P/Oth	(Various rare errors that could not be categorized)

Table 6: Distribution of the most common error types encountered during the human evaluation of 130 dialogues. Absolute counts of errors in the 50 erroneous dialogues are shown. The total error count is 61 as some dialogues contained multiple errors. The most likely source of the error (cf. Table 5) and a short description are given for each type.

	oracle		DST			NLG	
fine-tuned on	bs	db	joint acc.	slot acc.	F1	BLEU	ROUGE-L
MW 2.0	✗	✗	54.1	97.2	90.0	17.2	39.0
	✗	✓				17.4	39.3
	✓	✓				17.4	39.2
MW 2.1	✗	✗	56.5	97.2	90.6	17.4	38.6
	✗	✓				17.6	38.8
	✓	✓				17.6	38.8

Table 7: Performance of DST and NLG components. Joint and slot accuracies, as well as slot values F1 score, are used to evaluate DST. For NLG, BLEU and ROUGE-L metrics are used. Apart from using the generated belief states and database counts, we also evaluate the components with oracle values. Note that models were pre-trained on Taskmaster-1 and Schema-Guided Dialogue datasets.

Investigating Pretrained Language Models for Graph-to-Text Generation

Leonardo F. R. Ribeiro[†], **Martin Schmitt**[‡], **Hinrich Schütze**[‡] **and Iryna Gurevych**[†]

[†]Research Training Group AIPHES and UKP Lab, Technical University of Darmstadt
[‡]Center for Information and Language Processing (CIS), LMU Munich
www.ukp.tu-darmstadt.de

Abstract

Graph-to-text generation aims to generate fluent texts from graph-based data. In this paper, we investigate two recent pretrained language models (PLMs) and analyze the impact of different task-adaptive pretraining strategies for PLMs in graph-to-text generation. We present a study across three graph domains: meaning representations, Wikipedia knowledge graphs (KGs) and scientific KGs. We show that approaches based on PLMs BART and T5 achieve new state-of-the-art results and that task-adaptive pretraining strategies improve their performance even further. We report new state-of-the-art BLEU scores of 49.72 on AMR-LDC2017T10, 59.70 on WebNLG, and 25.66 on AGENDA datasets - a relative improvement of 31.8%, 4.5%, and 42.4%, respectively, with our models generating significantly more fluent texts than human references. In an extensive analysis, we identify possible reasons for the PLMs' success on graph-to-text tasks. Our findings suggest that the PLMs benefit from similar facts seen during pretraining or fine-tuning, such that they perform well even when the input graph is reduced to a simple bag of node and edge labels.[1]

1 Introduction

Graphs are important data structures in NLP as they represent complex relations within a set of objects. For example, semantic and syntactic structures of sentences can be represented using different graph representations (e.g., AMRs, Banarescu et al., 2013; semantic-role labeling, Surdeanu et al., 2008; syntactic and semantic graphs, Belz et al., 2011) and knowledge graphs (KGs) are used to describe factual knowledge in the form of relations between entities (Gardent et al., 2017; Vougiouklis et al., 2018; Koncel-Kedziorski et al., 2019).

Graph-to-text generation, a subtask of data-to-text generation (Gatt and Krahmer, 2018), aims to create fluent natural language text to describe an input graph (see Figure 1). This task is important for NLP applications such as dialogue generation (Moon et al., 2019) and question answering (Duan et al., 2017). Recently, it has been shown that structured meaning representation, such as AMR or KG, can store the internal state of a dialog system, providing core semantic knowledge (Bonial et al., 2020; Bai et al., 2021) or can be the result of a database query for conversational QA (Yu et al., 2019). Moreover, dialog states can be represented as KGs to encode compositionality and can be shared across different domains, slot types and dialog participators (Cheng et al., 2020).

Transfer learning has become ubiquitous in NLP and pretrained Transformer-based architectures (Vaswani et al., 2017) have considerably outperformed prior state of the art in various downstream tasks (Devlin et al., 2019; Yang et al., 2019a; Liu et al., 2020; Radford et al., 2019).

In this paper, we analyze the applicability of two recent text-to-text pretrained language models (PLMs), BART (Lewis et al., 2020) and T5 (Raffel et al., 2019), for graph-to-text generation. We choose these models because of their *encoder-decoder* architecture, which makes them particularly suitable for conditional text generation. Our study comprises three graph domains (meaning representations, Wikipedia KGs, and scientific KGs). We further introduce *task-adaptive* graph-to-text pretraining approaches for PLMs and demonstrate that such strategies improve the state of the art by a substantial margin.

While recent works have shown the benefit of explicitly encoding the graph structure in graph-to-text generation (Song et al., 2018; Ribeiro et al., 2019, 2020; Schmitt et al., 2020; Zhao et al., 2020a, to name a few), our approaches based on PLMs consistently outperform these models, even though PLMs – as sequence models – do not exhibit any

[1]Our code is available at https://github.com/UKPLab/plms-graph2text.

Proceedings of the Third Workshop on Natural Language Processing for Conversational AI, pages 211–227
November 10, 2021. ©2021 Association for Computational Linguistics

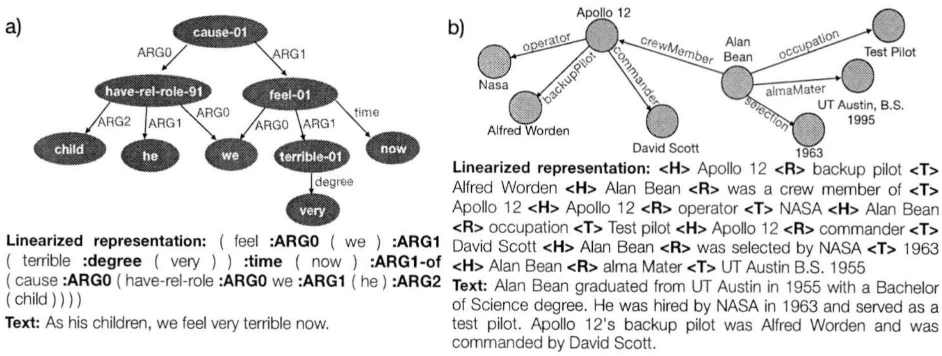

Figure 1: Examples of (a) AMR and (b) WebNLG graphs, the input for the models and the reference texts.

graph-specific structural bias.[2] Simply representing the graph as a linear traversal (see Figure 1) leads to remarkable generation performance in the presence of a strong language model. In our analysis we investigate to what extent fine-tuned PLMs make use of the graph structure represented in the graph linearization. We notably observe that PLMs achieve high performance on two popular KG-to-text benchmarks even when the KG is reduced to a mere bag of node and edge labels.

Our contributions are the following:

- We investigate and compare two PLMs, BART and T5, for graph-to-text generation, exploring *language model adaptation* (LMA) and *supervised task adaptation* (STA) pretraining, employing additional task-specific data.
- Our approaches consistently outperform the state of the art by significant margins, ranging from 2.6 to 12.0 BLEU points, on three established graph-to-text benchmarks from different domains, exceeding specialized graph architectures (e.g., Graph Neural Networks, GNNs, Kipf and Welling, 2017).
- In a crowdsourcing experiment, we demonstrate that our methods generate texts with significantly better fluency than existing works and the human references.
- We discover that PLMs perform well even when trained on a shuffled linearized graph representation without any information about connectivity (bag of node and edge labels), which is surprising since prior studies showed that explicitly encoding the graph structure improves models trained from scratch (e.g., Zhao et al., 2020a); and investigate the possible reasons for such a good performance.

[2]The model architecture does not explicitly encode the graph structure, i.e., which entities are connected to each other, but has to retrieve it from a sequence that tries to encode this information.

2 Related Work

Graph-to-text Learning. Various neural models have been proposed to generate sentences from graphs from different domains. Konstas et al. (2017) propose the first neural approach for AMR-to-text generation that uses a linearized input graph. Prior approaches for KG-to-text generation train text-to-text neural models using sequences of KG triples as input (Trisedya et al., 2018; Moryossef et al., 2019; Castro Ferreira et al., 2019; Ribeiro et al., 2021a).

Recent approaches (Marcheggiani and Perez Beltrachini, 2018; Song et al., 2018; Beck et al., 2018; Damonte and Cohen, 2019; Ribeiro et al., 2019; Zhao et al., 2020a; Schmitt et al., 2021; Ribeiro et al., 2021b) propose architectures based on GNNs to directly encode the graph structure, whereas other efforts (Ribeiro et al., 2020; Schmitt et al., 2020; Yao et al., 2020; Wang et al., 2020) inject the graph structure information into Transformer-based architectures. The success of those approaches suggests that imposing a strong relational inductive bias into the graph-to-text model can assist the generation.

Pretrained Language Models. Pretrained Transformer-based models, such as BERT (Devlin et al., 2019), XLNet (Yang et al., 2019b), or RoBERTa (Liu et al., 2020), have established a qualitatively new level of baseline performance for many widely used natural language understanding (NLU) benchmarks. Generative pretrained Transformer-based methods, such as GPT-2 (Radford et al., 2019), BART (Lewis et al., 2020), and T5 (Raffel et al., 2019), are employed in many natural language generation (NLG) tasks.

Mager et al. (2020) were the first to employ GPT-2, a decoder-only PLM, for AMR-to-text generation and use cycle consistency to improve the adequacy. In contrast, we are the first to investigate BART and T5 models, which have both a Transformer-based encoder and decoder, in AMR-to-text generation. Recently, Harkous et al. (2020) and Kale (2020) demonstrate state-of-the-art results in different data-to-text datasets, employing GPT-2 and T5 models respectively. Radev et al. (2020) propose DART, a new data-to-text dataset, and train a BART model gradually augmenting the WebNLG training data with DART data.

Hoyle et al. (2021) explore scaffolding objectives in PLMs and show gains in low-resource graph-to-text settings. Different from the above works, we focus on a general transfer learning strategies for graph-to-text generation, investigating task-adaptive pretraining approaches, employing additional collected task-specific data for different PLMs (BART and T5) and benchmarks. In addition, we provide a detailed analysis aimed at explaining the good performance of PLMs on KG-to-text tasks.

Recently, Gururangan et al. (2020) explored task-adaptive pretraining strategies for text classification. While our LMA (see §3) is related to their DAPT as both use a self-supervised objective on a domain-specific corpus, they notably differ in that DAPT operates on the model input while LMA models the output. We are the first to show the benefits of additional task-specific pretraining in PLMs for graph-to-text tasks.

3 PLMs for Graph-to-Text Generation

3.1 Models in this Study

We investigate BART (Lewis et al., 2020) and T5 (Raffel et al., 2019), two PLMs based on the Transformer *encoder-decoder* architecture (Vaswani et al., 2017), for graph-to-text generation. They mainly differ in how they are pretrained and the input corpora used for pretraining. We experiment with different T5 (*small* - 60M parameters, *base* - 220M, and *large* - 770M) and BART (*base* - 140M and *large* - 400M) capacity models.

We fine-tune both PLMs for a few epochs on the supervised downstream graph-to-text datasets. For T5, in the supervised setup, we add a prefix "translate from Graph to Text:" before the graph input. We add this prefix to imitate the T5 setup, when translating between different languages.

3.2 Task-specific Adaptation

Inspired by previous work (Konstas et al., 2017; Gururangan et al., 2020), we investigate whether leveraging additional task-specific data can improve the PLMs' performance on graph-to-text generation. Task-specific data refers to a pretraining corpus that is more task-relevant and usually smaller than the text corpora used for task-independent pretraining. In order to leverage the task-specific data, we add an intermediate adaptive pretraining step between the original pretraining and fine-tuning phases for graph-to-text generation.

More precisely, we first continue pretraining BART and T5 using language model adaptation (LMA) or supervised task adaptation (STA) training. In the supervised approach, we use pairs of graphs and corresponding texts collected from the same or similar domain as the target task. In the LMA approach, we follow BART and T5 pretraining strategies for language modeling, using the reference texts that describe the graphs. Note that we do not use the graphs in the LMA pretraining, but only the target text of our task-specific data collections. The goal is to adapt the decoder to the domain of the final task (Gururangan et al., 2020). In particular, we randomly mask text spans, replacing 15% of the tokens.[3] Before evaluation, we finally fine-tune the models using the original training set as usual.

4 Datasets

We evaluate the text-to-text PLMs on three graph-to-text benchmarks: AMR (LDC2017T10), WebNLG (Gardent et al., 2017), and AGENDA (Koncel-Kedziorski et al., 2019). We chose those datasets because they comprise different domains and are widely used in prior work. Table 10 in Appendix shows statistics for each dataset.

AMR. Abstract meaning representation (AMR) is a semantic formalism that represents the meaning of a sentence as a rooted directed graph expressing "who is doing what to whom" (Banarescu et al., 2013). In an AMR graph, nodes represent concepts and edges represent semantic relations. An instance in LDC2017T10 consists of a sentence annotated with its corresponding AMR graph. Following Mager et al. (2020), we linearize the AMR graphs

[3]Please, refer to Lewis et al. (2020) and Raffel et al. (2019) for details about the self-supervised pretraining strategies.

using the PENMAN notation (see Figure 1a).[4]

WebNLG. Each instance of WebNLG contains a KG from DBPedia (Auer et al., 2007) and a target text with one or multiple sentences that describe the graph. The test set is divided into two partitions: *seen*, which contains only DBPedia categories present in the training set, and *unseen*, which covers categories never seen during training. Their union is called *all*. Following previous work (Harkous et al., 2020), we prepend $\langle H \rangle$, $\langle R \rangle$, and $\langle T \rangle$ tokens before the head entity, the relation and tail entity of a triple (see Figure 1b).

AGENDA. In this dataset, KGs are paired with scientific abstracts extracted from proceedings of AI conferences. Each sample contains the paper title, a KG, and the corresponding abstract. The KG contains entities corresponding to scientific terms and the edges represent relations between these entities. This dataset has loose alignments between the graph and the corresponding text as the graphs were automatically generated. The input for the models is a text containing the title, a sequence of all KG entities, and the triples. The target text is the paper abstract. We add special tokens into the triples in the same way as for WebNLG.

4.1 Additional Task-specific Data

In order to evaluate the proposed task-adaptive pretraining strategies for graph-to-text generation, we collect task-specific data for two graph domains: meaning representations (like AMR) and scientific data (like AGENDA). We did not attempt collecting additional data like WebNLG because the texts in this benchmark do not stem from a corpus but were specifically written by annotators.

AMR Silver Data. In order to generate additional data for AMR, we sample two sentence collections of size 200K and 2M from the Gigaword[5] corpus and use a state-of-the-art AMR parser (Cai and Lam, 2020a) to parse them into AMR graphs.[6] For supervised pretraining, we condition a model on the AMR silver graphs to generate the corresponding sentences before fine-tuning it on gold AMR graphs. For self-supervised pretraining, we only use the sentences.[7]

Model	BLEU	M	BT
Ribeiro et al. (2019)	27.87	33.21	-
Zhu et al. (2019)	31.82	36.38	-
Zhao et al. (2020b)	32.46	36.78	-
Wang et al. (2020)	33.90	37.10	-
Yao et al. (2020)	34.10	38.10	-
based on PLMs			
Mager et al. (2020)	33.02	37.68	-
Harkous et al. (2020)	37.70	38.90	-
$\text{BART}_{\text{base}}$	36.71	38.64	52.47
$\text{BART}_{\text{large}}$	43.47	42.88	60.42
T5_{small}	38.45	40.86	57.95
T5_{base}	42.54	42.62	60.59
T5_{large}	**45.80**	**43.85**	**61.93**
with task-adaptive pretraining			
$\text{BART}_{\text{large}}$ + LMA	43.94	42.36	58.54
T5_{large} + LMA	46.06	44.05	62.59
$\text{BART}_{\text{large}}$ + STA (200K)	44.72	43.65	61.03
$\text{BART}_{\text{large}}$ + STA (2M)	47.51	44.70	62.27
T5_{large} + STA (200K)	48.02	44.85	63.86
T5_{large} + STA (2M)	***49.72***	***45.43***	***64.24***

Table 1: Results on AMR-to-text generation for the LDC2017T10 test set. M and BT stand for METEOR and BLEURT, respectively. **Bold** (***Italic***) indicates the best score without (with) task-adaptive pretraining.

Semantic Scholar AI Data. We collect titles and abstracts of around 190K scientific papers from the Semantic Scholar (Ammar et al., 2018) taken from the proceedings of 36 top Computer Science/AI conferences. We construct KGs from the paper abstracts employing DyGIE++ (Wadden et al., 2019), an information extraction system for scientific texts. Note that the AGENDA dataset was constructed using the older SciIE system (Luan et al., 2018), which also extracts KGs from AI scientific papers. A second difference is that in our new dataset, the domain is broader as we collected data from 36 conferences compared to 12 from AGENDA. Furthermore, to prevent data leakage, all AGENDA samples used for performance evaluation are removed from our dataset. We will call the new dataset KGAIA (KGs from AI Abstracts).[8] Table 11 in Appendix shows relevant dataset statistics.

5 Experiments

We modify the BART and T5 implementations released by Hugging Face (Wolf et al., 2019) in order to adapt them to graph-to-text generation. For the KG datasets, we add the $\langle H \rangle$, $\langle R \rangle$, and $\langle T \rangle$ tokens to the models' vocabulary. We add all edge labels seen in the training set to the vocabulary of the

[4]Details of the preprocessing procedure of AMRs are provided in Appendix A.

[5]https://catalog.ldc.upenn.edu/LDC2003T05

[6]We filter out sentences that do not yield well-formed AMR graphs.

[7]Gigaword and AMR datasets share similar data sources.

[8]We will release the collected additional task-specific data.

Model	BLEU A	BLEU S	BLEU U	METEOR A	METEOR S	METEOR U	chrF++ A	chrF++ S	chrF++ U
Castro Ferreira et al. (2019)	51.68	56.35	38.92	32.00	41.00	21.00	-	-	-
Moryossef et al. (2019)	47.24	53.30	34.41	39.00	44.00	37.00	-	-	-
Schmitt et al. (2020)	-	59.39	-	-	42.83	-	-	74.68	-
Ribeiro et al. (2020)	-	63.69	-	-	44.47	-	-	76.66	-
Zhao et al. (2020a)	52.78	64.42	38.23	41.00	46.00	37.00	-	-	-
based on PLMs									
Harkous et al. (2020)	52.90	-	-	42.40	-	-	-	-	-
Kale (2020)	57.10	63.90	52.80	44.00	46.00	41.00	-	-	-
Radev et al. (2020)	45.89	52.86	37.85	40.00	42.00	37.00	-	-	-
$BART_{base}$	53.11	62.74	41.53	40.18	44.45	35.36	70.02	76.68	62.76
$BART_{large}$	54.72	63.45	43.97	42.23	45.49	38.61	72.29	77.57	66.53
$T5_{small}$	56.34	**65.05**	45.37	42.78	45.94	39.29	73.31	**78.46**	67.69
$T5_{base}$	59.17	64.64	52.55	43.19	**46.02**	41.49	74.82	78.40	70.92
$T5_{large}$	**59.70**	64.71	**53.67**	**44.18**	45.85	**42.26**	**75.40**	78.29	**72.25**

Table 2: Results on WebNLG. A, S and U stand for *all*, *seen*, and *unseen* partitions of the test set, respectively.

models for AMR. Following Wolf et al. (2019), we use the Adam optimizer (Kingma and Ba, 2015) with an initial learning rate of $3 \cdot 10^{-5}$. We employ a linearly decreasing learning rate schedule without warm-up. The batch and beam search sizes are chosen from {2,4,8} and {1,3,5}, respectively, based on the respective development set. Dev BLEU is used for model selection.

Following previous works, we evaluate the results with BLEU (Papineni et al., 2002), METEOR (Denkowski and Lavie, 2014), and chrF++ (Popović, 2015) metrics. We also use MoverScore (Zhao et al., 2019), BERTScore (Zhang et al., 2020), and BLEURT (Sellam et al., 2020) metrics, as they employ contextual and semantic knowledge and thus depend less on the surface symbols. Additionally, we perform a human evaluation (cf. §5.4) quantifying the fluency, semantic adequacy and meaning similarity of the generated texts.

5.1 Results on AMR-to-Text

Table 1 shows our results for the setting without additional pretraining, with additional self-supervised task-adaptive pretraining solely using the collected Gigaword sentences (LMA), and with additional supervised task adaptation (STA), before fine-tuning. We also report several recent results on the AMR test set. Mager et al. (2020) and Harkous et al. (2020) employ GPT-2 in their approaches. Note that GPT-2 only consists of a Transformer-based decoder.

Only considering approaches without task adaptation, $BART_{large}$ already achieves a considerable improvement of 5.77 BLEU and 3.98 METEOR scores over the previous state of the art. With a BLEU score of 45.80, $T5_{large}$ performs best. The other metrics follow similar trends. See Table 13 in Appendix for evaluation with more metrics. The strong performance of both BART and T5 in the AMR dataset suggests that PLMs can infer the AMR structure by a simple linear sequence of the graph, in contrast to GNN-based models that explicitly consider the graph structure using *message-passing* between adjacent nodes (Beck et al., 2018).

Task-specific Adaptation. LMA already brings some gains with T5 benefitting more than BART in most metrics. It still helps less than STA even though we only have automatically generated annotations. This suggests that the performance increases with STA do not only come from additional exposure to task-specific target texts and that the models learn how to handle graphs and the graph-text correspondence even with automatically generated AMRs. After STA, T5 achieves 49.72 BLEU points, the new state of the art for AMR-to-text generation. Interestingly, gains from STA with 2M over 200K are larger in BART than in T5, suggesting that large amounts of silver data may not be required for a good performance with T5.

In general, models pretrained on the STA setup converge faster than without task-specific adaptation. For example, $T5_{large}$ without additional pretraining converges after 5 epochs of fine-tuning whereas $T5_{large}$ with STA already converges after 2 epochs.

5.2 Results on WebNLG

Table 2 shows the results for the WebNLG test set. Neural pipeline models (Moryossef et al., 2019; Castro Ferreira et al., 2019) achieve strong performance in the *unseen* dataset. On the other

Model	BLEU	M	BT
Koncel et al. 2019	14.30	18.80	-
An (2019)	15.10	19.50	-
Schmitt et al. (2020)	17.33	21.43	-
Ribeiro et al. (2020)	18.01	22.23	-
$BART_{base}$	22.01	23.54	-13.02
$BART_{large}$	**23.65**	**25.19**	**-10.93**
$T5_{small}$	20.22	21.62	-24.10
$T5_{base}$	20.73	21.88	-21.03
$T5_{large}$	22.15	23.73	-13.96
with task-adaptive pretraining			
$BART_{large}$ + LMA	25.30	25.54	-08.79
$T5_{large}$ + LMA	22.92	24.40	-10.39
$BART_{large}$ + STA	***25.66***	***25.74***	***-08.97***
$T5_{large}$ + STA	23.69	24.92	-08.94

Table 3: Results on AGENDA test set. **Bold** (***Italic***) indicates best scores without (with) task-adaptive pretraining.

Model	AMR	
	F	MS
Mager et al. (2020)	5.69^{A}	5.08^{A}
Harkous et al. (2020)	5.78^{A}	5.47^{AB}
$T5_{large}$	6.55^{B}	6.44^{C}
$BART_{large}$	6.70^{B}	5.72^{BC}
Reference	5.91^{A}	-
Model	**WebNLG**	
	F	**SA**
Castro Ferreira et al. (2019)	5.52^{A}	4.77^{A}
Harkous et al. (2020)	5.74^{AB}	6.21^{B}
$T5_{large}$	6.71^{C}	6.63^{B}
$BART_{large}$	6.53^{C}	6.50^{B}
Reference	5.89^{B}	6.47^{B}

Table 4: Fluency (F), Meaning Similarity (MS) and Semantic Adequacy (SA) obtained in the human evaluation. Differences between models which have a letter in common are not statistically significant and were determined by pairwise Mann-Whitney tests with $p < 0.05$.

hand, fully end-to-end models (Ribeiro et al., 2020; Schmitt et al., 2020) have strong performance on the *seen* dataset and usually perform poorly in *unseen* data. Models that *explicitly encode the graph structure* (Ribeiro et al., 2020; Zhao et al., 2020a) achieve the best performance among approaches that do not employ PLMs. Note that T5 is also used in Kale (2020). Differences in our T5 setup include a modified model vocabulary, the use of beam search, the learning rate schedule and the prefix before the input graph. Our T5 approach achieves 59.70, 65.05 and 54.69 BLEU points on *all*, *seen* and *unseen* sets, the new state of the art.

We conjecture that the performance gap between *seen* and *unseen* sets stems from the advantage obtained by a model seeing examples of relation-text pairs during fine-tuning. For example, the relation *party* (political party) was never seen during training and the model is required to generate a text that verbalizes the tuple: ⟨*Abdul Taib Mahmud, party, Parti Bumiputera Sarawak*⟩. Interestingly, BART performs much worse than T5 on this benchmark, especially in the *unseen* partition with 9.7 BLEU points lower compared to T5.

For lack of a suitable data source (cf. §4), we did not explore our LMA or STA approaches for WebNLG. However, we additionally discuss cross-domain STA in Appendix B.

5.3 Results on AGENDA

Table 3 lists the results for the AGENDA test set. The models also show strong performance on this dataset. We believe that their capacity to generate fluent text helps when generating paper abstracts, even though they were not pretrained in the scientific domain. $BART_{large}$ shows an impressive performance with a BLEU score of 23.65, which is 5.6 points higher than the previous state of the art.

Task-specific Adaptation. On AGENDA, BART benefits more from our task-adaptive pretraining, achieving the new state of the art of 25.66 BLEU points, a further gain of 2 BLEU points compared to its performance without task adaptation. The improvements from task-adaptive pretraining are not as large as for AMR. We hypothesize that this is due to the fact that the graphs do not completely cover the target text (Koncel-Kedziorski et al., 2019), making this dataset more challenging. See Table 12 in Appendix for more automatic metrics.

5.4 Human Evaluation

To further assess the quality of the generated text, we conduct a human evaluation on AMR and WebNLG via crowd sourcing on Amazon Mechanical Turk.[9] Following previous works (Gardent et al., 2017; Castro Ferreira et al., 2019), we assess three quality criteria: (i) *Fluency* (i.e., does the text flow in a natural, easy-to-read manner?), for AMR and WebNLG; (ii) *Meaning Similarity* (i.e., how

[9]We exclude AGENDA because its texts are scientific in nature and annotators are not necessarily AI experts.

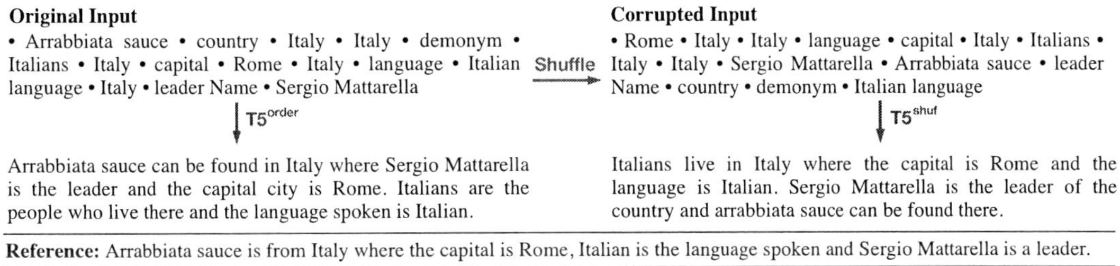

Figure 2: Example graph with 5 triples, from WebNLG dev linearized with the neutral separator tag, denoted •, (top left), its shuffled version (top right), texts generated with two fine-tuned versions of $T5_{small}$ and a gold reference (bottom). Note that T5 can produce a reasonable text even when the input triples are shuffled randomly.

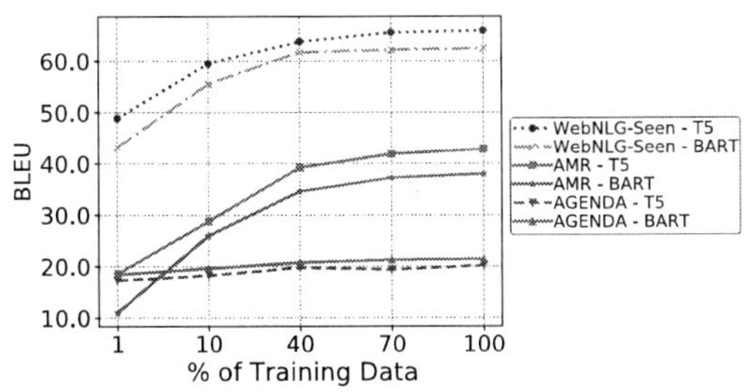

Figure 3: Performance of $BART_{base}$ and $T5_{base}$ in the dev set when experimenting with different amounts of training data.

close in meaning is the generated text to the reference sentence?) for AMR; (ii) *Semantic Adequacy* (i.e., does the text clearly express the data?) for WebNLG. We randomly select 100 generated texts of each model, which the annotators then rate on a 1-7 Likert scale. For each text, we collect scores from 3 annotators and average them.[10]

Table 4 shows the results. Our approaches improve the fluency, meaning similarity, and semantic adequacy on both datasets compared to other state-of-the-art approaches with statistically significant margins ($p<0.05$). Interestingly, the highest fluency improvement (+0.97) is on AMR, where our approach also has the largest BLEU improvement (+8.10) over Harkous et al. (2020). Finally, our models score higher than the references in fluency with statistically significant margins, highlighting their strong language generation abilities.[11]

5.5 Limiting the Training Data

In Figure 3, we investigate the PLMs' performance, measured with BLEU score, while varying (from 1% to 100%) the amount of training data used for fine-tuning. We find that, when fine-tuned with only 40% of the data, both BART and T5 already greatly improve the performance compared to using the entire training data in all three benchmarks. For example, BART fine-tuned on 40% of AMR training data achieves 91% of the BLEU score when fine-tuned on full data.

Note that in a low-resource scenario in AMR and WebNLG, T5 considerably outperforms BART. In particular, with only 1% of training examples, the difference between T5 and BART is 7.51 and 5.64 BLEU points for AMR and WebNLG, respectively. This suggests that T5 is more data efficient when adapting to the new task, likewise our findings in AMR-STA (cf. §5.1).

Model	AMR	WebNLG	AGENDA
$T5^{order}$	36.83	63.41	19.86
$T5^{shuf}$	15.56	61.54	19.08

Table 5: Impact (measured with BLEU) of using a bag of entities and relations (*shuf*) as input for $T5_{small}$.

6 Influence of the Graph Structure

We conduct further experiments to examine how much the PLMs consider the graph structure. To this end, we remove parentheses in AMRs and replace $\langle H \rangle$, $\langle R \rangle$, and $\langle T \rangle$ tokens with neutral separator tokens, denoted •, for KGs, such that the graph structure is only defined by the order of node and edge labels. If we shuffle such a sequence, the graph structure is thus completely obscured and the input effectively becomes a bag of node and edge labels. See Figure 2 for an example of both a correctly ordered and a shuffled triple sequence.

6.1 Quantitative Analysis

Table 5 shows the effect on T5's performance when its input contains correctly ordered triples ($T5^{order}$)

[10]Inter-annotator agreement for the three criteria ranged from 0.40 to 0.79, with an average Krippendorff's α of 0.56.

[11]Examples of fluent generations can be found in the Tables 15 and 16 in Appendix.

T/F	Input Fact	T5^{order}	T5^{shuf}
(1) S	• German language • Antwerp • Antwerp • Antwerp International Airport • Belgium • Belgium • Charles Michel • city Served • leader Name • Belgium • language • country	Antwerp International Airport serves the city of Antwerp. German is the language spoken in Belgium where Charles Michel is the leader.	Antwerp International Airport serves the city of Antwerp in Belgium where the German language is spoken and Charles Michel is the leader.
(2) T	• California • is Part Of • US • California • capital • Sacramento	California is part of the United States and its capital is Sacramento.	California is part of the United States and its capital is Sacramento.
(3) F	• US • is Part Of • California • California • capital • Sacramento	California's capital is Sacramento and the United States is part of California.	California is part of the United States and its capital is Sacramento.
(4) T	• Amarillo, Texas • is Part Of • United States	Amarillo, Texas is part of the United States.	Amarillo, Texas is part of the United States.
(5) F	• United States • is Part Of • Amarillo, Texas	Amarillo, Texas is part of the United States.	Amarillo, Texas is part of the United States.

Table 6: Example generations from shuffled (S), true (T), and corrupted (F) triple facts by T5$_{small}$, fine-tuned on correctly ordered triples (*order*) and randomly shuffled input (*shuf*).

vs. shuffled ones (T5^{shuf}) for both training and evaluation. We first observe that T5^{order} only has marginally lower performance (around 2-4%) with the neutral separators than with the $\langle H\rangle/\langle R\rangle/\langle T\rangle$ tags or parentheses.[12] We see that as evidence that the graph structure is similarly well captured by T5^{order}. Without the graph structure (T5^{shuf}), AMR-to-text performance drops significantly. Possible explanations of this drop are: (i) the relative ordering of the AMR graph is known to correlate with the target sentence order (Konstas et al., 2017); (ii) in contrast to WebNLG that contains common knowledge, the AMR dataset contains very specific sentences with higher surprisal;[13] (iii) AMRs are much more complex graph structures than the KGs from WebNLG and AGENDA.[14]

On the other hand, KG-to-text performance is not much lower, indicating that most of the PLMs' success in this task stems from their language modeling rather than their graph encoding capabilities. We hypothesize that a PLM can match the entities in a shuffled input with sentences mentioning these entities from the pretraining or fine-tuning phase. It has recently been argued that large PLMs can recall certain common knowledge facts from pretraining (Petroni et al., 2019; Bosselut et al., 2019).

6.2 Qualitative Analysis

The example in Figure 2 confirms our impression. T5^{shuf} produces a text with the same content as T5^{order} but does not need the correct triple structure to do so. Example (1) in Table 6 shows the output of both models with shuffled input. Interestingly, even T5^{order} produces a reasonable and truthful text. This suggests that previously seen facts serve as a strong guide during text generation, even for models that were fine-tuned with a clearly marked graph structure, suggesting that T5^{order} also relies more on language modeling than the graph structure. It does have more difficulties covering the whole input graph though. The fact that *Antwerp* is located in *Belgium* is missing from its output.

To further test our hypothesis that PLMs make use of previously seen facts during KG-to-text generation, we generate example true facts, corrupt them in a controlled setting, and feed them to both T5^{order} and T5^{shuf} to observe their output (examples (2)–(5) in Table 6). The model trained on correctly ordered input has learned a bit more to rely on the input graph structure. The false fact in example (3) with two triples is reliably transferred to the text by T5^{order} but not by T5^{shuf}, which silently corrects it. Also note that, in example (5), both models refuse to generate an incorrect fact. More examples can be found in Table 14 in the Appendix.

Our qualitative analysis illustrates that state-of-the-art PLMs, despite their fluency capacities (cf. §5.4), bear the risk of parroting back training sentences while ignoring the input structure. This issue can limit the practical usage of those models as, in many cases, it is important for a generation model to stay true to its input (Wiseman et al., 2017; Falke et al., 2019).

[12] See a more fine-grained comparison in Appendix C.

[13] Perplexities estimated on the dev sets of AMR and WebNLG datasets, with GPT-2 fine-tuned on the corresponding training set, are 20.9 and 7.8, respectively.

[14] In Appendix D, we present the graph properties of the datasets and discuss the differences.

7 Conclusion

We investigated two pretrained language models (PLMs) for graph-to-text generation and show that the pretraining strategies, language model adaptation (LMA) and supervised task adaptation (STA), can lead to notable improvements. Our approaches outperform the state of the art by a substantial margin on three graph-to-text benchmarks. Moreover, in a human evaluation our generated texts are perceived significantly more fluent than human references. Examining the influence of the graph structure on the text generation process, we find that PLMs may not always follow the graph structure and instead use memorized facts to guide the generation. A promising direction for future work is to explore ways of injecting a stronger graph-structural bias into PLMs, thus possibly leveraging their strong language modeling capabilities and keeping the output faithful to the input graph.

Acknowledgments

We thank our anonymous reviewers for their thoughtful feedback. Leonardo F. R. Ribeiro is supported by the German Research Foundation (DFG) as part of the Research Training Group "Adaptive Preparation of Information form Heterogeneous Sources" (AIPHES, GRK 1994/1) and as part of the DFG funded project UKP-SQuARE with the number GU 798/29-1. Martin Schmitt is supported by the BMBF as part of the project MLWin (01IS18050) and by the German Academic Scholarship Foundation (Studienstiftung des deutschen Volkes).

References

Waleed Ammar, Dirk Groeneveld, Chandra Bhagavatula, Iz Beltagy, Miles Crawford, Doug Downey, Jason Dunkelberger, Ahmed Elgohary, Sergey Feldman, Vu Ha, Rodney Kinney, Sebastian Kohlmeier, Kyle Lo, Tyler Murray, Hsu-Han Ooi, Matthew Peters, Joanna Power, Sam Skjonsberg, Lucy Wang, Chris Wilhelm, Zheng Yuan, Madeleine van Zuylen, and Oren Etzioni. 2018. Construction of the literature graph in semantic scholar. In *Proceedings of the 2018 Conference of the North American Chapter of the Association for Computational Linguistics: Human Language Technologies, Volume 3 (Industry Papers)*, pages 84–91, New Orleans - Louisiana. Association for Computational Linguistics.

Bang An. 2019. Repulsive bayesian sampling for diversified attention modeling. In *4th workshop on Bayesian Deep Learning (NeurIPS 2019)*.

Sören Auer, Christian Bizer, Georgi Kobilarov, Jens Lehmann, Richard Cyganiak, and Zachary Ives. 2007. Dbpedia: A nucleus for a web of open data. In *Proceedings of the 6th International The Semantic Web and 2nd Asian Conference on Asian Semantic Web Conference*, ISWC'07/ASWC'07, page 722–735, Berlin, Heidelberg. Springer-Verlag.

Xuefeng Bai, Yulong Chen, Linfeng Song, and Yue Zhang. 2021. Semantic representation for dialogue modeling. In *Proceedings of the 59th Annual Meeting of the Association for Computational Linguistics and the 11th International Joint Conference on Natural Language Processing (Volume 1: Long Papers)*, pages 4430–4445, Online. Association for Computational Linguistics.

Laura Banarescu, Claire Bonial, Shu Cai, Madalina Georgescu, Kira Griffitt, Ulf Hermjakob, Kevin Knight, Philipp Koehn, Martha Palmer, and Nathan Schneider. 2013. Abstract Meaning Representation for sembanking. In *Proceedings of the 7th Linguistic Annotation Workshop and Interoperability with Discourse*, pages 178–186, Sofia, Bulgaria. Association for Computational Linguistics.

Daniel Beck, Gholamreza Haffari, and Trevor Cohn. 2018. Graph-to-sequence learning using gated graph neural networks. In *Proceedings of the 56th Annual Meeting of the Association for Computational Linguistics (Volume 1: Long Papers)*, pages 273–283, Melbourne, Australia. Association for Computational Linguistics.

Anja Belz, Michael White, Dominic Espinosa, Eric Kow, Deirdre Hogan, and Amanda Stent. 2011. The first surface realisation shared task: Overview and evaluation results. In *Proceedings of the 13th European Workshop on Natural Language Generation*, pages 217–226, Nancy, France. Association for Computational Linguistics.

Claire Bonial, Lucia Donatelli, Mitchell Abrams, Stephanie M. Lukin, Stephen Tratz, Matthew Marge, Ron Artstein, David Traum, and Clare Voss. 2020. Dialogue-AMR: Abstract Meaning Representation for dialogue. In *Proceedings of the 12th Language Resources and Evaluation Conference*, pages 684–695, Marseille, France. European Language Resources Association.

Antoine Bosselut, Hannah Rashkin, Maarten Sap, Chaitanya Malaviya, Asli Celikyilmaz, and Yejin Choi. 2019. COMET: Commonsense transformers for automatic knowledge graph construction. In *Proceedings of the 57th Annual Meeting of the Association for Computational Linguistics*, pages 4762–4779, Florence, Italy. Association for Computational Linguistics.

Deng Cai and Wai Lam. 2020a. AMR parsing via graph-sequence iterative inference. In *Proceedings of the 58th Annual Meeting of the Association for Computational Linguistics*, pages 1290–1301, Online. Association for Computational Linguistics.

Deng Cai and Wai Lam. 2020b. Graph transformer for graph-to-sequence learning. In *The Thirty-Fourth AAAI Conference on Artificial Intelligence, AAAI 2020, The Thirty-Second Innovative Applications of Artificial Intelligence Conference, IAAI 2020, The Tenth AAAI Symposium on Educational Advances in Artificial Intelligence, EAAI 2020, New York, NY, USA, February 7-12, 2020*, pages 7464–7471. AAAI Press.

Thiago Castro Ferreira, Chris van der Lee, Emiel van Miltenburg, and Emiel Krahmer. 2019. Neural data-to-text generation: A comparison between pipeline and end-to-end architectures. In *Proceedings of the 2019 Conference on Empirical Methods in Natural Language Processing and the 9th International Joint Conference on Natural Language Processing (EMNLP-IJCNLP)*, pages 552–562, Hong Kong, China. Association for Computational Linguistics.

Jianpeng Cheng, Devang Agrawal, Héctor Martínez Alonso, Shruti Bhargava, Joris Driesen, Federico Flego, Dain Kaplan, Dimitri Kartsaklis, Lin Li, Dhivya Piraviperumal, Jason D. Williams, Hong Yu, Diarmuid Ó Séaghdha, and Anders Johannsen. 2020. Conversational semantic parsing for dialog state tracking. In *Proceedings of the 2020 Conference on Empirical Methods in Natural Language Processing (EMNLP)*, pages 8107–8117, Online. Association for Computational Linguistics.

Marco Damonte and Shay B. Cohen. 2019. Structural neural encoders for AMR-to-text generation. In *Proceedings of the 2019 Conference of the North American Chapter of the Association for Computational Linguistics: Human Language Technologies, Volume 1 (Long and Short Papers)*, pages 3649–3658, Minneapolis, Minnesota. Association for Computational Linguistics.

Michael Denkowski and Alon Lavie. 2014. Meteor universal: Language specific translation evaluation for any target language. In *Proceedings of the Ninth Workshop on Statistical Machine Translation*, pages 376–380, Baltimore, Maryland, USA. Association for Computational Linguistics.

Jacob Devlin, Ming-Wei Chang, Kenton Lee, and Kristina Toutanova. 2019. BERT: Pre-training of deep bidirectional transformers for language understanding. In *Proceedings of the 2019 Conference of the North American Chapter of the Association for Computational Linguistics: Human Language Technologies, Volume 1 (Long and Short Papers)*, pages 4171–4186, Minneapolis, Minnesota. Association for Computational Linguistics.

Nan Duan, Duyu Tang, Peng Chen, and Ming Zhou. 2017. Question generation for question answering. In *Proceedings of the 2017 Conference on Empirical Methods in Natural Language Processing*, pages 866–874, Copenhagen, Denmark. Association for Computational Linguistics.

Tobias Falke, Leonardo F. R. Ribeiro, Prasetya Ajie Utama, Ido Dagan, and Iryna Gurevych. 2019. Ranking generated summaries by correctness: An interesting but challenging application for natural language inference. In *Proceedings of the 57th Annual Meeting of the Association for Computational Linguistics*, pages 2214–2220, Florence, Italy. Association for Computational Linguistics.

Claire Gardent, Anastasia Shimorina, Shashi Narayan, and Laura Perez-Beltrachini. 2017. The WebNLG challenge: Generating text from RDF data. In *Proceedings of the 10th International Conference on Natural Language Generation*, pages 124–133, Santiago de Compostela, Spain. Association for Computational Linguistics.

Albert Gatt and Emiel Krahmer. 2018. Survey of the state of the art in natural language generation: Core tasks, applications and evaluation. *Journal of Artificial Intelligence Research*, 61(1):65–170.

Zhijiang Guo, Yan Zhang, Zhiyang Teng, and Wei Lu. 2019. Densely connected graph convolutional networks for graph-to-sequence learning. *Transactions of the Association for Computational Linguistics*, 7:297–312.

Suchin Gururangan, Ana Marasović, Swabha Swayamdipta, Kyle Lo, Iz Beltagy, Doug Downey, and Noah A. Smith. 2020. Don't stop pretraining: Adapt language models to domains and tasks. In *Proceedings of the 58th Annual Meeting of the Association for Computational Linguistics*, pages 8342–8360, Online. Association for Computational Linguistics.

Hamza Harkous, Isabel Groves, and Amir Saffari. 2020. Have your text and use it too! end-to-end neural data-to-text generation with semantic fidelity. In *Proceedings of the 28th International Conference on Computational Linguistics*, pages 2410–2424, Barcelona, Spain (Online). International Committee on Computational Linguistics.

Alexander Miserlis Hoyle, Ana Marasović, and Noah A. Smith. 2021. Promoting graph awareness in linearized graph-to-text generation. In *Findings of the Association for Computational Linguistics: ACL-IJCNLP 2021*, pages 944–956, Online. Association for Computational Linguistics.

Mihir Kale. 2020. Text-to-text pre-training for data-to-text tasks. *arXiv e-prints*.

Diederik P. Kingma and Jimmy Ba. 2015. Adam: A method for stochastic optimization. In *3rd International Conference on Learning Representations, ICLR 2015, San Diego, CA, USA, May 7-9, 2015, Conference Track Proceedings*.

Thomas N. Kipf and Max Welling. 2017. Semi-Supervised Classification with Graph Convolutional Networks. In *Proceedings of the 5th International Conference on Learning Representations*, ICLR 2017.

Rik Koncel-Kedziorski, Dhanush Bekal, Yi Luan, Mirella Lapata, and Hannaneh Hajishirzi. 2019. Text Generation from Knowledge Graphs with Graph Transformers. In *Proceedings of the 2019 Conference of the North American Chapter of the Association for Computational Linguistics: Human Language Technologies, Volume 1 (Long and Short Papers)*, pages 2284–2293, Minneapolis, Minnesota. Association for Computational Linguistics.

Ioannis Konstas, Srinivasan Iyer, Mark Yatskar, Yejin Choi, and Luke Zettlemoyer. 2017. Neural amr: Sequence-to-sequence models for parsing and generation. In *Proceedings of the 55th Annual Meeting of the Association for Computational Linguistics (Volume 1: Long Papers)*, pages 146–157, Vancouver, Canada. Association for Computational Linguistics.

Mike Lewis, Yinhan Liu, Naman Goyal, Marjan Ghazvininejad, Abdelrahman Mohamed, Omer Levy, Veselin Stoyanov, and Luke Zettlemoyer. 2020. BART: Denoising sequence-to-sequence pretraining for natural language generation, translation, and comprehension. In *Proceedings of the 58th Annual Meeting of the Association for Computational Linguistics*, pages 7871–7880, Online. Association for Computational Linguistics.

Yinhan Liu, Myle Ott, Naman Goyal, Jingfei Du, Mandar Joshi, Danqi Chen, Omer Levy, Mike Lewis, Luke Zettlemoyer, and Veselin Stoyanov. 2020. Roberta: A robustly optimized bert pretraining approach. *arXiv e-prints*.

Yi Luan, Luheng He, Mari Ostendorf, and Hannaneh Hajishirzi. 2018. Multi-task identification of entities, relations, and coreference for scientific knowledge graph construction. In *Proceedings of the 2018 Conference on Empirical Methods in Natural Language Processing*, pages 3219–3232, Brussels, Belgium. Association for Computational Linguistics.

Manuel Mager, Ramón Fernandez Astudillo, Tahira Naseem, Md Arafat Sultan, Young-Suk Lee, Radu Florian, and Salim Roukos. 2020. GPT-too: A language-model-first approach for AMR-to-text generation. In *Proceedings of the 58th Annual Meeting of the Association for Computational Linguistics*, pages 1846–1852, Online. Association for Computational Linguistics.

Diego Marcheggiani and Laura Perez Beltrachini. 2018. Deep graph convolutional encoders for structured data to text generation. In *Proceedings of the 11th International Conference on Natural Language Generation*, pages 1–9, Tilburg University, The Netherlands. Association for Computational Linguistics.

Seungwhan Moon, Pararth Shah, Anuj Kumar, and Rajen Subba. 2019. OpenDialKG: Explainable conversational reasoning with attention-based walks over knowledge graphs. In *Proceedings of the 57th Annual Meeting of the Association for Computational Linguistics*, pages 845–854, Florence, Italy. Association for Computational Linguistics.

Amit Moryossef, Yoav Goldberg, and Ido Dagan. 2019. Step-by-step: Separating planning from realization in neural data-to-text generation. In *Proceedings of the 2019 Conference of the North American Chapter of the Association for Computational Linguistics: Human Language Technologies, Volume 1 (Long and Short Papers)*, pages 2267–2277, Minneapolis, Minnesota. Association for Computational Linguistics.

Kishore Papineni, Salim Roukos, Todd Ward, and Wei-Jing Zhu. 2002. Bleu: A method for automatic evaluation of machine translation. In *Proceedings of the 40th Annual Meeting on Association for Computational Linguistics*, ACL '02, pages 311–318, Stroudsburg, PA, USA. Association for Computational Linguistics.

Fabio Petroni, Tim Rocktäschel, Sebastian Riedel, Patrick Lewis, Anton Bakhtin, Yuxiang Wu, and Alexander Miller. 2019. Language models as knowledge bases? In *Proceedings of the 2019 Conference on Empirical Methods in Natural Language Processing and the 9th International Joint Conference on Natural Language Processing (EMNLP-IJCNLP)*, pages 2463–2473, Hong Kong, China. Association for Computational Linguistics.

Maja Popović. 2015. chrF: character n-gram F-score for automatic MT evaluation. In *Proceedings of the Tenth Workshop on Statistical Machine Translation*, pages 392–395, Lisbon, Portugal. Association for Computational Linguistics.

Dragomir Radev, Rui Zhang, Amrit Rau, Abhinand Sivaprasad, Chiachun Hsieh, Nazneen Fatema Rajani, Xiangru Tang, Aadit Vyas, Neha Verma, Pranav Krishna, Yangxiaokang Liu, Nadia Irwanto, Jessica Pan, Faiaz Rahman, Ahmad Zaidi, Murori Mutuma, Yasin Tarabar, Ankit Gupta, Tao Yu, Yi Chern Tan, Xi Victoria Lin, Caiming Xiong, and Richard Socher. 2020. Dart: Open-domain structured data record to text generation. *arXiv e-prints*.

Alec Radford, Jeffrey Wu, Rewon Child, David Luan, Dario Amodei, and Ilya Sutskever. 2019. Language models are unsupervised multitask learners. *arXiv e-prints*.

Colin Raffel, Noam Shazeer, Adam Roberts, Katherine Lee, Sharan Narang, Michael Matena, Yanqi Zhou, Wei Li, and Peter J. Liu. 2019. Exploring the limits of transfer learning with a unified text-to-text transformer. *arXiv e-prints*.

Leonardo F. R. Ribeiro, Claire Gardent, and Iryna Gurevych. 2019. Enhancing AMR-to-text generation with dual graph representations. In *Proceedings of the 2019 Conference on Empirical Methods in Natural Language Processing and the 9th International Joint Conference on Natural Language Processing (EMNLP-IJCNLP)*, pages 3183–3194, Hong Kong, China. Association for Computational Linguistics.

Leonardo F. R. Ribeiro, Jonas Pfeiffer, Yue Zhang, and Iryna Gurevych. 2021a. Smelting gold and silver for improved multilingual amr-to-text generation. In *Proceedings of the 2021 Conference on Empirical Methods in Natural Language Processing, EMNLP 2021, Punta Cana, November 7-11, 2021.*

Leonardo F. R. Ribeiro, Yue Zhang, Claire Gardent, and Iryna Gurevych. 2020. Modeling global and local node contexts for text generation from knowledge graphs. *Transactions of the Association for Computational Linguistics*, 8:589–604.

Leonardo F. R. Ribeiro, Yue Zhang, and Iryna Gurevych. 2021b. Structural adapters in pretrained language models for amr-to-text generation. In *Proceedings of the 2021 Conference on Empirical Methods in Natural Language Processing, EMNLP 2021, Punta Cana, November 7-11, 2021.*

Martin Schmitt, Leonardo F. R. Ribeiro, Philipp Dufter, Iryna Gurevych, and Hinrich Schütze. 2021. Modeling graph structure via relative position for text generation from knowledge graphs. In *Proceedings of the Fifteenth Workshop on Graph-Based Methods for Natural Language Processing (TextGraphs-15)*, pages 10–21, Mexico City, Mexico. Association for Computational Linguistics.

Martin Schmitt, Leonardo F. R. Ribeiro, Philipp Dufter, Iryna Gurevych, and Hinrich Schütze. 2020. Modeling graph structure via relative position for better text generation from knowledge graphs. *arXiv e-prints*.

Thibault Sellam, Dipanjan Das, and Ankur Parikh. 2020. BLEURT: Learning robust metrics for text generation. In *Proceedings of the 58th Annual Meeting of the Association for Computational Linguistics*, pages 7881–7892, Online. Association for Computational Linguistics.

Linfeng Song, Yue Zhang, Zhiguo Wang, and Daniel Gildea. 2018. A graph-to-sequence model for AMR-to-text generation. In *Proceedings of the 56th Annual Meeting of the Association for Computational Linguistics (Volume 1: Long Papers)*, pages 1616–1626, Melbourne, Australia. Association for Computational Linguistics.

Mihai Surdeanu, Richard Johansson, Adam Meyers, Lluís Màrquez, and Joakim Nivre. 2008. The CoNLL 2008 shared task on joint parsing of syntactic and semantic dependencies. In *CoNLL 2008: Proceedings of the Twelfth Conference on Computational Natural Language Learning*, pages 159–177, Manchester, England. Coling 2008 Organizing Committee.

Bayu Distiawan Trisedya, Jianzhong Qi, Rui Zhang, and Wei Wang. 2018. GTR-LSTM: A triple encoder for sentence generation from RDF data. In *Proceedings of the 56th Annual Meeting of the Association for Computational Linguistics (Volume 1: Long Papers)*, pages 1627–1637, Melbourne, Australia. Association for Computational Linguistics.

Ashish Vaswani, Noam Shazeer, Niki Parmar, Jakob Uszkoreit, Llion Jones, Aidan N Gomez, Ł ukasz Kaiser, and Illia Polosukhin. 2017. Attention is all you need. In I. Guyon, U. V. Luxburg, S. Bengio, H. Wallach, R. Fergus, S. Vishwanathan, and R. Garnett, editors, *Advances in Neural Information Processing Systems 30*, pages 5998–6008. Curran Associates, Inc.

Pavlos Vougiouklis, Hady Elsahar, Lucie-Aimée Kaffee, Christophe Gravier, Frédérique Laforest, Jonathon Hare, and Elena Simperl. 2018. Neural wikipedian: Generating textual summaries from knowledge base triples. *Journal of Web Semantics*, 52-53:1 – 15.

David Wadden, Ulme Wennberg, Yi Luan, and Hannaneh Hajishirzi. 2019. Entity, relation, and event extraction with contextualized span representations. In *Proceedings of the 2019 Conference on Empirical Methods in Natural Language Processing and the 9th International Joint Conference on Natural Language Processing (EMNLP-IJCNLP)*, pages 5784–5789, Hong Kong, China. Association for Computational Linguistics.

Tianming Wang, Xiaojun Wan, and Hanqi Jin. 2020. Amr-to-text generation with graph transformer. *Transactions of the Association for Computational Linguistics*, 8:19–33.

Sam Wiseman, Stuart Shieber, and Alexander Rush. 2017. Challenges in data-to-document generation. In *Proceedings of the 2017 Conference on Empirical Methods in Natural Language Processing*, pages 2253–2263, Copenhagen, Denmark. Association for Computational Linguistics.

Thomas Wolf, Lysandre Debut, Victor Sanh, Julien Chaumond, Clement Delangue, Anthony Moi, Pierric Cistac, Tim Rault, Rémi Louf, Morgan Funtowicz, and Jamie Brew. 2019. Huggingface's transformers: State-of-the-art natural language processing.

Zhilin Yang, Zihang Dai, Yiming Yang, Jaime Carbonell, Russ R Salakhutdinov, and Quoc V Le. 2019a. Xlnet: Generalized autoregressive pretraining for language understanding. In *Advances in Neural Information Processing Systems*, volume 32, pages 5753–5763. Curran Associates, Inc.

Zhilin Yang, Zihang Dai, Yiming Yang, Jaime Carbonell, Russ R Salakhutdinov, and Quoc V Le. 2019b. Xlnet: Generalized autoregressive pretraining for language understanding. In H. Wallach, H. Larochelle, A. Beygelzimer, F. d'Alché-Buc, E. Fox, and R. Garnett, editors, *Advances in Neural Information Processing Systems 32*, pages 5753–5763. Curran Associates, Inc.

Shaowei Yao, Tianming Wang, and Xiaojun Wan. 2020. Heterogeneous graph transformer for graph-to-sequence learning. In *Proceedings of the 58th Annual Meeting of the Association for Computational*

Linguistics, pages 7145–7154, Online. Association for Computational Linguistics.

Tao Yu, Rui Zhang, Heyang Er, Suyi Li, Eric Xue, Bo Pang, Xi Victoria Lin, Yi Chern Tan, Tianze Shi, Zihan Li, Youxuan Jiang, Michihiro Yasunaga, Sungrok Shim, Tao Chen, Alexander Fabbri, Zifan Li, Luyao Chen, Yuwen Zhang, Shreya Dixit, Vincent Zhang, Caiming Xiong, Richard Socher, Walter Lasecki, and Dragomir Radev. 2019. CoSQL: A conversational text-to-SQL challenge towards cross-domain natural language interfaces to databases. In *Proceedings of the 2019 Conference on Empirical Methods in Natural Language Processing and the 9th International Joint Conference on Natural Language Processing (EMNLP-IJCNLP)*, pages 1962–1979, Hong Kong, China. Association for Computational Linguistics.

Tianyi Zhang, Varsha Kishore, Felix Wu, Kilian Q. Weinberger, and Yoav Artzi. 2020. Bertscore: Evaluating text generation with bert. In *International Conference on Learning Representations*.

Chao Zhao, Marilyn Walker, and Snigdha Chaturvedi. 2020a. Bridging the structural gap between encoding and decoding for data-to-text generation. In *Proceedings of the 58th Annual Meeting of the Association for Computational Linguistics*, pages 2481–2491, Online. Association for Computational Linguistics.

Wei Zhao, Maxime Peyrard, Fei Liu, Yang Gao, Christian M. Meyer, and Steffen Eger. 2019. MoverScore: Text generation evaluating with contextualized embeddings and earth mover distance. In *Proceedings of the 2019 Conference on Empirical Methods in Natural Language Processing and the 9th International Joint Conference on Natural Language Processing (EMNLP-IJCNLP)*, pages 563–578, Hong Kong, China. Association for Computational Linguistics.

Yanbin Zhao, Lu Chen, Zhi Chen, Ruisheng Cao, Su Zhu, and Kai Yu. 2020b. Line graph enhanced AMR-to-text generation with mix-order graph attention networks. In *Proceedings of the 58th Annual Meeting of the Association for Computational Linguistics*, pages 732–741, Online. Association for Computational Linguistics.

Jie Zhu, Junhui Li, Muhua Zhu, Longhua Qian, Min Zhang, and Guodong Zhou. 2019. Modeling graph structure in transformer for better AMR-to-text generation. In *Proceedings of the 2019 Conference on Empirical Methods in Natural Language Processing and the 9th International Joint Conference on Natural Language Processing (EMNLP-IJCNLP)*, pages 5459–5468, Hong Kong, China. Association for Computational Linguistics.

Appendices

In this supplementary material, we provide: (i) additional information about the data used in the experiments, and (ii) results that we could not fit into the main body of the paper.

A AMR Input Representation

We test three variants for the representation of the input AMR graph. Following previous work (Konstas et al., 2017; Mager et al., 2020), we evaluate (i) only node representation, where the edge information is removed from the linearization; (ii) depth-first search (DFS) through the graph and the (iii) PENMAN representation. An example for each representation is illustrated below:

only nodes
```
value interrogative commodity
true
```

DFS
```
value :mode interrogative
:ARG1 commodity :ARG1-of
true
```

PENMAN
```
( value :mode interrogative
:ARG1 ( commodity ) :ARG1-of
( true ) )
```

In this experiment we employ $T5_{small}$. Table 7 shows the results on the AMR development set. The PENMAN representation leads to best results. Therefore, this representation is used in the rest of the experiments.

Input	**BLEU**
only nodes	28.22
DFS	34.94
PENMAN	38.27

Table 7: Results on the AMR dev set using $T5_{small}$ for different AMR linearizations.

B Cross-domain Adaptation

For a given task, it is not always possible to collect closely related data – as we saw, e.g., for WebNLG. We therefore report STA in a cross-domain setting for the different KG-to-text benchmarks. Table 8 shows the results using $BART_{base}$ and $T5_{base}$. While the texts in KGAIA and AGENDA share thc domain of scientific abstracts, texts in WebNLG are more general. Also note that WebNLG graphs do not share any relations with the other KGs. For $BART_{base}$, STA increases the performance in the cross-domain setting in most of the cases. For $T5_{base}$, STA in KGAIA improves the performance on WebNLG.

In general, we find that exploring additional adaptive pretraining for graph-to-text generation can improve the performance even if the data do not come from the same domain.

STA on	**Fine-tuned & Evaluated on**	
	WebNLG-*Seen*	AGENDA
	$BART_{base}$	
None	58.71	22.01
KGAIA	63.20	23.48
WebNLG	-	21.98
AGENDA	61.25	-
	$T5_{base}$	
None	62.93	20.73
KGAIA	63.19	22.44
WebNLG	-	20.27
AGENDA	62.75	-

Table 8: Effect (measured with BLEU score) of cross-domain STA.

C Input Graph Size

Figure 4 visualizes $T5_{small}$'s performance with respect to the number of input graph triples in WebNLG dataset. We observe that $T5^{order}$ and $T5^{shuf}$ perform similarly for inputs with only one triple but that the gap between the models increases with larger graphs. While it is obviously more difficult to reconstruct a larger graph than a smaller one, this also suggests that the graph structure is more taken into account for graphs with more than 2 triples. For the *unseen* setting, the performance gap for these graphs is even larger, suggesting that the PLM can make more use of the graph structure when it has to.

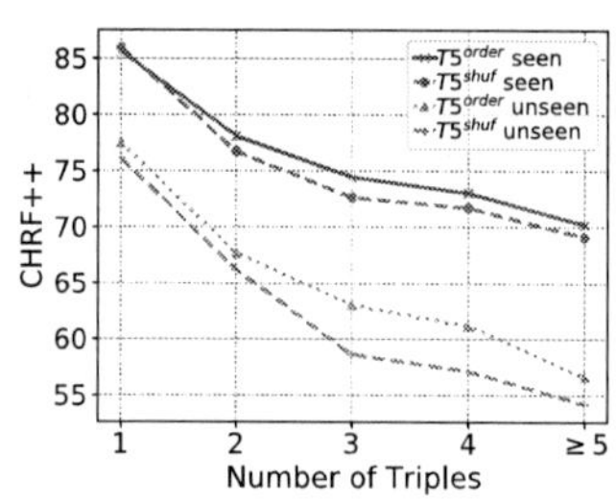

Figure 4: chrF++ scores with respect to the number of triples for WebNLG *seen* and *unseen* test sets.

D Graph Statistics

In Table 9, we present the graph properties of the three datasets. All statistics are calculated using

	AMR			WebNLG			AGENDA		
min, avg and max number of nodes	2	28.6	335	2	6.8	15	2	10.5	80
min, avg and max node degrees	1	2.2	21	1	1.7	7	1	1.67	15
min, avg and max number of edges	1	32.3	554	1	5.9	14	1	8.8	124
min, avg and max graph diameter	1	12.2	40	1	4.1	10	1	3.1	20
min, avg and max shortest path length	0	7.49	40	0	2.4	10	0	2.3	20

Table 9: Graph statistics of AMR, WebNLG and AGENDA datasets. The values are calculated using the training data. Note that AMR graphs contain a more complex structure than WebNLG and AGENDA graphs.

the Levi transformation (Beck et al., 2018) of the undirected version of the graphs, where edges are also considered nodes in the graph. WebNLG and AGENDA datasets contain disconnected graphs, and we use the largest subgraph to calculate the diameter. Note that AMR graphs have a much more complex structure: (i) they have more nodes and edges than WebNLG and AGENDA graphs; (ii) the average graph diameter and the average shortest path between nodes in AMRs are at least three times larger than in WebNLG and AGENDA graphs; (iii) nodes in AMRs have larger degrees than nodes in WebNLG and AGENDA graphs.

	AMR17	WebNLG	AGENDA
#Train	36,521	18,102	38,720
#Dev	1,368	872	1,000
#Test	1,371	1,862	1,000
#Relations	155	373	7
Avg #Tokens	16.1	31.5	157.9

Table 10: Statistics for the graph-to-text benchmarks.

	Title	Abstract	KG
Vocab	48K	173K	113K
Tokens	2.1M	31.7M	9.6M
Entities	-	-	3.7M
Avg Length	11.1	167.1	-
Avg #Nodes	-	-	19.9
Avg #Edges	-	-	9.4

Table 11: Statistics for the KGAIA dataset.

Model	chrF++	BS (F1)	MS
Schmitt et al. (2020)	44.53	-	-
Ribeiro et al. (2020)	46.37	-	-
$\text{BART}_{\text{base}}$	48.02	89.36	34.33
$\text{BART}_{\text{large}}$	**50.44**	88.74	32.24
T5_{small}	44.91	88.56	30.25
T5_{base}	48.14	88.81	31.33
T5_{large}	48.14	**89.60**	**35.23**
with task-adaptive pretraining			
$\text{BART}_{\text{large}}$ + LMA	51.33	89.12	33.42
T5_{large} + LMA	49.37	89.75	36.13
$\text{BART}_{\text{large}}$ + STA	***51.63***	89.27	34.28
T5_{large} + STA	50.27	***89.93***	***36.86***

Table 12: Results of the chrF++, BertScore (BS) and MoverScore (MS) scores for AGENDA test set. **Bold** (***Italic***) indicates best scores without (with) task-adaptive pretraining.

Model	chrF++	BS (F1)	MS
Guo et al. (2019)	57.30	-	-
Zhu et al. (2019)	64.05	-	-
Cai and Lam (2020b)	59.40	-	-
Wang et al. (2020)	65.80	-	-
Yao et al. (2020)	65.60	-	-
based on PLMs			
Mager et al. (2020)	63.89	-	-
$\text{BART}_{\text{base}}$	66.65	95.22	60.78
$\text{BART}_{\text{large}}$	71.06	96.08	65.74
T5_{small}	68.78	95.62	63.70
T5_{base}	70.81	95.99	65.63
T5_{large}	**72.57**	**96.27**	**67.37**
with task-adaptive pretraining			
$\text{BART}_{\text{large}}$ + LMA	71.14	95.94	64.75
T5_{large} + LMA	72.83	96.32	67.44
$\text{BART}_{\text{large}}$ + STA (200K)	72.26	96.21	66.75
$\text{BART}_{\text{large}}$ + STA (2M)	73.58	96.43	68.14
T5_{large} + STA (200K)	74.09	96.51	68.86
T5_{large} + STA (2M)	***74.79***	***96.59***	***69.53***

Table 13: Results of the chrF++, BertScore (BS) and MoverScore (MS) scores for the LDC2017T10 test set. **Bold** (***Italic***) indicates the best score without (with) task-adaptive pretraining.

T/F	Input Facts	$T5^{order}$	$T5^{shuf}$
(1) S	• capital • leader Name • London • Pound sterling • United Kingdom • leader Name • United Kingdom • Elizabeth II • United Kingdom • Boris Johnson • London • currency	The capital city is London, the currency is the Pound sterling and the leader is Elizabeth II. Boris Johnson is also a leader in the UK.	The capital of the United Kingdom is London, the currency is the Pound sterling and the country is lead by Elizabeth II and Boris Johnson.
(2) T	• Germany • capital • Berlin	Berlin is the capital of Germany.	Berlin is the capital of Germany.
(3) F	• Berlin • capital • Germany	Berlin's capital is Germany.	Berlin is the capital of Germany.
(4) F	• Leinster • is Part Of • Dublin	Leinster is part of Dublin.	Leinster is part of Dublin.
(5) F	• Rome • capital • Italy	Rome's capital is Italy.	Rome is the capital of Italy.
(6) T	• Italy • capital • Rome	Italy's capital is Rome.	Rome is the capital of Italy.
(7) T	• Texas • capital • Austin • Andrews County Airport • location • Texas	Austin is the capital of Texas where Andrews County Airport is located.	Austin is the capital of Texas where Andrews County Airport is located.
(8) F	• Austin • capital • Texas • Andrews County Airport • location • Texas	The capital of Austin is Texas and Andrews County Airport is located in Texas.	Andrews County Airport is located in Texas where Austin is the capital.

Table 14: Example generations from shuffled (S), true (T), and corrupted (F) triple facts by $T5_{small}$, fine-tuned on correctly ordered triples (*order*) and randomly shuffled input (*shuf*).

D	Model	Examples
AMR	Reference	I had to deal with verbal abuse from my dad for a long 8 years before I came to uni and honestly, the only reason why I'm here is because it was the only way out.
	T5	I had to deal with 8 years of verbal abuse from my dad before coming to university and honestly the only reason I'm here is because it's the only way out.
	BART	I had to deal with my dad's verbal abuse for 8 years long before coming to uni and honestly the only reason I'm here is because it's the only way out.
	Mager et al. (2020)	i've had to deal with verbal abuse from my dad for 8 years (before i came to uni i was honestly the only reason i was here) and it's only because of the way it is.
WebNLG	Reference	Aaron Turner is an electric guitar player who has played with the black metal band Twilight and with Old Man Gloom. Death metal is a musical fusion of black metal.
	T5	Aaron Turner plays the electric guitar and is associated with the band Twilight. He is also a member of the Old Man Gloom band. Black metal and death metal are both genres of music.
	BART	The black metal genre is a variation of the death metal genre. It is also where the band, Twilight, and the alternative rock band, Old Man Gloom, are from. One of the members of the band is Aaron Turner, who plays the electric guitar.
	Harkous et al. (2020)	Aaron Turner, a.k.a. Black Metal, is a member of the Twilight (band) and Old Man Gloom bands. He also plays electric guitar and has a strong connection with the Death Metal genre.

Table 15: Examples of text generated by the different models. D refers to the dataset.

Model	Examples
Reference	in this paper, a new array signal processing technique by using particle swarm optimization is proposed to identify multipath channel parameters. the proposed array signal processing technique provides estimates to the channel parameters by finding a global minimum of an optimization problem. since the optimization problem is formulated in the cross-ambiguity function (caf) domain of the transmitted signal and the received array outputs, the proposed array signal processing technique is called as particle swarm optimization. the performance of the particle swarm optimization is compared with the space alternating generalized expectation maximization technique and with another recently proposed pso based technique for various snr values. simulation results indicate the superior performance of the pso based technique over mentioned techniques for all snr values.
T5	this paper, we propose an array signal processing technique based on particle swarm optimization to estimate the multipath channel parameters from the received and the transmitted signal in a cross-ambiguity domain. the proposed array signal processing technique is formulated as an optimization problem and particle swarm optimization is compared with the generalized expectation maximization technique. simulation results show that the proposed particle swarm optimization outperforms the pso based technique for a wide range of snr values. in addition, the proposed particle swarm optimization is computationally more efficient than the gem based technique for small snr values.
BART	in this paper, a new array signal processing technique based on particle swarm optimization is proposed. the proposed array signal processing technique is used to estimate the multipath channel parameters from the transmitted signal. the proposed array signal processing technique is formulated as an optimization problem in the cross-ambiguity domain. the particle swarm optimization is compared with the generalized expectation maximization technique. simulation results show that the proposed particle swarm optimization outperforms the pso based technique for all snr values. furthermore, the proposed particle swarm optimization is able to estimate the channel parameters more accurately than the generalized expectation maximization technique.
Ribeiro et al. (2020)	in this paper, a novel array signal processing technique based on particle swarm optimization is proposed to estimate the multipath channel parameters from the transmitted signal. the proposed array signal processing technique uses particle swarm optimization to estimate the multipath channel parameters. the proposed array signal processing technique is formulated as an optimization problem. simulation results show that the proposed array signal processing technique outperforms the conventional generalized expectation maximization technique and the pso based technique is robust to the snr values.

Table 16: Examples of text generated by the different models trained on the AGENDA dataset.

Style Control for Schema-Guided Natural Language Generation

**Alicia Y. Tsai[1*], Shereen Oraby[2], Vittorio Perera[2], Jiun-Yu Kao[2],
Yuheng Du[2], Anjali Narayan-Chen[2], Tagyoung Chung[2], Dilek Hakkani-Tur[2]**
[1] University of California, Berkeley
[2] Amazon Alexa AI
aliciatsai@berkeley.edu
{orabys,pererv,jiunyk,yuhendu,
naraanja,tagyoung,hakkanit}@amazon.com

Abstract

Natural Language Generation (NLG) for task-oriented dialogue systems focuses on communicating specific content accurately, fluently, and coherently. While these attributes are crucial for a successful dialogue, it is also desirable to simultaneously accomplish specific stylistic goals, such as response length, point-of-view, descriptiveness, sentiment, formality, and empathy. In this work, we focus on stylistic control and evaluation for schema-guided NLG, with joint goals of achieving both semantic and stylistic control. We experiment in detail with various controlled generation methods for large pretrained language models: specifically, conditional training, guided fine-tuning, and guided decoding. We discuss their advantages and limitations, and evaluate them with a broad range of automatic and human evaluation metrics. Our results show that while high style accuracy and semantic correctness are easier to achieve for more lexically-defined styles with conditional training, stylistic control is also achievable for more semantically complex styles using discriminator-based guided decoding methods. The results also suggest that methods that are more scalable (with less hyper-parameters tuning) and that disentangle content generation and stylistic variations are more effective at achieving semantic correctness and style accuracy.

1 Introduction

Natural Language Generation (NLG) for task-oriented dialogue focuses on effectively generating responses based on inputs that are frequently in the form of a structured meaning representation (MR) (Moryossef et al., 2019; Dušek et al., 2018; Colin et al., 2016; Wen et al., 2015). Recent work has suggested a schema-guided paradigm for task-oriented dialogue by adding descriptions in natural language form (Lin et al., 2021; Du et al., 2020; Rastogi et al., 2019; Bapna et al., 2017). Compared to structured MRs, dialogue schemata contain much richer contextual information, leading to better generated outputs.

Although the primary aim of task-oriented NLG is to effectively generate outputs that realize system dialogue actions and communicate their associated contents correctly, it is often desirable to control the stylistic variations of an output. For example, recognizing and reacting to emotions has been shown to enhance task outcomes and user engagement in task-oriented conversations (Fraser et al., 2018). Language generation systems that use corpora and methods without awareness of emotions may generate callous, generic or even biased responses (Bender et al., 2021; Sheng et al., 2019). Depending on the use case or type of system, it may be useful to stylistically vary responses, e.g., using shorter responses for spoken dialogue systems, longer responses if the system includes visual modality through a screen, or emotion-specific responses that appropriately address user sentiment.

Previous work on controlled text generation aimed at achieving stylistic goals has not focused on a schema-guided paradigm where specific content must be communicated correctly; instead, most work focuses more on unconstrained text-to-text generation without explicit meaning representations (Liu et al., 2021; Krause et al., 2020; Keskar et al., 2019; Ghazvininejad et al., 2017). Meanwhile, work on schema-guided NLG has primarily focused on generating fluent outputs that achieve low semantic error rather than achieving stylistic goals (Kale and Rastogi, 2020; Peng et al., 2020; Du et al., 2020). In this paper, we hope to fill the gap on stylistic control and evaluation for schema-guided NLG. Our contributions in this paper are three-fold:

1. We describe how we pre-process and annotate style parameters within the Schema-guided Dialogue (SGD) dataset (Rastogi et al., 2019).

[*] Work done as an intern at Amazon Alexa AI.

Proceedings of the Third Workshop on Natural Language Processing for Conversational AI, pages 228–242
November 10, 2021. ©2021 Association for Computational Linguistics

2. We experiment with controlling different styles with various controlled text generation methods that aim to preserve fluency and semantic correctness.

3. We present results with a broad range of evaluation methods, including a detailed human evaluation.

Specifically, we consider three types of methods: *conditional training*, *guided fine-tuning*, and *guided decoding*. We show that conditional training (CT) can be used for both very lexically-defined (e.g., point-of-view) and more semantically complex styles (e.g., empathy). However, CT introduces the need to re-train new models per style and is more effective at learning styles with strong lexical characteristics (e.g., specific language patterns or vocabulary). For guided fine-tuning, we explore the Plug-and-Play Language Model (PPLM) (Dathathri et al., 2020), but show that it requires careful hyper-parameter turning and is prone to degeneration. For guided decoding, we evaluate the beam search weighted decoding (BSWD) method and show that it performs best overall on measures of style accuracy for semantically complex styles. The results suggest that unlike style control for unconstrained text generation where no specific content needs to be communicated, style control under the schema-guided paradigm has stronger restrictions on the degree of freedom allowed for content generation. We show that methods that disentangle content generation and style variations, especially for more semantically complex styles, result in better overall performance on semantic and stylistic control.

2 Related Work

Controllable text generation is an emerging research field. Current methods for controlling styles in text generation involve learning a conditional generative model or designing an appropriate decoding strategy. There are many methods proposed for learning a good conditional generative model. These include conditional training (Kikuchi et al., 2016; Ficler and Goldberg, 2017; Keskar et al., 2019; See et al., 2019), fine-tuning language models with external attribute models or side models (Dathathri et al., 2020; Zhang et al., 2020), fine-tuning models with reinforcement learning and human feedback (Ziegler et al., 2019), training generative adversarial models (Yu et al., 2017), and training variational auto-encoders (Yu et al., 2017; Hu et al., 2017).

Others have worked on designing a good decoding strategy to guide generation, where the decoding procedure is guided by a scoring function or discriminator. These include weighted decoding (Ghazvininejad et al., 2017; Holtzman et al., 2018; See et al., 2019) and guided generation (Krause et al., 2020). Other lines of work include curating training data with rich style markup to facilitate training models with explicit stylistic supervision Oraby et al. (2019, 2018). While this previous work does focus on controllable text generation, most work has been carried out in a text-to-text generation setting, without specific semantic constraints. Instead, we focus on the task-oriented dialogue framework where specific values must be communicated, and conduct a rigorous evaluation of different methods and their efficacy on different forms of style generation. Other recent work has explored adding additional information such as chit-chat data to task-oriented dialogue (Sun et al., 2021; Madotto et al., 2020) and could potentially provide new opportunities for stylistic control.

3 Data Collection and Annotation

3.1 Schema-to-Template pairs

We use the Schema-guided Dialogue (SGD) dataset[1] to create a rich corpus of schema-to-template pairs. This dataset is one of the largest publicly available corpora of annotated multi-domain, task-oriented dialogues (Rastogi et al., 2019). Each dialogue in the data is represented as a list of user and system utterances. We use only the system-side utterances and annotations since we are focused on system-side generation.

Table 1 shows an example pre-processed data instance and the final flattened input. To create schema-to-template pairs, we follow the preprocessing steps outlined in Du et al. (2020) with the following modifications: (1) we replace the slot values with generic slot values without any slot type by adding a `$` prefix and appending a increasing index (*e.g.*, `San Jose` → `$slot1`) for better generalization; and (2) we use only *domain*, *meaning representations (MRs)*, and *slot description* as input data. Domain provides the context of the conversation (*e.g.*, `Restaurants`); an

[1]The Schema-guided Dialogue Dataset: `https://github.com/google-research-datasets/dstc8-schema-guided-dialogue`

MR contains a dialog act, a slot and a value (*e.g.*, `OFFER(city=$slot2)`); and the slot description describes the meaning of the slot in natural language. Table 8 in Appendix A summarizes the full statistics for the final pre-processed SGD dataset. In summary, we have 1,698 MRs and 118,715 example templates in the training set and 1,137 MRs and 34,598 templates in the test set.

For a single example, there are usually multiple dialogue acts as shown in Table 1. An MR in the original data may also contain multiple values. In such cases, we flatten these MRs into multiple parts, each containing only one dialogue act. For instance, an MR that contains two values originally, *e.g.*, `REQUEST(cuisine=[Mexican, Italian])` becomes two separate dialogue acts, *e.g.*, `REQUEST(cuisine=$slot1)`, `REQUEST(cuisine=$slot2)`. Templates are obtained by delexicalizing the utterances with generic slot values (*e.g.*, `$slot1 is a good restaurant`). Finally, we flatten the input data into flat natural language strings similar to Budzianowski and Vulić (2019).

3.2 Style Parameters

In order to perform style control, we also need to annotate style parameters for the SGD dataset. Style parameters are features of text that are stylistically expressive. These parameters can be roughly identified at ***lexical*** (vocabulary and words), ***syntactic*** (sentence structure) and ***semantic*** (abstract meaning/emotion) levels (Verma and Srinivasan, 2019). We focus primarily on ***lexical*** and ***semantic*** features. Specifically, we characterize lexical style parameters as low-level linguistic features that can be derived from the text directly such as *word count* and *number of adjectives*, and semantic style parameters as high-level styles such as *sentiment* that are more complex to characterize.

Lexical style parameters Table 2 summarizes the lexical styles we annotate for the SGD data and the description of each parameter. In total, we automatically annotate six lexical style parameters for the SGD data. Similar to Zhang et al. (2018), the parameter "*has rare word*" uses the maximum Normalized Inverse Document Frequency (NIDF) to determine whether or not a template contains words that are used less frequently in the corpus.[2] The complete data distribution for all the style parameters is included in Table 10 in Appendix A.

Semantic style parameters Unlike lexical parameters which consider explicit features such as vocabulary, semantic parameters of style are less lexically-defined. As a result, it is generally harder to annotate these parameters directly from the original data without auxiliary information. In this work, we consider the following semantic parameters: ***formality***, ***negative sentiment***, ***positive sentiment*** and ***empathy***. Formality and sentiment are common stylistic parameters studied in the stylistic control NLG literature. We also include empathy as an interesting and complex style studied in recent work (Wang et al., 2021; Majumder et al., 2020; Lin et al., 2019; Zhou and Wang, 2018). We train a classifier for each of the four styles and annotate the utterances in SGD with these features. We include more details about the classifiers in Section 4 and show additional information about the dataset used to train each classifier in Table 9 of Appendix A.

4 Baseline Model

Language model Given a sequence of tokens $x = \{x_1, \cdots, x_t\}$, the goal of the language model is to model the joint probability of the sequence $p(x) = p(x_1, \cdots, x_t)$. The joint probability $p(x)$ is often factorized in terms of the product of conditional probabilities using the chain rule of probability $P(x) = \prod_{t=1}^{T} P(x_T|x_0, \cdots, x_{T-1})$ (Bengio et al., 2001). In recent years, transformer-based models have been used widely to model these conditional probabilities (Vaswani et al., 2017). In this work, we use GPT-2[3] as our baseline language model (Radford et al., 2019) and fine-tune the GPT-2 model with the processed SGD data using a flat representation with the beginning of sequence, separator, and end of sequence special tokens.[4]

Semantic style classifiers The classifiers used to annotate semantic parameters are single layer classifiers. To train each classifier, we encode the input $x = \{x_1, \cdots, x_t\}$ of length t using the baseline GPT-2 model described above and obtain the last hidden layer o_t for all time steps t. We then take the average representation across time, denoted $\bar{o}_t$, and train the classifier to predict the target label (*e.g.*, formal vs. informal) from the average repre-

[2]Appendix A includes the details of the NIDF calculation.

[3]GPT-2 small from HuggingFace: `https://huggingface.co/transformers/model_doc/gpt2.html`

[4]*e.g.*, "`[BOS]` flattened-schema-tokens `[SEP]` template-tokens `[EOS]`"

Original schema		Pre-processed schema	
Service	`Restaurants_1`	Domain	`Restaurants`
Act	`OFFER`	Act	`OFFER`
Slot	`restaurant_name`	Slot	`restaurant_name`
Slot Description	`Name of the restaurant`	Slot Description	`Name of the restaurant`
Values	`71 Saint Peter`	Value	`$slot1`
Act	`OFFER`	Act	`OFFER`
Slot	`city`	Slot	`city`
Slot Description	`City where the restaurant is located`	Slot Description	`City where the restaurant is located`
Values	`San Jose`	Value	`$slot2`
Utterance	`I see that at 71 Saint Peter there is a good restaurant which is in San Jose.`	Template	`I see that at $slot1 there is a good restaurant which is in $slot2.`
Flattened input after pre-processing	`restaurants offer restaurant_name name of the restaurant $slot1 offer city city where the restaurant is located $slot2`		

Table 1: Sample system-side schema and the flat natural language strings.

Style Parameter	Description	Condition
Short	Number of tokens in the template. The condition is based roughly on 25th percentile of the number of tokens per template in the training data.	≤ 7
Long	Number of tokens in the template. The condition is based roughly on 75th percentile of the number of tokens per template in the training data.	≥ 15
Has Rare Word	Whether or not the template contains very specific or rarely used words compared to other templates in the corpus	Max NIDF ≥ 0.5
First Person Pronouns	Whether or not the template contains first person pronouns: I, me, my, mine	-
Second Person Pronouns	Whether or not the template contains second person pronouns: you, your, yours	-
Descriptive	Number of adjectives in the template	> 2

Table 2: Lexical style parameters and possible values.

sentation: $f(\bar{o}_t) = f\Big(\sum_{t=1}^{T} \frac{o_t}{T}\Big)$. The classifiers are used for annotating the semantic parameters of the SGD data and for the style control models described in Section 5.

5 Style Controlled Text Generation

In this work, we require a controlled generation method that is able to simultaneously render the semantic content given the schemata while achieving the desired stylistic goals. We also require the method to be both stable (preserve the fluency of the response even when the stylistic goals are not met) and general-purpose (can be applied to many styles). Under these requirements and constraints, we discuss three types of controlled generation methods to achieve these goals: *conditional training*, *guided fine-tuning*, and *guided decoding*, and compare their performance in Section 6. To our knowledge, our work is the first to systematically study the effectiveness of these control methods for schema-guided NLG.

5.1 Conditional Training (CT)

Controllable generation entails modeling $p(x|a)$, where a is a control variable and x is the generated sequence. However, a pre-trained language model such as GPT-2 is only trained to learn $p(x)$. On the other hand, conditional training (Kikuchi et al., 2016; Peng et al., 2018; Fan et al., 2018; See et al., 2019) refers to directly learning the conditional generative model $p(x|a)$. The results are of high quality because the model is trained to directly maximize $p(x|a)$, but this comes at the expense of fixing the control variable upfront and of re-training the entire model for each new control variable.

To perform style control, we fine-tune the baseline GPT-2 with the conditional training method. Specifically, each input in the training set is annotated with the variable a that we wish to control, *e.g.,* the length (*short, long*) of the input. The value of the control variable a is then added to model vocabulary as a special token (*e.g.,* `[LENGTH_SHORT]`) and appended to the meaning representation after the `[BOS]` special token. The model then learns an embedding for each value of a and learns to generate $x = \{x_1, \cdots, x_t\}$ conditioned on a value of a and the given meaning representation by optimizing cross-entropy loss.

5.2 Guided Fine-tuning

Unlike conditional training that requires fine-tuning an entire GPT-2 model per style, guided fine-turning refers to methods that require only fine-tuning a smaller set of the parameters while the majority of the base model stays fixed. In this paper, we consider the recent Plug-and-Play Language Model (PPLM) (Dathathri et al., 2020). In guided fine-tuning methods, the conditional probability $p(x|a) \propto p(x)p(a|x)$ is obtained by fine-tuning the base language model (LM) using an auxiliary discriminator that explicitly models $p(a|x)$. In our work, we use the semantic style classifiers described in Section 4 for the discriminator $p(a|x)$ and the GPT-2 model for the base LM.

The major difficulty of the PPLM method is the problem of degeneration – output that is ungrammatical, incoherent, or repetitive. In practice, we observe that PPLM is prone to generating ungrammatical outputs or getting stuck in a repetitive loop if the hyper-parameters are not carefully tuned. We illustrate the effect of hyper-parameters tuning and the degeneration problem in Appendix B.

5.3 Guided Decoding

While conditional training and guided fine-tuning require fine-tuning the base language model, weighted decoding is applied only at decoding time, requiring no change to the base language model. To control the generation, it re-ranks the probability of words based on a scoring function or discriminator.

Weighted Decoding (WD) In weighted decoding (Ghazvininejad et al., 2017), at time step t, the distribution of the next token x_{t+1} is re-weighted by a semantic style classifier that models $p(a|x)$. The probability of each possible next word w in the vocabulary given the control variable a is then re-computed as

$$p(w|a) = \text{Softmax}\Big(p(w)\, p(a|w)\Big). \qquad (1)$$

Here $p(w)$ is the probability of the word w calculated by the base language model as the next token given the generated sequence $\{x_1, \cdots, x_t\}$, and $p(a|w)$ is the probability of the word w associated with the control variable a.

Beam search weighted decoding (BSWD) The weighted decoding method described above takes the highest scoring item at each time step. While this approach is effective, it is often non-optimal and can limit the diversity of the generated text. To mitigate this limitation, we can increase the search space at generation time using the beam search algorithm. Given a fixed beam width parameter B, the beam search algorithm selects B best alternatives with the highest probability for an input sequence at each time step. Therefore, the original weighted decoding approach described above is a special case of the beam search algorithm with $B = 1$.

Finally, we note that in Eq. 1, the style classifier is only conditioned on the next possible token w but not the entire past sequence, *i.e.,* the next possible token w plus the text that has been generated $\{x_1, \cdots, x_t, w\}$. Empirically, in both WD and BSWD, we observe that maximizing the probability of the desired style by greedily considering only the next generated token, rather than the entire sequence of previously generated tokens, yielded better performance on the SGD data. When the entire sequence representation is used, we find that the re-weighting of the distribution is usually not strong enough to successfully match the desired stylistic goal.

6 Experiments

In this section, we show the experimental results of the methods described in Section 5 for controlling the styles described in Section 3 on the SGD data. The baseline GPT-2 model is fine-tuned on the training set with no control variables, and the conditional training model is fine-tuned with control variable special tokens, *e.g.,* `LENGTH_SHORT`. Our evaluation is tested on the test set of 1,137 MRs. We focus on controlling a single style at a time in this experiment; however, it is also possible to control for multiple styles – we include details on multiple-style control experiments in Appendix C (with sample outputs in Appendix Table 14).

6.1 Automatic Evaluation Metrics

We focus on evaluating three key dimensions: style accuracy, fluency, and semantic correctness.

Style accuracy To evaluate how effective each controlled generation method is per style, we use the *style accuracy* metric, or the percentage of outputs that conform to the required input style. For lexical styles, this is simply computed using the conditions in Table 2. For semantic styles, we classify the generated text using the corresponding style classifier and check if the predicted style matches the desired style value. For instance, if the predicted sentiment for generated text with the "positive sentiment" control code does not match the "positive" label, then it is considered incorrect.

Response fluency We use *BLEU* score (n-gram precision with brevity penalty) (Papineni et al., 2002) as a measurement of the response fluency. We acknowledge that lexical overlap metrics are poor measures of quality (Novikova et al., 2017); however, we include BLEU for completeness and further evaluate quality through human judgments.

Semantic correctness We use *slot error rate (SER)* (Luong et al., 2015) to measure the semantic correctness of the generated response as compared to the given MR. SER measures the ratio of semantic errors that the model makes by finding the total number of slot mistakes (deletions, repetitions, and hallucinations) in the generated text (lower is better). SER here only considers slots that have explicit values that must be realized (e.g., `$slotN`).

6.2 Lexical Style Automatic Evaluation

We evaluate lexical styles with only conditional training as the rest of the methods include semantic style classifiers and are thus not applicable. Table 3 summarizes the performance of conditional training for the six lexical styles. The style accuracy for most styles is generally high, between 80% to nearly 100%, especially for styles marked explicitly by specific words, such as first and second person pronouns. However, we observe that "*descriptive*" has a particularly low accuracy. First, the majority of the references in the training data (95%) have less than two adjectives, making it difficult for the model to learn this kind of style effectively.[5] Secondly, we observe that conditional training is particularly effective when the style exhibits a clear syntactic characteristic (*e.g.*, length) or a particular set of vocabulary (*e.g.*, pronouns); however, this is not the case for the "*descriptive*" style.

The fluency of the generated text with style control drops slightly as compared to no style control. Having style control often makes the generated text different from its matching responses, *i.e.*, adding extra content or changing linguistic characteristics. Since BLEU score only considers lexical overlap, this behavior is expected. Finally, we see that there is not much of a performance drop in semantic correctness with respect to SER. The experimental results show that for lexical styles with a clear syntactic pattern or vocabulary, CT can be quite effective.

Table 4 illustrates example outputs using CT when controlling for "*short*", "*long*" and "*has rare word*" styles.[6] Interestingly, we see that when asked for a longer response, the model starts to hallucinate extra content (but not slots) not given in the MR in order to satisfy the control variable. This also translates to slightly lower BLEU scores and a higher SER. Methods to enforce better implicit constraints to increase fluency and semantic correctness are important points for future work.

Style	Style Acc.	BLEU ↑	SER ↓
Baseline (no style control)	-	0.480	0.010
Short	96.4%	0.205	0.009
Long	80.1%	0.381	0.012
Has Rare Word	89.5%	0.377	0.010
First Person Pronouns	99.9%	0.365	0.011
Second Person Pronouns	99.9%	0.447	0.011
Descriptive	19.6%	0.378	0.012

Table 3: Evaluation of lexical style parameters with conditional training.

6.3 Semantic Style Automatic Evaluation

Table 5 summarizes the main results for semantic style evaluation using CT, PPLM, and BSWD. Since CT is trained to directly maximize conditional probability, it frequently has a higher BLEU score and a lower SER across different styles with the exception of "*formal*" BLEU. We note that formality is rather lexically-defined, exhibiting characteristic keywords such as "**please**", which are frequently picked up by the model, resulting in a particularly high style accuracy for "*formal*" responses and a lower BLEU score.

For the three more semantically complex styles, "*positive sentiment*", "*negative sentiment*" and "*empathy*", we see that BSWD achieves a higher style accuracy than CT (at the cost of a lower BLEU and slightly higher semantic error). We note, however, that the drop in BLEU is expected: as the output is steered towards a certain style, its n-gram overlap with the references is more likely to decrease

[5]The full data distribution can be found in Appendix A Table 10.

[6]Example outputs for other lexical styles are included in Appendix C Table 12.

MR: OFFER(restaurant_name=$slot1), OFFER(city=$slot2)	
W/o Style Control	$slot1 is a nice restaurant in $slot2 that serves curry.
Short	$slot1 is a nice restaurant in $slot2.
Long	Okay! the restaurant, $slot1 located in $slot2 is a good one and serves Taiwanese dishes.
MR: OFFER(address=$slot1), OFFER(rating=$slot2)	
W/o Style Control	There is a nice house at $slot1 with a $slot2 rating.
Has Rare Word	There is a lovely residence located at $slot1. It has a rating of $slot2.

Table 4: Example outputs for conditional training with lexical styles *"short"*, *"long"* and *"has rare word"* (more content hallucinations for *"long"*). Example outputs for other lexical styles are included in Appendix C Table 12.

– thus, we use these automatic metrics as an evaluation guide, but leave a more rigorous evaluation to human judgment in the next section. Finally, with careful hyper-parameter tuning, PPLM can achieve similar performance to BSWD on BLEU and SER but does worse on style accuracy. Increasing the style accuracy for PPLM worsens the BLEU and SER score significantly and thus we do not consider it in our human evaluation. In summary, our automatic evaluation shows that for semantic styles, BSWD gives us a good trade-off between consistent style accuracy and semantic fidelity across styles.

Table 6 illustrates example outputs for the three semantic styles using BSWD (with additional examples including combining multiple styles in Appendix C). In general, styles that encapsulate complex phenomena such as *"empathy"* are harder to generate as shown by their lower style accuracy; nevertheless, we are able to preserve fluency and semantic correctness in most cases.

Style	Model	Style Acc.	BLEU ↑	SER ↓
Baseline	-	-	0.480	0.010
Formal	CT	**70.0%**	0.461	**0.009**
	PPLM	17.5%	0.390	0.016
	BSWD	42.5%	**0.496**	0.021
Negative	CT	7.5%	**0.409**	**0.012**
	PPLM	2.5%	0.373	0.017
	BSWD	**25.0%**	0.359	0.021
Positive	CT	17.5%	**0.442**	**0.009**
	PPLM	32.5%	0.371	0.026
	BSWD	**65.0%**	0.369	0.021
Empathy	CT	21.5%	**0.449**	**0.009**
	PPLM	11.0%	0.368	0.021
	BSWD	**31.0%**	0.394	0.017

Table 5: Evaluation of semantic styles.

6.4 Human Evaluation

We focus on human evaluation for our semantic styles since they are the most inherently subjective.[7] We pick a subset of our semantic styles to evaluate, specifically, *formal*, *negative* and *positive*. We also focus on the evaluation of CT and BSWD only since they have an overall better performance in the automatic evaluation and are simpler in nature (*e.g.,* less hyper-parameter tuning). To evaluate style, we ask three human annotators to rate:

- **Style Rating (Sty. Rat.)**: How closely the response matches the given style (1 being not at all, 5 being very closely).
- **Fluency (Flu.)**: The fluency of the generated response (1 being low, 5 being high).
- **Semantic Error**: Slot errors in the generated response using a 0/1 scale. For analysis purposes, we further break down the items marked "0" into four error types to understand the strengths and weaknesses of each method. For each type of error, the output is only marked "1" if there are no issues.
  - **Deletion (Del.)**: Whether the response drops any slot values from the MR.
  - **Repetition (Rep.)**: Whether the response repeats any slot values from the MR.
  - **Content Hallucination (Cont. Hal.)**: Whether the response includes extra content not given in the MR.
  - **Incorrect Slot Values (Inc. Slot)**: Whether the response includes any slot values not given in the MR (a specific type of hallucination).

Table 7 shows the aggregated evaluation (40 samples per style, with three judgments per sample). The results show that outputs generated by BSWD have a higher or comparable style rating

[7]More details on the human evaluation design are in Appendix D.

MR: `REQUEST(where_to=none)`	
W/o style control	What city are you staying?
Formal	What city are you planning to stay in?
MR: `OFFER(address=$slot1), OFFER(rating=$slot2)`	
W/o style control	There is a house at `$slot1` with a rating of `$slot2`.
Positive	There is a nice house with a `$slot2` rating located at `$slot1`.
MR: `INFORM(rating=$slot1), NOTIFY_FAILURE(null=none)`	
W/o style control	The rating is `$slot1`. I was unable to make a reservation.
Empathy	The rating is `$slot1`. I'm sorry, but I couldn't make the reservation.

Table 6: Example outputs of semantic styles using beam search weighted decoding (BSWD).

compared to CT, confirming its ability to control semantic styles. We also observe that outputs from BSWD have a higher fluency score across all styles. This means that even though BSWD showed lower BLEU scores in automatic evaluation, its outputs are considered to be more natural and fluent in human evaluation. Finally, we see an interesting difference in error types when comparing CT and BSWD. In general, BSWD is more prone to deleting and hallucinating slots, while CT more frequently generates incorrect slot values. Since BSWD requires no change to the base language model, it is able to obtain a lower incorrect slot value error rate as compared to CT, which requires re-training the language model with a control code. On the other hand, it has a higher deletion and hallucination error rate since during decoding time, BSWD is free to insert or drop content in order to achieve the desired style.

Style	Model	Sty. Rat.	Flu.	Semantic Error: Del.	Rep.	Cont. Hal.	Inc. Slot
Formal	CT	3.88	3.83	**15%**	0%	**13%**	3.75%
	BSWD	**3.95**	**4.30**	19%	0%	15%	**1.25%**
Negative	CT	2.78	3.54	20%	0%	12.5%	**2.5%**
	BSWD	**2.86**	**3.93**	20%	0%	12.5%	5%
Positive	CT	**3.48**	3.64	**22.5%**	0%	**22.5%**	12.5%
	BSWD	3.42	**3.84**	27.5%	0%	30%	**7.5%**

Table 7: Human evaluation results for selected semantic styles and methods.

7 Conclusion

In this work, we focus on stylistic control and evaluation of schema-guided NLG. We discuss three different types of methods for style controlled text generation: conditional training (CT), guided fine-tuning (PPLM), and guided decoding (BSWD). We present a rich set of evaluations to quantify each method's ability to achieve various styles while preserving language fluency and minimizing slot errors. Our analysis shows that, in general, styles that encapsulate abstract ideas are naturally harder to generate (*e.g.,* empathy), and methods that require careful hyper-parameters tuning may run into the problems of instability and degeneration (*e.g.,* PPLM) while under-performing in style accuracy. The automatic and human evaluations suggest that simultaneously achieving stylistic goals and realizing schema information requires methods that allow us to separate content generation and stylistic variations. We show that CT and BSWD overcome some of these challenges and are effective at controlling several styles while maintaining good fluency and semantic correctness in most cases. CT is effective for lexical styles with strong syntactic characteristics or distinctive vocabulary sets, while BSWD excels at semantic styles that are more complex to characterize.

For future work, we are interested in extending our analysis to a larger number of styles, and in exploring techniques for understanding and representing styles that are more abstract, such as "empathy", as well as methods for generating those styles under a task-oriented dialogue framework. Additionally, since abstract styles may be characterized by multiple features (*e.g.,* a combination of sentiment and descriptiveness), we are interested in studying how these underlying features can be represented and incorporated more accurately to improve overall semantic and stylistic control.

Acknowledgments

We would like to thank Sofia Scharfenberg, Jasmin Rehm, and the rest of the Alexa Data Services team for all of their help with preparing and performing the human evaluation study.

References

Ankur Bapna, Gokhan Tur, Dilek Hakkani-Tur, and Larry Heck. 2017. Towards zero shot frame semantic parsing for domain scaling. In *Interspeech 2017*.

Emily M. Bender, Timnit Gebru, Angelina McMillan-Major, and Shmargaret Shmitchell. 2021. On the dangers of stochastic parrots: Can language models be too big? In *Proceedings of the 2021 ACM Conference on Fairness, Accountability, and Transparency*, FAccT '21, page 610–623, New York, NY, USA. Association for Computing Machinery.

Yoshua Bengio, Réjean Ducharme, and Pascal Vincent. 2001. A neural probabilistic language model. In *Advances in Neural Information Processing Systems*, volume 13. MIT Press.

Paweł Budzianowski and Ivan Vulić. 2019. Hello, it's GPT-2 - how can I help you? towards the use of pretrained language models for task-oriented dialogue systems. In *Proceedings of the 3rd Workshop on Neural Generation and Translation*, pages 15–22, Hong Kong. Association for Computational Linguistics.

Sven Buechel, Anneke Buffone, Barry Slaff, Lyle Ungar, and João Sedoc. 2018. Modeling empathy and distress in reaction to news stories. In *Proceedings of the 2018 Conference on Empirical Methods in Natural Language Processing (EMNLP 2018)*.

Emilie Colin, Claire Gardent, Yassine M'rabet, Shashi Narayan, and Laura Perez-Beltrachini. 2016. The WebNLG challenge: Generating text from DBPedia data. In *Proceedings of the 9th International Natural Language Generation conference*, pages 163–167, Edinburgh, UK. Association for Computational Linguistics.

Sumanth Dathathri, Andrea Madotto, Janice Lan, Jane Hung, Eric Frank, Piero Molino, Jason Yosinski, and Rosanne Liu. 2020. Plug and play language models: A simple approach to controlled text generation. In *International Conference on Learning Representations*.

Yuheng Du, Shereen Oraby, Vittorio Perera, Minmin Shen, Anjali Narayan-Chen, Tagyoung Chung, Anushree Venkatesh, and Dilek Hakkani-Tur. 2020. Schema-guided natural language generation. In *Proceedings of the 13th International Conference on Natural Language Generation*, pages 283–295, Dublin, Ireland. Association for Computational Linguistics.

Ondřej Dušek, Jekaterina Novikova, and Verena Rieser. 2018. Findings of the E2E NLG challenge. In *Proceedings of the 11th International Conference on Natural Language Generation*, pages 322–328, Tilburg University, The Netherlands. Association for Computational Linguistics.

Angela Fan, David Grangier, and Michael Auli. 2018. Controllable Abstractive Summarization. In *Proceedings of the 2nd Workshop on Neural Machine Translation and Generation*, pages 45–54, Melbourne, Australia. Association for Computational Linguistics.

Jessica Ficler and Yoav Goldberg. 2017. Controlling Linguistic Style Aspects in Neural Language Generation. In *Proceedings of the Workshop on Stylistic Variation*, pages 94–104, Copenhagen, Denmark. Association for Computational Linguistics.

Jamie Fraser, Ioannis Papaioannou, and Oliver Lemon. 2018. Spoken Conversational AI in Video Games: Emotional Dialogue Management Increases User Engagement. In *Proceedings of the 18th International Conference on Intelligent Virtual Agents*.

Marjan Ghazvininejad, Xing Shi, Jay Priyadarshi, and Kevin Knight. 2017. Hafez: an interactive poetry generation system. In *Proceedings of ACL 2017, System Demonstrations*, pages 43–48, Vancouver, Canada. Association for Computational Linguistics.

Ari Holtzman, Jan Buys, Maxwell Forbes, Antoine Bosselut, D. Golub, and Yejin Choi. 2018. Learning to write with cooperative discriminators. *ArXiv*, abs/1805.06087.

Zhiting Hu, Zichao Yang, Xiaodan Liang, R. Salakhutdinov, and E. Xing. 2017. Toward controlled generation of text. In *ICML*.

Mihir Kale and Abhinav Rastogi. 2020. Template guided text generation for task-oriented dialogue. In *Proceedings of the 2020 Conference on Empirical Methods in Natural Language Processing (EMNLP)*, pages 6505–6520, Online. Association for Computational Linguistics.

Nitish Shirish Keskar, Bryan McCann, Lav R. Varshney, Caiming Xiong, and Richard Socher. 2019. Ctrl: A conditional transformer language model for controllable generation. *ArXiv*, abs/1909.05858.

Yuta Kikuchi, Graham Neubig, Ryohei Sasano, Hiroya Takamura, and Manabu Okumura. 2016. Controlling output length in neural encoder-decoders. In *Proceedings of the 2016 Conference on Empirical Methods in Natural Language Processing*, pages 1328–1338, Austin, Texas. Association for Computational Linguistics.

Ben Krause, Akhilesh Deepak Gotmare, B. McCann, N. Keskar, Shafiq R. Joty, R. Socher, and Nazneen Rajani. 2020. Gedi: Generative discriminator guided sequence generation. *ArXiv*, abs/2009.06367.

Zhaojiang Lin, Bing Liu, Seungwhan Moon, Paul Crook, Zhenpeng Zhou, Zhiguang Wang, Zhou Yu, Andrea Madotto, Eunjoon Cho, and Rajen Subba. 2021. Leveraging slot descriptions for zero-shot cross-domain dialogue StateTracking. In *Proceedings of the 2021 Conference of the North American Chapter of the Association for Computational Linguistics: Human Language Technologies*, pages 5640–5648, Online. Association for Computational Linguistics.

Zhaojiang Lin, Andrea Madotto, Jamin Shin, Peng Xu, and Pascale Fung. 2019. MoEL: Mixture of Empathetic Listeners. In *Proceedings of the 2019 Conference on Empirical Methods in Natural Language Processing and the 9th International Joint Conference on Natural Language Processing (EMNLP-IJCNLP)*, pages 121–132, Hong Kong, China.

Alisa Liu, Maarten Sap, Ximing Lu, Swabha Swayamdipta, Chandra Bhagavatula, Noah A. Smith, and Yejin Choi. 2021. Dexperts: Decoding-time controlled text generation with experts and anti-experts.

Thang Luong, Hieu Pham, and Christopher D. Manning. 2015. Effective approaches to attention-based neural machine translation. In *Proceedings of the 2015 Conference on Empirical Methods in Natural Language Processing*, pages 1412–1421, Lisbon, Portugal. Association for Computational Linguistics.

Andrea Madotto, Zhaojiang Lin, Chien-Sheng Wu, Jamin Shin, and Pascale Fung. 2020. Attention over parameters for dialogue systems. *ArXiv*, abs/2001.01871.

Navonil Majumder, Pengfei Hong, Shanshan Peng, Jiankun Lu, Deepanway Ghosal, Alexander Gelbukh, Rada Mihalcea, and Soujanya Poria. 2020. MIME: MIMicking emotions for empathetic response generation. In *Proceedings of the 2020 Conference on Empirical Methods in Natural Language Processing (EMNLP)*, pages 8968–8979, Online. Association for Computational Linguistics.

Amit Moryossef, Yoav Goldberg, and Ido Dagan. 2019. Step-by-step: Separating planning from realization in neural data-to-text generation. In *Proceedings of the 2019 Conference of the North American Chapter of the Association for Computational Linguistics: Human Language Technologies, Volume 1 (Long and Short Papers)*, pages 2267–2277, Minneapolis, Minnesota. Association for Computational Linguistics.

Jekaterina Novikova, Ondřej Dušek, Amanda Cercas Curry, and Verena Rieser. 2017. Why we need new evaluation metrics for NLG. In *Proceedings of the 2017 Conference on Empirical Methods in Natural Language Processing*, pages 2241–2252, Copenhagen, Denmark. Association for Computational Linguistics.

Shereen Oraby, Vrindavan Harrison, Abteen Ebrahimi, and Marilyn Walker. 2019. Curate and Generate: A Corpus and Method for Joint Control of Semantics and Style in Neural NLG. In *Proceedings of the 57th Annual Meeting of the Association for Computational Linguistics*, pages 5938–5951, Florence, Italy. Association for Computational Linguistics.

Shereen Oraby, Lena Reed, Shubhangi Tandon, Sharath T.S., Stephanie Lukin, and Marilyn Walker. 2018. Controlling Personality-Based Stylistic Variation with Neural Natural Language Generators. In *Proceedings of the 19th Annual SIGdial Meeting on Discourse and Dialogue*, pages 180–190, Melbourne, Australia. Association for Computational Linguistics.

Kishore Papineni, Salim Roukos, Todd Ward, and Wei-Jing Zhu. 2002. Bleu: a method for automatic evaluation of machine translation. In *Proceedings of the 40th Annual Meeting of the Association for Computational Linguistics*, pages 311–318, Philadelphia, Pennsylvania, USA. Association for Computational Linguistics.

Ellie Pavlick and Joel Tetreault. 2016. An Empirical Analysis of Formality in Online Communication. *Transactions of the Association for Computational Linguistics*, 4:61–74.

Baolin Peng, Chenguang Zhu, Chunyuan Li, Xiujun Li, Jinchao Li, Michael Zeng, and Jianfeng Gao. 2020. Few-shot natural language generation for task-oriented dialog. In *EMNLP*.

Nanyun Peng, Marjan Ghazvininejad, Jonathan May, and Kevin Knight. 2018. Towards Controllable Story Generation. In *Proceedings of the First Workshop on Storytelling*, pages 43–49, New Orleans, Louisiana. Association for Computational Linguistics.

Alec Radford, Jeff Wu, R. Child, David Luan, Dario Amodei, and Ilya Sutskever. 2019. Language models are unsupervised multitask learners.

Abhinav Rastogi, Xiaoxue Zang, Srinivas Sunkara, Raghav Gupta, and Pranav Khaitan. 2019. Towards scalable multi-domain conversational agents: The schema-guided dialogue dataset. *arXiv preprint arXiv:1909.05855*.

Abigail See, Stephen Roller, Douwe Kiela, and Jason Weston. 2019. What makes a good conversation? How controllable attributes affect human judgments. In *Proceedings of the 2019 Conference of the North American Chapter of the Association for Computational Linguistics: Human Language Technologies, Volume 1 (Long and Short Papers)*, pages 1702–1723, Minneapolis, Minnesota. Association for Computational Linguistics.

Emily Sheng, Kai-Wei Chang, Premkumar Natarajan, and Nanyun Peng. 2019. The woman worked as a babysitter: On biases in language generation. In *Proceedings of the 2019 Conference on Empirical Methods in Natural Language Processing and the 9th International Joint Conference on Natural Language Processing (EMNLP-IJCNLP)*, pages 3407–3412, Hong Kong, China. Association for Computational Linguistics.

Richard Socher, Alex Perelygin, Jean Wu, Jason Chuang, Christopher D. Manning, Andrew Ng, and Christopher Potts. 2013. Recursive deep models for semantic compositionality over a sentiment treebank. In *Proceedings of the 2013 Conference on Empirical Methods in Natural Language Processing*, pages 1631–1642, Seattle, Washington, USA. Association for Computational Linguistics.

Kai Sun, Seungwhan Moon, Paul Crook, Stephen Roller, Becka Silvert, Bing Liu, Zhiguang Wang, Honglei Liu, Eunjoon Cho, and Claire Cardie. 2021. Adding chit-chat to enhance task-oriented dialogues. In *Proceedings of the 2021 Conference of the North American Chapter of the Association for Computational Linguistics: Human Language Technologies*, pages 1570–1583, Online. Association for Computational Linguistics.

Ashish Vaswani, Noam Shazeer, Niki Parmar, Jakob Uszkoreit, Llion Jones, Aidan N Gomez, Ł ukasz Kaiser, and Illia Polosukhin. 2017. Attention is all you need. In *Advances in Neural Information Processing Systems*, volume 30. Curran Associates, Inc.

Gaurav Verma and Balaji Vasan Srinivasan. 2019. A Lexical, Syntactic, and Semantic Perspective for Understanding Style in Text. *arXiv:1909.08349 [cs]*. ArXiv: 1909.08349.

Yi-Hsuan Wang, Jia-Hao Hsu, Chung-Hsien Wu, and Tsung-Hsien Yang. 2021. Transformer-based empathetic response generation using dialogue situation and advanced-level definition of empathy. In *2021 12th International Symposium on Chinese Spoken Language Processing (ISCSLP)*, pages 1–5.

Tsung-Hsien Wen, Milica Gašić, Nikola Mrkšić, Pei-Hao Su, David Vandyke, and Steve Young. 2015. Semantically conditioned LSTM-based natural language generation for spoken dialogue systems. In *Proceedings of the 2015 Conference on Empirical Methods in Natural Language Processing*, pages 1711–1721, Lisbon, Portugal. Association for Computational Linguistics.

Lantao Yu, W. Zhang, J. Wang, and Y. Yu. 2017. Seqgan: Sequence generative adversarial nets with policy gradient. In *AAAI*.

J. Zhang, Alexander Sax, A. Zamir, L. Guibas, and J. Malik. 2020. Side-tuning: A baseline for network adaptation via additive side networks. In *ECCV*.

Ruqing Zhang, Jiafeng Guo, Yixing Fan, Yanyan Lan, Jun Xu, and Xueqi Cheng. 2018. Learning to Control the Specificity in Neural Response Generation. In *Proceedings of the 56th Annual Meeting of the Association for Computational Linguistics (Volume 1: Long Papers)*, pages 1108–1117, Melbourne, Australia. Association for Computational Linguistics.

Xianda Zhou and William Yang Wang. 2018. MojiTalk: Generating emotional responses at scale. In *Proceedings of the 56th Annual Meeting of the Association for Computational Linguistics (Volume 1: Long Papers)*.

Daniel M. Ziegler, Nisan Stiennon, Jeffrey Wu, T. Brown, A. Radford, Dario Amodei, Paul Christiano, and Geoffrey Irving. 2019. Fine-tuning language models from human preferences. *ArXiv*, abs/1909.08593.

A Statistics of Style Annotation for SGD Data

	Train	Dev	Test
System Turn	164,982	24,363	42,297
Meaning Representations	1,698	721	1,137
Templates	118,715	19,963	34,598

Table 8: Schema-Guided Dialogue dataset statistics.

Normalized inverse document frequency calculation For a word w in a template d, the Inverse Document Frequency (IDF) of w is

$$\mathrm{IDF}(w) = \log\left(\frac{N}{1 + \left|\{d \in D : w \in d\}\right|}\right) \quad (2)$$

where N is the total number of templates in the training data D, and $|\{d \in D : w \in d\}|$ is the number of those templates d in the training data that contain w. The Normalized IDF (NIDF) is obtained via the min-max normalization

$$\mathrm{NIDF}(w) = \frac{\mathrm{IDF}(w) - \min_{w' \in D}(\mathrm{IDF}(w'))}{\max_{w' \in D}(\mathrm{IDF}(w')) - \min_{w' \in D}(\mathrm{IDF}(w'))} \quad (3)$$

where $\max_{w' \in D}(\mathrm{IDF}(w'))$ and $\min_{w' \in D}(\mathrm{IDF}(w'))$ are the maximum and minimum IDF value of all the words in the training data. We use the maximum NIDF of all the words in a template to determine whether the template contains rarely used words.

Semantic style parameter annotation details The formality corpus[8] (Pavlick and Tetreault, 2016), which contains sentence-level formality annotations, is used for training the formality classifier. The Stanford sentiment treebank (SST)[9] (Socher et al., 2013) is used for training the sentiment classifier. The SST data consists of 5 classes – *very negative*, *negative*, *neutral*, *positive*, and *very positive*. We combine "*very negative*" and "*negative*" into one class and "*very positive*" and "*positive*" into one class. Finally, the empathetic reactions data[10] (Buechel et al., 2018) is used for training the empathy classifier. We use only the *empathy* label from the data.

[8] http://www.seas.upenn.edu/~nlp/resources/formality-corpus.tgz

[9] https://nlp.stanford.edu/sentiment/

[10] https://github.com/wwbp/empathic_reactions

Style parameters	Dataset
Formal	Formality corpus
Positive Negative	Stanford sentiment treebank (SST)
Empathy	Empathetic reactions

Table 9: Semantic style parameters with their possible values and associated training datasets.

Category	Style	Train	Dev	Test
Lexical styles	Short	31.42%	36.96%	32.23%
	Long	26.49%	25.13%	25.44%
	Has rare word	35.83%	37.76%	42.04%
	First person pron.	28.48%	28.88%	28.75%
	Second person pron.	52.89%	52.50%	60.18%
	Descriptive	5.00%	5.32%	3.88%
Semantic styles	Formal	30.59%	34.27%	29.76%
	Negative	6.55%	4.33%	4.95%
	Positive	39.70%	42.43%	37.41%
	Empathy	27.72%	30.04%	25.65%

Table 10: Data distribution for all of the style parameters we annotate in SGD.

B Hyper-parameters Tuning for PPLM

There are several hyper-parameters in PPLM models. We refer the readers to Dathathri et al. (2020) for the full model details. From Section 5.2, the PPLM model can be written as an optimization problem of the form:

$$\min_{\Delta H_t} \; L_{\mathrm{CE}}\Big(f\Big(\sum_{t=1}^{T} \widetilde{o}_t / T\Big)\Big) + \lambda D_{\mathrm{KL}}(\widetilde{o}_t \| o_t) \quad (4)$$

$$\text{s.t.} \quad \widetilde{o}_t = \mathrm{LM}(x_t, \widetilde{H}_t) \quad (5)$$

$$\widetilde{H}_t = H_t + \Delta H_t \quad (6)$$

$$o_t = \mathrm{LM}(x_t, H_t) \quad (7)$$

where λ is a hyper-parameter that scales the KL divergence and $f(\cdot)$ is the semantic style classifier learned to produce $p(a|x)$. We minimize the cross-entropy loss $L_{\mathrm{CE}}(\cdot)$ of the attribute model and the Kullback-Leibler (KL) divergence $D_{\mathrm{KL}}(\cdot\|\cdot)$ of the language model. For each time step t, the GPT-2 model generates a history of weight matrices H_t for all hidden layers. To control the generation, we shift the weight matrices H_t in the direction that accomplishes two goals: 1) minimize cross-entropy (CE) of the attribute a under the conditional attribute model $p(a|x)$ and 2) minimize the KL divergence between itself and the unmodified language model $p(x)$. Let ΔH_t be the small shift of H_t such that $\widetilde{H}_t = H_t + \Delta H_t$ can shift the last

MR: `OFFER(restaurant_name=$slot1), OFFER(city=$slot2)`	γ_{gm}	α	λ
`$slot1` is a nice restaurant in `$slot2`.	0.1	0.01	1
`$slot1` is a nice restaurant in `$slot2`.	0.1	0.1	1
`$slot1` is a good restaurant in `$slot2`.	0.1	1	1
`$slot1` is a nice restaurant in `$slot2`	0.3	0.01	0.01
`$slot1` is a restaurant in `$slot2`.	0.3	0.01	0.1
`$slot1` is a restaurant in `$slot2`.	0.3	0.01	1
There's the `$slot4` `$slot1` restaurant in `$slot2`. Do you like the same restaurant. Do you like this one more?	0.5	0.01	0.01
`$slot1` `$slot2` I have a restaurant has good rating restaurant has `$slot1`	0.5	0.01	0.1
`$slot1` `$slot2` I have a restaurant has good rating restaurant has a restaurant name is	0.5	0.01	1
`$slot1` is a nice restaurant in `$slot2`. Do i suggest you like that one I've found? You can have a nice meal.	0.5	0.1	1
I recommend mathemat, a `$slot1` is in `$slot2`.	0.5	1	1
`$slot4` `$slot4` `$slot4` there is `$slot4` there is	0.9	0.01	1

Table 11: Example outputs of PPLM for controlling *"positive sentiment"* with various hyper-parameters. Increasing γ_{gm} and α encourages style control but can lead to ungrammatical outputs or run into degeneration. Increasing λ encourages sentence fluency and semantic accuracy; however, careful hyper-parameters fine-tuning is required to ensure reasonable output quality.

layer (logit vector) to achieve the above two goals. The logit vector o_t is obtained by a forward pass of the LM, *i.e.* $o_t = \text{LM}(x_t, H_t)$. The next generated token x_{t+1} is sampled as $x_{t+1} \sim \text{softmax}(Wo_t)$ where W is a linear transformation that maps o_t to a probability distribution of vocabulary size.

The shift ΔH_t is then updated with gradient descent as follows:

$$\Delta H_t \leftarrow \Delta H_t - \alpha\Big(\nabla_{\Delta H_t} L_{\text{CE}}(\cdot) + \lambda \nabla_{\Delta H_t} D_{\text{KL}}(\cdot\|\cdot)\Big) \tag{8}$$

where α is the step size and the update can be repeated until it converges or up to a certain time step to obtain the shift ΔH_t. At generation time, a *post-norm fusion* that samples the next token x_{t+1} based on the shifted distribution $\widetilde{p}_{t+1}$ and the unmodified distribution p_{t+1} is done to increase the language fluency:

$$x_{t+1} \sim \frac{1}{\beta}\Big(\widetilde{p}_{t+1}^{\gamma_{gm}}\, p_{t+1}^{1-\gamma_{gm}}\Big) \tag{9}$$

β is a normalizing factor such that it forms a valid distribution. As $\gamma_{gm} \to 1$ this converges to the distribution from the shifted LM, and as $\gamma_{gm} \to 0$ it converges to the unmodified unconditional LM distribution. We observe that the hyper-parameters $\lambda, \alpha, \gamma_{gm}$ can be tuned to affect the generation. In practice, we found that increasing γ_{gm} led to non-sensical results very quickly as the generated text is no longer conformed to the given meaning representation. A larger step size α also led to unstable and nonsensical results compared to a smaller step size as it moves H_t further away from its original position. In practice, a larger λ helps keep the fluency and the semantic of the generated text. Nevertheless, its effect is less influential than α and γ_{gm}. Table 11 illustrates the effect of hyper-parameters on the model outputs.

C Additional Experimental Results

We include additional example outputs for lexical styles in Table 12.

Multiple Styles Control In this section, we demonstrate the possibility of controlling multiple styles with the methods described in Section 5. To control multiple styles with conditional training, we condition the CT model on multiple control variables $P(x|a_1, \cdots, a_n)$. The control variables are concatenated and then added to the input as special tokens after the `[BOS]` token. To control multiple styles with PPLM, we simply add the cross-entropy loss of each semantic style classifier to the objective function. Extra hyper-parameters can be introduced to control the significance of each style. Similarly, for (beam search) weighted decoding, the distribution is re-weighted by

$$p(w|a_1, \cdots, a_n) = \text{Softmax}\Big(p(w)\prod_{i=1}^{n} \lambda_i p(a_i|w)\Big) \tag{10}$$

where λ_i are hyper-parameters that allow us to determine the significance of each style a_i. Finally,

MR: `OFFER(address=$slot1), OFFER(rating=$slot2)`	
W/o Style Control	There is a nice house at `$slot1` with a `$slot2` rating.
Short	`$slot1` is rated `$slot2`.
Long	There is a house at `$slot1` with a rating of `$slot2`. Would you like that one?
Has Rare Word	There is a lovely residence located at `$slot1`. It has a rating of `$slot2`.
First Person Pron.	I found a house at `$slot1` with a `$slot2` rating.
Second Person Pron.	There is a house at `$slot1` with a `$slot2` rating. Would you like that one?
Descriptive	There is a nice house with a `$slot2` rating available at `$slot1`.

MR: `OFFER_INTENT(intent=intent)`	
W/o Style Control	Would you like to make a reservation for this house?
Short	Do you want to reserve it?
Long	Do you want me to go ahead and reserve a room at the hotel?
Has Rare Word	Would you like to continue with the hotel reservation?
First Person Pron.	Shall I book the rooms in that hotel now?
Second Person Pron.	Would you like to make a reservation for this house?
Descriptive	Would you like to reserve a room at this hotel?

Table 12: Example outputs using conditional training for the six lexical styles described in Section 3.

conditional training and (beam search) weighted decoding can be used simultaneously by training a CT model and then applying WD or BSWD on the trained CT model during decoding time. Example outputs and the style accuracy of multiple style control using CT and BSWD are shown in Tables 13 and 14.

Lexical Style	Lexical Sty. Acc.	Semantic Style	Semantic Sty. Acc.
Short	55.4%	Formal	2.0%
Long	95.2%	Formal	39.1%
Short	69.2%	Positive	20.3%
Long	84.4%	Positive	44.8%

Table 13: Style accuracy of multiple-style control using CT and BSWD with beam width $B = 2$. The parameter *length* is controlled by CT and the parameters *formality* and *sentiment* are controlled by the BSWD.

D Human Evaluation Design

The goal of the annotation task is to evaluate the style of the automatically generated templates that express specific information to the user. The templates follow a certain style value such as "*formal*". The annotators are asked to imagine that they are having a conversation with the system, and that the template presented to them is an example of something that the system may say to them. The template may be in the form of a question, statement, confirmation, etc. Table 15 illustrates two sample MRs and four generated templates, which we lexicalize with a map of values (one per slot) to make the annotation task more intuitive.

MR: `OFFER(restaurant_name=$slot), OFFER(city=$slot2)`	Lexical Sty.	Semantic Sty.
`$slot1` in `$slot2` is a very popular indian restaurant. `$slot1` is a restaurant in `$slot2` that serves pizza and pasta.	W/o Style Control	W/o Style Control
`$slot1` is a restaurant in `$slot2`. `$slot1` serves italian food in `$slot2`.	Short	W/o Style Control
Okay! The `$slot1` located in `$slot2`, as for the tofu, it has a pretty good rating. Would you like to try for a lunch or dinner reservation? Okay! The `$slot1` located in `$slot2`, as for the tofu, it has a pretty good rating. Would you like to try for a meal there?	Long	W/o Style Control
`$slot1` is a nice restaurant located in `$slot2`. `$slot1` might interest you, and it is located in `$slot2`.	W/o Style Control	Positive
`$slot1` is a good restaurant in `$slot2`. `$slot1` restaurant is also in `$slot2`.	Short	Positive
Okay! The restaurant `$slot1` located right inside `$slot2` is a good one and it has many vegetarian side dishes. Okay! The restaurant `$slot1` located right inside `$slot2` is a good one. Do you wish to have your lunch here?	Long	Positive

MR: `OFFER(address=$slot1), OFFER(rating=$slot2)`	Lexical Sty.	Semantic Sty.
There is a `$slot2` rated house at `$slot1`. There is a house at `$slot1` with a `$slot2` rating.	W/o Style Control	W/o Style Control
`$slot1` has a `$slot2` rating `$slot1` with a `$slot2` rating	Short	W/o Style Control
There is a house at `$slot1` with a `$slot2` rating. would you like to stay here? There is a house at `$slot1` that you might be interested in. It has a `$slot2` average rating.	Long	W/o Style Control
There is a lovely house at `$slot1` with a rating of `$slot2` There is a good house at `$slot1` with a rating of `$slot2`	W/o Style Control	Positive
`$slot1` has a rating of `$slot2` `$slot1` with rating of `$slot2`	Short	Positive
There is a lovely residence located at `$slot1` with a rating of `$slot2` There is a nice house located at `$slot1` with a rating of `$slot2`	Long	Positive

Table 14: Example outputs by combining CT and BSWD with beam width $B = 2$. Lexical style is controlled by CT and semantic style is controlled by the BSWD. Note how the lexical style "long" tends to yield outputs that include more hallucinated content in an attempt to fulfill the required style goal(s).

Domain	Simplified MR	Output template
Movies	*request city none* *request movie_name none*	What is the location and type of movie you are interested in?
		What movie do you want to see and in what location?
Restaurants	*confirm restaurant_name [Ala Romana]* *confirm date [March 1st]*	Please confirm: booking a table at [Ala Romana] on [March 1st].
		Please confirm the following: you want a table at [Ala Romana] on [March 1st].

Table 15: Example human evaluation worksheet.

Using Pause Information for More Accurate Entity Recognition

Sahas Dendukuri[1,*], **Pooja Chitkara**[†], **Joel Ruben Antony Moniz**[2], **Xiao Yang**[†], **Manos Tsagkias**[2], **Stephen Pulman**[2]
[1]University of Michigan, [2]Apple
sahasd@umich.edu, chitkarapooja@yahoo.com, joelrubenantony_moniz@apple.com, graceyx.scut@gmail.com, {etsagkias, spulman}@apple.com

Abstract

Entity tags in human-machine dialog are integral to natural language understanding (NLU) tasks in conversational assistants. However, current systems struggle to accurately parse spoken queries with the typical use of text input alone, and often fail to understand the user intent. Previous work in linguistics has identified a cross-language tendency for longer speech pauses surrounding nouns as compared to verbs. We demonstrate that the linguistic observation on pauses can be used to improve accuracy in machine-learnt language understanding tasks. Analysis of pauses in French and English utterances from a commercial voice assistant shows the statistically significant difference in pause duration around multi-token entity span boundaries compared to within entity spans. Additionally, in contrast to text-based NLU, we apply pause duration to enrich contextual embeddings to improve shallow parsing of entities. Results show that our proposed novel embeddings improve the relative error rate by up to 8% consistently across three domains for French, without any added annotation or alignment costs to the parser.

Index Terms: Natural Language Understanding, BERT, Shallow Parsing, Entity Recognition, Contextual Embeddings

1 Introduction and Related Work

Voice assistants are increasingly becoming a part of our daily lives as they empower us to complete diverse and complex tasks. Today, voice assistants are able to make phone calls, take notes, set alarms, narrate bed time stories, or even rap hip-hop. Given a user's request, the assistant transcribes the input audio to text, and a natural language understanding (NLU) system classifies and routes the transcribed text to components that handle the request (e.g., phone call, notes, alarm).

Typical conversational NLU systems rely on text, the output of an automatic speech recognition (ASR) system (Muralidharan et al., 2019). These systems have proven successful, but relying wholly on text means that some analyses may be inaccurate (Nygaard et al., 2009), since acoustic signals may be needed to arrive at the right intent. For example, in the utterance "play thank you next", the pause duration between "you" and "next" can help determine if the request is to play the specific song "thank you next" or to play the song "thank you" but next in the queue. This disambiguating function of pause information is well known, but the potential role of pause information in signalling different types of constituents, as described in Seifart et al. (2018), has not, to our knowledge, been investigated in this setting.

Our goal is two-fold. Our first objective is to analyze the findings of Seifart et al. (2018) in the context of spoken conversations typical of those processed by voice assistants. Specifically, we show that differences in pause length around named entity spans is a statistically reliable processing cue. Our second goal is to demonstrate that the intuitive role of pause duration in aiding language understanding can be used in practice. Specifically, we present novel pause-grounded contextual embeddings that consistently outperform text-based representations in a language understanding task across multiple domains.

A standard approach to a tighter integration between acoustic information and NLU has been to use end-to-end models that can consume acoustic waveforms directly and learn NLU labels (Haghani et al., 2018). However, this approach can be difficult to adapt to traditional text-based tasks since audio inputs need to be labeled with task-specific information, introducing additional annotation costs.

An alternative approach is suggested by the recent and growing body of research which encodes text along with other modalities, such as audio

*work done as an intern at Apple
†work done while at Apple

Proceedings of the Third Workshop on Natural Language Processing for Conversational AI, pages 243–250
November 10, 2021. ©2021 Association for Computational Linguistics

Table 1: Statistics for the dataset EngFrPauseData.

Measure	French	English
Number of utterances	17,799	22,388
Average # tokens in an utterance	3.67	4.71
% of tokens that are entities	24%	24.52%
Average pause duration per token	51.60ms	33.64ms

and video, in a single embedding, known as multi-modal grounded embeddings (Settle et al., 2019; Jeon et al., 2019; Rahman et al., 2020; Lan et al., 2020; Chuang et al., 2019; Chung et al., 2020). These models have proven successful in tasks like speech recognition (Settle et al., 2019) and sentiment analysis (Rahman et al., 2020). However, they require the data from different modalities to be aligned in order to produce the embeddings, again increasing the cost of generating training data.

We work within this paradigm of multi-modal grounded embeddings using pause markers in spoken utterances for the task of *shallow parsing* (Ladhak et al., 2016; Vijayakumar et al., 2017; Rahman et al., 2020; Liu et al., 2020; Lan et al., 2020). We propose a novel self-supervised architecture adding a pause prediction task to traditional text-based BERT-style language models (Devlin et al., 2019). To the best of our knowledge, this is the first study on grounding textual embeddings in spoken pause signals.

We pre-train our embeddings using token-level pauses from the ASR system, and consume the representations in the downstream parsing task without fine-tuning. We do not input pause duration in our downstream task and, therefore, do not require data from different modalities to be aligned. This sets our approach apart from end-to-end approaches that use speech signals as input during inference, requiring additional task-specific annotation (such as Chi et al. (2020); Liu et al. (2020); Ling et al. (2020)).

2 Analysis of Pause Duration

In Seifart et al. (2018), time-aligned spoken language corpora in multiple languages were compared in terms of speech rate and pause duration. The variable of interest was the difference between nouns and verbs, with the subtlety that nominalisations of verbs still counted as verbs, and (less frequent) verbalisings of nouns counted as nouns. This means the the distinction was close to the traditional semantic distinction of 'object' and 'action' words. Their main findings were that speech rate slows relatively before nouns, and for most languages, pauses are more likely before nouns than before verbs.

We are most interested in the observation about pauses before nouns, as a potential signal for an upcoming named entity sequence. Named entities may not be limited to single nouns, but may be a span of tokens with at least a head noun. We analyze if pauses are more likely and/or longer before (or after) the boundary of an entity span than within the span itself.

We investigate this as follows. We consider a set of utterances from a large internal, anonymous dataset, collected over several months and domains (referred to throughout as UsageData). Given the sampling methodology, it can be concluded that there are no speaker-dependent effects in our dataset. The utterances have been taken from an upstream ASR system which provides each utterance hypothesis with pause durations following each token, in milliseconds. In order to test the findings of Seifart et al. (2018) in the voice assistant setting, we randomly sample UsageData utterances from the sports, movies, and music domains in English and French (referred as EngFrPauseData); see Table 1 for an overview.

We manually annotate EngFrPauseData with BIO-style tags (Ramshaw and Marcus, 1995; Tjong Kim Sang and De Meulder, 2003); O for non-entity, B for beginning of an entity, I for inside an entity. Furthermore, if a token is tagged with a B or I, it contains an additional entity tag (e.g., Artist). We combine the pause information from ASR with the named entity tags to derive pauses before, during, and after an entity. We aggregate pause and token duration statistics across all utterances for all domains in a language and fit distributions for the following pairs of settings: O-B, B-I, I-I, B-O, I-O. For example, an O-B pair marks the pause duration between a token tagged O and the token following it tagged B, while an I-I pair denotes the pause between a token tagged I and the token following it

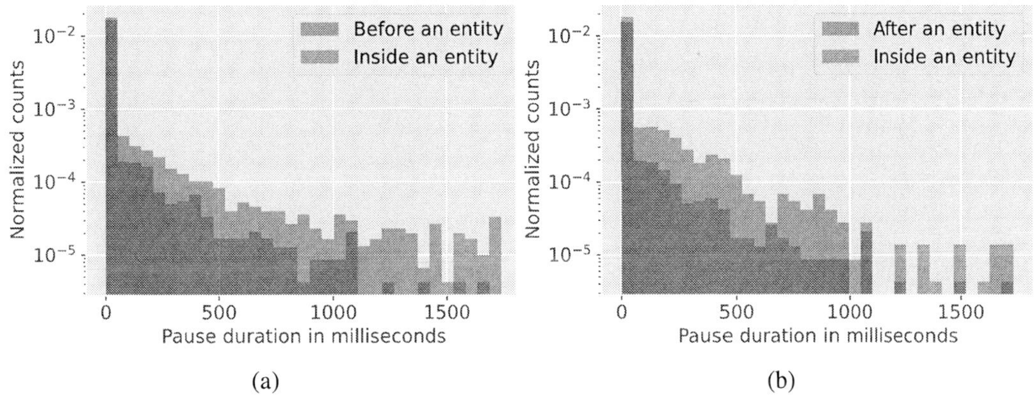

Figure 1: Histograms showing the normalized frequency distribution of the pause duration for French on the EngFrPause Data described in Table 1 across three domains: sports, movies, and music. x-axis marks pause duration in milliseconds (up to 3 standard deviations from the mean) for before (O-B) and inside (B-I and I-I) an entity (left), and after (B-O and I-O) and inside (B-I and I-I) an entity (right). y-axis shows log-normalized counts. Note that the deep purple-grey color is indicative of the red and blue histograms overlapping.

also tagged I.

To analyze whether the study in Seifart et al. (2018) can be extended to spoken entity sequences, we ask whether the pause duration before, within, and after an entity is different in a statistically significant way. To do this, we first log normalize the frequency of pauses before, inside, and after an entity to account for differences in their raw counts. In Fig. 1 and Fig. 2 we plot and compare histograms showing the normalized frequency distributions of pauses before an entity (O-B) and inside an entity (B-I and I-I), and inside an entity and after an entity (B-O and I-O) for French and English respectively. We observe that pauses before uttering and after uttering an entity are longer than pauses within the entity itself.

For French, the mean duration for pause within an entity is 18.17ms, for pause before an entity is 55.04ms, and for pause after an entity is 63.86ms. The differences in mean pause duration for both within and before an entity, and for within and after an entity are found statistically significant using a two sample statistical significance t-test; p-values are 4.59e-34 and 3.97e-20, respectively.

For English, the mean duration for pause within an entity is 15.21ms, for pause before an entity is 33.99ms, and for pause after an entity is 38.08ms. The differences in pause duration are again found to be statistically significant for both before and within an entity (p-value: 7.31e-33), and within and after an entity (p-value: 6.81e-36). These findings are in line with those from Seifart et al. (2018) and suggests that acoustic pauses are indeed a useful and complementary signal to text-based features.

Likewise, in Figure 3, we show the percentage frequency of pauses greater than or equal to 60ms for different types of entity labels. Here, too, we observe that such pauses are more frequent after or before entities (label types O-B, I-O, B-O) as compared to within entities (label types B-I, I-I), for both French (Figure 3a) and English (Figure 3b).

Note that the pause length difference within and outside an entity span tends to be greater in French than in English. Similarly, the difference in frequency of longer pauses at entity boundaries versus within entity spans is greater in French than in English, as can be visualized in Figure 3. We therefore carried out our further experiments on the French data (hereafter, FrPauseData), both for reasons of time, and on the grounds that any effects were more likely to show up there. [1]

3 Shallow Parsing

Our primary downstream setting that consumes contextual embeddings (described in Section 4) comprises of shallow parsing, as a sequence labelling task. It takes text output from an ASR system as the input, and produces an output label for each input token. The labels aim to recognize the intent of the spoken utterance, typically picking

[1] Regrettably, we could not find a public domain dataset with analogous properties so that our findings could be replicated by others, and so we have have presented results on this proprietary data and shared the statistics of our dataset.

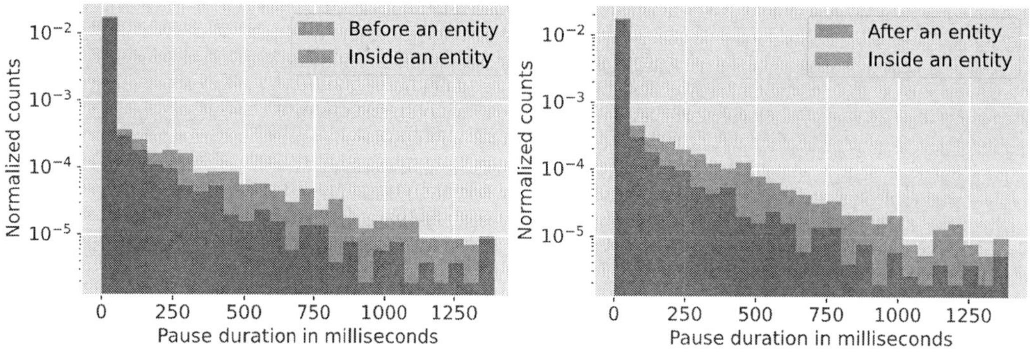

(a) (b)

Figure 2: Histograms showing the normalized frequency distribution of the pause duration for English on the EngFrPause Data described in Table 1 across three domains: sports, movies, and music. x-axis marks pause duration in milliseconds (up to 3 standard deviations from the mean) for before (O-B) and inside (B-I and I-I) an entity (left), and after (B-O and I-O) and inside (B-I and I-I) an entity (right). y-axis shows log-normalized counts. Note that the deep purple-grey color is indicative of the red and blue histograms overlapping.

out a verb and the phrases that could constitute arguments of the verb. For example, "play thank you next" would be parsed as "play/Verb thank/Song you/Song next/Song".[2]

In all experiments, we first pass the text output obtained from ASR into either a pre-trained baseline or pause-sensitive contextual embedding (refer Section 4). We pass the so-obtained contextual embedding representations into a relatively simple shallow parsing model. The shallow parser is a sequence tagger model that feeds the contextual embedding corresponding to each text token into a single-layered BiLSTM with a CRF on top, obtaining a predicted label for each token as the output (refer Fig. 4). During training, our shallow parser is optimized by minimizing the Negative Log Likelihood (NLL) over the data. Our shallow parser is identical to that of Muralidharan et al. (2021), except that we feed the output of the BiLSTM into a CRF layer, which we empirically observe boosts performance in all cases.

4 Pre-training Embeddings with Pause Information

The baseline version of the shallow parser uses a text-only embedding. This embedding is a BERT-style text-based language model (Devlin et al., 2019) trained without the next sentence prediction auxiliary task of the original BERT architecture.

To investigate the effect of pauses, we compare the baseline architecture with an identical BERT-based model extended with an additional spoken pause prediction task, as shown in Fig. 5. We are given, for each utterance, the pauses following each token in milliseconds, and we learn a model jointly optimizing a text-based language modeling task and a token-level pause duration prediction task. We add additional linear projections over intermediary representations from the encoder to predict pause durations following a token. We refer to the encoder as the "Joint Utterance Encoder", and to the linear projection as the "Pause Prediction Layer". We use negative log-likelihood (NLL) for categorical loss and mean squared error (MSE) for regression loss optimizations. We backpropagate the sum of the losses from both the text-based and the speech-based pause prediction tasks into the Joint Utterance Encoder.

We consider two variants of the prediction task:

Hierarchical Bin Classification [HBC]: The task is to perform hierarchical classification where the first linear projection predicts the boolean presence/absence of a pause and the second linear projection maps non-zero pauses (in the case of presence of a pause) into one of three labels: short, medium, and long, indicative of the pause durations.

Normalized Linear Regression [NLR]: The task is to linearly predict the length of pause (normalized into a range from zero to one) following a token.

More concretely, in a given utterance, let T_b be

[2]"thank you next" is the ASR recognition result for the song "Thank u, Next".

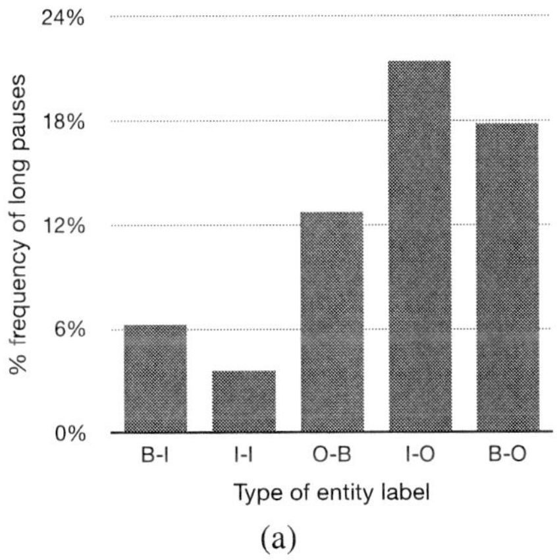

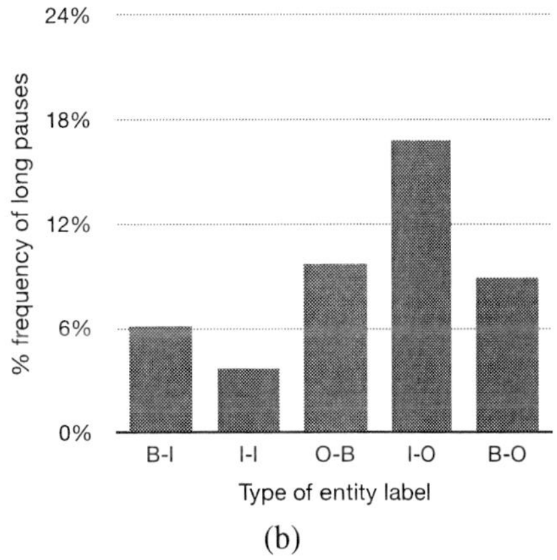

Figure 3: Histogram of percentage frequency of pause duration >=60ms on the EngFrPause Data (described in Table 1) per label type for (a) French and (b) English. x-axis marks entity label type and y-axis shows percentage frequency of long pauses. O-B, I-O, and B-O indicate label types at entity span boundaries (before/after entites), and B-I and I-I indicate label types within entity spans.

the set of tokens used to train the BERT-style model using a Masked Language Model (MLM) objective and l_i^b be the softmaxed LM prediction for the probability of the ith token t_i. Further, let T_s be the set of tokens on which the pause prediction tasks are to be trained, and for the t_i^{th} token, let l_i^c be the predicted probability of the true coarse-grained (presence/absence) label by HBC, let l_i^f be the predicted probability of the true fine-grained short (S), medium (M), or long (L) label by HBC, let l_i^r be the predicted pause by the NLR module, let $\mathbb{1}_{g_i^c}$ indicate the presence/absence of a pause, and let g_i^r be the true normalized pause duration. Then the baseline BERT-style encoder is trained by minimizing the loss

$$L_{\text{BERT}} = -\sum_{t_i \in T_b} \log l_i^b. \quad (1)$$

The loss for the HBC task is

$$L_{\text{HBC}} = -\sum_{t_i \in T_s} \left(\log l_i^c + \mathbb{1}_{g_i^c} \log l_i^f \right). \quad (2)$$

The loss for the NLR task is

$$L_{\text{NLR}} = \sum_{t_i \in T_s} (g_i^r - l_i^r)^2. \quad (3)$$

The joint loss is $L_{\text{BERT}} + \lambda L_{\text{HBC}}$ or $L_{\text{BERT}} + \lambda L_{\text{NLR}}$ respectively, where λ is a weighting factor set to 1 in our experiments.

5 Experimental Design

In our experiments, we compare the parser with the baseline version of text-only embeddings against a version using embeddings enhanced with pause information (HBC and NLR). This is the only dif ference between the two systems: the speech pause

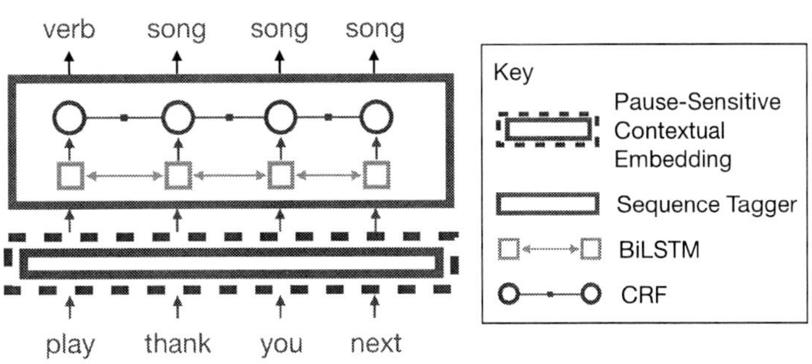

Figure 4: Illustration of our shallow parser module.

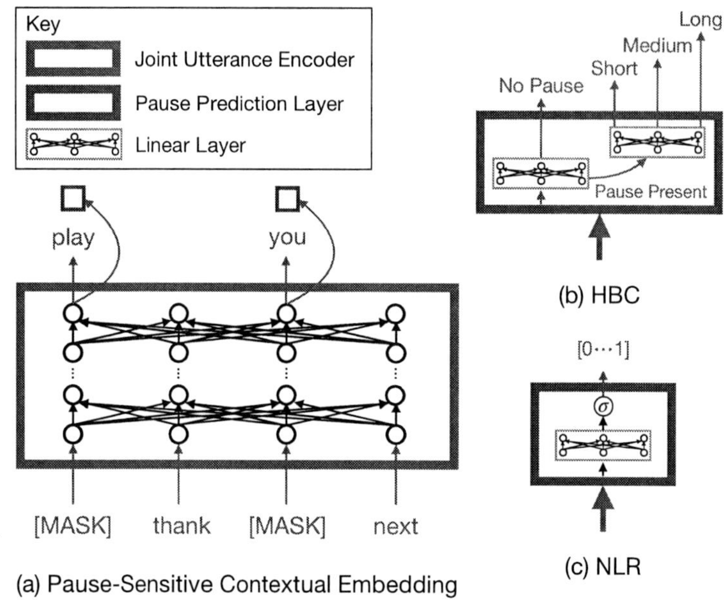

Figure 5: Pause-Sensitive Contextual Embedding. (a) Joint Utterance Encoder, in which the prediction layer can be (b) HBC, (c) NLR, or absent (baseline).

Table 2: Relative percent change in error rates for Shallow Parser with pause-sensitive embeddings. Boldface marks best performance for domain and metric.

Model	Domain	EER	TER	UER
HBC	Music	+0.47%	+0.22%	-2.34%
	Movies	-2.83%	-2.78%	-0.57%
	Sports	+0.70%	+0.71%	-1.12%
NLR	Music	**-2.94%**	**-3.32%**	**-4.10%**
	Movies	**-8.32%**	**-8.51%**	**-3.99%**
	Sports	**-2.63%**	**-2.67%**	**-3.22%**

signals used to pre-train the embeddings are not used directly in the parser. Neither the baseline version nor the pause-sensitive embeddings are fine-tuned in the parser.

For pre-training the BERT-style language models, we train over a random sample from the French section of UsageData without entity annotations ('FrTrainData'). FrTrainData contains about 50 million utterances with token-level ASR feature tuples consisting of recognized text and post-token pause duration (in milliseconds) for each input point.

To generate label boundaries for the HBC task, we sort pause durations in FrPauseData in ascending order and divide the resulting list of pauses into three parts with an equal number of data points. These serve as the label boundaries for the S, M, and L length labels for HBC. Empirically, pause durations less than 60ms are labeled as S, those between 60ms and 310ms are labeled as M, and those greater than 310ms are labeled as L. During training, we discard any pause greater than 10,000ms as noise from upstream ASR. For NLR, we normalize the pauses between 0 and 1 by dividing each duration by 10,000ms (the longest pause duration in the pruned dataset).

For the classification task, we opt for HBC to address the class imbalance problem in our data (Tsagkias et al., 2009) (see Figure 1, which shows a large proportion of tokens with zero pause detected). This coarse-to-fine approach helps with learning the presence/absence of pauses (coarse label) over the skewed dataset while also allowing the auxiliary S/M/L prediction (fine label) to be sufficiently fine-grained to prove useful in improving the feature representation.

To train the embeddings, we consider a vocabulary of the 100k most frequent tokens in FrTrainData. To train the pause prediction layers, we predict the labels over a subset of tokens per utterance. We randomly sample 15% of the tokens per utterance up to a maximum of 3 tokens, including at least one token with a non-empty label (words not contributing to the user intent are given a null label by the shallow parser). We backpropagate the sum of losses from the text-prediction and the pause-prediction tasks to the Joint Utterance Encoder.

We evaluate system performance on shallow parsing with three error rate measures at entity, token, and utterance levels:

Entity Error Rate (EER) measures the proportion of incorrectly labeled entities out of all entities.

Token Error Rate (TER) measures the proportion of incorrectly labeled entities out of all tokens (both entities and non-entities).

Utterance Error Rate (UER) measures the proportion of utterances with at least one mislabeled entity.

We report all metrics as means over 10 runs for each model configuration.

6 Results

We compare the performance of our pause-sensitive model with that of our baseline text-based BERT architecture in Table 2. Our best performing model consistently outperforms the baseline with an improvement in error rates on entity, token, and utterance levels across all three domains under study. We note that NLR consistently provides a greater improvement over HBC. This is in line with our expectations since user requests to a voice assistant are typically short utterances with small inter-token pauses (Table 1) across domains. Unlike the regression objective of the NLR model which is trained on exact pause durations scaled between 0 and 1, to train over the classification objective of HBC, we discretize these pause durations into four classes losing the granularity of small variations in these recorded pauses.

Looking at performance across domains, we observe that improvement in EER and TER for the Movies domain is consistently higher than that for Music and Sports. We look at FrPauseData to find that entity names in the Movies domain typically contain longer sequences of tokens than entities for the Music and Sports domains, where bynames and abbreviations are often used. On average, entity spans in the Movies domain are relatively longer than entity spans in Music by 49.64%, and in Sports by 39.71% in our dataset. For example, the majority entity span type in the Movies domain is 'movie title' which on average consists of 2.54 tokens and makes 34% of the domain. This token length is more than double that of the majority label type 'team name' in the Sports domain which makes 60% of the domain and contains 1.25 tokens on average. We note a similar pattern on observing the top-3 most frequent entity types per domain. For example, the mean token length for the top-3 most frequent labels in the Movies domain is 2.43 tokens compared with only 1.59 tokens in the Music domain. This relates with our earlier experiment with FrPauseData—we noted a longer mean pause duration of 120.23ms for Movies, compared with 39.06ms for Music, and 29.38ms for Sports. We hypothesize that longer sequences of entity names cause speakers to make longer pauses around these entity spans.

Finally, since the NLR model improves performance across all domains under study, we emphasize that it can be used in settings where a pre-trained set of embeddings are shared across multiple applications, which is particularly relevant in open-topic voice assistant NLU systems where the domain of a user request is ascertained at run time.

7 Conclusion

In this paper, we analyzed the statistically significant correlation of pause lengths with syntactic properties in real-world usage data for three entity-rich application domains. To exploit this property, we presented a novel pause-sensitive contextual embedding model. The model outperforms text-based representations in a language processing task across multiple domains. Our approach does not impose additional task-specific annotation requirements and can be extended to more text-based target tasks. To the best of our knowledge, this is the first study on grounding textual representations in pause signals for improved understanding in voice assistants.

Acknowledgements

The authors would like to thank Barry Theobald, Murat Akbacak, Lin Li, Sachin Agarwal, Anusha Kamath, John Bridle, Aaksha Meghawat, Melvyn

Hunt, and Ahmed Hussen Abdelaziz for their help and feedback.

References

Po-Han Chi, Pei-Hung Chung, Tsung-Han Wu, Chun-Cheng Hsieh, Shang-Wen Li, and Hung-yi Lee. 2020. Audio albert: A lite bert for self-supervised learning of audio representation. *arXiv preprint*.

Yung-Sung Chuang, Chi-Liang Liu, and Hung-Yi Lee. 2019. Speechbert: Cross-modal pre-trained language model for end-to-end spoken question answering. *arXiv preprint*.

Yu-An Chung, Chenguang Zhu, and Michael Zeng. 2020. Semi-supervised speech-language joint pre-training for spoken language understanding. *arXiv preprint*.

Jacob Devlin, Ming-Wei Chang, Kenton Lee, and Kristina Toutanova. 2019. BERT: Pre-training of deep bidirectional transformers for language understanding. In *NACL*, pages 4171–4186. ACL.

Parisa Haghani, Arun Narayanan, Michiel Bacchiani, Galen Chuang, Neeraj Gaur, Pedro Moreno, Rohit Prabhavalkar, Zhongdi Qu, and Austin Waters. 2018. From audio to semantics: Approaches to end-to-end spoken language understanding. In *2018 IEEE Spoken Language Technology Workshop (SLT)*, pages 720–726. IEEE.

W. Jeon, L. Liu, and H. Mason. 2019. Voice trigger detection from lvcsr hypothesis lattices using bidirectional lattice recurrent neural networks. In *ICASSP*, pages 6356–6360. IEEE.

Faisal Ladhak, Ankur Gandhe, Markus Dreyer, Lambert Mathias, Ariya Rastrow, and Björn Hoffmeister. 2016. Latticernn: Recurrent neural networks over lattices. In *Interspeech*, pages 695–699. ISCA.

Zhenzhong Lan, Mingda Chen, Sebastian Goodman, Kevin Gimpel, Piyush Sharma, and Radu Soricut. 2020. Albert: A lite bert for self-supervised learning of language representations. In *ICLR*.

Shaoshi Ling, Julian Salazar, Yuzong Liu, Katrin Kirchhoff, and AWS Amazon. 2020. Bertphone: Phonetically-aware encoder representations for utterance-level speaker and language recognition. In *The Speaker and Language Recognition Workshop*, pages 9–16. ISCA.

A. T. Liu, S. Yang, P. Chi, P. Hsu, and H. Lee. 2020. Mockingjay: Unsupervised speech representation learning with deep bidirectional transformer encoders. In *ICASSP*, pages 6419–6423. IEEE.

D. Muralidharan, J. Kao, X. Yang, L. Li, L. Viswanathan, M. Ibrahim, Kevin Luikens, Stephen Pulman, A. Garg, Atish Kothari, and J. Williams. 2019. Leveraging user engagement signals for entity labeling in a virtual assistant. *arXiv*.

Deepak Muralidharan, Joel Ruben Antony Moniz, Sida Gao, Xiao Yang, Justine Kao, Stephen Pulman, Atish Kothari, Ray Shen, Yinying Pan, Vivek Kaul, et al. 2021. Noise robust named entity understanding for voice assistants. In *Proceedings of the 2021 Conference of the North American Chapter of the Association for Computational Linguistics: Human Language Technologies: Industry Papers*, pages 196–204.

Lynne C Nygaard, Debora S Herold, and Laura L Namy. 2009. The semantics of prosody: Acoustic and perceptual evidence of prosodic correlates to word meaning. *Cognitive science*, 33(1):127–146.

Wasifur Rahman, Md Kamrul Hasan, Sangwu Lee, AmirAli Bagher Zadeh, Chengfeng Mao, Louis-Philippe Morency, and Ehsan Hoque. 2020. Integrating multimodal information in large pretrained transformers. In *ACL*, pages 2359–2369. ACL.

Lance Ramshaw and Mitch Marcus. 1995. Text chunking using transformation-based learning. In *Third Workshop on Very Large Corpora*, SIGDAT. ACL.

Frank Seifart, Jan Strunk, Swintha Danielsen, Iren Hartmann, Brigitte Pakendorf, Søren Wichmann, Alena Witzlack-Makarevich, Nivja H. de Jong, and Balthasar Bickel. 2018. Nouns slow down speech across structurally and culturally diverse languages. *Proceedings of the National Academy of Sciences*, 115(22):5720–5725.

Shane Settle, Kartik Audhkhasi, Karen Livescu, and Michael Picheny. 2019. Acoustically grounded word embeddings for improved acoustics-to-word speech recognition. In *ICASSP*, pages 5641–5645.

Erik F. Tjong Kim Sang and Fien De Meulder. 2003. Introduction to the conll-2003 shared task: Language-independent named entity recognition. In *HLT-NAACL*, CONLL, pages 142–147. ACL.

Manos Tsagkias, Wouter Weerkamp, and Maarten de Rijke. 2009. Predicting the volume of comments on online news stories. In *CIKM*, pages 1765–1768. ACM.

Ashwin Vijayakumar, Ramakrishna Vedantam, and Devi Parikh. 2017. Sound-Word2Vec: Learning word representations grounded in sounds. In *EMNLP*, pages 920–925. ACL.

Think Before You Speak: Learning to Generate Implicit Knowledge for Response Generation by Self-Talk

Pei Zhou[1*] Behnam Hedayatnia[2] Karthik Gopalakrishnan[2] Seokhwan Kim[2]
Jay Pujara[1] Xiang Ren[1] Yang Liu[2] Dilek Hakkani-Tur[2]
[1] Department of Computer Science, University of Southern California
[2] Amazon Alexa AI
{peiz, jpujara, xiangren}@usc.edu,
{behnam, karthgop, seokhwk, yangliud, hakkanit}@amazon.com

1 Introduction

End-to-end response generation (RG) models based on pre-trained transformer-based (Vaswani et al., 2017) language models (LM) have shown to produce human-like responses (Zhang et al., 2020; Lewis et al., 2020; Roller et al., 2020). Humans, however, not only "*just utter the right sentence*", but also contribute to the common ground consisting of mutual beliefs and common knowledge "*whose truth is taken for granted as part of the background of the conversation*" (Stalnaker, 1978; Clark and Schaefer, 1989; Clark and Brennan, 1991). For example, consider the utterance "*I need to buy some flowers for my wife*", a potential appropriate response is "*Perhaps you'd be interested in red roses*". To produce this response, the participant needs to understand relevant background knowledge such as "*rose is a type of flower*". Note that this background knowledge is *implicit* in the dialogue turns, meaning that an end-to-end RG system that takes utterances as input and outputs responses will omit this intermediate process that is crucial for humans in communications.

To fill the gap between current model's RG process and how humans use implicit background knowledge in conversations, we focus on *commonsense inference* as a type of background knowledge and aim to *train RG models that first generate implicit commonsense inferences before producing a response given previous utterances.* Inspired by inquiry-based discovery learning (Bruner, 1961) and the self-talk procedure (Shwartz et al., 2020), we encourage the RG model to talk with itself to elicit implicit knowledge before making a response.

Collecting training data is challenging for our purpose since commonsense knowledge is by definition often omitted in conversations. We use ConceptNet triples (Speer et al., 2017) as the knowledge schema to represent knowledge and align common sense-focused dialogues (Zhou et al., 2021) with knowledge to train RG models. We conduct extensive human evaluation on different variants of our training procedure and find that models that generate implicit background knowledge before responding produce more grammatical, coherent, and engaging responses compared to RG models that directly generate responses. Further analysis shows that models can sometimes even learn to distinguish *when it is necessary to self-talk to generate implicit knowledge*, i.e., be aware of potential knowledge gaps in dialogues. We hope our findings encourage more future studies on making RG models better emulate human communication process and produce better-quality responses.

[*] Work done while Pei Zhou was an intern at Amazon Alexa AI

2 Task Formulation and Setup

Given a dialogue history (multi-turn or single-turn) U, the task is to generate implicit background knowledge I and then produce a response R given both U and I. Extending most neural RG models that treat this as a *conditional language modeling* problem, we aim to learn the conditional probability distribution $P(I, R|U)$ by training on human dialogues.

2.1 Data Preparation

Knowledge Schema We consider *ConceptNet* (Speer et al., 2017) as our knowledge schema, which is a large-scale crowdsourced commonsense knowledge base consisting of triples such as "*buy, RelatedTo, money*". We have explored several other sources such as LMs trained to generate knowledge (Hwang et al., 2021; Becker et al., 2021) but observe much noise while aligning knowledge to dialogue turns.

Dialogues We use dialogue datasets from Zhou et al. (2021) as they propose "*common sense-focused dialogues*" by filtering three existing di-

Proceedings of the Third Workshop on Natural Language Processing for Conversational AI, pages 251–253
November 10, 2021. ©2021 Association for Computational Linguistics

alogue datasets DailyDialog (Li et al., 2017), EmpatheticDialogues (Rashkin et al., 2019), MuTual (Cui et al., 2020) using ConceptNet triples, and also crowdsourced SocialIQA-prompted dialogues (Zhou et al., 2021). We extract dialogues that each has at least one matched triple from ConceptNet in one of its consecutive turn pairs, resulting in around 31k dialogues and 159k turns we can use for training instances (excluding the first turn). The total number of turn pairs that have at least one matched triple is around 57k.

2.2 Training Setup

Each of our training instance is a sequence of tokens with three components: a dialog history U, implicit knowledge (empty or non-empty) I, and a response R. We enclose the implicit knowledge I with special symbols "<implicit>" and "< \implicit>" and add it between U and R. For example: "*<bos> <speaker1> I need to buy some flowers for my wife. <implicit> rose is a type of flower < \implicit> <speaker2> Perhaps you'd be interested in red roses <eos>*". We train the models to generate everything after <implicit> till <eos>, i.e. generate I and R conditioned on U. We use GPT2-medium (Radford et al.) and train the model for 3 epochs with batch size 4 and learning rate 6.25e-5.

Training Variations We also explore different ways to better train a model that can both self-talk and respond in dialogues. 1). **Two-Step training** Instead of jointly modeling $P(I, R|U)$ in a one-shot fashion, we consider split the instance to first train the model to generate I only based on U and then train it to generate R based on both I and U, i.e. $P(I|U)$ and then $P(R|U, I)$. 2). **Learning to distinguish when knowledge is needed.** In addition to using only the 57k instances where there is always non-empty implicit knowledge, we also evaluate using all dialogue instances, some of which have empty implicit knowledge. This allows us to evaluate if models can determine when to self-talk and when it is not needed (e.g., for simple chitchat utterances). 3). **Imbalanced VS balanced training set** Since we have more instances with empty implicit knowledge than non-empty knowledge (102k vs. 57k), we consider an imbalanced training set where we include all 159k instances and a balanced version where we randomly sample the same number of empty knowledge instances as non-empty ones (114k total).

	Grammatical	Coherent	Engaging
Prefers Self-Talk	**134**	**152**	**148**
Prefers Vanilla	116	121	120
Not Sure	50	27	32

Table 1: Human evaluation on three criteria by comparing vanilla RG model versus the *imbalanced* version

	Grammatical	Coherent	Engaging
Prefers Balanced	**145**	**139**	**154**
Prefers Imbalanced	128	128	128
Not Sure	27	33	18

Table 2: Human evaluation on three criteria by comparing self-talk models trained on *balanced* data versus the *imbalanced* version

3 Preliminary Results

For evaluation, we randomly sample 300 instances from unseen test dialogues for human evaluation. We provide a dialogue history and two model responses and ask three workers on Amazon Mechanical Turk (AMT) platform to select which one is better or not sure. We consider three criteria following most previous RG evaluation: which response is more *grammatical*, *coherent*, and *engaging*.

We generally find trained models follow the template of first generating implicity knowledge and then respond. Some example outputs to the utterance "*I need to buy some flowers for my wife*" are "*(buy is related to expensive) Can you afford the expensive flowers?*" and "*(buy is related to money) How much money do you want to spend?*".

Self-Talk models produce higher quality responses than vanilla RG models Table 1 shows that when comparing with a vanilla RG trained on dialogues, the two-step self-talk models improve on all three aspects, especially on coherence and engagingness.

Balanced training data results in better model Table 2 shows that although imbalanced self-talk model contains 45k more training instances than the balanced version, models trained on balanced data perform better on all three criteria, posing interesting phenomenon for later studies.

Due to page limit, we will summarize results for other model comparisons. We find two-step training outperforms one-step and learning to distinguish outperforms always outputs some implicit knowledge. We also find interesting new knowledge generated from models (not included in ConceptNet we used), e.g. "*bus is located at airport*".

References

Maria Becker, Siting Liang, and Anette Frank. 2021. Reconstructing implicit knowledge with language models. In *Proceedings of Deep Learning Inside Out (DeeLIO): The 2nd Workshop on Knowledge Extraction and Integration for Deep Learning Architectures*, pages 11–24.

Jerome S Bruner. 1961. The act of discovery. *Harvard educational review*.

Herbert H Clark and Susan E Brennan. 1991. Grounding in communication.

Herbert H Clark and Edward F Schaefer. 1989. Contributing to discourse. *Cognitive science*, 13(2):259–294.

Leyang Cui, Yu Wu, Shujie Liu, Yue Zhang, and Ming Zhou. 2020. Mutual: A dataset for multi-turn dialogue reasoning. In *Proceedings of the 58th Annual Meeting of the Association for Computational Linguistics*, pages 1406–1416.

Jena D. Hwang, Chandra Bhagavatula, Ronan Le Bras, Jeff Da, Keisuke Sakaguchi, Antoine Bosselut, and Yejin Choi. 2021. Comet-atomic 2020: On symbolic and neural commonsense knowledge graphs. In *AAAI*.

Mike Lewis, Yinhan Liu, Naman Goyal, Marjan Ghazvininejad, Abdelrahman Mohamed, Omer Levy, Veselin Stoyanov, and Luke Zettlemoyer. 2020. BART: Denoising sequence-to-sequence pre-training for natural language generation, translation, and comprehension. In *Proceedings of the 58th Annual Meeting of the Association for Computational Linguistics*, pages 7871–7880, Online. Association for Computational Linguistics.

Yanran Li, Hui Su, Xiaoyu Shen, Wenjie Li, Ziqiang Cao, and Shuzi Niu. 2017. Dailydialog: A manually labelled multi turn dialogue dataset. In *Proceedings of the Eighth International Joint Conference on Natural Language Processing (Volume 1: Long Papers)*, pages 986–995.

Alec Radford, Jeffrey Wu, Rewon Child, David Luan, Dario Amodei, Ilya Sutskever, et al. Language models are unsupervised multitask learners.

Hannah Rashkin, Eric Michael Smith, Margaret Li, and Y-Lan Boureau. 2019. Towards empathetic open-domain conversation models: A new benchmark and dataset. In *Proceedings of the 57th Annual Meeting of the Association for Computational Linguistics*, pages 5370–5381.

Stephen Roller, Emily Dinan, Naman Goyal, Da Ju, Mary Williamson, Yinhan Liu, Jing Xu, Myle Ott, Kurt Shuster, Eric M Smith, et al. 2020. Recipes for building an open-domain chatbot. *arXiv preprint arXiv:2004.13637*.

Vered Shwartz, Peter West, Ronan Le Bras, Chandra Bhagavatula, and Yejin Choi. 2020. Unsupervised commonsense question answering with self-talk. In *Proceedings of the 2020 Conference on Empirical Methods in Natural Language Processing (EMNLP)*, pages 4615–4629.

Robyn Speer, Joshua Chin, and Catherine Havasi. 2017. Conceptnet 5.5: An open multilingual graph of general knowledge. In *Thirty-first AAAI conference on artificial intelligence*.

Robert C Stalnaker. 1978. Assertion. In *Pragmatics*, pages 315–332. Brill.

Ashish Vaswani, Noam Shazeer, Niki Parmar, Jakob Uszkoreit, Llion Jones, Aidan N Gomez, Łukasz Kaiser, and Illia Polosukhin. 2017. Attention is all you need. In *Advances in neural information processing systems*, pages 5998–6008.

Yizhe Zhang, Siqi Sun, Michel Galley, Yen-Chun Chen, Chris Brockett, Xiang Gao, Jianfeng Gao, Jingjing Liu, and Bill Dolan. 2020. DIALOGPT : Large-scale generative pre-training for conversational response generation. In *Proceedings of the 58th Annual Meeting of the Association for Computational Linguistics: System Demonstrations*, pages 270–278, Online. Association for Computational Linguistics.

Pei Zhou, Karthik Gopalakrishnan, Behnam Hedayatnia, Seokhwan Kim, Jay Pujara, Xiang Ren, Yang Liu, and Dilek Hakkani-Tur. 2021. Commonsense-focused dialogues for response generation: An empirical study. In *Proceedings of the 21th Annual Meeting of the Special Interest Group on Discourse and Dialogue*.

Teach Me What to Say and I Will Learn What to Pick: Unsupervised Knowledge Selection Through Response Generation with Pretrained Generative Models

Ehsan Lotfi, Maxime De Bruyn, Jeska Buhmann, Walter Daelemans
CLiPS Research Center
University of Antwerp, Belgium
firstname.lastname@uantwerpen.be

Abstract

Knowledge Grounded Conversation Models (KGCM) are usually based on a selection/retrieval module and a generation module, trained separately or simultaneously, with or without having access to a 'gold' knowledge option. With the introduction of large pre-trained generative models, the selection and generation part have become more and more entangled, shifting the focus towards enhancing knowledge incorporation (from multiple sources) instead of trying to pick the best knowledge option. These approaches however depend on knowledge labels and/or a separate dense retriever for their best performance. In this work we study the unsupervised selection abilities of pre-trained generative models (e.g. BART) and show that by adding a score-and-aggregate module between encoder and decoder, they are capable of learning to pick the proper knowledge through minimising the language modelling loss (i.e. without having access to knowledge labels). Trained as such, our model - K-Mine - shows competitive selection and generation performance against models that benefit from knowledge labels and/or separate dense retriever.

1 Introduction

The ability to properly ground conversations in structured and unstructured data, has become an increasingly important feature in designing conversational agents. By generating more informative and specific responses, such models can establish human-machine interactions that are more engaging and less prone to producing bland and common responses. The task of modelling knowledge-grounded conversations is traditionally decomposed into two sub-tasks: 1) knowledge selection (**KS**), i.e. picking the proper knowledge piece(s) from a provided pool based on dialogue history, and 2) response generation (**RG**), i.e. producing a response to the user's utterance conditioned on both dialogue history and selected knowledge piece(s). Therefore and because of this sequential dependency, the generation performance is directly affected by model's selection/retrieval ability and the way this knowledge is being incorporated in the generation process.

Early examples of knowledge grounded conversation models mainly tried to diffuse the external knowledge as an extra hidden state into the decoder part of a recurrent seq-to-seq architecture (Liu et al., 2018; Ghazvininejad et al., 2018). With the release of large knowledge grounded conversational datasets like Wizard of Wikipedia (Dinan et al., 2019), Topical-chat (Gopalakrishnan et al., 2019) and Holl-E (Moghe et al., 2018), the field witnessed numerous studies aimed to best coordinate the KS and RG sub-tasks to improve the overall performance of models. As an early standard baseline Dinan et al. (2019) proposed variations of Transformer MemNet, a generative model trained to do KS and RG using a memory network for selecting the most relevant knowledge piece.

Attempts to improve on these benchmarks can mostly be divided into two categories, based on their point of focus. **Selection oriented methods** focus on enhancing the KS task, usually by introducing additional learning signals like the prior-posterior discrepancy (Lian et al., 2019; Chen et al., 2020) or long-term structural traits of conversations like flow and initiative changes (Kim et al., 2020; Meng et al., 2020; Zhan et al., 2021; Meng et al., 2021; Zheng et al., 2020). **Generation oriented methods** on the other hand, try to mitigate the selection bottleneck by employing more powerful methods to incorporate knowledge in the generation process, thus reformulating the KS problem as an adaptive fine-grained selection to be dealt with in decoding (Zheng and Zhou, 2019). This was especially encouraged with the introduction of large pretrained generative models like GPT2 (Radford et al., 2019), BART (Lewis et al., 2019) and T5

Proceedings of the Third Workshop on Natural Language Processing for Conversational AI, pages 254–262
November 10, 2021. ©2021 Association for Computational Linguistics

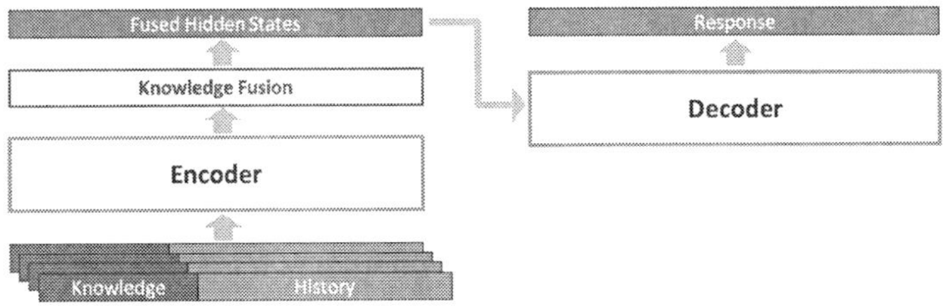

Figure 1: General overview of our model based on a pretrained encoder-decoder like BART

(Raffel et al., 2020) which allow leveraging their ability in conditional text generation (Zhao et al., 2020; De Bruyn et al., 2020). More recently RAG (Lewis et al., 2021) and FiD (Izacard and Grave, 2021) models have been proposed (primarily in the QA context) to ease the computational costs and limitations of these big models, especially if the supporting passage(s) needs to be retrieved from a huge unstructured corpus. Since these models integrate the KS and RG tasks, they do not need labeled knowledge for training, although a knowledge pool of manageable size is provided often via a parametric or non-parametric retrieval module.

In this study we propose K-Mine (Knowledge Mixing in encoder); a model that bridges between the two aforementioned paradigms by doing unsupervised knowledge selection with and within pretrained generative models (e.g. BART). Using a simple score-and-aggregate module between the encoder and decoder of such a model, K-Mine learns to (soft-) select the most relevant passage without needing knowledge labels or a separate retriever, while maintaining the generative skills of the original pretrained model. Our experiments show very competitive performances on two knowledge grounded conversation datasets and state of the art results in integrated unsupervised knowledge selection.

2 Related Work

Like most NLP tasks, knowledge grounded conversation has been significantly influenced by the introduction of large pretrained language models, which have helped generative models beat retrieval models in both automatic and human evaluations (Roller et al., 2020). Thanks to their language modeling skills, these models have shown the ability to use the provided context (e.g. history, knowledge, persona, etc.) on a per-demand basis, thus alleviating the knowledge selection bottleneck. Adapting them to the specifics of the problem, usually requires modifications in such a way that would still allow for leveraging model's pretrained skills. Zhao et al. (2020) employed reinforcement learning to jointly optimize KS and RG with unlabeled dialogues in a BERT-GPT2 based architecture. De Bruyn et al. (2020) opted for BART by modifying the encoder to do the supervised KS task and showed that providing the decoder with more knowledge pieces (top-k instead of 1), leads to a lower RG perplexity. Izacard and Grave (2021) proposed Fusion in Decoder (FiD) which passes a selection of individually encoded question-knowledge pairs as a single concatenated sequence to decoder, hence reducing the computational cost of self-attention over all knowledge options at once. RAG (Lewis et al., 2021) is another (more general) framework to incorporate knowledge in text generation which allows the (pretrained) decoder to choose content from top-k retrieved knowledge pieces via token-wise or sequence-wise marginalization. In principle FiD and RAG replace the KS step with a pool retrieval task that provides the pretrained model with multiple (top-k) relevant passages to attend to (FiD) or marginalize over (RAG) during generation. In particular RAG benefits from a DPR retriever which is updated (only the query encoder part) during training through the back-propagation of generation error. Recently Shuster et al. (2021) adopted FiD and RAG (originally introduced mainly for QA tasks) for knowledge grounded conversation and tried to improve the performance with a variety of general and task-inspired modifications, e.g. using poly encoders (Humeau et al., 2020) or extending the marginalized decoding idea to dialog turns.

Our work has similarities with both FiD and RAG in the sense of learning knowledge grounded generation with pretrained models and without the need to have labeled knowledge. It is however different in some key aspects. The retrieval/selection part in K-Mine is truly and completely integrated

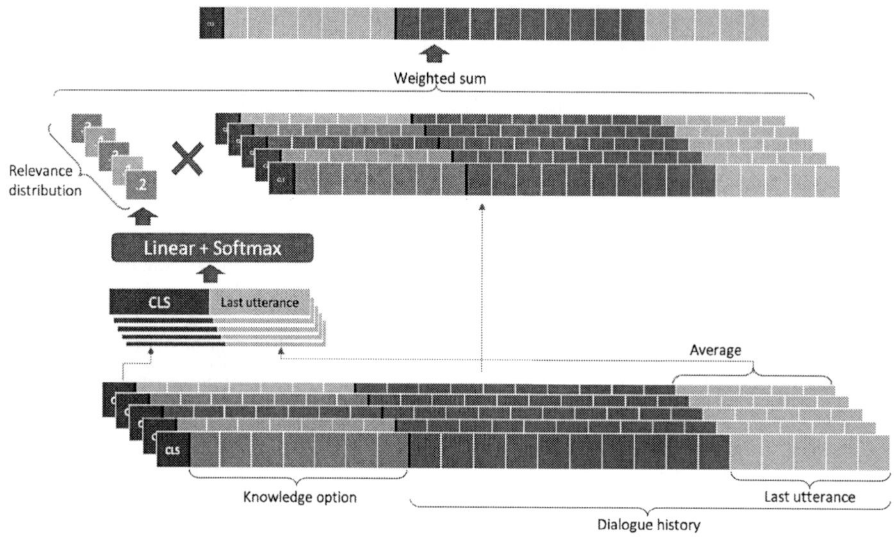

Figure 2: Inside the knowledge fusion module: Inputs are the encoded knowledge-history pairs (same history with different (in this case 5) knowledge options) from which the [CLS] embedding and the average last utterance embedding are concatenated and fed to a linear layer to calculate relevance scores. The scores are converted to a distribution via a normalizing function like Softmax. Finally the normalized scores are used to produce a weighted sum of the inputs which will be passed to the decoder as the encoder output.

inside the pretrained model, so unlike RAG, it does not require a separate parametric retriever, and unlike FiD, it is not totally disentangled from the retriever. Moreover, unlike both FiD and RAG, K-Mine aggregates over encoded knowledge options before passing them to the decoder. We will discuss the advantages and disadvantages of these choices at the end of the paper.

3 Methodology

3.1 Problem Definition and Formalization

In general the question of knowledge grounded conversation modelling is defined over dialog and knowledge datasets $\mathcal{D}_d = \{(C_i, r_i)\}_{i=1}^{N}$ and $\mathcal{D}_k = \{(k_j)\}_{j=1}^{M}$ where $\forall i \in \{1, ..., N\}$, C_i and r_i represent context and response for a specific dialog turn, and $\forall j \in \{1, ..., M\}$, k_j is a knowledge piece (e.g. a sentence or paragraph). $\mathcal{D}_d$ and $\mathcal{D}_k$ usually are connected through a retrieval function:

$$f_{ret} : \mathcal{D}_d \rightarrow \mathcal{D}_k^m \; ; \; m \in \{0, ..., M\} \, , m << M$$

f_{ret} can be part of the trained model or a non-parametric module which does a preliminary filtering by narrowing down the knowledge options from M to m, based on some similarity metric. In most knowledge grounded conversation datasets, $\mathcal{D}_d$ and $\mathcal{D}_k$ are provided as parallel, which allows for a simpler formalization over $\mathcal{D} = \{(C_i, K_i, r_i)\}_{i=1}^{N}$, where $K_i \in \mathcal{D}_k^m$; $m \in \{0, ..., M\}$ is the narrowed down subset of the original $\mathcal{D}_k$, and often includes a 'gold truth', i.e. the knowledge piece which has been picked by the (human) participant during data curating. We consider the model to be 'Fully-supervised' if this gold truth is used in training. Otherwise, it will be referred to as 'RG-supervised'.

3.2 Approach and model

Figure 1 shows a general overview of our model which is built by adding a 'knowledge fusion' module between the encoder and decoder of a pretrained generative model like BART. The encoder receives the input sequence as the concatenation of the $[CLS]$ token, a knowledge option and the dialog history which includes the last u utterances, each pre-pended by special identifier tokens $<user>$ or $<agent>$ based on the speaker. One learning sample contains m such sequences (padded to the same length) with different knowledge options and same history, which allows the encoder to create m contextualized encodings for each knowledge-history pair. These encodings then are passed to the knowledge manager module which fuses them and creates a single sequence of hidden states to be fed to the decoder as the final encoder output. In order to make the manipula-

Dataset	Train		Valid		Test		#Kn
	All	w/ Kn	All	w/ Kn	All	w/ Kn	
Wizard of Wikipedia	82965	77332	8814	8270	4336/4370	4073/4119	63
HOLL-E	36584	34632	4654	4399	4602	4339	58

Table 1: Overview of datasets used in the study. Numbers are for turns with access to knowledge and *w/ Kn* refers to the number of such turns for which a knowledge option has been chosen to generate the response. WoW test set is divided into seen/unseen subsets and *#Kn* is the (average) number of knowledge options provided for each turn.

tion and modification of hidden states easier in the knowledge fusion module, we pad-truncate knowledge options to the same length, decided by the dataset statistics.

Figure 2 shows a detailed overview of how the fusion is done. The module receives the encoded knowledge-history pairs (created by the pretrained encoder), from which the [CLS] token embedding and the average embedding of the last utterance are concatenated and fed to a linear layer to calculate relevance scores for each pair. The scores then are converted into a distribution by a normalizing function (e.g. Softmax). Finally the normalized scores are used to produce a weighted sum of the inputs which will be passed to the pretrained decoder as the encoder hidden states. Empirically the fused output can be written as:

$$h_j^{fus} = \sum_{i=1}^{m} \alpha_i H_{ij}^{enc}$$

$$\alpha_i = f([CLS_i; mean(LU_i)])$$

where m is the number of knowledge options for each sample, H_i^{enc} is the encoded hidden states for the i_{th} knowledge-history pair, LU is the last utterance and f is the $Softmax(Linear)$ operator. The training is done by minimizing the usual NLL loss over the generated response in decoder. The knowledge fusion module can be also supervised by introducing a BCE loss with respect to the gold truth (when available). So in general:

$$\mathcal{L} = (1 - \lambda)\mathcal{L}_{RG} + \lambda\mathcal{L}_{KS} \qquad (1)$$

although the RG-supervised case ($\lambda = 0$) is of more interest to us.

4 Experiments

4.1 Data

We study our model on 2 publicly available datasets for knowledge grounded conversation (KGC):

Wizard of Wikipedia (WoW)(Dinan et al., 2019) is a widely used dataset for open-domain KGC created by crowd-sourcing dialogues between an *apprentice* and a *wizard* who has access to a retrieved pool of Wikipedia passages which he/she can use in conversing with the apprentice. WoW consists of 22311 conversations (split into train, valid and test) over 1365 general topics. The validation and test set are further split into *seen* and *unseen* versions where the latter contains dialogues with new topics not discussed in the training data, for out-of-distribution topic evaluations. The knowledge pool size varies and on average each wizard turn is provided with ~63 Wikipedia passages, although not all wizard turns make use of these options in generating the response[1].

HOLL-E (Moghe et al., 2018) is another KGC dataset that contains 7228, 930 and 913 dialogues for training, validation and test. Each conversation is about a specific movie and both parties have access to a document which contains the plot and a fact table besides a selection of viewer comments and reviews. The original dataset provides a list of spans in the document as knowledge options and indicates the one (if any) that has been used to generate the response. We use the processed version provided by Kim et al. (2020) which changed it to the WoW format by redefining the spans as complete sentences.

Table 1 summarizes important information for these datasets. To have a more detailed evaluation, we do the experiments under two data settings: **w/Kn**; i.e. only including turns which use knowledge and **All**; i.e. including all turns.

4.2 Evaluation metrics

Following the related literature, we employ commonly used automatic metrics; **R@1** for knowl-

[1]We use the pre-processed dataset provided by Zheng and Zhou (2019) in `https://github.com/ChuanMeng/DukeNet/`.

edge selection, and unigram **F1**, **ROUGE** and **PPL** (perplexity) for response generation. When comparing with variations (Table 4) we also use **KF1** or Knowledge-F1 introduced by Shuster et al. (2021) which measures the unigram word overlap between the model's generation and the ground-truth knowledge. Whereas F1 can be seen as measuring conversational ability, KF1 attempts to capture whether a model is speaking knowledgeably by using relevant knowledge as judged by humans. This provides an easy way to distinguish between general language modeling skills and knowledge incorporation.

4.3 Architecture and baselines

In theory K-Mine can be implemented using any pretrained encoder-decoder model including the two most commonly used ones, BART(Lewis et al., 2019) and T5 (Raffel et al., 2020). Exploring both options, BART turned out to yield better results so we opted for this model. We compared K-Mine with the following models:

TMemNet (Dinan et al., 2019): Combines a transformer (not pretrained) with an external memory network to select the knowledge. TMemNet+BERT, uses BERT as encoder.

DukeNet (Zheng and Zhou, 2019): Explicitly models knowledge tracking and knowledge shifting as dual tasks to address the prior-posterior gap. It uses a BERT encoder.

MIKe (Meng et al., 2021): Further improves KS by explicitly distinguishing between user-initiative and system-initiative knowledge selection. It uses a BERT encoder.

BFKGC (De Bruyn et al., 2020): Uses a BART-based model to do both KS and RG in a fully supervised manner (shared encoder).

FiD-RAG (Shuster et al., 2021): Augments FiD by using a separate DPR-based retriever trained with RAG which results in state of the art performance on WoW.

In addition, we also include a few specialized baselines/variations to better assess the performance. These include:

K-Mine-mean: Instead of the weighted fusion, the decoder receives the average of knowledge-context encodings.

K-Mine-max: Instead of the weighted fusion, the decoder receives the argmax; i.e. the knowledge-context encoding with the highest relevance score.

K-Mine-max-full: Fully supervised K-Mine-max; i.e. with access to knowledge labels.

K-Mine-full: Fully supervised K-Mine; i.e. with access to knowledge labels ($\lambda = .5$ in Equation 1).

KS-RoBERTa: A RoBERTa model trained (only) on the knowledge selection task as a ranking problem with KS labels.

4.4 Implementation details

We use HuggingFace's Transformers library (Wolf et al., 2020) to implement our models. Training was done with an effective batch size of 64 and learning rates of 2e-5 and 5e-4 for the pretrained and raw parts respectively, with linear decay applied to both. For WoW dataset, we considered the last 3 utterances as the history, whereas for HOLL-E we just kept the last one since utterances mostly stand alone in this dataset. Passages were truncated or padded to the fixed length of 32 tokens before being concatenated with the history tokens, so that the weighted summation would not perturb the knowledge-history division in the input sequence.

5 Results and discussion

Tables 2 and 3 show the performance of K-Mine in knowledge selection and response generation for the WoW (Seen and Unseen) and HOLL-E test sets against baselines. As one can see, K-Mine shows very competitive results, especially in knowledge selection accuracy (R@1) although it does not benefit from knowledge labels in training, or a separate retrieval module. Adding KS supervision (K-Mine-full) enhances the knowledge selection performance by $\sim$3% although it negatively affects the RG performance. Regarding the data, the KS performance boosts by more than 2% when only the 'w/Kn' turns (turns that use knowledge to generate response) are used for training and testing, which shows that in the absence of explicit (KS) labels, the model prefers to select something than nothing[2].

Table 4 shows the performance of standard K-Mine models against some variations. Evidently the performance drops significantly when instead of the weighted mix, only the highest scored knowledge-history pair is passed to decoder (K-Mine-max vs. K-Mine), which shows that the full

[2]This might also depend on the way the 'empty' or 'no-knowledge' option is being represented. However in our experiments, using various choices including the original 'no_passages_used' string, PAD tokens and the pool average, showed no difference. We also tried using certainty thresholds and gating mechanisms to link the 'no-knowledge' case with the relevance distribution but these too proved ineffective.

Model	Test Seen R@1	PPL	F1	ROUGE-L	Test Unseen R@1	PPL	F1	ROUGE-L
TMemNet (E2E)†	21.6	63.5	16.9	16.8	12.1	97.3	14.4	15.4
TMemNet+BERT (E2E)†	23.9	53.2	17.7	17.0	16.3	137.8	13.6	15.6
DukeNet†	26.4	-	-	18.5	19.6	-	-	17.0
MIKe †	28.4	-	-	18.8	21.5	-	-	17.4
BFKGC† (BART-large)	26.0	12.2	20.1	-	19.9	14.9	19.3	-
FID-RAG‡ (BART-large)	29.3*	10.5	23.2	24.2	26.9*	10.7	23.2	24.4
K-Mine (BART-base)	27.9	16.3	20.9	19.6	27.0	20.3	20.1	19.2
K-Mine -w/Kn (BART-base)	29.2	16.1	21.4	19.9	28.4	20.3	20.3	19.4
K-Mine (BART-large)	28.3	13.2	21.8	20.1	28.4	16.4	21.1	19.7
K-Mine -w/Kn (BART-large)	30.4	13.1	22.2	20.1	30.8	16.5	21.5	20.0

Table 2: Results on WoW test sets for K-Mine and baselines. R@1 is the KS accuracy and the other metrics assess the response generation performance. Models with † next to their names benefit from KS labels in training and ‡ identifies pretrained models which use a separate retriever. Results with ∗ are for retrieval from 21M 100-word passages in Wikipedia so they are not directly comparable. K-Mine-w/Kn has been trained and tested on the w/Kn subsets; i.e. turns which have used knowledge (see Table 1 for statistics)

Model	R@1	ROUGE-1	ROUGE-L
TMemNet+BERT†	28.4	31.6	25.9
DukeNet†	30.0	36.5	31.5
MIKe†	31.9	37.8	32.8
K-Mine (BART-base)	28.7	36.1	32.6
K-Mine -w/Kn (BART-base)	30.7	37.3	33.8
K-Mine (BART-large)	31.7	38.5	35.1
K-Mine -w/Kn (BART-large)	32.8	39.3	36.0

Table 3: Results on HOLL-E test set (single reference) for K-Mine and baselines. R@1 is the KS accuracy and the other metrics assess the response generation performance. Models with † next to their names, benefit from KS labels in training. K-Mine-w/Kn has been trained and tested on the w/Kn subsets; i.e. turns which have used knowledge (see Table 1 for statistics)

Model	Data	Test Seen R@1	PPL	F1	R-L	KF1	Test Unseen R@1	PPL	F1	R-L	KF1
K-Mine	All	27.9	16.3	20.9	19.6	18.2	27.0	20.3	20.1	19.2	17.5
K-Mine	w/Kn	29.2	16.1	21.4	19.9	19.1	28.4	20.3	20.3	19.4	18.6
K-Mine-mean	All	-	19.7	18.7	18.2	14.4	-	26.6	17.0	17.2	12.3
K-Mine-mean	w/Kn	-	19.5	18.9	18.2	15.4	-	27.0	17.2	17.3	13.1
K-Mine-max	All	3.2	18.5	18.5	18.2	14.1	2.6	24.2	16.9	17.2	12.1
K-Mine-max	w/Kn	1.2	18.5	18.8	18.3	15.0	0.9	24.7	17.3	17.6	12.9
K-Mine-max-full†	All	29.7	17.2	20.8	19.4	19.8	27.2	20.8	19.9	18.9	18.7
K-Mine-max-full†	w/Kn	31.2	17.0	21.4	19.8	22.2	29.0	20.7	20.5	19.4	21.1
K-Mine-full†	All	29.7	17.8	20.6	19.2	18.2	28.3	21.0	20.0	19.0	17.2
K-Mine-full†	w/Kn	30.9	17.6	21.1	19.5	19.9	29.5	20.9	20.1	19.1	19.7
KS-RoBERTa†	All	25.9	-	-	-	-	25.5	-	-	-	-
KS-RoBERTa†	w/Kn	28.3	-	-	-	-	27.5	-	-	-	-

Table 4: Results on WoW test sets for K-Mine and some extreme variations/baselines. R@1 is the KS accuracy and the other metrics assess the response generation performance (R-L = ROUGE-L). Models with † next to their names, benefit from KS labels in training. All models use the base version of the pretrained transformer.

aggregated gradient is essential for the unsupervised KS learning. Adding KS supervision to K-Mine-max (K-Mine-max-full), boosts the performance in both KS and RG tasks, surpassing the standard K-Mine model. Here the KF1 metric is of special importance as it shows that although the fully supervised version (K-Mine-max-full) does slightly worse than K-Mine in terms of conversational ability and language modeling (F1, R-L and PPL), it generates significantly more knowledgeable responses, which can be attributed to passing a less noisy representation to decoder (as confirmed by the results from the K-Mine-full model). Finally, comparing the two fully supervised models (K-Mine-max-full and K-Mine-full) shows that in the presence of knowledge labels, fusion actually hurts the model's performance.
Another interesting result is the higher discrepancy between the seen/unseen KS performance (R@1) in the presence of supervision (1.4-2.5 vs. 0.9) which indicates a lower ability to generalize when the task has been learned via explicit signals. Finally the inferior performance of the pure selection model (KS-RoBERTa) compared to K-Mine, K-Mine-max-full and K-Mine-full, reflects the broadly studied prior-posterior gap in KGCMs; i.e. the model can benefit from (or even exclusively rely on) responses for selecting the relevant knowledge[3].

To have a better understanding of the way knowledge selection happens under the hood, we introduce a localization metric to measure the level by which the knowledge distribution vector $\boldsymbol{p}$ deviates from the uniform distribution $\boldsymbol{u}$ towards a one-hot distribution $\boldsymbol{o}$. Defined as:

$$Loc = \frac{1 - cos(\angle(\boldsymbol{p}, \boldsymbol{u}))}{1 - cos(\angle(\boldsymbol{o}, \boldsymbol{u}))}$$

Loc varies between 0 ($\boldsymbol{p} = \boldsymbol{u}$; zero certainty) and 1 ($\boldsymbol{p} = \boldsymbol{o}$; absolute certainty) and provides a good way to track the average knowledge distribution. Figure 3 shows how this metric changes during training for the standard K-Mine model along with K-Mine-max and K-Mine-max-full. We can see that for K-Mine-max the localization stays close to zero (~1e-4) whereas when knowledge labels are provided, it surges rapidly in less than 100 iterations. K-Mine shows a delayed (starting around 500 iterations) but more extreme surge. This can

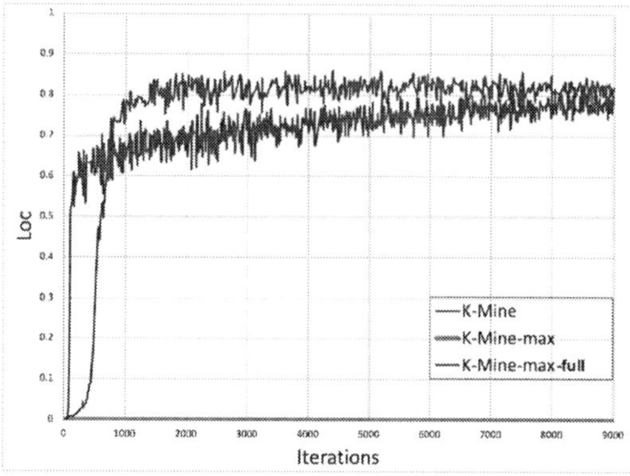

Figure 3: Evolution of the Localization metric during training for K-Mine and 2 variations. K-Mine-max is the (almost) flat line in the bottom.

be attributed to the weighted fusion which forces the model to localize the distribution as soon as possible -and thus at the cost of a less accurate distribution- in order to pass a less noisy representation to the decoder. The model seems to partly re-evaluate and improve this process subsequently as can be seen in the slightly descending behaviour of Loc in later steps, eventually converging to the ascending supervised values.

6 Conclusion and future work

In this work we introduced K-Mine (Knowledge Mixing in encoder), which provides a simple way to train knowledge grounded conversation models based on pretrained generative models without knowledge labels or a separate retriever. K-Mine uses a weighted aggregation method to fuse different encoded knowledge-context pairs into one sequence of the same length before passing it to the decoder, which has its advantages and disadvantages in comparison to models like RAG and FiD. It significantly reduces the computational cost in the decoder (at least by a factor of m= number of encoded knowledge options) but this naturally comes with the cost of a noisier and less rich input for the decoder which affects the response generation performance. This was partly confirmed by the relatively low KF1 values of K-Mine compared with the fully supervised version in Table 4 but a qualitative assessment of K-Mine's response generation can shed more light on this.

Another interesting topic is the relationship between the KS and RG performance in K-Mine. In our experiments we saw that in later iterations, the KS performance often keeps improving while the

[3]Comparing RoBERTa and BART in this manner is not trivial but it is also not unsound considering that the number of parameters are close (139M vs. 125M) and the selection task in K-Mine is 'mainly' done via the BART encoder.

RG performance (according to automatic metrics) starts to suffer. A more comprehensive study can determine whether it is possible to reconcile the two, or K-Mine actually serves better as an auxiliary retriever or re-ranker module. Either way, the potentials and limitations of this approach (i.e. selection via generation) in similar tasks and problems is worth exploring.

7 Acknowledgement

This research received funding from the Flemish Government under the "Onderzoeksprogramma Artificiële Intelligentie (AI) Vlaanderen" program.

References

Xiuyi Chen, Fandong Meng, Peng Li, Feilong Chen, Shuang Xu, Bo Xu, and Jie Zhou. 2020. Bridging the gap between prior and posterior knowledge selection for knowledge-grounded dialogue generation. In *Proceedings of the 2020 Conference on Empirical Methods in Natural Language Processing (EMNLP)*, pages 3426–3437, Online. Association for Computational Linguistics.

M. De Bruyn, E. Lotfi, Jeska Buhmann, and W. Daelemans. 2020. Bart for knowledge grounded conversations. In *Converse@KDD*.

Emily Dinan, Stephen Roller, Kurt Shuster, Angela Fan, Michael Auli, and Jason Weston. 2019. Wizard of wikipedia: Knowledge-powered conversational agents.

Marjan Ghazvininejad, Chris Brockett, Ming-Wei Chang, Bill Dolan, Jianfeng Gao, Wen tau Yih, and Michel Galley. 2018. A knowledge-grounded neural conversation model.

Karthik Gopalakrishnan, Behnam Hedayatnia, Qinlang Chen, Anna Gottardi, Sanjeev Kwatra, Anu Venkatesh, Raefer Gabriel, and Dilek Hakkani-Tür. 2019. Topical-Chat: Towards Knowledge-Grounded Open-Domain Conversations. In *Proc. Interspeech 2019*, pages 1891–1895.

Samuel Humeau, Kurt Shuster, Marie-Anne Lachaux, and Jason Weston. 2020. Poly-encoders: Transformer architectures and pre-training strategies for fast and accurate multi-sentence scoring.

Gautier Izacard and Edouard Grave. 2021. Leveraging passage retrieval with generative models for open domain question answering.

Byeongchang Kim, Jaewoo Ahn, and Gunhee Kim. 2020. Sequential latent knowledge selection for knowledge-grounded dialogue.

Mike Lewis, Yinhan Liu, Naman Goyal, Marjan Ghazvininejad, Abdelrahman Mohamed, Omer Levy, Ves Stoyanov, and Luke Zettlemoyer. 2019. Bart: Denoising sequence-to-sequence pre-training for natural language generation, translation, and comprehension.

Patrick Lewis, Ethan Perez, Aleksandra Piktus, Fabio Petroni, Vladimir Karpukhin, Naman Goyal, Heinrich Küttler, Mike Lewis, Wen tau Yih, Tim Rocktäschel, Sebastian Riedel, and Douwe Kiela. 2021. Retrieval-augmented generation for knowledge-intensive nlp tasks.

Rongzhong Lian, Min Xie, Fan Wang, Jinhua Peng, and Hua Wu. 2019. Learning to select knowledge for response generation in dialog systems.

Shuman Liu, Hongshen Chen, Zhaochun Ren, Yang Feng, Qun Liu, and Dawei Yin. 2018. Knowledge diffusion for neural dialogue generation. In *Proceedings of the 56th Annual Meeting of the Association for Computational Linguistics (Volume 1: Long Papers)*, pages 1489–1498, Melbourne, Australia. Association for Computational Linguistics.

Chuan Meng, Pengjie Ren, Zhumin Chen, Z. Ren, Tengxiao Xi, and M. Rijke. 2021. Initiative-aware self-supervised learning for knowledge-grounded conversations. *Proceedings of the 44th International ACM SIGIR Conference on Research and Development in Information Retrieval.*

Chuan Meng, Pengjie Ren, Zhumin Chen, Weiwei Sun, Zhaochun Ren, Zhaopeng Tu, and Maarten de Rijke. 2020. Dukenet: A dual knowledge interaction network for knowledge-grounded conversation. In *Proceedings of the 43rd International ACM SIGIR Conference on Research and Development in Information Retrieval*, SIGIR '20, page 1151–1160, New York, NY, USA. Association for Computing Machinery.

Nikita Moghe, Siddhartha Arora, Suman Banerjee, and Mitesh M. Khapra. 2018. Towards exploiting background knowledge for building conversation systems.

Alec Radford, Jeff Wu, R. Child, David Luan, Dario Amodei, and Ilya Sutskever. 2019. Language models are unsupervised multitask learners.

Colin Raffel, Noam Shazeer, Adam Roberts, Katherine Lee, Sharan Narang, Michael Matena, Yanqi Zhou, Wei Li, and Peter J. Liu. 2020. Exploring the limits of transfer learning with a unified text-to-text transformer.

Stephen Roller, Y-Lan Boureau, Jason Weston, Antoine Bordes, Emily Dinan, Angela Fan, David Gunning, Da Ju, Margaret Li, Spencer Poff, Pratik Ringshia, Kurt Shuster, Eric Michael Smith, Arthur Szlam, Jack Urbanek, and Mary Williamson. 2020. Open-domain conversational agents: Current progress, open problems, and future directions.

Kurt Shuster, Spencer Poff, Moya Chen, Douwe Kiela, and Jason Weston. 2021. Retrieval augmentation reduces hallucination in conversation.

Thomas Wolf, Lysandre Debut, Victor Sanh, Julien Chaumond, Clement Delangue, Anthony Moi, Pierric Cistac, Tim Rault, Rémi Louf, Morgan Funtowicz, Joe Davison, Sam Shleifer, Patrick von Platen, Clara Ma, Yacine Jernite, Julien Plu, Canwen Xu, Teven Le Scao, Sylvain Gugger, Mariama Drame, Quentin Lhoest, and Alexander M. Rush. 2020. Huggingface's transformers: State-of-the-art natural language processing.

Haolan Zhan, Hainan Zhang, Hongshen Chen, Zhuoye Ding, Yongjun Bao, and Yanyan Lan. 2021. Augmenting knowledge-grounded conversations with sequential knowledge transition. In *Proceedings of the 2021 Conference of the North American Chapter of the Association for Computational Linguistics: Human Language Technologies*, pages 5621–5630, Online. Association for Computational Linguistics.

Xueliang Zhao, Wei Wu, Can Xu, Chongyang Tao, Dongyan Zhao, and Rui Yan. 2020. Knowledge-grounded dialogue generation with pre-trained language models. In *Proceedings of the 2020 Conference on Empirical Methods in Natural Language Processing (EMNLP)*, pages 3377–3390, Online. Association for Computational Linguistics.

Chujie Zheng, Yunbo Cao, Daxin Jiang, and Minlie Huang. 2020. Difference-aware knowledge selection for knowledge-grounded conversation generation.

Wen Zheng and Ke Zhou. 2019. Enhancing conversational dialogue models with grounded knowledge. In *Proceedings of the 28th ACM International Conference on Information and Knowledge Management*, CIKM '19, page 709–718, New York, NY, USA. Association for Computing Machinery.

Influence of user personality on dialogue task performance: A case study using a rule-based dialogue system

Ao Guo[1], Atsumoto Ohashi[1], Ryu Hirai[2]
Yuya Chiba[3], Yuiko Tsunomori[1], and Ryuichiro Higashinaka[1]
[1]Graduate School of Informatics, Nagoya University
[2]School of Informatics, Nagoya University, [3]NTT Communication Science Laboratories
{guo.ao@a,ohashi.atsumoto@g,hirai.ryu@a,tsunomori.yuiko@b}
.mbox.nagoya-u.ac.jp, yuuya.chiba.ax@hco.ntt.co.jp
higashinaka@i.nagoya-u.ac.jp

Abstract

Endowing a task-oriented dialogue system with adaptiveness to user personality can greatly help improve the performance of a dialogue task. However, such a dialogue system can be practically challenging to implement, because it is unclear how user personality influences dialogue task performance. To explore the relationship between user personality and dialogue task performance, we enrolled participants via crowdsourcing to first answer specified personality questionnaires and then chat with a dialogue system to accomplish assigned tasks. A rule-based dialogue system on the prevalent Multi-Domain Wizard-of-Oz (MultiWOZ) task was used. A total of 211 participants' personalities and their 633 dialogues were collected and analyzed. The results revealed that sociable and extroverted people tended to fail the task, whereas neurotic people were more likely to succeed. We extracted features related to user dialogue behaviors and performed further analysis to determine which kind of behavior influences task performance. As a result, we identified that average utterance length and slots per utterance are the key features of dialogue behavior that are highly correlated with both task performance and user personality.

1 Introduction

Personality is the characteristics of behavior, cognition, and emotional patterns that evolve from biological and environmental factors (Corr and Matthews, 2020). As a fundamental difference between individuals, personality has been found to influence the performance of task-oriented dialogue systems, such as the user satisfaction to dialogue systems (Cassell and Bickmore, 2003). Endowing a task-oriented dialogue system with adaptiveness to user personality is therefore essential to achieve better dialogue task performance.

In a previous study, Mairesse and Walker analyzed the differences between introverts and extroverts in dialogue behavior, such as extroverts being more talkative and using fewer words per utterance than introverts (Mairesse and Walker, 2007). They further designed a parameterized natural language generation system named "PERSONAGE." Increasing applications of personality have been put forward on a dialogue system that is able to generate natural, coherent, and personalized utterances (Zheng et al., 2020). However, two problems remain that hinder the dialogue system adapting to user personality to achieve better task performance: (1) what kind of personality traits are correlated with task performance and (2) how the personality influences the task performance.

In this work, we performed a case study analysis of user personality and task performance using a rule-based dialogue system on the prevalent Multi-Domain Wizard-of-Oz (MultiWOZ) task (Budzianowski et al., 2018; Eric et al., 2020). Specifically, we enrolled participants via crowdsourcing to first take several personality questionnaires and then interact with the dialogue system via text chat to accomplish assigned tasks. Participants' personality and dialogue data were collected. We then analyzed the correlation between personality and task performance to identify the personalities highly correlated with task performance. Considering that the task performance largely depends on the user's dialogue behavior, we further examined the main features of dialogue behavior influenced by the identified personalities.

For data collection, we selected four mainstream personality questionnaires that could possibly influence the dialogue task performance and use a rule-based dialogue system for the MultiWOZ task (Zhu et al., 2020). In total, 211 participants were enrolled, and their personalities and 633 dialogues were collected and analyzed. Five task performance metrics are used.

Our contributions are two-fold:

- The correlation of user personality and task

Proceedings of the Third Workshop on Natural Language Processing for Conversational AI, pages 263–270
November 10, 2021.

performance is clarified by performing a large-scale data collection experiment and analysis.

- By revealing the correlation between personality and dialogue behavior, the influence of user personality on task performance is clarified.

The remainder of this paper is organized as follows. The related work on personality and dialogue systems is presented in the next section. Section 3 describes the research approach and analysis procedures. The data collection and data analysis are presented in Sections 4 and 5. Conclusions and future work are addressed in the last section.

2 Related Work

Related studies can be classified into: (1) the exploration of correlations between personality and dialogue system performance, (2) the application of personality to a dialogue system, and (3) user-adaptive dialogue system.

In the past decades, Nass and Lee (2000) explored the differences between extroverts and introverts in speaking, such as pitch and volume. Cassell and Bickmore (2003) further identified that extroverts feel extroverted voices are generally more credible, whereas introverts feel the opposite. Conscientiousness (the tendency to act in an organized or thoughtful way) and agreeableness (the tendency to be compassionate and cooperative toward others) have been found to be important factors influencing the dialogue in customer service (Blignaut et al., 2014; Sackett and Walmsley, 2014). Qiu et al. (2017) examined the consistency of the correlation between personality and word usage in different languages and found that such correlation is independent of language. Wang et al. (2020) recently found that people with different personalities use different persuasion strategies, which can potentially be used by a personalized persuasion dialogue system. Although numerous studies have found that personality is more or less related to dialogue behaviors, few studies have comprehensively investigated the influences of user personality on dialogue task performance.

As for applying personality to a dialogue system, Mairesse and Walker (2007) applied extraversion as the parameter of a natural language generation system, so as to generate personalized and natural dialogue. Specifically, they used an extraversion parameter to control the communication content and the template sentence with different syntactic styles. Qian et al. (2018) applied a profile as personality into an encoder-decoder dialogue system to increase the coherence of generated utterances. Zhang et al. (2018) proposed a dataset named "Persona-Chat" containing a corpus with a corresponding persona description to help build an end-to-end chit-chat dialogue system with consistent personality and coherent utterance generation.

Towards a more user-adaptive dialogue system, several researchers have investigated user-adaptive dialogue systems. Komatani et al. (2003) focused on a system that generates the responses to users' information queries in accordance with their skill with regard to the system, domain-related knowledge, and the degree of hastiness. Dohsaka et al. (2010) developed a dialogue system that adapts to users' behavior regarding pause duration preceding system utterance and gaze to reduce user's discomfort during conversation. To increase user engagement, Liang et al. (2020) proposed a system that is able to select a chat topic in accordance with user interests.

The aim of our research is to find out the influences of personality on task performance to benefit further development of a dialogue system that can adapt to user personality to achieve better dialogue task performance.

3 Approach

To explore the correlation between user personality and dialogue task performance, a dataset is needed that contains a variety of user personality traits (e.g., extraversion), dialogue data, and the corresponding dialogue task performances (e.g., task success rate).

The data to be analyzed is collected via crowdsourcing, and various features of dialogue behavior related to task feature, utterance feature, and action/utterance intent are extracted from the dialogue data.

After collecting a sufficient amount of data, user personality and task performance are explored in three steps: (1) correlation analysis of user personality and dialogue task performance to identify the personality traits highly correlated with task performance; (2) correlation analysis of behavior feature and dialogue task performance to determine their relevance; and (3) analysis of highly correlated personalities, behaviors, and task performances to figure out how a person's personality influences task performance through dialogue behavior.

4 Data Collection

We designed a data collection task to obtain user personality and dialogue data on the Amazon Mechanical Turk (AMT), a Human-Intelligence Task (HIT) crowdsourcing platform. The task has been approved by the ethical review of the relevant organization.

4.1 Description of HIT

Our HIT consisted of two main parts: personality questionnaire and conversation with a dialogue system. Each enrolled participant (Turker) followed a three-step procedure to chat with the dialogue system:

1. The Turker carefully reads the description of the assigned task before starting the conversation.

2. The Turker chats with the dialogue system within 30 turns and tries his/her best to finish the assigned task; once the Turker has covered all the items and accomplished the tasks, he/she sends a "success" message to the dialogue system to finish the current conversation.

3. The Turker rates the performance of the dialogue system on the metrics of language understanding, response appropriateness, and satisfaction with the dialogue system.

The eligible Turkers should have (1) a HIT accomplishment number greater than 100, (2) a HIT approval rate greater than 95%, and (3) have passed our designed qualification test. The qualification test contains two common-sense questions written in English aiming at selecting English native speakers. Each Turker who finished our HIT received $10 as a reward.

4.2 Description of Personality Questionnaire

Some personality recognition tools can be adopted to measure the user personality directly from their dialogue text, e.g., IBM Watson's personality insights (Mostafa et al., 2016), but these tools can only measure a few dimensions of personality with lower accuracy than personality questionnaires. Therefore, all users' personalities were measured through personality questionnaires in this research.

Category	Item
Gender	• Male • Female • Other
Age	• ~19 • 20~29 • 30~39 • 40~49 • 50~59 • 60~69 • 70~
Education	• Less than four-year college • Four-year college • Postgraduate
Employment status	• Out of work • Employed • Homemaker • Student • Unable to work • Retired
How often use a dialogue system	• Never • Rarely • Sometimes • Often • Very often • Always

Table 1: Demographic categories

To cover a wide spectrum of user personality dimensions, we prepared four prevalent personality questionnaires considering their potential correlations with task performance.

- Inclusion of Others in the Self (IOS) Scale: IOS corresponds to how close the respondent feels to another person or group (Aron et al., 1992). The IOS scales from 1 to 7 in terms of closeness.

- Big Five Personality Traits (BF-44): BF-44 contains 44 questions to identify five common parameters of human personality: extraversion, neuroticism, agreeableness, conscientiousness, and openness to experience (Raad, 2000).

- Kikuchi's Scale of Social Skills (KISS-18): KISS-18 contains 18 questions to identify six social skills (Takahashi et al., 2013): basic skill, advanced skill, emotional management skill, offense management skill, stress management skill, and planning skill.

- Adult Temperament Questionnaire (ATQ): ATQ contains 77 questions to measure 13 user temperaments with regard to four dimensions: negative affect, extraversion, effortful control, and orienting sensitivity (Evans and Rothbart, 2007).

User's demographic information regarding age, gender, final education, occupation, and dialogue system usage frequency were also collected, as presented in Table 1.

Domain	Info Slot	Request Slot
Restaurant	Area : South Food : Indian Price Range : Expensive	Address Phone
Hotel	Name : Gonville Hotel	Area Postcode Address Phone
Attraction	Area : Centre Type : Theatre	Entrance Fee Address Phone
Taxi	Departure : Hotel Destination : Attraction Leave At : 12:30	Phone Car Type

Table 2: An example task with very hard difficulty. Note that these pieces of information are presented to users in the form of a textual scenario so as to elicit natural interaction from users.

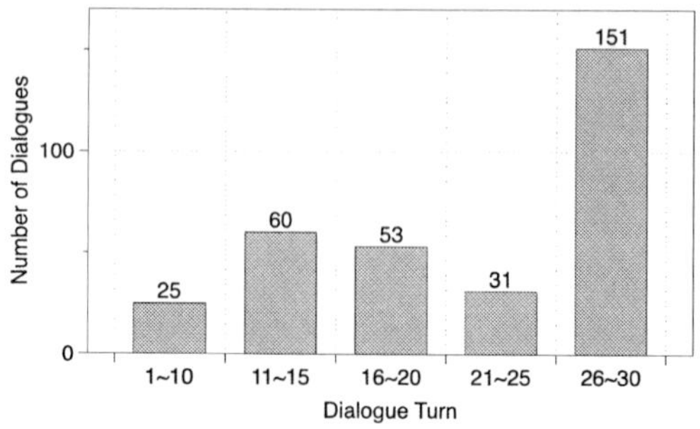

Figure 1: Distribution of successful dialogue turns

Dataset Statistics	
Participants	211
Dialogues	633
Avg. questionnaire time	905s
Avg. dialogue time	583s
Avg. task time	2654s
Avg. slots per dialogue	14.8
Avg. words per utterance	7.9
Avg. time per utterance	21s
Success rate per dialogue	51%
Avg. satisfaction score	2.3/5
Avg. understanding score	2.6/5
Avg. appropriateness score	2.7/5
Total unique tokens	2281

Table 3: Statistics of collected data

4.3 Description of Dialogue System

We utilized ConvLab-2, an open-source toolkit by Zhu et al. (2020), in order to build the system for data collection. The best performing rule-based dialogue system built by the ConvLab-2 on MultiWOZ 2.1 task (Eric et al., 2020) was selected. The rule-based dialogue system consists of four modules in a pipeline structure: joint-BERT as natural language understanding (NLU) (Zhang et al., 2019), rule-based dialogue state tracking, rule-based dialogue policy, and template-based natural language generation (NLG). For the system to smoothly chat with the users, we further (1) limited the utterance to contain a maximum of three sentences and (2) revised the grammar mistakes and a few inappropriate texts of the NLG module's template utterances.

The MultiWOZ task requires the Turkers to play the role of a tourist searching for information about Cambridge, UK, and the dialogue system acts as an information desk clerk to help the tourist plan their tour. Four domains of MultiWOZ were selected to generate the dialogue tasks, i.e., hotel, restaurant, train, and attraction. Each domain contains five slots regarding user request. Below is an example task description on the restaurant domain:

"*You are looking for a restaurant called 'Mahal of Cambridge'. Once you find the restaurant, make sure you get its address and phone number. You want to book a table for 19:00 on Tuesday.*"

The difficulty of the task should be balanced to ensure a task success rate per dialogue of about 50% because the influences of user personality on task performance will be revealed less if the task is too easy or too hard for the majority of Turkers to accomplish. To balance the difficulty to ensure a 50% success rate per dialogue, we performed a small scale test with four levels of difficulty by changing the number of domains and corresponding slots: easy (1 domain), normal (2 domains), hard (3 domains), and very hard (4 domains). As a result, we selected the task with the very hard level, which consists of four domains with 20 slots in total. We designed three very hard tasks, one of which is shown in Table 2. We use the three tasks in the following data collection. We use this fixed set of tasks to examine behaviors/task performance with the same stimuli.

4.4 Data Statistics

The statistics of the collected data are presented in Table 3. In total, 211 participants were enrolled in our tasks, and 633 dialogues were collected. We observed that the average task (including four personality questionnaires and three rounds of conversation with the same level of difficulty) took about 44 minutes, and the success rate per dialogue was about 51%. We present the distribution of dialogue turns only from successful dialogues, as shown in Figure 1. We observed that there are two types of users: one kind of user finished the dialogue tasks rapidly (within 11 to 15 turns), whereas the

	Task Success Rate	Slot Filling Rate	Satisfaction	Understanding	Appropriateness
Education	.01	.06	−.07	**−.13***	−.10
Usage Frequency	**−.14***	−.10	.02	.00	−.10
IOS	−.07	−.09	**.16***	**.15***	.08
Extraversion	−.10	**−.13***	.07	.03	−.02
Sociability	−.08	−.10	.06	.06	.01
Neuroticism	.06	**.12***	−.01	.04	.02
Sadness	.06	**.14***	.07	.11	.11
Neutral Perceptual Sensitivity	.00	**.13***	.00	.06	.08

$^*p < .05$

Table 4: Correlation between user personality and task performance (selected by $r \geq 0.1$)

other kind finished the task slowly (within 25 to 30 turns).

5 Data Analysis

The Pearson correlation coefficient r (range from -1 to 1) is used for analysis. We first extracted a variety of dialogue behaviors and task performances to be analyzed. We then analyzed the correlation between user personalities and task performances. We further clarified the influences of user personalities on task performances through dialogue behaviors that are highly correlated with personalities and task performance.

5.1 Data Processing

The user dialogue behavior and task performance parameter are necessary for our analysis. The dialogue behaviors extracted from the task data were categorized into three aspects:

- Task Feature: Task feature contains questionnaire time, dialogue time, average utterance time, and average slots covered per utterance.
- Utterance Feature: Utterance feature contains average utterance length, the richness of word token variability (reflecting vocabulary), and part-of-speech tags.
- Action Intent: Action intent refers to user intent that is recognized by the dialogue system from user utterances. In the rule-based dialogue system, the action intents are classified into greet, inform, request, recommend, request more, thank, and say goodbye.

The values to represent task performance are categorized into two aspects:

- Objective Task Performance: Objective task performance covers the task success rate and slot filling rate rate_{slot} as formulated below:

$$\text{rate}_{slot} = \frac{\text{num}_{filled\_slot}}{\text{num}_{total\_slot}} \quad (1)$$

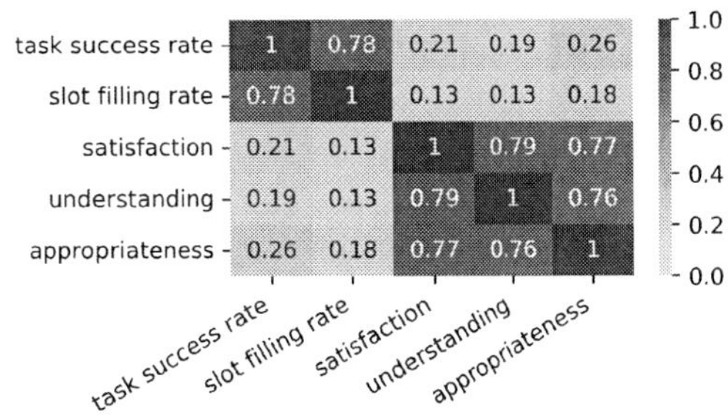

Figure 2: Correlation heatmap of task performances

where num_{filled_slot} denotes the slots user filled in three rounds of tasks, and num_{total_slot} implies the total slots of three rounds of tasks (60 slots in our tasks).

- Subjective Task Performance: Subjective task performance contains the values of the evaluation metrics of dialogue system language understanding, appropriateness of the generated utterances, and user satisfaction with the dialogue system. The values scale from 1 (strongly disagree) to 5 (strongly agree).

To compare different task performance parameters, a heatmap is provided in Figure 2, in which we can see that there is a high correlation between task success rate and slot filling rate, and a high correlation between satisfaction, understanding, and appropriateness scores. However, the objective and subjective task performance values do not show a high correlation.

5.2 Analysis between User Personality and Task Performance

To identify the user personalities highly correlated with task performance, we performed the correlation analysis between user personality and five task performances, as presented in Table 4. The five task performances are task success rate, slot filling

	Task Success Rate	Slot Filling Rate	Satisfaction	Understanding	Appropriateness
Slots per Utt.	.70**	.72**	.29**	.30**	.33**
Avg Utt. Length	.28**	.41**	.01	.12	.11
User Vocabulary	−.14*	−.02	−.18**	−.16*	−.21**
Request	.58**	.58**	.23**	.17*	.19**
Recommend	−.16*	−.35**	.21**	.16*	.16*

$^{*}p < .05$, $^{**}p < .01$

Table 5: Correlation between dialogue behavior and task performance (selected by $r \geq 0.1$)

rate, and average task performance over three dialogues with regard to satisfaction, understanding, and appropriateness. Only those user personalities correlated to task performances with correlation value r no less than 0.1 are shown in Table 4. User personality showed a weak correlation with task performance; the highest correlation was determined between the IOS score and the satisfaction with the dialogue system, reaching .16 (significance level $p < .05$).

Table 4 shows that: (1) the higher a person's final education level, the lower he/she rates the response appropriateness of the dialogue system; (2) the more frequently a person uses the dialogue system, the less likely he/he is to succeed in the task; (3) extroverted and sociable people tend to fail the task; and (4) neurotic and sensitive people who often feel sad are more likely to succeed in the task. The correlation could be categorized into intuitive correlations (e.g., highly educated people are unsatisfied with the dialogue system) and counter-intuitive correlations (e.g., extroverted and sociable people tend to fail the task). User personality and task performance are further analyzed in view of dialogue behavior in the next subsections to better understand the intuitive and counter-intuitive correlations.

5.3 Analysis between Dialogue Behavior and Task Performance

As shown in Table 5, the selected dialogue behavior exhibited a moderate or strong correlation with the task performance. The correlation coefficient r between slots per utterance and filled slots reached .72 ($p < .01$). The request intent (e.g., "*What is the price for a ticket?*") and recommend intent (e.g., "*How about Lensfield hotel?*") recognized by the dialogue system are highly correlated with filled slots.

To better illustrate the correlation between dialogue behavior and task performance, comparisons among average utterance time, slots per utterance, and user utterance length depending on the number

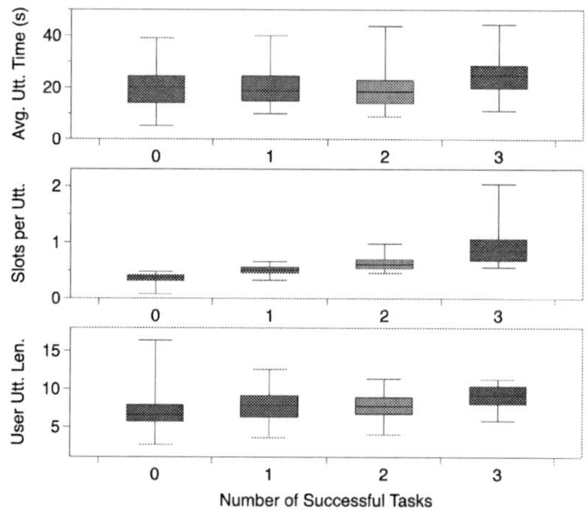

Figure 3: Average utterance time, slots per utterance and user utterance length on number of successful tasks

of successful tasks are plotted in Figure 3. The plot-box shows the maximum, 75 percentile, average, 25 percentile, and the minimum value. Apparently, the users who succeeded in more tasks have an upward trend in the parameters of the plot-box, which shows that their average utterance time and user utterance length are longer, and their slots per utterance are larger.

5.4 Analysis of User Personality and Task Performance through Dialogue Behavior

Since a set of dialogue behaviors was identified to be highly correlated with dialogue performance, we further explored the influences of user personality on task performance through dialogue behavior. The dialogue behaviors highly correlated with those personalities ($r \geq 0.1$) and task performances ($r \geq 0.2$) in Table 4 are selected in the subsequent analysis.

The selected personality, dialogue behavior, task performance, and correlations of $corr_{ps,be}$, and $corr_{be,pf}$ are shown in Table 6. $corr_{ps,be}$ and $corr_{be,pf}$ are correlations of dialogue behavior respectively with personality and task performance. The table shows that: (1) people with higher final education levels use a more enriched vocabulary

Personality	$corr_{ps,be}$	Behavior	$corr_{be,pf}$	Performance
education	.13*	vocabulary	−.21**	appropriateness
usage frequency	−.10	slots per utt	.42**	task success rate
sociability	−.13	slots per utt	.44**	slot filling rate
extraversion	.15*	recommend	−.35**	slot filling rate
neuroticism	.11	average utt length	.41**	slot filling rate
sadness	.14*	average utt length	.41**	slot filling rate
neutral perceptual sensitivity	.13*	average utt length	.41**	slot filling rate
neutral perceptual sensitivity	.10	slots per utt	.44**	slot filling rate

$^*p < .05$, $^{**}p < .01$

Table 6: Associations among personality, dialogue behavior and task performance

and thereby tend to negatively evaluate the appropriateness of the dialogue system generating utterances by fixed templates; (2) people who usually use a dialogue system or are social or insensitive to external stimuli use utterances containing fewer slots in our designed task, which thus results in failure of the task; (3) extroverted people are more likely to use sentences like "*How about*" (with an underlying recommendation intent); and (4) neurotic and sensitive people who often feel sad tend to use longer utterances that are likely to contain more slots.

6 Conclusion and Future Work

We presented a case study analysis using a rule-based system on the Multi-Domain Wizard-of-Oz (MultiWOZ) task to explore the correlation between user personality and task performance. We identified the user personalities highly correlated with task performances and found that sociable and extroverted people tended to fail the task, while neurotic people were more likely to succeed. We further selected user personalities, dialogue behaviors, and task performance having high correlations with each other to understand the correlation of personality and task performance in view of dialogue behavior. As a result, we clarified that average utterance length and slots per utterance are the two key dialogue behaviors influenced by the personality, affecting the task performance in the case of our data collection using MultiWOZ.

Our work is an initial step to enable a dialogue system to adapt to user personality. Since the analyzed correlation results are based on a rule-based system, more dialogue systems, e.g., end-to-end dialogue systems such as SimpleTOD (Hosseini-Asl et al., 2020) and UBAR (Yang et al., 2020), and different task domains will need to be considered for the analysis to derive more general correlations. The effect of personality and task performance should also be qualitatively explored to better interpret the correlations we observed in the experiment. Furthermore, the dialogue system adapting to user personality should be implemented to ascertain its dialogue task performance.

7 Acknowledgments

Funding was provided by a Grant-in-Aid for Scientific Research (Grant No. JP19H05692).

References

Arthur Aron, Elaine N Aron, and Danny Smollan. 1992. Inclusion of other in the self scale and the structure of interpersonal closeness. *Journal of personality and social psychology*, 63:596–612.

Linda Blignaut, Leona M Ungerer, and Helene Muller. 2014. Personality as predictor of customer service centre agent performance in the banking industry: An exploratory study. *South African Journal of Human Resource Management*, 12:16.

Paweł Budzianowski, Tsung-Hsien Wen, Bo-Hsiang Tseng, Inigo Casanueva, Stefan Ultes, Osman Ramadan, and Milica Gašić. 2018. MultiWOZ: A large-scale multi-domain Wizard-of-Oz dataset for task-oriented dialogue modelling. *arXiv preprint arXiv:1810.00278*.

Justine Cassell and Timothy Bickmore. 2003. Negotiated collusion: Modeling social language and its relationship effects in intelligent agents. *User Modelling and User-Adapted Interaction*, 13:89–132.

Philip J Corr and Gerald Matthews. 2020. *The Cambridge handbook of personality psychology*. Cambridge University Press.

Kohji Dohsaka, Atsushi Kanemoto, Ryuichiro Higashinaka, Yasuhiro Minami, and Eisaku Maeda. 2010. User-adaptive coordination of agent communicative behavior in spoken dialogue. In *Proceedings of the SIGDIAL 2010 Conference*, pages 314–321.

Mihail Eric, Rahul Goel, Shachi Paul, Adarsh Kumar, Abhishek Sethi, Anuj Kumar Goyal, Peter Ku, Sanchit Agarwal, Shuyang Gao, and Dilek Hakkani-Tür. 2020. MultiWOZ 2.1: A consolidated multi-domain dialogue dataset with state corrections and state tracking baselines. In *Proceedings of the 12th International Conference on Language Resources and Evaluation*, pages 422–428.

David E. Evans and Mary K. Rothbart. 2007. Developing a model for adult temperament. *Journal of Research in Personality*, 41:868–888.

Ehsan Hosseini-Asl, Bryan McCann, Chien-Sheng Wu, Semih Yavuz, and Richard Socher. 2020. A simple language model for task-oriented dialogue. *arXiv preprint arXiv:2005.00796*.

Kazunori Komatani, Shinichi Ueno, Tatsuya Kawahara, and Hiroshi G Okuno. 2003. Flexible guidance generation using user model in spoken dialogue systems. In *Proceedings of the 41st Annual Meeting of the Association for Computational Linguistics*, pages 256–263.

Kaihui Liang, Austin Chau, Yu Li, Xueyuan Lu, Dian Yu, Mingyang Zhou, Ishan Jain, Sam Davidson, Josh Arnold, Minh Nguyen, et al. 2020. Gunrock 2.0: A user adaptive social conversational system. *arXiv preprint arXiv:2011.08906*.

François Mairesse and Marilyn Walker. 2007. Personage: Personality generation for dialogue. In *Proceedings of the 45th Annual Meeting of the Association for Computational Linguistics*, pages 496–503.

Mohamed Mostafa, Tom Crick, Ana C Calderon, and Giles Oatley. 2016. Incorporating emotion and personality-based analysis in user-centered modelling. In *Proceedings of the International conference on innovative techniques and applications of artificial intelligence*, pages 383–389.

Clifford Nass and Kwan Min Lee. 2000. Does computer-generated speech manifest personality? An experimental test of similarity-attraction. In *Proceedings of the Conference on Human Factors in Computing Systems*, pages 329–336.

Qiao Qian, Minlie Huang, Haizhou Zhao, Jingfang Xu, and Xiaoyan Zhu. 2018. Assigning personality/profile to a chatting machine for coherent conversation generation. In *Proceedings of the 27th International Joint Conference on Artificial Intelligence*, pages 4279–4285.

Lin Qiu, Jiahui Lu, Jonathan Ramsay, Shanshan Yang, Weina Qu, and Tingshao Zhu. 2017. Personality expression in Chinese language use. *International Journal of Psychology*, 52(6):463–472.

Boele De Raad. 2000. *The big five personality factors: The psycholexical approach to personality.* Hogrefe & Huber Publishers.

Paul R Sackett and Philip T Walmsley. 2014. Which personality attributes are most important in the workplace? *Perspectives on Psychological Science*, 9:538–551.

Junichi Takahashi, Koju Tamaki, Nozomi Yamawaki, et al. 2013. Autism spectrum, attachment styles, and social skills in university student. *Creative Education*, 4:514–520.

Xuewei Wang, Weiyan Shi, Richard Kim, Yoojung Oh, Sijia Yang, Jingwen Zhang, and Zhou Yu. 2020. Persuasion for good: Towards a personalized persuasive dialogue system for social good. In *Proceedings of the 57th Annual Meeting of the Association for Computational Linguistics, Proceedings of the Conference*, pages 5635–5649.

Yunyi Yang, Yunhao Li, and Xiaojun Quan. 2020. UBAR: Towards fully end-to-end task-oriented dialog systems with GPT-2. *arXiv preprint arXiv:2012.03539*.

Saizheng Zhang, Emily Dinan, Jack Urbanek, Arthur Szlam, Douwe Kiela, and Jason Weston. 2018. Personalizing dialogue agents: I have a dog, do you have pets too? In *Proceedings of the 56th Annual Meeting of the Association for Computational Linguistics*, page 2204–2213.

Zhichang Zhang, Zhenwen Zhang, Haoyuan Chen, and Zhiman Zhang. 2019. A joint learning framework with BERT for spoken language understanding. *IEEE Access*, 7:168849–168858.

Yinhe Zheng, Rongsheng Zhang, Minlie Huang, and Xiaoxi Mao. 2020. A pre-training based personalized dialogue generation model with persona-sparse data. In *Proceedings of the AAAI Conference on Artificial Intelligence*, volume 34, pages 9693–9700.

Qi Zhu, Zheng Zhang, Yan Fang, Xiang Li, Ryuichi Takanobu, Jinchao Li, Baolin Peng, Jianfeng Gao, Xiaoyan Zhu, and Minlie Huang. 2020. ConvLab-2: An open-source toolkit for building, evaluating, and diagnosing dialogue systems. *arXiv preprint arXiv:2002.04793*, pages 142–149.

Towards Code-Mixed Hinglish Dialogue Generation

Vibhav Agarwal, Pooja Rao S B*, Dinesh Babu Jayagopi
International Institute of Information Technology Bangalore, India
* University of Lausanne, Switzerland
{vibhav.agarwal,jdinesh}@iiitb.ac.in, pooja.rao@unil.ch

Abstract

Code-mixed language plays a crucial role in communication in multilingual societies. Though the recent growth of web users has greatly boosted the use of such mixed languages, the current generation of dialog systems is primarily monolingual. This increase in usage of code-mixed language has prompted dialog systems in a similar language. We present our work in Code-Mixed Dialog Generation, an unexplored task in code-mixed languages, generating utterances in code-mixed language rather than a single language that is more often just English. We present a new synthetic corpus in code-mix for dialogs, CM-DailyDialog, by converting an existing English-only dialog corpus to a mixed Hindi-English corpus. We then propose a baseline approach where we show the effectiveness of using mBART like multilingual sequence-to-sequence transformers for code-mixed dialog generation. Our best performing dialog models can conduct coherent conversations in Hindi-English mixed language as evaluated by human and automatic metrics setting new benchmarks for the Code-Mixed Dialog Generation task.

1 Introduction

Due to the popularity of different social media and messaging platforms over the last decade, there has been a significant increase in internet users, mainly from multilingual societies. Multilingual speakers regularly combine languages in what is commonly called code-mixing or code-switching while communicating with other multilingual speakers. This has resulted in a substantial influx of mixed language data in the form of comments, conversations, and other forms of communication. Traditional natural language processing tasks like tokenization and tagging, semantic processing, machine translation, and text generation face new and interesting challenges due to this language mixing.

Dialog Systems have been of great interest amongst the natural language processing community for widespread applications. These systems are broadly categorized into three categories: task-oriented dialog system (Wen et al., 2017; Williams and Zweig, 2016), open-ended conversational systems (Shang et al., 2015; Xing et al., 2017), and interactive question answering system. Traditional Dialog Systems have mostly relied on a rule or template-based approach (Williams et al., 2013).

The success of deep neural networks with a considerable amount of training data has led towards end-to-end trained sequence-to-sequence (seq2seq) (Sutskever et al., 2014) models that enhance the generality and diversity of the text generated. Recent advances in attention-based mechanisms (Bahdanau et al., 2015) and Transformers (Vaswani et al., 2017) have shown significant performance improvement and shifted the communities' approach and interest in training larger models. However, all of these prior works use monolingual data and specifically English.

The increasing use of code-mixed languages and ubiquitous nature of multilingual speakers call for catering to the needs of such users in a multilingual fashion with a dialog system, the need for a Code-Mixed Dialog Generational System. A recent study by Bawa et al. (2020) shows that in a real-life setting, people prefer chatbots that engage in code-mixed language.

Code-mixing in informal contexts like newsgroups, tweets, comments and blogs has made it difficult to define a uniform structure to the language. However, linguists have formulated various hypotheses (Belazi et al., 1994; Pfaff, 1979; Poplack, 1981) and constraints (Sankoff and Poplack, 1981; Sciullo et al., 1986; Joshi, 1982) that can define a general rule for code-mixing.

With the rise of large pretrained language models like (Devlin et al., 2019; Radford et al., 2019; Conneau et al., 2020), there's been a lot of improve-

Proceedings of the Third Workshop on Natural Language Processing for Conversational AI, pages 271–280
November 10, 2021.

ment in machine translation and multilingual models. Prior works (Khanuja et al., 2020b; Gupta et al., 2020) show the effectiveness of large multilingual pretrained language models like mBERT (Devlin et al., 2019) and XLM (Conneau and Lample, 2019) on code-mixed data.

Our work attempts to utilize these large seq2seq pre-trained multilingual transformer-based models for the code-mixed dialog generation task. Specifically, our contributions are as follows.

- We propose a synthetic code-mixed dialog dataset, CM-DailyDialog. This is the first benchmark dataset in Hindi-English mixed language for dialog generation generated from translating DailyDialog (Li et al., 2017) to code-mix.

- We set new benchmarks for the code-mixed dialog generation task on the CM-DailyDialog. We finetune the mBART model for the dialog generation in two ways to generate coherent dialog, as seen from both automatic and human evaluation metrics.

- To create CM-DailyDialog, we train a machine translation model. We use monolingual English data as our input instead of a parallel English and Hindi corpus. This differs from earlier work on code-mixed Machine Translation (Gupta et al., 2020; Garg et al., 2018) where they process a parallel corpus for training, making our approach less resource-intensive.

2 Related Work

Code-mixing refers to the interleaving of words belonging to different languages. Code-mixing is most common in multilingual cultures, and it is becoming more common as the number of people using social media and messaging services on the internet grows (Ansaldo et al., 2008). This has lead to a rising research interest in recent years, and several tasks have been conducted as part of code-switching workshops (Diab et al., 2014, 2016). There has been a lot of advancements in solving different code-mixed tasks like language identification (Solorio et al., 2014; Molina et al., 2016), named-entity recognition (Rao and Devi, 2016; Aguilar et al., 2018), question answering (Chandu et al., 2018), part-of-speech tagging (Jamatia et al., 2018), and information retrieval (banerjee et al., 2016). Very recently, a code-mixed version of the GLUE benchmark was proposed by Khanuja et al. (2020b) which introduced a common benchmark for all the tasks.

2.1 Code-Mixed Machine Translation

Machine Translation on Code-Mixed language is a relatively less explored area. There are only a few studies on English to Hinglish Code-Mixed language despite a large population of Code-Mixed speakers in South Asian countries. Dhar et al. (2018) collects a dataset of 6,096 Hinglish-English bitexts and proposes a pipeline where they identify the languages involved in the code-mixed sentence, compute the matrix language and then translate the resulting sentence into a target language. Srivastava and Singh (2020) collects a diversified large parallel corpus called PHINC, consisting of 13,738 Hinglish-English bitexts. Gupta et al. (2020) propose a code-mixed text generator built upon the encoder-decoder framework. They propose using features from a pre-trained cross-lingual transformer based model XLM (Conneau and Lample, 2019) along with Pointer-Generator (See et al., 2017) model as its decoder for the code-mixed text generation.

2.2 Conversational Dialog Systems

This work focuses on open-ended conversational dialog systems, which are interchangeably also called dialog systems here. Conversational systems engage in more open-ended conversations with no specific objective or task to solve in contrast to a task-oriented dialog system. In the open domain, conversational dialog systems fall again into two categories: retrieval-based and generative dialog systems. We take the generative model approach for a code-mixed dialog model rather than retrieve them from a fixed set as it is more dynamic and interactive.

Traditional dialog systems have mostly relied on hand-crafted rules or templates (Williams et al., 2013). Recently, a more data-driven approach is used to enhance the generality and diversity of the text generated in other domains. Researches used RNN (Rumelhart et al., 1986) and LSTM (Hochreiter and Schmidhuber, 1997) based encoder-decoder architectures for the dialog systems. Since the popularity of attention-based mechanisms (Bahdanau et al., 2015), these also have been widely adapted to boost performance. Recent works like DialoGPT (Zhang et al., 2020), Blender-

Bot (Smith et al., 2020) and Meena (Adiwardana et al., 2020) are just a few examples of the open domain conversational agents.

Although much work has been done in dialog systems, mostly all of it is for English conversations. This is because, in most of the work, the dataset used is monolingual. The only recent work involving a multilingual conversational system is by Chen et al. (2019) which performs dialog generation on English and Chinese data. It uses a shared memory mechanism with a seq2seq encoder-decoder like architecture and is trained using multi-task learning (Caruana, 1997).

3 System Overview

This section describes the benchmark dataset for code-mixed dialog generation: CM-DailyDialog, the English to Hinglish translation model used to generate this dataset, and our mBART based dialog generation model.

3.1 CM-DailyDialog dataset

There is no standardized dataset available for multilingual dialog generation; therefore, we choose to generate a synthetic dataset to train our model for code-mixed dialog. We use a standardized and popular English dialog dataset called DailyDialog (Li et al., 2017) and translate the utterances and conversations from English to Code-Mixed using our mBART model (**mBART-en_cm**) defined in Section 3.1.1. This results in the CM-DailyDialog dataset consisting of 11,118 conversations in the training set and 1,000 conversations in both test and validation sets.

We also use the Code-Mixed NLI conversation dataset from the GLUECoS benchmark (Khanuja et al., 2020a). This dataset contains roughly 1,800 training and roughly 500 test conversations extracted from movies.

We first process the multi-turn conversations from the CM-DailyDialog dataset into triplets of utterances using a sliding window approach. The first two utterances in that triplet are served as contextual inputs to the model, while the third utterance is served as the ground truth on which the loss is calculated. This processing of conversations into triplets of utterances increased the size of our dialog dataset from 13,118 to 76,745 data points. Similarly, we process the Code-Mixed NLI dataset into similar triplets, expanding our working dataset from 1,800 to 2,128 unique dialog triplets in the train set and by roughly 500 triplets in the test set. We choose to process these multi-turn conversations into splits of 3 and not say 5 or any other number because of increased computational costs for the mBART model to process such long conversations.

We describe our English to Hinglish translation model mBART-en_cm and the dataset used for its training in the following section.

3.1.1 Machine Translation model

We use an mBART model finetuned on English to Code-Mixed data described in Section 3.1.2 as our machine translation model to convert the English DailyDialog dataset to Code-Mixed form. We denote this model as **mBART-en_cm**. mBART is a multilingual seq2seq denoising bidirectional auto-encoder pre-trained using the same objective as BART (Lewis et al., 2020) but on large-scale monolingual corpora of 25 languages. It is based on the transformer (Vaswani et al., 2017) architecture and consists of 12 encoder and decoder layers, each with 16 attention heads and model dimensions being 1024 resulting in roughly 680 million parameters.

3.1.2 Dataset for Translation

We use the following datasets to finetune and test our *mBART-en_cm* model for English to Hinglish translation task:

- **CMU Hinglish** is an extended Code-Mixed form of the Document Grounded Conversation dataset by Zhou et al. (2018). It consists of roughly 10,000 English and Hinglish Code-Mixed sentences.

- **Reverse PHINC** is the reverse version of the PHINC (Srivastava and Singh, 2020) dataset but we switch the source and target pairs for our task. It contains roughly 13,000 Hinglish and parallel English translations.

- **LinCE** (Aguilar et al., 2020) Benchmark provides an English to Hinglish Code-Mixed dataset as part of their Code-Mixing benchmark for Machine Translation and GLUE. The dataset consists of roughly 10,000 English and Code-Mixed pairs.

We use these datasets individually and in conjunction to see any improvement with increased data.

Dataset	BLEU	Perplexity	CMI_{test}
mBART-dialog			
CM-DailyDialog	4.11	17.4	27.5
CM-DailyDialog + Code-Mixed NLI	1.54	13.6	22.6
mBART-dialog^{+}			
CM-DailyDialog	**8.11**	20.54	**28.9**
CM-DailyDialog + Code-Mixed NLI	5.74	12.93	26.8

Table 1: mBART performance on Dialog Generation

3.2 Code-Mixed Dialog Model

We use the end-to-end multilingual training of the mBART. In literature, there is minimal work utilizing the BART architecture for dialog generation. De Bruyn et al. (2020) is one such work. It utilizes BART for knowledge grounding and knowledge retrieval in dialogs. Our approach attempts to leverage multilingualism by using the pre-trained BART for multilingual dialog generation and presents a few baselines for future work. We compare two strategies for finetuning mBART model for dialog generation:

- **mBART-dialog:** We finetune the mBART model on a Code-Mixed dialog dataset. In our case, we use triplet utterances to train our model.
- **mBART-dialog^{+}:** We finetune the mBART model in a dual curriculum learning method where we first finetune the mBART on an English to Code-Mixed translation task and then on a Code-Mixed dialog dataset.

4 Experimental Setup

In this section, we describe our experimental setup for both our mBART-en_cm model and the dialog model described in Section 3.1.1 & 3.2 respectively.

Our proposed approach is written in Pytorch (Paszke et al., 2019), and the mBART model weights and architecture used are from the HuggingFace's Transformer (Wolf et al., 2020) package. We use only the *mbart-cc-25* weights in all our modeling. All the mBART based models were trained using the AdamW optimizer with weight decay. We used all the default hyperparameters except the number of training epochs. We finetuned all our mBART models for five epochs only. As discussed in Section 2, there is extremely limited prior work and literature on multilingual dialogs. Therefore, there is no baseline for us to compare our model to and we report our numbers as it is.

Datasets	BLEU	CMI_{test}
LinCE Benchmark	11	28.3
CMU Hinglish	**11.53**	**32.5**
CMU Hinglish + LinCE Benchmark + Reverse PHINC	11.25	31.9

Table 2: BLEU score on test set for English to Hinglish Translation using mBART-en_cm model

As discussed in Section 3.1, we process our datasets from English to Code-Mixed and then into triplets. We split our processed CM-DailyDialog dataset into 8:1:1 splits for training, validation, and test set and use the additional Code-Mixed NLI dataset in conjunction with the CM-DailyDialog dataset to see any performance improvement with the increased data. We evaluate both our mBART-dialog and mBART-dialog^{+} models on BLEU and perplexity metric and report our scores in the Table 1. To gauge the language mixing performance of our models, we also use the Code-Mixing Index (CMI) (Gambäck and Das, 2016). We report sacrebleu as our BLEU metric using the HuggingFace's Dataset package.

We also show the performance of our *mBART-en_cm* model on different datasets for the monolingual English to Hinglish translation task using metrics like sacrebleu(reported as BLEU) and Code-Mixing Index in Table 2.

5 Results

Table 1 shows that the model trained using the dual curriculum learning method (mBART-dialog^{+}) performs better both on the BLEU as well as the CMI

English Dialogs to Code-Mixed Translation		
S1: Good afternoon. This is Michelle Li speaking, calling on behalf of IBA. Is Mr Meng available at all?		**S1:** Accha afternoon. Ye Michelle Li speaking hai, IBA ka on behalf calling. Kya Mr Meng available hai?
S2: This is Mr Meng speaking, Michelle.	→	**S2:** Ye hai Mr Meng speaking, Michelle.
S1: Oh, hello! Sorry about that. I'm just calling to say that we've received your new Corporate Credit Card from HQ.		**S1:** Oh, hello! Sorry iske bare mein. Main bas kah raha hoon ki hamen apna new Corporate Credit Card mil gaya hai HQ.

Table 3: Translating DailyDailog dataset from English to Code-Mixed. Blue tokens refer to the Hindi tokens in the Roman script. S1 and S2 refer to Speaker 1 and 2 respectively.

Code-Mixed Dialogs
S1: actually, fruits aur veggies tumhe ache lagte hain
S2: haan, muje patha hein, lekin chicken ke baare mein kya?
S1(generated): Mujhe lagta hai I'm going to make a slice of it.
S1: Mike! Tumhare se sunke accha laga. Aap kaise hain?
S2: everything is fine , aur tum kaise ho?
S1(generated): Main thik hoon. Tumhare sath baat krke accha laga.

Table 4: Examples of the response generated by mBART-dialog$^+$ on the CM-DailyDialog. S1 and S2 refer to Speaker 1 and 2 respectively.

metric. This boost in performance might be due to the model understanding code-mixed language after the first finetune and, as a result, adapting better over the code-mixed dialogs in the second finetune. We show some of the examples of our dialog model in Table 4. We also observe that simply increasing the data does not necessarily increase the model performance and leads to a significant drop in this case. This drop might be due to the inconsistent Hindi vocabulary in the romanized form in different datasets. The same Devanagari token can be represented in various Roman scripts in different datasets. This can cause the model not to have a fixed code-mixed vocabulary, causing this confusion and, hence, a drop in model performance.

Table 2 shows our mBART-en_cm model performance on different datasets. As observed previously, increasing the data leads to a drop in performance, which may be due to different datasets' vocabulary discrepancies. We use the best performing model, i.e. trained on the CMU Hinglish dataset and use that to generate our CM-DailyDialog dataset as described in Section 3.1. Table 3 shows some of the translation examples from English DailyDialog to CM-DailyDialog.

Table 5 shows some of the statistics of the CM-DailyDialog dataset. The CMI scores for all the splits for our generated dataset are close to that of the real world code-mixed datasets like Dhar et al. (2018). This strengthens our intent to utilize this synthetic code-mixed dialog dataset for our dialog generation model.

5.1 Error Analysis of mBART-en_cm Translations

Considering BLEU and CMI ratings do not give insight into translation errors, we use error analysis to further assess the quality of our CM-DailyDialog dataset. We assess the quality of our mBART-en_cm model's translations on the test set by grouping the different errors generated by the model into three error categories and a no error category. We randomly sample 50 sentences from our test set and bucket them into categories. We follow the error analysis categories from Gautam et al. (2021). We employ three human raters that classify the sampled translations into the error buckets. Graduate students (non-native English speakers) familiar with the usage of code-mixed language, specifically Hinglish, in everyday life are the human annotators involved in this research. We report our numbers as a mode of three rater evalu-

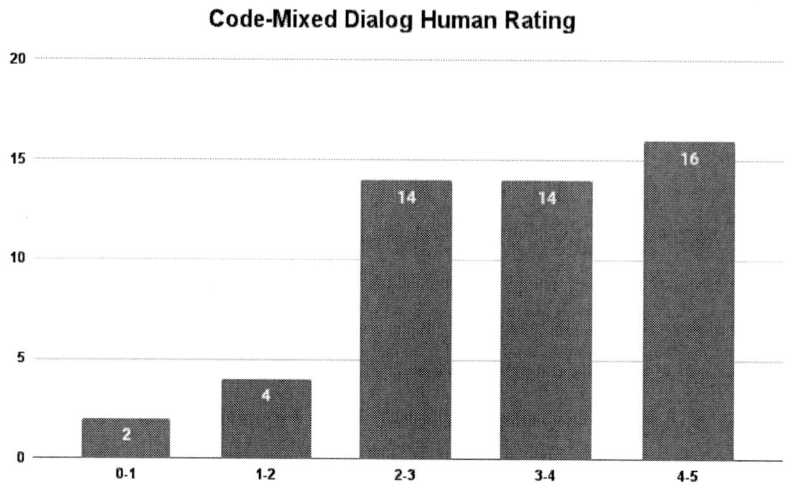

Figure 1: Bucketed average rating of 3 raters over the Code-Mixed dialogs quality from the range of 1-5

	Train set	Dev set	Test set
# of English tokens	295,565	54,150	32,676
# of Hindi tokens	546,535	86,231	67,505
# of Other tokens	77,519	13,493	10,721
Code-Mixing Index (CMI)	35	38.5	32.6

Table 5: Statistics of the generated CM-DailyDialog dataset

ations to account for the subjectivity among the raters. Mistranslated/Partially translation category indicates if the translation has low or no semantic resemblance with the source sentence. Morphological/Syntactical errors indicate if the translation has the same semantic meaning as the source sentence but has minor grammatical or syntax errors. NER mistranslations refer to the situation where the model translates the named entities in the generated output.

Table 6 shows the results of the error analysis over the described errors categories for the 50 test translations. We observe that the model makes 12 syntactical errors and 13 partial/mistranslations out of the 50 samples. After a more nuanced analysis of these numbers, we find that most of the syntax errors were 1-2 token errors or misalignment of those tokens. We also found that out of the 13 partial/mistranslations, only 15% of the translations were complete mistranslations. Most of the sentences in this error category were partial translations where the model failed to translate and code-mix simultaneously.

Error Category	Freq.
Mistranslated/Partially Translated	13
Morphology/Syntax Issues	12
NER mistranslation	1
No error	24

Table 6: Error Analysis on 50 randomly sampled test translated sentences from our best performing mBART-en_cm model on CMU Hinglish Dataset

5.2 Human Evaluation of Code-Mixed Dialog

To further strengthen the assessment of the generated code-mixed dialog, we perform a human evaluation of our best performing dialog model (mBART-dialog$^+$ trained on CM-DailyDialog). We employ three human raters who rate the generated follow-up dialog given prior contextual dialogs. These contextual dialogs refer to the first two utterances in the triplets that we processed in Section 3.1. As previously stated, the raters here are Graduate students familiar with the usage of Hinglish. The raters were instructed to rate the quality of the dialog on a scale of 1-5, with 1 being the lowest. The quality was assessed in terms of both the coherence in the dialog and the code-mixing. We do this analysis on 50 randomly sampled dialog generations from the test set. The results of the human ratings can be seen in Figure 1 as the mean of all three raters.

As it can be seen from Figure 1, 60% of the dialog utterances achieve a score greater than 3. 88% of the dialog utterance are scored above 2. These numbers indicate that our machine-generated code-mixed dialog followups are of good quality both in terms of coherence as well as code-mixing.

6 Conclusion

We introduce a new benchmark dataset for code-mixed dialog generation, CM-DailyDialog, a code-mixed version of the DailyDialog. Our work proposes using multilingual Transformers (mBART) and demonstrates how they help in code-mixed dialog generation. We also introduce a new monolingual English to Code-Mixed machine translation model using mBART. With our comprehensive experiments, we show the effectiveness of our approach in terms of machine translation and dialog generation and set new benchmarks in the Code-Mixed dialog generation task. The manual error analysis illustrates the quality of the new dataset, although it is synthetically generated. In terms of both automatic and human evaluation metrics, we show that the dialog generated from our model is of high quality.

As part of the future work, we would like to improve our machine translation model to improve our CM-DailyDialog data that further boosts our dialog generation. Another huge scope of improvement is in the vocabulary discrepancy in different datasets, and we wish to resolve this to further boost our modeling and performance.

References

Daniel Adiwardana, Minh-Thang Luong, David R. So, Jamie Hall, Noah Fiedel, Romal Thoppilan, Zi Yang, Apoorv Kulshreshtha, Gaurav Nemade, Yifeng Lu, and Quoc V. Le. 2020. Towards a Human-like Open-Domain Chatbot. *arXiv:2001.09977 [cs, stat]*. ArXiv: 2001.09977.

Gustavo Aguilar, Fahad AlGhamdi, Victor Soto, Thamar Solorio, Mona Diab, and Julia Hirschberg, editors. 2018. *Proceedings of the Third Workshop on Computational Approaches to Linguistic Code-Switching*. Association for Computational Linguistics, Melbourne, Australia.

Gustavo Aguilar, Sudipta Kar, and Thamar Solorio. 2020. LinCE: A centralized benchmark for linguistic code-switching evaluation. In *Proceedings of the 12th Language Resources and Evaluation Conference*, pages 1803–1813, Marseille, France. European Language Resources Association.

Ana Inés Ansaldo, Karine Marcotte, Lilian Scherer, and Gaelle Raboyeau. 2008. Language therapy and bilingual aphasia: Clinical implications of psycholinguistic and neuroimaging research. *Journal of Neurolinguistics*, 21(6):539–557.

Dzmitry Bahdanau, Kyunghyun Cho, and Yoshua Bengio. 2015. Neural machine translation by jointly learning to align and translate. In *3rd International Conference on Learning Representations, ICLR 2015, San Diego, CA, USA, May 7-9, 2015, Conference Track Proceedings*.

Somnath banerjee, Kunal Chakma, Sudip Kumar Naskar, Amitava Das, Paolo Rosso, Sivaji Bandyopadhyay, and Monojit Choudhury. 2016. Overview of the Mixed Script Information Retrieval (MSIR). In *Proceedings of FIRE 2016*. FIRE.

Anshul Bawa, Pranav Khadpe, Pratik Joshi, Kalika Bali, and Monojit Choudhury. 2020. Do multilingual users prefer chat-bots that code-mix? let's nudge and find out! *Proc. ACM Hum.-Comput. Interact.*, 4(CSCW1).

Hedi M. Belazi, Edward J. Rubin, and Almeida Jacqueline Toribio. 1994. Code switching and x-bar theory: The functional head constraint. *Linguistic Inquiry*, 25(2):221–237.

Rich Caruana. 1997. Multitask Learning. *Machine Learning*, 28(1):41–75.

Khyathi Chandu, Ekaterina Loginova, Vishal Gupta, Josef van Genabith, Günter Neumann, Manoj Chinnakotla, Eric Nyberg, and Alan W. Black. 2018. Code-mixed question answering challenge: Crowd-sourcing data and techniques. In *Proceedings of the Third Workshop on Computational Approaches to Linguistic Code-Switching*, pages 29–38, Melbourne, Australia. Association for Computational Linguistics.

Chen Chen, Lisong Qiu, Zhenxin Fu, Dongyan Zhao, Junfei Liu, and Rui Yan. 2019. Multilingual Dialogue Generation with Shared-Private Memory. *arXiv:1910.02365 [cs]*. ArXiv: 1910.02365.

Alexis Conneau, Kartikay Khandelwal, Naman Goyal, Vishrav Chaudhary, Guillaume Wenzek, Francisco Guzmán, Edouard Grave, Myle Ott, Luke Zettlemoyer, and Veselin Stoyanov. 2020. Unsupervised cross-lingual representation learning at scale. In

Proceedings of the 58th Annual Meeting of the Association for Computational Linguistics, pages 8440–8451, Online. Association for Computational Linguistics.

Alexis Conneau and Guillaume Lample. 2019. Cross-lingual language model pretraining. In *Advances in Neural Information Processing Systems 32: Annual Conference on Neural Information Processing Systems 2019, NeurIPS 2019, December 8-14, 2019, Vancouver, BC, Canada*, pages 7057–7067.

Maxime De Bruyn, Ehsan Lotfi, Jeska Buhmann, and Walter Daelemans. 2020. Bart for knowledge grounded conversations. In *Converse@ KDD*.

Jacob Devlin, Ming-Wei Chang, Kenton Lee, and Kristina Toutanova. 2019. BERT: Pre-training of deep bidirectional transformers for language understanding. In *Proceedings of the 2019 Conference of the North American Chapter of the Association for Computational Linguistics: Human Language Technologies, Volume 1 (Long and Short Papers)*, pages 4171–4186, Minneapolis, Minnesota. Association for Computational Linguistics.

Mrinal Dhar, Vaibhav Kumar, and Manish Shrivastava. 2018. Enabling code-mixed translation: Parallel corpus creation and MT augmentation approach. In *Proceedings of the First Workshop on Linguistic Resources for Natural Language Processing*, pages 131–140, Santa Fe, New Mexico, USA. Association for Computational Linguistics.

Mona Diab, Pascale Fung, Mahmoud Ghoneim, Julia Hirschberg, and Thamar Solorio, editors. 2016. *Proceedings of the Second Workshop on Computational Approaches to Code Switching*. Association for Computational Linguistics, Austin, Texas.

Mona Diab, Julia Hirschberg, Pascale Fung, and Thamar Solorio, editors. 2014. *Proceedings of the First Workshop on Computational Approaches to Code Switching*. Association for Computational Linguistics, Doha, Qatar.

Björn Gambäck and Amitava Das. 2016. Comparing the level of code-switching in corpora. In *Proceedings of the Tenth International Conference on Language Resources and Evaluation (LREC'16)*, pages 1850–1855, Portorož, Slovenia. European Language Resources Association (ELRA).

Saurabh Garg, Tanmay Parekh, and Preethi Jyothi. 2018. Code-switched language models using dual RNNs and same-source pretraining. In *Proceedings of the 2018 Conference on Empirical Methods in Natural Language Processing*, pages 3078–3083, Brussels, Belgium. Association for Computational Linguistics.

Devansh Gautam, Prashant Kodali, Kshitij Gupta, Anmol Goel, Manish Shrivastava, and Ponnurangam Kumaraguru. 2021. CoMeT: Towards code-mixed translation using parallel monolingual sentences. In *Proceedings of the Fifth Workshop on Computational Approaches to Linguistic Code-Switching*, pages 47–55, Online. Association for Computational Linguistics.

Deepak Gupta, Asif Ekbal, and Pushpak Bhattacharyya. 2020. A semi-supervised approach to generate the code-mixed text using pre-trained encoder and transfer learning. In *Findings of the Association for Computational Linguistics: EMNLP 2020*, pages 2267–2280, Online. Association for Computational Linguistics.

Sepp Hochreiter and Jürgen Schmidhuber. 1997. Long short-term memory. *Neural Comput.*, 9(8):1735–1780.

Anupam Jamatia, Björn Gambäck, and Amitava Das. 2018. Collecting and Annotating Indian Social Media Code-Mixed Corpora. In *Computational Linguistics and Intelligent Text Processing*, pages 406–417, Cham. Springer International Publishing.

Aravind K. Joshi. 1982. Processing of sentences with intra-sentential code-switching. In *Coling 1982: Proceedings of the Ninth International Conference on Computational Linguistics*.

Simran Khanuja, Sandipan Dandapat, Sunayana Sitaram, and Monojit Choudhury. 2020a. A new dataset for natural language inference from code-mixed conversations. In *Proceedings of the The 4th Workshop on Computational Approaches to Code Switching*, pages 9–16, Marseille, France. European Language Resources Association.

Simran Khanuja, Sandipan Dandapat, Anirudh Srinivasan, Sunayana Sitaram, and Monojit Choudhury. 2020b. GLUECoS: An evaluation benchmark for code-switched NLP. In *Proceedings of the 58th Annual Meeting of the Association for Computational Linguistics*, pages 3575–3585, Online. Association for Computational Linguistics.

Mike Lewis, Yinhan Liu, Naman Goyal, Marjan Ghazvininejad, Abdelrahman Mohamed, Omer Levy, Veselin Stoyanov, and Luke Zettlemoyer. 2020. BART: Denoising sequence-to-sequence pre-training for natural language generation, translation, and comprehension. In *Proceedings of the 58th Annual Meeting of the Association for Computational Linguistics*, pages 7871–7880, Online. Association for Computational Linguistics.

Yanran Li, Hui Su, Xiaoyu Shen, Wenjie Li, Ziqiang Cao, and Shuzi Niu. 2017. DailyDialog: A manually labelled multi-turn dialogue dataset. In *Proceedings of the Eighth International Joint Conference on Natural Language Processing (Volume 1: Long Papers)*, pages 986–995, Taipei, Taiwan. Asian Federation of Natural Language Processing.

Giovanni Molina, Fahad AlGhamdi, Mahmoud Ghoneim, Abdelati Hawwari, Nicolas Rey-Villamizar, Mona Diab, and Thamar Solorio.

2016. Overview for the second shared task on language identification in code-switched data. In *Proceedings of the Second Workshop on Computational Approaches to Code Switching*, pages 40–49, Austin, Texas. Association for Computational Linguistics.

Adam Paszke, Sam Gross, Francisco Massa, Adam Lerer, James Bradbury, Gregory Chanan, Trevor Killeen, Zeming Lin, Natalia Gimelshein, Luca Antiga, Alban Desmaison, Andreas Köpf, Edward Yang, Zachary DeVito, Martin Raison, Alykhan Tejani, Sasank Chilamkurthy, Benoit Steiner, Lu Fang, Junjie Bai, and Soumith Chintala. 2019. Pytorch: An imperative style, high-performance deep learning library. In *Advances in Neural Information Processing Systems 32: Annual Conference on Neural Information Processing Systems 2019, NeurIPS 2019, December 8-14, 2019, Vancouver, BC, Canada*, pages 8024–8035.

Carol W. Pfaff. 1979. Constraints on language mixing: Intrasentential code-switching and borrowing in spanish/english. *Language*, 55(2):291–318.

Shana Poplack. 1981. *Syntactic structure and social function of code-switching*, pages 169–184.

Alec Radford, Jeff Wu, Rewon Child, David Luan, Dario Amodei, and Ilya Sutskever. 2019. Language models are unsupervised multitask learners.

Pattabhi R. K. Rao and S. Devi. 2016. Cmee-il: Code mix entity extraction in indian languages from social media text @ fire 2016 - an overview. In *FIRE*.

David E. Rumelhart, Geoffrey E. Hinton, and Ronald J. Williams. 1986. Learning representations by back-propagating errors. *Nature*, 323(6088):533–536.

David Sankoff and Shana Poplack. 1981. A formal grammar for code-switching. *Papers in Linguistics - International Journal of Human Communication*, 14:3–46.

Anne-Marie Di Sciullo, Pieter Muysken, and Rajendra Singh. 1986. Government and code-mixing. *Journal of Linguistics*, 22(1):1–24.

Abigail See, Peter J. Liu, and Christopher D. Manning. 2017. Get to the point: Summarization with pointer-generator networks. In *Proceedings of the 55th Annual Meeting of the Association for Computational Linguistics (Volume 1: Long Papers)*, pages 1073–1083, Vancouver, Canada. Association for Computational Linguistics.

Lifeng Shang, Zhengdong Lu, and Hang Li. 2015. Neural responding machine for short-text conversation. In *Proceedings of the 53rd Annual Meeting of the Association for Computational Linguistics and the 7th International Joint Conference on Natural Language Processing (Volume 1: Long Papers)*, pages 1577–1586, Beijing, China. Association for Computational Linguistics.

Eric Michael Smith, Mary Williamson, Kurt Shuster, Jason Weston, and Y-Lan Boureau. 2020. Can you put it all together: Evaluating conversational agents' ability to blend skills. In *Proceedings of the 58th Annual Meeting of the Association for Computational Linguistics*, pages 2021–2030, Online. Association for Computational Linguistics.

Thamar Solorio, Elizabeth Blair, Suraj Maharjan, Steven Bethard, Mona Diab, Mahmoud Ghoneim, Abdelati Hawwari, Fahad AlGhamdi, Julia Hirschberg, Alison Chang, and Pascale Fung. 2014. Overview for the first shared task on language identification in code-switched data. In *Proceedings of the First Workshop on Computational Approaches to Code Switching*, pages 62–72, Doha, Qatar. Association for Computational Linguistics.

Vivek Srivastava and Mayank Singh. 2020. PHINC: A parallel Hinglish social media code-mixed corpus for machine translation. In *Proceedings of the Sixth Workshop on Noisy User-generated Text (W-NUT 2020)*, pages 41–49, Online. Association for Computational Linguistics.

Ilya Sutskever, Oriol Vinyals, and Quoc V. Le. 2014. Sequence to sequence learning with neural networks. In *Advances in Neural Information Processing Systems 27: Annual Conference on Neural Information Processing Systems 2014, December 8-13 2014, Montreal, Quebec, Canada*, pages 3104–3112.

Ashish Vaswani, Noam Shazeer, Niki Parmar, Jakob Uszkoreit, Llion Jones, Aidan N. Gomez, Lukasz Kaiser, and Illia Polosukhin. 2017. Attention is all you need. In *Advances in Neural Information Processing Systems 30: Annual Conference on Neural Information Processing Systems 2017, December 4-9, 2017, Long Beach, CA, USA*, pages 5998–6008.

Tsung-Hsien Wen, David Vandyke, Nikola Mrkšić, Milica Gašić, Lina M. Rojas-Barahona, Pei-Hao Su, Stefan Ultes, and Steve Young. 2017. A network-based end-to-end trainable task-oriented dialogue system. In *Proceedings of the 15th Conference of the European Chapter of the Association for Computational Linguistics: Volume 1, Long Papers*, pages 438–449, Valencia, Spain. Association for Computational Linguistics.

Jason Williams, Antoine Raux, Deepak Ramachandran, and Alan Black. 2013. The dialog state tracking challenge. In *Proceedings of the SIGDIAL 2013 Conference*, pages 404–413, Metz, France. Association for Computational Linguistics.

Jason D. Williams and Geoffrey Zweig. 2016. End-to-end LSTM-based dialog control optimized with supervised and reinforcement learning. *arXiv:1606.01269 [cs]*. ArXiv: 1606.01269.

Thomas Wolf, Lysandre Debut, Victor Sanh, Julien Chaumond, Clement Delangue, Anthony Moi, Pierric Cistac, Tim Rault, Remi Louf, Morgan Funtowicz, Joe Davison, Sam Shleifer, Patrick von Platen,

Clara Ma, Yacine Jernite, Julien Plu, Canwen Xu, Teven Le Scao, Sylvain Gugger, Mariama Drame, Quentin Lhoest, and Alexander Rush. 2020. Transformers: State-of-the-art natural language processing. In *Proceedings of the 2020 Conference on Empirical Methods in Natural Language Processing: System Demonstrations*, pages 38–45, Online. Association for Computational Linguistics.

Chen Xing, Wei Wu, Yu Wu, Jie Liu, Yalou Huang, Ming Zhou, and Wei-Ying Ma. 2017. Topic aware neural response generation. In *Proceedings of the Thirty-First AAAI Conference on Artificial Intelligence, February 4-9, 2017, San Francisco, California, USA*, pages 3351–3357. AAAI Press.

Yizhe Zhang, Siqi Sun, Michel Galley, Yen-Chun Chen, Chris Brockett, Xiang Gao, Jianfeng Gao, Jingjing Liu, and Bill Dolan. 2020. DIALOGPT : Large-scale generative pre-training for conversational response generation. In *Proceedings of the 58th Annual Meeting of the Association for Computational Linguistics: System Demonstrations*, pages 270–278, Online. Association for Computational Linguistics.

Kangyan Zhou, Shrimai Prabhumoye, and Alan W Black. 2018. A dataset for document grounded conversations. In *Proceedings of the 2018 Conference on Empirical Methods in Natural Language Processing*, pages 708–713, Brussels, Belgium. Association for Computational Linguistics.

Towards Zero and Few-shot Knowledge-seeking Turn Detection in Task-orientated Dialogue Systems

Di Jin, Shuyang Gao, Seokhwan Kim, Yang Liu, Dilek Hakkani-Tur
Amazon Alexa AI, Sunnyvale, CA, USA
{djinamzn,shuyag,seokhwk,yangliud,hakkanit}@amazon.com

Abstract

Most prior work on task-oriented dialogue systems is restricted to supporting domain APIs. However, users may have requests that are out of the scope of these APIs. This work focuses on identifying such user requests. Existing methods for this task mainly rely on fine-tuning pre-trained models on large annotated data. We propose a novel method, REDE, based on adaptive representation learning and density estimation. REDE can be applied to zero-shot cases, and quickly learns a high-performing detector with only a few shots by updating less than 3K parameters. We demonstrate REDE's competitive performance on DSTC9 data and our newly collected test set.

1 Introduction

Current task-oriented dialog systems often rely on pre-defined APIs to complete target tasks (Williams et al., 2017; Eric et al., 2017) and filter out any other requests beyond the APIs as out-of-domain cases. However, some in-domain user requests can be addressed by incorporating external domain knowledge from the web or any other sources (Kim et al., 2020). To address this problem, Kim et al. (2021) recently organized a benchmark challenge on task-oriented conversational modeling with unstructured knowledge access in DSTC9 (Gunasekara et al., 2020). This challenge includes the knowledge-seeking turn detection task to determine whether to invoke a knowledge-driven responder or just rely on available API functions. One data sample is provided in Table 1. The state-of-the-art systems (He et al., 2021; Tang et al., 2021; Mi et al., 2021; Jin et al., 2021) implemented this detector by fine-tuning a large pre-trained model on the training dataset (about 72K samples) as a binary classifier, and achieved an F1 score of over 95% on the benchmark test set. However, after close investigation, we find those user queries in the test set are very limited in topic coverage and language variation. To evaluate the detector performance on real-world user queries, we specially curate a new contrast set following Gardner et al. (2020) by manually collecting questions posted by real users on Tripadvisor forums. We found that the detector trained on DSTC9 Track 1 training samples had a large performance degradation on this contrast set (F1 score dropped by over 15%), suggesting the need for methods with better generalization.

In this work, we propose a method that can quickly learn a knowledge-seeking turn detector with much fewer out-of-domain samples, such as only a few shots or even zero shot. Our method is composed of two stages: **RE**presentation learning and **DE**nsity estimation (REDE). First, we learn a representation model via fine-tuning a pre-trained sentence encoder on all non-knowledge-seeking turns (utterances that can be supported by APIs) via masked language modeling (MLM). Then we learn a density estimator using these representation vectors. During inference, the density estimator produces a density score for a given user utterance. If it is above a threshold, this utterance is counted as an in-domain API turn, otherwise as a knowledge-seeking turn.

To incorporate out-of-domain examples, we propose to use principle component analysis to quickly learn a projection matrix with few knowledge-seeking turn samples and then use this matrix to linearly transform the representation vectors. We conduct experiments on the DSTC9 Track 1 data as well as our new contrast test set. We demonstrate that REDE can achieve competitive performance as other supervised methods in the full-shot setting and outperform them by a large margin in the low-resource setting. More importantly, our approach generalizes much better in the new contrast test set that we created.

Overall, our contributions are summarized as follows:

- We propose a new approach, REDE, for

Proceedings of the Third Workshop on Natural Language Processing for Conversational AI, pages 281–288
November 10, 2021.

Turn	Speaker	Utterance	Sampled Knowledge Snippets from FAQs
1	User	I'm looking for a place to stay in the south of town. It doesn't need to have free parking.	
2	Agent	There are 4 hotels that are in the area you are looking for. Would you prefer a 3 or 4 star rated hotel?	
3	User	I don't care about the star rating as long as it's expensive.	
4	Agent	The ***Lensfield Hotel*** is the only expensive hotel in the south area. Would you like any more information on this location?	
5	User	I'm interested in knowing, do they have a workout facility on the premises?	
6	Agent	There are both a fitness center and gym available on the premises. Does this sound ok?	Q1: Do you have room service for your guests? A1: Yes, the Lensfield Hotel provides room services. **Q2: Is there a gym available at your location? A2: There is both a fitness center and gym available on the premises.** Q3: Can I bring my dog? A3: Pets are not allowed at the Lensfield Hotel.
7	User	That is perfect can you book that for me please.	
8	Agent	The Lensfield Hotel is located in the South. It has a 3 star rating and is expensive. There is free parking and internet. I have booked it for you.	
9	User	Great, thank you!	

Table 1: One example of task-oriented conversations with unstructured knowledge access. The user utterance of turn 5 is beyond the coverage of API and needs external knowledge support, therefore it is a knowledge-seeking turn while other user turns are non-knowledge-seeking turns. To address turn 5, three sampled FAQ pairs for the entity "Lensfield Hotel" extracted from the external knowledge are listed in the rightmost column. The most appropriate FAQ pair is highlighted in bold font.

knowledge-seeking turn detection that be applied to zero or few shot cases. It can be quickly adapted to new knowledge-seeking turns data with much less training samples, which can achieve over 90% F1 score with only five shots;

- Once the continuous pretraining stage on non-knowledge-seeking turns data is finished, our model can be quickly adapted to any kinds of knowledge-seeking turns data within seconds with only a few parameters to be learned.
- We curate and release a contrast set to examine the generalization capability of the knowledge seeking-turn detectors.[1] We demonstrate that our model is better at generalizing to this contrast set than the previous best models.

2 Related Work

Our work is closely related to those participating systems in DSTC9 Track 1 (Kim et al., 2020, 2021). All the systems proposed to treat the problem of knowledge-seeking turn detection as a binary classification task and fine-tuned pre-trained models such as RoBERTa, UniLM, PLATO, GPT2, on the whole training set (He et al., 2021; Tang et al., 2021; Mi et al., 2021), which yielded around 99% and 96% F1 scores on the development and test sets, respectively. Our method differs in two aspects: 1) We do not need to fine-tune the pre-trained model on the training set; 2) Our model is at least 5 times smaller and we need less than 5% of training data to achieve similar performance.

Our method is inspired by previous work for out-of-domain (OOD) detection (Ren et al., 2019; Gangal et al., 2020; Hendrycks et al., 2019) and one-class classification (Sohn et al., 2021). Kim et al. (2020) also tried tackling this problem by applying an unsupervised anomaly detection algorithm, Local Outlier Factor (LOF) (Breunig et al., 2000), which compares the local densities between a given input instance and its nearest neighbors, but did not obtain good results (F1 score is less than 50%). Sohn et al. (2021) proposed to first learn a representation model via contrastive learning, then learn a density estimator on the obtained representations. They showed decent performance for one-class classification. All these previous work assumed no access to OOD samples, however, we would like to make use of those OOD samples efficiently when they are available. Therefore we extend the general representation learning framework by proposing a novel representation transformation method to learn OOD samples, which leads to significantly boosted detection performance.

Our work is also related to few/zero-shot learn-

[1]https://github.com/jind11/REDE

ing, which has been widely studied previously (Gao et al., 2020; Jin et al., 2020c,b). Transfer learning (Zhou et al., 2019c; Jin et al., 2020a; Zhou et al., 2019a,b; Yan et al., 2020) and data augmentation (Jindal et al., 2020b,a) have been two major methods for this direction, while our work focuses on manipulation of learned representations, which provides a new perspective.

3 Methods

Our method includes three steps: encoder adaptation, representation transformation, and density estimation. The representation transformation step is only applicable when there are OOD examples (i.e., knowledge-seeking turns).

3.1 Encoder Adaptation

In this step, we adapt a pre-trained sentence encoder E to the in-domain data, i.e., non-knowledge-seeking turns, $X^{NK} = \{x_1^{NK}, ..., x_N^{NK}\}$, via masked language modeling (Devlin et al., 2019). Specifically, 15% of tokens of x_i^{NK} are masked and E is trained to predict these masked tokens.

3.2 Representation Transformation

To incorporate the knowledge-seeking turns $X^K = \{x_1^K, ..., x_M^K\}$, a standard solution is to fine-tune E on the combined data of knowledge-seeking and non-knowledge-seeking turns, $X = X^K \cup X^{NK}$, as a supervised binary classifier. However, in few-shot settings where $M << N$, there is an extreme class imbalance problem. In addition, fine-tuning large models may take a long time and much computation power with large data size. Instead, we propose a simple linear transformation to the sentence representation $e = E(x)$ without updating the model parameters, following (Su et al., 2021):

$$\tilde{e} = T(e) = (e - \mu)W \quad (1)$$

where $\mu = \frac{1}{M}\sum_{i=1}^{M} E(x_i^K)$. To calculate W, we first calculate the covariance matrix, $\Sigma = \frac{1}{M}\sum_{i=1}^{M}(E(x_i^K) - \mu)^T(E(x_i^K) - \mu)$, then perform Singular Value Decomposition (SVD) over Σ such that: $\Sigma = U\Lambda U^T$, and finally we obtain $W = U\sqrt{\Lambda^{-1}}$.

The elements in diagonal matrix Λ derived from SVD are sorted in descending order. Therefore, we can retain the first L columns of W to reduce the dimension of transformed vectors $\tilde{e}$, which is theoretically equivalent to Principal Component Analysis (PCA). However, to be noted, both μ and W parameters are obtained using those knowledge-seeking turns instead of non-knowledge-seeking turns and the number of knowledge-seeking turns is much smaller, which can be as small as just a few shots. In another word, we only need a very small size of out-of-domain samples to learn the parameters needed for our representation transformation as defined in Eq. 1 to transform the representations of in-domain data. This is in contrast to the conventional PCA based density estimation method that assumes only having access to in-domain data, i.e. non-knowledge-seeking turns, and needs to learn and perform PCA transformation both on a good amount of those in-domain data.

This step of transformation can be viewed as another round of unsupervised representation learning with knowledge-seeking turns, which helps us obtain a better representation and is extremely critical to our claimed great performance for few-shot learning, as analyzed in Section 5.2.2.

3.3 Density estimation

In this step, we encode all the non-knowledge-seeking turns in the training set and transform them to obtain $\{\tilde{e}_1^{NK}, ..., \tilde{e}_N^{NK}\}$, normalize them into unit vectors, and then learn a shallow density estimator D over them, such as Gaussian Mixture Model (GMM). Note that in the zero-shot setting when no knowledge-seeking turns are available, the representation transformation step (in Section 3.2) is skipped.

During inference, given a test sample x, we encode it with the encoder E, transform it with T defined in Eq. 1, and then use the learned density estimator D to produce a density score $D(T(E(x)))$. If it is above a pre-set threshold η, x is considered as a non-knowledge-seeking turn, otherwise as a knowledge-seeking turn. This whole pipeline is motivated by the assumption that the well learned representations of in-domain (non-knowledge-seeking turns) and OOD samples (knowledge-seeking turns) should be distributed separately in the latent space, and thus the estimated density of in-domain data by the density estimator should be higher than that of OOD data.

4 Experiments

4.1 Dataset

We use the DSTC9 Track 1 competition data (Kim et al., 2020, 2021), and focus on the sub-task of binary knowledge-seeking turn detection. The data statistics are summarized in Table 2.[2] We further curate a new contrast test set by first collecting questions posted by real users in the Tripadvisor forums[3], then obtain the questions as knowledge-seeking turns that cannot be addressed by Multi-WOZ API schema (Eric et al., 2019) (this schema was also used for constructing the DSTC9 Track 1 dataset), and finally manually paraphrasing them to make them more like dialogue utterances. We obtained 617 knowledge-seeking turns and mixed them with those non-knowledge-seeking turns in the original test set to form the contrast set.

Table 3 shows several data samples for the newly curated contrast set. These user queries collected from real users are much more diverse than those in the benchmark test set of DSTC9 Track 1 dataset. Among these examples, the user query of "How much do you charge for parking?" is actually quite challenging for knowledge-seeking turn detection since this query is very close to one of the available API functions that is responsible for checking whether there is free parking. However, in order to answer this query, we still need to invoke the knowledge module to retrieve external unstructured knowledge.

	Pos	Neg	All
Train Set	19,184	52,164	71,348
Valid Set	2,673	6,990	9,663
Test Set	1,981	2,200	4,181
Contrast Set	617	2,200	2,817

Table 2: Statistics of the knowledge-seeking turn detection benchmark dataset. Pos: knowledge-seeking turns; Neg: non-knowledge-seeking turns.

4.2 Baselines and Settings

The baselines are 1) the best performing model in the DSTC9 Track 1 competition (Kim et al., 2021), which is a fine-tuned RoBERTa-Large model (Liu et al., 2019) on the training set. 2) Fine-tuned RoBERTa-Large-NLI (obtained by fine-tuning RoBERTa-Large on SNLI and MultiNLI datasets) and DistilBERT-Base-NLI-STSB (obtained by fine-tuning DistilBERT-Base on SNLI, MultiNLI, and STS-B datasets) on the training set.

The sentence encoder E we used is DistilBERT-Base-NLI-STSB (Reimers and Gurevych, 2019).[4]

[2]Data can be downloaded from: https://github.com/alexa/alexa-with-dstc9-track1-dataset

[3]https://www.tripadvisor.com

[4]https://github.com/UKPLab/sentence-transformers

Domains	Examples
Attraction	Is it necessary to buy tickets in advance?
Attraction	How long it could take to see it all ? 4 hours it would be enough?
Hotel	Is there a minimum check in age?
Hotel	How much do you charge for parking?
Restaurant	Would there be room for a stroller with a sleeping baby during dinner?
Restaurant	Can I order crab cakes take out for eight servings ?

Table 3: Examples of newly collected user questions in the contrast set. These user queries collected from real users are much more diverse than those in the benchmark test set of DSTC9 Track 1 dataset.

The threshold η is chosen based on the highest F1 score on the development set. For the density estimator, we have tried OC-SVM, KDE with various kinds of kernels, and GMM, and we find GMM performs the best and its inference time is the lowest. We set the number of components to 1 for GMM. Dimensionality L is set as 650 for PCA transformation by tuning on the development set. Details of comparison and tuning results are in the appendix. For evaluation metrics, we report precision (P), recall (R), and F1 scores.

5 Results & Discussion

5.1 Main Results

Full supervised setting Table 4 summarizes the comparison of our method REDE with baselines where all knowledge-seeking turn samples in the DSTC9 Track 1 training set are used for training. REDE has two advantages: (1) Once the first step of adaptive pre-training on non-knowledge-seeking turns is done, it only needs to update less than 3K parameters of the density estimator for learning the knowledge-seeking turns, but it can still achieve superior performance on the test set; (2) It can be better generalized to the new contrast set that has distribution shift with respect to the training data.

Low-resource setting We are more interested in exploring how our method performs under the low-resource setting compared with baselines. Therefore, we sub-sampled different numbers of knowledge-seeking turn samples and kept using all non-knowledge-seeking turn samples. We then trained the model and obtained F1 scores on the test set. We performed five times of random sub-sampling and report the average and standard deviation in Figure 1. Since the error bar of REDE is

Learning Schema	Sentence Encoder	Model size	Trainable Parameters	Test Set (%)			Contrast Set (%)		
				P	R	F1	P	R	F1
Standard Fine-tuning	RoBERTa-Large	355M	355M	99.19	92.88	95.93	96.61	69.37	80.75
	RoBERTa-Large-NLI	355M	355M	99.46	92.28	95.73	97.54	64.18	77.42
	DistilBERT-Base-NLI-STSB	66M	66M	98.92	92.78	95.75	95.36	66.67	78.44
REDE	DistilBERT-Base-NLI-STSB	66M	3K	97.76	94.65	**96.18**	86.98	94.17	**90.43**

Table 4: Performance on the original test set and contrast set when all knowledge-seeking turns data are used for training. Trainable parameters refer to those parameters that are updated for learning knowledge-seeking turns.

too small to be seen, we further provide the complete results in Table 5. As we can see, REDE is always superior than baselines for all sub-sampling ratios. The performance gap is larger when fewer examples are used. Most notably, for the zero-shot setting without using any knowledge-seeking turns, REDE can still achieve 85.95% of F1 score. For comparison, in the zero-shot setting, we also tested Local Outlier Factor (LOF) (Breunig et al., 2000), which was used in (Kim et al., 2020), and obtained an F1 score of 73.78% on the test set, which is much lower than our proposed density estimation method. Under the few-shots setting such as 5-shots and 10-shots, REDE can obtain more than 90% of F1, whereas other supervised baselines' scores are under 20%.

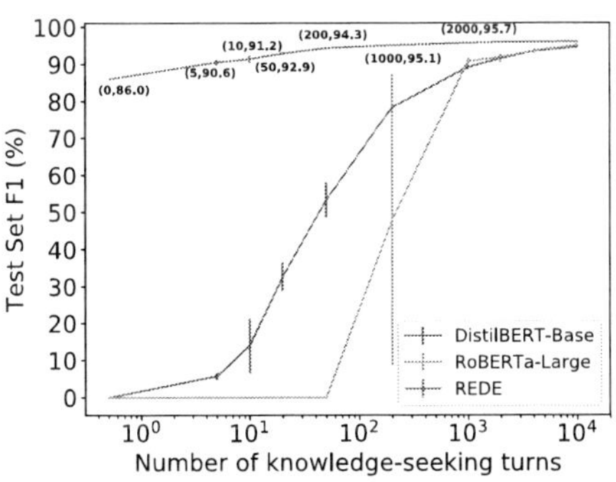

Figure 1: F1 score plots with error bar on the test set with different numbers of knowledge-seeking turns used for training Full name of DistilBERT-Base is DistilBERT-Base-NLI-STSB.

5.2 Analysis

5.2.1 Effect of MLM Adaptation

As shown in Table 6, after removing the MLM adaptation step, our method has significant performance degradation, especially for the contrast set, indicating the importance of adapting the general pre-trained model to the target dataset via unsupervised learning. We have also tried adopting contrastive learning for such unsupervised adaptation

Samples	DistillBERT	RoBERTa	REDE
5	5.70 ± 0.99	0.00 ± 0.00	90.56 ± 0.69
10	13.88 ± 7.37	0.00 ± 0.00	91.34 ± 0.92
20	32.51 ± 3.84	0.00 ± 0.00	92.85 ± 0.26
50	53.22 ± 4.70	0.00 ± 0.00	94.29 ± 0.35
200	78.35 ± 2.57	47.87 ± 39.28	95.05 ± 0.20
1,000	89.14 ± 0.49	90.76 ± 0.94	95.74 ± 0.13
2,000	91.49 ± 0.97	91.92 ± 0.79	95.97 ± 0.12
4,000	93.49 ± 0.53	93.55 ± 0.49	95.95 ± 0.18
10,000	94.56 ± 0.32	95.06 ± 0.46	96.07 ± 0.17

Table 5: Averaged F1 score and standard deviation under the low-resource setting by randomly sub-sampling different number of knowledge-seeking turns for five times. DistillBERT is DistillBERT-Base-NLI-STSB while RoBERTa is RoBERTa-Large.

(i.e., SimCSE), which has shown state-of-the-art performance for unsupervised representation learning (Gao et al., 2021). Results in Table 6 show that it is worse than MLM. The reason could be that contrastive learning used in SimCSE would lead to more uniform and dispersed distribution over the latent space, however, the density estimation based OOD detection favors more dense and collapsed distribution for in-domain data.

Settings	Test Set F1 (%)	Contrast Set F1 (%)
REDE	**96.18**	**90.43**
no MLM	93.49	75.65
MLM $\rightarrow$ SimCSE	92.00	74.39

Table 6: Ablation study for MLM adaptation by removing it or replacing it with SimCSE (a contrastive learning method). All training samples are used here.

Dimensions	Zero-shot	Ten-shot	Full-shot
Top 5	65.67	76.64	78.38
Top 50	71.04	82.23	92.40
Top 500	77.16	91.73	96.32
All (768)	77.05	92.37	96.09

Table 7: F1 score on test set for top 5, 50, 500, and all principle components under three different settings: zero-shot (PCA over non-knowledge-seeking turns), ten-shot (PCA over ten knowledge-seeking turns), and full-shot (PCA over all knowledge-seeking turns).

Estimator	Test Set (%)				Contrast Set (%)		
	P	R	F1	Inference Time (s)	P	R	F1
OC-SVM	92.30	88.34	90.28	74.36	68.81	88.33	77.36
KDE-Gaussian	92.81	91.17	91.98	377.43	72.49	88.82	79.83
KDE-Exponential	92.29	91.87	92.08	373.76	73.18	88.01	79.91
GMM	**97.76**	**94.65**	**96.18**	**0.07**	**86.98**	**94.17**	**90.43**

Table 8: Comparison of different density estimators. Inference time is measure on the whole test set using the same machine. We have also tried other kernels for the KDE estimator, such as 'tophat', 'epanechnikov', 'linear', and 'cosine', but they all perform poorly.

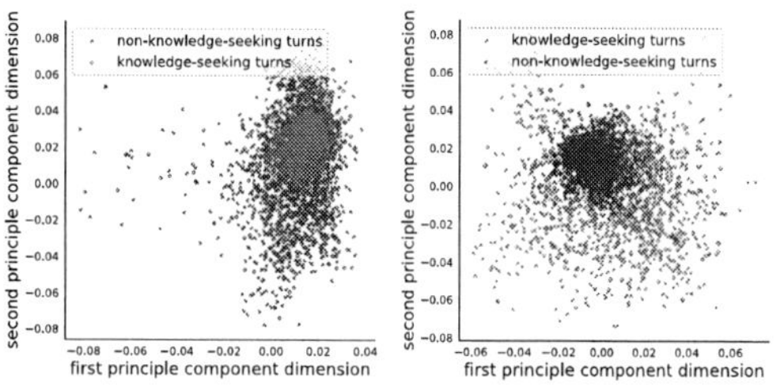

(a) PCA with non-knowledge-seeking turns, F1 = 68.59%. (b) PCA with knowledge-seeking turns, F1 = 78.49%.

Figure 2: Scatter plot using top two principle components of PCA on test samples. F1 score is measured on the test set with top two dimensions only.

5.2.2 Understanding PCA Transformation

In Section 3.2, the sentence representation is transformed with PCA learned from knowledge-seeking turns. Table 7 shows the F1 score on the test set using top L principle components with PCA learned using different data. Overall, we can see that PCA with knowledge-seeking turns achieves better performance, and using more principle components is always beneficial. PCA is well-known to help construct new subspaces by maximizing the global variance. Intuitively, by learning PCA over knowledge-seeking turns, we expect the manifolds on knowledge-seeking turns to spread out and non-knowledge seeking turns condense. Figure 2 shows the scatter plot of the top two principle components of transformed features. In Figure 2a, we learn PCA from non-knowledge-seeking turns, which results in the manifold of knowledge-seeking turns (red dots) to be within that of non-knowledge-seeking turns (blue dots). It hurts the performance since the density estimation is performed over non-knowledge-seeking turns, as confirmed by the zero shot result in Table 7 in comparison to that in Fig 1. In contrast, in Figure 2b, we learn PCA with knowledge-seeking turns, which makes knowledge-seeking turns (red dots) spread out and non-knowledge-seeking turns (blue dots) condense. By estimating the density of this condensed blue area, we obtain higher F1 score because all the red dots falling outside of the region of blue dots will be classified as out-of-distribution correctly.

Components #	Dev Set F1	Test Set F1	Contrast Set F1
1	98.71	96.18	90.43
2	98.88	95.82	90.61
3	98.97	96.12	90.35
4	99.03	96.04	89.72

Table 9: Comparison of performance (in percentage) by using different number of components for the GMM estimator.

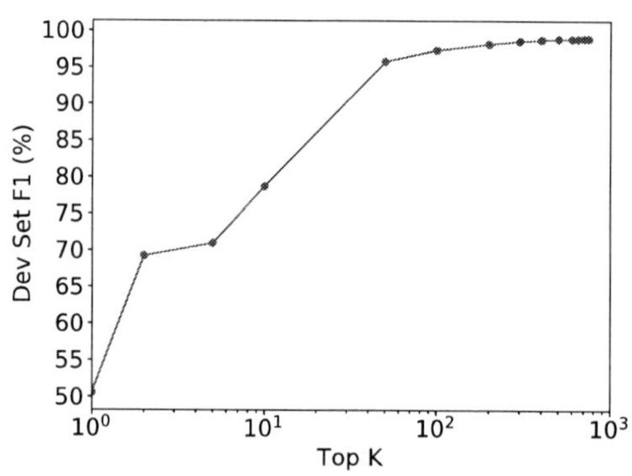

Figure 3: Development set F1 scores by retraining different values of first L columns of W. Full dimension is 768.

5.2.3 Comparison of Density Estimators

For the density estimator, we have tried OC-SVM, KDE with various kinds of kernels, and GMM, which are summarized in Table 8. All these estimators are implemented using Scikit-Learn library.[5] From Table 8, we see that GMM performs the best while being the fastest for inference, therefore we chose it as the density estimator in our work.

[5]https://scikit-learn.org/stable/

Table 9 shows the performance under different number of components for the GMM density estimator. From it, we see that the number of components has minor influence on the performance so we decide to use 1 as the number of components in this work.

5.2.4 Effects of L

We can retrain only the first L columns of W for the PCA transformation, which can help us reduce the dimension of transformed representation vector $\tilde{e}$. Figure 3 shows the development set performance under different values of L when all knowledge-seeking turns are used for training. We see that the first 50 dimensions can achieve over 95% F1 score and 300 dimensions are already enough to realize the peak performance, whereas the full dimension is 768.

6 Conclusion

In this work, we propose a novel method REDE based on domain-adapted representation learning and density estimation for knowledge-seeking turn detection in tasked-orientated dialogue systems. Compared with previous SOTA models, REDE can achieve comparable performance in the full supervised setting and significantly superior performance for the low-resource setting. Besides, REDE has much better generalization capability onto a new contrast set we curated.

References

Markus M Breunig, Hans-Peter Kriegel, Raymond T Ng, and Jörg Sander. 2000. Lof: identifying density-based local outliers. In *Proceedings of the 2000 ACM SIGMOD international conference on Management of data*, pages 93–104.

Jacob Devlin, Ming-Wei Chang, Kenton Lee, and Kristina Toutanova. 2019. BERT: Pre-training of deep bidirectional transformers for language understanding. In *Proceedings of the 2019 Conference of the North American Chapter of the Association for Computational Linguistics: Human Language Technologies, Volume 1 (Long and Short Papers)*, pages 4171–4186, Minneapolis, Minnesota. Association for Computational Linguistics.

Mihail Eric, Rahul Goel, Shachi Paul, Adarsh Kumar, Abhishek Sethi, Peter Ku, Anuj Kumar Goyal, Sanchit Agarwal, Shuyang Gao, and Dilek Hakkani-Tur. 2019. Multiwoz 2.1: A consolidated multi-domain dialogue dataset with state corrections and state tracking baselines. *arXiv preprint arXiv:1907.01669*.

Mihail Eric, Lakshmi Krishnan, Francois Charette, and Christopher D. Manning. 2017. Key-value retrieval networks for task-oriented dialogue. In *Proceedings of the SIGDIAL 2017 Conference*, pages 37–49.

Varun Gangal, Abhinav Arora, Arash Einolghozati, and Sonal Gupta. 2020. Likelihood ratios and generative classifiers for unsupervised out-of-domain detection in task oriented dialog. In *Proceedings of the AAAI Conference on Artificial Intelligence*, volume 34, pages 7764–7771.

Shuyang Gao, Sanchit Agarwal, Tagyoung Chung, Di Jin, and Dilek Hakkani-Tur. 2020. From machine reading comprehension to dialogue state tracking: Bridging the gap. *arXiv preprint arXiv:2004.05827*.

Tianyu Gao, Xingcheng Yao, and Danqi Chen. 2021. Simcse: Simple contrastive learning of sentence embeddings. *arXiv preprint arXiv:2104.08821*.

Matt Gardner, Yoav Artzi, Victoria Basmov, Jonathan Berant, Ben Bogin, Sihao Chen, Pradeep Dasigi, Dheeru Dua, Yanai Elazar, Ananth Gottumukkala, Nitish Gupta, Hannaneh Hajishirzi, Gabriel Ilharco, Daniel Khashabi, Kevin Lin, Jiangming Liu, Nelson F. Liu, Phoebe Mulcaire, Qiang Ning, Sameer Singh, Noah A. Smith, Sanjay Subramanian, Reut Tsarfaty, Eric Wallace, Ally Zhang, and Ben Zhou. 2020. Evaluating models' local decision boundaries via contrast sets. In *Findings of the Association for Computational Linguistics: EMNLP 2020*, pages 1307–1323, Online. Association for Computational Linguistics.

R. Chulaka Gunasekara, Seokhwan Kim, Luis Fernando D'Haro, Abhinav Rastogi, Yun-Nung Chen, Mihail Eric, Behnam Hedayatnia, Karthik Gopalakrishnan, Yang Liu, Chao-Wei Huang, Dilek Hakkani-Tür, Jinchao Li, Qi Zhu, Lingxiao Luo, Lars Liden, Kaili Huang, Shahin Shayandeh, Runze Liang, Baolin Peng, Zheng Zhang, Swadheen Shukla, Minlie Huang, Jianfeng Gao, Shikib Mehri, Yulan Feng, Carla Gordon, Seyed Hossein Alavi, David R. Traum, Maxine Eskénazi, Ahmad Beirami, Eunjoon Cho, Paul A. Crook, Ankita De, Alborz Geramifard, Satwik Kottur, Seungwhan Moon, Shivani Poddar, and Rajen Subba. 2020. Overview of the ninth dialog system technology challenge: DSTC9. *CoRR*, abs/2011.06486.

Huang He, Hua Lu, Siqi Bao, Fan Wang, Hua Wu, Zhengyu Niu, and Haifeng Wang. 2021. Learning to select external knowledge with multi-scale negative sampling. *arXiv preprint arXiv:2102.02096*.

Dan Hendrycks, Mantas Mazeika, and Thomas Dietterich. 2019. Deep anomaly detection with outlier exposure. In *International Conference on Learning Representations*.

Di Jin, Shuyang Gao, Jiun-Yu Kao, Tagyoung Chung, and Dilek Hakkani-tur. 2020a. Mmm: Multi-stage multi-task learning for multi-choice reading comprehension. In *Proceedings of the AAAI Conference on Artificial Intelligence*, volume 34, pages 8010–8017.

Di Jin, Zhijing Jin, Joey Tianyi Zhou, Lisa Orii, and Peter Szolovits. 2020b. Hooks in the headline: Learning to generate headlines with controlled styles. In *Proceedings of the 58th Annual Meeting of the Association for Computational Linguistics*, pages 5082–5093, Online. Association for Computational Linguistics.

Di Jin, Zhijing Jin, Joey Tianyi Zhou, and Peter Szolovits. 2020c. A simple baseline to semi-supervised domain adaptation for machine translation. *arXiv preprint arXiv:2001.08140*.

Di Jin, Seokhwan Kim, and Dilek Hakkani-Tur. 2021. Can I be of further assistance? using unstructured knowledge access to improve task-oriented conversational modeling. In *Proceedings of the 1st Workshop on Document-grounded Dialogue and Conversational Question Answering (DialDoc 2021)*, pages 119–127, Online. Association for Computational Linguistics.

Amit Jindal, Arijit Ghosh Chowdhury, Aniket Didolkar, Di Jin, Ramit Sawhney, and Rajiv Ratn Shah. 2020a. Augmenting NLP models using latent feature interpolations. In *Proceedings of the 28th International Conference on Computational Linguistics*, pages 6931–6936, Barcelona, Spain (Online). International Committee on Computational Linguistics.

Amit Jindal, Narayanan Elavathur Ranganatha, Aniket Didolkar, Arijit Ghosh Chowdhury, Di Jin, Ramit Sawhney, and Rajiv Ratn Shah. 2020b. Speechmix-augmenting deep sound recognition using hidden space interpolations. In *INTERSPEECH*, pages 861–865.

Seokhwan Kim, Mihail Eric, Karthik Gopalakrishnan, Behnam Hedayatnia, Yang Liu, and Dilek Hakkani-Tur. 2020. Beyond domain APIs: Task-oriented conversational modeling with unstructured knowledge access. In *Proceedings of the 21th Annual Meeting of the Special Interest Group on Discourse and Dialogue*, pages 278–289, 1st virtual meeting. Association for Computational Linguistics.

Seokhwan Kim, Mihail Eric, Behnam Hedayatnia, Karthik Gopalakrishnan, Yang Liu, Chao-Wei Huang, and Dilek Hakkani-Tur. 2021. Beyond domain apis: Task-oriented conversational modeling with unstructured knowledge access track in dstc9. *arXiv preprint arXiv:2101.09276*.

Yinhan Liu, Myle Ott, Naman Goyal, Jingfei Du, Mandar Joshi, Danqi Chen, Omer Levy, Mike Lewis, Luke Zettlemoyer, and Veselin Stoyanov. 2019. Roberta: A robustly optimized BERT pretraining approach. *CoRR*, abs/1907.11692.

Haitao Mi, Qiyu Ren, Yinpei Dai, Yifan He, Jian Sun, Yongbin Li, Jing Zheng, and Peng Xu. 2021. Towards generalized models for beyond domain api task-oriented dialogue. *AAAI-21 DSTC9 Workshop*.

Nils Reimers and Iryna Gurevych. 2019. Sentence-bert: Sentence embeddings using siamese bert-networks. In *Proceedings of the 2019 Conference on Empirical Methods in Natural Language Processing*. Association for Computational Linguistics.

Jie Ren, Peter J. Liu, Emily Fertig, Jasper Snoek, Ryan Poplin, Mark Depristo, Joshua Dillon, and Balaji Lakshminarayanan. 2019. Likelihood ratios for out-of-distribution detection. In *Advances in Neural Information Processing Systems*, volume 32. Curran Associates, Inc.

Kihyuk Sohn, Chun-Liang Li, Jinsung Yoon, Minho Jin, and Tomas Pfister. 2021. Learning and evaluating representations for deep one-class classification. In *International Conference on Learning Representations*.

Jianlin Su, Jiarun Cao, Weijie Liu, and Yangyiwen Ou. 2021. Whitening sentence representations for better semantics and faster retrieval. *arXiv preprint arXiv:2103.15316*.

Liang Tang, Qinghua Shang, Kaokao Lv, Zixi Fu, Shijiang Zhang, Chuanming Huang, and Zhuo Zhang. 2021. Radge relevance learning and generation evaluating method for task-oriented conversational system-anonymous version. *AAAI-21 DSTC9 Workshop*.

Jason D. Williams, Kavosh Asadi, and Geoffrey Zweig. 2017. Hybrid code networks: practical and efficient end-to-end dialog control with supervised and reinforcement learning. In *Proceedings of the 55th Annual Meeting of the Association for Computational Linguistics (ACL 2017)*.

Ming Yan, Hao Zhang, Di Jin, and Joey Tianyi Zhou. 2020. Multi-source meta transfer for low resource multiple-choice question answering. In *Proceedings of the 58th Annual Meeting of the Association for Computational Linguistics*, pages 7331–7341, Online. Association for Computational Linguistics.

Joey Tianyi Zhou, Hao Zhang, Di Jin, and Xi Peng. 2019a. Dual adversarial transfer for sequence labeling. *IEEE transactions on pattern analysis and machine intelligence*, 43(2):434–446.

Joey Tianyi Zhou, Hao Zhang, Di Jin, Xi Peng, Yang Xiao, and Zhiguo Cao. 2019b. Roseq: Robust sequence labeling. *IEEE transactions on neural networks and learning systems*, 31(7):2304–2314.

Joey Tianyi Zhou, Hao Zhang, Di Jin, Hongyuan Zhu, Meng Fang, Rick Siow Mong Goh, and Kenneth Kwok. 2019c. Dual adversarial neural transfer for low-resource named entity recognition. In *Proceedings of the 57th Annual Meeting of the Association for Computational Linguistics*, pages 3461–3471, Florence, Italy. Association for Computational Linguistics.

Association for Computational Linguistics
209 N. Eighth Street
Stroudsburg, Pennsylvania 18360

ISBN 978-1-7138-9177-2

9 781713 891772

CURRAN ASSOCIATES INC.
proceedings.com